INTRODUCTION

TO SOCIOLOGY

3rd Edition

HENRY L. TISCHLER
FRAMINGHAM STATE COLLEGE

INTRODUCTION

TO SOCIOLOGY

3rd Edition

Holt, Rinehart and Winston, Inc.

Fort Worth   Chicago   San Francisco   Philadelphia
Montreal   Toronto   London   Sydney   Tokyo

Publisher   Ted Buchholz
Aquisitions Editor   Chris Klein
Developmental Editor   Carol Einhorn
Project Editor   Kristen Costen
Production Manager   Kenneth A. Dunaway
Art & Design Supervisor   Hal Lockwood
Text Designer   Gloria Gentile
Cover Designer   Guy Jacobs
Cover Illustration   Connie Connally

Printed in the United States of America

0 1 2 3   039   9 8 7 6 5 4 3 2 1

Library of Congress Cataloging-in-Publication Data

Tischler, Henry L.
   Introduction to sociology/Henry L. Tischler.
   —3rd ed.
      p. cm.
   Includes bibliographical references.
   ISBN 0-03-22717-8
   1. Sociology. I. Title.
HM51.T625   1990
301—dc20   89-29227
                                             CIP

To Melissa and Ben.

*May their generation help to make
the world a better place.*

H.L.T.

Back in the 1960s, as a new freshman at Temple University, my first experience with a college textbook was in my sociology course. I dutifully read the assigned chapter during my first week of class hoping to become familiar with the subject matter of this required course. The only problem was I had no idea what the author was saying. The writing level was advanced, the style dense, and the book downright threatening, without photos or illustrations. After several hours of reading I felt frustrated, stupid, and knew no more about sociology than when I started. If this was what college was going to be like, I was not going to make it, I thought. I remember commuting home, looking out at the slums of North Philadelphia, and thinking to myself that I was probably not what guidance counselors in that day referred to as "college material." I could already picture myself dropping out after the first semester and looking for a job selling furniture or driving a cab. My family would be disappointed, but my father was a factory worker, and there was no family history of college attendance to live up to. I continued to struggle with the book and earned a D on the mid-term exam. After much effort, I managed to finish the course with a C and a burning disinterest in the field of sociology. I did not take another sociology course for two years, and when I did it was "Marriage and the Family," the easiest course on campus.

I often wonder how I came from this inauspicious beginning to becoming a sociology professor, let alone the author of a widely used introductory sociology textbook. Then again, maybe it is not all that unusual, because that experience continues to have an effect on me each day. Those fifteen weeks helped to develop my view that little is to be gained by presenting knowledge in an incomprehensible or unnecessarily complicated way or by making yourself unapproachable. Learning should be an exciting, challenging, eye-opening experience and not a threatening one. I have taught my courses with this viewpoint in mind, and I hope that it comes through in this book as well.

One of the real benefits of writing three editions of this textbook is that I have been forced to reexamine every concept and theory presented in an introductory course. In doing so, I have approached the subject matter through a new set of eyes and have tried to find better ways of presenting the material. As professors we rarely venture into each others' classrooms, and hardly ever do we receive honest, highly detailed, and constructive criticism of how well we are transmitting the subject matter. In the writing of a textbook we do receive this type of information, and we can radically restructure or fine-tune our presentation, as the case may be. It is quite an education for those of us who have devoted our career to teaching sociology.

NEW IN THIS EDITION

This is no ordinary revision but the product of 2 years' work. Every aspect of the book has been updated and a great deal changed; the information is as current and up-to-date as it can be. The chapter order has been changed to reflect a more logical progression of topics.

My goal is to demonstrate the vitality, interest, and utility associated with sociology. Examining society, social institutions, and social processes is an exciting and absorbing undertaking. I do not set out to make sociologists of the readers (although if that is an outcome I will be delighted) but rather to show how sociology applies to many areas of life and how it is used in day-to-day activities. In meeting this objective I focused on two basic ideas: first, that sociology is a rigorous scientific discipline; and second, that a basic knowledge of sociology is essential for understanding social interactions in many different settings, whether they be work or social environments. In order to understand society, we must understand how society shapes people — and how people in turn shape society. We must develop a new way of understanding the world we have experienced for so many years.

The chapters together build from a micro- to a macro-level analysis of society, each part introducing increasingly more comprehensive factors necessary for a broad-based understanding of social organization. Great care has been taken to structure the book in a way that permits flexibility in the presentation of the material. Each chapter is self-contained, so the chapters may be taught in any order.

A COMPARATIVE AND CROSS-CULTURAL PERSPECTIVE

Sociology is a highly organized discipline shaped by several theoretical perspectives, or schools of thought. It is not merely the study of social problems or the random voicing of opinions. No single perspective is given greater emphasis in this book; a balanced presentation of both functionalist theory and conflict theory is supplemented whenever possible by the symbolic interactionist viewpoint.

The book has received a great deal of praise for being cross-cultural in approach and bringing in examples from a wide variety of other cultures. Sociology is concerned with the interactions of people wherever and whenever they occur. It would be shortsighted, therefore, to concentrate on only our own society. Often, in fact, the best way to appreciate our own situation is through comparison with other societies. We use our cross-cultural focus as a basis for comparison and contrast with U.S. society.

NEW CHAPTERS

There are two new chapters in this third edition. In addition to a chapter on social

stratification, a new chapter called *Social Class in the United States* deals with a wide variety of issues not covered in other books. Many myths about both the poor and the wealthy are refuted with ample data. The professor will find much material here for lively class discussions.

Deviant behavior and social control, discussed together in most books, have been divided into two chapters. The chapter on deviant behavior deals only with deviance and the reasons for its existence; the chapter on law and social control deals with the criminal justice system and various topics related to crime.

FEATURES
Opening Vignettes

Each chapter begins with a lively vignette that introduces the student to the subject matter of the chapter. Many of these vignettes are from real life events that the students can relate to, such as television talk shows (Chapter 1), recruitment by religious cults (Chapter 4), or the meaning of eye contact in large cities (Chapter 5). Other vignettes refer to current situations that have received media attention, such as Masters and Johnson's flawed AIDS research (Chapter 2), the death of a navy recruit during training (Chapter 6), principal Henry Wilson and his approach as portrayed in the film "Lean on Me" (Chapter 14), or Willie Horton and the Bush/Dukakis election (Chapter 17). Still others deal with unusual circumstances that will cause the student to realize that sociology applies to a broad scope of events. Examples include nude bathing on Cape Cod (Chapter 7), whites who claim to be black (Chapter 10), and the belief in harmonic convergence (Chapter 13).

Controversies in Sociology

A special feature at the end of each chapter is designed to show students two sides of an issue. This section will help students see that most social events require close analysis and that hastily drawn conclusions are often wrong. Students will learn that to be a good sociologist one must be knowledgeable about disparate positions and must be willing to question the validity of statements made by the interested parties.

This section presents such controversies as "Is Daycare Harmful to Children?" (Chapter 4); "What is the Origin of the Black Underclass?" (Chapter 8); "Does Television Make Kids Stupid?" (Chapter 14); "Does Capital Punishment Deter Murderers?" (Chapter 15); "Should We Have a Higher Minimum Wage?" (Chapter 16); "How Many Homeless are There?" (Chapter 19); and "Should Sex Selection Abortions be Permitted?" (Chapter 21).

Taking the Sociological Perspective

Another feature within each chapter expands on a concept, theory, or issue discussed in the chapter, allowing the professor and student to examine a specific situation in depth and see its application to sociology. Some of the features in this section are "Fraternities: The Ultimate In-Group" (Chapter 6); "Prisons for Profit" (Chapter 7); "The Gap Between the Rich and the Poor Continues to Widen" (Chapter 8); "The Black Middle Class" (Chapter 9); "International Adoption and Interracial Families" (Chapter 10); "Sexual Harassment on Campus" (Chapter 11); and "Who Will Bear the Burden of AIDS?" (Chapter 18).

What This Means to You

Each chapter also has a section designed to show students how the topic under discussion relates specifically to their lives. This is often done by way of a table or graph that lets students see where they fall within the general population. This section also gives the student an opportunity to interpret data from a table or chart. Some of the topics discussed in this section are "Is Smoking a Sign of an Unhealthy Lifestyle?" (Chapter 1); "What Language Should You Study in College?" (Chapter 3); "Is Drunk Driving Deviant Behavior?" (Chapter 7); "The Poor Pay More for Food" (Chapter 9); "Who Attends Religious Services?" (Chapter 13); "What are Your Chances of Being the Victim of a Crime?" (Chapter 15); and "Where the Jobs Will Be in the Year 2010" (Chapter 19).

Sociology at Work

In selected chapters, special interviews highlight people whose lives are directly influenced by the topic under discussion. Some of these individuals are well-known sociologists doing current research, such as Judith S. Wallerstein on divorce and children (Chapter 12) and William H. Whyte on urban environments (Chapter 19). Others are people working within the area being discussed, such as Peggy Charren (of Action for Children's Television) on socialization and TV (Chapter 4), Roger Fisher on negotiating (Chapter 5), Shirley Hoover on women in the ministry (Chapter 13), and Cheryl Gould on producing television news (Chapter 17).

THE ANCILLARY PACKAGE

The primary objective of a textbook is to provide clear information in a format that promotes learning. In order to assist the instructor in using *Introduction to Sociology,* an extensive ancillary package has been developed to accompany the book.

Instructor's Manual

Both the new and the experienced instructor will find plenty of ideas in the instructor's manual, written by Edward Kick of the University of Utah (Salt Lake City). The manual corresponds to the text and to the student study guide. Each chapter of the manual includes teaching objectives, key terms, lecture outlines, activities, discussion questions, and a section on computer exercises.

Test Bank

The Test Bank, created by Jeffrey Rosenfeld of Nassau Community College, contains approximately 2000 multiple-choice, true/false, matching, and essay questions. These test items are page referenced to the text and are coded as either knowledge or application questions.

Computerized Test Bank

The Computerized Test Bank, available for IBM, Apple, and Macintosh computers, allows the instructor to modify and add questions, as well as to create, scramble, and print tests and answer keys. A telephone hotline is available to assist those who experience difficulty with the program or its interface with a particular printer.

Study Guide

The Student Study Guide, written by Herb Haines of the State University of New York (Cortland) is designed to reinforce the learning of key concepts presented in the text. Each chapter includes a synopsis and outline, learning objectives, a list of key terms, and a self-test section that includes multiple choice, true/false, and fill-in-the-blank exercises.

Interactive Computer Program

Users of this book will also be able to obtain *The Social Scene,* an interactive computer program specifically designed for sociology students. This program familiarizes students with the basic procedures of survey data analysis by allowing them to actually manipulate data sets drawn from the General Social Survey (GSS). *The Social Scene* moves the learning of sociology into the twenty-first century.

Overhead Transparencies

To help the instructor with the lectures, a package of overhead transparencies has been developed to illustrate various subjects in the sociology curriculum. These transparencies are based on the latest available data.

Sociology Videos

Holt, Rinehart and Winston offers five *Currents* videos to accompany the third edition of *Introduction to Sociology. Currents* is the highly acclaimed series produced by a PBS affiliate in New York City, WNET. The main focus of this series is to provide a forum in which important changes in our society can be evaluated.

ACKNOWLEDGMENTS

Anyone who has written an introductory textbook realizes that at various points a project of such magnitude becomes a team effort, with many people devoting enormous amounts of time to ensure that the final product is as good as it can possibly be.

The manuscript was reviewed and commented on by professors from many institutions. I would like to thank the following reviewers for their thoughtful reading of the chapters:

Larry Perkins
Oklahoma State University
Pat Ashton
Indiana University-Purdue University
Chuck Carselowey
Oklahoma City Community College
Richard Gale
University of Oregon
Gregg L. Carter
Bryant College
Martin Epstein
Middlesex Community College
Thomas Regulus
University of Illinois, Chicago
Dennis Nagi
Hudson Valley Community College

Brenda VanderMey
Clemson University

Gerald Stott
Southeast Missouri State University

Peter Chroman
College of San Mateo

Shirley Pigman
Fullerton College

Philip Nyden
Loyola University

Roger Barnes
University of Texas, San Antonio

Ali Eminov
Wayne State College

David Medina
Mount San Antonio College

David Petty
Stephen F. Austin State University

Carole Beveridge
Middle Tennessee State University

Richard McMann
Ohio University

Jarvis Gamble
Owens Technical College

Jane Baumgarden
Illinois Benedictine College

David Edwards
San Antonio College

William Schwab
University of Arkansas

V.V. Prakava Roa
Jackson State University

Lee Dodson
Rockingham Community College

William Snizek
Virginia Polytechnic Institute and State
  University

Juanita Firestone
University of Texas, San Antonio

Dwayne Smith
Tulane University

Alice Kemp
University of New Orleans

David Van Mierlo
St. Charles County Community College

Jeffrey Davidson
University of Delaware

Christopher Ezell
Vincennes University

Ernest Brandewie
Indiana University, South Bend

Orin Solloway
University of Oklahoma

Many people at Holt, Rinehart and Winston provided valuable assistance. Sociology editor Chris Klein ushered the project through many difficult stages and managed to keep it on schedule despite various obstacles. It was a privilege to have his support and assistance. I would also like to thank Ted Buchholz, editor-in-chief for his involvement and concern with this book.

I am also grateful to Hal Lockwood of Bookman Productions and the many others who helped to make this book possible.

Henry L. Tischler

Henry L. Tischler grew up in Philadelphia and received his bachelor's degree from Temple University and his masters and doctorate degrees from Northeastern University. He pursued post-doctoral studies at Harvard University.

His first venture into textbook publishing took place while he was a graduate student in sociology, when he wrote the fourth edition of *Race and Ethnic Relations* with Brewton Berry. The success of that book led to his authorship of the three editions of *Introduction to Sociology.*

Tischler has been a professor at Framingham State College (in Framingham, Massachusetts) since 1969. He continues to teach introductory sociology every semester, and his encouragement has been instrumental in the decision of many students to major in the field. His other areas of interest are race and ethnicity, urban sociology, and organizational behavior.

Professor Tischler has also been active in making sociology accessible to the general population as the host of a radio talk show on sociological issues. Currently he writes a weekly newspaper column called "Society Today," which deals with a wide variety of sociological topics. Tischler is also producing a documentary that examines the life developments of a group of former student activists who are currently reaching middle age.

Tischler lives in Sudbury, Massachusetts, with his wife, Linda (a journalist), a teenage daughter, Melissa, and a grade-school son, Ben.

CONTENTS IN BRIEF

CONTENTS

Chapter 7
Deviant Behavior   187

PART 3
SOCIAL INEQUALITY   213

Chapter 8
Social Stratification   215

Chapter 9
Social Class in the United States   241

FEATURES

INTRODUCTION TO SOCIOLOGY

3rd Edition

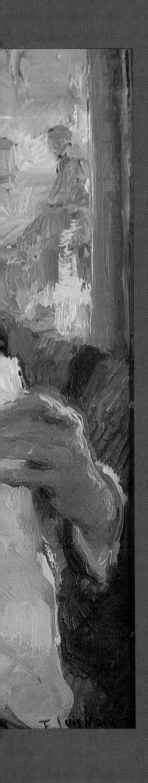

Part 1

THE STUDY OF SOCIETY

Chapter 1

THE SOCIOLOGICAL PERSPECTIVE

SOCIOLOGY AS A POINT OF VIEW

The Sociological Imagination
Is Sociology Common Sense?
Sociology and Science
Sociology as a Social Science

THE DEVELOPMENT OF SOCIOLOGY

Comte and Saint-Simon
Classical Theorists
The Development of Sociology in the United States

THEORETICAL PERSPECTIVES

Functionalism
Conflict Theory
The Interactionist Perspective
Contemporary Sociology
Theory and Practice

SUMMARY

Are Phil Donahue, Oprah Winfrey, or Geraldo Rivera sociologists? Of course not. But that does not stop these television talk show hosts from acting as if they were when they investigate social issues. Here are a few examples:

• The topic was a marriage that no longer worked. When "Barbara," a guest who preferred to disguise her identity, went on "The Oprah Winfrey Show" to talk about her celibate marriage, the discussion was captivating to the audience and the host. The trouble was that "Barbara" was an impostor, staging a media event. She fooled everyone, including Oprah, who had no idea she was being duped.

• Geraldo Rivera did a program on racist skinhead groups and stacked the show with a variety of guests guaranteed to produce an inflammatory discussion. Not only was the discussion heated, but it erupted into an outright brawl during which Geraldo had his nose broken by a chair thrown into the group of combatants. Geraldo's bandaged face appeared in magazines and newspapers for weeks thereafter, and the event boosted the show's ratings.

• Phil Donahue went so far as to write a book, *The Human Animal,* and did a five-part series related to the book's investigation of a wide variety of contemporary concerns. At times the book could be mistaken for an introductory sociology text, as it examined family issues and life in the United States, and throughout the world.

It would seem that sociology is everywhere. Sociological information has become so much a part of our lives that most of us have informed opinions on drug abuse, homelessness, welfare, high school dropout rates, or white-collar crime. Yet, if Phil Donahue can discuss sociological topics, and journalists can write sociological articles, why is it necessary for sociologists to spend many years earning graduate degrees in this field? If professional sociologists do not claim any close affinity to talk show hosts or journalists, what is it we actually do that is so different from these two professions?

A simple way to begin answering that question is to note that sociologists have very different goals in mind when they investigate a problem. A television talk show host needs to make the program entertaining and maintain high ratings or the show will be cancelled. This will certainly limit the choice of topics, as well as the manner in which an issue is investigated. On the other hand, a sociologist must answer to the scientific community as she or he tries to further our understanding of a topic. This means that the goal is not high ratings, but an accurate and scientific approach to the topic under investigation.

As you will see throughout this text, we will ask you to go beyond pop sociology and investigate issues more scientifically than you did before. We will ask you to look at major events, as well as everyday things around you, a little differently and start to notice patterns you may have never seen before. After you are equipped with the tools of sociology you will come back to Phil Donahue, Oprah Winfrey, and Geraldo Rivera and see their programs very differently. You will realize they often do not help to bring about an accurate understanding of a particular topic. You will also understand how sociology represents both a body of knowledge, as well as a scientific approach to the study of social issues, that goes beyond most popular presentations.

Whenever people come together, social interactions and social relationships take place that form the basis of what sociologists study. We will ask you to look at major events, as well as everyday situations around you, a little differently and start to notice patterns you may have never seen before.

SOCIOLOGY AS A POINT OF VIEW

Sociology is the scientific study of human society and social interactions. As sociologists our main goal is to *understand* social situations and look for repeating patterns in society. We do not have to use facts selectively to make for a lively talk show, sell newspapers, or support one particular point of view. Instead, we are engaged in a rigorous scientific endeavor, which requires objectivity and detachment.

The main focus of sociology is the group, not the individual. Sociologists attempt to understand the forces that operate throughout society—forces that mold individuals, shape their behavior, and thus determine social events.

When you walk into an introductory physics class, you may know very little about the subject, and hold very few opinions about the various topics within the field. On the other hand, when you enter your introductory sociology class for the first time, you will feel quite familiar with the subject matter. You have the advantage of coming to sociology with a substantial amount of information that you have gained simply by being a member of society. Ironically, this knowledge can leave you at a disadvantage also, because these views have not been gathered in a scientific fashion and may not be accurate.

Over the years we have developed a set of deeply ingrained views of the world and how it operates. This perspective influences how we look at the world, and guides us in our understanding of social life. As we try to answer questions about our identity, and the actions and reactions of others, we rely on information gathered from our own backgrounds and experiences with others. Even though we accept the premise that individuals are unique, we tend to categorize or even stereotype people in order to interpret and predict behavior and events.

Is this individual perspective adequate for bringing about an understanding of ourselves and society? Even though it may serve us quite well in our day-to-day lives, sociologists would answer that it does not give us enough accurate information to develop an understanding of the broader social picture. This picture only becomes clear when we know something about the society in which we live, the social processes that affect us, and the typical patterns of interaction that characterize our lives.

Let us take a major-league baseball game as an example. If you were asked to go to the game and prepare a report on your observations of the spectators at that game, your notes might contain comments about the woman next to you who carefully recorded each play on a scorecard, the man behind you who seemed more interested in the offerings of the various food vendors than in the game, and the seven-year-old boy clutching his mitt in the hope of catching a foul ball. Sociologists, on the other hand, would more likely be interested in the age, socioeconomic level, and ethnic backgrounds of the crowd and the ballplayers as well. They might want to compare the

sociology The scientific study of human society and social interactions.

Bullfights are a part of Spanish culture but not American culture. Consequently, our attitudes toward such events are likely to be quite different from those of someone who has grown up with this activity. Sociology asks us to try to understand the value differences that may exist between cultures.

Vast differences often exist within the same society. In this scene from the Hong Kong harbor, the merchants who ply their trade on the water have very little contact with the people who live in the high-rise buildings in the background.

background and behavior of spectators at a baseball game with the characteristics of spectators at a tennis match and ask such questions as: Are there differences? If so, what kinds and why?

We all have different perceptions of what is going on in the world. These different perceptions of reality produce many different life-styles, and different life-styles in turn produce different perceptions of reality.

While studying sociology you will be asked to look at the world a little differently than you usually do. Because you will be looking at the world through other people's eyes—using new perspectives—you will start to notice things you may never have noticed before. When you look at life in a middle-class suburb, for instance, what do you see? How does your view differ from that of a poor slum resident? How does the suburb appear to a recent immigrant from the Soviet Union or Cuba or Haiti? How does it appear to a burglar? Finally, what does the sociologist see?

Sociology asks you to broaden your perspective on the world. You will start to see that the reason people act in markedly different ways is not because one person is "sane" and another is "crazy." Rather, it is because they all have different perceptions of what is going on in the world. These different perceptions of reality produce many different life-styles, and different life-styles in turn produce different perceptions of reality. In order to understand other people, we must begin to look at the world from a perspective that is broader than one based only on our own individual experiences.

THE SOCIOLOGICAL IMAGINATION

Whereas people often interpret social events on the basis of their individual experiences, sociologists look for *relationships* among these events to understand the broader forces in society. They are willing to step back and view society more as an outsider than as a personally involved and possibly biased participant. C. Wright Mills (1959) realized that there are different levels on which social events can be perceived and interpreted. He used the term *sociological imagination* to refer to this relationship between individual experiences and the larger society.

Indeed, the sociological imagination looks at all types of human behavior patterns, discerning unseen connections among events, noting similarities in the actions of individuals with no direct knowledge of one another, and finding subtle forces that mold people's actions. Like a museum-goer who draws back from a painting in order to see how the separate strokes and colors form subtly shaded images, sociologists stand back in their imagination from individual events in order to see why and how they occurred. In so doing, they discern patterns that govern our social existence.

For example, although we assume that most people in the United States marry because of love, sociologists remind us that the decision to marry—or not to marry—is influenced by a variety of social values taught to us since early childhood. That is, we select our mates according to the social values we internalize from family, peers, neighbors, community leaders, and even our television heroes. As a result we are less likely to marry someone from a different socioeconomic class, from a different race or religion, or from a markedly different educational background. Thus, as we pair off, we follow somewhat predictable patterns: In most cases the man is older, earns more money, and has a higher occupational status than the woman. These patterns may not be evident to the two people who are in love with each other—indeed, they may not be aware that anything other than romance played a role in their choice of a mate.

By stepping back along with the sociologist we can begin to discern marriage patterns. We may note that marriage rates are different in different parts of the country; that the average age of marriage is related to educational level; that social class is related to marital stability. These patterns (which are discussed in Chapter 12) show us that there are forces at work influencing marriage that may not be evident to the individuals who fall in love and marry. The sociological imagination encourages us to look for these patterns and to try to explain why they exist.

The sociologist would look at alcoholism in a different way than, for instance, the

To the average person this wedding may be quite unusual. To the sociologist it is also very interesting, because certain expected behaviors are being followed at the same time that other common norms are being violated.

psychologist. Whereas the psychologist might view alcoholism as a personal problem that has the potential to destroy an individual's physical and emotional health, as well as marriage, career, and friendships, the sociologist would look for patterns in alcoholism. Although each alcoholic personally makes the decision to take each drink—and each suffers the pain of addiction—the sociologist would remind us that to think of alcoholism as being merely each alcoholic's personal problem is to misunderstand the issue. Sociologists encourage us to look at the social causes of alcoholism. They want to know who drinks excessively, when they drink, where they drink, and under what conditions they drink. Sociologists also want to know the social costs of chronic drinking—costs in terms of families torn apart, jobs lost, children severely abused and neglected; in terms of highway accidents and deaths; in terms of drunken quarrels leading to violence and to murder. Noting the startling increase in heavy alcohol use by adolescents over the last 10 years and the rapid rise of chronic alcoholism among women, sociologists ask: At this moment in history, what forces are at work to account for these patterns?

Sociologists force us to recognize the enormous impact alcohol has on all of us—whether we drink or not. This knowledge mobilizes us to treat the problem as a societal issue and to deal with it on a number of different levels.

The sociological imagination focuses on every aspect of society and every relationship among individuals. It studies the behavior of crowds at ball games and racetracks; shifts in styles of dress and popular music; changing patterns of courtship and marriage; the emergence and fading of different life-styles, political movements, and religious sects; the distribution of income and access to resources and services; decisions made by the Supreme Court, by congressional committees, and by local zoning boards; and so on. Every detail of social existence is food for sociological thought and relevant to sociological analysis.

The broad spectrum of areas into which sociology delves is reflected in the number of articles related to sociological subjects that appear in the mass media—newspapers, magazines, books, and television and radio programs. From predictions and analyses of voting behavior of various groups such as blacks, women, and union members, to reports on school busing and why it works in some places and not in others, to surveys of people's attitudes and opinions on different issues—the popular media are full of stories based on sociology.

It is necessary to exercise caution when examining media polls and reports on studies because many of them do not use acceptable sociological research methods (see Chapter 2). Reports in the media may be used as a source of basic information about research, as a springboard for thinking about what further studies are needed, and for searching for patterns among events. Media reports should not be viewed as sociological gospel however.

The potential for sociology to be put to use—applied to the solution of "real-world" problems—is very great. Proponents of the idea of applied sociology believe the work of sociologists can and should be used to help bring about an understanding of, and perhaps even guidelines for changing, the complexities of modern society. (We will examine the issue of applying sociology in our Sociological Controversy "Should Sociology Aim to Improve Society?")

The demand for applied sociology is growing, and many sociologists work directly with government agencies or private businesses in an effort to apply sociological knowledge to real-world problems. For example, they might investigate such questions as how the building of a dam on a particular site will affect the residents of the area, how busing to integrate schools affects the children involved, why voters select one candidate over another, how a company can boost employees' morale, and how relationships among administrators, doctors, nurses, and patients affect hospital care. The answers to these questions have practical applications. The growing demand for sociological information provides many new career areas for sociology students (see *What This Means to You* box, "What Do You Do With a B.A. in Sociology?").

IS SOCIOLOGY COMMON SENSE?

Common sense is what people develop through living everyday lives. In a very real sense, it is the set of expectations about society and people's behavior that guides our own behavior. Unfortunately, these expectations are not always reliable or accurate, because we tend to believe what we want to believe, to see what we want to see, and to accept as fact whatever appears to be logical, without further investigation. The "common sense" approach to sociology is one of the major dangers the new student encounters.

Whereas common sense is often vague, oversimplified, and frequently contradictory, sociology as a science attempts to be

WHAT DO YOU DO WITH A B.A. IN SOCIOLOGY?

Frequency of Selected Position Titles Held by B.A. Graduates

Employer	Percentage	
Professions:	33.7	
Social Work		9.9
Counseling		5.4
Researcher		5.4
Elementary/Secondary Teacher		4.7
Nursing		1.1
Management/Administration	12.5	
Sales	13.3	
Retail Sales		7.4
Insurance		1.6
Service Occupations	23.5	
Restaurant Service		2.2
Planning		2.1
Parole/Probation Agent/Officer		1.9
Police Officer		1.4
Day Care/Child Care Worker		1.8
Clerical	11.3	
Secretary		2.6
Construction and Trades	3.2	
Miscellaneous	2.4	
TOTAL (Number of Cases)	100.0 (759)	

T he American Sociological Association tracked studies asking that question and found that there are a range of careers open to people who graduate college with a bachelor's degree in sociology. As you can see from the following table, B.A. graduates use their skills in many different ways. One-third hold professional jobs (social work is the most popular) and one-fourth are employed in the service sector.

Source: Bettina J. Huber, "Career Possibilities for Sociology Graduates," American Sociological Association, 1984.

specific, to qualify its statements, and to prove its assertions. Upon closer inspection, we find that the proverbial words of wisdom rooted in common sense are often illogical. Why, for example, should you "look before you leap" if "he who hesitates is lost"? How can "absence make the heart grow fonder" when "out of sight, out of mind"? Why should "opposites attract" when "birds of a feather flock together"? Sociologists as scientists would attempt to qualify these statements by specifying, for example, under what conditions "opposites tend to attract" or "birds of a feather flock together."

Although common sense gleaned from personal experience may help us in certain types of interactions, it will not help us understand why and under what conditions these interactions are taking place. Sociology as a science is oriented toward gaining knowledge about why and under what conditions they do take place, thus to understand human interactions better (Vernon, 1965).

SOCIOLOGY AND SCIENCE

Sociology is commonly described as one of the social sciences. **Science** refers to a body of systematically arranged knowledge that shows the operation of general laws.

Sociology also employs the same general methods of investigation that are used in the natural sciences. Like the natural scientists, sociologists use the **scientific method.** They attempt to build a body of scientific knowledge through the four components of the scientific method: observation, experimentation, generalization, and verification. The collection of data is an important aspect of the scientific method, but facts alone do not constitute a science. To have any meaning, facts must be ordered in some way, analyzed, generalized, and related to other facts. This is known as theory construction. Theories help us to organize and interpret facts and relate them to previous findings of other researchers.

Science is only one of the ways in which human beings study the world around them. Unlike other means of inquiry that depend on a logical discussion of abstract concepts such as religion or philosophy, science for the most part limits its investigations to things that can be observed directly or that produce directly observable events. Things that can be observed in this way are termed empirical entities; therefore, one of the basic features of science is **empiricism.** For example, theologians might discuss the role of faith in producing "true happiness"; philosophers might deliberate over what happiness actually encompasses; but sociologists would note, analyze, and predict the consequences of such measurable items as job satisfaction, the relationship between income and stated contentment, and the role of social class in the incidence of depression.

SOCIOLOGY AS A SOCIAL SCIENCE

The **social sciences** consist of all those disciplines that apply scientific methods to the study of human behavior. Although there is some overlap, each of the social sciences has its own areas of investigation. It is helpful to understand each of the social sciences and to examine sociology's relationship to them.

Cultural Anthropology

Cultural anthropology is the social science most closely related to sociology. The two have many theories and concepts in common and often overlap. The main difference is in the groups they study and the research methods they use. Sociologists tend to study groups and institutions within large, modern, industrial societies, using research methods that enable them rather quickly to gather specific information about large numbers of people. In contrast, cultural anthropologists often immerse themselves in another society for a long period of time, trying to learn as much as possible about that society and the relationships among its people. Thus, anthropologists tend to focus on the culture of small, preindustrial societies because they are less complex and more manageable with this method of study.

Psychology

Psychology is the study of brain functioning, mental processes, and individual behavior. It is concerned with such issues as motivation, perception, cognition, creativity, mental disorders, and personality. More than any other social science, psychology uses laboratory experiments. Psychology and sociology overlap in a subdivision of each field known as *social psychology*—the study of how human behavior is influenced and shaped by various social situations. Social psychologists study such issues as how individuals in a group solve problems and reach a consensus or what factors might produce nonconformity in a group situation. For the most part, however, psychology studies the individual, and sociology

---

science A body of systematically arranged knowledge that shows the operation of general laws. The term also refers to the logical, systematic methods by which that knowledge is obtained.

scientific method The approach to research that involves observation, experimentation, generalization, and verification.

empiricism The view that generalizations are valid only if they rely on evidence that can be observed directly or verified through our senses.

social sciences All those disciplines that apply scientific methods to the study of human behavior. The social sciences include sociology, cultural anthropology, psychology, economics, history, and political science.

Sociologists and anthropologists share many theories and concepts. Whereas sociologists tend to study groups and institutions within large, modern, industrial societies, anthropologists tend to focus on the culture of small, preindustrial societies.

studies groups of individuals, as well as society's institutions.

Economics

Economics studies the creation, distribution, and consumption of goods and services. Economists have developed techniques for measuring such things as prices, supply and demand, money supplies, rates of inflation, and employment. The economy, however, is just one part of society. It is each individual in society who decides whether to buy an American car or a Japanese import, whether she or he is able to handle the mortgage payments on a dream house, and so on. Whereas economists study price and availability factors, sociologists are interested in the social factors that influence the resulting economic behavior. Is it peer pressure that results in the buying of the large flashy car, or is it concern about gas mileage that leads to the purchase of a small, fuel-efficient modest vehicle? What social and cultural factors contribute to the differences in the portion of income saved by the average wage earner in different societies? What effect does the unequal allocation of resources have on social interaction? These are examples of the questions sociologists seek to answer.

History

History looks at the past in an attempt to learn what happened, when it happened, and why it happened. Sociology also looks at historical events within their social contexts to discover why things happened and, more important, to assess what their social significance was and is. Historians provide a narrative of the sequence of events during a certain period and may use sociological research methods to try to learn how social forces have shaped historical events. Sociologists, on the other hand, examine historical events to see how they influenced later social situations. Historians focus on individual events—the American Revolution or slavery, for example.

When considering the subject of slavery in the United States, historians typically focus on when the first slaves arrived or how many slaves there were in 1700 or 1850 and the conditions under which they lived. Sociologists and modern social historians would use these data to ask many questions: What were the social and economic forces that shaped the institution of slavery in the United States? How did the Industrial Revolution affect slavery? How has the experience of slavery affected the black family? Although history and sociology have been moving toward each other over the last 20 years, each discipline still retains a somewhat different focus: sociology on the present, history on the past.

The changes that grew out of the French Revolution contributed to an environment in which the systematic study of society could emerge.

Political Science

Political science concentrates on three major areas: political theory, the actual operation of government, and, in recent years, political behavior. In its emphasis on political behavior, political science overlaps with sociology. The primary distinction between the two disciplines is that sociology focuses on how the political system affects other institutions in society, while political science devotes more attention to the forces that shape political systems and theories for understanding these forces. However, both disciplines share an interest in why people

vote the way they do, why they join political movements, how the mass media are changing political parties and processes, and so on.

Social Work

Much of the theory and research methods of social work are drawn from sociology and psychology, but social work focuses to a much greater degree on application and problem solving. The disciplines of sociology and social work are often confused with each other. The main goal of social work is to help people directly with their problems, while the aim of sociology is to understand why the problems exist. Social workers provide help for individuals and families who have emotional and psychological problems or who experience difficulties that stem from poverty or other ongoing problems that are rooted in the structure of society. They also organize community groups to tackle local issues such as housing problems and try to influence policymaking bodies and legislation. Sociologists provide many of the theories and ideas that can be used to help others. Although sociology is not social work, it is a useful area of academic concentration for those interested in entering the helping professions.

THE DEVELOPMENT OF SOCIOLOGY

It is hardly an accident that sociology emerged as a separate field of study in Europe during the nineteenth century. That was a time of turmoil, a period in which the existing social order was being shaken by the growing Industrial Revolution and by violent uprisings against established rulers (the American and French revolutions). People were also affected by world exploration and colonialization, and discoveries of how others lived. At the same time, the declining power of the church and religion to impose its views of right and wrong on whole nations left a void. A new social class of industrialists and business people emerged to challenge the rule of the feudal aristocracies. Many peasants became industrial workers. Tightly knit communities, held together by centuries of tradition and well-defined social relationships, were strained by dramatic changes in the social environment. Factory cities began to replace the rural estates of nobles as a center for society at large. People with different backgrounds were brought together under the same factory roof to work for wages in-

stead of exchanging their services for land and protection. Families now had to protect themselves, to buy food rather than grow it, and to pay rent for their homes. These new living and working conditions led to the development of an industrial, urban life-style, which, in turn, produced new social problems.

Many people were frightened by what was going on and wanted to find some way of understanding and dealing with the changes taking place. The need for a systematic analysis of society coupled with acceptance of the scientific method resulted in the emergence of sociology. Henri Saint-Simon (1760–1825) and Auguste Comte (1798–1857) were among the pioneers in the science of sociology.

COMTE AND SAINT-SIMON

Born in the French city of Montpellier on January 19, 1798, Auguste Comte grew up in the period of great political turmoil that followed the French Revolution of 1789–1799.

In August 1817 Comte met Henri Saint-Simon and became his secretary and eventually his close collaborator. Under Saint-Simon's influence Comte converted from an ardent advocate of liberty and equality to a supporter of an elitist conception of society. During their association the two men collaborated on a number of essays, most of which contained the seeds of Comte's major ideas. Their alliance came to a bitter end in 1824, when Comte broke with Saint-Simon for both financial and intellectual reasons.

Saint-Simon and Comte rejected the lack of empiricism in the social philosophy of the day. Instead, they turned for inspiration to the methods and intellectual framework of the natural sciences, which they perceived as having led to the spectacular successes of industrial progress. They set out to develop a "science of man" that would reveal the underlying principles of society, much as the sciences of physics and

August Comte coined the term sociology. *He wanted to develop a "science of man" that would reveal the underlying principles of society much as the sciences of physics and chemistry explained nature and guided industrial progress.*

chemistry explained nature and guided industrial progress.

Financial problems, lack of academic recognition, and marital difficulties combined to force Comte into a shell. Eventually he reached the point that for reasons of "cerebral hygiene" he would no longer read any scientific work related to the fields about which he was writing. Living in isolation at the periphery of the academic world, Comte concentrated his efforts between 1830 and 1842 on writing his major work, *Cours de Philosophie Positive,* in which he coined the term *sociology.*

After Comte's wife left him, he met and fell in love with Clothilde de Vaux. Although she died of tuberculosis soon after they met, Comte vowed to devote the rest of his life to her memory. He thus began writing *Le Système de Politique Positive,* which proclaimed the importance of emotion over intellect and of feelings over ideas and established the Religion of Humanity based

on universal love. Published between 1851 and 1854, the *Système* lost Comte his few remaining followers, who could not support the idea that love was the answer to all the problems of the time.

Auguste Comte devoted a great deal of his writing to describing the contributions he expected sociology would make in the future. He was much less concerned with defining sociology's subject matter than with showing how it would improve society. Although Comte was reluctant to specify subdivisions of sociology, he identified two major areas that sociology should concentrate on: social statics—the study of how the various institutions of society are interrelated, focusing on order, stability, and harmony; and social dynamics—the study of complete societies and how they develop and change over time. Comte believed all societies move through certain fixed stages of development, eventually reaching perfection (as exemplified in his mind by industrial Europe). The idea of a perfect society, however, no longer is accepted by sociologists today.

CLASSICAL THEORISTS

During the nineteenth century sociology developed rapidly under the influence of four scholars of highly divergent temperaments and orientations. Despite their differences in aims and theories, however, these men—Karl Marx, Herbert Spencer, Émile Durkheim, and Max Weber—were responsible for shaping sociology into a relatively coherent discipline.

Karl Marx (1818–1883)

Because the name Karl Marx triggers thoughts of communism, those who are unfamiliar with his writings often think of him as a revolutionary proponent of the political and social system we see in the Soviet Union today. Yet Marx was not Russian, and although he was committed to social change, he did not espouse the type of government and social structure that we now see in those countries that today are labeled communist.

Marx lived during a period when the overwhelming majority of people in industrial societies were poor. This was the early period of industrialization in such nations as England, Germany, and the United States. Those who owned and controlled the factories and other means of production exploited the masses who worked for them. The rural poor were forced or lured into cities where employment was available in the factories and workshops of the new industrial economies. In this way the rural poor were converted into an urban poor. In the United States, children, some as young as 5 or 6 years old, were employed in the cotton mills of the South. They worked 12-hour days, 6 and 7 days a week (Lipsey and Steiner, 1975), and received only a subsistence wage. "The iron law of wages"—the philosophy that justified paying workers only enough money to keep them alive—prevailed during this early period of industrialization. Meanwhile, those who owned the means of production possessed great wealth, power, and prestige. Marx tried to understand the institutional framework that produced such conditions and looked for a means to change it in order to improve the human condition.

Marx stated that the entire history of human societies may be seen as the history of class conflict: the conflict between those who own and control the means of production and those who work for them—the exploiters and the exploited. He believed that ownership of the means of production in any society determines the distribution of wealth, power, and even ideas in that society. The power of the wealthy is derived not just from their control of the economy but from their control of the political, educational, and religious institutions as well. According to Marx, capitalists construct and enforce laws that serve their interests and act against the interests of workers. Their control over all institutions enables them to create ideologies that justify to the workers

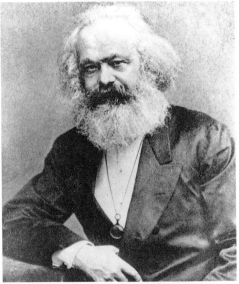

Karl Marx's views on class conflict were shaped by the Industrial Revolution. He believed that capitalist societies produce greater conflict because of the deep divisions between the social classes.

the worth of the existing system. These economic, political, and religious ideologies make the masses loyal to the very institutions that are the source of their exploitation and that also are the source of the wealth, power, and prestige of the ruling class. Thus, the prevailing ideologies of any society are those of its dominant group.

Marx predicted that capitalist society eventually would be polarized into two broad classes — the capitalists and the increasingly impoverished workers. Intellectuals like himself would show the workers that the capitalist institutions of production were the source of exploitation and poverty. Gradually, the workers would become unified and organized, and then through revolution they would take over control of the economy. The means of production would then be owned and controlled by the workers in a workers' socialist state. Once the capitalist elements of the society had been eliminated, the government would wither away. Pure communism would evolve — a society in which people may work according to their ability and take according to their need. For Marx the seeds of societal conflict and social change through revolution would come to an end once the means of production no longer were privately owned.

In many capitalist societies today regulatory mechanisms have been introduced to prevent some of the excesses of capitalism. Unions have been integrated into the capitalist economy and the political system, giving their members a legal, legitimate means through which they can benefit from the capitalist system. Contrary to Marx's predictions, most revolutions have not taken place in the industrialized Western nations but rather in agrarian nations — the Soviet Union, China, Cuba, and Vietnam, for example.

Marx's interests focused on the stresses and strains of society. His perspective thus is often called **conflict theory,** to which he is considered the major contributor. From his point of view, the social order of society is determined by the control exercised by a dominant group over subordinate groups through control of social institutions. The subordinate groups in a stable society tend to be socialized to conform to the prevailing ideologies of the ruling group. Marx's conflict theory is thought to be as applicable to communist nations as it is to capitalist nations. In communist nations, it is the Communist party that is the source of control over the economy and other institutions.

Herbert Spencer (1820–1903)

Herbert Spencer was a largely self-educated Briton who had a talent for synthesizing information. In 1860 he undertook the work of organizing all human knowledge into one system. The result was his *Principles of Sociology* (1876, 1882), the first sociology textbook. Unlike Comte, Spencer was precise in defining the subject matter of sociology. He stated that the field of sociology includes the study of the family, politics, religion, social control, work, and stratification.

Herbert Spencer helped to define the subject matter of sociology. Spencer also became a proponent of a doctrine known as social Darwinism.

Herbert Spencer believed society was analogous to a living organism. Just as the individual organs of the body are interdependent and ultimately must be understood in terms of their specialized contributions to the living whole, so, too, are the various component structures of society. Every part of society serves a specialized function necessary to ensure society's survival as an integrated entity.

Spencer also became a proponent of a doctrine known as **social Darwinism.** Darwin's notion of "survival of the fittest," those species of animals best adapted to the environment survived and prospered, while those poorly adapted died out, was applied to human adjustment to society. Spencer reasoned that people who could not successfully compete in the industrial society were poorly adapted to their environment and therefore inferior. Lack of success was viewed as an individual failing that was in no way related to barriers (such as racism) created by society.

Social Darwinism had a significant effect on those who believed in the inequality of the races. They now claimed that those who had difficulty succeeding in the white world were really members of inferior races. The fact that they lost out in the competition was proof of their poor adaptability to the environment. The survivors were clearly of superior stock (Berry and Tischler, 1978).

White society accepted social Darwinism because it served as a justification for their control over institutions. It enabled them to oppose reforms or social welfare programs, which they viewed as interfering with nature's plan to do away with the unfit. Social Darwinism thus became a justification for the repression and neglect of U.S. blacks following the Civil War. It also justified policies that had resulted in the decimation of North American Indian populations and the complete extinction of the native people of Tasmania (near Australia) by white settlers (Fredrickson, 1971).

Spencer's ties to social Darwinism have led many scholars to disregard his original contributions to the discipline of sociology. However, many of the standard concepts and terms still current in sociology today were formulated by Spencer first, and their use derives directly from his works.

Émile Durkheim (1858–1917)

A student of law, philosophy, and social science, Émile Durkheim was the first professor of sociology at the University of Bordeaux in France. Whereas Spencer wrote the first textbook of sociology, it was Durkheim who produced the first true sociological study. Durkheim's work moved sociology fully out of the realm of social philosophy and charted the discipline's course as a social science.

Durkheim believed that individuals are exclusively the product of their social environment, that society shapes people in every possible way. In order to prove his point, Durkheim decided to study suicide. He believed that if he could take what was

social Darwinism The attempt to apply the evolutionary theories of animal and plant development proposed by Charles Darwin to social phenomena.

Emile Durkheim produced the first true sociological study. Durkheim's work moved sociology fully out of the realm of social philosophy and charted the discipline's course as a social science.

perceived to be a totally personal act and show that it was patterned by social factors rather than exclusively by individual mental disturbances, he would be able to verify his view.

Durkheim began with a theory—that the industrialization of Western society was undermining the social control and support that communities had historically provided for individuals. Industrialization forced or induced individuals to leave rural communities for urban areas, where there were usually greater economic opportunities. The anonymity and impersonality of urban areas, however, caused many people to become isolated from both family and friends. In addition, in industrial societies people are frequently encouraged to aspire to goals that are often unclearly defined and difficult to attain. Durkheim suspected that this trend would affect the suicide rate and wanted to prove the importance of sociology by demonstrating how what was believed to be a totally personal act, suicide, was in fact a product of social forces. He thus refined his theory to state that suicide rates are influenced by the degree of solidarity or integration in society. He believed that low levels of solidarity—which involve more individual choice, more reliance on self, and less adherence to group standards —would mean high rates of suicide.

To test his idea Durkheim narrowed his focus and decided to study the suicide rates of Catholic versus Protestant countries. He assumed the suicide rate in Catholic countries would be lower than in Protestant countries because Protestantism emphasizes the individual's relationship to God over community ties. He then compared the suicide records in Catholic and Protestant countries, communities, and provinces in Europe to see if he was right. The results of these comparisons supported his theory by showing the probability of suicide to be higher in Protestant than in Catholic communities.

Recognizing that his results did not necessarily prove his theory, because the fact that Catholics had lower suicide rates

than Protestants could be caused by factors other than solidarity, Durkheim proceeded to test other groups. Reasoning that married people would be more integrated into a group than single people, people with children more than people without children, noncollege-educated people more than college-educated people (because college tends to break group ties and encourage individualism), and Jews more than non-Jews, Durkheim tested each of these groups, and in each case his theory held up.

Then, Durkheim extended his theory by identifying three types of suicide— *egoistic, altruistic,* and *anomic*—that take place under different types of conditions.

Egoistic suicide comes from low solidarity, an underinvolvement with others. Durkheim argued that loneliness and a commitment to personal beliefs rather than group values can lead to egoistic suicide. He found that single and divorced people had higher suicide rates than did married people and that Protestants, who tend to stress individualism, had higher rates of suicide than did Catholics.

Altruistic suicide derives from a very high level of solidarity, an overinvolvement with others. The individual and the moral order are so close that the person is willing to die for the sake of the community. This type of suicide, Durkheim noted, still exists in the military as well as in societies based on ancient codes of honor and obedience. Perhaps the best-known examples of altruistic suicide come from Japan: the ceremonial rite of *segguku,* in which a disgraced person rips open his own belly, and the *kamikaze* attacks by Japanese pilots at the end of World War II. Today we often see examples of altruistic suicide with terrorists. These individuals are willing to sacrifice their lives for their cause as they blow up a plane, restaurant, or military installation.

Anomic suicide results from a sense of disorientation and a lack of values experienced when people lose their social moorings. A person may know what goals to strive for but not have the means of attaining them, or a person may not know what

Émile Durkheim believed suicide rates were related to the degree of solidarity or cohesiveness in society. He studied suicide in order to show that something which is seen as a purely personal act is really patterned by social factors.

goals to pursue. Durkheim found that times of rapid social change or economic crisis are associated with high rates of anomic suicide.

Durkheim's study was noteworthy not only because it proved that the most personal of all acts, suicide, is in fact a product of social forces but also because it was one of the first examples of a scientifically conducted, sociological study. Durkheim systematically posed theories, tested them, and drew conclusions that led to further theories. He also published his results for everyone to see and criticize.

Durkheim's interests were not limited to suicide. His mind ranged over the entire spectrum of social activities. He published studies on *The Division of Labor in Society* (1893) and *The Elementary Forms of Religious Life* (1917). In both these works he drew on what was known about nonliterate societies, following the lead of Comte and Spencer in viewing them as evolutionary precursors of the contemporary industrial societies of Europe.

Because Durkheim was primarily interested in how society molds the individual, he focused on the forces that hold society together—that is, on the functions of various social structures. This point of view, often called the *functionalist theory* or *perspective,* remains today one of the dominant approaches to the study of society.

Max Weber (1864–1920)

Much of the work of Weber is an attempt to clarify, criticize, and modify the works of Marx. For that reason we shall discuss Weber's ideas as they relate to and contrast with those of Marx. Unlike Marx, who was not only an intellectual striving to understand society but also a revolutionary conspiring to overturn the capitalist social system, Weber was much more an academic attempting to understand human behavior than a revolutionary who sought change. Weber believed the role of the intellectual should be simply to describe and explain what is true, whereas Marx believed that the scholar also should tell people what they ought to do.

Marx believed that ownership of the means of production resulted in the control of wealth, power, and ideas in a society. Weber showed that economic control does not necessarily result in prestige and power. For example, the wealthy president of a chemical company whose toxic wastes have been responsible for the pollution of the local water supply might have very little prestige in the community. Moreover, the company's board of directors may well deprive the president of real power.

Although Marx maintained that the control of production inevitably results in the control of ideologies, Weber stated that the opposite may happen: ideologies sometimes influence the economic system. When Marx called religion "an opiate to the people," he was referring to the ability of those in control to create an ideology that would justify the exploitation of the masses. Weber, however, showed that religion could be a belief system that contributed to the

Much of the work of Max Weber was an attempt to clarify, criticize, and modify the works of Karl Marx. He also showed how religion contributed to the creation of new economic conditions and institutions.

creation of new economic conditions and institutions. In *The Protestant Ethic and the Spirit of Capitalism* (1904–1905), Weber tried to demonstrate how the Protestant Reformation of the seventeenth century provided an ideology that gave religious justification to the pursuit of economic success through rational, disciplined, hard work. This ideology, called the Protestant Ethic, ultimately helped transform northern European societies from feudal agricultural to industrial capitalist.

On the other hand, Weber also predicted that science—the systematic, rational description, explanation, and manipulation of the observable world—would lead to a gradual demythologizing and disenchantment of the population and hence to a gradual turning away from religion. The apparent decline in the influence of organized religion in the highly industrialized societies seems to support Weber's prediction. (We shall look at this question more deeply in Chapter 13.)

Weber also was interested in understanding the development of bureaucracy as the means by which people and material resources could be organized for the pursuit of specific goals. Whereas Marx saw capitalism as the source of control, exploitation, and alienation of human beings and believed that socialism and communism would ultimately bring an end to this exploitation, Weber believed that bureaucracy would characterize both socialist and capitalist societies. He anticipated and feared the domination of individuals by large bureaucratic structures. As he foresaw, our modern industrial world, both capitalist and socialist, is now ruled by bureaucracies —economic, political, military, educational, and religious. Given the existing situation, it is easy to appreciate Weber's anxiety. As he put it,

> . . . each man becomes a little cog in the machine and, aware of this, his one preoccupation is whether he can become a bigger cog. . . . The problem which besets us now is not: how can this evolution be changed?—for that is impossible, but what will become of it. (Quoted in Coser, 1977)

Max Weber was interested in understanding the means by which people and material resources could be organized for the pursuit of specific goals. Advances in space travel could not take place without bureaucracies.

THE DEVELOPMENT OF SOCIOLOGY IN THE UNITED STATES

Sociology has its roots in Europe and did not really become recognized in the United States until the twentieth century. The early growth of American sociology took place at the University of Chicago. That setting provided a context in which a large number of scholars and their students could work closely together to refine their views of the discipline. It was there that the first graduate department of sociology in America was founded in the 1890s. From the 1920s to the 1940s the so-called Chicago school of sociologists led American sociology in the study of communities, with particular emphasis on urban neighborhoods and ethnic areas. Many of America's leading sociologists from this period were members of the Chicago school, including Robert E. Park, W. I. Thomas, and Ernest W. Burgess. Most of these men were Protestant ministers or sons of ministers, and as a group they were deeply concerned with social reform.

Perhaps the single most influential American sociologist was Talcott Parsons (1902–1979). He presided over the Department of Social Relations at Harvard University from the 1930s until he retired in 1973. Parsons's early research was quite empirical, but he later turned to the philosophical and theoretical side of sociology. In *The Structure of Social Action* (1937) Parsons presented English translations of the writings of European thinkers, most notably Weber and Durkheim. In his best-known work, *The Social System* (1951), Parsons portrayed society as a stable system of well-ordered, interrelated parts. His viewpoint elaborated on Durkheim's functionalist perspective.

Contemporary sociologist Robert K. Merton also has been an influential proponent of functionalist theory. He is concerned with understanding the structures and functions of social systems, whatever their forms. In his classic work, *Social*

Talcott Parsons portrayed society as a stable system of well-ordered, interrelated parts.

Theory and Social Structure (1968), first published in 1949, Merton spelled out the functionalist view of society. One of his main contributions to sociology was to distinguish between two forms of social functions—manifest functions and latent functions. By **social functions** Merton meant those social processes that contribute to the ongoing operation or maintenance of society. **Manifest functions** are the intended and recognized consequences of those processes. For example, one of the manifest functions of going to college is to obtain knowledge, training, and a degree in a specific area. **Latent functions** are the unintended or not readily recognized consequences of such processes. Therefore, college may also offer the opportunity of making lasting friendships and finding potential marriage partners.

Under the leadership of Parsons and Merton, sociology in America moved away from a concern with social reform and adopted a so-called value-free perspective.

social function A social process that contributes to the ongoing operation or maintenance of society.

manifest function One of two types of social functions identified by Robert Merton referring to an *intended* and recognized consequence of a social process.

latent function One of two types of social functions identified by Robert Merton referring to the *unintended* or not readily recognized consequences of a social process.

This perspective, which was advocated by Max Weber, requires description and explanation rather than prescription: people should be told what is, not what should be. As critics of Parsons and Merton point out, however, interpretations of what exists may differ depending on the perspective from which reality is viewed and on the values of the viewer (Gouldner, 1970; Lee, 1978; Mills, 1959).

THEORETICAL PERSPECTIVES

Scientists need a set of working assumptions to guide them in their work. These assumptions suggest which problems are worth investigating and offer a framework for interpreting the results of studies. Such sets of assumptions are known as **paradigms.** They are models for explaining events that provide frameworks for the questions that generate and guide research. Of course, not all paradigms are equally valid, even though at first they may seem to be. Sooner or later, some will be found to be rooted in fact, whereas others will remain abstract and unusable, finally to be discarded. We shall examine those paradigms that have withstood the scrutiny of major sociologists.

FUNCTIONALISM

Functionalism, or **structural functionalism,** as it is often called, is rooted in the writings of Spencer and Durkheim and the work of such scholars as Parsons and Merton. Functionalists view society as a system of highly interrelated structures, or parts, that function or operate together rather harmoniously. Functionalists analyze society by asking what each different part of society contributes to the smooth functioning of the whole. For example, we may assume the education system serves to teach students specific subject matter. However, functionalists might also note that it acts as a system for the socialization of the young and as a means for producing conformity. The education system acts as a gatekeeper to the rewards society offers to those who follow the rules.

From the functionalist perspective, society appears quite stable and self-regulating. Much like a biological organism, society is normally in a state of equilibrium or balance. Most of a society's members share a value system and know what to expect from one another.

The best-known proponent of the structural-functionalist perspective was Talcott Parsons. He, more than anyone else, helped develop this viewpoint in sociology. His theory centered on the view that there were interrelated social systems consisting of the major areas of social life, such as the family, religion, education, politics, and economics. These systems were then analyzed according to the functions they performed for society as a whole and for one another.

Functionalism is a very broad theory in that it attempts to account for the complicated interrelationships of all the elements that make up human societies, including the complex societies of the industrialized (and industrializing) world. In a way it is impossible to be a sociologist and not be a functionalist, because most parts of society do serve some stated or unstated purpose. Functionalism is limited in one regard, however: the preconception that societies normally are in balance or harmony makes it difficult for proponents of this view to account for how social changes come about.

A major criticism of functionalist theory is that it has a very conservative bias. That is, if all the parts of society fit together smoothly, we can assume that the social system is working well. Conflict is then seen as something that disrupts the essential orderliness of the social structure and produces disequilibrium between the parts and the whole.

paradigm A basic model for explaining events that provides a framework for the questions that generate and guide research.

functionalism (structural functionalism) One of the major sociological perspectives which assumes that society is a system of highly interrelated parts that operate (function) together rather harmoniously.

CONFLICT THEORY

Conflict theory is rooted in the work of Marx and other social critics of the nineteenth century. This approach sees society as constantly changing in response to social inequality and social conflict. For the conflict theorists, social change pushed forward by social conflict is the normal state of affairs. Static periods are merely temporary way stations along the road.

Marx and his contemporaries saw the main source of conflict as the struggle among social classes for access to, and control over, the means of production and the distribution of resources. Conflict theorists believe social order results from dominant groups making sure that subordinate groups are loyal to the institutions that are the dominant groups' sources of wealth, power, and prestige. The dominant groups will use coercion, constraint, and even force to help control those people who are not voluntarily loyal to the laws and rules they have made. When this order cannot be maintained and the subordinate groups rebel, change comes about.

Conflict theorists are concerned with the issue of who benefits from particular social arrangements and how those in power maintain their positions and continue to reap benefits from them. In this sense Randall Collins (1975) sees the conflict perspective as an attempt to study how those in power maintain and enlarge their sphere of influence over many aspects of the social structure, including values and beliefs. The ruling class is seen as a group that spreads certain values, beliefs, and social arrangements in order to enhance its power and wealth. The social order, then, reflects the outcome of a struggle among those with unequal power and resources.

Proponents of conflict theory are often criticized for concentrating too much on conflict and change and too little on what produces stability in society. They are also criticized for being too ideologically biased and making little use of research methods or objective statistical evidence. The conflict theorists counter that the complexities of modern social life cannot be reduced to statistical analysis, that doing so has caused many sociologists to become detached from their object of study and removed from the real causes of human problems.

Both functionalist and conflict theories are descriptive and predictive of social life. Each has its strengths and weaknesses, and each emphasizes an important aspect of society and social life. Table 1.1 compares the approaches of functionalist and conflict theory.

THE INTERACTIONIST PERSPECTIVE

Functionalism and conflict theory can be thought of as the opposite sides of the same coin. Although quite different from each other, they share certain similarities. Both approaches focus on major structural features of entire societies and attempt to give us an understanding of how societies survive and change. Social life, however, occurs on an intimate scale between individuals. The interactionist perspective focuses on how individuals make sense of— or interpret—the social world they are part of. As such, this approach is primarily concerned with human behavior on a person-to-person level. Interactionists criticize functionalists and conflict theorists for implicitly assuming that social processes and social institutions somehow have a life of their own apart from the participants. Interactionists remind us that the educational system, the family, the political system, and indeed all of society's institutions are ultimately created, maintained, and changed by people interacting with one another. Understanding the nature of this day-to-day interaction is of vital importance.

The interactionist perspective includes several loosely linked approaches. George Herbert Mead devised a *symbolic interactionist* approach that focuses on signs, gestures, shared rules, and written and spoken language. Harold Garfinkel used *ethno-*

conflict theory This label applies to any of a number of theories which assume that society is in a constant state of social conflict, with only temporarily stable periods, and that social phenomena are the result of this conflict.

TABLE 1.1
Comparison of Functionalist and Conflict Theory

Functionalist Theory	Conflict Theory
1. The various parts of society are interdependent and functionally related.	1. Society is a system of accommodations among competing interest groups.
2. Each part of the social system contributes positively to the continued operation of the system.	2. The social system may at any time become unbalanced because of shifts in power.
3. The various parts of the social system fit together harmoniously.	3. The various parts of the social system do not fit together harmoniously.
4. Social systems are highly stable.	4. Social systems are unstable and are likely to change rapidly.
5. Social life is governed by consensus and cooperation.	5. Social life involves conflict because of differing goals.
6. Functionalist sociologists are concerned with the role each part of society contributes to the smooth functioning of the whole.	6. Conflict sociologists are concerned with who benefits from particular social arrangements.
7. Social order is achieved through cooperation.	7. Social order is achieved through coercion and even force.

methodology to show how people create and share their understanding of social life. Erving Goffman took a *dramaturgical* approach in which he saw social life as a form of theater. Of these three, the symbolic interactionist approach has received the widest attention and presents us with a well-formulated theory.

Symbolic Interactionism

symbolic interactionism
A theoretical approach that stresses the meanings people place on their own and one another's behavior.

Symbolic Interactionism as developed by George Herbert Mead (1863–1931) is concerned with the meanings that people place on their own and one another's behavior. Human beings are unique in that most of what they do with one another has meaning beyond the concrete act. According to Mead, people do not act or react automatically but carefully consider and even rehearse what they are going to do. They take into account the other people involved and the situation in which they find themselves.

The expectations and reactions of other people greatly affect each individual's actions. In addition, people give things meaning and act or react on the basis of these meanings. For example, when the flag of the United States is raised, people stand because they see the flag as representing their country.

Because most human activity takes place in social situations—in the presence of other people—we must fit what we as individuals do with what other people in the same situation are doing. We go about our lives with the assumption that most people share our definitions of basic social situations. This agreement on definitions and meanings is the key to human interactions in general, according to symbolic interactionists. For example, a staff nurse in a mental hospital unlocking a door for an inpatient is doing more than simply enabling the patient to pass from one ward to another. He or she also is communicating a

Interactionists recognize that there are symbolic meanings attached to many social events.

position of social dominance over the patient (within the hospital) and is carrying a powerful symbol of that dominance — the key. The same holds true for a professor writing on a blackboard or a company vice-president dictating to a secretary. Such interactions, therefore, although they appear to be simple social actions, also are laden with highly symbolic social meanings. These symbolic meanings are intimately connected with our understanding of what it is to be and to behave as a human being. This includes our sense of self; how we experience others and their views of us; the joys and pains we feel at home, at school, at work, and among friends and colleagues; and so on.

Ethnomethodology

Many of the social actions we engage in on a day-to-day basis are quite commonplace events. They tend to be taken for granted

In order to create an impression, people play roles, and their performance is judged by others who are alert to any slips that might reveal the actors' true character.

TAKING THE SOCIOLOGICAL PERSPECTIVE

IF YOU ARE THINKING ABOUT SOCIOLOGY AS A CAREER, READ THIS

Speaking from this side of the career-decision hurdle, I can say that being a sociologist has opened many doors for me. It gave me the credentials to teach at the college level and to become an author of a widely used sociology text. It also enabled me to be a newspaper columnist and a talk-show host. Would I recommend this field to anyone else? I would, but not blindly. Realize before you begin that sociology can be an extremely demanding discipline and, at times, an extremely frustrating one.

As in many other fields, the competition for jobs in sociology can be fierce. If you really want this work, do not let the herd stop you. Anyone with motivation, talent, and a determined approach to finding the job will do well. But be prepared for the long haul: To get ahead in many areas you will need to spend more than 4 years in college. Consider your bachelor's degree as just the beginning. Fields like teaching at the college level and advanced research often *require* a Ph.D., which means at least 4 to 6 years of school beyond the B.A.

Now for the job possibilities. As you read through these careers, remember that right now your exposure to sociology is limited (you are only on Chapter 1 in your first college sociology text), so do not eliminate any possibilities right at the start. Spend some time thinking about each one as the semester progresses and you learn more about this fascinating discipline.

Most people who go into sociology become teachers. You will need a Ph.D. to teach in college, but you can get away with less if you teach on the high-school level. With the number of college-age students declining, teaching positions currently are scarce, despite the popularity of sociology courses. However, the college-age population is expected to rise in the 1990s, which would open more opportunities for teaching in college.

Second in popularity to teaching are nonacademic research jobs in government agencies, private research institutions, and the research departments of private corporations. Researchers carry on many different functions, including conducting market research, public opinion surveys, and impact assessments. Evaluation research, as the latter field is known, has become more popular in recent years as the federal government has passed laws requiring environmental impact studies on all large-scale federal projects. For example, before a new interstate highway is built, evaluation researchers attempt to determine the effect the highway will have on communities along the proposed route.

---

ethnomethodology The study of the sets of rules or guidelines people use in their everyday living practices. This approach provides information about a society's unwritten rules for social behavior.

and rarely are examined or considered. Harold Garfinkel (1967) has proposed that it is important to study the commonplace. Those things we take for granted have a tremendous hold over us because we accept their demands without question or conscious consideration. **Ethnomethodology** seeks to discover and describe the sets of rules or guidelines that individuals use to initiate behavior, respond to behavior, and modify behavior in social settings. For ethnomethodologists, all social interactions are equally important because they all provide information about a society's unwritten rules for social behavior, the shared knowledge of which is basic to social life.

Garfinkel asked his students to participate in experiments in which the researcher would violate some of the basic understandings among people. For example, when a conversation is held between two people, each assumes that certain things are perfectly clear and obvious and do not need further elaboration. Examine the following

This is only one of many opportunities available in government work. Sociologists are also hired by federal, state, and local governments in policymaking and administrative functions. For example, a sociologist employed by a community hospital provides needed data on the population groups being served and on the health-care needs of the community. Another example: sociologists working in a prison system can devise plans to deal with the social problems that are inevitable when people are put behind bars. Here are a few additional opportunities in government work: community planner, correction officer, environmental analyst, equal opportunity specialist, probation officer, rehabilitation counselor, resident director, and social worker.

A growing number of opportunities also exist in corporate America, including market researchers, pollsters, human resource managers, affirmative action coordinators, employee assistance program counselors, labor relations specialists, and public information officers, just to name a few. These jobs are available in nearly every field from advertising to banking, from insurance to publishing. Although your corporate title will not be "sociologist," your educational background will give you the tools you need to do the job — and do it well, which, to corporations, is the bottom line.

Whether you choose government or corporate work, you will have the best chance of finding the job you want by specializing in a particular field of sociology while you are still in school. You can become an urban or family specialist or knowledgeable in organizational behavior before you enter the job market. For example, many demographers, who compile and analyze population data, have specialized in this aspect of sociology. Similarly, human ecologists, who investigate the structure and organization of a community in relation to its environment, have specialized educational backgrounds as well. Keep in mind that many positions require a minor or some course work in other fields such as political science, psychology, ecology, law, or business. By combining sociology with these fields, you will be well prepared for the job market.

What next? Be optimistic and start planning. As the American Sociological Association observed, few fields are as relevant to today and as broadly based as sociology. Yet, ironically, its career potential is just beginning to be tapped. Start planning by reading the *Occupational Outlook Quarterly,* published by the U.S. Bureau of Labor Statistics, as well as academic journals to keep abreast of career trends. Then study hard and choose your specialty. With this preparation, when the time comes to find a job, you will be well prepared.

conversation and notice what happens when one individual violates some of these expectations:

BOB: That was a very interesting sociology class we had yesterday.

JOHN: How was it interesting?

BOB: Well, we had a lively discussion about deviant behavior, and everyone seemed to get involved.

JOHN: I'm not certain I know what you mean. How was the discussion lively? How were people involved?

BOB: You know, they really participated and seemed to get caught up in the discussion.

JOHN: Yes, you said that before, but I want to know what you mean by lively and interesting.

BOB: What's wrong with you? You know what I mean. The class was interesting. I'll see you later.

Bob's response is quite revealing. He is puzzled and does not know whether or not John is being serious. The normal expectations and understandings around which day-to-day forms of expression take place have been challenged. Still, is it not reasonable to ask for further elaboration of certain statements? Obviously not when it goes beyond a certain point.

Another example of the confusion brought on by the violation of basic understandings was shown when Garfinkel asked his students to act like boarders in their own homes. They were to ask whether they could use the phone, take a drink of water, have a snack, and so on. The results were quite dramatic:

> Family members were stupefied. They vigorously sought to make the strange actions intelligible and to restore the situation to normal appearances. Reports were filled with accounts of astonishment, shock, anxiety, embarrassment, and anger and with charges by various family members that the student was mean, inconsiderate, selfish, nasty, or impolite. Family members demanded explanations: What's the matter? What's gotten into you? Did you get fired? Are you sick? What are you being so superior about? Why are you mad? Are you out of your mind or are you stupid? One student acutely embarrassed his mother in front of her friends by asking if she minded if he had a snack from the refrigerator. "Mind if you have a little snack? You've been eating little snacks around here for years without asking me. What's gotten into you?" (Garfinkel, 1972)

Ethnomethodology seeks to make us more aware of the subtle devices we use in creating the realities to which we respond. These realities are often more inside than outside us. Ethnomethodology addresses questions about the nature of social reality and how we participate in its construction.

Dramaturgy

People create impressions, and others respond with their own impressions. Erving Goffman (1959, 1963, 1971) concluded that a central feature of human interaction

is impression formation—the attempt to present oneself to others in a particular way. Goffman believed that much human interaction can be studied and analyzed on the basis of principles derived from the theater. This approach, known as **dramaturgy,** is based on the assumption that in order to create an impression, people play roles, and their performance is judged by others who are alert to any slips that might reveal the actors' true character. For example, a job applicant at an interview tries to appear composed, self-confident, and capable of handling the position's responsibilities. The interviewer is seeking to find out whether the applicant is really able to work under pressure and perform the necessary functions of the job.

Most interactions require some type of playacting to present an image that will bring about the desired behavior from others. Dramaturgy sees these interactions as governed by planned behavior designed to enable an individual to present a particular image to others.

The interactionist perspective and its various offshoots have been criticized for paying too little attention to the larger elements of society. Interactionists respond that societies and institutions are made up of individuals who interact with one another and do not exist apart from these basic units. They believe that an understanding of the process of social interaction will lead to an understanding of larger social structures. In fact, interactionists still have to bridge the gap between their studies of social interaction and those of the broader social structures. Nevertheless, symbolic interactionism does complement functionalism and conflict theory in important ways and gives us profound insights into how people interact.

CONTEMPORARY SOCIOLOGY

Contemporary sociological theory continues to build on the original ideas proposed in the interactionist perspective, functionalism, and conflict theory. It would be difficult to call contemporary sociological theory either conflict theory or functionalism in the original sense. Much of it has been modified to include important aspects of each. Even symbolic interactionism has not been wholeheartedly embraced, and aspects of it have instead been absorbed into general sociological writing.

Very little contemporary sociological theory can still be identified as functionalism, partly because sociologists today have abandoned trying to develop all-inclusive theories and instead have opted for what Merton (1968) referred to as **middle-range theories.** These theories are concerned with explaining specific issues or aspects of society instead of trying to explain how all of society operates. A middle-range theory might be one that explains why divorce rates rise and fall with certain economic conditions, or how crime rates are related to residential patterns.

Modern conflict theory was initially refined by such sociologists as C. Wright Mills (1959), Ralf Dahrendorf (1958), Randall Collins (1975, 1979), and Lewis Coser (1956) to reflect the realities of contemporary society. Mills and Dahrendorf did not see conflict as confined to class struggle. Rather, they viewed it as applicable to the inevitable tensions that arise between groups: parents and children, suppliers and producers, producers and consumers, professional specialists and their clients, environmentalists and industrialists, unions and employers, the poor and the materially comfortable, and minority and majority ethnic groups (and among minority groups as well). Members of these groups have both overlapping and competing interests, and their shared needs keep all parties locked together within one society. At the same time the groups actively pursue their own ends, thus constantly pushing the society to change in order to accommodate them.

Lewis Coser incorporated aspects of both functionalism and conflict theory, seeing conflict as an inevitable element of all societies and as both functional and dysfunctional for society. Conflict between two groups tends to increase their internal cohesion. For example, competition between two divisions of two computer companies to be the first to produce a new product may draw the members closer to each other as they strive to reach the desired goal. This feeling might not have occurred had it not been for the sense of competition, as the conflict itself becomes a form of social interaction. Conflict could also lead to cohesion by causing two or more groups to form alliances against a common enemy. For example, a political contest may cause several groups to unite to defeat a common opponent.

middle-range theories
Theories concerned with explaining specific issues or aspects of society instead of trying to explain how all of society operates.

Sociology helps us to understand the highly complex world in which we live.

Should Sociology Aim to Improve Society?

Shortly after the French Revolution when Auguste Comte was writing, he dreamed of a harmonious society run by social scientists according to principles evolved from a science of society. This science he named *sociology.* The social scientists would solve social problems and determine the proper balance between the interests of the many competing groups. Comte believed the people would accept the judgment of the social scientists as authoritative in much the same way as the teachings of the Church were accepted in the Middle Ages. The end result would be peace, prosperity, and solidarity.

Over 150 years have passed since Comte's utopian vision. Will Comte's dream of a scientifically managed society come true? It hardly seems likely. How much does sociology have to contribute to make society a better place to live in? For that matter, should sociology, in fact, attempt to improve society? Whose vision of that perfect society should we adopt? Sociologist Jack D. Douglas and writer Richard P. Appelbaum have conflicting opinions on this question.

Douglas challenges the notion that the goal of sociology is simply to understand society. He believes that the rapid increase in the complexity of American society and the rate of social change have meant that most people are ignorant of what is going on in those segments of society beyond their own immediate experience. The insight of the sociologist is essential. Casual observation by the outsider will not reveal the truth of events in urban ghettos or in corporate boardrooms. Policy makers are bound to be ever more dependent on the objective and specialized knowledge of the social scientists. Sociologists must provide policy makers with reliable predictions based on information about social trends. In fact, sociologists have an obligation, Douglas believes, to not leave the field of policy advising to self-appointed specialists whose ignorance of the complexity of the problems leads them to promise certain superficial solutions.

Richard Appelbaum disagrees with this view and believes there has been a mystification of expert scientific knowledge that is not justified. He notes that there is

During the last twenty-five years conflict theory has been influenced by a generation of neo-Marxists. These people have helped produce a more complex and sophisticated version of conflict theory that goes beyond the original emphasis on class conflict and instead shows that conflict exists within almost every aspect of society (Gouldner, 1970, 1980; Skocpol, 1979; Starr, 1982; Tilly, 1978, 1981; Wallerstein, 1974, 1979, 1980).

THEORY AND PRACTICE

It is sociological theory that gives meaning to sociological practice. The mere assembling of countless descriptions of social facts may keep bookbinders busy, but it has no scientific value, just as personal experiences are inadequate for an understanding of society as a whole. If we rely only on our own experiences, we are like the blind men of Hindu legend trying to describe an elephant: the first man, feeling its trunk, asserted, "It is like a snake"; the second, trying to reach around the beast's massive leg argued, "No, it is like a tree"; and the third, feeling its powerful side, disagreed, saying, "It is more like a wall." In a small way, each man was right, but not one of them was able to understand or describe what the whole elephant was like. So, too, with sociology. Only when data are collected within the

a marked lack of theories in the social sciences generally, and particularly as they are employed for the purposes of social planning. In the physical sciences the researcher knows what to look for and how to measure it. This situation is not true in sociology. In the absence of adequate theories, we must pick and choose the important explanatory variables. This is often done according to subjective criteria determined by the political or other predispositions of the sociologist. The resulting solutions may or may not reflect the way things really are. Important factors may be omitted or not considered important. Yet this uncertainty does not deter the sociologist from confidently putting all the facts into the hopper, processing them, and presenting

the results as scientifically correct.

Given the underdeveloped state of sociology, Appelbaum believes that any attempt to provide information to policy makers should acknowledge that condition and proceed accordingly. This means that sociologists should make it clear that their information represents an informed, but by no means accurate, guess about the situation. Any other guess is almost as good as that of the sociologist. Appelbaum believes the role of the expert needs to be deprofessionalized, and ordinary people must be given the confidence and skills required to understand the forces that mold their lives.

In Appelbaum's view, the sociologist is another expert who serves influential groups by turning

political issues into technical problems and removing them from public debate. He sees the only role for the sociologist as one in which he or she informs the citizenry in order to aid the democratic process. Instead of solving social problems, the sociologist should merely provide people with information they need in their quest for a democratic and just society.

Sources: Jack D. Douglas, *The Relevance of Sociology* (New York: Appleton-Century Crofts, 1970). Richard P. Appelbaum, "The Future is Made, Not Predicted: Technocratic Planners versus Public Interests," *Society,* May/June 1977.

conceptual framework of a theory—in order to answer the specific questions growing out of that theory—is it possible to draw conclusions and make valid generalizations. This is the ultimate purpose of all science.

Theory without practice (research to

test it) is at best poor philosophy, not science, and practice uninformed by theory is at best trivial and at worst a tremendous waste of time and resources. Therefore, in the next chapter we shall move from theory to practice—to the methods and techniques of social research.

SUMMARY

Each of us has a personal perspective that we use to interpret the world around us. Even though it may serve us quite well in

our day-to-day lives, it does not provide us with enough information to develop an accurate understanding of the broader social picture. The focus of sociology is the group and not the individual. The sociologist tries to understand the forces that operate throughout society: forces that mold individuals, shape their behavior, and thus determine social events. To do this, the sociologist must depend on a more scientific form of observation than just individual experience. To achieve their goals, sociologists rely on the sociological imagination, a term C. Wright Mills used to refer to the different levels on which social events can be perceived and interpreted.

Commonsense ideas often interfere with the study of sociology. We tend to believe what we want to believe, to see what we want to see, and to accept as fact whatever appears to be logical. Sociologists strive to gather and analyze facts in an objective fashion.

Sociology is one of the social sciences, which encompass all those disciplines that apply scientific methods to the study of human behavior. Although there is some overlap in goals and procedures, each of the social sciences has its own areas of concern. Cultural anthropology, psychology, economics, history, political science, and social work all have some things in common with sociology, but each has its own distinct focus, objectives, theories, and methods.

The science of sociology began to emerge during the nineteenth century—a time of dramatic social change. In an effort to understand the effects of the Industrial Revolution on the fabric of society and on the life-style of individuals, scholars such as Henri Saint-Simon and Auguste Comte turned to the methods of the natural sciences to discover the underlying principles of society.

Karl Marx, Herbert Spencer, Émile Durkheim, and Max Weber were all instrumental in shaping the development of sociology.

Marx believed that the entire history of human societies could be viewed as a history of class struggle—the conflict between those who own and control the means of production and those who work for them. He believed not only in investigating social problems but also in working to change the social system.

Spencer was the first to define the subject matter of sociology. Although he has been criticized for his adherence to social Darwinism, his original contributions to the discipline still form the basis for many of today's standard concepts.

Durkheim, believing individuals are exclusively the product of their social environment, set out to prove his point through the study of suicide. He identified three major types of suicide: altruistic, egoistic, and anomic. All types, he stated, were a result of some type of social influence.

Weber was interested in understanding rather than changing human behavior and interaction. He challenged Marx on many of his ideas and proposed that ideologies could influence groups and that power over the means of production did not automatically lead to power in other areas.

It was in the twentieth-century United States that the goals and methods of sociology were refined uner the leadership of the Chicago school and such other distinguished sociologists as Talcott Parsons and Robert Merton.

Scientists need a set of working assumptions to guide them in their work. Such sets of assumptions are known as paradigms. Sociologists have developed several paradigms to help them view social events. Functionalism sees society as a system of highly interrelated structures that work together harmoniously. Conflict theory regards society as being pushed forward by the struggle between classes for control over the means of production and distribution of resources. Modern conflict theorists such as C. Wright Mills and Ralf Dahrendorf do not see conflict as confined to class struggle. Rather, they view it as applicable to the inevitable tensions that arise in families, businesses, racial groups, and a variety of other settings. Symbolic interactionism is concerned with the meanings people place on their own and one another's behavior. This perspective looks beyond the concrete act itself to the symbolic meanings of the act. Ethnomethodology tries to discover and describe unwritten rules that guide the behavior of individuals and groups in society, and dramaturgy looks at the roles people play in order to create a desired impression among others.

Chapter 2

DOING SOCIOLOGY:

RESEARCH METHODS

THE RESEARCH PROCESS

Define the Problem
Review Previous Research
Develop One or More Hypotheses
Determine the Research Design
Define the Sample and Collect Data
Analyze the Data and Draw Conclusions
Prepare the Research Report

OBJECTIVITY AND ETHICS IN SOCIOLOGICAL RESEARCH

Objectivity
Ethical Issues
Research Fraud

SUMMARY

AIDS (Acquired Immune Deficiency Syndrome) has become one of the most frightening diseases of the last decade. Little wonder, then, that when respected sex therapists William H. Masters and Virginia E. Johnson and colleague Robert C. Kolodny announced the results of their study on the transmission of AIDS to the heterosexual community, many people took notice.

The conclusions were startling. Masters and Johnson contended that the AIDS virus was "running rampant" among heterosexuals in the United States. In their view the AIDS virus was well established among the ranks of heterosexuals and the spread of the disease would escalate at an alarming pace (*Newsweek,* March 14, 1988).

AIDS experts responded with outrage. U.S. Surgeon General C. Everett Koop called the work "irresponsible." An epidemiologist noted, "This is the AIDS equivalent of shouting 'Fire!' in a crowded theater" (*Time,* March 21, 1988).

Why were the experts so upset? In large part, the intensity of the reaction was brought about because of improper research procedures. Masters and Johnson used a sample of 400 men and 400 women who volunteered for the study after responding to notices in churches, childbirth classes, colleges, and singles meeting places.

The first problem here is that they allowed the subjects to decide if they wanted to be part of this study, without attempting to get a cross section of the population.

Next, there was no attempt to verify the truthfulness of the information they obtained from the subjects. Researchers need to know if their subjects are being honest, particularly when dealing with personal information.

They also went overboard with such claims as it is theoretically possible to contract AIDS through the bite of a mosquito, kissing, and toilet seats and that 3 million Americans are infected with the virus. This kind of false information is dangerous because it could produce unfounded fears in people who read the study.

Finally, the authors did not submit their work for scientific review by their peers before they published their book. Many saw this as an admission that their methods were flawed. It is only through the careful review of research methods and results by panels of experts that findings achieve validity in the scientific community.

What called into question the validity of the Masters and Johnson study, and many other studies that we hear about, is the failure to conduct research properly—to devise a research study that adheres to strict standards and to follow these standards precisely.

As you will see in this chapter, the research process involves a number of specific steps that must be followed to produce a valid study. Only when this is done faithfully can we have any confidence in the results of the study. In this chapter we shall examine some of the methods used by scientists in general—and sociologists in particular—to collect data to test their ideas.

research process A sequence of steps in the design and implementation of a research study, including defining the problem, reviewing previous research, determining the research design, defining the sample, and collecting data, analyzing and interpreting the data, and preparing the final research report.

THE RESEARCH PROCESS

How, then, should you conduct a research study? After reading Chapter 1, you would know that you should not approach a study and draw conclusions on the basis of your personal experience and perceptions; rather, you should approach the study scientifically.

To approach a study scientifically you should keep in mind that science has two main goals: (1) to describe in detail particular things or events and (2) to propose and test general principles by which these things or events can be understood.

There is a great deal of similarity between what a detective does in attempting to solve a crime and what a sociologist does in answering a research problem. In the course of their work, both detectives and sociologists must gather and analyze information. For detectives, the object is to identify and locate criminals and to collect enough evidence to ensure that their identification is correct. Sociologists, on the other hand, develop hypotheses, collect data, and develop theories to help them understand social behavior. Although their specific goals differ, both sociologists and detectives try to answer two general questions: "Why did it happen?" and "Under what circumstances is it likely to happen again?"—that is, to explain and predict.

All research problems require their own special emphasis and approach. Every research problem is unique in some ways, so the research procedure is usually custom-tailored. Nonetheless, there is a sequence of steps called the **research process** that is followed when designing a research project. The sequence of steps in this process and the typical questions asked at each step are illustrated in Table 2.1. If there are any terms in this table that you are not familiar with, do not become concerned. We will define them as we move through the various steps.

We begin the research process by defining the problem, then we review previous research on the topic, develop one or more hypotheses, determine the research design, define the sample and collect data, analyze and interpret the data, and finally prepare our research report. We will now examine each of these steps.

---- **TABLE 2.1**
The Research Process

Steps in the Process	Typical Questions
Define the problem	What is the purpose of the study? What information is needed? How can we operationalize the terms? How will the information be used?
Review previous research	What studies have already been done on this topic? Is additional information necessary before we begin? From what perspective should this issue be approached?
Develop one or more hypotheses	What are the independent and dependent variables? What is the relationship among the variables? What types of questions need to be answered?
Determine the research design	Can existing data be used? What is to be measured or observed? What research methods should be used?
Define the sample and collect data	Is there a specific population we are interested in? How large should the sample be? Who will gather the data? How long will it take?
Analyze the data and draw conclusions	What statistical techniques will be used? Have our hypotheses been proven or disproven? Is our information valid and reliable? What are the implications of our study?
Prepare the research report	Who will read the report? What is their level of familiarity with the subject? How should the report be structured?

DEFINE THE PROBLEM

"Love leads to marriage." Suppose you were given this statement as a subject for sociological research. How would you proceed to gather data to prove or disprove it? To investigate whether or not it is true, you must begin by defining "love." This in itself

would pose a serious problem, because to this day people are still grappling with the question "How do you know when you are in love?"

To be sure, you could define love as an intense emotional state in which positive feelings for another person are present. You would then have to find some way of deter-

Although their specific goals differ, both sociologists and detectives try to answer two general questions: "Why did it happen?" and "Under what circumstances is it likely to happen again?"—that is, to explain and predict.

empirical question A question that can be answered by observation and analysis of the world as it is known.

operational definition A definition of an abstract concept in terms of the observable features that describe the things being investigated.

mining whether this condition exists. You must also decide whether both people have to be in love for marriage to take place. (You may already have noticed that in this case it may be difficult to achieve the level of precision necessary for a useful research project.) Once you accurately define your terms and provide details to clarify your descriptions, you can begin to test the statement we proposed.

Even after arriving at a careful definition of your terms and a detailed description of love, your may still have trouble answering the question empirically. An **empirical question** can be answered by observing and analyzing the world as it is known. Examples: How many students in this class have an A average? How many millionaires are there in the United States? Scientists pose empirical questions in order to collect information, to add to what is already known, and to test hypotheses. To turn the statement about love into an empirical question, you must ask: How do we measure the existence of love?

In trying to define and measure love, one researcher (Rubin, 1970) used an interesting approach. He prepared a large number of self-descriptive statements that re-

flected various aspects of love relationships as mentioned by writers, philosophers, and social scientists. After administering these statements to a variety of subjects, he was able to isolate nine items that best reflected feelings of love for another. Three of these items are shown in the next paragraph. In each sentence, the person is to fill in the blank with the name of a particular person and indicate the degree to which the item describes the relationship.

The following statements reflect three components of love. The first is attachment-dependency: "If I were lonely, my first thought would be to seek ——— out." The second component is caring: "If ——— were feeling badly, my first duty would be to cheer him (her) up." The final component is intimacy: "I feel that I can confide in ——— about virtually everything." These three statements show the strong aspect of mutuality in love relationships.

Using Rubin's scale you can begin to make some headway toward clarifying an important component of your research problem. In the language of science you have begun to operationalize your definition of love. An **operational definition** is a statement of the features that describe the thing that is being investigated. Attachment-dependency, caring, and intimacy can then be three features of your operational definition of love and can indicate the presence of love in your research study.

REVIEW PREVIOUS RESEARCH

Which questions are the "right" questions? Although there are no inherently correct questions, some are better suited to investigation than others. To decide what to ask, researchers must first learn as much as possible about the subject. We would want to familiarize ourselves with as many of the previous studies on the topic as possible, particularly those that are closely related to what we want to do. By knowing as much as possible about previous research, we can avoid duplicating a previous study, and we are able to build on the contributions that others have made to our understanding of the topic.

DEVELOP ONE OR MORE HYPOTHESES

Our original statement, "love leads to marriage," is presented in the form of a hypotheses. A **hypothesis** is a testable statement about the relationships between two or more empirical variables.

A **variable** is anything that can change (vary). The number of highway deaths on Labor Day weekends, the number of divorces that occur each year in the United States, the amount of energy the average American family consumes in the course of a year, the daily temperature in Dallas, the number of marathoners in Boston or in Knoxville, Tennessee—all these are variables. The following are not variables: the distance from Los Angeles to Las Vegas, the altitude of Denver, and the number of children who were abused in Ohio in 1987. These are fixed, unchangeable facts.

As we review the previous research on the topic on love, we find that we are able to develop additional hypotheses that will help us investigate the issue further. For example, our reading might show that a common stereotype people hold is that women are more romantic than men. After all, it appears that women enjoy love movies and romantic novels more than men.

But wait a minute. We begin to suspect that the common stereotypes may be all wrong, and that they are related to traditional gender-role models. We note that in a traditional society, the male is the breadwinner, and the female is dependent on him for her economic support, status, and financial security. Therefore, it would seem that when a man marries, he chooses a companion and perhaps a helpmate, and when a woman marries, she chooses a companion as well as a standard of living. This leads us to hypothesize that in traditional societies men are more likely to marry for love, whereas women marry for economic security.

There is support for this hypothesis. In one study a scale was designed to measure belief in a romantic ideal in marriage. Males were more likely than females to agree with statements such as the following: "A person should marry whomever he loves regardless of social position" and "As long as they love one another, two people should have no difficulty getting along together in marriage." Men also were more likely to disagree than women with the statement "Economic security should be carefully considered before selecting a marriage partner" (Rubin, 1973).

Additional cross-cultural research shows that romantic love is likely to be strong in societies where one member of the couple has primary responsibility for the economic well-being of the family (Rosenblatt, 1974). This evidence could lead us to hypothesize further that as gender-role stereotyping declines in the United States and as more and more families come to depend on the income of both spouses, one of two things could happen. Either the impor-

hypothesis A testable statement about the relationship between two or more empirical variables.

variable Anything that can change (vary).

statement of causality A proposition that one thing brings about, influences, or changes something else.

statement of association A proposition that changes in one thing are related to changes in another, but that one does not necessarily cause the other.

dependent variable A variable that changes in response to changes in the independent variable.

independent variable A variable that changes for reasons that have nothing to do with the dependent variable.

tance of romantic love as a basis for marriage will begin to fade away, or it could become stronger for both men and women as they now come together on the basis of mutual attraction, as opposed to economic considerations.

Hypotheses involve statements of causality or association. A **statement of causality** says that something brings about, influences, or changes something else. "Love between a man and a woman always produces marriage" is a statement of causality.

A **statement of association,** on the other hand, says that changes in one thing are related to changes in another but that one does not necessarily cause the other. Therefore, if we propose that "the greater the love relationship between a man and a woman, the more likely the chance that they will marry," we are making a statement of association. We are noting that there is a connection between love and marriage, but that one does not necessarily always cause the other.

Often hypotheses propose relationships between two different kinds of variables—a dependent variable and an independent variable. A **dependent variable** changes in response to changes in the independent variable. An **independent variable** changes for reasons that have nothing to do with the dependent variable. For example, we might propose the following hypothesis: Men who live in cities are more likely to marry young than men who live in the country. In this hypothesis the independent variable is the location: some men live in the city, some live in the country, but presumably their choice of where to live is not influenced by whether they marry young. The dependent variable is the age of marriage, because it is possible it is dependent on where the men live. If research shows that age of marriage (the dependent variable) is indeed younger among urban men than among rural men, the hypothesis probably is correct. If there is no difference in the age of marriage among urban and rural men—or if it is earlier among rural men—

then the hypothesis is not supported by the data. Keep in mind that proving a hypothesis false can be scientifically useful: it eliminates unproductive avenues of thought and suggests other, more productive approaches to understanding a problem.

Even if research shows that a hypothesis is correct, it does not mean that the independent variable necessarily produces or causes the dependent variable. For example, if it turns out that we can show that love leads to marriage, we still may not know why. In principle, at least, it is possible to be in love without getting married. We still do not know what causes people to take the next step.

DETERMINE THE RESEARCH DESIGN

Once we have developed our hypotheses, we must design a project in which they can be tested. This is a difficult task and frequently causes researchers a great deal of trouble. If a research design is faulty, it may be impossible to conclude whether the hypotheses are true or false, and the whole project will have been a waste of time, resources, and effort, as was the case with the Masters and Johnson study.

A research design must provide for the collection of all necessary and sufficient data to test the stated hypotheses. The important word here is "test." The researcher must not try to prove a point; rather, the goal is to test the validity of the hypotheses.

Although it is important to gather as much information as needed, research designs must guard against the collection of unnecessary information, which can lead to a waste of time and money.

When we design our research project, we will decide on which of several research approaches to use. There are three main methods of research used by sociologists: surveys, participant observation, and experiments. Each has its own advantages and limitations. Therefore, the choice of method depends on the questions the researcher hopes to answer.

Surveys

A **survey** is a research method in which a population, or a portion thereof, is questioned in order to reveal specific facts about itself. Surveys are used when it is desirable to discover the distribution and interrelations of certain variables among large numbers of people.

The largest survey in the United States takes place every 10 years when the government takes its census. The U.S. Constitution requires this census in order to determine the apportionment of members to the House of Representatives. In theory, at least, a representative of every family and every unmarried adult responds to a series of questions about his or her circumstances.

From the answers, it is possible to construct a picture of the social and economic facts that characterize the American public at one point in time. Such a view, which cuts across a population at a given time, is called a **cross-sectional study.** Surveys, by their nature, usually are cross-sectional. If the same population is surveyed two or more times at certain intervals, a comparison of cross-sectional research can give a picture of changes in variables over time. Research that investigates a population over a period of time is called **longitudinal research.** (For a look at how Americans have changed their attitudes over time about the family and women's place in society, see the *What This Means To You* box entitled "Public Opinion Polls Reflect Who We Are.")

Survey research usually deals with large numbers of subjects in a relatively short time. One of the shortcomings resulting from this is that investigators are not able to capture the full richness of feelings, attitudes, and motives underlying people's responses. Some surveys are designed to gather this kind of information through interviewing. An **interview** consists of a conversation between two (or occasionally more) individuals in which one party attempts to gain information from the other(s) by asking a series of questions.

Sociologists use interviews for three

Certain groups, such as these battered women, may be difficult to interview because of their personal fears and distress. A sociologist trying to conduct research with these women would have to be sensitive to a variety of issues, not the least of which is maintaining some measure of objectivity.

purposes: (1) to explore a subject in order to identify important variables and relationships and to develop hypotheses, (2) as a research tool to obtain core data, and (3) as a supplementary research tool to follow up unexpected findings or to pursue certain issues in greater depth (Kerlinger, 1973).

It would, of course, be ideal to gather exactly the same kinds of information from each research subject. One way researchers attempt to achieve this is through interviews in which all questions are carefully worked out to get at precisely the information that is wanted. Sometimes subjects also are forced to choose from among a limited number of responses to the questions (as in multiple-choice tests). This process results in very uniform data that are easily subjected to statistical analysis.

A research interview entirely predetermined by a questionnaire (or so-called interview schedule) that is followed rigidly is called a **structured interview.** Structured interviews tend to produce uniform or replicable data that can be elicited time after time by different interviewers.

The use of this method, however, may also allow useful information to slip into the "cracks" between the predetermined ques-

survey A research method in which a population or a sample is studied in order to reveal specific facts about it.

cross-sectional study A comparison of two or more similar groups that differ only with respect to the factor being studied.

longitudinal research A research approach in which a population is studied at several intervals over a relatively long period of time.

interview A conversation between an investigator and a subject for the purpose of gathering information.

structured interview An interview with a predetermined set of questions that are followed precisely with each subject.

PUBLIC OPINION POLLS REFLECT WHO WE ARE

R eading a public opinion poll is like looking in the mirror; we see reflections of our thoughts and beliefs staring right back at us. Sometimes the image is not complimentary; others times we have every right to feel proud. Just as we see changes in ourselves as we age over the years, we also can track our changing attitudes over time. Norval D. Glenn, professor of sociology at the University of Texas at Austin, did just this and came up with some telling results. As you can see in the following table, attitudes about the family and women's place in society changed significantly between 1969 and 1986. How do you feel about these changes?

Source: Norval D. Glenn, "Social Trends in the United States: Evidence from Sample Surveys," *Public Opinion Quarterly,* Spring 1987, p. S120.

Trends in Family-Related Attitudes Shown by U.S. National Survey Data, 1969–1986

	Percentages of Respondents Who Said:			
Year	*Women Should Take Care of Running Their Homes and Leave Running the Country to Men* (GSS)*	*They Disapprove of a Married Woman Earning Money in Business or Industry If She Has a Husband Who Can Support Her* (GSS)	*Ideal Number of Children For a Family Is Three or More* (Gallup)	(GSS)
1969	— %	— %	— %	— %
1972	—	35	—	50
1973	—	—	47	—
1974	36	31	—	44
1975	36	29	—	42
1976	—	—	—	37
1977	38	34	—	42
1978	32	27	43	41
1980	—	—	—	—
1982	27	25	—	37
1983	23	23	37	39
1984	—	—	—	—
1985	26	14	—	36
1986	24	22	30	41

Source: The General Social Survey (GSS) data are from Davis (1982, 1986); the Gallup data are from The Gallup Organization (1985b, 1986). All percentages were calculated with "no opinion" and similar neutral responses removed from the base.

* GSS = General Social Survey.

tions. For example, a questionnaire being administered to married individuals might ask about their age, family background, and what role love played in their reasons for getting married. If, however, we do not ask about social class or ethnicity, we may not find out that these characteristics are very important for our study. If such questions were not built into the questionnaire from the beginning, it is impossible to recover this "lost" information later in the process when its importance may become apparent.

One technique that can prevent this kind of information loss is the **semistructured,** or **open-ended, interview,** in which the investigator asks a list of questions but is free to vary them or even to make up new questions on topics that take on importance in the course of the interview. This means that each interview will cover those topics important to the research project but, in addition, will yield additional data that are somewhat different for each subject. Analyzing such diverse and complex data is difficult, but the results are often rewarding.

Interviewing, although it may produce very valuable information, is a complex, time-consuming art. Some research studies try to get similar information by distributing questionnaires directly to the subjects and asking them to complete and return them. This is the way the federal government obtains much of its census data. Although it is perhaps the least expensive way of doing social research, it is often difficult to assess the quality of data obtained in this manner. For example, people may not answer honestly or seriously for a variety of reasons: they may not understand the questions, they may fear the information will be used against them, and so on. But even data gained from personal interviews may be unreliable. In one study student-interviewers were embarrassed to ask subjects preassigned questions on sexual habits. So they left these questions out of the interviews and filled them in themselves afterward. In another study, follow-up research found that the subjects had consistently lied to the interviewers.

One important use of surveys is to predict elections—especially every four years when we elect a new president. As you will see when you read this chapter's Controversial Issue, "Do Early Calls of Election Results Influence Voter Behavior?" a research study can have a major effect on the issue being studied.

Participant Observation

Participant observation requires that researchers enter into a group's activities and also observe the group members at the same time. Unlike the usual practice in survey research, participant observers do not try to make sure they are studying a carefully chosen sample. Rather, they attempt to get to know all the members of the group in question personally to whatever degree possible.

This research method generally is used to study relatively small groups over an extended period of time. The intention is to obtain a detailed portrait of the way of life of the group, to observe individual and group behavior, and to interview selected informants. Participant observation depends for its success on the nature of the relationship that develops between the researchers and research subjects. The closer and more trusting the relationship is, the more information will be revealed to the researcher—especially the kind of personal information that often is crucial if the research is to be successful.

One of the first and still most famous studies employing the technique of participant observation was a study of Cornerville, a lower-class Italian neighborhood in Boston. William Foote Whyte moved into the neighborhood and lived for three years with an Italian family. He published his results in a book called *Street Corner Society* (1943). All the information for the book came from his field notes, which described the behavior and attitudes of the people whom he came to know by living with them and participating in their day-to-day activities.

Several years after Whyte's study, Herbert Gans conducted a participant ob-

semistructured (open-ended) interview An interview in which the investigator asks a list of questions but is free to vary them or make up new ones that become important during the course of the interview.

participant observation A research technique in which the investigator enters into a group's activities while, at the same time, studying the group's behavior.

Participant observation research in a prison would be nearly impossible. The difficulty in obtaining accurate information, as well as the danger involved in gathering the data, has made prisons unlikely settings for this research method.

experiment An investigation in which the variables being studied are controlled and the researcher obtains the results through precise observation and measurement.

servation study, published as *The Urban Villagers* (1962), of another Italian neighborhood in Boston. The picture Gans drew of the West End was broader than Whyte's study of Cornerville. Gans included descriptions of the family, work experience, education, medical care, relationships with social workers, and other aspects of life in the West End. Although he covered a wider range of activities than Whyte, his observations were not as detailed.

On rare occasions, participant observers hide their identities while doing research and join groups under false pretenses. Leon Festinger and his students hid their identities when they studied a religious group preaching the end of the world and the arrival of flying saucers to save the righteous (Festinger, Riecken, and Schacter, 1956). However, most sociologists consider this deception unethical. They believe it is better for participant observers to be honest about their intentions and work together with their subjects to create a situation that is satisfactory to all concerned. By declaring their positions at the outset, sociologists can then ask appropriate questions, take notes, and carry out research tasks without fearing the risk of detection.

Participant observation is a highly subjective research approach. In fact, some

scholars reject it because different researchers often produce different results. However, this method has the virtue of revealing the social life of a group in far more depth and detail than surveys or interviews alone. The participant observer who is able to establish good rapport with the subjects is likely to uncover information that would never be revealed to a survey taker. The participant observer is in a difficult position. He or she will be torn between the need to become trusted and, therefore, also emotionally involved in the group's life and the need to remain a somewhat detached observer striving for scientific objectivity.

Experiments

The most precise research method available to sociologists is the controlled **experiment.** In a controlled experiment, inside or outside a laboratory, researchers can make observations while recording information in detail. Under these circumstances, it is possible to have more control over the variables of the study.

Because of their precision, experiments are an attractive means of doing research. Many researchers have used experiments to study patterns of interaction in small groups under different conditions, such as stress, fatigue, limited access to information, and prestructured channels of communication among group members. Although experimentation is appropriate for small-group research, most of the issues that interest sociologists cannot be investigated in totally controlled situations. Social events usually cannot be studied in controlled experiments because, very simply, they cannot be controlled. For these reasons experiments remain the least-used research method in sociology.

DEFINE THE SAMPLE AND COLLECT DATA

After determining how the needed information will be collected, the researchers must decide what group will be observed or

TAKING THE SOCIOLOGICAL PERSPECTIVE

HOW PEOPLE METERS DETERMINE WHAT YOU WATCH ON TV

What do random selection, representative samples, and sample bias have to do with your day-to-day routine? A great deal if you watch television. The connection is this: about 2000 randomly selected families all over America are tied into people meters, electronic devices that track what they are watching on television. Because these families are supposed to represent all the rest of us (here is where the representative sample comes in), what they watch—and do not watch—determines what *you* will see on television next season. From people meters come the ratings—the numbers that determine whether a show will be cancelled or renewed and how much advertisers will have to pay for each commercial minute.

A. C. Nielsen, the nation's largest television rating company, is responsible for finding just the right people to monitor and for putting the people meters in place. They are also the ones to tell us what the numbers all mean. People meters are high tech compared to the "diary" system Nielsen used to use. In Nielsen's view, it made a great deal of sense to go electronic—to leave nothing to chance or to the viewer's faulty memory. People meters do this with multibutton remote control devices.

Nielsen keys demographic information about each family member to the appropriate button so that it knows exactly who is watching what. All household members push their buttons whenever they turn on the set, make viewing choices, and leave and reenter the room.

Although the high-tech system may be efficient, it rapidly becomes a boring routine for those who have to use it. Those who circumvent the system, either intentionally or because they are too young to use it (how can we blame the 4-year-old, sitting down to 2 hours of cartoons on Saturday morning, who forgets to punch in and out everytime he puts on the set or leaves the room?) give Nielsen results that are far from accurate. Many subjects who simply do not want to deal with the system any more, place tape over the flashing lights so they can watch in peace. Ac-

cording to some reports, as many as 25 percent of all people-meter households are guilty of circumventing the recording device in this way.

When the sample does not cooperate, that is trouble enough, but many network executives believe that the original design of the sample was also flawed—that it contained too many households in the western states and too many viewers under 35. This sample bias affected CBS more than the other two networks or cable channels because CBS traditionally has a relatively older, more southern audience.

Despite these glitches, the results are what the networks and advertisers live by. For now, at least, Dan Rather is running ahead of Tom Brokaw and Peter Jennings, even though he was trailing under the old diary system. This should not upset anyone, because it will probably change next week.

Sources: "The Networks' Big Headache," *Business Week,* July 6, 1987, pp. 26–28; Edwin Diamond, "Attack of the People Meters," *New York,* August 24, 1987, pp. 39–41; "Networks' Newest Nemesis," *U.S. News & World Report,* February 1, 1988, p. 47; "People Meter Faulted on Counting Children," *New York Times,* April 4, 1988, p. D9.

questioned. Depending on the study, this group might be college students, Texans, or baseball players. The particular subset of the population chosen for study is known as a **sample.**

Sampling is a research technique through which investigators study a manageable number of people, called a sample, selected from a larger population or group. If the procedures are carried out correctly,

sample The particular subset of a larger population that has been selected for study.

sampling A research technique in which a manageable number of subjects (a sample), are selected for study from a larger population.

representative sample A sample that has the same distribution of characteristics as the larger population from which it is drawn.

sampling error The failure to select a representative sample.

stratified random sample A technique to make sure that all significant variables are represented in a sample in proportion to their numbers in the larger population.

random sample A sample selected purely on the basis of chance.

These elderly people are enjoying themselves in Florida. Would they be considered representative of the elderly in the United States as a whole? Why or why not?

the sample will show, in equivalent proportion, the significant variables that characterize the population as a whole. In other words, the sample will be representative of the larger population, and the findings of the research thus will generalize to the larger group. Such a sample is called a **representative sample,** and failure to achieve a representative sample is called **sampling error.**

Suppose you wanted to sample the attitudes of the American public on some issue such as military spending or federal aid for abortions. You could not limit your sample to only New Yorkers or Republicans or Catholics or blacks or homeowners. These groups do not represent the nation as a whole, and any findings you came up with would contain a sampling error.

How do researchers make sure their samples are representative? The basic technique is to use a **random sample** — to select subjects so that each individual in the population has an equal chance of being chosen. For example, if we wanted a random sample of all college students in the United States, we might choose every fifth or tenth or hundredth person from a comprehensive list of all college students registered in this country. Or we might assign each student a number and have a computer pick a sample randomly. However, there is a possibility that, simply by chance, a small segment of the total college student population would fail to be represented adequately. This might happen with Native American students, for instance, who account for less than 1 per-

cent of all college students in America. For some research purposes this might not matter, but if ethnicity is an important aspect of the research, it would be important to make sure Native American students were included.

The method used to prevent certain groups from being under- or overrepresented in a sample is to choose a **stratified random sample.** With this technique the population being studied is first divided into two or more groups (or strata) according to some common denominator, such as age, sex, or ethnicity. A simple random sample is then taken within each group. Finally, the subsamples are combined (in proportion to their numbers in the population) to form a total sample. In our example of college students, the researcher would identify all ethnic groups represented among college students in America. Then the researchers would calculate the proportion of the total number of college students represented by each group and draw a random sample separately from each ethnic group. The number chosen from each group should be proportional to its representation in the entire college student population. The sample would still be random, but it would be stratified for ethnicity.

For a study to be accurate, it is crucial that a sample be chosen with care. The most famous example of sampling error occurred in 1936, when *Literary Digest* magazine incorrectly predicted that Alfred E. Landon would win the presidential election. Using telephone directories and automobile registration lists to recruit subjects, *Literary Digest* pollsters sent out more than 10 million straw vote ballots and received 2.3 million completed responses. The survey gave the Republican candidate Landon 55 percent of the vote and Roosevelt only 41 percent (the remaining 4 percent went to a third candidate). From this poll the *Digest* confidently predicted Landon's victory, which never came about. Instead, Alfred E. Landon has become known as the candidate who was buried in a landslide vote for Franklin D. Roosevelt (Squire, 1988).

How could this happen? Two major flaws in the sample accounted for the mistake. First, although the *Literary Digest* sample was large, it was not representative of the nation's voting population because it contained a major sampling error. During the Depression years, only the well-to-do could afford telephones and automobiles, and these people were likely to vote Republican.

The second problem with the study was the response rate. Interestingly, of those who claimed to have received a *Literary Digest* ballot, 55 percent claimed they would have voted for Roosevelt and 44 percent for Landon. If these people had actually voted in the poll, the *Digest* would have predicted the correct winner. As it turned out, there was a low response rate, and those who did respond were generally better-educated, wealthier people, who tended to be Landon supporters (Squire, 1988).

The outcome of the election was not entirely a surprise to everyone. A young pollster by the name of George Gallup forecast the results accurately. He realized that the majority of Americans supported the New Deal policies proposed by the Democrats. Gallup's sample was much smaller but far more representative of the American public than that of the *Literary Digest*. This points out that the representativeness of the sample is more important than the sample size.

There are many other, more recent examples of surveys with unrepresentative samples. *USA Today* informed its readers about a survey reporting that 39 percent of women with a college degree were earning more than $30,000 a year. This information was obtained from a subscriber survey done by *Working Woman* magazine. This subscriber survey is not representative of American women, however, and the information is incorrect. According to the Census Bureau, only 7 percent of women with college degrees earn more than $30,000 a year (*American Demographics,* February 1986).

Just as misleading is a recent survey that columnist Ann Landers did. She asked her readers to let her know if their sex lives had gone downhill after marriage. "The verdict was clear," noted Landers. "Eighty-two percent said sex after marriage was less exciting."

Lending the illusion of accuracy to this survey was the fact that 141,000 readers from all fifty states, every Canadian province, Asia, and Europe responded to the survey. Yet, despite this large response, the fact that no attempt was made to make the sample representative, or to ask the questions in an unbiased fashion, makes the information useless and irrelevant for providing any real understanding of sex after marriage.

Landers noted: "I found the results of the survey disturbing. These people are saying more than they realize. . . . They are talking about the state of their marriage" (*Editor and Publisher,* February 4, 1989). What is really disturbing, however, is that Ann Landers is presenting herself as a researcher and interpreter of information about the family and that this survey, which has little, if any, real value, is taken seriously by large numbers of people.

Researcher Bias

Researcher bias is one of the most serious problems in data collection. It is the tendency for researchers to select data that support, and to ignore data that seem to go against, their hypotheses. We see this quite often in mass media publications. They may structure their study to produce the results they wish to obtain. Or they may only publicize information that supports their viewpoint.

Researcher bias often takes the form of a self-fulfilling prophecy. A researcher who is strongly inclined toward one point of view may communicate that attitude through questions and reactions in such a way that the subject fulfills the researcher's expectations. Most often this phenomenon is seen in the classroom where a teacher, treating a child as intellectually inferior,

researcher bias The tendency for researchers to select data that support their hypothesis and to ignore data that appear to contradict it.

double-blind investigator
A researcher who does not know either the kind of subject being investigated or the hypothesis being tested.

elicits from that child behavior that conforms to the teacher's view (Rosenthal and Jacobson, 1966). Researchers in sociology can also fall into this trap and pull the subjects in with them. For example, a researcher who is trying to prove an association between poverty and antisocial behavior might question low-income subjects in a way that would indicate a low regard for their social attitudes. The subjects, perceiving the researcher's bias, might react with hostility and thus fulfill the researcher's expectations.

Writer Shere Hite (1987), fell into the trap of researcher bias on the topic of love and marriage, which we have been discussing in this chapter. She set out to find out how women today feel about men and relationships. Hite sent out 100,000 questionnaires to women in forty-three states who belonged to a variety of women's groups ranging from feminist organizations to church groups and garden clubs. She based her findings on the 4,500 responses she received. This is an unacceptably low response rate.

analysis The process through which scientific data are organized so that comparisons can be made and conclusions drawn.

Hite's interpretation of the results led her to state that women are extremely dissatisfied with men. To support her view she pointed to the fact that almost all women reported "emotional and psychological harassment" from the men they love. Seventy percent of those married more than 5 years said that they had had extramarital affairs. Only 19 percent of the respondents defined their relationships with men as the most important thing in their lives.

These results were startling because they were so one-sided—an indication of researcher bias in the design of the project. In effect, the respondents were a self-selected sample of malcontents, said psychologist June Reinisch. "Unhappy people are more willing to answer these questions than happy people." Columnist Ellen Goodman added that Hite "goes in with a prejudice and comes out with a statistic" (*Time,* October 12, 1987).

blind investigator A researcher who does not know whether a specific subject belongs to the group of actual cases being investigated or to a comparison group. This is done to eliminate researcher bias.

One of the standard means for dealing with researcher bias is to use **blind investi-**

gators, who do not know whether a specific subject belongs to the group of actual cases being investigated or to a comparison group. For example, in a study on the causes of child abuse, the investigator looking at the children's family background would not be told which children had been abused and which were in the nonabused comparison group. Sometimes **double-blind investigators** are used. They are kept uninformed not only of the kinds of subjects (case subjects or comparison group subjects) they are studying but also of the hypotheses being tested. This eliminates any tendency on their part to find cases that support—or disprove—the research hypothesis.

ANALYZE THE DATA AND DRAW CONCLUSIONS

In its most basic sense, **analysis** is the process through which large and complicated collections of scientific data are organized so that comparisons can be made and conclusions drawn. It is not unusual for a sociological research project to result in hundreds of thousands of individual pieces of information. By itself this vast array of data has no particular meaning. The analyst must find ways to organize such data into useful categories so that the kinds of relationships that exist between the categories of data can be determined. In this way the hypotheses that are the core of the research can be tested, and new hypotheses can be formulated for further investigation. (One important device to aid in the analysis of data is the table, which is explained in Box 2.1, "How to Read a Table.")

Sociologists often summarize their data by calculating central tendencies, or averages. Actually, there are three different types of averages used by sociologists: the mean, the median, and the mode. Each type is calculated differently, and each can result in a different figure.

Suppose you are studying a group of ten college students and you find that their verbal SAT scores were as follows:

450	690	280	450	760
540	520	450	430	530

Although you can report the information in this form, a more meaningful presentation would give some indication of the central tendency of the ten SAT scores.

The mean is what is commonly called the average. To calculate the mean, you add up all the figures and divide by the number of items. In our example the SAT scores add up to 5100. Dividing by 10 gives a mean of 510.

The median is the figure that falls midway in a series of numbers—there are as many numbers above it as below it. Because we have ten scores—an even number—in our example, the median is the mean (the average) of the fifth and sixth figures, the two numbers in the middle. To calculate the median, rearrange the data in order from the lowest to highest (or vice versa). In our example you would list the scores as follows: 280, 430, 450, 450, 450, 520, 530, 540, 690, 760. The median is 485—midway between the fifth score (450) and the sixth score (520).

The mode is the number that occurs most often in the data. In our example the mode is 450.

The three types of averages are used for different reasons, and each has its advantages and disadvantages. The mean is most useful when there is a narrow range of figures, because it has the advantage of including all the data. It can be misleading, however, when there are one or two scores much higher or lower than the rest. The median deals with this problem by not allowing extreme figures to distort the central tendency. The mode enables researchers to show which number occurs most often. Its disadvantage is that it does not give any idea of the entire range of data. Realizing the problems inherent in each average, sociologists often state the central tendency in more than one form.

It is important to caution at this point against an overreliance on statistical methodology. To say that a finding has statistical significance does not necessarily mean that this finding is important. **Statistical significance** is only a mathematical statement about the probability that some event or relationship is not due to chance alone. It has meaning (and thus importance) only to the extent that it is relevant to the context of the research and to the world as we understand it. For example, a British study found a statistically significant relationship between the presence of emotional depression in mothers of young children and where they lived in their apartment buildings. The higher the apartment floor, the greater the incidence of depression.

Alone, this finding is not important because it does not seem to be relevant to anything we know about depression. However, if we know that few of these apartment buildings have elevators, and if we imagine the difficulty of negotiating two, three, or four flights of stairs with one or more youngsters several times a day, we can construct a new hypothesis: the higher the floor, the less likely the parent is to go outside with the child. And then another hypothesis suggests itself: the more a parent is confined to the apartment with a young child, the greater the stress of parenthood and hence the greater the likelihood of emotional depression. In this context the research findings acquire meaning as well as statistical significance.

This example also illustrates a very important aspect of scientific research—namely, the analysis of data raises new questions and leads to further investigation.

Scientists usually are careful in drawing conclusions from their research. One of the purposes of drawing conclusions from data compiled in the course of doing research is to be able to apply the information gathered to other, similar situations. Problems thus may develop if there are faults in the research design. For example, the study must show **validity**—that is, the study must actually test what it was intended to test. If you want to say that one event is the cause of another, you must be able to rule out other explanations to show that your research is

statistical significance A mathematical statement about the probability that some event or relationship is not due to chance alone.

validity The ability of a research study to test what it was designed to test.

BOX 2.1

HOW TO READ A TABLE

Statistical tables are used frequently by sociologists both to present the findings of their own research and to study the data of others. We will use the accompanying table to outline the steps to follow in reading and interpreting a table.

1. *Read the title.* The title tells you the subject of the table. This table presents data on life expectancy at birth in various countries for people of both sexes.

2. *Check the source.* At the bottom of a table you will find its source. In this case the source is the *Statistical Abstract of the United States: 1988.* Knowing the source of a table can help you decide whether the information it contains is reliable. It also tells you where to look to find the original data and how recent the information is. In our example the source is both reliable and recent. If the source were the 1958 *Abstract,* it would be of limited value in telling you about life expect-

ancy in those countries today. Improvements in health care, control of epidemic diseases, or national birth-control programs all are factors that may have altered life expectancy drastically in several countries since 1958. Likewise, consider a table of data about the standard of living of black people in South Africa.

If its source were an agency of the South African government (which might be trying to "prove" how well off blacks are in that country), you might well be skeptical about the reliability of the information in the table.

3. *Look for headnotes.* Many tables contain headnotes directly

Life Expectancy at Birth by Sex for Selected Countries

Country	Expectation of Life at Birth, 1986	
	Males	*Females*
Afghanistan	42	40
Burma	52	55
Canada	73	81
Ghana	56	60
India	55	57
Japan	75	80
Kenya	58	62
Poland	66	74
Soviet Union	63	73
Syria	66	67
United States	71	79

Source: *Statistical Abstract of the United States: 1988,* 108th edition (Washington, D.C.: U.S. Bureau of the Census, 1987), p. 800.

---

replication Repetition of the same research procedure or experiment to determine whether earlier results can be duplicated.

reliability The ability to repeat the findings of a research study.

valid. Suppose you conclude that marijuana use leads to heroin addiction. You must show that it is marijuana use and not some other factor such as peer pressure that leads to heroin addiction.

The study must also demonstrate **reliability**—that is, the findings of the

study can be repeated (known as **replication**). Suppose you conclude from a study that whites living in racially integrated housing projects, who have contact with blacks in the project, have more favorable attitudes toward them than do whites living in racially segregated housing projects. If

below the title. These may explain how the data were collected, why certain variables (and not others) were studied, why the data are presented in a particular way, whether some data were collected at different times, and so on. In our table on life expectancy the headnote explains that the numbers in the table refer to the average number of years a person born in 1986 can expect to live.

4. *Read the labels or headings for each row and column.* The labels will tell you exactly what information is contained in the table. It is essential that you understand the labels—both the row headings on the left and the column headings at the top. Here the row headings tell you the names of the countries being compared for life expectancy. The column headings are broken down into two groups: males and females. For each group, life expectancy is given. Note the units being used in the table. In this case the units are years. Often the figures represent percentages or rates. Many population and crime statistics are given in rates per 100,000 people.

5. *Examine the data.* Suppose you want to find the life expectancy of a newborn baby boy in the United States. First look down the row at the left until you come to "United States." Then look across the columns until you come to "Males." Reading across you discover that, on average, a newborn baby boy in the United States can expect to live another 71 years. By contrast, a newborn baby girl can look forward to another 79 years.

6. *Compare the data.* Compare the data in the table both horizontally and vertically. Suppose you want to find in which country males can expect to live longest from birth. Looking down the Males column we find that males born in Japan can expect to live longest—75 years. Among these eleven nations the United States males rank third, behind Japan and Canada. A girl born in Afghanistan has the shortest life expectancy—only 40 years.

Now suppose you want to compare the life expectancy at birth of men versus women. Look down the Males and Females columns. We find that in ten of the eleven countries in the table women can expect to live longer than men. Only in Afghanistan is a man's life expectancy (at birth) longer than a woman's.

7. *Draw conclusions.* Draw conclusions about the information in the table. After examining the data in the table, you might conclude that women generally live longer than men do. You might also conclude that a person born in a relatively developed country (Canada, Japan, Poland, United States) is likely to live much longer than someone born in a poorer nation (Afghanistan, Burma, Ghana, India, Kenya).

8. *Pose new questions.* The conclusions you reach might well lead to new questions that could prompt further research. Why, you might want to know, do women tend to live longer than men? Why do women in Afghanistan have shorter life expectancies than men? What causes the gap in life expectancy between the rich and poor nations?

you or other researchers carry out the same study in housing projects in various cities throughout the country and get the same results, then the study is reliable.

It is highly unlikely that any single piece of research will provide all the answers to a given question. In fact, good research frequently leads to the discovery of unanticipated information requiring further research. One of the pleasures of research is that ongoing studies keep opening up new perspectives and posing further questions that require originality and creativity in the design of fresh research to answer them.

PREPARE THE RESEARCH REPORT

Research that goes unreported is wasted. Scientific progress is made through the accumulation of research that tests hypotheses and contributes to the ongoing process of bettering our understanding of the world. Therefore, it is usual for agencies that fund research to insist that scientists agree to share their findings.

Scientists generally publish their findings in technical journals. If the information is relevant to the public, many popular and semiscientific publications will report on these findings as well. It is especially important that research in sociology and the other social sciences be made available to the public, because much of this research has a bearing on social issues and public policies.

Unfortunately, the general public is not always cautious in interpreting research findings. Special-interest groups, politicians, and others who have a cause to plead are often too quick to generalize from specific research results—frequently distorting them beyond recognition. This happens most often when the research focuses on something of national or emotional concern. It is therefore important to double-check reports of sociological research appearing in popular magazines with the original research—or, at least, with discussions of the research by the investigators themselves.

OBJECTIVITY AND ETHICS IN SOCIOLOGICAL RESEARCH

Max Weber believed that the social scientist should describe and explain what is rather than prescribe what should be. His goal was a value-free approach to sociology. More and more sociologists today, however, are admitting that completely value-free research may not be possible.

OBJECTIVITY

Sociology, like any other science, is molded by factors that impose values on research. Gunnar Myrdal (1969) lists three such influential factors: (1) the scientific tradition within which the scientist has been educated, (2) the cultural, social, economic, and political environment within which the scientist is trained and engages in research, and (3) the scientist's own temperament, inclinations, interests, concerns, and experiences. These factors are especially strong in sociological research because the researcher usually is part of the society being studied.

Does this mean that all science—and sociology in particular—is hopelessly subjective? Is objectivity in sociological research an impossible goal? There are no simple answers to these questions. The best sociologists can do is to strive to become aware of the ways in which these factors influence them and to make such biases explicit when sharing the results of their research. We think of this as disciplined, or "objective," subjectivity, and it is a reasonable goal for sociological research.

Another problem of bias in sociological research relates to the people being studied rather than to the researchers themselves. The mere presence of investigators or researchers may distort the situation and produce unusual reactions from subjects who now feel special because they were selected for study.

ETHICAL ISSUES

In 1919 Franz Boas, the father of American anthropology, incurred the anger of the United States government by publicly denouncing spying done under the guise of social research. Boas's criticism did not result in any changes, however. In the ensuing years social scientists have continued to engage in research projects that—with or without their knowledge—are used for political purposes by governments. Project Camelot, organized in 1964, is an example of government-controlled research that backfired on its planners.

The aim of that project, as described by the United States Army, was "to devise procedures for assessing the potential for internal war within national societies." It sought to "predict and influence politically significant aspects of social change in . . . Latin American countries" and "to identify . . . actions which a government might take to relieve conditions which are assessed as giving rise to a potential for internal war." In plain English, the army wanted to know how to predict revolutions in Latin America and how to nip them in the bud.

The complete story of Project Camelot has been detailed by Irving Louis Horowitz in *The Rise and Fall of Project Camelot* (1976). It started with a budget of some $6 million and the army's recruitment of some top social scientists in the United States. According to Horowitz, these participants saw themselves as "reformers" with an opportunity to influence government policy, to help eradicate poverty, and to "educate" the army. None actually believed, however, that the army would act on their policy recommendations. Enticed by the lure of almost limitless funds, the social scientists simply ignored the ethical issue of how their research would be used.

Project Camelot never really got off the ground. News of the project and the source of its funding were leaked to newspapers in Chile, and a hue and cry erupted immediately throughout South America. Both the State Department and Congress, unwilling to risk the nation's already strained relations with our neighbors to the south, pressured the army to cancel the project. Only a year after it was conceived, Project Camelot was aborted.

All research projects raise fundamental questions. In whose interest is the research? Who will benefit from it? How might people be hurt? To what degree do subjects have the right to be told about the research design, its purposes, and possible applications? Who should have access to and control over research data after a study is completed—the agency that funded the study, the scientists, the subjects? Should research subjects have the right to participate in the planning of projects? Is it ethical to manipulate people without their knowledge in order to control research variables? To what degree do researchers owe it to their subjects not to invade their privacy and to keep secret (and, therefore, not report anywhere) things that were told them in strict confidence? What obligations do researchers have to the society in which they are working? What commitments do researchers have to supporting or subverting a political order? Should researchers report to legal authorities any illegal behavior discovered in the course of their investigations? Is it ethical to expose subjects to such risk by asking them to participate in a study?

In the 1960s the federal government began to prescribe regulations for "the protection of human subjects." These regulations force scientists to think about one central issue: how to judge and balance the intellectual and societal benefits of scientific research against the actual or possible physical and emotional costs paid by the people who are being studied. This issue arises in at least three types of situations.

The first situation concerns the degree of permissible risk, pain, or harm. Suppose a study that temporarily induces severe emotional distress promises significant benefits. The researcher may justify the study. However, we may wonder whether the benefits will be realized or whether they justify the potential dangers to the subjects, even if they are volunteers who know what to expect and all possible protective measures have been taken.

A second dilemma is the extent to which subjects should be deceived in a study. It is now necessary for researchers to obtain, in writing, the "informed consent" of the people they study. Questions still arise, however, about whether subjects are informed about the true nature of the study and whether, once informed, they could freely decline to participate.

A third problem in research studies concerns the disclosure of confidential or personally harmful information. Is the researcher entitled to delve into people's personal lives? What if the researcher uncovers some information that should be brought to the attention of the authorities? Should confidential information be included in a published study (Gans, 1979)?

Every sociologist must grapple with these questions and find answers that apply to particular situations. However, two general points are worth noting. The first is that social research rarely benefits the research subjects directly. Benefits to subjects tend to be indirect and delayed by many years — as when new government policies are developed to correct problems discovered by researchers. Second, most subjects of sociological research belong to groups with little or no power. It is hardly an accident that poor people are the most studied, rich people the least. Therefore, research subjects typically have little control over how research findings are used, even though such applications may affect them greatly. This means that sociologists must accept responsibility for the fact that they have recruited research subjects who may be made vulnerable as a result of their cooperation. It is important that researchers establish safeguards limiting the use of their findings, protecting the anonymity of their data, and honoring all commitments to confidentiality made in the course of their research.

The ideal relationship between scientist and research participant is characterized by openness and honesty. Deliberate lying in the interest of manipulating the participant's perceptions and actions goes directly against this ideal. Yet often researchers must choose between carrying out the deception and abandoning the research. With few, if any, exceptions social scientists regard deception of research participants as a questionable practice to be avoided if at all possible. It diminishes the respect due to others and violates the expectations of mu-

tual trust on which organized society is based. When the deceiver is a respected scientist, it may have the undesirable effect of modeling deceit as an acceptable practice. Conceivably, it may contribute to the growing climate of cynicism and mistrust bred by widespread use of deception by important public figures. Obviously, planned deception of research subjects presents the sociologist with a serious ethical dilemma.

RESEARCH FRAUD

The history of science is replete with examples of frauds. Some of these were quickly discovered and forgotten, and others have damaged the reputations of individuals or even entire fields of study. One hoax that had devastating consequences for the social sciences was the IQ fraud perpetrated by the British psychologist Sir Cyril Burt.

Over a period of 60 years, beginning in 1912, Burt published a great many books and articles "proving" that intelligence is largely inherited. The basis of this co-called proof was his analysis and comparison of some fifty-three pairs of identical twins who had been orphaned and raised apart.

Although Burt's work was attacked by sociologists, anthropologists, and geneticists, he was defended by his fellow psychologists and in 1946 was knighted for his service to British education. When he died in 1971, at the age of 88, colleagues called him "a born nobleman" and "a man of Renaissance proportions." The *London Times* eulogized him, stating: "For over forty years he had been the leading figure in . . . the application of psychology to education and the development of children, and to the assessment of mental qualities."

When Arthur Jensen published an article in the *Harvard Educational Review* in 1969, in which he implied that blacks are innately less intelligent than whites, he acknowledged his great debt to Burt by citing ten of Burt's studies. It now is known that all ten studies were fraudulent. Apparently, Burt was so convinced that intelligence was determined mainly by a person's genetic endowment, and that upper-class Britons were the most generously endowed of all, that he simply invented the existence of pairs of twins raised in different environments to prove his point.

Burt's prestige was so great that it was not until five years after his death that accusations of fraud were raised publicly. It was then discovered that no one except Burt's colleague, a Ms. Conway, had ever seen any of the twins who figured in Burt's studies. An investigation revealed that Ms. Conway never existed.

Why Burt—a man of undoubted intelligence and ability—spent a lifetime deliberately publishing fraudulent studies is a question that no one can really answer. Whatever the reason, the fraud Burt perpetrated has had an incalculably negative impact on thousands, perhaps even millions, of young children. In Britain Burt's research was used to develop a national education policy that "tracked" youngsters from a very early age and systematically excluded many of them from obtaining the necessary skills that would lead them up the social and economic ladder. In the United States Burt's studies were cited over and over again as a justification for shifting federal funds away from day-care and Head Start programs. Many programs were closed down, and thousands of children were deprived of what might have been enriching educational experiences.

It is useful for human beings to seek to understand themselves and the social world in which they live. Sociology has a great contribution to make to this endeavor, both in promoting understanding for its own sake and in providing social planners with scientific information with which well-founded decisions can be made and sound plans for future development adopted. However, sociologists must also shoulder the burden of self-reflection—of seeking to understand the role they play in contemporary social processes and at the same time of assessing how these social processes affect their findings (Gouldner, 1970).

SUMMARY

Science has two main goals: (1) to describe in detail particular things or events and (2) to propose and test general principles by means of which these things and events can be understood.

We begin the research process by defining the problem. To begin a project, the researcher must first try to find out as much as possible about the work that has already been done on the subject. The next step is to develop one or more hypotheses. In developing a hypothesis, the researcher should keep in mind the difference between a statement of causality and a statement of association: an event may be caused by another event, or it may merely be related to another event. Empirical questions are ones that can be answered by observation and analysis of the world as it is known. Such questions are often asked in order to test hypotheses—statements about relationships among things or events—which are useful only if their terms are defined operationally.

Hypotheses often propose a relationship between a dependent variable and an independent variable. A dependent variable changes in response to changes in the independent variable, and an independent variable changes for reasons that have nothing to do with the dependent variable. Once the hypotheses have been developed, the researcher designs a project in which they can be tested.

After we have developed our hypotheses we determine the research design, define the sample, and collect data.

When researchers collect data, they must be on the alert for any distortions that may arise from researcher bias or sampling error. The first problem is sometimes

Do Early Calls of Election Results Influence Voter Behavior

I t is 6 P.M. in California and 9 P.M. in New York on the first Tuesday in November in 1992—election day with the office of the president of the United States up for grabs. As the polls close in each state, the three major networks and the Cable News Network project the winner of the presidential race. Within a short time—minutes at most—it becomes clear to voters on the West Coast that the race has been decided—that one candidate has enough electoral votes to be the next president. Trouble is, millions of West Coast voters have not yet gone to the polls. Although polls have closed in New York, Boston, Miami, and Hartford, closing time in Los Angeles, Portland, Tacoma, and San Diego is three hours away. On the basis of network news projections, millions of people who might have voted for the president do not bother because they already know who won.

Are these early calls of election results fair in a society that gives nearly every adult an equal voice at the polls? As you will see, opinions are divided, although the law is clear: Networks have the right to make projections as polls close in each state—even in national races where projections are made before polls close in the West. "That's how we elect a president—by going across the electoral college," said Mary Klette, Director of Election Unit Operations at NBC. "There are no restrictions in place on the federal or state level to prevent networks from making these projections on a state-by-state basis. If there were, these laws would violate the constitutional right to freedom of the press" (Interview with Klette, June 23, 1988).

When the state of Washington passed a law preventing the press from conducting exit polls, which ask people for whom they voted as they leave the voting place, the law was overturned as a violation of this basic freedom. In 1985, the networks signed a pledge to avoid "projections, characterizations, or any other uses of exit polling data that would indicate the winner of the election before polls in a given state were closed." Although this agreement went a long way toward minimizing the influence network projections have on voter behavior, it still did not solve the problem faced by West Coast voters in a presidential election year.

The main argument against early calls of elections based on polling data is that the calls will discourage voters from showing up at the polls; it is human nature not to bother to vote if you already know who won. But the effect may be limited. According to Seymour

avoided by the use of blind investigators, the second by the use of a representative sample. A sampling error can occasionally be overcome by weighing the results of a survey. Researchers can ensure a representative sample through the technique of choosing a random sample. A further refinement of the technique is choosing a stratified random sample.

After the data have been collected, the researcher analyzes the many pieces of information and then determines what conclusions can be drawn. It is important to make clear whether research findings are generalizable—that is, applicable to the wider society because the research population adequately reflects the characteristics of the wider society. Finally, the research report is prepared.

There are three research methods used by sociologists: surveys, participant observation, and experiments. A survey is a research method in which a population is studied in order to reveal specific facts about it. The survey can be conducted through the use of questionnaires or interviews. An interview can be structured or semistructured (open-ended).

Participant observation researchers enter into a group's activities and observe the behavior of the group's members. Although some participant observers conceal

Sudman, professor of marketing at the University of Illinois, studies have shown that "the only time the exit polls can have an effect is when they change voters' perceptions about the closeness of the race.

Exit polls, in particular, are subject to error and manipulation. Many voters lie to the pollsters or refuse to answer pollsters' questions, thus limiting the size of the sample. Or political hacks may try to stack the deck by finding out where the poll is being conducted, hiring people to go in and out of voting places without actually voting, and then telling the pollster that they voted for a particular candidate. Realizing the possibility of this type of manipulation, many polling organizations do not base their calls on exit polls, but rely instead on projections, which are based on votes actually cast as the count is tabulated in different pre-

cincts throughout a state. Unlike exit polls, projections have nothing to do with what voters tell the pollsters.

Freedom of the press aside, the arguments against the restraint of early election calls are substantial. Burns W. Roper, chairman of The Roper Organization, makes these points:

"I have never seen any convincing evidence that demonstrates that an early call here affects the outcome of an election there. Moreover, logic . . . argues against the thesis that an early call will change the outcome. If in 1980 you were for Ronald Reagan and I was for Jimmy Carter and we both heard early calls before we went to the polls, it seems to me the effect on us would be equal. You might be tempted not to vote because it is now clear that Ronald Reagan

no longer needs your vote. I might be tempted not to vote because it is now clear my vote for Carter can't help him.

To deal with the public perception that West Coast voters are being cheated of their right to participate fully in the election of the president, legislation has been proposed for a uniform poll closing time throughout the country. That is, if the polls close at 9 P.M. in California, they would close at 6 P.M. in New York. Meanwhile, voters can take some comfort in knowing that there is little solid research on exactly what the effect of early calls is.

Sources: Seymour Sudman, "Do Exit Polls Influence Voting Behavior?" *Public Opinion Quarterly,* Spring 1985, pp. 332–333; Burns W. Roper, "Early Election Calls: The Larger Dangers," *Public Opinion Quarterly,* Spring 1985, pp. 5–6.

---

their identities while doing research, most sociologists argue that this tactic is unethical.

An experiment is carried out in a controlled situation that permits close observation through the use of videotape or other recording instruments. Although laboratory experiments are an attractive means of doing research, sociologists seldom use them because most of the issues that interest sociologists cannot be investigated within the confines of a laboratory.

Even though sociologists strive for objectivity in their research, a completely value-free approach may be impossible; however, it is a goal toward which all social

scientists strive. All scientists bring to bear on their work their cultural, social, economic, political, and educational backgrounds as well as their interest, concerns, and personalities.

Of major concern to social scientists is the question of ethics in research. In whose interest is the research? Who will benefit from it? Will anyone be hurt? While struggling to answer these questions, researchers must also keep in mind that social research rarely benefits the subjects directly and that most subjects of sociological research belong to groups with little or no power. These conditions place an added responsibility on researchers to protect their subjects.

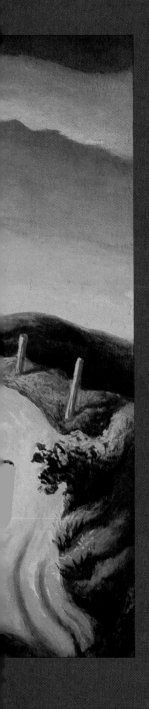

Part 2

THE INDIVIDUAL IN SOCIETY

Chapter 3

CULTURE

In 1830 the British exploring vessel *Beagle* reached Tierra del Fuego at the southern tip of South America. The crew of the *Beagle* represented the most highly developed industrial society of the time, whereas the Fuegian Indians were members of one of the simplest New World societies. The captain of the *Beagle* thus decided to take back with him four Fuegian Indians in the hope of educating them and eventually returning them to their community so that they could introduce "civilized cultural" ways.

The four were reduced to three after one contracted smallpox. These three included two men, Jemmy and York, and one woman, Fuegia Basket. The three spent one year with a minister near London who taught them the English language and culture. They were even granted an audience with King William IV, who gave them a variety of gifts representative of the industrial age. At the end of 1831 the *Beagle* sailed back to South America carrying the three Anglicized Fuegian Indians and Charles Darwin. Darwin was very impressed with the experiment, which seemed to have supplanted one set of cultural ways with another.

Once they reached Tierra del Fuego, Jemmy, York, and Fuegia Basket were dropped off. York was met by his mother and several brothers. Darwin noted,

> The meeting was less interesting than that between a horse, turned out into a field, when he joins an old companion. There was no demonstration of affection; they simply stared for a short time at each other; and the mother immediately went to look after her canoe.

Darwin and the crew then departed, expecting the cultural transformation of the community to begin under the leadership of the three Fuegian Indians.

A year later Darwin and the crew of the *Beagle* again returned to the area. Soon a canoe paddled by Jemmy approached. Darwin had been enormously impressed by Jemmy's Anglicized manner acquired during his year in England. However, Darwin now noted that Jemmy was

> . . . a thin haggard savage, with long disordered hair, and naked, except a bit of blanket around his waist. We did not recognize him till he was close to us; . . . We had left him plump, fat,

clean, and well dressed; . . . I never saw so complete and grievous a change.

Over the years further information about the three showed that the experiment in cultural change had failed. Jemmy eventually instigated the massacre of six missionaries who had come to the area; York was murdered after he killed another man; and Fuegia Basket returned to her previous cultural ways (Farb, 1978).

The failure of this experiment demonstrates to us how deeply ingrained the cultural customs and beliefs are that have been transmitted to us since birth as members of a society.

THE CONCEPT OF CULTURE

In the nineteenth century, anthropologists inspired by Darwin's work on evolution began to describe the complex rules of behavior, linguistic structures, and other aspects of the lives of primitive peoples. Old assumptions that these peoples were living a life in pure nature or as "noble savages" were discarded. It was recognized that all human societies had complex ways of life that differed greatly from one society to another. These ways of life came to be referred to as *culture,* and in 1871 Edward Tylor gave us the first definition of the concept, which to this day remains one of the most widely quoted. Culture, he noted, is that complex whole that includes knowledge, belief, art, law, morals, custom, and other capabilities and habits acquired by man as a member of society" (Tylor, 1958). Robert Bierstadt then simplified Tylor's definition by stating, "Culture is the complex whole that consists of all the ways we think and do and everything we have as members of society" (Bierstadt, 1974).

Most definitions of culture emphasize certain features, namely, culture is shared; it is acquired, not inborn; the elements make up a complex whole; and it is transmitted from one generation to the next (Sagarin, 1978).

We will define **culture** as all that human beings learn to do, to use, to produce, to know, and to believe as they grow to maturity and live out their lives in the social groups to which they belong. Culture is basically a blueprint for living in a particular society. In common speech, people often refer to a "cultured person" as someone with an interest in the arts, literature, or music, suggesting that the individual has a highly developed sense of style or aesthetic appreciation of the "finer things." To sociologists, however, every human being is "cultured." All human beings participate in a culture, whether they are Harvard educated and upper class, or illiterate and living in a primitive society. Culture is crucial to human existence.

When sociologists speak of culture, they are referring to the general phenomenon that is a characteristic of all human groups. However, when they refer to *a* culture, they are pointing to the specific culture of a particular group. In other words, all human groups have a culture, but it often varies considerably from one group to the next. Take the concept of time, which we accept as entirely natural. To Westerners, time "marches on" steadily and predictably, with past, present, and future divided into units of precise duration (minutes, hours, days, months, years, and so on). In the culture of the Sioux Indians, however, the concept of time simply does not exist apart from ongoing events: nothing can be early or late—things just happen when they happen. For the Navajo Indians, the future is a meaningless concept—immediate obligations are what count. For natives of the Pacific island of Truk, however, the past has no independent meaning—it is a living part of the present. These examples of cultural differences in the perception of time point to a basic sociological fact—each culture must be investigated and understood on its own terms before it is possible to make valid cross-cultural comparisons (Hall, 1981).

In every social group, culture is transmitted from one generation to the next. Unlike other creatures, human beings do not pass on many behavioral patterns through their genes. Rather, culture is taught and learned through social interaction.

CULTURE AND BIOLOGY

Human beings, like all other creatures, have basic biological needs. We must eat, sleep, protect ourselves from the environment, reproduce, and nurture our young—or else we could not survive as a species. In most other animals, such basic biological needs are met in more or less identical ways by all the members of a species. This is a result of inherited behavior patterns or instincts, which are unlearned and specific for a given species as well as universal for all members of that species. Thus, instinctual behaviors, such as the web spinning of specific species of spiders, are constant and do not vary significantly from one individual member of a species to another.

culture All that human beings learn to do, to use, to produce, to know, and to believe as they grow to maturity and live out their lives in the social groups to which they belong.

When these Hopi Indians experience a conflict, they wish to follow the traditional practices and customs of their culture. At the same time the culture of the larger society urges them to adopt the conventions of mainstream American society.

A CASE OF CULTURE SHOCK

Culture shock can be a problem for sociologists who wish to study foreign countries or social groups whose life-styles are very different from those in their own country. For example, anthropologist Napoleon A. Chagnon experienced culture shock when he went to live with a group of people known as the Yąnomamö (pronounced "Yah-no-mama" and nasalized). The Yąnomamö are approximately ten thousand South American Indians who live in 125 villages in southern Venezuela and northern Brazil. When Chagnon first visited them, they had had almost no contact with the outside world. The Yąnomamö are known as the "fierce people" because of the importance aggression and fighting play in their culture. Each village is in a constant state of warfare with others. Men often beat their wives and engage in chest-pounding duels and club fights with one another.

Here Chagnon describes his first encounter with the Yano-mamö:

My first day in the field illustrated to me what my teachers meant when they spoke of "culture shock." I had traveled in a small, aluminum rowboat propelled by a large outboard motor for two and a half days. . . . We arrived at the village, Bissaai-teri, about 2:00 P.M. and docked the boat along the muddy bank at the [end] of the path used by the Indians to fetch their drinking water. It was hot and muggy, and my clothing was soaked with perspiration. . . . The small, biting gnats were out in astronomical numbers, for it was the beginning of the dry season. My face and hands were swollen from the venom of their numerous stings. In just a few moments I was to meet my first Yąnomamö, my first primitive man. What would it be like? . . . Would they like me? This was important to me; I wanted them to be so fond of me that they would adopt me into their kinship system and way of life. I was determined to become a member of their society. My heart began to pound as we approached the village and heard the buzz of activity within the circular compound. . . .

The entrance to the village was covered over with brush and dry palm leaves. We pushed them aside to expose the low opening to the village. The excitement of meeting my first Indians was almost unbearable as I duck-waddled through the low passage into the village clearing.

I looked up and gasped when I saw a dozen burly, naked, filthy, hideous men staring at us down the shafts of their drawn arrows! Immense wads of green tobacco were stuck between their lower teeth and lips, making them look even more hideous, and strands of dark green slime dripped or hung from their noses. We arrived at the village while the men were blowing a hallucinogenic drug up their nose. The mucus is always saturated with the green powder and the Indians usually let it run freely from their nostrils. My next discovery was that there were a dozen or so vicious, underfed dogs snapping at my legs, circling me as if I were going to be their next meal. I just stood there holding my notebook, helpless and pathetic. Then the stench of the decaying vegetation and filth struck me and I almost got sick. I was horrified. What sort of welcome was this for the person who came here to live with you and learn your way of life, to become friends with you? They put their weapons down when they recognized [my companion] and returned to their chanting, keeping a nervous eye on the village entrances. . . .

[By evening,] I had not eaten all day, I was soaking wet from perspiration, the gnats were biting me, and I was covered with red pigment, the result of a dozen or so complete examinations I had been given by as many burly Indians. These examinations capped an

This is not true of humans, whose behaviors are highly variable and changeable, both individually and culturally. It is through culture that human beings acquire the means to meet their needs. For example,

the young, or larvae, of hornets and yellow jackets are housed in paper-walled, hexagonal chambers that they scrape against with their heads when hungry. This is a signal to workers to immediately feed the young tiny

otherwise grim day. The Indians would blow their noses into their hands, flick as much of the mucus off that would separate in a snap of the wrist, wipe the residue into their hair, and then carefully examine my face, arms, legs, hair, and the contents of my pockets. I asked Mr. Barker how to say "Your hands are dirty"; my comments were met by the Indians in the following way: They would "clean" their hands by spitting a quantity of slimy tobacco juice into them, rub them together, and then proceed with the examination. . . .

The thing that bothered me most was the incessant, passioned, and aggressive demands the Indians made. It would become so unbearable that I would have to lock myself in my mud hut every once in a while just to escape from it: Privacy is one of Western culture's greatest achievements. But I did not want privacy for its own sake; rather, I simply had to get away from the begging. Day and night for the entire time I lived with the Yąnomamö I was plagued by such demands as: "Give me a knife, I am poor!"; "If you don't take me with you on your next trip to Widokaiya-teri I'll chop a hole in your canoe!"; "Don't point your camera at me or I'll hit you!" "Share your food with me!"; "Take me across the river in your canoe and be quick about it!"; "Give me a cooking pot!"; "Loan me your flashlight so I can go hunting tonight!"; "Give me medi-

cine . . . I itch all over!"; "Take us on a week-long hunting trip with your shotgun!"; and "Give me an axe or I'll break into your hut when you are away visiting and steal one!" And so I was bombarded by such demands day after day, months on end, until I could not bear to see an Indian.

It was not as difficult to become calloused to the incessant begging as it was to ignore the sense of urgency, the impassioned tone of voice, or the intimidation and aggression with which the demands were made. It was likewise difficult to adjust to the fact that the Yąnomamö refused to accept "no" for an answer until or unless it

seethed with passion and intimidation—which it did after six months. Giving in to a demand always established a new threshold; the next demand would be for a bigger item or favor, and the anger of the Indians ever greater if the demand was not met. I soon learned that I had to become very much like the Yąnomamö to be able to get along with them on their terms: sly, aggressive, and intimidating. . . .
(Chagnon, 1977).

Source: Excerpted from Napoleon A. Chagnon, *Yąnomamö: The Fierce People,* 2d ed. (New York: Holt, Rinehart and Winston, 1977), pp. 4–10, 140–143.

Napolean Chagnon's attempt to study the Yąnamamö produced several problems. Yąnamamö culture prohibits using the name of the deceased. When Chagnon asked the Yąnamamö about their ancestors, they gave him fictitious and obscene names. Without realizing it, Chagnon was uttering obscenities as he tried to interview the Indians and gain further information.

bits of undigested insect parts (Wilson, 1975). Neither the larvae nor the workers learn these patterns of behavior: they are instinctual. In contrast, although human infants cry when hungry or uncomfortable,

the responses to those cries vary from group to group and even from person to person within the same group. In some groups, infants are breast-fed; in others, they are fed prepared milk formulas from bottles; and in still others they are fed according to the mother's preference. Some groups breast-feed children for as long as 5 or 6 years; others for no more than 10 to 12 months. Some mothers feed their infants on demand—whenever they seem to be hungry; other mothers hold their infants to a rigid feeding schedule. In some groups, infants are picked up and soothed when they seem unhappy or uncomfortable. Other groups believe that infants should be left to "cry it out." In the United States, mothers differ in their approaches to feeding and handling their infants, but most are influenced by the practices they have observed among members of their families and their social groups. Such habits, shared by the members of each group, express the group's culture. They are learned by group members and are kept more or less uniform by social expectations and pressures.

culture shock The reaction people may have when encountering cultural traditions different from their own.

CULTURE SHOCK AND ETHNOCENTRISM

Every social group has its own specific culture, its own way of seeing, doing, and making things, its own traditions. Some cultures are quite similar to one another; others are very different. When individuals travel

ethnocentrism The tendency to judge other cultures in terms of one's own customs and values.

abroad to countries with cultures that are very different from their own, the experience can be quite upsetting. Meals are scheduled at different times of day, "strange" or even "repulsive" foods are eaten, and the traveler never quite knows what to expect from others or what others in turn may expect. Local customs may seem "charming" or "brutal." Sometimes travelers are unable to adjust easily to a foreign culture; they may become anxious, lose their appetites, or even feel sick. Sociologists call these reactions **culture shock** to describe what happens when people have difficulty adjusting to a new culture that differs markedly from the one they are used to.

Culture shock can also be experienced within a person's own society. Picture the army recruit, fresh from civilian life, having to adapt to a whole new set of behaviors, rules, and expectations in basic training—a new cultural setting.

People often make judgments about other cultures according to the customs and values of their own, a practice sociologists call **ethnocentrism.** Thus, for example, an American might call the floor of a Guatemalan peasant's home filthy because it is constructed of packed dirt or believe that the family organization of the Watusi (of East Africa) is immoral because it allows a husband to have several wives. Ethnocentrism can lead to prejudice and discrimination and can become ugly when it results in the repression or domination of one group by another.

Immigrants, for instance, often encounter hostile ethnocentrism when their manners, dress, eating habits, or religious beliefs differ markedly from those of their new neighbors. Because of this hostility and because of their own ethnocentrism, immigrants often establish their own communities in their adopted country. Cuban-Americans, for example, have settled in Miami, where they have built a power base through strength in numbers. In Dade County, which includes Miami, there are about 652,000 Cubans—a number that made

Hasidic Jews represent a unique culture within the larger American society as well as among mainstream Jews. Their appearance and ways of practicing their religion originated in nineteenth-century Poland.

possible the election of the country's first Cuban-American mayor, Xavier Suarez.

Sociologists recognize that social groups and cultures must be studied and understood on their own terms before valid comparisons can be made. This perspective is termed **cultural relativism,** a position that frequently is taken to mean that social scientists never should judge the relative merits of any group or culture. This is not the case. Cultural relativism is an approach to doing objective cross-cultural research. It does not require researchers to abdicate their personal standards. In fact, good social scientists will take the trouble to spell out exactly what their standards are so that both the researchers and the readers will be alert to possible bias in their studies.

Cultural relativism requires that behaviors and customs be viewed and analyzed within the context in which they occur. The packed-dirt floor of the Guatemalan house should be noted in terms of the culture of the Guatemalan peasant, not in terms of suburban America. Researchers, however, may find that dirt floors contribute to the incidence of parasites in young children and may therefore judge such construction to be less desirable than wood or tile floors.

COMPONENTS OF CULTURE

The concept of culture is not easy to understand, perhaps because every aspect of our social lives is an expression of it and also because familiarity produces a kind of near-sightedness toward our own culture, making it difficult for us to take an analytical perspective toward our everyday social lives. Sociologists find it helpful to break down culture into two separate components: material culture (having and using objects) and nonmaterial culture (doing, thinking, and feeling).

MATERIAL CULTURE

Material culture consists of human technology—all the things human beings make and use, from small hand-held tools to skyscrapers. Without material culture our species could not survive long, for material culture provides a buffer between humans and their environment. Using it, human beings can protect themselves from environmental stresses, as when they build shelters and wear clothing to protect themselves from the cold or from strong sunlight. Even more important, humans use material culture to modify and exploit the environment. They build dams and irrigation canals, plant fields and forests, convert coal and oil into energy, and transform ores into versatile metals. Using material culture, our

material culture All the things human beings make and use, from small hand-held tools to skyscrapers.

cultural relativism The position that social scientists doing cross-cultural research should view and analyze behaviors and customs within the cultural context in which they occur.

The King of Akure in Nigeria appears in the palace court with some of his 156 wives during the festival of Ifa. The mores of our society do not allow this type of behavior. Cultural relativism would require that we not judge this practice from the standpoint of our culture alone.

Housing is an aspect of material culture that can vary widely, as can be seen by comparing this elaborate home in Saudi Arabia, and these thatched huts in Nigeria.

nonmaterial culture The totality of knowledge, beliefs, values, and rules for appropriate behavior that specify how a people should interact and how they may solve their problems.

normative culture One of the two categories of nonmaterial culture. Normative culture consists of the rules people follow for doing things. Norms, mores, and folkways are the central elements of normative culture.

norms Specific rules of behavior that are agreed upon and shared within a culture to prescribe limits of acceptable behavior.

species has learned to cope with the most extreme environments and to survive and even to thrive on all continents and in all climates. Human beings have walked on the floor of the ocean and on the surface of the moon. No other creature can do this: none has our flexibility. Material culture has made human beings the dominant life form on earth.

NONMATERIAL CULTURE

Nonmaterial culture is the totality of knowledge, beliefs, values, and rules for appropriate behavior (norms) that specify how a people should interact and how they may solve their problems. Nonmaterial culture is ordered through the institutions of family, religion, education, economy, and government. Most people acquire culture through these institutions.

Whereas the elements of material culture are things that have a physical existence (they can be seen, touched, and so on), the elements of nonmaterial culture are the ideas associated with their use. Although

engagement rings and birthday flowers have a material existence, they also reflect attitudes, beliefs, and values that are part of our culture. There are rules for their appropriate use in specified situations. Nonmaterial culture is separated into two categories: normative culture and cognitive culture.

Normative Culture

Normative culture consists of the rules for doing things. **Norms** are central elements of normative culture. They are rules of behavior that are agreed upon and shared within a culture to prescribe limits of acceptable behavior. They define "normal" expected behavior in a given situation and help human beings achieve organization and predictability in their lives. For example, Edward T. Hall (1966) has found that Americans follow an unwritten rule concerning public behavior. As soon as an individual stops or is seated in a public place, a small, invisible sphere of privacy that is considered inviolate swells around the person. The size will vary with the degree of crowding, the age, sex, and importance of the person, and the general surroundings. Anyone who enters this zone and stays there is intruding. To overcome this personal-space barrier, a person who intrudes for a specific purpose will usually acknowledge the intrusion by beginning with a phrase like "Pardon me, but can you tell me? . . ."

On the other hand, pushing and shoving in public places is a characteristic of Middle Eastern culture, a characteristic that, unlike the attitude in Western cultures, is not considered a rude behavior. For the Arab, there is no such thing as an intrusion of space in public. Occupying a given spot does not give you any special rights to that area at all. If, for example, person A is standing on a street corner and person B wants that spot, it is perfectly all right for person B to try to make person A uncomfortable enough to move.

Arabs have a completely different set of assumptions regarding the body and the rights associated with it than do Westerners. Certainly the Arab tendency to shove and push one another in public and to touch and pinch women in public vehicles would not be tolerated by Westerners. Arabs do not have any concept of a private zone outside the body. In the Western world, the person is synonymous with an individual inside a skin, and in many places the skin and even the clothes are inviolate. You need permission to touch if you are strangers. For the Arab, however, the location of the person in relation to the body is quite different. The person exists somewhere down inside the body, protected from touch. Touching the outside of the body—skin and clothes —is not really touching the person.

Although Arabs do not mind being crowded by people, they hate to be hemmed in by walls. They avoid partitions because they do not like to be alone. When searching for a home, Arabs look for plenty of unobstructed space in which to move around. Because physical privacy is relatively unknown in the Arab world, they simply stop talking to be alone. Arabs believe that if you

are not with people, you are deprived of life. This attitude makes their choice of a home an extension of, and consistent with, their approach to the body.

Arabs also believe that sharing smells is an act of friendship and to deny the smell of your breath to your friends is interpreted as an act of shame. So it is that Americans, trained as they are not to breathe in people's faces, automatically communicate shame to the Arabs (Hall, 1966).

Mores (pronounced "more-ays") are strongly held norms that usually have a moral connotation and are based on the central values of the culture. Violations of mores produce strong negative reactions, which are often supported and expressed through the legal system. Desecration of a church or temple, sexual molestation of a child, rape, murder, incest, and child beating all are violations of American mores.

Not all norms command such absolute conformity. Much of day-to-day life is governed by traditions, or **folkways,** which are norms that permit a rather wide degree of individual interpretation as long as certain limits are not overstepped. People who violate folkways are seen as peculiar or possibly eccentric, but rarely do they elicit strong public response. For example, a wide range of dress is now acceptable in theaters and restaurants. A man may wear clothes ranging from a business suit, shirt, and tie to

mores Strongly held norms that usually have a moral connotation and are based on the central values of the culture.

folkways Norms that permit a rather wide degree of individual interpretation as long as certain limits are not overstepped. Folkways change with time and vary from culture to culture.

According to the norms of American culture, a common way for people to greet each other is to shake hands. In Japan, people greet each other by bowing.

A CONTRAST BETWEEN AMERICAN AND ARAB VALUES

The following situation described by Moshe Rubinstein provides an excellent example of contrasting values between American culture and Arab culture.

One summer my wife and I became acquainted with an educated, well-to-do Arab named Ahmed in the city of Jerusalem. Following a traditional Arabic dinner one evening, Ahmed decided to test my wisdom with his fables. One of them caught me in a rather awkward setting. "Moshe," he said as he put his fable in the form of a question, "imagine that you, your mother, your wife, and your child are in a boat and it capsizes. You can save yourself and only one of the remaining three. Whom will you save?" For a moment I froze, while thoughts raced through my mind. Did he have to ask this of all questions? And in the presence of my wife yet? No matter what I might say, it would not be right

from someone's point of view, and if I refused to answer I might be even worse off. I was stuck. So I tried to answer by thinking aloud as I progressed to a conclusion, hoping for salvation before I said what came to my mind as soon as he posed the question, namely, save the child.

Ahmed was very surprised. I flunked the test. As he saw it, there was one correct answer and a corresponding rational argument to support it. "You see," he said, "you can have more than one wife in a lifetime, you can have more than one child, but you have only one mother. You must save your mother!"

I told the story to a class of one hundred freshmen and asked for their responses. Sixty would save the child, and forty the wife. When I asked who would save his mother, there was a roar of laughter. No one raised his hand. They thought the question was funny. They were also quite amazed to learn of Ahmed's response. A group of about forty executives whom I addressed on problem solving and decision making responded as follows: More than half would save the child, less than half would save the wife. One reluctantly raised his hand in response to "Who would save his mother?" (I believe he had an ac-

cent. . . .) I promised the group to send the mothers sympathy cards.

The executives were apparently impressed by the story because, at a dinner party that followed the lectures, Ahmed's question was ringing all over the place. Across the table from me sat one of the course instructors and his wife. Both came from Persia and spent the last 7 years in the United States. She wanted to know what the conversation about mother, wife, child was all about. Her husband related the story, and she came up with a response immediately: "Of course I would save my mother, you have only one mother." Here her values were a perfect match to Ahmed's culture. But then she turned to her husband and added: I hope you won't do that." The influence of new values in the U.S.A., or did she mean specifically her mother-in-law. . . ?

Most of our friends reacted as if it was natural to save the child. One, an artist, said that she would probably drown before she could ever decide what to do. . . .

Source: Moshe Rubinstein, *Patterns of Problem Solving* (Englewood Cliffs, N.J.: Prentice-Hall, 1975), pp. 1–2.

informal jeans, open-necked shirt, and sweater. A woman may choose a cocktail dress and high-heeled shoes or, like the man, the casual-jeans look. However, extremes in either direction will cause a reac-

tion. Many establishments limit the extent of informal dress: signs may specify that no one with bare feet or without a shirt may enter. On the other hand, a person in extremely formal attire might well attract attention and elicit amused comments in a fast-food restaurant.

Good manners in our culture also show a range of acceptable behavior. A man may or may not open a door or hold a coat for a woman, who also may choose whether or not to open a door or hold a coat for a man—all four options are acceptable behavior and cause neither comment nor other negative reactions from people.

These two examples illustrate another aspect of folkways: they change with time. Not too long ago a man was *always* expected to hold a door open for a woman, and a woman was *never* expected to hold a coat for a man.

Folkways also vary from one culture to another. In the United States, for example, it is customary to thank someone for a gift. Not to do so is to be ungrateful and ill-mannered. Subtle cultural differences can make international gift giving, however, a source of anxiety or embarrassment to well-meaning business travelers. For example, if you give a gift on first meeting an Arab businessman, it may be interpreted as a bribe. If you give a clock in China, it is considered bad luck. In Latin America you will have a problem if you give knives or handkerchiefs. The former connote the end of a friendship; the latter are associated with sadness.

The Japanese are maniacal gift givers. Gift giving is so prevalent in the Japanese culture that they often practice something called *taraimawashi,* which involves giving a gift of something utterly useless that the recipient can then give to someone else, who in turn can pass it on (*New York Times,* December 6, 1981).

Norms are specific expectations about social behavior, but it is important to add, they are not absolute. Even though we learn what is expected in our culture, there is room for what might be called "slippage" in individual interpretations of these norms that deviate from the ideal.

Ideal norms are expectations of what people should do under perfect conditions. These are the norms we first teach our chil-

Each culture allows for a wide degree of interpretation of customs. Even though it may be common for children to carve a pumpkin at Halloween or ask Santa Claus for gifts at Christmas, not following these customs does not usually produce any strong sanctions.

dren. They tend to be simple, making few distinctions and allowing for no exceptions. Drivers "stop at red lights" is an ideal norm in American society. So is the norm that a marriage will last "until death do us part."

In reality, however, nothing about human beings is ever that dependable. For example, if you interviewed Americans

ideal norms Expectations of what people should do under perfect conditions. The norm that marriage will last "until death do us part" is an ideal norm in American society.

cognitive culture The thinking component of culture consisting of shared beliefs and knowledge of what the world is like—what is real and what is not, what is important and what is trivial. One of the two categories of nonmaterial culture.

real norms Norms that allow for differences in individual behavior. Real norms specify how people actually behave, not how they should behave under ideal circumstances.

values A culture's general orientations toward life—its notion of what is good and bad, what is desirable and undesirable.

about how drivers respond to red lights, you would get answers something like this: "Ideally, drivers should stop at red lights. But in actual fact, drivers sometimes run red lights. So, even though you can pretty much count on a driver stopping for a red light, it pays to be careful. And if it looks like a driver is not going to stop for a light, better play it safe and slow down." In other words, people recognize that drivers usually do feel they should stop when a traffic light is red, but they also acknowledge that as things really are, there are times when a driver will not stop for a red light. The driver may be in a hurry, drunk, upset, or simply not paying attention. Norms expressed in this way—with qualifications and allowances for differences in individual behavior—are what sociologists call **real norms,** and they specify how people actually behave. They reflect the fact that people's behavior is a function not only of norm guidance but also of situational elements, as exemplified by the driver who does not always stop at a red light if no car appears to be coming from the other direction.

The concepts of ideal and real norms are useful for distinguishing between mores and folkways. For mores, the ideal and the real norms tend to be very close, whereas for folkways they can be much more loosely connected: our mores say *thou shalt not kill* and really mean it, but you might forget to follow folkways and neglect to say thank you without provoking general outrage. More important, the very fact that a culture

Certain aspects of the material culture, such as the invention of the telephone, produce profound and lasting changes.

legitimizes the difference between ideal and real expectations allows the individual some room to interpret norms according to his or her own personal disposition.

Cognitive Culture

Cognitive culture, the thinking component of culture, consists of shared beliefs and knowledge of what the world is like—what is real and what is not, what is important and what is trivial. The beliefs need not even be true or testable as long as they are shared by a majority of the people. Cognitive culture is like a map in that it is a representation of the world around us. Think of a scout troop on a hike in the wilderness. The troop finds its way by studying a map showing many of the important features of the terrain. The scouts who use the map share a mental image of the area as it is represented by the map. Yet, just as maps differ, each perhaps emphasizing different details of the terrain or using different symbols to represent them, so do cultures differ in the ways in which they represent the world. It is important not to confuse any culture's representation of reality with what ultimately is real—just as a map is not the actual terrain it charts.

Values are a culture's general orientations toward life—its notions of what is good and bad, what is desirable and undesirable. Values themselves are abstractions. They can best be found by looking for the recurring patterns of behavior that express them. Values are not the same in every culture. See *Taking the Sociological Perspective* box entitled "A Contrast between American and Arab Values."

THE RELATIONSHIP BETWEEN MATERIAL AND NONMATERIAL CULTURE

Material culture and nonmaterial culture are very closely related. People produce and use things the way their cognitive culture instructs them to. Living side by side, culturally different groups may produce and use very different things. In Israel, for example, Bedouin nomads live in felt tents, whereas their farming neighbors live in concrete prefabricated apartments.

It would be wrong, however, to think of material culture simply as the expression of cognitive culture. Once created, material culture can result in changes in a people's cognitive culture. Thus, for instance, the invention of the plow and irrigation ditches were relatively modest achievements in themselves, but the development of agriculture helped make possible the rise of civilization as we know it. Computers originally were developed simply as a means to perform high-speed calculations, but within a generation they have contributed to developments in the sciences, the arts, and even philosophy no one even dreamed of.

CULTURE AND ADAPTATION

Over time cultures adjust to the demands of the environment. Although **environmental determinism**—the belief that the environment dictates cultural patterns—is no longer accepted, there must be some degree of "fit" between environment and culture. Whereas other animal species must rely on the long, slow process of evolution in order to adapt to their environment, culture has allowed humans to adapt to many different habitats and become the most flexible species on earth. In Arctic regions, generation after generation of animal life developed the fur, feathers, and fat layers necessary to survive. In the deserts only those life forms that could cope with intense heat and little water have remained. Adaptation to the environment among other animal species is a slow biological process. Among humans, it is a relatively fast series of developments in knowledge, behavior, and toolmaking. For example, the hammock allows air to circulate freely around the sleeper; surely it was

no accident that it was invented and used by tropical peoples. Using culture, humans do not simply adapt to their environment, they also change it.

HUMAN EVOLUTION: BIOLOGICAL AND CULTURAL

Because most human behavior is not instinctive but is learned (see Chapter 4) and depends on culture, much can be learned about human development by tracing the evolution of culture.

The earliest evidence of culture found thus far is in Africa. In Tanzania, Kenya, and Ethiopia, fist-sized stone tools have been found dating from 1.5 million to 2.9 million years ago. These are very simple tools made by knocking several flakes off pieces of flint to produce an implement with which animals could be killed and butchered. The creatures that produced these tools stood upright and walked on their hind legs as we do, were 4 feet to 5 feet tall, and weighed from 80 pounds to 150 pounds. However, their heads were still very apelike.

These ancestors of ours subsisted on a varied diet of plants and small game, and there is evidence that they also were able to hunt larger animals. To protect themselves against dangerous meat-eating predators and to hunt big-game successfully, they probably developed some form of communication system and social organization. (This is a reasonable assumption, because our closest primate relatives, also live in organized social groups.)

Sometime between 1 million and 1.5 million years ago our immediate ancestors —called *Homo erectus*—evolved. *Homo erectus* resembled the modern human in all respects except for its head, which still was quite primitive. The jaws were large, the eyes protected by heavy ridges, the forehead still slanted sharply back. However, the brain had grown significantly. It averaged 1000 cubic centimeters, which is a little over two-thirds that of modern humans.

environmental determinism The belief that the environment dictates cultural patterns.

Homo erecti were very versatile. Groups of them moved out of the tropics and subtropics, venturing forth across the vast expanses of Africa, Europe, and Asia as far north as Germany in Europe and Peking in China. They lived in caves and skin huts on windswept plains, braving cold winters in their pursuit of big game — mammoth, horse, rhinoceros, deer, and oxen. *Homo erecti* lived in nomadic, well-organized bands, and their tools and weapons were well adapted to the different environments they inhabited.

Human culture and subsistence activities changed significantly around 70,000 years ago. By this time the Neanderthal, an early form of our own species, had already been in existence for several hundred thousand years. The cultural changes that came about at this time seem to have been in response to human populations moving ever farther north, right up to thu Ice Age glaciers. Here humans became even more skillful hunters than their ancestors were. Stone tools were made in a new process that involved shaping a piece of flint carefully before the final tool was split off. The process resulted in the production of a great variety of specialized tools, including spear points. But the most dramatic cultural developments were in other areas. There is evidence that Neanderthals practiced crude

surgery, cared for the aged and crippled, and buried their dead according to rituals that included tying corpses into a fetal position, sprinkling them with red powder, placing offerings of food beside them, and sometimes even covering them with flower petals (Solecki, 1971). This evidence suggests that Neanderthal people were intelligent, developed strong feelings for each other, and had ideas about death and possibly even about an afterlife.

By 35,000 to 40,000 years ago, stone-tool technology had reached its highest stage of development. Tool kits featured many forms of choppers, scrapers, chisels, points, and blades. In southern Europe, beginning around 25,000 B.C., we find the emergence of sophisticated art forms: engravings, wall paintings, abstract designs, and even three-dimensional sculptures of animals and humans. Hunter-gatherers — nomadic people who moved around in small groups living off whatever game or plants they happened to come upon — were responsible for these advances. It was bands of these versatile and creative hunter-gatherers that crossed the last frontiers into Australia and the Americas (where they arrived probably around 40,000 years ago).

By 10,000 B.C. the agricultural revolution was beginning, and on this base civilizations were built — societies that were to push forward the evolution of culture at an ever-accelerating pace. As the agricultural revolution progressed, the remaining hunting and gathering bands were driven into increasingly marginal territories, where their life-styles were doomed to extinction.

MECHANISMS OF CULTURAL CHANGE

Cultural change takes place at many different levels within a society. Some of the radical changes that have taken place often become obvious only in hindsight. When the airplane was invented, few people could visualize the changes it would produce. Not only did it markedly decrease the impact of distance on cultural contact, but it also had

We have learned a great deal about primitive cultures from cave paintings such as this one found in Niaux, France.

an enormous impact on such areas as economics and warfare.

It is generally assumed that the number of cultural items in a society (including everything from toothpicks to structures as complex as government agencies) has a direct relation to the rate of social change. A society that has few such items will also tend to have few innovations. As the number of cultural items increases, so do the innovations, as well as the rate of social change. For example, an inventory of the cultural items —from tools to religious practices— among the hunting and gathering Shoshone Indians totals a mere three thousand. Modern Americans who inhabit the same territory in Nevada and Utah are part of a culture with items numbering well into the millions. Social change in American society is proceeding rapidly, while Shoshone culture, as revealed by archeological excavations, appears to have changed scarcely at all for thousands of years.

Two simple mechanisms are responsible for cultural evolution: innovation and diffusion. **Innovation** is the source of all new **cultural traits**—that is, items of a culture such as tools, materials used, beliefs, values, and typical ways of doing things. Innovation takes place in several different ways, including recombining in a new way elements already available to a society (invention), discovering new concepts, finding new solutions to old problems, and devising and making new material objects.

Diffusion is the movement of culture traits from one culture to another. It almost inevitably results when people from one group or society come into contact with another, as when immigrant groups take on the dress or manners of already established groups and in turn contribute new foods or art forms to the dominant culture. Rarely does a trait diffuse from one culture into another without being modified in some way so that it fits better in its new context. This process of modification, called **reformulation,** can be seen in the transformation of black folk-blues into commercial music such as rhythm and blues and rock 'n roll.

When people of one society come in contact with people of another society, cultural diffusion takes place, as evidenced by this display of Valentine's Day candy representing a holiday indigenous to the United States.

Or, consider moccasins—the machine-made, chemically waterproofed, soft-soled cowhide shoes (with or without thongs)— which today differ from the Native American originals and usually are worn for recreation and not as a part of basic dress, as they originally were. Sociologists would say, therefore, that the culture trait of moccasins was reformulated when it diffused from Native American culture to the culture of industrial America.

CULTURE AS AN ADAPTIVE MECHANISM

Culture probably has been part of human evolution since the time, some 15 million years ago, when our ancestors first began to live on the ground. As we have stressed throughout this chapter, humans are extraordinarily flexible and adaptable. This adaptability, however, is not the result of being biologically fitted to the environment; in fact, human beings are remarkably unspecialized. We do not run very fast, jump very high, climb very well, or swim

innovation One of the two mechanisms responsible for cultural evolution. Innovation is the source of all new cultural traits.

cultural traits Items of a culture such as tools, materials used, beliefs, values, and typical ways of doing things.

diffusion One of the two mechanisms responsible for cultural evolution. Diffusion is the movement of cultural traits from one culture to another.

reformulation The process in which traits passed from one culture to another are modified to fit better in their new context.

adaptation The process by which human beings adjust to the changes in their environment.

specialization One of the two forms of adaptation. Specialization is developing ways of doing things that work extremely well in a particular environment or set of circumstances.

generalized adaptation One of the two forms of adaptation. Generalized adaptation involves developing more complicated yet more flexible ways of doing things.

cultural lag A situation that develops when new patterns of behavior conflict with traditional values. Cultural lag may occur when technological change (material culture) is more rapid than changes in norms and values (nonmaterial culture).

very far. But we are specialized in one area: we are culture producing, culture transmitting, and culture dependent. This unique specialization is rooted in the size and structure of the human brain and in our physical ability both to speak and to use tools.

Culture, then, is the primary means by which human beings adapt to the challenges of their environment. Thus, using enormous machines we strip away layers of the earth to extract minerals, and using other machines we transport their minerals to yet other machines, where they are converted to a staggering number of different products. Take away all our machines and American society would cease to exist. Take away all culture and the human species would perish. Culture is as much a part of us as our skin, muscles, bones, and brains.

Adaptation is the process by which human beings adjust to changes in their environment. Adaptation can take two different forms: specialization and generalized adaptability. Most cultures make use of both these means. **Specialization** involves

developing ways of doing things that work extremely well in a particular environment or set of circumstances. For example, the Inuit (Eskimo) igloo is a specialized way of building a shelter. It works in the Arctic but would fail miserably in the Sahara desert or in a Florida swamp. An American brick apartment building also is specialized. It is fine where the ground is solid and bricks can be delivered by truck or train, but in swamps, deserts, or where people must move around a great deal to subsist, the brick apartment building is of no use whatsoever.

Generalized adaptability involves developing more complicated yet more flexible ways of doing things. For example, industrial society has very elaborate means of transportation, including trucks, trains, planes, and ships. Industrialized transportation is complex, much more so than, say, the use of camels by desert nomads. At the same time, industrial transportation is a much more flexible transportation system, adaptable to every climate on earth. As such, it displays the quality of generalized adaptability as long as our environment continues to provide enough resources to meet its needs. Should we ever run out of rubber, metals, oil, and the other resources necessary for the operation of this technology, suddenly it will have lost its adaptive value. Then the camel might look like a very tempting means of transportation, and our "adaptable" technology would be as overspecialized as the dinosaur, with about the same probability of survival.

CULTURAL LAG

Although the diverse elements of a culture are interrelated, some may change rapidly and others lag behind. Thus, new patterns of behavior may emerge, even though they conflict with traditional values. William F. Ogburn (1964) coined the term **cultural lag** to describe this phenomenon. Ogburn observed that technological change (material culture) typically is faster than changes in nonmaterial culture—a culture's norms

The extraordinary conditions of the Andes produced a specialized type of cultural adaptation (seen in these ancient ruins) known as Machu Picchu. The terraces were built into the nearly vertical mountainside so that they could collect soil and moisture for gardening. The beveled building stones were so well fitted that they survived many earthquakes.

and values—and technological change often results in cultural lag. Consequently, stresses and strains among elements of a culture are more or less inevitable. For example, although it is now possible to determine if a baby is genetically normal before birth through procedures known as amniocentesis and chorion vills tissue sampling, the Catholic Church, as well as other religious groups, is opposed to using this technology. Similarly, although some three thousand babies have been born through *in vitro* fertilization, a process in which the egg and sperm are joined outside the mother's body, the Catholic Church also opposes this type of human reproduction.

Or, consider the warning recently issued to commuters between Kuala Lumpur, the capital of Malaysia, and the town of Port Kelang. Workers building a modern bridge apparently consulted local religious leaders, who declared that human heads were needed to appease dangerous spirits during the construction, and commuters were alerted that headhunters had been busy trying to supply them.

Other instances of cultural lag have considerably greater and more widespread negative effects. Advances in medicine have led to lowered infant mortality and greater life expectancy, but there has been no corresponding rapid worldwide acceptance of birth-control methods. The result is a potentially disastrous population explosion—our planet may not be able to support all the people who are being born and who are living longer.

THE SYMBOLIC NATURE OF CULTURE

Our discussion so far has stressed several qualities of culture: it is *learned,* it is *shared,* and it is *adaptive.* There is yet a fourth quality of culture, which is equally important: culture is *symbolic.*

All human beings respond to the world around them. They may decorate their bodies, make drawings on cave walls or canvases, or mold likenesses in clay. These all act as symbolic representations of their society. All complex behavior is derived from the ability to use symbols for people, events, or places. Without the ability to use symbols, culture could not exist.

SIGNS, SYMBOLS, AND CULTURE

What does it mean to say that culture is symbolic? To answer this we first must distinguish between signs and symbols. **Signs** are objects or things that can represent other things because they share some important quality with them. A clenched fist can be a sign of anger, because when people are angry they may use their fists to beat one another. Wrinkling one's nose can be a sign that something is undesirable because that is what people do when something smells bad.

Few travelers would think of going abroad without taking along a dictionary or phrase book to help them communicate with the people in the countries they visit. Although most people are aware that gestures are the most common form of cross-cultural communication, they do not realize that the language of gestures can be just as different, just as regional, and just as likely to cause misunderstanding as the spoken word can.

After a good meal in Naples, a well-meaning American tourist expressed his appreciation to the waiter by making the "A-okay" gesture with his thumb and forefinger. The waiter was shocked. He headed for the manager. The two seriously discussed calling the police and having the hapless tourist arrested for obscene behavior in a public place.

What had happened? How could such a seemingly innocent and flattering gesture have been so misunderstood?

Although we all recognize the differences in language and even colloquial

signs Objects or things that can represent other things because they share some important quality with them. A clenched fist, for example, can be a sign of anger because fists are used in physical arguments.

The communication system of many animals involves a series of signs, as does this courtship dance of the male seagull. The little boy's shrug is a symbol because it conveys an agreed-upon meaning.

"thumbs up" always a positive gesture? It is in the United States and in most of western Europe. And when it was displayed by the emperor of Rome, the upright thumb gesture spared the lives of gladiators in the Coliseum. But do not try it in Sardinia or northern Greece. There the gesture means the insulting phrase "Up yours."

The same naivete that can lead Americans into trouble in foreign countries also may work in reverse. After paying a call on Richard Nixon, Soviet leader Leonid Brezhnev stood on a balcony at the White House and saluted the American public with his hands clasped together in a gesture many people interpreted as meaning "I am the champ," or "I won." What many Americans perceived as a belligerent gesture was really just the Russian gesture for friendship (Ekman, Friesen, and Bear, 1984).

The communication systems of many animal species consist of more or less complicated systems of signs. For example, a worker bee returning to its hive can communicate accurately to other bees the location of pollen-rich plants by performing a complicated dance. Careful research by the German biologist Karl von Frisch (1967) showed that this is accomplished when the bee, in effect, acts out a miniature version of its flight. The direction of the dance is the direction of the flight, and the duration of the dance is proportional to the distance of the pollen-rich flowers from the hive. Most important, a bee can dance only to communicate where pollen is to be found, not about anything else, such as imminent danger from an approaching bear.

Symbols are objects that, like signs, represent other things. However, unlike signs, symbols need not share any quality at all with whatever they represent. Symbols stand for things simply because people agree that they do. Hence, when two or more individuals agree about the things a particular object represents, that object becomes a symbol by virtue of its shared meaning for those individuals. When Betsy Ross sewed the first American flag, she was creating a symbol.

symbols Objects that represent other things. Unlike signs, symbols need not share any of the qualities of whatever they represent.

phrases between countries, few of us are aware that the meaning of gestures may vary remarkably from culture to culture. Take the "A-okay" symbol, for example. In American culture it is used confidently in public by everyone from astronauts to politicians to signify that "everything is fine." In France and Belgium, however, it means "You're worth zero," but in Greece and Turkey it is an insulting or vulgar sexual invitation. And in parts of southern Italy, it is an offensive and graphic reference to a part of the anatomy. Small wonder that the waiter was shocked.

There are, in fact, dozens of gestures that take on totally different meanings as you move from one country to another. Is

The important point about the meanings of symbols is that they are entirely arbitrary, a matter of cultural convention. Each culture attaches its own meanings to things. Thus, in the United States mourners wear black to symbolize their sadness at a funeral. In the Far East people wear white. In this case the symbol is different but the meaning is the same. On the other hand, the same object can have different meanings in different cultures. Among the Sioux Indians the swastika (a cross made with ends bent at right angles to its arms) was a religious symbol; in Nazi Germany its meaning was political.

Looking at culture from this point of view, we would have to say that all aspects of culture—nonmaterial and material—are symbolic. Thus, culture may be said to consist of shared patterns of meanings expressed in symbols (Geertz, 1973). This means that virtually everything we say and do and use as group members has some shared meaning beyond itself. For example, wearing liptick is more than just coloring one's lips; smoking a cigarette is more than just filling one's lungs with smoke; and wearing high-heeled shoes is more than just trying to be taller. All these actions and artifacts are part of American culture and are symbolic of sexuality and adulthood, among other things. Even a person's clothes and home—material possessions—represent more than just means of protection from the environment; they are also symbolic of that person's status in the social class structure. An automobile for many people is more than just a means of transportation—it is symbolic of their socioeconomic status.

LANGUAGE AND CULTURE

Of all symbols, words are the most important. Using the symbols of language, humans organize the world around them into labeled cognitive categories and use these labels to communicate with one another. Language, therefore, makes possible the teaching and sharing of cognitive and normative culture. It provides the principal means through which culture is transmitted and the foundation on which the complexity of human thought and experience rests.

Language allows humans to transcend the limitations imposed by their environment and biological evolution. It has taken tens of millions of years of biological evolution to produce human beings. On the other hand, in a matter of decades, cultural evolution has made it possible for us to travel to the moon. Biological evolution had to work slowly through genetic changes, but cultural evolution works quickly through the transmission of information from one generation to the next. In terms of knowledge and information, each human generation, because of language, is able to begin where the previous one left off. Each generation does not have to begin anew, as is the case in the animal world.

It is important that we remember that culture is selective: in each culture some aspects of the world are viewed as important and others are virtually neglected. The language of a culture reflects this **selectivity** in its vocabulary and even in its grammar. Therefore, as children learn a language, they are being molded to think and even to experience the world in terms of one particular cultural perspective.

This view of language and culture, known as the **Sapir-Whorf hypothesis,** argues that the language a person uses determines his or her perception of reality (Whorf, 1956; Sapir, 1961). This idea caused some alarm among social scientists at first, for it implied that people from different cultures never quite experience the same reality. Although more recent research has modified this extreme view, it remains true that different languages classify experiences differently—that language is the lens through which we experience the world. The prominent anthropologist Ruth Benedict (1961) pointed out, "We do not see the lens through which we look."

The category corresponding to one word and one thought in language A may be regarded by language B as two or more cate-

selectivity A process that defines some aspects of the world as important and others as unimportant. Selectivity is reflected in the vocabulary and grammar of language.

Sapir-Whorf hypothesis A hypothesis that argues that the language a person uses determines his or her perception of reality.

WHAT LANGUAGE SHOULD YOU STUDY IN COLLEGE?

There are nearly three thousand languages spoken throughout the world today. One-half of the world's population, however, speaks only fifteen of those languages. English is the most common language, spoken in forty or more countries. French is spoken in twenty-seven, Arabic in twenty-one, and Spanish in twenty.

When it comes to sheer numbers of people who speak a particular language, Chinese is the clear winner with 806 million people speaking Mandarin Chinese, compared to 426 million English speakers. Among the other most commonly spoken languages there are 313 million Hindi speakers, 308 million Spanish speakers, 287 million Russian speakers, 182 million Arabic speakers, and 123 million Japanese speakers.

When American students study foreign languages their choices are somewhat out of sync with these facts. Spanish, French, and German still continue to be the most popular foreign languages. Ironically, more American students study Latin than Japanese, and more struggle with ancient Greek than Chinese. In the 1986–1987 academic year only 23,454 American college students were studying Japanese, and only 17,608 were studying Chinese. In contrast, the Japanese and Chinese are learning English in large numbers. At least 250,000 Chinese are studying English. Every Japanese student begins to study English in the seventh grade and continues to do so for at least six years.

Source: Stephen Karel, "On Language," *American Demographics,* May 1989, p. 54.

College students studying foreign languages

1968–1969	1,127,363
1970–1971	1,111,505
1977–1978	933,478
1980–1981	924,837
1983–1984	966,013
1986–1987	1,003,234

	1986–1987	Change since 1980–1981
Spanish	411,293	+8.4%
French	275,328	+10.9%
German	121,022	−4.6%
Italian	40,945	+17.7%
Russian	33,961	+41.6%
Latin	25,038	0%
Japanese	23,454	+103.8%
Ancient Greek	17,608	−20.4%
Chinese	16,891	+48.6%
Hebrew	15,630	−19.6%

College Students Registered for Foreign Language Courses 1986–1987.
Source: U.S. News & World Report, *December 28, 1987/January 4, 1988,* p. 114. Basic data from Modern Language Association.

gories corresponding to two or more words or thoughts. For example, we have only one word for water but the Hopi Indians have two words—*pāhe* (for water in a natural state) and *kēyi* (for water in a container). On the other hand, the Hopi have only one word to cover every thing or being that flies, except birds. Strange as it may seem to us, they call a flying insect, an airplane, and a pilot by the same word. Inuit (Eskimos) must find it very odd indeed to learn that we have only one word for snow. For them falling snow, slushy snow, loose snow, hard-packed snow, wind-driven snow, and so on clearly are different, and the Inuit language uses different words for each of them. In contrast, the ancient Aztecs of Mexico used only one word for cold, ice, and snow. Verbs also are treated differently in different cultures. In English we have one verb *to go.* In New Guinea, however, the Manus language has three verbs—depending on direction, distance, and whether the going is up or down.

A little bit closer to home, consider today's urban American youngsters, who casually use many words and expressions pertaining to technology. Technological terms even are used to describe states of mind—*tuned in, tuned out,* or *turned on* or *turned off,* for instance. This use of language reflects the preoccupation of American culture with technology. In contrast, many Americans are at a loss for words when they are asked to describe nature: varieties of snow, wind, or rain; kinds of forests; rock formations; earth colors and textures; vegetation zones. Why? Because these things are not of great importance in urban American culture.

The translation of one language into another often presents problems. Direct translations are often impossible because (1) words may have a variety of meanings and (2) many words and ideas are culture-bound and are not natural to another culture.

An extreme example of the first type of these translation problems occurred near the end of World War II. After Italy and Germany had surrendered, the Allies sent Japan an ultimatum to surrender also. Japan's premier responded that his government would *mokusatsu* the surrender ultimatum. *Mokusatsu* can be translated into English as either "to consider" or "to take notice of." The premier meant that the government would consider the surrender ultimatum. The English translators, however, used the second interpretation, "to take notice of," and assumed that Japan had rejected the ultimatum. This belief that Japan was unwilling to surrender led to the atomic bombing of Hiroshima and Nagasaki. Most

The Inuit Eskimos would have a much easier time describing the subtleties of this snow scene than would the average American. With nearly forty words for snow, it is clear that snow is much more important to them than it is to us.

likely the bombing would still have taken place even with the other interpretation, but this example does demonstrate the problems in translating words and ideas from one language into another (Samovar, Porter, and Jain, 1981).

These examples demonstrate the uniqueness of language. No two cultures represent the world in exactly the same manner, and this cultural selectivity or bias is expressed in the form and content of a culture's language.

DO ANIMALS HAVE CULTURE?

All human beings have culture. It is the foundation on which all human achievements rest and is perhaps the defining characteristic of our species. But do animals have culture too? Not long ago most scholars would have said "no," but in the last two decades a variety of research has challenged this view. For example, Jane van Lawick-Goodall (1971) discovered that chimpanzees living in nature not only use tools but produce them first and then carry them to where they will use them. The chimps break twigs off trees, strip them of leaves and bark, then carry them to termite mounds where, after wetting them with spit, they poke them into tunnels and pull them out again all covered with delicious termites ready to be licked off. Sea otters search out flat pieces of rock and, while floating on their backs, place them on their stomachs and crack shellfish open against them.

Language is often cited as the major behavioral difference between humans and animals. It is said we possess language, whereas animals do not. For years scientists reported that animals used their calls simply to announce their identity, sex, species, location, and readiness to fight or mate. Some scientists claimed that it is all animals need to express, as life in the wild is simple. Or is it? Could it be that animals use symbols in other ways that we have overlooked? Is it possible to find the roots of human language in animal language?

Several experiments—the earliest dating back to the mid-1960s—have shown that apes are able to master some of the most fundamental aspects of language. Apes, of course, cannot talk. Their mouths and throats simply are not built to produce speech, and no ape has been able to approximate more than four human words. However, efforts to teach apes to communicate by other means have met with a fair amount of success.

The first and most widely known experiment in ape language research began in 1966, under the direction of Alan and Beatrix Gardner of the University of Nevada, with a chimpanzee named Washoe. This experiment consisted of teaching Washoe American Sign Language (ASL), the hand-gesture language used by deaf people. Washoe learned more than 130 distinct signs and was able to ask for food, name objects, and make reference to her environment. The Gardners replicated their results with four other chimpanzees.

Today Washoe lives with four other signing chimpanzees at Central Washington University under the direction of Roger

and Debbie Fouts. She now has an adopted son named Loolis. Loolis is not being taught any signs by humans, and the Fouts are observing him to see whether he will acquire signs from the other chimps. To date he has learned forty-one signs.

Another female chimp, Lana, has been taught to communicate by pressing different-shaped buttons in a particular series to obtain a desired goal. These buttons represent individual words, and Lana has mastered quite a few of them. She can even distinguish between nouns, verbs, adjectives, and adverbs.

One of the most successful experiments involves a female gorilla named Koko. Francine Patterson has been working with Koko for the last 17 years. Koko uses approximately 400 signs regularly and another 300 occasionally. She also understands several hundred spoken words (so much so that Patterson has to spell such words as "candy" in her presence). In addition, Koko also invents signs or creates sign combinations to describe new things. She tells Patterson when she is happy or sad, refers to past and future events, defines objects, and insults her human companions by calling them such things as "dirty toilet," "nut," and "rotten stink."

Koko has taken several IQ tests, including the Stanford-Binet, and scores just below average for a human child—between 85 and 95 points. However, as Patterson points out, the IQ tests have a cultural bias toward humans, and the gorilla may be more intelligent than the test indicates. For example, one item instructs the child: "Point to two things that are good to eat." The choices are a block, an apple, a shoe, a flower, and an ice cream sundae. Reflecting her tastes, Koko pointed to the apple and the flower. She likes to eat flowers and has never seen an ice cream sundae. Although these answers are correct for Koko, they are wrong for humans and were scored incorrect.

Patterson claims that Koko uses signs to swear, gossip, rhyme, and lie. If she is right, then these findings represent the most sophisticated results anyone has ever achieved with an ape.

Recently, however, some social scientists have raised serious questions as to whether apes truly are using language (Terrace et al., 1979; Greenberg, 1980). They argue that although apes can acquire large vocabularies, they cannot produce a sentence and are not using the equivalent of human language. For now the implications of language use by apes remains unresolved, and the evidence continues to mount on both sides.

Language and the production and use of tools are central elements of nonmaterial and material culture. So, does it make sense to say that culture is limited to human beings? Although scientists disagree in their answers to this question, they do agree that humans have refined culture to a far greater degree than have any other animals and also that humans depend on culture for their existence much more completely than do any other creatures.

———— SUBCULTURES

To function, every social group must have a culture of its own — its own goals, norms, values, and typical ways of doing things. As Thomas Lasswell (1965) pointed out, such a group culture is not just a "partial" or "miniature" culture. It is a full-blown, complete culture in its own right. Every family, clique, shop, community, ethnic group, and society has its own culture. Hence, every individual participates in a number of different cultures at the same time or in sequence in the course of a day. Meeting social expectations of various cultures is often a source of considerable stress for individuals in complex, heterogeneous societies like ours. Many college students, for example, find that the culture of the campus varies significantly from the culture of their family or neighborhood. At home they may be criticized for their musical taste, their clothing, their antiestablishment

ideas, and for spending too little time with the family. On campus they may be pressured to open up their minds and experiment a little or to reject old-fashioned values.

Sociologists use the term **subculture** to refer to the distinctive life-styles, values, norms, and beliefs of groups that nevertheless participate in the culture of a whole society. The concept of subculture originated in studies of juvenile delinquency and criminality (Sutherland, 1924), and in some contexts the *sub* in *subculture* still has the meaning "inferior." However, sociologists increasingly use *subculture* to refer to the cultures of discrete population segments within a society (Gordon, 1947). The term is primarily applied to the culture of ethnic groups (Italian-Americans, Jews, Native Americans, and so on) as well as to social classes (lower or working, middle, upper, and so on). Certain sociologists reserve the term *subculture* for marginal groups — that is, for groups that differ significantly from the so-called dominant culture.

Some theorists, stressing the adaptive function of culture, view subcultures as specialized approaches to solving the particular problems faced by specific groups (Cohen, 1955). For example, they note that chronic unemployment or underemployment among inner-city residents evokes criminal behavior that is reinforced by social interactions and eventually becomes normal for certain inner-city groups. Once this happens, a deviant subculture has begun to flourish.

TYPES OF SUBCULTURES

Several groups have been studied at one time or another by sociologists as examples of subcultures. These can be classified roughly as follows.

Ethnic Subcultures

Many immigrant groups have maintained their group identities and sustained their traditions while at the same time adjusting

subculture The distinctive life-styles, values, norms, and beliefs of certain segments of the population within a society.

to the demands of the wider society. Although originally distinct and separate cultures, they have become American subcultures in the context of our society. America's newest immigrants, Asians from Vietnam, Japan, the Philippines, Taiwan, India, and Cambodia, have maintained their values by living together in tight-knit communities in New York, Los Angeles, and other large cities while, at the same time, encouraging their children to achieve success in American terms.

Occupational Subcultures

Certain occupations seem to involve people in a distinctive life-style even beyond their work. For example, New York's Wall Street is not only the financial capital of the world; it also is identified with such values as materialism, greed, and power. Construction workers, police, entertainers, and many other occupational groups involve people in distinctive subcultures.

Religious Subcultures

Certain religious groups, although continuing to participate in the wider society, nevertheless practice life-styles that set them apart. These include Christian evangelical groups, Mormons, Muslims, Jews, and many religious splinter groups.

Sometimes the life-style may separate the group from the culture as a whole, as well as from the subculture of their immediate community. In a drug-ridden area of Brooklyn, New York, for example, a group of Muslims follows an antidrug religious creed in a community filled with addicts, drug dealers, and crack houses. The Muslims' religious beliefs set them apart from the general society, and their attitude toward drugs divides them from many other community members.

Political Subcultures

Small, marginal political groups may so involve their members that their entire way of life is an expression of their political convictions. Often these are so-called left-wing and right-wing groups that reject much of what they see in American society but remain engaged in the society by their constant efforts to change it to their liking.

Geographical Subcultures

Large societies often show regional variations in culture. America has several geo-

These wranglers working in the mountains of Montana are part of an occupational as well as geographic subculture.

graphical areas known for their distinctive subcultures. For instance, the South is known for its leisurely approach to life, its broad dialect, and its hospitality. The North is noted for "Yankee ingenuity," commercial cunning, and a crusty standoffishness. California, or "the Coast," is known for its trendiness and ultrarelaxed, or "laid-back," life-style. And New York stands as much for an anxious, elitist, arts-and-literature-oriented subculture as for a city.

Social Class Subcultures

Although social classes cut horizontally across geographical, ethnic, and other subdivisions of society, to some degree it is possible to discern cultural differences among the classes. Sociologists have documented that linguistic styles, family and household forms, and values and norms applied to child rearing are patterned in terms of social class subcultures. (See Chapter 9 for a discussion of social class in the United States.)

Deviant Subcultures

As we have mentioned, sociologists first began to study subcultures as a way of explaining juvenile delinquency and criminality. This interest has expanded to include the study of a wide variety of groups that are marginal to society in one way or another and whose life-styles clash with that of the wider society in important ways. Some of the deviant subcultural groups studied by sociologists include prostitutes, strippers, swingers, pool hustlers, pickpockets, drug users, and various kinds of criminals.

UNIVERSALS OF CULTURE

In spite of their individual and cultural diversity, their many subcultures and coun-tercultures, human beings are members of one species with a common evolutionary heritage. Therefore, people everywhere must confront and resolve certain common, basic problems, such as maintaining their group organization and overcoming difficulties originating in their social and natural environments. To resolve such problems, our species has developed certain forms or patterns that are found in all cultures and, therefore, are called **cultural universals.**

Among those universals that fulfill basic human needs are the division of labor; the incest taboo, marriage, and the family; rites of passage; and ideology. It is important to keep in mind that although these *forms* are universal, their specific *contents* are particular to each culture.

cultural universals Forms or patterns for resolving the common, basic human problems that are found in all cultures. Cultural universals include the division of labor, the incest taboo, marriage, the family, rites of passage, and ideology.

THE DIVISION OF LABOR

Many primates live in social groups in which it is typical for each adult member to meet most of his or her own needs. The adults find their own food, prepare their own sleeping places, and, with the exceptions of infant care, mutual grooming, and some defense-related activities, generally fend for themselves (DeVore, 1965; Kummer, 1971).

This is not true of human groups. In all societies—from the simplest bands to the most complex industrial nations—groups divide the responsibility for completing necessary tasks among their members. This means that humans constantly must rely on one another; hence, they are the most cooperative of all primates (Lancaster and Whitten, 1980).

The variety of ways in which human groups divide their tasks and choose the kind of tasks they undertake reflects differences in environment, history, and level of technological development. Yet there are certain commonalities in the division of labor. All cultures distinguish between females and males and between adults and children, and these distinctions are used to organize the division of labor. Thus, in every society there are adult-female tasks, adult-male tasks, and children's tasks. In the last two decades in America, these role distinctions have been changing quite rapidly, a topic we shall explore in Chapter 11.

THE INCEST TABOO, MARRIAGE, AND THE FAMILY

All human societies regulate sexual behavior. Sexual mores vary enormously from one culture to another, but all cultures apparently share one basic value: sexual relations between parents and their children are to be avoided. (There is evidence that some primates also avoid sexual relations between males and their mothers.) In most societies it is also held to be wrong for brothers and sisters to have sexual contact (notable exceptions being the brother-sister marriages among royal families in ancient Egypt and Hawaii, and among the Incas of Peru). The term for sex within families is **incest,** and because in most cultures very strong feelings of horror and revulsion are attached to incest, it is said to be forbidden by **taboo.**

The presence of the incest taboo means that individuals must seek socially acceptable sexual relationships outside their families. All cultures provide definitions of who is or is not an acceptable candidate for sexual contact. They also provide for institutionalized marriages—ritualized means of publicly legitimizing sexual partnerships and the resultant children. Thus, the presence of the incest taboo and the institution of marriage results in the creation of families. Depending on who is allowed to marry whom—and how many spouses each person is allowed to have—the family will differ from one culture to another. However, the basic family unit consisting of husband, wife, and children (called the nuclear family) seems to be a recognized unit in almost every culture, and sexual relations among its members (other than between husband and wife) are almost universally taboo. For one thing, this helps keep sexual jealousy under control. For another, it prevents the confusion of authority relationships within the family. But perhaps most important, the incest taboo ensures that family offspring will marry into other families, thus recreating in every generation a network of social bonds among families that knits them together into larger, more stable social groupings.

RITES OF PASSAGE

All cultures recognize stages through which individuals pass in the course of their lifetimes. Some of these stages are marked by biological events, such as appearance of menstruation in girls. However, most of these stages are quite arbitrary and culturally defined. All such stages—whether or not corresponding to biological events—are meaningful only in terms of each group's culture.

Rarely do individuals just drift from one such stage to another; every culture has standardized rituals marking each transition. These rituals are called **rites of passage.** The most widespread—if not universal—rites of passage are those marking the arrival of puberty (often resulting in the individual's taking on adult status), marriage, and death. Typical rites of passage celebrated in American society include baptisms, bar and bas mitzvahs, confirmations, major birthdays, graduations, showers (for brides-to-be), stag parties (for grooms-to-be), wedding ceremonies and receptions, major anniversaries, retirement parties, and funerals and wakes. Such rituals accomplish several important things, including helping the individual achieve a sense of social identity, mapping out the individual's life course, and aiding the individual in making appropriate life plans. Finally, rites of passage provide people with a context in which to share common emo-

incest The term used to describe sexual relations within families. Most cultures have strict taboos against incest, which is often associated with strong feelings of horror and revulsion.

taboo The prohibition against a specific action. Incest taboos are found in most cultures.

rites of passage Standardized rituals that mark the transition from one stage of life to another.

tions, particularly with regard to events that are sources of stress and intense feelings, such as marriage and death.

ists, environmentalists. These and countless other groups have marched behind their ideological banners, and in the name of their ideologies they have changed the world, often in major ways.

ideologies Strongly held beliefs and values to which group members are firmly committed and which cement the social structure.

IDEOLOGY

A central challenge that every group faces is how to maintain its identity as a social unit. One of the most important ways that groups accomplish this is by promoting beliefs and values to which group members are firmly committed. Such strongly held beliefs and values, called **ideologies,** are the cement of social structure.

Ideologies are universal in that they are found in every culture. Some are religious, referring to things and events beyond the perception of the human senses. Others are more secular—that is, nonreligious and concerned with the everyday world. In the end, all ideologies rest on untestable ideas that are rooted in the basic values and assumptions of each culture. There is a story (Geertz, 1973) about a researcher who challenged the assertion of a native of India that the world is supported on the back of an elephant. "Well," he snorted, "what's the elephant standing on?"

"He's standing on the back of a turtle," came the confident reply.

"And what's the turtle standing on?"

"From there"—the Indian smiled— "it's turtles . . . turtles all the way down."

Even though ideologies rest on untestable assumptions, their consequences are very real. They give direction and thrust to our social existence and meaning to our lives. The power of ideologies to mold people's passions and behavior is well known. History is filled with both horrors and noble deeds people have performed in the name of some ideology: thirteenth-century Crusaders, fifteenth-century Inquisitors, pro–states rights and pro–union forces in nineteenth-century America, abolitionists, prohibitionists, trade unionists, nazis and fascists, communists, segregationists, civil rights activists, feminists, consumer activ-

Certain patterns of behavior, such as marriage, are found in every culture but take various forms. The marriage ceremony, for example, varies greatly among different cultures.

Japanese Culture: To Be Emulated or Rejected?

It should not surprise anyone if we claim that Japanese culture is unique. We are willing to admit that the past 250 years of American history, which include revolution, settling the frontier, subjugating Indians, slavery, and absorbing vast numbers of immigrants, have given the United States a distinctive set of values. Therefore, it is certainly conceivable that 2500 years of isolation on a few small islands might have given the Japanese a peculiar culture.

In recent years we have come to admire aspects of Japanese society and to contrast them with facets of American society. Beyond the much discussed successes of the Japanese economy, Japan seems different and better in those details of daily life that reflect consideration and duty. A thousand times a day in modern society your life is made easier or harder, depending on the care with which someone else has done his or her job. In general, can you count on others to do their best? In Japan you can.

From bureaucrats at the Ministry of Foreign Affairs to department-store package-wrappers, the Japanese seem invulnerable to the idea that discharging one's duty to others might be considered "just a job." Tipping is virtually unknown in Japan; from the Japanese perspective it seems vulgar, because it implies that the recipient will not do his best unless he is bribed.

Most of Japan is extremely crowded. It is common for one hundred thousand people to live within a half mile radius. Yet, in the evening one can walk through the alleyways and notice that the neighborhoods are totally quiet. The restraint and reserve of Japanese life can seem suffocating if you are used to something different, but they are also admirable and necessary, if so many people are to coexist so harmoniously in such close quarters.

With a very low crime rate and its economic miracle, is this not truly Japan's golden age? Everything is working, Japan is taking a proud place in the world, there are no serious domestic divisions, and the drugs, corruption, and similar disorders that blight the rest of the world barely exist there. It appears that Japan has figured out what is still puzzling everybody else.

The same culture that produces so many of the above-mentioned admirable traits also has some very deeply ingrained dilemmas. The most serious of these is an attitude of racial exclusion. Rather than talking about race—as white Americans did when enslaving blacks and excluding "inferior" immigrants—the Japanese talk about "purity." Their society is different from others in being purer; it consists of practically none but Japanese. What makes the subject so complicated is the overlap between two different kinds of purity, that of culture and that of blood.

The significant point is that as

CULTURE AND INDIVIDUAL CHOICE

Very little of human behavior is instinctual or biologically programmed. In the course of human evolution, culture gradually was substituted for genetic programming as the source of instructions about what to do, how to do it, and when it should be done. This means that humans have a great deal of individual freedom of action—probably more than any other creature.

However, as we have seen, individuals' choices are not entirely free. By being born

far as the Japanese are concerned, they are inherently different from other people, and are all bound together by birth and blood. The United States is built on the principle of a voluntary fraternity; in theory, anyone can become an American. A place in Japanese society is open only to those who are born Japanese. Being born Japanese means with the right racial background, not merely on rocky Japanese soil. One of Japan's touchiest problems is the second- and third-generation Koreans, descended from the people who were brought to Japan for forced labor in the fascist days. They are still known as Koreans even though they were born in Japan, speak the language like natives, and in many cases are physically indistinguishable from everyone else. They have long-term "alien residence" permits but are not citizens—and in principle they and their descendants never will be (obtaining naturalized Japanese citizenship is nearly impossible). They must register as aliens and be fingerprinted by the police.

The Japanese public has a voracious appetite for *Nihonjinron*—the study of traits that distinguish them from everyone else. Hundreds of works of self-examination are published each year. This discipline involves perfectly reasonable questions about what makes Japan unique as a social system, but it easily slips into inquiries about what makes the Japanese people special as a race. One popular book was *The Japanese Brain.* This book contends that the Japanese have brains that are organized differently from those of the rest of humanity. Many Japanese believe that their thoughts and emotions are different from those of anyone else in the world.

The United States has tried, albeit inconsistently and with limited success, to assimilate people from different backgrounds and parts of the world. It could be argued that this ethnic mixture has helped us in our dealings with other countries. The Japanese, in contrast, have suffered grievously from their lack of any built-in understanding of foreign cultures. Sitting off on their own, it is easy for them to view the rest of the world as merely a market. A homogeneous population with no emotional ties to the rest of the world acts even more narcissistically than others.

Professor Edward Seidensticker, after living in Japan many years, noted that the Japanese "are not like other people. They are infinitely more clannish, insular, parochial, and one owes it to one's self-respect to preserve a feeling of outrage at the insularity." Even as Japan steadily rises in influence, the idea that it should be the new world model is difficult to accept.

Source: Excerpted and adapted from James Fallows, "The Japanese Are Different from You and Me," *Atlantic Monthly,* September 1986, pp. 35–41.

into a particular society with a particular culture, every human being is presented with a limited number of recognized or socially valued choices. Every society has means of training and of social control that are brought to bear on each person, making it difficult for individuals to act or even think in ways that deviate too far from their culture's norms. To get along in society, people must keep their impulses under some control and express feelings and gratify needs in a socially approved manner at a socially approved time. This means that human beings inevitably feel somewhat dissatisfied, no matter to which group they belong (Freud, 1930).

Coming to terms with this central truth about human existence is one of the great tasks of living. Perhaps it is especially important to consider at the present time, for a society that sets out to meet all personal needs is doomed to failure.

Sociology, therefore, has an opportunity to make a contribution to setting goals for the future, for only if these goals are grounded solidly on the nature of society and culture will it be possible to make realistic plans that have a chance of succeeding in the long run.

SUMMARY

Sociologists define culture as all that humans learn to do, to use, to produce, to know, and to believe as they live out their lives in the social groups to which they belong. Although all human groups have culture, it often varies considerably from one group to another.

Whereas other animals rely on instincts to pass on behavioral patterns, humans rely on culture, which is transmitted from one generation to the next.

Interaction between cultures can result in difficult adjustments known as culture shock. When sociologists study various cultures, they must view them objectively and perceive their customs in the context of the situation in which they occur. Such a perspective is called cultural relativism.

The concept of culture is best understood when it is separated into two components: material culture and nonmaterial culture.

Material culture consists of all the things that human beings learn to use and produce. Humans use material culture to modify and exploit the environment. Because of their ability to control and fit into the environment, human beings have prevailed as the most flexible species on earth.

Nonmaterial culture consists of the totality of knowledge, beliefs, vaules, and rules for appropriate behavior in a particular society. One part of nonmaterial culture is normative culture, which includes norms, mores, and folkways. Norms are rules of behavior that are agreed upon and shared within a culture. They define normal behavior. Mores define moral behavior, and folkways (or conventions) reflect custom and habit. Ideal norms are expectations of what people should do if conditions were perfect, and statistical norms provide qualifications and allowances for differences in individual behavior.

Another aspect of nonmaterial culture is cognitive culture, the shared conceptions of what the world is like—what is real, important, and correct. Included in this conception are values, a culture's orientations toward life, and its notions of what is good and what is bad.

Innovation and diffusion are responsible for our cultural evolution. Innovation, comprising invention and discovery, is the source of all new culture traits, such as tools and materials, beliefs and values. Diffusion is the movement of cultural traits from one culture to another. When, as sometimes happens, the material culture surges forward, the normative culture does not always keep up. This results in cultural lag.

Culture is learned, shared, adaptive, and symbolic. Symbols are objects that represent other things but need not share any quality with what they represent. Signs, on the other hand, can represent other things because they share some important quality with them. Of all the symbols in human culture, words are the most important because they enable us to organize the world into labeled cognitive categories and use these labels to communicate with one another.

A subculture is a segment of society that has a distinctive life-style, value system, norms, and beliefs. Subcultures have been categorized as ethnic, occupational, religious, political, geographical, social, and deviant.

Certain forms and patterns that are found in all cultures are termed cultural universals. Those universals that directly promote the organization of group life are the division of labor; the incest taboo, marriage, and the family; rites of passage; and ideology.

Chapter 4

SOCIALIZATION

AND DEVELOPMENT

It all starts innocently enough. Young people are approached on the street by recruiters from Sun Myung Moon's Unification Church who bear messages of love and emotional awareness. Seen as potential converts to the church, the young people are flattered, made to feel important, and finally convinced to learn more about the church by attending a weekend workshop.

The workshop is a retreat held at a Unification Church mansion — a strange world that bears little resemblance to normal life. Once there, the potential converts experience a "lovefest" that disguises the true purpose of the encounter — resocialization and ultimate acceptance of the church as the one true force in their lives. In no uncertain terms, the Moonies are after new members.

The conversion process begins as soon as the young people arrive. They are welcomed by banners expressing brotherly and sisterly love and are hugged by everyone in sight. At work is a subtle form of intimidation designed to make the skeptics among them feel self-conscious and guilty about their doubts.

They are worn down further by the pace of activity that follows. Each day is 16 to 18 hours long, with every minute planned. There are games, sing-alongs, discussions, lectures, and prayers — each designed to communicate a sense of community and mission. Time away is forbidden. Potential converts who try to find moments alone to reflect on, and perhaps reject, the Moonie philosophy are drawn back into the group by church members whose job it is to eliminate dissent. After two or three days, the recruits lose track of time and place. Their grueling schedule has left them confused, numb, and emotionally drained.

The Moonies take advantage of this mental and physical exhaustion by bombarding the recruits with lectures and discussions. Their presentation is persuasive and doubts are further discouraged by sidestepping questions and making private conversations among skeptics impossible. The Moonies dole out information in bits and pieces and avoid all harshness and criticism.

Their conversion message is delivered by highly trained lecturers who deal in resocialization. Immaculately dressed and groomed, these lecturers are the only persons allowed to wear shoes in the house — a sign of their special authority. Over and over, they stress the goodness of the church and the church's supremacy in life. Self-interest is belittled and relationships with parents, friends, and lovers outside the church are discouraged. Their primary tool is guilt. Recruits are made to feel that they have wronged God if they question the doctrine set before them.

In this way, recruits are isolated from the life they left behind. Above all, the Moonies want the young people to feel that they are now part of a warm, communal family that is far better than the one they knew. Exhausted by the continuing ordeal, recruits ultimately lose their sense of self and become one in the communal spirit. When this happens, the resocialization process — and the conversion — takes hold (MacRobert, 1977a, 1977b).

Here a religious cult is using methods of mind control to resocialize young adults, to make them accept values and ideas that differ from those they learned as children. Although this is an extreme example of the resocialization process, it proves a point: Socialization and, in this case, resocialization, can take place throughout life. Although most socialization occurs during childhood, social learning is lifelong; but, as you will see next, we do not come to it with a blank slate.

BECOMING A PERSON: BIOLOGY AND CULTURE

A human being takes 10 to 15 years to reach sexual maturity and usually even longer to come of age socially. This long period of dependency allows children time to learn things they need to know to care for themselves and become members of society. The long and complicated processes of social interaction through which a child learns the intellectual, physical, and social skills needed to function as a member of society are known as **socialization.** It is through socialization experiences that children learn the culture of the society into which they have been born. It is in the course of this process that each child slowly acquires a **personality** — that is, the patterns of behavior and ways of thinking and feeling that are distinctive for each individual. Contrary to popular wisdom, nobody is a "born" business genius, criminal, or leader. These things all are learned as part of the socialization process.

socialization The long and complicated processes of social interaction through which a child learns the intellectual, physical, and social skills needed to function as a member of society.

personality The patterns of behavior and ways of thinking and feeling that are distinctive for each individual.

NATURE VERSUS NURTURE: A FALSE DEBATE

Every human being is born with a set of inherited units of biological material called **genes.** Half are inherited from the mother, half from the father. No two people have exactly the same genes, except for identical twins. Genes are made up of complicated chemical substances, and a full set of genes is found in every body cell. Scientists still do not know how many different genes a human being has, but certainly they number in the tens of thousands.

What makes genes so special is that they influence the chemical processes in our bodies and even control some of these processes completely. For example, such things as blood type, the ability to taste the pres-

ence of certain chemicals, and some people's inability to distinguish certain shades of green and red are completely under the control of genes. Most of our body processes are not controlled solely by genes, however, but are the result of the interaction of genes and the environment (physical, social, and cultural). Thus, how tall you are depends on the genes that control the growth of your legs, trunk, neck, and head and also on the amount of protein, vitamins, and minerals in your diet. Genes help determine your blood pressure, but so do the amount of salt in your diet, the frequency with which you exercise, and the amount of stress under which you live.

For more than a century, sociologists, educators, and psychologists have argued about which is more important in determining a person's qualities: inherited char-

genes The set of inherited units of biological material with which each individual is born.

It is through the process of socialization that the young learn the culture of the society they have been born into. Just as the young are socialized to accept the values of American society, they were also socialized into accepting those that were part of the Nazi society. This poster (right) proclaims the glory of the Nazi youth movement as it seeks to rid Germany of those people who are seen as disruptive. Notice how the people representing the threatening groups are made to seem like fleeing rodents or insects.

acteristics (nature) or socialization experiences (nurture). After Charles Darwin (1809–1882) published *On the Origin of Species* in 1859, human beings were seen to be a species similar to all the others in the animal kingdom. Because most animal behavior seemed to the scholars of that time to be governed by inherited factors, they reasoned that human behavior similarly must be determined by **instincts** — biologically inherited patterns of complex behavior. Instincts were thought to lie at the base of all aspects of human behavior, and eventually more than 10,000 human instincts were catalogued by researchers (Bernard, 1924).

Then, at the turn of the century, a Russian scientist named Ivan Pavlov (1849–1936) made a startling discovery. He found that if a bell were rung just before dogs were fed, eventually they would begin to salivate at the ringing of the bell itself, even when no food was served. The conclusion was inescapable: So-called instinctual behavior could be molded or, as Pavlov (1927) put it, **conditioned.** Dogs could be taught to salivate. Pavlov's work quickly became the foundation on which a new view of human beings was built — one that stressed their infinite capacity to learn and be molded. The American psychologist John B. Watson (1878–1958) taught a little boy to be afraid of a rabbit by startling him with a loud noise every time he was allowed to see it. What he had done was to link a certain reaction (fear) with an object (the rabbit) through the repetition of the experience. He also claimed that if he were given complete control over the environment of a dozen healthy infants, he could train each one to be whatever he wished — doctor, lawyer, artist, merchant, even beggar or thief (Watson, 1925). Among certain psychologists, conditioning became the means through which they explained human behavior.

Sociobiology

The debate over nature versus nurture has taken a new turn with the emergence of sociobiology. The discipline of **sociobiology**

tries to use biological principles to explain the behavior of all social beings, both animal and human. For example, when an especially harsh and prolonged winter leaves an Inuit (Eskimo) family without food supplies, they must break camp and quickly find a new site in order to survive. Frequently an elderly member of the family, often a grandmother, who may slow down the others and require some of the scarce food, will stay behind and face certain death. From the viewpoint of a sociobiologist such as Edward O. Wilson (1975, 1979), this would be an example of altruism, which might ultimately have a biological component.

Wilson believes that behavior can be explained in terms of the ways in which individuals act to increase the probability that their genes and the genes of their close relatives will be passed on to the next generation. Proponents of this view, known as sociobiologists, believe that social science will one day be a mere subdivision of biology. Sociobiologists would claim that the grandmother, in sacrificing her own life, is improving her kin's chances of survival. She has already made her productive contribution to the family. Now the younger members of the family must survive to ensure the continuation of the family and its genes into future generations.

Many researchers disagree with the sociobiological viewpoint. Biologist-geologist Stephen Jay Gould (1976) proposed another, equally plausible scenario, one that discounts the existence of a particular gene programmed for altruism. He perceives the grandmother's sacrifice as an adaptive cultural trait. (It is widely acknowledged that culture is a major adaptive mechanism for humans.) Gould posits that the elders remain behind because they have been socially conditioned from earliest childhood to the possibility and appropriateness of this choice. They grew up hearing the songs and stories that praised the elders who stayed behind. Such self-sacrificers were the greatest heroes of the clan. Families whose elders rose to such an occasion survived to cele-

instincts Biologically inherited patterns of complex behavior.

conditioning The molding of behavior through a series of repeated experiences that link a desired reaction with a particular object or event.

sociobiology An approach that tries to use biological principles to explain the behavior of social beings.

brate the self-sacrifice, but those families without self-sacrificing elders died out.

Wilson nonetheless makes several major concessions to Gould's viewpoint, acknowledging that among human beings, "the intensity and form of altruistic acts are to a large extent culturally determined" and that "human social evolution is obviously more cultural than genetic." He also leaves the door open to free will: Admitting that even though our genetic coding may have a major influence, we still have the ability to choose an appropriate course of action (Wilson, 1978). However, Wilson insists that the underlying motivation remains genetic, no matter how it is altered or reinforced by cultural influences.

Gould agrees that human behavior has a biological, or genetic, base, but stresses that which of these numerous possibilities a particular person displays depends on his or her experience in the culture.

Although both nature and nurture are important, the debate over the relative contribution of each continues. However, just as a winter snowfall is the result of both the temperature and the moisture in the air, so must the human organism and human behavior be understood in terms of both genetic inheritance and the effects of environment. **Nurture**—that is, the entire socialization experience—is as essential a part of "human nature" as our genes. It is from the interplay between genes and environment that each human being emerges.

DEPRIVATION AND DEVELOPMENT

Some unusual events and interesting research indicate that human infants need more than just food and shelter if they are to function effectively as social creatures.

Extreme Childhood Deprivation

There are only a few recorded cases of human beings who have grown up without any real contact with other humans. One such case took place in the winter of 1799, when hunters in Aveyron, in southern France, captured a boy who was running naked through the forest. He seemed to be about 11 years old and apparently had been living alone in the forest for at least 5 or 6 years. He appeared to be thoroughly wild and was subsequently exhibited in a cage from which he managed to escape several times. Finally, he was examined by "experts" who found him to be an incurable "idiot." But a young doctor, Jean Itard, thought differently. He believed that the boy's wild behavior, lack of speech, highly developed sense of smell, and poor visual attention span all were the result of having been deprived of human contact. He took the boy into his house, named him Victor, and tried to socialize him. He had little success. Although Victor slowly learned to wear clothes, to speak and write a few simple words, and to eat with a knife and fork, he ignored human voices unless they were associated with food, developed no relationships with people other than Dr. Itard and the woman who cared for him, and died at the age of 40 (Itard, 1932; Shattuck, 1980).

Psychologist Bruno Bettleheim (1967) believes that children such as Victor are really autistic—that is, they have never developed the capacity to relate to others in a human way because of a prolonged early period of deprivation. The case of Anna sheds more light on this subject.

Anna, who grew up in the 1930s, had the misfortune of being born illegitimately to the daughter of an extremely disapproving family. Her mother was unable to place Anna with foster parents and so brought her home. To quiet the family's harsh criticisms, the young mother hid Anna away in a room in the attic, where she could be out of sight and even forgotten by the family. Anna remained there for almost 6 years, ignored by the whole family, including her mother, who did the very minimum to keep her alive. Finally, Anna was discovered by social workers. The 6-year-old girl was unable to sit up, to walk, or to talk. In fact, she was so withdrawn from human beings that

nurture The entire socialization experience.

at first she appeared to be deaf, mute, and brain damaged. However, after she was placed in a special school, Anna did learn to communicate somewhat, to walk (awkwardly), to care for herself, and even to play with other children. Unfortunately, she died at the age of 10 (Davis, 1940).

A more recent case is that of a girl named Genie, who came to the attention of authorities in California in 1970. From the age of 20 months until age 13½, Genie lived in nearly total isolation. Genie's 70-year old father kept her restrained day and night in a harness he fashioned for her. She had nothing to do and could only move her hands and feet. Her brother fed her milk and baby food and followed his father's instructions not to talk to her.

When Genie was hospitalized, she was malformed, unsocialized, and severely malnourished. She was unable to speak or even stand upright. After 4 years of good care, Genie had learned some social skills, was able to take a bus to school, had begun to express some feelings toward others, and had achieved the intellectual development of a 9-year-old. There were still, however, serious problems with her language development that could not be corrected no matter how involved the instruction (Curtiss et al., 1977).

These examples of extreme childhood isolation point to the fact that none of the behavior we think of as typically human arises spontaneously. Humans must be taught to stand up, to walk, to talk, even to think. Human infants must learn to have feelings for others and must see evidence that other people care for them — that is, they need to develop **social attachments.** This seems to be a basic need of all primates, as the research by Harry F. Harlow shows.

In a series of experiments with rhesus monkeys, Harlow and his coworkers demonstrated the importance of body contact in social development (Harlow, 1959; Harlow and Harlow, 1962). In one experiment, infant monkeys were taken from their mothers and placed in cages where they were raised in isolation from other mon-

social attachments The emotional bonds that infants form with others that are necessary for normal development. Social attachments are a basic need of human beings and all primates.

keys. Each cage contained two substitute mothers: one was made of hard wire and contained a feeding bottle; the other was covered with soft terry cloth but did not have a bottle. Surprisingly, the baby monkeys spent much more time clinging to the cloth mothers than to the wire mothers, even though they received no food at all from the cloth mothers. Apparently, the need to cling to and to cuddle against even this miserable substitute for a real mother was more important to them than being fed.

Other experiments with monkeys have confirmed the importance of social contact in behavior. Monkeys raised in isolation *never* learn how to interact with other monkeys or even how to mate. If placed in a cage with other monkeys, they either withdraw or become violent and aggressive — threatening, biting, and scratching the others.

Monkeys that are raised without affection make wretched mothers themselves. After being artificially impregnated and giving birth, such monkeys either ignored their infants or displayed a pattern of behavior described by Harlow as "ghastly":

> When an infant attempted to make contact with its mother, she would literally scrape it from her body and abuse it by various sadistic devices. The mother would push the baby's face against the floor and rub it back and forth. Not infrequently, the mother would encircle the infant's head with her jaws, and in one case an infant's skull was crushed in this manner. (*Science News,* 1972)

Most times the researchers were able to stop the battering and abuse, but in a few instances the mothers were so violent that the infants were killed before the researchers could intervene. For obvious ethical reasons, similar experiments have never been carried out with human babies.

As with all animal studies, we must be very cautious in drawing inferences for human behavior. After all, we are not monkeys. Yet, Harlow's experiments show that

WHAT KIDS DO WHEN THEY COME HOME FROM SCHOOL

Not all socialization of children takes place within the family or the school. There are many outside sources that parents have little control over. The following table gives us an idea of how influential these outside sources of socialization may be when we see what children do typically do when they come home from school.

Source: U.S. News & World Report, May 9, 1988, p. 84. Basic data from M/E Report by M/E Marketing and Research, Inc.

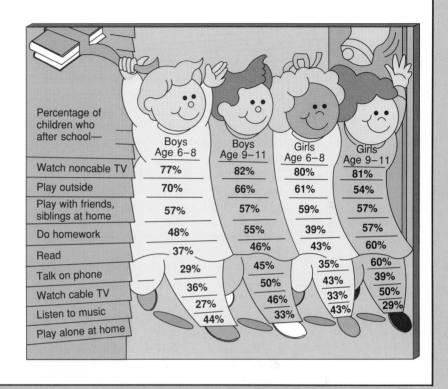

Percentage of children who after school—	Boys Age 6–8	Boys Age 9–11	Girls Age 6–8	Girls Age 9–11
Watch noncable TV	77%	82%	80%	81%
Play outside	70%	66%	61%	54%
Play with friends, siblings at home	57%	57%	59%	57%
Do homework	48%	55%	39%	57%
Read	37%	46%	43%	60%
Talk on phone	29%	45%	35%	60%
Watch cable TV	36%	50%	43%	39%
Listen to music	27%	46%	33%	50%
Play alone at home	44%	33%	43%	29%

without socialization, monkeys do not develop normal social, emotional, sexual, or maternal behavior. Because human beings rely on learning even more than monkeys do, it is likely that the same is true of us.

Infants in Institutions

Studies of infants and young children in institutions confirm the view that human beings' developmental needs include more than the mere provision of food and shelter. Psychologist Rene Spitz (1945) visited orphanages in Europe and found that in those dormitories where children were given routine care but were otherwise ignored, they were slow to develop and were withdrawn and sickly. In sociological language, these children's needs for **affiliation** (meaningful interaction with others) were not met.

In another example, seventy-five children in an American institution were studied (Provence and Lipton, 1962). The infants who received minimal physical care but were otherwise neglected in their first year of life became severely retarded socially and emotionally. Although they improved when they were given more attention or when they were brought back into their families, they continued to show some long-lasting emotional problems. Like Harlow's monkeys, they found it difficult to form relationships with others, and they were unable to control their aggressive impulses adequately.

In 1987 there were 300 abandoned infants, most of whose mothers were drug addicts, living in New York City hospitals for extended periods of time because no foster homes were available. Many of the older

affiliation Meaningful interaction with others.

babies were placed in cagelike cribs to keep them from climbing out, and staff shortages made proper care and nurturing virtually impossible. In response to the problems that institutionalized babies face, several child advocacy groups forced New York City to develop a plan to deal with abandoned babies in city hospitals. The city responded by raising payments to foster families and making efforts to return the babies to their natural mothers whenever possible (Oreskes, 1987).

As the studies we have cited show, human infants need more than just food and shelter if they are to grow and develop normally. Every human infant needs frequent contact with others who demonstrate affection, who respond to attempts to interact, and who themselves initiate interactions with the child. Infants also need contact with people who find ways to interest the child in his or her surroundings and who teach the child the physical and social skills and knowledge that are needed to function. In addition, in order to develop normally, children need to be taught the culture of their society—to be socialized into the world of social relations and symbols that are the foundation of human experience.

statuses The culturally and socially defined positions occupied by individuals throughout their lifetime.

social identity The statuses that define an individual. Social identity is determined by how others see us.

self The personal identity of each individual that is separate from his or her social identity.

The process of socialization involves trying on a variety of roles that will eventually make up the self.

THE CONCEPT OF SELF

Every individual comes to possess a social identity by occupying culturally and socially defined positions—called **statuses**—in the course of his or her socialization. This social identity changes as the person moves through the various stages of childhood and adulthood recognized by the society. New statuses are occupied; old ones are abandoned. Picture a teenage girl who volunteers as a "candy striper" in a community hospital. She leaves that position to attend college, joins a sorority, becomes a premedical major, and graduates. She goes to medical school, completes an internship, becomes engaged, and then enters a program for specialized training in surgery. Perhaps she marries; possibly she has a child. All along the way she is moving through different social identities, often assuming several at once. When, many years later, she returns to the hospital where she was a teenage volunteer, she will have an entirely new social identity: adult woman, surgeon, wife (perhaps), mother (possibly).

The foregoing description of the developing girl was from the outside, the way that other members of the society experience her social transitions, or what sociologists would call changes in her **social identity.** But what of the person herself? How does this human being, who is growing and developing physically, emotionally, intellectually, and socially, experience these changes? Is there something constant about a person's experience that allows one to say, "I am that changing person—changing, but yet somehow the same individual?" In other words, do all human beings have personal identities separate from their social identities? Most social scientists believe that the answer is yes. This changing yet enduring personal identity is called the **self.**

The self develops when the individual becomes aware of his or her feelings, thoughts, and behaviors as separate and distinct from those of other people. This usually happens at a young age when children begin to realize that they have their own history, habits, and needs and begin to imagine how these might appear to others. By adulthood the concept of self is fully developed.

Most researchers would agree that the concept of self includes (1) an awareness of the existence, appearance, and boundaries of one's own body (you are walking among the other members of the crowd, dressed appropriately for the occasion, and trying to avoid bumping into people as you chat); (2) the ability to refer to one's own being by using language and other symbols ("Hi, as you can see from my name tag, I'm Harry Hernandez from Gonzales, Texas"); (3) knowledge of one's personal history ("Yup, I grew up in Gonzales; my folks own a small farm there, and since I was a small boy I've wanted to study farm management"); (4) knowledge of one's needs and skills ("I'm good with my hands all right, but I need the intellectual stimulation of doing large-scale planning"); (5) the ability to organize one's knowledge and beliefs ("Let me tell you about planning crop rotation . . ."); (6) the ability to organize one's experiences ("I know what I like and what I don't like"); and (7) the ability to take a step back and look at one's being as others do, to evaluate the impressions one is creating, and to understand the feelings and attitudes one stimulates in others ("It might seem a little funny to you that a farmer like me would want to come to a party for the opening of a new art gallery. Well, as far back as I can remember, I always kinda enjoyed art, and now that I can afford to indulge myself, I thought maybe I'd buy some paintings"). (See Cooley, 1909; Erikson, 1964; Gardner, 1978; Mead, 1934.)

DIMENSIONS OF HUMAN DEVELOPMENT

Clearly, the development of the self is a complicated process. It involves many in-

George Bush may be best known as President of the United States, but to his family he has a variety of other social identities, such as father and husband.

teracting factors, including the acquisition of language and the ability to use symbols. There are three dimensions of human development tied to the emergence of the self: cognitive development, moral development, and gender identity.

Cognitive Development

For centuries most people assumed that a child's mind worked in exactly the same way as an adult's. The child was thought of as a miniature adult who was simply lacking information about the world. Swiss philosopher and psychologist Jean Piaget (1896–1980) was instrumental in changing that view through his studies of the development of intelligence in children. His work has been significant to sociologists because the processes of thought are central to the development of identity and, consequently, to the ability to function in society.

Piaget found that children move through a series of predictable stages on their way to logical thought, and some never attain the most advanced stages. From birth to age 2, the sensorimotor stage, the infant relies on touch and the manipulation of objects for information about the world, slowly learning about cause and effect. At about the age of 2, the child begins to learn that words can be symbols for objects. In this, the preoperational stage of development, the child cannot yet see the world from another person's point of view.

The operational stage is next and lasts from the age of 7 to about the age of 12. During this period the child begins to think with some logic and can understand and work with numbers, volume, shapes, and spatial relationships. With the onset of adolescence, the child progresses to the most advanced stage of thinking—formal logical thought. People at this stage are capable of abstract, logical thought and can develop ideas about things that have no concrete reference, such as infinity, death, freedom, and justice. In addition, they are able to anticipate possible consequences of their acts and decisions. Achieving this stage is crucial to developing an identity and an ability to enter into mature interpersonal relationships (Piaget and Inhelder, 1969).

Moral Development

moral order A society's shared view of right and wrong.

Every society has a **moral order**—that is, a shared view of right and wrong. Without moral order a society would soon fall apart.

Seventy-five-year-old Roswell Gilbert killed his ailing wife, who was suffering from Alzheimer's disease. He was found guilty of first-degree murder and sentenced to life in prison. Which of Kohlberg's stages of reasoning do you think Gilbert used in arriving at his decision to murder his wife?

People would not know what to expect from themselves and one another, and social relationships would be impossible to maintain. Therefore, the process of socialization must include instruction about the moral order of an individual's society.

The research by Lawrence Kohlberg (1969) suggests that not every person is capable of thinking about morality in the same way. Just as our sense of self and our ability to think logically develop in stages, our moral thinking develops in a progression of steps as well. To illustrate this, Kohlberg asked children from different societies (including Turkey, Mexico, China, and the United States) to resolve moral dilemmas such as the following: A man's wife is dying of cancer. A rare drug might save her, but it costs $2000. The man tries to raise the money but can come up with only $1000. He asks the druggist to sell him the drug for $1000, and the druggist refuses. The desperate husband then breaks into the druggist's store to steal the drug. Should he have done so? Why or why not?

Kohlberg was more interested in the *reasoning* behind the child's judgment than in the answer itself. From his analysis of this reasoning, he believed that changes in moral thinking progress step by step through six qualitatively distinct stages (although most people never go beyond stages 3 or 4):

Stage 1: Orientation toward punishment. Those who thought the man should steal (pros) said he could get into trouble if he just let his wife die. Those who said he should not steal (cons) stressed that he might be arrested for the crime.

Stage 2: Orientation toward reward. The pros said that if the woman lived, the man would have what he wanted. If he got caught in the act of stealing the drug, he could return the drug and would probably be given only a light sentence. The cons said that the man should not blame himself if his wife died; and if he got caught, she might die before he got out of jail, so he would have lost her anyway. Stealing just would not pay.

Stage 3: Orientation toward possible disapproval by others. The pros observed that nobody would think the man was bad if he stole the drug but that his family would never forgive him if his wife died and he had done nothing to help her. The cons pointed out that not only would the druggist think of the man as a criminal, but the rest of society would, too.

Stage 4: Orientation toward formal laws and fear of personal dishonor. The pros said that the man would always feel dishonored if he did nothing and his wife died. The cons said that even if he saved his wife by stealing, he would feel guilty and dishonored for having broken the law.

Stage 5: Orientation toward peer values and democracy. The pros said that failure to steal the drug would cost the man his peers' respect because he would have acted out of fear rather than out of consideration of what was the logical thing to do. The cons countered that the man would lose the respect of the community if he were caught because he would show himself to be a person who acted out of emotion rather than according to the laws that govern everybody's behavior.

Stage 6: Orientation toward one's own set of values. The pros focused on the man's conscience, saying he would never be able to live with himself if his wife died and he had done nothing. The cons argued that although others might not blame the man for stealing the drug, in doing so he would have failed to live up to his own standards of honesty.

Kohlberg found that although these stages of moral development correspond roughly to other aspects of the developing self, most people never progress to stages 5 and 6. In fact, Kohlberg subsequently dropped stage 6 from his scheme because it met with widespread criticism that he could not deny. It was felt by critics that stage 6 was elitist and culturally biased. Kohlberg himself could find no evidence that any of his long-term subjects ever reached this stage (Muson, 1979). At times people regress from a higher state to a lower one. For

example, when Kohlberg analyzed the explanations that Nazi war criminals of World War II gave for their participation in the systematic murder of millions of people who happened to possess certain religious (Jewish), ethnic (gypsies), or psychological (mentally retarded) traits, he found that none of the reasons were above stage 3 and most were at stage 1 —"I did what I was told to do, otherwise I'd have been punished" (Kohlberg, 1967). However, many of these war criminals had been very responsible and successful people in their prewar lives and presumably in those times had reached higher stages of moral development.

Gender Identity

One of the most important elements of the sense of self is our view of ourselves resulting from our sex — what sociologists call **gender identity.** Certain aspects of gender identity are rooted in biology. Males tend to be larger and stronger than females are, but females tend to have better endurance than males do. Females also become pregnant and give birth to infants and (usually) can nurse infants with their own milk. However, gender identity is mostly a matter of cultural definition. There is nothing inherently male or female about a teacher, a pilot, a carpenter, or a typist other than what our culture tells us. As we shall see in Chapter 11, "Gender Roles" are far more a matter of nurture than of nature.

gender identity The view of ourselves resulting from our sex.

———— THEORIES OF DEVELOPMENT

Among the scholars who have devised theories of development, Charles Horton Cooley, George Herbert Mead, Sigmund Freud, and Erik Erikson stand out because of the contributions they have made to the way sociologists today think about socialization. Cooley and Mead saw the individual and society as partners. They were symbolic interactionists (see Chapter 1) and as such believed that the individual develops a self solely through social relationships— that is, through interaction with others. They believed that all our behaviors, our attitudes, even our ideas of self, arise from our interactions with other people. Hence, they were pure environmentalists in that they believed that social forces rather than genetic factors shape the individual.

Freud, on the other hand, tended to picture the individual and society as enemies. He saw the individual as constantly having to yield reluctantly to the greater power of society, to keep internal urges (especially sexual and aggressive ones) under strict control.

Erikson presented something of a compromise position. He thought of the individual as progressing through a series of stages of development that express internal urges, yet are greatly influenced by societal and cultural factors.

looking-glass self A theory developed by Charles Horton Cooley to explain how individuals develop a sense of self through interaction with others. The theory has three stages: (1) we imagine how our actions appear to others, (2) we imagine how other people judge these actions, and (3) we make some sort of self-judgment based on the presumed judgments of others.

If a child's need for meaningful interaction with others is not met, the development of a social identity will be delayed.

CHARLES HORTON COOLEY (1864–1929)

Cooley believed that the self develops through the process of social interaction with others. This process begins early in life and is influenced by such primary groups as the family. Later on, peer groups become very important as we continue to progress as social beings. Cooley used the phrase **looking-glass self** to describe the three-stage process through which each of us develops a sense of self. First, we imagine how our actions appear to others. Second, we imagine how other people judge these actions. Finally, we make some sort of self-judgment based on the presumed judgments of others. In effect, other people become a mirror or looking glass for us (1909).

In Cooley's view, therefore, the self is entirely a social product—that is, a product of social interaction. Each individual acquires a sense of self in the course of being socialized and continues to modify it in each new situation throughout life. Cooley believed that the looking-glass self constructed early in life remains fairly stable and that childhood experiences are very important in determining our sense of self throughout our lives.

One of Cooley's principal contributions to sociology was his observation that although our perceptions are not always correct, what we believe is more important to determining our behavior than what is real. This same idea was also expressed by sociologist W. I. Thomas (1928) when he noted, "If men define situations as real, they are real in their consequences." If we can understand the ways in which people perceive reality, then we can begin to understand their behavior.

GEORGE HERBERT MEAD (1863–1931)

Mead was a philosopher and a well-known social psychologist at the University of Chicago. His work led to the development of the school of thought called symbolic interactionism (described in Chapter 1). Mead was a student of Cooley. He built on Cooley's ideas, tracing the beginning of a person's awareness of self to the relationships between the care giver (usually the mother) and the child (1934). The self becomes the sum total of a person's beliefs and feelings about themselves. The self is composed of two parts, the "I" and the "me." The **I** portion of the self wishes to have free expression, to be active, and to be spontaneous. The "I" wishes to be free of the control of others and to take the initiative in situations. It is the part of the individual that is unique and distinctive. The **me** portion of the self is made up of those things learned through the socialization process from the family, peers, school, and so on. The "me" makes normal social interaction possible, while the "I" prevents it from being mechanical and totally predictable.

The "I" and the "me" are shaped through the socialization process as we interact with others. Mead used the term **significant others** to refer to those individuals who are most important in our development, such as parents, friends, and teachers. As we continue to be socialized we learn to be aware of the views of the **generalized others** also. These are the viewpoints, attitudes, and expectations of society as a whole or of a general community of people that we are aware of and who are important to us. We may believe it is important to go to college, for example, because significant others have instilled this viewpoint in us. While at college we may be influenced by the views of selected generalized others who represent the community of lawyers whom we hope to join one day.

Mead believed that the self develops in three stages (1934). The first or *preparatory stage* is characterized by the child's imitating the behavior of others, which prepares the child for learning social-role expectations. In the second or *play stage,* the child has acquired language and begins not only to imitate behavior but also to formulate role expectations: playing house, cops and robbers, and so on. In this stage the play will feature many discussions among playmates about the way things "ought" to be. "I'm the boss," a little boy may announce. "The daddy is the boss of the house." "Oh no," his friend might counter, "mommies are the real bosses. . . ." In the third or *game stage,* the child learns that there are rules that specify the proper and correct relationship among the players. For example, in a baseball game there are rules that apply to the game in general as well as to a series of expectations about how each position should be played. During the game stage, according to Mead, we learn the expectations, positions, and rules of society at large. Throughout life, in whatever position we occupy, we must learn the expectations of the various positions with which we interact as well as the expectations of the general audience, if our performance is to go smoothly.

Thus, for Mead the self is rooted in, and begins to take shape through, the social play of children and is well on its way to being formed by the time the child is 8 or 9 years old. Therefore, like Cooley, Mead regarded childhood experiences as very important in charting the course of development.

SIGMUND FREUD (1856–1939)

Freud was a pioneer in the study of human behavior and the human mind. He was a doctor in Vienna, Austria, who gradually became interested in the problem of understanding mental illness. Once he turned his attention to this area, he charted new pathways of scholarship and thought, and today he is regarded as one of the most creative and original thinkers of the nineteenth and twentieth centuries.

Over his lifetime, Freud developed a body of thought about the mind that is called **psychoanalysis.** (The same term is used to refer to the form of treatment Freud developed to treat patients suffering from mental illnesses.) Psychoanalysis rests on two basic hypotheses. The first is psychic determinism, or the view that every human

I The portion of the self that wishes to have free expression, to be active, and to be spontaneous.

me The portion of the self that is made up of those things learned through the socialization process from the family, peers, school, and so on.

significant others Those people who are most important in our development, such as parents, friends, and teachers.

generalized others The viewpoints, attitudes, and expectations of society as a whole or of a general community of people that we are aware of and who are important to us.

psychoanalysis A body of thought developed by Sigmund Freud that rests on two basic hypotheses: (1) every human act has a psychological cause or basis, and (2) every person has an unconscious mind.

ego In Freudian theory, one of the three separately functioning parts of the self. The ego tries to mediate in the conflict between the id and the superego and to find socially acceptable ways for the id's drives to be expressed. This part of the self constantly evaluates social realities and looks for ways to adjust to them.

reality principle A Freudian principle that explains the ego's attempts to adjust to the socially appropriate demands of the real world.

id In Freudian theory, one of the three separately functioning parts of the self. The id consists of the unconscious drives or instincts that Freud believed every human being inherits.

libido One of the two basic instincts of the id. According to Freud, the libido controls the erotic or sexual drive.

superego In Freudian theory, one of the three separately functioning parts of the self. The superego consists of society's norms and values, learned in the course of a person's socialization, which often conflict with the impulses of the id. The superego is the internal censor.

pleasure principle A Freudian principle that explains the id's impulsive attempts to satisfy its drive for sexual expression.

act has a psychological cause or basis. Because no human behavior comes about as the result of chance, "slips" of the tongue, moments of clumsiness, and unexpected moods all are explainable as events in the person's mind. The second hypothesis supposes the existence of the unconscious, or the view that people are aware of only a small part of the thoughts and feelings that exist in their minds.

In Freud's view, the self has three separately functioning parts: the id, the superego, and the ego. The **id** consists of the drives or instincts that Freud believed every human being inherits but for the most part remain unconscious. Of these instincts two are most important: the aggressive drive and the erotic or sexual drive (called **libido**). Every feeling emerges from these two drives. The **superego** is the internal censor. It is not inherited biologically, like the id, but is learned in the course of a person's socialization. The superego keeps trying to put the brakes on the id's impulsive attempts to satisfy its drives (the so-called **pleasure principle**). Put another way, the superego in each of us represents society's norms and moral values as learned primarily from our parents. So, for instance, the superego must hold back the id's unending drive for sexual expression (Freud, 1920, 1923). The id and superego, then, are eternally at war with each other. Fortunately,

Sigmund Freud believed that even though the individual needs society, society's restrictive norms are a constant source of discontent.

there is a third functional part of the self that tries not only to mediate in the eternal conflict between id and superego but also to find socially acceptable ways for the id's drives to be expressed. This part of the self, which constantly is evaluating social realities and looking for ways to adjust to them, is called the **ego.** For example, the ego finds socially appropriate sexual partners with whom the individual can discharge sexual drives. Thus, just as the id works on the pleasure principle, the ego works on the **reality principle** (Freud, 1920, 1923).

Freud pictured the individual as constantly in conflict: the instinctual drives of the id (essentially sex and aggression) push for expression, while at the same time the demands of society set certain limits on the behavior patterns that will be tolerated. Even though the individual needs society, society's restrictive norms and values are a source of ongoing discontent (Freud, 1930). Freud's theories suggest that society and the individual are enemies, with the latter yielding to the former reluctantly and only out of compulsion.

ERIK H. ERIKSON (1902–)

In 1950 Erikson, an artist-turned-psychologist who studied with Freud in Vienna, published an influential book called *Childhood and Society* (1963). In it he built on Freud's theory of development but added two important elements. First, he stressed that development is a lifelong process and that a person continues to pass through new stages even during adulthood. Second, he paid greater attention to the social and cultural forces operating on the individual at each step along the way.

In Erikson's view, human development is accomplished in eight separate stages (see Table 4.1). Each stage amounts to a crisis of sorts brought on by two factors: biological changes in the developing individual and social expectations and stresses. At each stage the individual is pulled in two opposite directions to resolve the crisis. In normal development the individual re-

—————————————————— **TABLE 4.1**
Erikson's Eight Stages of Human Development

Stage	Age Period	Characteristic to Be Achieved	Major Hazards to Achievement
Trust versus mistrust	Birth to 1 year	Sense of trust or security—achieved through parental gratification of needs and affection.	Neglect, abuse, or deprivation; inconsistent or inappropriate love in infancy; early or harsh weaning.
Autonomy versus shame and doubt	1 to 4 years	Sense of autonomy—achieved as child begins to see self as individual apart from his/her parents.	Conditions that make the child feel inadequate, evil, or dirty.
Initiative versus guilt	4 to 5 years	Sense of initiative—achieved as child begins to imitate adult behavior and extends control of the world around him/her.	Guilt produced by overly strict discipline and the internalization of rigid ethical standards that interfere with the child's spontaneity.
Industry versus inferiority	6 to 12 years	Sense of duty and accomplishment—achieved as the child lays aside fantasy and play and begins to undertake tasks and school work.	Feelings of inadequacy produced by excessive competition, personal limitations, or other events leading to feelings of inferiority.
Identity versus role confusion	Adolescence	Sense of identity—achieved as one clarifies sense of self and what he/she believes in.	Sense of role confusion resulting from the failure of the family or society to provide clear role models.
Intimacy versus isolation	Young adulthood	Sense of intimacy—the ability to establish close personal relationships with others.	Problems with earlier stages that make it difficult to get close to others.
Generativity versus stagnation	30s to 50s	Sense of productivity and creativity—resulting from work and parenting activities.	Sense of stagnation produced by feeling inadequate as a parent and stifled at work.
Integrity versus despair	Old age	Sense of ego integrity—achieved by acceptance of the life one has lived.	Feeling of despair and dissatisfaction with one's role as a senior member of society.

According to Erik Erikson, adolescence is a time when the teenager must develop an identity, as well as the ability to establish close personal relationships with others.

body at all. Most of us are able to trust at least some other people and thereby form enduring relationships while at the same time staying alert to the possibility of being misled.

Erikson's most valuable contribution to the study of human development has been to show that socialization continues throughout a person's life and does not stop with childhood. There is indeed development after 30 — and after 60 and 70 as well. The task of building the self is lifelong; it can be considered our central task from cradle to grave. We construct the self — our identity — using the materials made available to us by our culture and our society.

solves the conflict experienced at each stage somewhere toward the middle of the opposing options. For example, very few people are entirely trusting, and very few trust no-

The elderly in our society run the risk of feelings of despair and dissatisfaction with their role as senior members of the community.

DANIEL LEVINSON (1920–)

A fascinating blend of sociology and psychology has taken place in the area of adult development. Through research in this field we have come to recognize that there are predictable age-related developmental periods in the adult life cycle, just as there are in the developmental cycles of children and adolescents. These periods are marked by a concerted effort to resolve particular life issues and goals.

Important research in this area has been done by Daniel Levinson and his colleagues (1978). Levinson recruited forty men, aged 35 to 45, from four occupational groups: factory workers, novelists, business executives, and academic biologists. Each subject was interviewed several times during a 2- to 3-month period and again, if possible, in a follow-up session 2 years later.

From this study Levinson developed the foundation of his theory. He proposed that adults are periodically faced with new but predictable developmental tasks throughout their life and that working through these challenges is the essence of adulthood. Levinson believes the adult life course is marked by a continual series of building periods, followed by stable periods, and then followed again by periods in which attempts are made to change some of the perceived flaws in the previous design.

Levinson's model describes the periods in the adult life cycle:

I. *Early Adult Period (Age 18 to 22)*
Leaving the family of origin is the major task of this period. A great deal of energy is expended in trying to reduce dependence on the family for support or authority. Peer support often becomes critical to this task.

II. *Getting into the Adult World (Age 22 to 28)*
This period is marked by the exploration and beginning commitment to adult roles, responsibilities, and relationships. Career advancement may become a major focal point. This period produces an initial life structure including marriage and occupation. The individual may also form a *dream* that serves as a guiding force and provides images of future life structures.

III. *Age 30 Transitional Period (Age 28 to 32)*
At this point the individual begins to perceive some of the "flaws" in his or her initial life structure and sets out to correct them. Divorce and job changes are common during this period. This is a time of internal instability, in which many aspects of the individual's life are questioned and examined.

IV. *Settling Down (Age 33 to 40)*
Having reworked some of the aspects of one's life during the previous period, the individual is now ready to seek order and stability. There is a strong desire for achievement and an earnest attempt to make the dream a reality. The individual wants to "sink roots."

V. *Age 40 Transitional Period (Age 38 to 42)*
This is a major transitional period and

Daniel Levinson believes that the period from age 22 to 28 is marked by a beginning commitment to adult roles, responsibilities, and relationships.

represents the turning point between young and middle adulthood. The individual starts to see a difference between the dream and the reality of his or her life, leading to a great deal of soul-searching. Divorce and career changes once again become real possibilities. The individual may start to give up certain aspects of the dream and become less achievement and advancement oriented.

VI. *Beginning of Middle Adulthood (Age Mid-40s)*
The previous period of turmoil has produced a greater acceptance of oneself. The individual is less dominated by the need to win or to achieve external rewards and more concerned with enjoying his or her life and work. The individual also has a greater concern for other people than before.

Levinson did not study people beyond age 45, although he does believe that the developmental process continues throughout the entire life course. The model is particularly interesting to sociologists because it appears to show us that there is a close relationship between individual development and one's position in society at a particular time.

There are, however, problems with being too quick to embrace this type of theory. Levinson's theory of adult development is what is commonly referred to as a "stage theory." Stage theories describe a series of changes that follow an orderly sequential pattern. These theories have been criticized for being too rigid; for assuming that the changes are always in one direction; and for assuming that the stages are universal. Critics note that we can apply stages of development to children, but when we do so with adults, we leave little room for individual differences, social change, and specific cohort experiences (Neugarten, 1979).

Levinson's theory has also been criticized as not being relevant to women. Because the model is based on a study that included only men, it is not clear whether all the stages also apply to women. Barnett and Baruch (1979) argue that women's roles involve various life structures that are not so centrally tied to chronological age as men's. Women may experience various combinations of career, marriage, and children throughout their lives. A woman may not enter the world of work until her children have started school. Her ability to reassess her career commitments at age 40 may involve different issues than those important to men.

Rossi (1985) notes that the stage theorists may have merely described the life pattern of a particular cohort. Most of the subjects in these studies were born before and during the Depression, were predominantly white and upper middle class. What was true for this group may not hold for today's 30- and 40-year-olds, born after World War II. She points out that the men in the studies may just have "burned out at a premature age, rather than reflecting a normal developmental process all men go through" (Neugarten and Rossi, 1985).

EARLY SOCIALIZATION IN AMERICAN SOCIETY

Children are brought up very differently from one society to another. Each culture has its own child-rearing values, attitudes, and practices. No matter how children are raised, however, each society must provide certain minimal necessities to ensure normal development. The infant's body must, of course, be cared for. But more than that is required. Children need speaking social partners (some evidence suggests that a child who has received no language stimulation at all in the first five to six years of life will be unable ever to acquire speech [Chomsky, 1975]). They also need physical stimulation; objects that they can manipulate; space and time to explore, to initiate activity, and to be alone; and finally, limits and prohibitions that organize their options and channel development in certain culturally specified directions (Provence, 1972).

Every society provides this basic minimum care in its own culturally prescribed ways. A variety of agents are used to mold the child to fit into the society. Once again, these agents vary from culture to culture. Here we consider some of the most important agents of socialization in American society.

THE FAMILY

For young children in most societies—and certainly in American society—the family is the primary world for the first few years of life. Children are also having significant early experiences in day-care centers with nonfamily members. The values, norms, ideals, and standards presented are accepted by the child uncritically as correct—indeed, as the only way things could possibly be. Even though later experiences lead children to modify much of what they have learned within the family, it is not unusual for individuals to carry into the social relationships of adult life the role expectations that characterized the family of their childhood. It is hardly insignificant that we joke about such things as a newlywed wife not being able to cook her husband's favorite meal as well as his mother did or that a daughter may take on many of the characteristics of her mother.

Every family, therefore, socializes its children to its own particular version of the society's culture. In addition, however, each family exists within certain subcultures of the larger society: it belongs to a geographical region, a social class, one (or two) ethnic groups, and possibly a religious group or other subculture. Families differ with regard to how important these factors are in determining their life-style and their child-rearing practices. For example, some families are very deeply committed to an ethnic identification, such as black, Hispanic, Chinese, Native American, Italian-American, Polish-American, or Jewish. Much of family life may revolve around participation in social and religious events of the community and may include speaking a language other than English.

There is also evidence that social class and parents' occupation influence the ways in which children are raised in America. Parents who have white-collar occupations are used to dealing with people and solving problems. As a consequence, white-collar parents value intellectual curiosity and flexibility. Blue-collar parents have jobs that involve machines and require the obeying of orders and being on time. They are likely to reward obedience to authority, punctuality, and mechanical ability in their children (Kohn and Schooler, 1983; Kohn and Schooler, 1983.)

The last two decades have seen major changes in the structure of the American family. High divorce rates, the dramatic increase in single-parent families, and the common phenomenon of two-worker families has meant that the family as the major source of socialization of children is being

Every family socializes its children to its own particular version of the society's culture. The values and world view of a boy raised on a dairy farm in Wisconsin are likely to be different from those of a child born and raised in an urban center such as Los Angeles or New York City.

challenged. Child-care providers have become a major influence in the lives of many young children. (For a discussion of the effects of day care on the socialization of children, see Controversies in Sociology, "Is Day-Care a Threat to Children?")

THE SCHOOL

The school is an institution intended to socialize children in selected skills and knowledge. In recent decades, however, the school has been assigned additional tasks. For instance, in poor communities and neighborhoods, school lunch (and breakfast) programs are an important source of balanced nutrition for children. There is also a more basic problem the school must confront. As an institution the school must resolve the conflicting values of the local community and of the state and regional officials whose job it is to determine what should be taught. For example, in many schools of the rural American South, the theory of evolution is not taught, even though it represents a body of knowledge that most American scholars accept as valuable and important. In other

ARE GENIUSES BORN OR CREATED?

On approximately six Sundays a year, a new group of eighty people arrives on the campus of The Institute for the Advancement of Human Potential in Philadelphia to take a week-long course on how to turn their children into geniuses. About half of them are from the United States. About a dozen are Canadians, with the rest coming from Europe, Asia, the South Pacific, the Middle East, South America, and Africa.

Marjorie Bennett has been using the regime taught in this course with her son Jeremy, age 6. While many of Jeremy's peers are struggling through their first primer, Jeremy is breezing through the *Wall Street Journal, Newsweek,* and selected works by Longfellow. He likes knock-knock jokes in addition to history, paleontology, geography, and astronomy.

Jeremy's interests are not confined to books. He just signed up for an advanced gymnastics class, and he plays the piano and sings.

Since Jeremy was barely out of the womb, his mother has been teaching him reading, math, science, and music. Marjorie Bennett recently quit her job so she can spend even more time leading Jeremy to what she hopes will be the fast track to success.

Not so long ago, most parents wanted their children to be like everybody else. They were often as upset if their children were advanced as they were if the children were slow. Now all that appears to have changed. For many parents today there is no such thing as going too fast, and their major concern is that their children stay ahead of the pack.

Perhaps the most controversial and evangelical proponent of the "start-them-young-and-push-them-hard" philosophy is Glenn Doman, founder of the Philadelphia institute mentioned above. He has written such books as *Teach Your Baby Math, How To Teach Your Baby to Read,* and *How to Multiply Your Baby's Intelligence.*

At Doman's institute, children as young as 7 months are "reading" in three languages, 1-year-olds study musical notation, and 18-month-olds begin violin lessons. Doman, who has been teaching parents how to teach their babies for the past 40 years, believes that early education can lead to a "golden age" for society and an end to war, poverty, and hunger.

David Elkind believes the major consequence of this new parenting is that many contemporary parents are putting tremendous pressure on children to perform at ever-earlier ages. Clearly, there is nothing wrong with wanting children to do their

instances, education officials are able to ramrod curriculum changes into the classroom despite the complaints of parents, whose objections are dismissed as ignorant or tradition-bound.

An example of schools deciding what issues should be presented to children involves the addition of AIDS education to the curriculum in many schools. Some parents have objected to teaching young children about condoms and homosexuality, despite the health risk that ignorance could pose. Many school boards have taken the position that the schools have a responsibility to provide this information even when large numbers of parents object.

In coming to grips with their multiple responsibilities, many schools have established a philosophy of education that encompasses socialization as well as academic instruction. According to the philosophy adopted by one school, for instance, its aim is to help students develop to their fullest capacity, not only intellectually, but also emotionally, culturally, morally, socially, and physically. By exposing the student to a variety of ideas, the teachers attempt to guide the development of the whole student

best. It is not the normal healthy desire of parents to have successful children that is the problem but the excessive pressure some parents are putting on children.

What is behind this push for excellence? Elkind believes it is related to the fact that parents today are having fewer children. The pressure to have "a child to be proud of" is therefore greater. Parents who have been successful in their own careers see no reason why they should not ensure the same success for their children. The gifted children become proof of their own success.

Elkind believes many parents become far too intrusive and rob the children of the opportunity to take the initiative for their own education. The children are deprived of the opportunity to take responsibility for their mistakes and credit for their achievements. These parents run the risk of producing children who are dependent and lack self-esteem. Instead of superkids, Elkind notes,

the parents may end up with super problems.

Glenn Doman disagrees. He believes that every human infant has within him or her the seeds of genius. He notes, "Genius is available to each human infant both genetically . . . and environmentally (because intelligence can be either created or throttled, increased or decreased, in each individual human infant)."

Doman believes that what we call genius, a uniquely human capacity, is no gift at all but is instead a human birthright common to us all, out of which we have been cheated by our lack of knowledge—a superb opportunity which has been stolen from us. Every human mother has the capacity to nurture the seeds of genius within her infant.

Studies of gifted and successful adults give no support to the idea that early formal instruction creates intellectual giftedness or creative talent. Autobiographical

statements from such adults note that their parents were careful not to impose their own priorities on them. Instead, these parents allowed their children to lead and then provided the necessary support and encouragement.

We must also ask "What is gained by ballet lessons?" The child is forced to adjust to another adult, another set of standards, another group of people, another set of rules. Is this activity being done for the convenience of the parents or out of interest for the child? We should remember that childhood is the springtime of life, not spring training.

Sources: Glenn Doman, *How to Multiply Your Baby's Intelligence* (Garden City, New York: Doubleday, 1984); David Elkind, "Superkids and Super Problems," *Psychology Today,* May 1987, pp. 60–61; David Elkind, *Miseducation: Preschoolers at Risk* (New York: Alfred A. Knopf, 1987).

---

in areas of interest and ability unique to each. Students are expected to learn how to analyze these ideas critically and reach their own conclusions. The ultimate goal of the school is to produce a "well-integrated" person who will become socially responsible and a good neighbor and citizen. Two questions arise: Is such an ambitious, all-embracing educational philosophy working? And is it an appropriate goal for our schools?

In a way, the school is a model of much of the adult social world. Interpersonal relationships are not based on individuals' love and affection for one another. Rather, they are impersonal and predefined by the society with little regard for each particular individual who enters into them. Children's process of adjustment to the school's social order is a preview of what will be expected as they mature and attempt to negotiate their way into the institutions of adult society (job, political work, organized recreation, and so on). Of all the socializing functions of the school, this may be the most important. (The role of the school in socialization will be discussed more extensively in Chapter 14).

PEER GROUPS

peers Individuals who are social equals.

Peers are individuals who are social equals. From early childhood until late adulthood we encounter a wide variety of peer groups. No one will deny that they play a powerful role in our socialization. Often their influence is greater than any other socialization source.

Within the family and the school, children are in socially inferior positions relative to figures of authority (parents, teachers, principals). As long as the child is small and weak, this social inferiority seems natural, but by adolescence a person is almost fully grown, and arbitrary submission to authority is not so easy to accept. Hence, many adolescents withdraw into the comfort of social groups composed of peers. In the United States, school-age children spend twice as much time with their peers, on the average, as they do with their parents (Bronfenbrenner, 1970).

It appears that parents play a major role in teaching basic values and the desire to achieve long-term goals. Peers have the greatest influence in life-style issues, such as appearance, social activities, and dating (Sebald, 1986).

Peer groups provide valuable social support for adolescents.

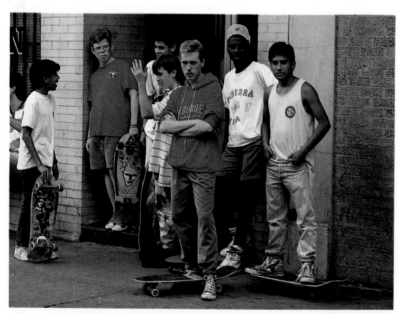

Peer groups provide valuable social support for adolescents who are moving toward independence from their parents. As a consequence, their peer-group values often run counter to those of the older generation. New group members are quickly socialized to adopt symbols of group membership, such as styles of dress, use and consumption of certain material goods, and stylized patterns of behavior. It is ironic that although adolescents often proclaim their freedom from the conformity of their parents, within their peer groups they are themselves slaves to group fashion.

Many studies have documented the increasing importance of peer-group socialization in America. One reason for this is that parents' life experiences and accumulated wisdom may not be very helpful in preparing young people to meet the requirements of life in a society that is changing constantly. Not infrequently, adolescents are better informed than their parents about such things as sex, drugs, and technology. In her study of the generation gap, Margaret Mead (1970) likened youth to pioneers exploring not a new land but rather a new time (Sebold, 1986).

Peer-group influence for many inner-city youths can lead to wasted lives and violence. For many, joining gangs—kids banding together for identity, status, petty criminal activity, and mutual protection—often involves drug abuse. In Dallas, for example, cocaine is traded in many high schools, and attempts to emphasize the dangers of drugs fall on deaf ears. According to Lloyd Johnston, a survey researcher at the University of Michigan's Institute of Social Research, which conducts an annual survey of high school seniors, drug use is well entrenched in the ghetto. "If anything," says Johnston, "it [drug use] is a badge of courage" (*Newsweek,* November 23, 1987).

The negative effects of peer pressure are felt on college campuses as well as in the ghetto. Peer pressure has caused deaths from hazing activities in college fraternities. An 18-year-old freshman at Rutgers University in New Jersey died when he consumed more than 20 ounces of liquor in less than 45 minutes as part of a hazing ritual to initiate new members into the fraternity. The student's need for being accepted by his peers overcame his sense of reason, even when he realized that the alcohol was making him sick (Rangel, 1988).

As the authority of the family diminishes under the pressures of social change, peer groups move into the vacuum and substitute their own morality for that of the older generation. Peer groups are most effective in molding the behavior of those adolescents whose parents do not provide consistent standards, a principled moral code, guidance, and emotional support (Baumrind, 1975; Elder, 1975). Elkins (1981) has expressed the view that the power of the peer group is in direct proportion to the extent that the adolescent feels ignored by the parents. In fact, four decades ago sociologist David Riesman, in his classic work *The Lonely Crowd* (1959), already thought that the peer group had become the single most powerful molder of many adolescents' behavior and that striving for peer approval had become the dominant concern of an entire American generation — adults as well as adolescents. He coined the term *other directed* to describe those who are overconcerned with finding social approval (Elkind, 1981).

THE MASS MEDIA

It is possible that today Riesman would review his thinking somewhat. Over the past 25 to 30 years, the mass media — television, radio, magazines, films, newspapers — have become important agents of socialization in America. It is almost impossible in our society to escape from the images and sounds of television or radio; even in most private homes, especially those with children, the media are constantly visible or audible.

The mass media are an impersonal means of transmitting information to great numbers of people in a very short time. For the most part, the communication is one way, creating an audience that is conditioned to receive passively what is sometimes called *mass culture* (Rosenberg and White, 1971), consisting of whatever news, messages, programs, or events are brought to them. Television has been criticized because it often deals with trivial events and does not encourage us to think critically (Postman, 1985).

Because young children are so impressionable and because in so many American households the television is used as an unpaid mechanical babysitter, social scientists have become increasingly concerned about the socializing role played by the mass media in our society.

Today 99 percent of all households in the United States have a television set. The average household has the television on for more than 7 hours each day. Most children become regular watchers of television between the ages of 3 and 6. One study concluded that by the time most people reach the age of 18, they will have spent more waking time watching television than doing anything else — talking with parents, spending time with friends, or even going to school (*Statistical Abstract of the United States: 1988, 1987*). What effect does this have on children?

For one thing, today's children receive an enormous amount of information. They are instantly informed of new fads and styles, new activities, and new products through television programs and cartoon shows. Many people consider this blatant exploitation, because young children have no way of evaluating the merits of advertising programs. (For a critical view of the current state of children's television, see our interview with Peggy Charon, founder of Action for Children's Television, in this chapter.)

This is not to say that all children's television programming is exploitive. Programs such as Sesame Street, a production of the Children's Television Workshop, are designed to help preschoolers develop the intellectual, social, and emotional skills needed to succeed in school. Although Sesame Street teaches children their letters and numbers, an equally important aim is to help young children understand and adjust to the relationships around them. For example, after Sesame Street researchers interviewed ninety preschoolers and found that the children did not understand the connection between love and marriage, they developed an on-screen romance between Maria and Luis, partners in the program's Fix-It Shop. Even though, ideally, love and romance are subjects best learned from a family's everyday experiences, many Sesame Street viewers come from broken and single-parent homes where the traditional stability of love and marriage are not part of their lives. For many of these children, seeing marriage as a good and natural thing — one that comes from love and commitment — was a totally new experience (*Christian Science Monitor,* May 17, 1988).

The influence of television on behavior is of special concern to those who believe that the prevalence of violence depicted on television and in films produces violent crime and aggression in children. A study by the National Institute of Mental Health (1982) came to the conclusion that there was "overwhelming" evidence that there was a clear relationship between televised violence and antisocial behavior. The study concluded that television is not innocuous entertainment, and that we must be aware of its negative impact.

More recent research places in doubt some of the views about this relationship. Cullingford (1984) believes that children are not really paying that much attention to what they watch and that they are better at separating fact from fiction than we may think. We now believe that the relationship between violent acts and antisocial behavior is much more complicated than we originally thought. For both adults and children, social context, peer influence, values, and attitudes all play at least as important a role in determining their behavior as television does.

Children are also exposed to attitudes toward authority figures and criminal behavior on television. Two researchers (Lichter and Lichter, 1984) analyzed 3 decades of television programming and found that contemporary television is laced with antiestablishment and antiauthority themes. The public is being socialized to a particular view of society through entertainment programming.

The Lichters found that criminals on prime time television are usually middle- or upper-class white males over 30. In fact, wealthy individuals are portrayed as criminals twice as often as those who are middle class or poor. The criminals we are less likely to see on television are the juvenile delinquents or the youth gangs. We are infrequently exposed to the culture of poverty that is directly or indirectly responsible for a great deal of crime.

There is also a possible link between homicides and suicides and television presentations of these acts. It has been shown (Bollen and Phillips, 1982) that homicides tend to increase immediately after a widely publicized boxing match, and that suicides increase during the 10 days after the reported suicide of a well-known person.

Recent waves of adolescent suicides have focused attention on the effects of fictional accounts of suicide and television news coverage of subsequent "imitation suicides." At the moment it is not clear that there is a proven statistical link between these suicides and the television programs. According to Harvard Medical School psychiatrist Leon Eisenberg however, it is time "to ask whether there are measures that should be undertaken to limit media coverage of suicide" (*Science News,* October 3, 1987).

ADULT SOCIALIZATION

A person's **primary socialization** is completed when he or she reaches adulthood.

primary socialization The process by which children master the basic information and skills required of members of society.

SOCIALIZATION AND TELEVISION

Since its inception 20 years ago, Action for Children's Television (ACT) has acted as a watchdog agency to monitor children's programming. Under the leadership of founder Peggy Charren, ACT has protested the overcommercialization of children's television, the advertising of candy-shaped vitamins, cartoon shows such as "He-Man" and "Captain Power," which ACT claims are 30-minute commercials for toy products, and more.

We spoke with Peggy Charren about children's television, and the role of parents, government, and the television industry in the socialization of our young.

Q *uestion:* How important is television as an influence in children's lives?

Answer: You don't have to know a lot about children to understand that something they spend four hours a day doing will influence how they think, feel, and grow up. When kids spend this much time watching TV at the very least, they're not kicking stones or looking at clouds or even talking with family and friends.

Q: You have noted that children are "TV's most vulnerable constituency." Why?

A: Most TV executives still try to figure out how to benefit from children rather than how to benefit children. For example, children's advertising is very manipulative and is targeted to an audience, some of whom are too young to cross the street. How can we expect them to understand the vagaries of the marketplace and why they have to listen to commercials with a third — critical — ear. Young children just can't deal with sophisticated concepts like these, and TV executives know it.

Q: What should parents do?

A: First, they should monitor what their children watch. Research shows that the involvement of caring adults counters the negative effects of TV. Parents should steer their children toward quality programming and encourage them to turn off the set when enough is enough.

Q: What about children who are home alone and the television serves the role of babysitter?

A: Some things we cannot fix. If you think about it, a child alone in a house may be better off watching television than being

Peggy Charren

frightened by an empty, silent home.

Q: Haven't programs like Sesame Street and The Electric Company encouraged the networks to improve their children's programming?

A: No. Anything that's good gives TV executives an excuse to do nothing. Sesame Street was supposed to be a model for educating children while entertaining them. Instead, network executives took the position that since public television was producing this kind of programming, they didn't have to.

Q: What should our attitude be toward television?

A: ACT believes — and I believe — that TV is a delivery system. It can be wonderful, but children have to learn how to use it.

This means that adults have mastered the basic information and skills required of members of a society. They have (1) learned a language and can think logically to some degree, (2) accepted the basic norms and values of the culture, (3) developed the ability to pattern their behavior in terms of these norms and values, and (4) assumed a culturally appropriate social identity.

There is still much to learn, however,

adult socialization The process by which adults learn new statuses and roles. Adult socialization continues throughout the adult years.

and there are many new social identities to explore. Socialization, therefore, continues during the adult years. However, **adult socialization** differs from primary socialization in two ways.

First, adults are much more aware than young people of the processes through which they are being socialized. In fact, they deliberately engage in programs such as advanced education or on-the-job training in which socialization is an explicit goal. Second, adults often have more control over how they wish to be socialized and therefore can mobilize more enthusiasm for the process. Whether going to business school, taking up a new hobby, or signing up for the Peace Corps, adults can decide to channel their energy into making the most effective use of an opportunity to learn new skills or knowledge.

An important aspect of adult socialization is **resocialization,** which involves being exposed to ideas or values that in one way or another conflict with what was learned in childhood. This is a common experience for college students who leave their homes for the first time and encounter a new environment in which many of their family's cherished beliefs and values are held up to critical examination. Changes in religious and political orientation are not uncommon during the college years, which often lead to a time of stress for students and their parents.

Erving Goffman (1961a) discussed the major resocialization that takes place in **total institutions**—environments such as prisons or mental hospitals in which the participants are physically and socially isolated from the outside world. Goffman noted several factors that make for effective resocialization. These include (1) isolation from the outside world, (2) spending all one's time in the same place with the same people, (3) shedding individual identity by giving up old clothes and possessions for standard uniforms, (4) a clean break with the past, and (5) loss of freedom of action. Under these circumstances there usually is a major change in the individual along the

resocialization An important aspect of adult socialization that involves being exposed to ideas or values that in one way or another conflict with what was learned in childhood.

total institutions Environments such as prisons or mental hospitals in which the participants are physically and socially isolated from the outside world.

lines prescribed by those doing the resocialization.

In the next section we will discuss four events in adult socialization: marriage, parenthood, work, and aging.

MARRIAGE AND RESPONSIBILITY

As Ruth Benedict (1938) noted in a now-classic article on socialization in America, ". . . our culture goes to great extremes in emphasizing contrasts between the child and the adult." We think of childhood as a time without cares, a time for play. Adulthood, on the other hand, is marked by work and taking up the burden of responsibility. One of the great adult responsibilities in our society is marriage.

Indeed, many of the traditional role expectations of marriage no longer are accepted uncritically by today's young adults. For both men and women choices loom large: How much should they devote themselves to a career, how much to self-improvement and personal growth, how much to a spouse? Ours is a time of uncertainty and experimentation. Even so, marriage still retains its primacy as a life choice for adults. Although divorce has become acceptable in most circles, marriage still is treated seriously as a public statement that both partners are committed to each other and to stability and responsibility. (We will discuss marriage and alternative lifestyles in greater detail in Chapter 12).

Once married, the new partners must define their relationships to each other and in respect to the demands of society. This is not as easy today as it used to be when these choices largely were determined by tradition. Although friends, parents, and relatives usually are only too ready to instruct the young couple in the "shoulds" and "should nots" of married life, increasingly such attempts at socialization are resented by young people who wish to chart their own courses. One choice they must make is whether or not to become parents.

PARENTHOOD

Once a couple has a child, their responsibilities increase enormously. They must find ways to provide the care and nurturing necessary to the healthy development of their baby, and at the same time they must work hard to keep their own relationship intact, because the arrival of an infant inevitably is accompanied by stress. This requires a reexamination of the role expectations each partner has of the other, both as a parent and as a spouse.

Of course, most parents anticipate some stresses and try to resolve them even before the baby is born. Financial plans are made, living space is created, baby care is studied. Friends and relatives are asked for advice, and their future baby-sitting services are secured. However, not all the stresses of parenthood are so obvious. One that is frequently overlooked is the fact that parenthood is itself a new developmental phase.

The psychology of being and becoming a parent is extremely complicated. Already during the pregnancy both parents experience intense feelings—some expected, others quite surprising. Some of these feelings may even be very upsetting: for instance, the fear that one will not be an adequate parent or that one might even harm the child. Sometimes such feelings lead people to reconsider their decision to become parents.

The birth of the child brings forth new feelings in the parents, many of which can be traced to the parents' own experiences as infants. As their child grows and passes through all the stages of development we have described, parents relive their own development. In psychological terms parenthood can be viewed as a "second chance": adults can bring to bear all that they have learned in order to resolve the conflicts that were not resolved when they were children. For example, it might be possible for some parents to develop a more trusting approach to life while observing their infants grapple with the conflict of basic trust and mistrust (Erikson's first stage).

CAREER DEVELOPMENT: VOCATION AND IDENTITY

Taking a job is more than finding a place to work. It means stepping into a new social context with its own statuses and roles, and it requires that a person be socialized to meet the needs of the situation. This may even include learning how to dress appropriately. For example, a young management trainee in a major corporation was criticized for wearing his keys on a ring snapped to his belt. "Janitors wear their keys," his supervisor told him. "Executives keep them in their pockets." The keys disappeared from his belt.

To some, choosing a career means rejecting the traditions of the past. Young Navajo women, for example, are no longer willing to take up rug weaving—a traditional occupation that has been practiced by Navajo women for more than two centuries. Instead they want office jobs where they will have higher status and wages (Matthews, 1988).

Aspiring climbers of the occupational ladder may even have to adjust their personalities to fit the job. In the 1950s and 1960s, corporations looked for quiet, loyal, tradition-oriented men to fill their management positions—men who would not "upset the applecart" (Whyte, 1956)—and most certainly not women. Since the late 1960s, however, the trend has been toward recruiting men and women who show drive and initiative and a capacity for creative thinking and problem solving.

Some occupations require extensive resocialization. Individuals wishing to become doctors or nurses, for example, must overcome their squeamishness about blood, body wastes, genitals, and the inside of the body. They must also accept the undemocratic fact that they will receive much of their training while caring for poor patients (usually ethnic minorities). More well-to-do patients receive care mostly from fully trained personnel.

The armed forces use basic training of recruits to socialize them to obey orders

Is Day Care Harmful to Children?

Our culture sends conflicting messages to mothers about child rearing. On the one hand mothers are still viewed as the principal caretakers of children. Yet, on the other hand they are now also expected to expand fully as individuals and develop their own potentials and needs (Rubinstein, 1988).

A variety of demographic and social changes have produced serious conflicts for parents with respect to child-care arrangements. The mothers who were born after World War II are far more likely to be working when their children are preschoolers than women were in the past. In 1987 there were 13.4 million two-worker families in the United States where the wife was 18 to 44. This was up from 8.3 million in 1976. Of all women who gave birth in 1987, 51 percent were employed after the birth, well above the 31 percent recorded in 1976 (Bureau of the Census, 1988).

There are 8.2 million children under 5 whose mothers work. These children are usually in one of three types of child care. About 31 percent of the children are cared for in their own homes (principally by their fathers). In the second type of arrangement, usually referred to as "family day care," a woman takes four to six unrelated young children into her home on a regular basis. Thirty-seven percent of child care is of this type. The remaining 23 percent of the children are enrolled in day-care centers. Another 8 percent are cared for by their mothers while the mothers are working (see Figure 4.1) (Bureau of the Census, Statistical Brief, May 1987).

Nearly one in four parents, then, put their preschoolers in organized child care. This is more than double the number of parents who did so 20 years ago. However, is this development serving the children as well as traditional child rearing did?

Sociologists and psychologists begin to answer this question by noting that just as all parenting is not uniformly good, neither is all day care mediocre. High-quality day care does exist, and can be a suitable substitute for home parenting. Unfortunately, poor quality care that threatens the child with serious physical and psychological harm is also readily available.

According to Edward Zigler, one of the architects of Project Head Start, we have the knowledge necessary to provide absolutely first-rate child care, but what is missing is the commitment and the will. Zigler believes we must convince people that when a family uses a day-care center, they are not just dropping the child off so they can work. These families are selecting an environment that will have an enormous impact on the development of their child (Trotter, 1987).

Many experts agree that one way to improve child-care standards is to insure that no adult should be allowed to care for more than three infants at a time. Currently there are only three states — Kansas, Massachusetts, and Maryland—that adhere to this standard. Kinder-Care, a national chain of day-care centers, staffs its centers according to state-mandated ratios, which for infants in Connecticut, for example, is one to four; in Alabama this ratio is one to six; and in Ohio, it is one to eight. For 3-year-olds, some states allow a ratio of one worker to fifteen children (Magnet, 1983).

Problems also arise in centers where the staff is underpaid, where there is a high staff turnover, and where there is a high child-to-worker ratio. For example, a teacher with a college degree and a teaching certificate will start at Kinder-Care at the minimum wage and will average just over $8,000 for a full year's work. At some centers the staff turnover is consequently quite high.

Working mothers are also providing their children with a different model of what a woman's role in society is. This is particularly important to women who have daughters, as research has shown that the daughters of working women see the world in a less sex-stereotypical fashion than daughters of nonworking women. They have a higher regard for their own sex and a greater sense of competence (Hoffman, 1974).

In addition to the impact that two-worker families have on children and child-care arrangements, there is also a substantial effect on the parents themselves. Women are likely to experience considerable role conflict and role strain as they try to meet the obligations of the job and the family. In the traditional role of mother, women are considered to be responsible for the well-being of the children. If a woman's children have problems, it is assumed to be her fault. Mothers are vulnerable to self-blame when their children show signs of distress (Barnett and Baruch, 1987). One way to alleviate this guilt is to have the father take a more active role in the child care.

When fathers do take an active role in child care, however, new problems may arise. In one study (Baruch and Barnett, 1986) of 160 fathers, their wives, and their children, it was found that although fathers who participated in child care and home chores extensively

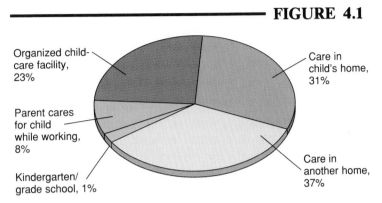

FIGURE 4.1

Organized child-care facility, 23%

Care in child's home, 31%

Parent cares for child while working, 8%

Kindergarten/grade school, 1%

Care in another home, 37%

Primary Child-Care Arrangements of Preschool Children (8 million children). Source: Bureau of the Census, *Statistical Brief,* May 1987.

felt more competent as parents, they also were likely to report having too little time for their careers and to complain that their family responsibilities were interfering with their work. These fathers were also more critical of their wife's performance as a mother.

At least in the short run, then, one of the costs of changing family-care arrangements is increased marital strain.

Because day care is now becoming a reality for a large segment of the nation's preschoolers, the issue that needs to be addressed is how to make it a positive socialization experience. Clearly this requires well-trained staff and a properly supervised environment. If we can create that type of envi-

ronment, then the fear of damaging experiences will be minimized.

Sources: Mark Rubinstein, *The Growing Years* (New York: Atheneum, 1988); Bureau of Census, *United States Department of Commerce News,* June 16, 1988; Bureau of the Census, "Who's Minding the Kids?" *Statistical Brief,* May 1987; Robert J. Trotter, "Project Day-Care," *Psychology Today,* December 1987, pp. 32–38; Grace Baruch and Rosalind Barnett, "Consequences of Fathers' Participation in Family Work: Parents' Role-strain and Well-being," *Journal of Personality and Social Psychology* 51, pp. 578–585; Rosalind C. Barnett and Grace Baruch, "Social Roles, Gender, and Psychological Distress," in *Gender and Stress* (New York: The Free Press, 1987); Louis W. Hoffman, "The Effects of Maternal Employment on the Child: A Review of the Research," *Developmental Psychology* 10 (1974), pp. 204–228; Myron Magnet, "What Mass-Produced Child Care Is Producing," *Fortune,* November 28, 1983, pp. 157–174.

without hesitating and to accept killing as a necessary part of their work. For many people such resocialization can be quite painful.

For some, career and identity are so intertwined that job loss can lead to personal crisis. This occurred for many young investment bankers and others in the financial community after the stock market crash of October 1987. Some 15,000 workers—many of whom were earning six-figure salaries—were laid off. For many, unemployment meant reevaluation and a new direction. For others, it meant spending months looking for a new job and realizing that it would be difficult to earn as much as they did before.

AGING AND SOCIETY

In many societies age itself brings respect and honor. Older people are turned to for advice, and their opinions are valued because they reflect a full measure of experience. Often, older people are not required to stop their productive work simply because they have reached a certain age. Rather, they work as long as they are able to, and their tasks may be modified to allow them to continue to work virtually until they die. In this way people maintain their social identities as they grow old—and their feelings of self-esteem as well.

This is not the case in the United States. Most employers retire their employees arbitrarily once they have reached age 70, and social security regulations restrict the amount of nontaxable income that retired persons may earn.

Perhaps the biggest concern of the elderly is where they will live and who will take care of them when they get sick. The American family is not ordinarily prepared to accommodate an aging parent who is sick or whose spouse has recently died. Apartment rents are high, and the cost of an extra room may be more than the family can afford. Most suburban houses are not designed to meet the needs of the elderly. In the typical house, for example, none of the bedrooms is at the same level as the kitchen or living room, and the family room frequently is down a flight of stairs. As a result, those older people who have trouble moving around or caring for themselves often find themselves with no choice but to live in homes for the aged and nursing homes. They have little access to their families and are deprived of the pleasure of seeing their grandchildren grow up. (The grandchildren also are deprived of the pleasure of getting to know their grandparents.)

This means that late in life, many people are forced to acquire another social identity. Sadly, it is not a valued one, but rather one of social insignificance (de Beauvoir, 1972). This can be very damaging to older people's self-esteem, and it may even hasten them to their graves. The last few years have seen some attempts at reform to address these issues. Age discrimination in hiring is illegal, and some companies have extended or eliminated arbitrary retirement ages. However, the problem will not be resolved until the elderly achieve once again a position of respect and value in American culture.

Even though aging is itself a biological process, becoming old is a social and cultural one: only society can create a "senior citizen." From infancy to old age, both biology and society play important parts in determining how people develop over the course of their lives.

In many societies, older people are turned to for advice, and their opinions are valued because they are based on life experiences.

SUMMARY

Socialization is the long and complicated process of social interaction through which a child learns the intellectual, physical, and social skills needed to function as a member of society. It is through socialization experiences that children learn the culture of the society into which they have been born. During this process each child acquires a personality—the patterns of behavior and ways of thinking and feeling that are distinctive for each individual.

The long-standing debate over nature versus nurture has taken a new turn with the emergence of sociobiology. The discipline of sociobiology tries to use biological principles to explain the behavior of all social beings, both animal and human.

Studies of extreme childhood deprivation have shown that humans need more than just food and shelter to develop into fully functioning social beings.

Every individual acquires a social identity by occupying culturally and socially defined positions. In addition, the individual acquires a personal identity called the self. The self develops when the individual becomes aware of his or her feelings, thoughts, and behaviors as separate and distinct from those of other people.

The work of Piaget has been important for sociologists because the processes of thought are central to the development of identity and therefore to the ability to function in society. Piaget found that children move through a series of predictable stages on their way to logical thought: from objects to symbols to concepts to logic. Kohlberg studied the moral development of individuals and proposed that it takes place in six stages. Most people never progress beyond stage 3 or 4, and those who do sometimes regress. In addition to the development of thought processes and moral orientation, the development of a gender identity is crucial to the sense of self.

Cooley, Mead, Freud, and Erikson developed theories of development that have been useful to sociologists in helping them view socialization. Cooley and Mead were symbolic interactionists who believed that the individual can develop only through social relationships. Freud saw the individual and society as enemies in a constant struggle, explaining this struggle through his concept of the id, ego, and superego. Erikson emphasized that development is a lifelong process and that even in adulthood a person continues to pass through new stages. Levinson showed that there are predictable age-related developmental periods in the adult life cycle, just as there are in the developmental cycles for children and adolescents.

The most important early socializing influences on the American child are the family, the school, peer groups, and the mass media. These factors have an impact on the concept of self as well as on the individual's interaction with others.

A person's primary socialization is completed when he or she reaches adulthood. It does not mark the end of learning and developing, though. Often, adults are required to go through a process of resocialization in which they are exposed to ideas or values that conflict with what they learned in childhood. Among the important issues involved in adult socialization, marriage, parenthood, vocation choice, and aging stand out as pivotal points in adult development.

Chapter 5

SOCIAL INTERACTION AND SOCIAL STRUCTURE

Wayne Farrell had only arrived in New York City two days ago, but he had already had his fill of strange experiences. It was almost as if panhandlers, con artists, and a host of individuals pushing unusual causes could sense that he was an easy mark. No sooner would he walk down the street and notice someone distributing leaflets than the person would pick him out of the crowd and engage him in a conversation. He tried to be polite and listen, but found himself repeatedly in the midst of uncomfortable situations. He was starting to wonder whether he was doing anything to contribute to these encounters, or whether this was just part of living in a large urban environment.

Without realizing it Wayne was engaging in a pattern of social interaction with these strangers. Coming from a small town in Wyoming, he was unaware of the fact that he was looking at passersby for a second or two longer than the typical person walking down the street. Just enough to signal to those looking for just such a cue that he was ripe for their approach.

Most Americans use four main distances in their business and social relations: intimate, personal, social, and public. Intimate distance varies from direct physical contact with another person to a distance of 6 to 18 inches and is used for private activities with a close acquaintance.

Personal distance varies from $2\frac{1}{2}$ to 4 feet, and is the most common spacing used by people in conversation.

The third zone — social distance — is employed during business transactions or interactions with a clerk or repairman. People as they work with each other tend to use this distance, which is usually between 4 and 7 feet.

The fourth zone — public distance — is used by teachers in classrooms or speakers at public gatherings and can be anywhere from 7 to 50 feet or more.

As Wayne walks down the busy urban street he is within the fourth zone. Eye contact in this environment has some specific rules attached to it. For urban whites once they are within definite recognition distance (usually 16 to 32 feet), there is mutual avoidance of eye contact — unless they want something specific: a proposition, a handout, or information of some kind. In small towns, however, people are much more likely to look at each other, even if they are strangers.

Panhandlers and others seeking to establish contact exploit the unwritten, unspoken conventions of eye contact. They take advantage of the fact that once explicit eye contact is established, it is rude to look away, because to do so means to brusquely dismiss the other person and his needs. Once having caught the eye of his mark, the individual locks on, not letting go until he moves through the public zone, the social zone, the personal zone, and, finally, the intimate zone, where people are most vulnerable.

Wayne's experiences were not just a coincidence. He was actually engaging in a social interaction with others in his environment that he was not aware of. He started to make a conscious attempt to avoid prolonged eye contact with strangers and the unwanted encounters began to subside.

As Wayne discovered, there is no way *not* to interact with others. Social interaction has no opposite. If we accept the fact that all social interaction has a message value, then it follows that no matter how one may try, one cannot *not* send a message. Activity or inactivity, words or silence all contain a message. They influence others and others respond to these messages. The mere absence of talking or taking notice of each other is no exception, because there is a message in that behavior also.

When sociologists study human behavior, they are primarily interested in how people's behavior affects other people and in turn is affected by others. They look at the overt actions that produce responses from others as well as the subtle cues that may result in unintended consequences. In this respect human social interaction is very flexible and quite unlike that of the more social animals.

WHAT SOCIAL INTERACTION IS

Max Weber (1922) was one of the first sociologists to stress the importance of social interaction in the study of sociology. He argued that the main goal of sociology was to explain what he called *social action*. He used this term to refer to anything people are conscious of doing because of other people. Weber claimed that in order to interpret social actions, we have to put ourselves in the position of the people we are studying and try to understand their thoughts and motives. The German word Weber used for this is *Verstehen,* which can be translated as "sympathetic understanding."

It is easier to understand social actions than it is to understand social interactions. A **social action** involves one individual taking others into account before acting. A **social interaction** involves two or more people taking each other into account. It is the interplay between the actions of one individual and those of one or more other people. In this respect, social interaction is a central concept to understanding the nature of social life.

In this chapter we shall explain how sociologists investigate social interaction phenomena. We shall start with the basic components of social interaction, such as the goals, norms, contexts, and motivations that produce it. Next we shall examine how social interaction affects those involved in it. Then we shall look at social interactions in social groups. The web of all patterned social interactions in a society makes up its social organization. Finally, we shall describe the means by which society maintains its patterns of interaction through the social institutions that make social life possible and that ultimately make up the social structure. In other words, we shall start with social behavior at the most basic level and show how human beings are tied together into ever more complicated and abstract levels of interaction as we move outward from the individual to the society as a whole.

WHAT INFLUENCES SOCIAL INTERACTION

Can the picking up of a glass of wine at a social event be thought of as a social interaction? A social interaction has four major components: (1) the ends or goals it is intended to achieve; (2) the motivation for its being undertaken; (3) the situation or context within which it takes place; and (4) the norms or rules that govern or regulate it (Parsons and Shils, 1951). Hence, picking up a glass of wine has a number of goals— refreshment, reduction of anxiety, interaction with others at a particular social event, conformity to the actions of these others, and the like. The context may be the opening of an art gallery. The norms governing such an event may dictate that not too much wine be consumed and that it be consumed in an appropriate manner over a certain period of time. The motivation for the behavior may be to appear relaxed and to achieve the previously described goals. Let us examine more closely each of the components of a social interaction.

Goals and Motivations

When a doctor taps your leg just below the kneecap, the lower portion of your leg is likely to jerk forward. This action is a normal reflex, a normal physical response. It is obviously not a social interaction, as it lacks both a goal and a motivation. Goals and

social action Anything people are conscious of doing because of other people.

social interaction The interplay between the actions of one individual and those of one or more other people.

Social interaction is a central concept to understanding the nature of social life.

goal The intended result of an action.

motivations are closely related and often confused. The **goal** is the state of affairs one wishes to achieve. For many actions the goal may seem obvious: One eats to satisfy one's hunger, sleeps to rid one's body of fatigue, and runs for exercise. Even in such obvious cases, however, there can be more than one goal for an action. For example, one can eat to be polite to one's host as well as to satisfy hunger; one can sleep (perhaps with the aid of a pill) to get through a boring (or anxiety-producing) experience, such as a transatlantic airplane flight, as well as to eliminate fatigue; and one may run as much for the social prestige of being a marathoner as for the exercise itself. Therefore, it is important to remember that social interactions often have less obvious goals that may or may not be related to the obvious goals.

motivation A person's wish or intention to achieve a goal.

A **motivation** is a person's wish or intention to achieve a goal. Hence, a behavior such as a reflex has no goal and consequently no motive. In our example, the doctor's behavior does have a motive — the desire to find out whether the patient's reflexes are normal.

Social interactions may have numerous goals and a variety of motivations as well. For example, consider a young man running to catch a bus. His goal is to catch the bus, but his motivations may be quite complex: he may want to be on time for work; he may have seen one of his co-workers through the window; or he may run for the bus every morning because he needs the exercise.

The goals of a social interaction may often be obvious, although human motivations are often very complicated — so much so that we often are unaware of all the motivations that prompt us.

Contexts

context The conditions under which an action takes place, including the physical setting or place, the social environment, and the other activities surrounding the action.

Where a social interaction takes place makes a difference in what it means. Edward T. Hall (1974) identified three elements that, taken together, define the **context** of a social interaction: (1) the physical setting or place, (2) the social environment,

Where a social interaction takes place makes a difference in what it means.

and (3) the activities surrounding the interaction — preceding it, happening simultaneously with it, and coming after it. For example, consider a kiss, an interaction that can have many different meanings.

What is its physical setting — does it happen in the back seat of a parked car, in the bleachers of a football stadium, in the grand ballroom of the Plaza Hotel, on a Hawaiian beach, at the airport, in the living room, in the bedroom, or in a motel room? What is the social context — two teenagers alone, a married couple at a party, a father with his young son at a football game, a family welcoming a relative at the airport, a married couple at home, or a couple at a secret rendezvous? And then, what else is happening — is the kiss preceded by a handshake, a hug, a sigh? Is it accompanied by fondling, a pat on the back, laughter? Does it lead to another kiss, to a wink and a smile, to more fondling, to a wave good-bye? The context of an interaction is a complicated whole that consists of the various interrelated elements, as we can see from the above example. Without knowledge of these elements it is impossible to know the meaning of even the simplest interaction. It follows, then, that the context of an interaction is also closely tied to cultural learning.

For example, Germans and Americans treat space very differently. Hall (1969) noted that in many ways the difference between German and American doors gives us a clue about the space perceptions of these two cultures. In Germany public and private buildings usually have double doors that create a soundproof environment. Germans feel that American doors, in contrast, are flimsy and light, inadequate for providing the privacy that Germans require. In American offices doors are usually kept open; in German offices they are kept closed. In Germany the closed door does not mean that the individual wants to be left alone or that something is being planned that should not be seen by others. Germans simply think that open doors are sloppy and disorderly. As Hall explained it:

> I was once called in to advise a firm that has operations all over the world. One of the first questions asked was, "How do you get the Germans to keep their doors open?" In this company the open doors were making the Germans feel exposed and gave the whole operation an unusually relaxed and unbusinesslike air.
> Closed doors, on the other hand, gave the Americans the feeling that there was a conspiratorial air about the place and that they were being left out. The point is that whether the door is open or shut, it is not going to mean the same thing in the two countries. (Hall, 1969)

The English, particularly those of the middle and upper classes, are at the opposite extreme from the Germans in their requirements for privacy. They are usually brought up in a nursery shared with brothers and sisters. The oldest has a room to himself or herself that is vacated when he or she leaves for boarding school. Children in England may never have a room of their own and seldom expect one or feel entitled to one. Even members of Parliament have no offices and often conduct their business in the open. The English are consequently puzzled by the American need for a secure place in which to work — an office. Americans working in England often are annoyed that they are not given an appropriately enclosed workplace (Hall, 1969). These markedly different views of the use of space are culturally determined, and it is important to be aware of these differences in order to interpret correctly the context of an interaction.

Norms

Human behavior is not random. It is patterned and, for the most part, quite predictable. What makes human beings act predictably in certain situations? For one thing, there is the presence of **norms** — specific rules of behavior that are agreed upon and shared and prescribe limits of acceptable behavior. Norms tell us the things we should both do and not do. In fact, our society's norms are so much a part of us that we often are not aware of them. In the United States our norms tells us that it is proper to drive on the right, to look at someone when speaking to him or her, and to stand up for the national anthem. Likewise, they tell us that when two people meet, one of the ways of greeting people is by shaking hands. Yet in most Asian countries, people have learned to bow to express this same idea.

We also have norms that guide us in how we present ourselves to others. We realize that how we dress, how we speak, and the objects we possess relay information about us. In this respect North Americans are a rather outgoing group of people. The Japanese have learned that it is a sign of weakness to disclose too much of oneself by overt actions. They are taught very early in life that touching, laughing, crying, or speaking loudly in public are not acceptable ways of interacting.

norms Specific rules of behavior that are agreed upon and shared, which prescribe limits of acceptable behavior.

Not only can the norms for behavior differ considerably from one culture to another, but they also can differ within our own society. Conflicting interpretations of an action have been shown to exist among men and women in our society when a stranger joins them at a public table they may be using, such as in a library. It has been found that men prefer to position themselves across from others they like, whereas women prefer to position themselves next to someone they like (Byrne, 1971). On the basis of this information Fisher and Byrne (1975) reasoned that females thus would respond more negatively than males would to a side-by-side invasion of their personal space, and males would respond more negatively to face-to-face invasions.

An experiment was set up using males and females who were sitting alone in a library. An "invader" was sent to sit either across or next to the subjects. After five minutes, the invader left and an experimenter arrived to ask the subjects some questions. Regardless of the invader's sex, the males felt negatively about the invader when he or she sat across from them but did not seem to have those feelings about a side-by-side invader. The females responded negatively when the invader sat next to them but not when he or she sat across from them.

It was hypothesized this difference results from gender-role socialization, in which males are taught to be relatively competitive and hence more sensitive to competitive cues. Sitting across from a male may tend to signal a competitive situation, and males tend to prefer a trusted or nonthreatening person in that location. Females were thought to be more sensitive to affiliative cues. Sitting adjacent to a female tends to be interpreted as an affiliative demand, and so females tend to respond negatively to this cue when the person occupying the seat is a stranger or someone with whom they do not wish to be intimate.

Sociologists thus need to understand the norms that guide people's behavior, because without this knowledge it is impossible to understand social interaction.

TYPES OF SOCIAL INTERACTION

When two individuals are in each other's presence, they inevitably affect each other. They may do so intentionally, as when one person asks the other for change for a quarter, or they may do so unintentionally, as when two people drift toward opposite sides of the elevator in which they are riding. Whether intentional or unintentional, they both represent types of social interaction.

NONVERBAL BEHAVIOR

In recent years many researchers have focused our attention on how we communicate with one another by using body movements. This study of body movements is known as *kinesics*. It attempts to examine how such things as slight head nods, yawns, postural shifts, and other nonverbal cues, whether spontaneous or deliberate, affect communication.

Many of our movements relate to an attitude that our culture has, consciously or unconsciously, taught us to express in a specific manner. In the United States, for example, we show a status relationship in a variety of ways. The ritualistic nonverbal movements and gestures in which we engage to see who goes through a door first or who sits or stands first are but a few ways our culture uses movement to communicate status. In the Middle East, status is underscored nonverbally by which individual you turn your back to. In Oriental cultures, the bow and backing out of a room are signs of status relationships. Humility might be shown in the United States by a slight downward bending of the head, but in many European countries this same attitude is manifested by dropping one's arms

THE SOCIAL LIFE OF THE STREET

W hen you have a conversation with a friend you have met in a public place, do you move out of the flow of pedestrian traffic? Before you answer yes, think again. William H. Whyte has written extensively about cities and how social interactions take place within them. He focused time-lapse cameras on several street corners and recorded the activity for two weeks.

The activity was not as expected. To his surprise, the people who stopped to talk did not move out of the main pedestrian flow. In fact, if they had been out of it, they moved into it. Observers in other countries have also noted this trend.

Why do people do this? One possible reason Whyte proposes is that in the center of the crowd you have maximum choice—to break off the conversation, to include other people, or to continue the interaction. The crowd can always be used as an excuse to not continue the discussion.

Source: William H. Whyte, *City* (New York: Doubleday, 1988), pp. 8–9).

---

and sighing. In Samoa humility is communicated by bending the body forward.

The use of hand and arm movements as a means of communicating also varies among cultures. We all are aware of the different gestures for derision. For some European cultures it is a closing fist with the thumb protruding between the index and middle fingers. The Russian expresses this same attitude by moving one index finger horizontally across the other.

In the United States, we can indicate that things are okay by making a circle with one's thumb and index finger while extending the others. In Japan this gesture signifies "money." Among Arabs if you accompany this gesture with a baring of the teeth, it displays extreme hostility.

In the United States you say good-bye or farewell by waving the hand and arm up and down. If you wave in this manner in South America, you may discover that the

The use of hand and arm movements, eye contact, and norms of nonverbal behavior are markedly different for these Arab Bedouins than they are for Americans, such as tennis pro John McEnroe.

other person is not leaving, but moving toward you. That is because in many countries what we use as a sign of leaving is a gesture that means "come."

Eye contact is another area in which some interesting findings have appeared. In the United States the following has been noted: (1) We tend to look at the person we are speaking to more when we are listening than when we are talking. If we are at a loss for a word we frequently look into space, as if to find the words imprinted somewhere out there. (2) The more rewarding we find the speaker's message to be, the more intensely we will look at that person. (3) How much eye contact we maintain with other people is determined in part by how high we perceive their status to be. When we address someone we regard as having high status, we maintain a modest-to-high degree of eye contact. On the other hand, when we address a person of low status, we make very little effort to maintain eye contact. (4) Eye contact must be regularly broken, because we feel uncomfortable if someone gazes at us for longer than 10 seconds at a time.

These notions of eye contact found in the United States differ from those of other societies. In Japan and China, for example, it is considered rude to look into another person's eyes during conversation. Arabs, on the other hand, use personal space very differently and stand very close to the person they are talking to and stare directly into the person's eyes. Arabs believe the eyes are a key to a person's being, and looking deeply into another's eyes allows one to see that person's soul.

The proscribed relationships between males and females in a culture also influence eye behavior. Asian cultures, for example, consider it taboo for women to look straight into the eyes of men. Therefore, most Asian men, out of respect for this cultural characteristic, do not stare directly at women. French men accept staring as a cultural norm and often stare at women in public (Samovar, Porter, and Jain, 1981).

Nonverbal behavior can even be used to signal government political response. When, for example, Libyan leader Col. Muammar el Quaddafi attended a summit meeting of seventeen Arab kings, emirs, and presidents in 1988, he showed his displeasure with the group in nonverbal ways. When Jordan's King Hussein began to speak, Quaddafi pulled a white hood down over his face as a sign of disgust for the king. When King Hassan of Morocco entered the conference hall, Quaddafi turned his back to the king, a deliberate gesture in response to the king's having greeted Shimon Peres, the Israeli prime minister, 2 years earlier. Quaddafi also wore a single white glove on his right hand to avoid touching the hands of other Arab leaders. He also blew cigar smoke in the direction of King Fahd of Saudi Arabia as yet another sign of his displeasure (*New York Times,* June 10, 1988).

UNFOCUSED AND FOCUSED INTERACTION

Some interactions occur simply because two or more people happen to be in each other's presence. For example, two people in a doctor's waiting room cannot help noticing each other. Usually they will look at each other's clothing, posture, behavior, and other characteristics while at the same time adjusting their own behavior because they assume the other person is also doing the same thing. Sociologist Erving Goffman (1961b) called such actions, which have little by way of goals other than to catalog other people and make a decent impression on them, **unfocused interaction.** Although such interaction is an ongoing, almost unconscious part of daily life, it is important because through it we monitor how others are reacting to what we are doing. With this constant stream of feedback we can adjust our behavior to try to achieve our goals. Unfocused interactions were included in our discussion of ethnomethodology and dramaturgy in Chapter 1.

When two or more individuals agree (explicitly or implicitly) to sustain an interaction with one or more particular goals in

unfocused interaction An interaction that occurs simply because two or more people happen to be in each other's presence.

mind, they are engaged in a **focused interaction** (Goffman, 1961b). People playing cards, watching home movies, or simply enjoying a conversation are involved in focused interaction. Focused interactions are the basic building blocks of all social organization.

TYPES OF FOCUSED INTERACTION

Social interactions are not random but occur in predictable patterns. There are four basic types of focused social interaction: exchange, cooperation, conflict, and competition.

Exchange

When people do something for each other with the express purpose of receiving a reward or return, they are involved in an **exchange**. Most employer–employee relationships are exchange relationships. The employee does the job and is rewarded with a salary. The reward in an exchange interaction, however, need not always be material; it may be based on emotions such as gratitude. For example, if you visit a sick friend, help someone with a heavy package at the supermarket, or assist a blind person across a busy intersection, you probably will expect that person to feel grateful to you.

Sociologist Peter Blau pointed out that exchange is the most basic form of social interaction.

> Social exchange can be observed everywhere once we are sensitized . . . to it, not only in market relations but also in friendship and even in love. . . . Neighbors exchange favors; children, toys; colleagues, assistance; acquaintances, courtesies; politicians, concessions; discussants, ideas; housewives, recipes (Blau, 1964).

Cooperation

A form of social interaction in which people act together to promote common interests or achieve shared goals is **cooperation.** The members of a basketball team pass to one another, block off opponents for one another, rebound, and assist one another to achieve a common goal—winning the game. Likewise, family members cooperate to promote their interests as a family—husband and wife both may hold jobs as well as share in household duties, and children may help out by mowing the lawn and washing the dishes. College students often cooperate by studying together for tests. Tenants in Cochran Gardens, a public housing development in St. Louis, cooperated to improve their living conditions. A decade ago Cochran Gardens was filthy, dilapidated, and overrun by drug dealers. Today, thanks to tenant action, it is a showcase of cooperative action. The change was masterminded by tenant Bertha Gilkey, who founded the tenants' organization. "People threw garbage out of the windows, and the hallways were lined with garbage bags stuffed with month-old food and mice jumping out of the trash," said Gilkey. "The abnormal became normal." Gilkey

focused interaction A purposeful interaction between individuals who have particular goals in mind.

cooperation A form of social interaction in which people act together to promote common interests or achieve shared goals.

exchange An interaction involving one person doing something for another with the express purpose of receiving a reward or return.

Spontaneous cooperation, which arises from the needs of a particular situation, is the oldest and most natural form of cooperation. An Amish barn raising is an example of traditional cooperation that carries the weight of custom and is passed on from one generation to the next.

A REUNION OF CAMPUS RADICALS

An unusual college reunion took place at Harvard University during the second weekend in April 1989. Students who had been part of the seizure and occupation of Harvard's University Hall assembled on campus to mark the twentieth anniversary of that event. On that date in 1969, student radicals took over the dean's office and refused to leave until the university met their demands, which included abolishing R.O.T.C. Twenty-four hours later, as the media watched, police cleared out the demonstrators, beating many and arresting 184. In response to the arrests, Harvard students went on strike, becoming one of the sixties' leading symbols of student protest.

While student uprisings had taken place on other campuses, Harvard's ivied halls had always seemed above the fray. But when students themselves ejected Dean Archie Epps from his office, it became clear that even Harvard was not immune to the turmoil of the times. The image of Harvard University under siege was so compelling that the story made news across the country. The *New York Times* ran photos and stories on the front page for several days.

Responding to the reunion, some current students found the protesters from the sixties anachronistic.

"My initial reaction was that all the kooks were out again, banging their heads, screaming and yelling, trying to recapture something from the sixties," said Steven C. Papkin, a senior from Washington who called himself a conservative. Others, such as Robert F. Sanfillipo noted, "As long as it doesn't interfere with my life, it's okay."

Two decades have passed and the era of the sixties, marked by protests and demonstrations, has taken on an air of nostalgia. People often wonder what happened to the student radicals of that period who were so passionate and committed to their causes. How have the lives of these individuals evolved as a result of their involvement in the student movement, and what effect has that action subsequently had on their careers, marriages, and children?

There is an image out there that they have become either Porsche drivers or paranoid schizophrenics. People think that they have shed their politics to fill their wallets or have become burned-out misfits who could not adjust to a changing society.

This would be a simplistic misreading of the situation.

---

traditional cooperation
Cooperation that is tied to custom and is passed on from one generation to the next.

spontaneous cooperation
Cooperation that arises from the needs of a particular situation.

decided she could no longer live like this and took action. "We wanted to build accountability and standards and self-esteem." Today Cochran Gardens is clean and well kept and rules are strictly enforced. The building has become such a success because the impetus for change came from within and was built on a spirit of cooperation (*New York Times,* June 11, 1988).

Sociologists Robert A. Nisbet and Robert Perrin (1977) describe four types of cooperation: spontaneous, traditional, directed, and contractual. The oldest, most natural, and most common form of cooperation is **spontaneous cooperation,** which arises from the needs of a particular situation. For example, when the calm of a rainy May evening in Chepachet, Rhode Island, was broken by the sound and sight of a girl being dragged into the woods by a masked abductor, five of the girl's neighbors pursued and cornered the kidnapper until the police arrived. Said one of the rescuers, who may have saved the young girl's life, "It all went click, click, with everybody doing their part. Around here, people notice if something's not right" (*Newsweek,* July 4, 1988).

Traditional cooperation, which held together earlier (preindustrial) societies, carries the weight of custom and is passed on from one generation to the next. Examples of this form of cooperation are the barn raisings and quilting bees of American farming communities.

Values are not trendy fashions that are easily traded in. There is often an intricate merging of values and ethics.

In one sense, most of the former student radicals have become more conservative in that they have relatively conventional jobs as teachers, computer programmers, college professors, and lawyers. They have families, mortgages, and houses in the suburbs.

In another sense, however, they have not changed. In their odyssey from student protest to middle age, there is little evidence that any have done an about-face and become investment bankers or real estate developers. Many seem to have retained the ideals of the sixties and continue to express them in their daily work. They continue to wrestle with ethical and political questions.

Carl Offner, a graduate student in mathematics at the time of the takeover, was one of the people featured in the *New York Times.* He was kicked out of Harvard as a result of attacking Dean Epps. Harvard proceeded to prosecute him for assault and battery, although his case was eventually dismissed on appeal 3 years later. He married a woman who was in S.D.S. at M.I.T. during the takeover and was also involved in the strike. With his graduate studies having been cut short, Carl turned to the Peace Corps and teaching junior high school. He became active in the teachers union, eventually becoming its president. After a number of years as a teacher, he tried to resume his studies. Once the required two-thirds of the entire Harvard faculty voted to allow his readmission, he completed his degree. Today he is a software engineer who writes compilers. He is still active in a number of causes, including the sanctuary movement, which aids Central American refugees who have entered the United States illegally.

John St. George, a teacher for special-needs children is running for city council in Cambridge, Massachusetts. He is a long-time housing advocate and hopes to lend continuing support to the city's strict rent-control laws, which are threatened with change.

Ellen Messing is a lawyer who has been actively involved in efforts to shut down the Seabrook, New Hampshire, Nuclear Power Plant. Aldyn McKean has become an AIDS activist.

The former radicals of the sixties do not long for a return to the political activism and sense of community of the past. Older and wiser, they have moved on but continue to be what they once were — society's idealists.

Modern societies rely less on traditional cooperation than on directed and contractual cooperation. **Directed cooperation** is a joint activity that is under the control of people in authority. It is planned in advance and requires leadership. When President John F. Kennedy announced that the United States would put a person on the moon before 1970, he initiated large-scale directed cooperation that achieved its goal. After the Challenger space shuttle disaster killed seven astronauts in January 1986, more than $2 billion was spent over a 2-year period to rebuild the system and make it safer. There were approximately 600 system improvements, which involved workers in dozens of private aerospace corporations, as well as in governments agencies.

Contractual cooperation is also planned, but here people agree to cooperate in certain specified ways, with each person's obligations clearly spelled out. The author of this text and the publisher signed a formal contract and met their specific obligations to produce the book you are now reading.

Conflict

In a cooperative interaction, people join forces to achieve a common goal. By contrast, people in **conflict** struggle with one

directed cooperation
Cooperation characterized by a joint effort that is under the control of people in authority.

contractual cooperation
Cooperation in which each person's specific obligations are clearly spelled out.

conflict The opposite of cooperation. People in conflict struggle against one another for some commonly prized object or value.

another for some commonly prized object or value (Nisbet and Perrin, 1977). In a conflict relationship, a person can gain only at someone else's expense. Conflicts arise when people or groups have incompatible values or when the rewards or resources available to a society or its members are limited. Thus, conflict always involves an attempt to gain or use power.

The fact that conflict often leads to unhappiness and violence causes many people to view it negatively. However, conflict appears to be inevitable in human society. A stable society is not a society without conflicts but one that has developed methods for resolving its conflicts by justly or brutally suppressing them temporarily. For example, Lewis Coser (1956, 1967) pointed out that conflict can be a positive force in society. The American civil rights movement in the 1950s and 1960s may have seemed threatening and disruptive to many people at the time, but it helped bring about important social changes that may have led to a greater social stability.

Coercion is a special kind of conflict that can occur when one of the parties in a conflict is much stronger than the other. The stronger party can impose its will on the weaker, as in the case of a parent using the threat of punishment to impose a curfew on

an adolescent child. Coercion rests on force or the threat of force, but usually it operates more subtly.

Competition

The fourth type of social interaction, **competition,** is a form of conflict in which individuals or groups confine their conflict within agreed-upon rules. Competition is a common form of interaction in the modern world — not only on the sports field but in the marketplace, the education system, and the political system as well. During the 1988 political primaries in which presidential candidates were chosen by the Republican and Democratic parties, George Bush and Michael Dukakis outlasted a field of competitors through months of grueling campaigning to become their party's standard-bearer. During the presidential campaign itself, in which the nation eventually chose George Bush to be president, the stakes were even higher and the competition even more intense.

One type of relationship may span the entire range of focused interactions: an excellent example is marriage. Husbands and wives cooperate in household chores and responsibilities (an interaction discussed earlier). They also engage in exchange interactions. Married people often discuss their problems with each other—the partner whose role is listener at one time will expect the other spouse to provide a sympathetic ear at another time. Married people also experience conflicts in their relationship. A couple may have a limited amount of money set aside, and each may want to use it for a different purpose. Unless they can agree on a third, mutually desirable use for the money, one spouse will gain at the other's expense, and the marriage may suffer. The husband and wife whose marriage is irreversibly damaged may find themselves in direct competition. If they wish to separate or divorce, their conflict will be regulated according to legal and judicial rules.

competition A form of conflict in which individuals or groups confine their conflict within agreed-upon rules.

coercion A form of conflict where one of the parties in a conflict is much stronger than the other and imposes its will because of that strength.

Competition is a common type of social interaction. It is a form of conflict in which the individuals confine their conflict to agreed-upon rules.

Through the course of a lifetime people are involved in many types of social interaction because most of our time is spent in some kind of group situation. How we behave in these situations is generally determined by two factors—the statuses we occupy and the roles we play—which together constitute the main components of what sociologists call social organization.

COMPONENTS OF SOCIAL INTERACTION

People do not interact with each other as anonymous beings. They come together in the context of specific environments, and with specific purposes. Their interactions involve behavior associated with defined statuses and particular roles. These statuses and roles help to pattern our social interactions and provide predictability.

STATUSES

Statuses are socially defined positions that people occupy in a group or society and in terms of which they interact with one another. Common statuses may pertain to religion, education, ethnicity, and occupation—for example, Protestant, college graduate, black American, and teacher. Statuses exist independent of the specific people who occupy them (Linton, 1936). For example, our society recognizes the status of race car driver. Many people occupy that status, including Mario Andretti, Paul Newman, and Richard Petty. New racers are trained; old racers retire (or are killed). But the status, as the culture defines it, remains essentially unchanged. The same is true for all other statuses: occupational statuses, such as doctor, computer analyst, bank teller, police officer, butcher, insurance adjuster, thief, and prostitute; and nonoccupational statuses, such as son

and daughter, jogger, friend, Little League coach, neighbor, gang leader, and mental patient.

It is important to keep in mind that from a sociological point of view, status does not refer—as it does in common usage—to the idea of prestige, even though different statuses often do contain differing degrees of prestige. In America, for example, research has shown that the status of physician has more prestige than that of lawyer, which in turn has more prestige than that of sociologist (Base and Rossi, 1983).

People generally occupy more than one status at a time. Consider yourself, for example: you are someone's daughter or son, a full-time or part-time college student, perhaps also a worker, a licensed car driver, perhaps a member of a church or synagogue, and so forth. Sometimes one of the multiple statuses a person occupies seems to dominate the others in patterning that person's life. Such a status is called a **master status.** For example, George Bush has occupied a number of diverse statuses: husband, father, vice-president, and presidential candidate. After January 20, 1989, however, his master status was that of president of the United States, because it governed his actions more than any other status he occupied at the time.

A person's master status will change many times in the course of his or her life cycle. Right now your master status probably is that of college student. Five years from now it may be graduate student, artist, lawyer, spouse, or parent. Figure 5.1 illustrates the different statuses occupied by a 35-year-old woman who is an executive at a major television network. Although she occupies many statuses at once, her master status is that of vice-president for programming.

In some situations, a person's master status may have a negative influence on that person's life. For example, people who have followed a deviant life-style may find that their master status is labeled according to this deviant behavior. Those who have been identified as former convicts are likely to be

master status One of the multiple statuses a person occupies that dominates the others in patterning that person's life.

statuses Socially defined positions that people occupy.

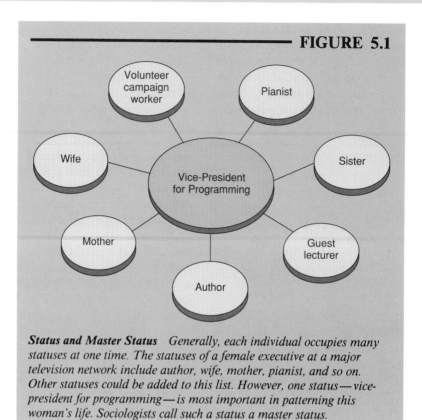

FIGURE 5.1

Status and Master Status *Generally, each individual occupies many statuses at one time. The statuses of a female executive at a major television network include author, wife, mother, pianist, and so on. Other statuses could be added to this list. However, one status—vice-president for programming—is most important in patterning this woman's life. Sociologists call such a status a master status.*

so classified no matter what other statuses they occupy: they will be thought of as former convict–painters, former convict–machinists, former convict–writers, and so on. Their master status has a negative effect on their ability to fulfill the roles of the statuses they would like to occupy. Former convicts who are good machinists or house painters may find employers unwilling to hire them because of their police records. Because the label "criminal" can stay with individuals throughout their lives, the criminal justice system is reluctant to label juvenile offenders or to open their records to the courts. Juvenile court files are usually kept secret and often permanently sealed when the person reaches age 18.

Some statuses are conferred on us by virtue of birth or other socially significant factors not controlled by our own actions or decisions. These are called **ascribed statuses,** and people occupy them regardless of

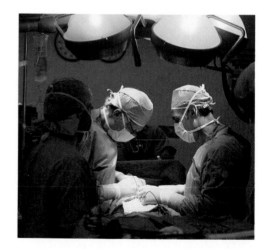

These surgeons have the ascribed status of "male." Their achieved status is "doctor."

their intentions. Certain family positions—daughter, son—are typical ascribed statuses, as are one's sex and ethnic or racial identity. Other statuses are occupied as a

ascribed statuses Statuses that are conferred on an individual at birth or on other occasions by circumstances beyond the individual's control.

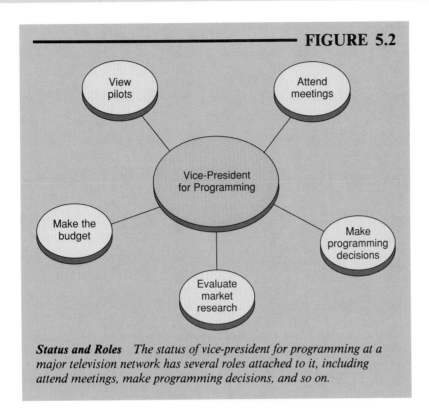

FIGURE 5.2

Status and Roles *The status of vice-president for programming at a major television network has several roles attached to it, including attend meetings, make programming decisions, and so on.*

result of the individual's actions. These are called **achieved statuses**—student, professor, garage mechanic, race car driver, hobo, artist, prisoner, bus driver, husband, wife, mother, or father.

ROLES

Statuses alone are static—nothing more than social categories into which people are put. Roles bring statuses to life, making them dynamic. As Linton (1936) observed, you occupy a status but you play a role. **Roles** are the culturally defined rules for proper behavior that are associated with every status. Roles may be thought of as collections of rights and obligations. To return to our example of race car drivers, every driver has the *right* to expect other drivers not to try to pass when the race has been interrupted by a yellow flag because of danger. Turned around, each driver has the *obligation* not to pass other drivers under

yellow-flag conditions. A driver also has a *right* to expect race committee members to enforce the rules and spectators to stay off the raceway. On the other hand, a driver has an *obligation* to the owner of the car to try hard to win.

In the case of our television executive, she has the *right* to expect to be paid on time, to be provided with good-quality scripts and staff support, and to make decisions about the use of her budget. On the other hand, she has the *obligation* to act in the best interests of the network, to meet schedules, to stay within her budget, and to treat her employees fairly. What is important is that all these rights and obligations are part of the roles associated with the status of vice-president for programming. They exist without regard to the particular individuals whose behavior they guide (see Figure 5.2).

A status may include several roles, and each role will be appropriate to a specific

achieved statuses Statuses that are obtained as a result of the individual's efforts.

roles Culturally defined rules for proper behavior associated with every status.

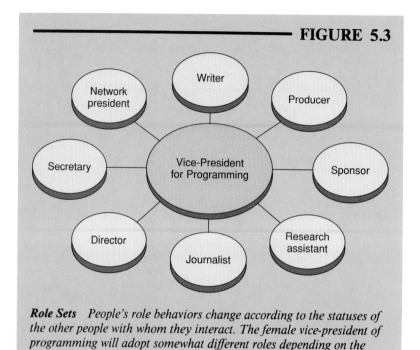

FIGURE 5.3

Role Sets *People's role behaviors change according to the statuses of the other people with whom they interact. The female vice-president of programming will adopt somewhat different roles depending on the statuses of the various people with whom she interacts at the station: a writer, a journalist, her secretary, and so on.*

social context. For example, the president of the United States must be a host at diplomatic dinners, a leader at cabinet sessions, and a policy setter for his staff. Sociologists use the concept of role sets to explain this phenomenon.

Role Sets

All the roles attached to a single status are known collectively as a **role set.** However, not every role in a particular role set is enacted all the time. An individual's role behaviors depend on the statuses of the other people with whom he or she is interacting. For example, as a college student you behave one way toward other students and another way toward professors. Similarly, professors behave one way toward other professors, another way toward students, and yet a third way toward deans. So the role behavior we expect in any given situa-

role set The roles attached to a single status.

tion depends on the pairs of statuses occupied by the interacting individuals. This means that role behavior really is defined by the rights and obligations that are assigned to statuses when they are paired with one another (see Figure 5.3).

It would be difficult to describe the wide-ranging, unorganized assortment of role behaviors associated with the status of television vice-president for programming. Sociologists find it more useful to describe the specific behavior expected of a network television vice-president for programming interacting with different people. Such a role set would include:

vice-president for programming/network president
vice-president for programming/other vice-presidents
vice-president for programming/ scriptwriter
vice-president for programming/secretary

vice-president for programming/television
   star
vice-president for programming/journalist
vice-president for programming/producer
vice-president for programming/sponsor

The vice-president's role behavior in each case would be different, meshing with the role behavior of the individual(s) occupying the other status in each pairing (Merton, 1968).

Role Strain

Even though most people try to enact their roles as they are expected to, they sometimes find it difficult. When a single role has conflicting demands attached to it, individuals who play that role experience **role strain** (Goode, 1960). For example, the captain of a freighter is expected to be sure the ship sails only when it is in safe condition, but the captain also is expected to meet the company's delivery schedule, because a day's delay could cost the company thousands of dollars. These two expectations may exert competing pulls on the captain, especially when some defect is reported, such as a malfunction in the ship's radar system. The stress of these competing pulls is not due to the captain's personality but rather is built into the nature of the role expectations attached to the captain's status. Therefore, sociologists describe the captain's experience of stress as role strain.

Role Conflict

An individual who is occupying more than one status at a time and who is unable to enact the roles of one status without violating those of another status is encountering **role conflict.**

Military wives who want to pursue their own careers are often in a role conflict situation. Traditionally, military wives volunteer for a variety of activities on the base and take part in an endless number of social events to help further their husbands' careers. When a wife has a career of her own,

she no longer has the time for volunteer work—the makings of role conflict. The role conflict was so great for the wife of Col. Michael Langston that the colonel resigned from the Air Force and left 20 years of service and a promising career behind. The colonel felt he had no choice but to resign when his wife, a top media consultant, refused to relocate overseas along with him (*U.S. News & World Report,* August 18, 1988).

Or consider the problems faced by the woman who occupies at the same time the statuses of business executive, wife, and mother. In the status of business executive, the woman's role is to work long hours, entertain clients, and travel. As wife her role is to be a stimulating companion to her husband and help keep the household running smoothly. As mother she is expected to spend time with the children, go places with them, do things with them, and take pleasure in nurturing and teaching them. The people with whom she interacts in each status expect her to consider their needs first—clearly an impossible task.

As society becomes more complex, individuals occupy increasingly more statuses. This increases the chances for role conflict, which is one of the major sources of stress in modern society.

Role Playing

The roles we play can have a profound influence on both our attitudes and our behavior. Playing a new social role often feels awkward at first, and we may feel we are just acting—pretending to be something that we are not. However, many sociologists feel that the roles a person plays are the person's only true self. Peter Berger's (1963) explanation of role playing goes further—the roles we play can transform not only our actions but ourselves as well:

> One feels more ardent by kissing, more humble by kneeling, and more angry by shaking one's fist. That is, the kiss not only expresses ardor but manufactures it. Roles carry with them both certain

role strain The stress that results from conflicting demands within a single role.

role conflict The situation in which an individual who is occupying more than one status at the same time is unable to enact the roles of one status without violating those of another.

THE ART OF NEGOTIATION

Roger Fisher's skill as a negotiator has brought him in contact with Menachim Begin, Yassir Arafat, various terrorists, and the Ayatollah Khomeni. In the 40 years he has spent hammering out agreements between adversaries, he has taken on disputes between auto workers and companies, teachers and school boards, Arabs and Israelis, the contras, the Iranians, and the IRA. Fisher thinks the same skills he uses in negotiating cease-fires can be used

equally well in resolving common conflicts. In the following interview we will see how most social interactions involve a negotiation of different points of view.

"People tell me they do not have relationships to deal with differences. However, a small but crucial aspect of every successful relationship is an ability to deal well with differences," notes Fisher. "Whatever reason you have for the relationship— for profit, for comfort, for pleasure, for companionship, for sex —it is extremely important to your ability to get what you want that you can handle differences."

To explain how techniques used in business or diplomatic negotiations can also be used in everyday relationships, Fisher has distilled his strategy into a few main points:

Balance emotion with reason. "You do not want to make decisions when you are angry, or when you are euphoric. If my wife and I are feeling very passionate and the checking account comes up, I am liable to say, 'Oh, don't bother to keep the stubs!' That is not the time to make decisions."

Try to understand. "When dealing with your mother-in-law, you want to be able to understand her point of view. Does she think she has lost a daughter? Does she think her daughter puts me above her? What are her perceptions, because maybe we can deal with them."

Inquire, consult, and listen. "The best advice is to ask for advice. The right decision will not necessarily produce a good relationship if the other parties have not been consulted."

Be reliable. "Reliability enhances a relationship enormously. The easiest way to be reliable is to make very few promises—and keep the ones you do make."

Accept the other person as someone worth dealing with. "It is easier to have a relationship with people with whom you share values, but the reason you want a working relationship is to deal with differences. Don't define a good road as one that is easy to build."

Source: Linda Tischler, "Dealing with Terrorists—or Mom-in-Law," *The Boston Herald,* July 5, 1988, pp. 27, 30.

actions and emotions and attitudes that belong to these actions. The professor putting on an act that pretends to wisdom comes to feel wise.

In an attempt to gauge the degree to which social roles affect attitudes and behavior, Stanford social psychologist Philip G. Zimbardo (1972) created his own prison. An ad was placed in a local newspaper asking for volunteers for an experiment. Two dozen young men described by Zimbardo as "mature, emotionally stable, normal intelligent college students" were selected. The students were paid fifteen dollars a day for their participation. Half were arbitrarily given the role of prisoner by a flip of a coin, and the other half were assigned the role of guard in the simulated prison.

Zimbardo allowed his guards to make up their own formal rules for maintaining law, order, and respect. The prisoners were treated like any other prisoners. Picked up at their homes by a city police officer, they were "searched, handcuffed, fingerprinted, and booked. . . ." They were then taken blindfolded to Zimbardo's jail, where they were stripped, deloused, given a number and a uniform, and placed in a cell with two other "prisoners."

The experiment was expected to last for 2 weeks, but at the end of only 6 days Zimbardo had to stop it. It was no longer apparent to most of the subjects—or even to Zimbardo himself—where reality ended and the "artificial" roles began. Zimbardo explained:

The majority had indeed become prisoners or guards, no longer able to clearly differentiate between role playing and self. There were dramatic changes in virtually every aspect of their behavior, thinking and feeling. In less than a week the experience of imprisonment undid (temporarily) a lifetime of learning; human values were suspended, self-concepts were challenged and the ugliest, most base pathological side of human nature surfaced. We were horrified because we saw some boys (guards) treat others as if they were despicable animals, taking pleasure in cruelty, while other boys (prisoners) became servile, dehumanized robots who thought only of escape, of their own individual survival and of their mounting hatred for the guards.

We had to release three prisoners in the first four days because they had such acute situational traumatic reactions as hysterical crying, confusion in thinking and severe depression. Others begged to be paroled. By then . . . they had been so programmed to think of themselves as

prisoners that when their request for parole was denied, they returned docilely to their cells. . . .

About a third of the guards became tyrannical in their arbitrary use of power, in enjoying their control over other people. They were corrupted by the power of their roles and became quite inventive in their techniques of breaking the spirit of the prisoners and making them feel they were worthless (Zimbardo, 1972).

The technique of role playing is often used to help people understand another person's attitude or behavior—to see the world from the other person's perspective. Often conflict can be resolved when we are made to stand in our adversary's shoes.

Role Enactment

No two people are exactly alike in how they enact their roles. Some are skillful, others awkward; some enthusiastic, others reluctant; some happy, others ashamed; some involved, others detached. Therefore, although two individuals may occupy the same status, their behavior is not likely to be identical. People interpret the roles they enact through their own unique personalities, much as two actors bring to the stage very different interpretations of the same dramatic role. For example, Chris Evert and John McEnroe both are professional tennis players, but they enact their roles very differently. Evert shows little emotion, whether she is winning or losing. McEnroe, on the other hand, has been fined for his displays of anger and disgust and his arguments with umpires' decisions.

Interestingly, as McEnroe has grown older and taken on the responsibilities of a wife and family, he has calmed down considerably and even ridiculed others for the antics that used to be his trademark.

Statuses and roles, together with values and norms, are the basic threads that make up the fabric of society. As these elements vary, so, too, does the social structure that evolves.

—— INSTITUTIONS AND SOCIAL ORGANIZATION

group A collection of specific, identifiable people.

institution A system for organizing standardized patterns of social behavior.

Anyone who has traveled to foreign countries knows that different societies have different ways of doing things. The basic things that get done actually are quite similar—food is produced and distributed; people get married and have children; and children are raised to take on the responsibilities of adulthood. The vehicle for accomplishing the basic needs of any society is the social institution.

SOCIAL INSTITUTIONS

Sociologists usually speak of five areas of society in which basic needs have to be fulfilled: the family sector, the education sector, the economic sector, the religious sector, and the political sector. For each of these areas there are social groups and associations that carry out the goals and meet the needs of society. The behavior of people in these groups and associations is organized or patterned by the relevant **social institutions**—that is, the ordered social relationships that grow out of the values, norms, statuses, and roles that organize those activities that fulfill society's fundamental needs. Thus, economic institutions organize the ways in which society produces and distributes the goods and services it needs; educational institutions determine what should be learned and how it should be taught; and so forth.

social institutions The ordered social relationships that grow out of the values, norms, statuses, and roles that organize those activities that fulfill society's fundamental needs.

Of all social institutions, the family is perhaps the most basic. A stable family unit is the main ingredient necessary for the smooth functioning of society. For instance, sexual behavior must be regulated and children must be cared for and raised to fit into society. Hence, the institution of the family provides a system of continuity from one generation to the next.

Although nothing in society is completely static, social institutions normally are among the most slowly changing aspects of any society. Thus, particular businesses may come and go, but basic economic institutions persist. Political power may change hands, but usually according to the rules and within the context of a society's political institution. It is important, therefore, to keep clear the distinction between the concept of group and the concept of institution. A **group** is a collection of specific, identifiable people. An **institution** is a system for organizing standardized patterns of social behavior. In other words, a group consists of people, and an institution is the standardized ways in which people do certain things. For example, when sociologists discuss *a* family (say, the Smith family), they are referring to a particular group of people. When they discuss *the* family, they are referring to the family as an institution—a cluster of statuses and roles and values and norms that organize the standardized patterns of behavior that we expect to find within family groups. Thus, the family as an American institution typically embodies several master statuses: husband, wife, and, possibly, father, mother, and child. It also includes the statuses son, daughter, brother, and sister. These statuses are organized into well-defined, patterned relationships: Parents have authority over their children; spouses have a sexual relationship with each other (but not with the children); and so on. However, specific family groups may not conform entirely to the ideals of the institution. There are single-parent families, families in which the children appear to be running things, and families in which there is an incestuous parent–child relationship. Although a society's institutions provide what can be thought of as a "master plan" for human interactions in groups, *actual* behavior and *actual* group organization often deviate in varying degrees from this plan.

We should make it clear that in common speech there are several different uses of the term *institution* that could be confused with the sociological one we have pre-

Relatively rapid social change is making less predictable the types of behavior that should go along with gender roles.

sented. Sometimes the term is used to refer to an association like the Smithsonian Institution in our nation's capital. Sometimes —more popularly—it is applied to hospitals for mental patients or homes for the aged. In adjective form it is used to denote a style of architecture: cold, formal, "functional," large, impersonal, and without a trace of esthetic virtue. In everyday speech each of these uses is valid, although sociologists confine their use of the term to the specific definition we have offered.

SOCIAL ORGANIZATION

If we step back from a mosaic, the many multicolored stones are seen to compose a single, coordinated pattern or picture. Similarly, if we step back and look at society, the many actions of all its members fall into a pattern or series of interrelated patterns. These consist of social interactions and relationships expressing individual decisions and choices. These choices, however, are not random; rather, they are an outgrowth

of a society's social organization. **Social organization** consists of the relatively stable pattern of social relationships among individuals and groups in society. These relationships are based on systems of social roles, norms, and shared meanings that provide regularity and predictability in social interaction. Social organization differs from one society to the next. Thus, Islam allows a man to marry up to four wives at any given time, whereas in our society with its Judeo-Christian religious tradition, such plural marriage is not an acceptable family form.

Just as statuses and roles exist within ordered relationships to one another, social institutions also exist in patterned relationships with one another in the context of society. All societies have their own patterning for these relationships. For example, a society's economic and political institutions often are closely interrelated. So, too, are the family and religious institutions. Thus, a description of American social organization would indicate the presence of

social organization The relatively stable pattern of social relationships among individuals and groups in society.

monogamy along with Judeo-Christian values and norms and the institutionalization of economic competition and of democratic political organizations.

A society's social organization tends to be the most stable aspect of society. The American social organization, however, may not be as static as that of many other societies. Our society is undergoing relatively rapid social change because of its complexity and because of the great variety in the types of people that are part of it. This complexity makes life less predictable because new values and norms being introduced from numerous quarters result in changes in our social organization. For example, ideas about the behavior that should go along with female sex roles have changed considerably over the last decade or two. Not long ago it was assumed that most married women would not work but would stay home and attend to the rearing of children. Today the majority of American women are working outside the home, and views on what roles mothers should play in the lives of their children are in flux.

hunting and food-gathering societies The earliest human societies, whose members survived by foraging for vegetable foods and small game, fishing, collecting shellfish, and hunting larger animals.

society The largest and most inclusive social system that exists.

————— SOCIETIES

The most complex structures sociologists examine are societies. A **society** is a grouping of people who share the same territory and participate in a common culture. Organized and long-lasting societies are rare among most mammals, with the wolf pack, the prairie dog town, and the baboon troop representing some of the notable exceptions. Society, however, is universal among humans. For this to be so, it must have performed major adaptive functions that have increased the chances of human survival. Among certain species of animals, great speed, powerful jaws, or brute strength may be the key adaptive advantage. Among humans, the social organization that results in society has enabled our survival.

Among humans, the members of a particular society are so mutually interdependent that often the very survival of each member depends on the behavior of the other members. There have been a variety of different types of societies throughout history. Let us examine these.

TYPES OF SOCIETIES

In this section we shall trace the development of the major types of societies. In tracing this development we shall look at hunting and food-gathering societies, horticultural societies, pastoral societies, agricultural societies, and, finally, industrial and postindustrial societies.

Hunting and Food-Gathering Societies

The members of the earliest human societies — **hunting and food-gathering societies** — survived by foraging for vegetable foods and small game, fishing, collecting shellfish, and hunting larger animals. They did not plant crops or raise animals for future needs; rather, they subsisted from day to day on whatever was at hand. In modern times a few of the world's simplest societies — in Australia, Africa, and South America — still subsist using these methods and depend to a large degree on tools made of stone, wood, and bone.

If we were to consider the evolutionary cycle during which human beings have been on this earth, we would find that most of it has been marked by hunting and gathering societies. Anthropologists have estimated that humans hunted for at least 1 million years, but it has been a mere 10,000 years since the first people began to experiment with the possibilities of organized agriculture. Richard Leakey (Leakey and Lewin, 1977) believes that hunting is the key characteristic in the development of human social organization. Our close primate cousins are primarily vegetarians. Primates are social animals, but a plant-eating existence tends to make the individual members very self-centered and uncooperative. To be a vegetarian is essentially to be solitary. Each member tears a leaf from a branch, or plucks fruit from a tree, and promptly eats it. There is little communal eating or sharing of food.

When our ancestors organized their hunting and gathering, the adoption of sharing opened a behavioral gulf between us and our primate relatives. Sharing was one of a group of traits acquired through hunting and gathering that helped produce an increasingly adaptable way of life. This adaptability enabled the human species to thrive in practically every corner of the globe.

The San tribe is a hunting and gathering society that migrates throughout the Kalahari Desert in southern Africa.

Horticultural Societies

Some 12,000 to 15,000 years ago, coinciding with the retreat of the last glaciers, a drying trend took place in what previously had been rich, subtropical climates, and the giant deserts of Africa, Asia, and the Middle East took shape. Even beyond the deserts' constantly expanding borders, new arid conditions made precarious the age-old hunting and food-gathering way of life. Some groups continued to eke out an existence using the old subsistence techniques. Others crowded together in the more abundant regions, harvesting wild grains until population pressures drove them out into less favorable environments. There they attempted to recreate the rich environments they had left. In doing so, they created a new form of subsistence—**horticultural societies**—using human muscle power and hand-held tools (such as digging sticks and hoes) to cultivate gardens and fields (Flannery, 1965, 1968). It is generally agreed that women invented this new and revolutionary form of food production—deliberately planting seeds with the idea of having a sure source of food later on—through their observations of the relationships between seeds and the growth of plants.

The movement from hunting and gathering to farming also represented a dramatic social change. Hunters as a people must have faith in the resources of their physical world and in their ability to exploit them. They live in small, intimate, cooperative groups moving from camp to camp as their food supplies dictate. As they roam the land that they may share with other bands, they may encounter confrontations, but they do not search them out.

An agricultural existence produces the exact opposite of this way of life. Because crops must be tended and harvested, farmers are confined to a certain area. A sedentary way of life also offers the possibility of accumulating material possessions. In turn, the land bearing the crops and the farmers' possessions must be defended. A whole new outlook on life thus develops. Agriculture also can support a much greater density of people, therefore giving rise to villages and towns. The possibility of expanding possessions and the ability to have power over others in turn produces the urge to accumulate still more and brings about the necessity of protecting what has already been won. The stage is thus set for conflict and wars.

horticultural societies
The first societies whose members used human muscle power and hand-held tools to cultivate gardens and fields.

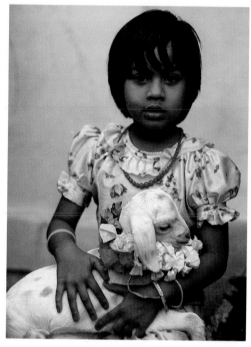

The Lapps lead a nomadic existence in northern Scandinavia, while this Banjara girl of India is part of a group that has given up its nomadic lifestyle.

To hunting and gathering tribes, it made little sense to appropriate the territory of a neighboring band. In contrast, agriculture allowed local populations to grow. If one village decided to take over the crops of another, it would benefit because its own population could then expand with the extra food. In this respect anthropologists would argue that the violence and destruction peculiar to modern times is an outgrowth of the agricultural way of life, and not a biological remnant from our hunting ancestors (Leakey and Lewin, 1977).

Pastoral Societies

Pastoral societies rely on herding and the domestication and propagation of animals for food and clothing to satisfy the bulk of the group's needs. Animal herds provide milk, dung (for fuel), skin, sheared fur, and even blood (which is drunk as a major source of protein in East Africa).

Pastoral societies appear in many regions that are not suitable for plant domestication, such as semiarid desert regions and the northern tundra plains of Europe and

Asia. They are also found in less severe climates, including East African savannas and mountain grasslands. Pastoralism, however, almost never occurs in forest or jungle regions. It is an interesting fact, which scholars have not been able to explain, that no true pastoral societies ever emerged in the Americas before the arrival of the Europeans.

Agricultural Societies

Agricultural societies are distinguished from other groups by their use of the plow in food production. Agriculture is more efficient than horticulture: Plowing turns the topsoil far deeper than hoeing, allowing for better aerating and fertilizing of the ground and thus improving the yield. Interestingly, early agriculture probably did not yield much more than the food-gatherers were able to harvest in naturally rich environments. However, by about 5500 B.C. farmers in the Middle East were not only using the plow but irrigation (the channeling of water for crops) as well. With irrigation, farmers became capable of producing

agricultural societies Societies that use the plow in food production.

pastoral societies Societies that rely on herding and the domestication and propagation of animals for food and clothing to satisfy the bulk of the group's needs.

huge surpluses—enough to feed large numbers of people who did not produce food themselves.

Reliance on agriculture had dramatic and interrelated consequences for society. Ever-growing populations came together in broad river valleys like those of the Nile in Egypt, the Tigris and Euphrates in the Middle East, the Huang Ho (Yellow River) in China, and the Danube and Rhine in Europe. This rapidly rising and geographically compressed population density gave rise to cities and to new social forms. For the first time society was *not* organized principally in terms of kinship. Rather, occupational diversity and institutional specialization (including differentiated political, economic, and religious institutions) predominated.

As populations grew and cities developed, the need arose for a central organization that could administer the ever-widening and increasingly complex activities that accompanied this growth. Such a central authority could serve the interests of the priest-kings by enabling them to collect taxes; it also provided the means to maintain a permanent military force with military leaders to protect the new centers of population. These developments led to the emergence of the centralized state.

Industrial Societies

Industrialism consists of the use of mechanical means (machines and chemical processes) for the production of goods. The Industrial Revolution at first developed slowly. It had begun in a small way by the mid-eighteenth century and gained momentum by the turn of the nineteenth century. (In 1798, Eli Whitney built the first American factory for the mass production of guns near New Haven, Connecticut.) By the mid-1800s the Industrial Revolution had swung into high gear with the invention of the steam locomotive and Henry Bessemer's development of large-scale production techniques at his steelworks in England in 1858. It is called a revolution because of the enormous changes it brought about in society.

Industrial societies are characterized by more than just the use of mechanical means for production. They constitute an entirely new form of society that requires an immense, mobile, diversely specialized, highly skilled, and well-coordinated labor force. To meet the demand for people with specialized and complex skills, many members of the labor force must be educated, at least able to read and write. Hence, an educational system open to all is a hallmark of industrial societies—something that was not necessary in preindustrial times. Industrialism also requires the creation of highly organized systems of exchange between the suppliers of raw materials and industrial manufacturers on the one hand, and between the manufacturers and consumers on the other.

Industrial societies are inevitably divided along class lines. The nature of the division varies, depending on whether the society allows private ownership of capital (capitalism) or puts all capital in the hands of the state (socialism). All industrial societies have at least two social classes: (1) a large labor force that produces goods and services but has little or no influence on what is done with them, and (2) a much smaller class that determines what will be produced and how it will be distributed.

Postindustrial Society

The world has continued to change since the beginning of industrialization. These changes have prompted some sociologists to adopt the concept of the **postindustrial society** (Bell, 1973). Whereas industrial societies depend on inventions and advances made by craftspeople, postindustrial societies depend on specialized knowledge to bring about continuing progress in technology. The computer industry, which has experienced such phenomenal growth, is an integral part of postindustrial society. Advances in this field are made by highly trained specialists who work to increase the

industrial societies Societies characterized by the use of machines, exchange relationships, division along class lines, secularization, and bureaucracy. They require a large, mobile, diversely specialized, highly skilled, and well-coordinated labor force.

industrialism The use of mechanical means (machines and chemical processes) for the production of goods.

postindustrial society A society that depends on specialized knowledge to bring about continuing progress in technology.

capabilities of computers. Knowledge and information are the hallmarks of the postindustrial society.

Some theorists like Daniel Bell (1973) have speculated on the characteristics of postindustrial society. The trends they see are based on changes already under way in industrial societies, particularly in the United States. The economies of postindustrial society will be service oriented. Already in the United States more than half of all jobs are in the service sector, and the proportion is expected to increase as computers direct automation in industry and as agriculture becomes more and more mechanized. In fact, some theorists believe that eventually all heavy industry will be located in nonservice-oriented societies. Advanced technology, on which postindustrial society is based, is in turn dependent on well-educated, well-informed scientists, technologists, and social theorists. Intellectual and technical knowledge and access to the quantities of information made possible by computers are crucial to this kind of society.

Government at all levels will play a larger and larger role in society, both as employer and as the seat of policy making. Residence patterns will change, with people moving from the more crowded cities and suburbs in search of space, a trend already substantiated by recent census data. At the same time, people will be more segregated according to their age and family status.

It is evident from the impact on society of the computer alone that there will be major and far-reaching changes in industrial society and that these changes are already in evidence. We shall discuss social change in a postindustrial society further in Chapter 21.

Using the concepts we have discussed in this chapter, sociologists study the ways in which individuals interact with one another as individuals and within gatherings and groups and the ways in which they organize themselves into the large mosaic that makes up modern society. The rest of this book consists of an extended analysis of these processes.

SUMMARY

There is no way *not* to interact with others. Social interaction has no opposite. If we accept the fact that all social interaction has a message value, then it follows that no matter how one may try, one cannot *not* send a message. Activity or inactivity, words or silence all contain a message.

Max Weber was one of the first sociologists to stress the importance of social interaction in the study of sociology. He argued that the main goal of sociology was to explain what he called *social action*. He used this term to refer to anything people are conscious of doing because of other people.

Social interaction involves two or more people taking each other into account. Although the goals of social interaction may

often be obvious, the motivations may be quite obscure and complicated.

Human behavior is not random. It is patterned and, for the most part, quite predictable. There is the presence of norms — specific rules of behavior that are agreed upon and shared and which prescribe limits of acceptable behavior.

Erving Goffman called actions that have little by way of goals other than to catalog other people and make a decent impression on them "unfocused interaction."

There are four basic types of focused social interaction: exchange, cooperation, conflict, and competition.

Statuses are socially defined positions that people occupy in a group or society and in terms of which they interact with one another. Sometimes one of the multiple statuses a person occupies seems to dominate the others in patterning that person's life. Such a status is called a master status. The statuses that are conferred upon a person (usually at birth) are called ascribed statuses; those that are occupied as a result of an individual's actions are called achieved statuses.

Roles are the culturally defined rules for proper behavior that are associated with every status. A status may contain a number of roles, which collectively are known as a role set. When a single role has conflicting demands attached to it, people who play that role often experience role strain. When an individual is unable to enact the roles of one status without violating those of another status, role conflict results. The roles individuals play can have a dramatic influence on their attitudes and behavior. Deliberately playing the role of someone with whom we are in conflict can often help us resolve that conflict by letting us see the other person's point of view or experiencing that person's emotions. No two people are exactly alike in the way they enact their roles. The differences in role enactment are the result of differences in personality.

Sociologists usually speak of five areas of society in which basic needs have to be fulfilled: the family sector, the education sector, the economic sector, the religious sector, and the political sector. For each of these areas there are social groups and associations that carry out the goals and meet the needs of society. The behavior of people in these groups and associations is organized or patterned by the relevant social institutions—that is, the ordered social relationships that grow out of the values, norms, statuses, and roles that organize those activities that fulfill society's fundamental needs.

Social organization consists of the relatively stable pattern of social relationships among individuals and groups in society. These relationships are based upon systems of social roles, norms, and shared meanings that provide regularity and predictability in social interaction.

Social institutions consist of the ordered social relationships that grow out of the values, norms, statuses, and roles that organize the activities that fulfill society's basic needs. The patterned relationships among people in a society that grow out of the choices they make because of the society's institutions compose its social oganization. The patterned relationships among a society's social institutions make up its social structure. Although social structure tends to be the most stable aspect of society, the American social structure has undergone relatively rapid change because of its complexity and because of the many types of people that are part of it.

A society is the largest and most inclusive social system that exists. A society recruits most of its members from within, sustains itself across generations, shares a culture, and occupies a territory. Organized and long-lasting societies are rare among most mammals.

When we examine individual social interaction, we are adopting a microsociological view; when we focus on the larger aspects of social systems, we are taking a macrosociological view.

Forms of social organization depend on a society's technological development and on the social relationships that arise from it. Hunting and food-gathering groups are subsistence societies that forage for vegetables and game on the basis of what is needed for each day's existence. Horticultural societies are those that plant gardens and fields using only human muscle power and hand-held tools.

Pastoral societies rely on the domestication and propagation of animals for existence, whereas agricultural societies cultivate plants with the use of a plow. The introduction of irrigation helped agricultural societies flourish.

Industrial societies arose as a result of the Industrial Revolution. These societies

CONTROVERSIES IN SOCIOLOGY
Does Birth Order Influence How You Interact with Others?

We have all heard that birth order affects our interactions with others. Why does it take place, and what are the results? Most children develop certain behaviors peculiar to a specific birth-order position in order to help them cope with their particular place in the family. For example, they may try very hard to please, to gain attention, to be strong, or to excel in certain areas.

Most of these coping strategies are developed in response to siblings rather than to parents. With the exception of the first born and only child, children develop birth-order characteristics as a result of coping strategies designed to deal with the next older child. The second born must deal with the overachieving first born, the third born must contend with a perfectionistic second born, and the fourth born must grapple with a strong-willed third born. The first born must deal with the possible loss of attention to the second born, and the only child must deal with playing alone often. These situations help to produce birth-order characteristics that are readily identifiable to the trained eye. Below are statements that are typical of specific birth-order positions.

THE FIRST BORN: I don't know. What do you think?

The first born's desire for approval, admiration, and respect causes him to lose track of what he wants or thinks. He needs to know where others stand before they are aware of their own position. The first born tries to tune in to the needs and feelings of other people.

THE SECOND BORN: That won't work. It's not good enough.

In order to keep the first born from outperforming her and making her feel inadequate, the second born tries to find fault. If the first born tries to impress the parents by achieving good grades, the second born will point out that he is not good in sports.

By saying "That won't work," the second born puts people on the defensive. By pointing out that "It's not good enough," the second born is trying to humble the arrogant-appearing first born.

THE THIRD BORN: No problem. It doesn't bother me any.

When the second born tried to intimidate the third born by saying something would not work, the third born responded with "No problem," and did it anyway. The second born's continuing criticism produced the response "It doesn't bother me any." The third born is characterized by the desire to become impervious to the put-down strategies of the second born.

THE FOURTH BORN: Life isn't easy. You have to try hard.

The fourth born feels frustrated at being made to feel immature by the third born. Life was not easy when it came to playing with the older children. In order to cope, the fourth born learned "You have to try hard." The fourth born tries hard to be part of the world from which he feel excluded.

THE ONLY CHILD: Leave me alone. I'd rather do it myself.

These statements represent the only child's reaction to the excessive attention she received from her parents. As a result, the only child wants to keep others from intruding into her life. The only child wants to do it her way.

Source: Clifford E. Isaacson, *Understanding Yourself Through Birth Order* (Algona, Iowa: Upper Des Moines Counseling Center, 1988).

require an immense, mobile, diversely specialized, skilled, and well-coordinated labor force. They have brought about tremendous shifts in population and have led to the establishment of bureaucracy.

Some theorists see drastic changes already in progress that will lead to postindustrial societies, which will be based on technology, information, and knowledge. The computer is the symbol of the postindustrial society. Life-styles will change: Most people will work in the service, or white-collar, sectors of the economy and live in smaller, less-crowded cities and suburban areas, segregated according to age and family status. Although this view of the future is open to debate — other theorists as well as actual events indicate that many of these trends may change or be reversed — it seems that major changes in modern societies are inevitable.

Chapter 6

GROUP STRUCTURES

Like so many other 19-year-olds, Lee William Mirecki joined the Navy in the hope of becoming a pilot. He was one of twenty-seven members in the airmen recruit class at the Naval Air Station in Pensacola, Florida —a class that was put through rigorous naval training to prepare for duty.

The most difficult exercise for Mirecki was a search-and-rescue mission for drowning victims known as "sharks and daisies." The goal of this exercise was to prepare recruits for actual air disasters in which they had to jump from a hovering helicopter to rescue downed fliers or shipwrecked sailors. Instructors played the role of panicky drowning victims while the trainees took the part of their rescuers. To pass, trainees had to carry victims to safety at the side of a training facility swimming pool.

Mirecki failed the drill once. Even though he was a good swimmer, he panicked under stress in the water. But he was motivated to try again. His second attempt was no better. Realizing that he could not go on — that he was just too scared — Mirecki swam to the side of the pool, exhausted and terrified.

Although he told his instructors that he could not finish and clutched an equipment rack for dear life, they would not let him quit. As one shouted, "Get him, put Mirecki back in the water," three others forced him back into the pool and one pushed his head below the surface. As this was happening, the twenty-six other recruits were instructed to stand with their backs to the pool and sing the "Star-Spangled Banner" in their loudest voices. Still the din could not drown out Mirecki's screams. "D-O-R! . . . D-O-R!" he shouted. Using his last breaths, he pleaded with his instructors in the Navy's own shorthand to "drop on request" the exercise that would soon kill him.

Mirecki's shouts soon stopped. He was dead. When the other airmen recruits turned around, they saw their instructors dragging the body from the pool. Mirecki's lips were blue; his eyes rolled back. According to one recruit, the incident never should have happened. "He was panicked. He was scared. He was yelling. It was obvious he didn't want to be back in the pool." Another recruit overheard one of the instructors admit that "maybe we used too much force." (*New York Times,* May 18, June 6, June 9, 1988; *Newsweek,* May 23, 1988)

How could a human life be taken in the name of training and "military discipline?" The answer lies, in part, in the nature of group interaction. To Mirecki, becoming a naval pilot was a goal he had long held. Succeeding — becoming part of a group of chosen men — motivated him to attempt the exercise a second time, despite his fears. To his instructors, pushing recruits to the

limits of their endurance was their mandate. They walked the fine line of training inexperienced recruits for dangerous missions without jeopardizing their health or safety. Nearly 1600 sailors had passed the air–sea rescue course before Mirecki, and they were determined that Mirecki would pass too. Group standards had to be met, despite Mirecki's panic.

The situation that caused Airman Mirecki's death is shocking because it was so unnecessary. Yet group interactions are at the very heart of human relationships. We are dependent on one another for our lives, our happiness, our well-being. From the smallest, personal groups — family, friends, schoolmates, and work companions — to the large, often anonymous groups who provide us with goods and services, our ability to function in society is related to our interactions with others. This chapter will focus on group interactions and the effects that they have on our lives.

THE NATURE OF GROUPS

In common speech the word *group* is often used for almost any occasion when two or more people come together. In sociology, however, there are several terms we use for various collections of people, not all of which are considered groups. A **social group** consists of a number of people who have a common identity, some feeling of unity, and certain common goals and shared norms.

In any social group the individuals interact with one another according to established statuses and roles. The members develop expectations of proper behavior for people occupying different positions in the social group. The people have a sense of identity and realize they are different from others who are not members. Social groups

social group A number of people who have a common identity, some feeling of unity, and certain common goals and shared norms.

have a set of values and norms that may or may not be similar to those of the larger society.

Our description of a social group contrasts with our definition of a **social aggregate,** which is made up of people who temporarily happen to be in physical proximity to each other, but share little else. Consider passengers riding together in one car of a train. They may share a purpose (traveling to Des Moines) but do not interact or even consider their temporary association to have any meaning. It hardly makes sense to call them a group—unless something more happens. If it is a long ride, for instance, and several passengers start a card game, the cardplayers will have formed a social group: they have a purpose, they share certain role expectations, and they attach importance to what they are doing together. Moreover, if the cardplayers continue to meet one another every day (say, on a commuter train), they may begin to feel special in contrast with the rest of the passengers, who are "just riders."

A social group, unlike an aggregate, does not cease to exist when its members are away from one another. Members of social groups carry the fact of their membership with them and see the group as a distinct entity with specific requirements for membership. A social group has a purpose and is therefore important to its members, who know how to tell an "insider" from an "outsider." It is a social entity that exists for its members apart from any other social relationships that some of them might share. Members of a group interact according to established norms and traditional statuses and roles. As new members are recruited to the group, they move into these traditional statuses and adopt the expected role behavior—if not gladly, than as a result of group pressure.

Consider, for example, a tenants' group that consists of the people who rent apartments in a building. Most such groups are founded because tenants feel a need for a strong, unified voice in dealing with the landlord on problems with repairs, heat, hot water, and rent increases. Many members of a tenants' group may never have met one another before; others may be related to one another; and some may also belong to other groups such as a neighborhood church, the PTA, a bowling league, or political associations. The group's existence does not depend on these other relationships for its existence, nor does it cease to exist when members leave the building to go to work or to go away on vacation. The group remains even when some tenants move out of the building and others move in. Newcomers are recruited, told of the group's purpose, and informed of its meetings; they are encouraged to join committees, take leadership responsibilities, and participate in the actions the group has planned. Members who fail to support the group action (such as withholding rent) will be pressured and criticized and may even receive threats of violence or be expelled from the group.

People are sometimes defined as being part of a specific group because they share certain characteristics. If these characteristics are unknown or unimportant to those in the category, it is not a social group; involvement with other people cannot develop unless one is aware of them. People with similar characteristics do not become a social group unless concrete, dynamic interrelations develop among them (Lewin,

social aggregate People who happen to be in the same place but share little else.

If these people have only come together temporarily to be part of this parade, then we would consider them a social aggregate, not a social group.

Even if people are aware of one another, it is still not enough to make them a social group. In a social group, people are involved with each other in some patterned way.

primary group A group that is characterized by intimate face-to-face association and cooperation. Primary groups involve interaction among members who have an emotional investment in one another and who interact as total individuals rather than through specialized roles.

1948). For example, although all left-handed people fit into a group, they are not a social group just because they share this common characteristic. A further interrelationship must also exist. They may, for instance, belong to Left-handers International, an organization that champions the rights of left-handers by addressing issues of discrimination and analyzing new products designed for use by left-handers. About 23,000 left-handers belong to this social group.

Even if people are aware of one another, it is still not enough to make them a social group. We may be classified as Democrats, college students, upper class, or suburbanites. Yet, for many of us who fall into these categories, there is no group. We may not be involved with the others in any patterned way that is an outgrowth of that classification. In fact, we personally may not even define ourselves as members of the particular category, even if someone else does.

Social groups can be large or small, temporary or long-lasting. Your family is a social group, as is your bowling club, any association to which you belong, or the clique with which you "hang around." In fact, it is difficult for you to participate in society without belonging to several different groups.

In general, social groups, regardless of

their nature, have the following characteristics: (1) permanence beyond the meetings of members — that is, even when members are dispersed, (2) means for identifying members, (3) mechanisms for recruiting new members, (4) goals or purposes, (5) social statuses and roles (that is, norms for behavior), and (6) means for controlling members' behavior.

The traits we described are features of many groups. A baseball team, a couple about to be married, a work unit, a weekly poker game, members of a family, or a town planning board all may be described as groups. Yet, being a member of a family is significantly different from being a member of a work unit. The family is a primary group, whereas most work units are secondary groups.

PRIMARY AND SECONDARY GROUPS

The difference between primary and secondary groups lies in the kinds of relationships their members have with one another. Charles Horton Cooley (1909) defined **primary groups** as groups that are characterized by

> intimate face-to-face association and cooperation. They are primary in several senses, but chiefly in that they are fundamental in forming the social nature and ideas of the individual. The result of intimate association, . . . so that one's very self, for many purposes at least, is the common life and purpose of the group. Perhaps the simplest way of describing this wholeness is by saying that it is a "we"; it involves the sort of sympathy and mutual identification for which "we" is the natural expression. (p. 23)

Cooley called primary groups the nursery of human nature, because they have the earliest and most fundamental impact on the individual's socialization and development. He identified three basic primary groups: the family, children's play groups, and neighborhood or community groups.

Primary groups involve interaction

TABLE 6.1
Relationships in Primary and Secondary Groups

	Primary	*Secondary*
Physical Conditions	Small number	Large number
	Long duration	Shorter duration
Social Characteristics	Identification of ends	Disparity of ends
	Intrinsic valuation of the relation	Extrinsic valuation of the relation
	Intrinsic valuation of other person	Extrinsic valuation of other person
	Inclusive knowledge of other person	Specialized and limited knowledge of other person
	Feeling of freedom and spontaneity	Feeling of external constraint
	Operation of informal controls	Operation of formal controls
Sample Relationships	Friend–friend	Clerk–customer
	Husband–wife	Announcer–listener
	Parent–child	Performer–spectator
	Teacher–pupil	Officer–subordinate
Sample Groups	Play group	Nation
	Family	Clerical hierarchy
	Village or neighborhood	Professional association
	Work-team	Corporation

Source: Kingsley Davis, *Human Society* (New York: Macmillan, 1949).

among members who have an emotional investment in one another and in a situation, who know one another intimately and interact as total individuals rather than through specialized roles. For example, members of a family are emotionally involved with one another and know one another well. In addition, they interact with one another in terms of their total personalities, not just in terms of their social identities or statuses as breadwinner, student, athlete, or community leader.

A **secondary group,** in contrast, is characterized by much less intimacy among its members. It usually has specific goals, is formally organized, and is impersonal. Secondary groups tend to be larger than primary groups, and their members do not necessarily interact with all other members.

In fact, many members often do not know one another at all; to the extent that they do, rarely do they know more about one another than about their respective social identities. Members' feelings about, and behavior toward, one another are patterned mostly by their statuses and roles rather than by personality characteristics. The chairman of the board of General Motors, for example, is treated respectfully by all General Motors employees—regardless of the chairman's sex, age, intelligence, habits of dress, physical fitness, temperament, or qualities as a parent or spouse. In secondary groups, such as political parties, labor unions, and large corporations, people *are* very much what they *do*. Table 6.1 outlines the major differences between primary and secondary groups.

secondary group A group that is characterized by an impersonal, formal organization with specific goals. Secondary groups are larger and much less intimate than primary groups, and the relationships among members are patterned mostly by statuses and roles rather than by personality characteristics.

FRATERNITIES: THE ULTIMATE IN-GROUPS

For many, fraternities are the ultimate in-group. They give young men, many of whom are living away from home for the first time, a sense of belonging—of being part of a group that serves as a surrogate family. Although there are many good reasons to join a fraternity and many good fraternities, the in-group mentality that is the basis of fraternity life is frought with problems.

First, many fraternities are exclusionary; they reject applicants who do not measure up to their standards—whatever those standards may be. "We were, after all, chiefly in the excluding business," said novelist Richard Ford, recalling his fraternity days. "This guy had 'the breath of death'; . . . This guy 'had the handshake of a fish.' We didn't want Jews, blacks, Orientals, gays, women, big fatties, or cripples. Steven Spielberg couldn't have been a Sigma Chi. Neither could . . . Justice Marshall" (Richard Ford, *Esquire,* June 1986).

This "us" against "them" mentality is often an excuse for racism, anti-Semitism, and sexism. Here are two examples: At the University of Pennsylvania, black students have been verbally abused as they walked down fra-ternity row, especially on party nights. And at the University of Michigan, a "nonmalicious" prank resulted in three students from a white Christian fraternity stealing a mock jail cell built to show Jewish students' solidarity with Soviet Jews.

The second problem with Greek life is that fraternity initiations often involve hazing—rituals in which out-group members willingly degrade themselves to be accepted by the in-group. The degradation can be extreme, and some hazing methods are akin to those used by torturers. According to the researchers, Janice T. Gibson and Mika Haritos-Fatouros, fraternities use the following training techniques to instill unquestioning obedience in fraternity members and pledges: (1) After screening to find the best candidates, they isolate pledges and introduce them to fraternity life, which has a differ-ent set of rules and values than the rest of college society. (2) Elitist attitudes and in-group language further accentuate the difference between "us" and "them." (3) To encourage obedience, fraternity members blame and dehumanize pledges, a process that makes harming them less disturbing. In addition, harassment of them through physical and psychologi-cal intimidation prevents logical thinking that might motivate pledges to reject the group. Fra-ternity members are encouraged to degrade pledges by watching other group members do the same and then receive rewards. Mem-bers become desensitized to these acts through gradual exposure. After awhile, say the researchers, even violence seems routine.

This is not to say that frater-nities are driven solely by these in-group versus out-group pres-sures. Fraternities provide friend-ship and belonging in a new envi-ronment, without which many students would not adjust as well to college life. They also contrib-ute to society by raising money for charity and working for good causes.

To many, the abuses of fra-ternity life are isolated incidents. To others, they are a symptom of something terribly wrong with a system that divides college stu-dents into in-groups and out-groups. With fraternity member-ship having doubled in the past ten years (during the same period the undergraduate student popu-lation increased by only 20 per-cent), these organizations are having a greater impact on college life. Whether fraternities can overcome divisions and bring stu-dents together is an issue that needs further examination.

Sources: Janice T. Gibson and Mika Har-itos-Fatouros, "The Education of a Tor-turer," *Psychology Today,* November 1986, pp. 50–58; M. G. Lord, "The Greek Rites of Exclusion," *The Nation,* July 4/11, 1987, pp. 10–13.

IN-GROUPS AND OUT-GROUPS

Some groups go a long way toward distinguishing between themselves and other groups. These distinctions may be based on unique racial, ethnic, religious, or social-class characteristics or on special interests, residential location, or unique common experiences. William Graham Sumner (1906) referred to this type of group as an **in-group** —a group that members use as a point of reference. Their definition of who they are is very closely linked to the in-group. There is a "we" feeling generated among the members of the group, who are immediately aware of those who do not belong—the "they" groups. For example, I am a member of the Lions Club, you are not; I am a Tri Delt, you are not; I live on the hill, you live in the valley; I am an alumnus of Harvard, you are not.

Those who do not belong to the in-group are part of the **out-group**. In-group members use the out-group as a negative point of reference. As an in-group member, you reject out-group people or at least do not think of them as having a standing equal to that of your in-group members. High school peer groups often act as in-groups, "putting down" those schoolmates who do not belong—that is, who are "out."

CHARACTERISTICS OF GROUPS

To function properly, all groups—both primary and secondary—must (1) define their boundaries, (2) choose leaders, (3) make decisions, (4) set goals, (5) assign tasks, and (6) control members' behavior.

Defining Boundaries

Group members must have ways of knowing who belongs to their group and who does not. Sometimes devices for marking boundaries are obvious symbols, such as the uniforms worn by athletic teams, lapel pins worn by Rotary Club members, rings worn by Masons, and styles of dress. Other ways in which group boundaries are marked include the use of gestures (think of the special handshakes often used by many American blacks) and language (dialect differences often mark people's regional origin and social class). In some societies (including our own), skin color also is used to mark boundaries between groups. The idea of the British school tie that, by its pattern and colors, signals exclusive group membership, has been adopted by businesses ranging from banking to brewing.

Choosing Leaders

All groups must grapple with the issue of leadership. A **leader** is someone who occupies a central role or position of dominance and influence in a group. In some groups, such as large corporations, leadership is assigned to individuals by those in positions of authority. (**Authority** combines leadership and legitimized power—the ability to force people to act in certain ways.) In other groups, such as adolescent peer groups, individuals move into positions of leadership through the force of personality or through particular skills such as athletic ability,

in-group A group that members use as a point of reference. The identity of in-group members is very closely linked to their sense of belonging to the group.

out-group A group that exists in the perceptions of in-group members and takes on a social reality as a result of behavior by in-group members who use the out-group as a negative point of reference.

leader Someone who occupies a central role or position of dominance and influence in a group.

authority A combination of leadership and legitimized power, which confers the ability to force people to act in certain ways.

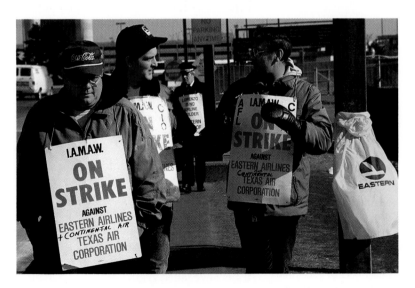

A strike has the effect of creating a clear-cut line between those who are part of the in-group and those who are the out-group.

Bear Bryant, former football coach at the University of Alabama, was both an instrumental and an expressive leader.

instrumental leadership A form of leadership in which a leader actively proposes tasks and plans to guide the group toward achieving its goals.

expressive leadership A form of leadership in which a leader works to keep relations among group members harmonious and morale high.

authoritarian leader A type of instrumental leader who makes decisions and gives orders.

democratic leader A type of instrumental leader who attempts to encourage group members to reach a consensus.

fighting, or debating. In still other groups, including political organizations, leadership is awarded through the democratic process of nominations and voting. Think of the long primary process that presidential candidates must endure to amass enough votes to carry their party's nomination for the November election.

Leadership need not always be held by the same person within a group. It can shift from one individual to another in response to problems or situations that the group encounters. In a group of factory workers, for instance, leadership may fall on different members depending on what the group plans to do — complain to the supervisor, head toward a tavern after work, or organize a picnic for all members and their families.

Politicians and athletic coaches often like to talk about individuals who are "natural leaders." Although attempts to account for leadership solely in terms of personality traits have failed again and again, personality factors may determine what kinds of leadership functions a person assumes. Re-

searchers (Bales, 1958; Slater, 1966) have identified two types of leadership roles: (1) **instrumental leadership** in which a leader actively proposes tasks and plans to guide the group toward achieving its goals, and (2) **expressive leadership,** in which a leader works to keep relations among group members harmonious and morale high. Both kinds of leadership are crucial to the success of a group.

Sometimes both functions are fulfilled by one person, as they were in the case of Bear Bryant, former football coach at the University of Alabama. Ken Stabler, who went on to become quarterback of the Oakland Raiders and New Orleans Saints, described Bryant's leadership style this way:

> Coach Bryant had a way of being very, very tough, while still making you love him. He was doing it to make you a better player and ultimately a better man. . . . He was the sort of man who had his own way of doing things, and that was the only way things got done. . . . I think Coach Bryant's strong suit was motivation. He knew how to make an overachiever out of everybody. . . . There was a certain amount of intimidation in his style, but the main thing always was respect. He kept his distance, yet somehow you felt close to him. I still don't know how he managed to do that. (Stabler, 1986)

When one person cannot be found to take on both leadership functions, these functions are often distributed among several group members. The individual with knowledge of the terrain who leads a group of airplane crash survivors to safety is providing instrumental leadership. The group members who think of ways to keep the group from giving in to despair are providing expressive leadership. The group needs both to survive.

There are three types of instrumental leaders: an **authoritarian leader** makes decisions and gives orders; a **democratic leader** attempts to encourage group members to

King Juan Carlos of Spain has inherited his lifetime leadership position. He believes in a parliamentary type of democracy. What type of leader whould you call him?

reach a consensus; and a **laissez-faire leader** is a leader in name or title only and does little actively to influence group affairs.

When former Pakistan President Gen. Mohammed Zia ul-Haq decided unilaterally in 1988 to dismiss the civilian government and dissolve the national assembly, he demonstrated the power of an authoritarian leader. Several months after this decision, Zia ul-Haq was killed when the airplane in which he was riding was destroyed by a bomb. In the corporate arena, Lee Iacocca, chairman of Chrysler Corporation, also tends to exercise an authoritarian form of leadership. Says Iacocca: "You have to be a decision maker. After all the information has been gathered, somebody has to decide. That's what being in charge is all about" (*U.S. News & World Report,* May 20, 1985).

On the whole, Americans are biased toward democratic leaders. Much of this is due to an ideological opposition to authoritarian political systems.

In most situations a democratic style of leadership promotes greater satisfaction among group members and more effective group functioning than either the authoritarian or laissez-faire style. The authoritarian type of leader may be generally disliked in times of normal operations. However, there are certain group situations in which the authoritarian form of leadership is more effective than the democratic form. For example, when speed and efficiency are important, an authoritarian leader can be quite useful. An authoritarian leader may take charge very effectively during emergencies, whereas the democratic leader, highly valued during routine operations, might find it more difficult to assume a strong leadership role when the situation demands it.

Making Decisions

Closely related to the problem of leadership is the way in which groups make decisions. In many early hunting and food-gathering societies, important group decisions were reached by consensus—talking about an issue until everybody agreed on what to do (Fried, 1967). Today, occasionally, town councils and other small governing bodies operate in this way. Because this takes a great deal of time and energy, many groups opt for efficiency by taking votes or simply letting one person's decision stand for the group as a whole. Bales and Strodtbeck (1951) identified four stages in group decision making: (1) *orientation*—in which a situation that has disrupted the group's equilibrium is identified and information is gathered, (2) *evaluation*—in which the information is assessed and possible courses of action are proposed, (3) *decision*—in which the group chooses a course of action, and (4) *restoration of equilibrium*—in which the group once more takes up its normal activities.

laissez-faire leader A type of instrumental leader who is a leader in name or title only and does little actively to influence group affairs.

Setting Goals

As we pointed out before, all groups must have a purpose, a goal, or a set of goals. The goal may be very general, such as spreading peace throughout the world, or it may be very specific, such as playing cards on a railroad train. Group goals may change. For example, the cardplayers might discover that they all share a concern about the use of nuclear energy and decide to organize a political action group.

Assigning Tasks

Establishing boundaries, defining leadership, making decisions, and setting goals are not enough to keep a group going. To endure, a group must do something, if nothing more than ensure that its members continue to make contact with one another. Therefore, it is important that group members know what needs to be done and who is going to do it. This assigning of tasks in itself can be an important group activity—think of your family discussions about sharing household chores. By taking on group tasks, members not only help the group reach its goals but also show their commitment to one another and to the group as a whole. This leads members to appreciate one another's importance as individuals and the importance of the group in all their lives—a process that injects life and energy into a group.

Controlling Members' Behavior

If a group cannot control its members' behavior, it will cease to exist. For this reason, failure to conform to group norms is seen as dangerous or threatening, whereas conforming to group norms is rewarded—if only by others' friendly attitudes. Groups not only encourage but often depend for survival on conformity of behavior. A member's failure to conform is met with responses ranging from coolness to criticism or even ejection from the group. Anyone who has ever tried to introduce changes

into the constitution of a club or to ignore long-standing conventions, such as ways of dressing, rituals of greeting, or the assumption of designated responsibilities, probably has experienced group hostility.

Primary groups tend to be more tolerant of members' deviant behavior than secondary groups (Lee, 1966). For example, families often will conceal the problems of a member who suffers from chronic alcoholism or drug abuse. Even primary groups, however, must draw the line somewhere, and they will invoke negative sanctions (see Chapter 7) if all else fails to get the deviant member to show at least a willingness to *try* to conform. When this does happen and primary groups finally act, their punishments can be far more severe or harsh than those of secondary groups. Thus, an intergenerational conflict in a family can result in excluding the teenager from the family altogether.

Secondary groups tend to use formal, as opposed to informal, sanctions and are much more likely than primary groups simply to expel, or push out, a member who persists in violating strongly held norms: corporations fire unsatisfactory employees, the army discharges soldiers who violate regulations, and so on.

Even though primary groups are more tolerant of their members' behavior, people tend to conform more closely to their norms than to those of secondary groups. This is because people value their membership in a primary group, with its strong interpersonal bonds, for its own sake. Secondary group membership is valued mostly for what it will do for the people in the group, not because of any deep emotional ties. Because primary group membership is so desirable, its members are more reluctant than secondary group members to risk expulsion by indulging in behavior that might violate the group's standards, or norms.

Usually group members will want to conform as long as the group is seen as important. Solomon Asch (1955) showed just how far group members will go to promote group solidarity and conformity. In a series of experiments, he formed groups of eight people and then asked each member to match one line against three other lines of varied lengths (see Figure 6.1). Each judgment was announced in the presence of the other group members. The groups were composed of one real subject and seven of Asch's confederates, whose identity was kept secret from the real subject. The confederates had previously met with Asch and had been instructed to give a unanimous but incorrect answer at certain points throughout the experiment. Asch was interested in finding out how the individual who had been made a minority of one in the presence of a unanimous majority would respond. The subject was placed in a situation in which a group unanimously contradicted the information of his or her senses. Asch repeated the experiment many times. He found that 32 percent of the answers by the real subjects were identical with, or in the direction of, the inaccurate estimates of the majority. This was quite remarkable, because there were virtually no incorrect answers in the control groups that lacked Asch's accomplices, which rules out the possibility of optical illusion. What we have here is an instance in which individuals are willing to give incorrect answers in order not to appear out of step with the judgments of the other group members. Although groups must fulfill certain functions to continue to exist, they serve primarily as a point of reference for their members.

REFERENCE GROUPS

Groups are more than just bridges between the individual and society as a whole. We spend much of our time in one group or another, and the impact that these groups have on us continues even when we are not actually in contact with the other members. The norms and values of groups to which we belong or with which we identify serve as the basis for evaluating our own and others' behavior.

A **reference group** is a group or social

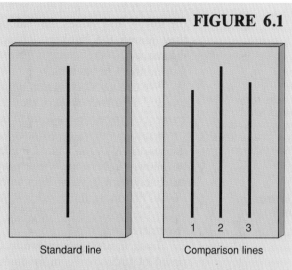

FIGURE 6.1

Standard line   Comparison lines

Group Pressure *In Solomon Asch's experiment on conformity to group pressure, groups of eight students were asked to decide which of the comparison lines (right) was the same length as the standard line (left).*

category that an individual uses to help define beliefs, attitudes, and values and to guide behavior. They provide a comparison point against which persons measure themselves and others. A reference group is often a category with which we identify, rather than a specific group to which we belong. For example, a communications major may identify with individuals in the media without having any direct contact with them. In this respect, anticipatory socialization is taking place, in that the individual may alter his or her behavior and attitudes toward those perceived to be part of the group the individual plans to join. For example, people who become bankers soon feel themselves part of a group—bankers —and assume ideas and life-styles that help them identify with that group. They tend to dress in a conservative, "bankerish" fashion, even buy their clothes in shops that other bankers patronize to make sure they have the "right" clothes from the "right" stores. They join certain clubs and other organizations such as country clubs and alumni associations so that they can mingle

reference group A group or social category that an individual uses to help define beliefs, attitudes, and values, and to guide behavior.

with other bankers and clients. Eventually, the norms and values they adopted when they joined the bankers' group become internalized — they see and judge the world around them as bankers.

We can also distinguish between positive and negative reference groups. Positive reference groups are made up of people that we want to emulate. Negative reference groups provide a model that we do not wish to follow. Therefore, a writer may identify positively with those writers who produce serious fiction, while thinking of journalists who write for gossip publications as a negative reference group.

Even though groups are in fact composed of individuals, individuals are also created to a large degree by the groups to which they belong through the process of socialization (see Chapter 4). Of these groups, the small group usually has the strongest direct impact on an individual.

small group A relative term that refers to the many kinds of social groups that actually meet together and contain few enough members so that all members know one another.

dyad A small group containing two members.

triad A small group containing three members.

SMALL GROUPS

The term **small group** is relative. It refers to the many kinds of social groups, such as families, peer groups, and work groups, that actually meet together and contain few enough members so that all members know one another. The smallest possible group contains only two members, and its technical label is **dyad**. An engaged couple is a dyad, as are the pilot and copilot of an aircraft.

Georg Simmel (1950) was the first sociologist to emphasize the importance of the size of a group on the interaction process. He suggested that small groups have distinctive qualities and patterns of interaction that disappear when the group grows larger. For example, dyads resist change in their group size: on the one hand, the loss of one member destroys the group, leaving the other member alone; but on the other hand, the addition of a third member, creating a **triad,** adds uncertainty because it introduces the possibility of two-against-one alliances and group pressure directed at one member.

Triads can sometimes be more adaptable than dyads. However, on occasions they can be more unstable. "Two's company, three's a crowd" derived from this view. Triads are more stable in those situations when one member can help resolve quarrels between the other two. When three diplomats are negotiating offshore fishing rights, for example, one member of the triad may offer a concession that will break the deadlock between the other two. If that does not work, the third person may try to analyze the arguments of the other two in an effort to bring about a compromise. The formation of shifting pair-offs within triads can help stabilize the group. When it appears that one group member is weakening, one of the two paired members often will break the alliance and form a new one with the individual who had been isolated (Hare,

Triads are usually unstable groups because there is always the possibility of two-against-one alliances.

1976). This is often seen among groups of children engaged in games. In triads in which there is no shifting of alliances and the configuration constantly breaks down into two against one, the group will become unstable and may eventually break up. In Aldous Huxley's novel *Brave New World,* the political organization of the earth was organized into three eternally warring political powers. As one power seemed to be losing, one of the others would come to its aid in a temporary alliance, thereby ensuring worldwide political stability while also making possible endless warfare. No power could risk the total defeat of another because the other surviving power might then become the stronger of the surviving dyad.

As a group grows larger, the number of relationships within it increases, which often leads to the formation of **subgroups** —splinter groups within the larger group. Once a group has more than five to seven members, spontaneous conversation becomes difficult for the group as a whole. Then there are two solutions available: the group can split into subgroups (as happens informally at parties), or it can adopt a formal means of controlling communication (use of *Robert's Rules of Order,* for instance). For these reasons, small groups tend to resist the addition of new members because increasing size threatens the nature of the group. In addition, there may be a fear that new members will resist socialization to group norms and thereby undermine group traditions and values. On the whole, small groups are much more vulnerable than large groups are to disruption by new members, and the introduction of new members often leads to shifts in patterns of interaction and group norms.

THE STUDY OF SMALL GROUPS

Small groups are everywhere. More than a decade ago one researcher estimated that there were as many as four or five billion small groups functioning around the world

(Mills, 1967). Sheer numbers, however, do not alone account for sociologists' interest in small groups.

Small Groups and the Course of History

It is important to understand how small groups function because they play an important part in determining the course of history. During the summer and fall of 1941, for example, the commander in chief of the U.S. Pacific Fleet, Admiral Husband Kimmel, received many warnings that war with Japan was imminent. He discussed these warnings with his staff but was assured again and again that his decision to ignore them was correct. As late as November 27, Admiral Kimmel received an official "war warning" from Washington, but because the message did not specifically mention the naval base at Pearl Harbor as a possible target of attack, Kimmel and the other officers in his in-group decided that no special defensive preparations were needed. On December 3, Kimmel was informed that Washington had intercepted a secret message from Tokyo to all Japanese diplomatic missions abroad ordering staff immediately to destroy their secret codes—a very strong sign of last-minute war preparations. Again Kimmel's group refused to take defensive action (such as sending out scout planes and dispersing the ships of the fleet anchored in the harbor). Finally, on December 6, the signs of war were too many to ignore, but by then Kimmel and his staff were paralyzed: they felt unable to choose among their few remaining options. On the next day the Japanese attacked Pearl Harbor with bombs and torpedoes and succeeded in destroying or incapacitating much of the U.S. Pacific Fleet as it rode at anchor. The internal group process that kept Kimmel and his staff from acting appropriately, even though they had more than enough information, is called **defensive avoidance** (or more popularly, "groupthink"). This same small-group process also characterized the administration of President Richard M.

subgroups Splinter groups within the larger group.

defensive avoidance An internal group process that keeps an in-group from acting appropriately despite the evidence before it; also known as "groupthink."

Nixon and eventually led to his downfall after the Watergate scandal (Janis and Mann, 1976). Clearly, it is important to understand under what conditions defensive avoidance emerges in small groups (especially in groups with important responsibilities) and to know how to intervene and bring such processes to a halt.

Small Groups and Experiments

Because of their convenient size, small groups can be studied in the laboratory and their variables subjected to tight experimental control (see Chapter 2). For example, it is possible to study how all-female groups compare with all-male groups in coping with stress and frustration or how limiting the distribution of information to certain arbitrary flow channels affects a group's ability to reach decisions.

COHESIVENESS IN SMALL GROUPS

One facet of small groups that is of particular interest to sociologists is the impact that group members have on one another. Research indicates that working on a task with several other people may, in fact, reduce individual effort. Although increases in group size may produce greater total output, the gains may not be as great as expected. They may even represent a clear example of the law of diminishing returns, as each of the people participating in a joint task expends less effort on it than if he or she worked alone.

Three researchers (Latane, Williams, and Harkins, 1979) wanted to test this idea for simple small-group tasks. They selected shouting and hand clapping as the tasks to be observed.

In one experiment, six subjects were seated in a semicircle in a soundproof laboratory. They were told that on a signal they were to clap or cheer as loudly as they could for 5 seconds. Each subject clapped and shouted twice alone, four times each in pairs and foursomes, and six times in groups of six. A sound-level meter recorded their performances in dynes/cm^2 — the physical unit of work involved in producing sound pressure.

The results showed that individual performance decreased as the size of the group increased. Alone, each subject's performance averaged 3.7 dynes/cm^2. In pairs, individual performance dropped to 2.6 dynes/cm^2. Foursomes averaged 1.8 dynes/cm^2 for each subject; groups of six, 1.5 dynes/cm^2 per subject. The sound of twelve hands clapping is not even three times as intense as the sound of two hands clapping. The experimenters identified this tendency of individual performances to decrease as the number of coperformers increased as social loafing.

These findings seem to violate both common stereotype and social organizational theory. Common stereotype holds that team participation leads to increased effort, that group morale and cohesiveness spur individual enthusiasm, that by pulling together groups can achieve any goal, that in unity there is strength. Organizational theory holds that, at least for simple, well-learned tasks, the presence of coworkers should facilitate performance. The contrary evidence of social loafing requires further thinking and investigation into small-group dynamics.

The quality of interaction of group members and the cohesiveness that develops can determine the success of the group as a whole. An example of the importance of group cohesiveness can be found in an examination of morale in the military forces.

During World War II the American soldier's morale generally was high. While fighting, they took great risks, and when captured, they constantly sought to escape. In the 1960s in Vietnam, military morale sank to all all-time low. It finally reached the point at which some soldiers joined protest movements against the war — risking imprisonment rather than continuing to fight or to train others to fight. The use of drugs, including heroin, reached epidemic proportions, and many soldiers have testified that they were "high" for much of their active tour of duty—including the times they were out on patrol (Moskos, 1975).

What happened to American soldiers in the 20 to 25 years between World War II and Vietnam? Many things changed, of course. The issues and goals in World War II seemed much more clear-cut than they did in the war in Vietnam, and society as a whole backed military involvement in the war of the 1940s much more so than in that of the 1960s. But sociologists have found another—perhaps even more powerful—difference. In World War II it was understood that soldiers generally stayed with the same unit to which they were originally assigned for the duration of the war. As a result each soldier knew that the sooner the war was won, the sooner he could return home. Also, because he would stay with the same unit until the war was over, a soldier quickly came to identify his own safety with the survival of the unit. The men ate, slept, and fought side by side for years. They went on leave together, read one another's mail from home, and formed close friendships. In other words, American fighting units in World War II became primary groups as well as in-groups—with commitment to and pride in their membership (Shils, 1950).

In Vietnam a soldier was assigned for a 1- or 2-year tour of duty. In all fighting units, the members came and went constantly, and each member had his own number of days left to stay. Group loyalties never could develop the way they did in World War II because each soldier tried desperately to play it safe so that he would survive until the end of his tour. Whereas it is true that soldiers everywhere are motivated by a concern for their own survival, the way in which the U.S. armed forces were organized in Vietnam prevented the soldiers from identifying the survival of their fighting units as groups with their own survival (Moskos, 1975).

NETWORK ANALYSIS

The goal of **network analysis** is to explain the complicated interactions people have with each other. Network analysis is similar to a traffic engineer using photography to estimate traffic flows. If you were to take a night-time aerial photo every 30 seconds, without advancing the film, of a city's traffic, you would get a pattern of thicker and thinner lines of light (from car headlights). The thick and thin lines of light are representative of the volume of traffic. Network analysts do something similar to this with social relationships.

Some network analysts use the notion of cognitive balance in looking at small-group relationships. In their view it is difficult for people to maintain "unbalanced" relationships—or, in other words, to remain friendly with two people who detest each other. Such a situation would exist in a triad relationship, in which an individual wishes to maintain a friendship and interact with two people who dislike each other.

This relationship is unstable because it is unbalanced. The group is likely to break up. The assumption is that relationships will become more balanced over time. People who like each other will strengthen their relationships gradually and break off friendships with people whom their friends abhor. These points also cause us to realize that over time groups will become more segmented, and cliques are likely to develop.

Network analysis is also useful in explaining what is going on in large-scale social institutions. In a large work setting, for example, it often is difficult to explain what is going on at the personal level. Why is it that three workers seem to have a difficult time working with three other workers? The network analyst looks beyond the work environment to see how and where the lives of the various participants intersect. Do they get together after work within a bowling league? Are they members of the same church? Has there been a major dispute be-

network analysis The collection of data explaining the complicated interactions people have with each other.

THE MOST IMPORTANT INSTITUTIONS IN AMERICAN LIFE

How do our institutions stack up against one another? What is the impact each has on decisions affecting the nation as a whole? Is the family, as an institution, more important than big business, television more influential than organized religion? *U.S. News & World Report* asked prominent leaders to rank thirty institutions and organizations by the influence they exert. The ranking scale ranged from a low of 1 to a high of 7. Here is the list. Put them in your own order and then check the answer key to see how your assessment compares to that of the experts.

Source: "Institutions That Influence American Life," *U.S. News & World Report*, May 20, 1985, p. 64. Reprinted by permission.

Banks
Family
Advertising
The White House
Labor unions
Lobby, pressure groups
Newspapers
Big business
Movies
Oil industry
State, local government
Federal bureaucracy
Educational institutions
Public opinion polls
Medical profession
Supreme Court
Republican party
Wall Street
Radio
Cabinet
Television
Civil rights groups
Small business
U.S. Senate
Magazines
U.S. House
Legal profession
Organized religion
Democratic party
Military

Answer Key:

		Average Rating
1.	The White House	6.71
2.	Big business	5.92
3.	Supreme Court	5.78
4.	Television	5.77
5.	U.S. Senate	5.53
6.	Banks	5.47
7.	Wall Street	5.31
8.	U.S. House	5.19
9.	Cabinet	5.10
10.	Lobby, pressure groups	5.03
11.	Oil industry	4.99
12.	Newspapers	4.85
13.	Federal bureaucracy	4.82
14.	Advertising	4.69
15.	Military	4.44
16.	Republican party	4.41
17.	Family	4.33
18.	State, local government	4.16
19.	Radio	4.15
20.	Public opinion polls	4.11
21.	Educational institutions	4.10
22.	Legal profession	4.09
23.	Magazines	4.07
24.	Organized religion	4.02
25.	Labor unions	3.71
26.	Medical profession	3.58
27.	Democratic party	3.45
28.	Civil rights groups	3.25
29.	(Tie) Small business and movies	3.22

tween the families of certain workers? All these can give us a clearer insight into how people are interacting with each other on the job.

One weakness of network analysis is that it can require an extremely detailed and time-consuming collection of information. The researcher may actually at times engage in extensive participant observation work. However, the insights gleaned from network analysis can often be quite valuable and not easily obtained in another manner.

LARGE GROUPS: ASSOCIATIONS

Although all of us probably would be able to identify and describe the various small groups to which we belong, we might find it difficult to follow the same process with the large groups that affect us. As patrons or employees of large organizations and governments, we function as part of large groups all the time. Thus, sociologists must study large groups as well as small groups to understand the workings of society.

Much of the activity of a modern society is carried out through large and formally organized groups. Sociologists refer to these groups as **associations.** These are purposefully created special-interest groups that have clearly defined goals and official ways of doing things. Associations include such organizations as government departments and agencies, businesses and factories, labor unions, schools and colleges, fraternal and service groups, hospitals and clinics, and clubs for various hobbies from gardening to antique collecting. Their goals may be very broad and general, such as helping the poor, healing the sick, or making a profit, or quite specific and limited, such as manufacturing automobile tires or teaching people to speak Chinese. Although an enormous variety of associations exist, they all are characterized by some degree of formal structure with an underlying informal structure.

THE FORMAL STRUCTURE

For associations to function, the work that must be accomplished is assessed and broken down into manageable tasks that are assigned to specific individuals. In other words, associations are run according to some type of **formal organizational structure** that consists of planned, highly institutionalized, and clearly defined statuses and role relationships (see Chapter 5). The formal organizational structure of large associations in contemporary society is best exemplified by the organizational structure called bureaucracy.

A college or university must have a highly developed organizational structure. Fulfilling its main purpose of educating students requires far more than simply bringing together students and teachers. Funds must be raised, buildings constructed, qualified students and instructors recruited, programs and classes organized, materials ordered and distributed, grounds kept up, and buildings maintained. Messages need

to be typed, copied, and filed; lectures must be given; and seminars must be led. To accomplish all these tasks the school must create many different positions: president, deans, department heads, registrars, public relations staff, grounds keepers, maintenance personnel, purchasing agents, secretaries, faculty, and students. Every member of the school has clearly spelled-out tasks that are organized in relation to one another: students are taught and evaluated by faculty, faculty are responsible to department heads or deans, deans to the president, and so on. Yet, underlying these clearly defined assignments are procedures that are never written down but are worked out and understood by those who have to get the job done.

THE INFORMAL STRUCTURE

Sociologists recognize that formal associations never operate entirely according to their stated rules and procedures. Every association has an **informal structure** consisting of networks of people who help out one another by "bending" rules and taking procedural shortcuts. No matter how carefully plans are made, no matter how clearly and rationally roles are defined and tasks assigned, every situation and its variants cannot be anticipated. Sooner or later, then, individuals in associations are confronted with situations in which they must improvise and even persuade others to help them do so.

As every student knows, no school ever runs as smoothly as planned. For instance, "going by the book" — that is, following all the formal rules — often gets students tied up in long lines and red tape. Enterprising students and instructors find shortcuts. For example, a student who wants to change from Section A of Sociology 100 to Section E might find it very difficult or time-consuming to change sections ("add-and-drop") officially. However, it may be possible to work out an informal deal — the student stays registered in Section A but attends and is evaluated in Section E. The

associations Purposefully created special-interest groups that have clearly defined goals and official ways of doing things, such as government agencies.

informal structure The structure within an association that is made up of networks of people who help one another by "bending" rules and taking procedural shortcuts.

formal organizational structure The planned, highly institutionalized, and clearly defined statuses and role relationships that characterize associations.

instructor of Section E then turns the grade over to the instructor of Section A, who hands in that grade with all the other Section A grades—as if the student had attended Section A all along. The formal rules have been "bent," but the major purposes of the school (educating and evaluating students) have been served.

In addition, human beings have their own individual needs even when they are on "company time," and these needs are not always met by attending single-mindedly to assigned tasks. To accommodate these needs, people often try to find extra break time for personal business by getting jobs done faster than would be possible if all the formal rules and procedures were followed. To accomplish these ends, individuals in associations find it useful to help one another by "covering" for one another, "looking the other way" at strategic moments, and offering one another useful information about office politics, people, and procedures. Gradually, the reciprocal relationships among members of these informal networks become institutionalized: "unwritten laws" are established, and a fully functioning informal structure evolves (Selznick, 1948).

At the same time as the goals of associations have given rise to an informal structure for job performance, they have also spawned an organizational structure that often increases the formality of procedures. This formal organizational structure is called bureaucracy and has an impact on the informal structure.

ideal type A simplified, exaggerated model of reality used to illustrate a concept.

BUREAUCRACY

bureaucracy A formal, rationally organized social structure with clearly defined patterns of activity in which, ideally, every series of actions is fundamentally related to the organization's purpose.

Associations evolved along with literacy and the rise of cities some 5500 years ago, but **bureaucracy** emerged as the organizational counterpart of the Industrial Revolution only two centuries ago. Although in ordinary usage the term suggests a certain rigidity and red tape, it has a somewhat different meaning to sociologists. Robert K. Merton (1968) defined bureaucracy as "a formal, rationally organized social structure [with] clearly defined patterns of activity in which, ideally, every series of actions is functionally related to the purposes of the organization."

Max Weber, the German sociologist we introduced in Chapter 1, provided the first detailed study of the nature and origins of bureaucracy. Although much has changed in society since he developed his theories, Weber's basic description of bureaucracy remains essentially accurate to this day.

WEBER'S MODEL OF BUREAUCRACY: AN IDEAL TYPE

Weber viewed bureaucracy as the most efficient—although not necessarily the most desirable—form of social organization for the administration of work. He studied examples of bureaucracy in history and in contemporary times and noted the elements that they had in common. From this work he developed a model of bureaucracy, which is known as an **ideal type.** Weber believed it useful to accentuate or even exaggerate reality in certain situations in order to understand an idea better. An ideal type is just such an exaggeration. When Weber presented his ideal type of bureaucracy, he combined into one those characteristics that could be found in one form or another in a variety of organizations. It is unlikely that we ever would find a bureaucracy that has all the traits presented in Weber's ideal type. However, his presentation can help us understand what is involved in bureaucratic systems. It is also important to recognize that Weber's ideal type is in no way meant to be "ideal" in the sense that it presents a desired state of affairs. In short, an ideal type is an exaggeration of a situation that is used to convey a set of ideas. Weber outlined six characteristics of bureaucracies:

1. *A clear-cut division of labor.* The activities of a bureaucracy are broken down into clearly defined, limited tasks, which are attached to formally defined positions (statuses) in the organization. This permits a great deal of specialization and a high degree of expertise. For example, a small-town police department might consist of a chief, a lieutenant, a detective, several sergeants, and a dozen officers. The chief issues orders and assigns tasks; the lieutenant is in charge when the chief is not around; the detective does investigative work; the sergeants handle calls at the desk and do the paper work required for formal "booking" procedures; and the officers walk or drive through the community, making arrests and responding to emergencies. Each member of the department has a defined status and duty as well as specialized skills appropriate to his or her position.

2. *Hierarchical delegation of power and responsibility.* Each position in the bureaucracy is given sufficient power that the individual who occupies it can do assigned work adequately and also compel subordinates to follow instructions. Such power must be limited to what is necessary to meet the requirements of the position. For example, a police chief can order an officer to walk a specific beat but cannot insist that the officer join the Lions Club.

3. *Rules and regulations.* The rights and duties attached to various positions are clearly stated in writing and govern the behavior of all individuals who occupy them. That way, all members of the organizational structure know what is expected of them, and each person can be held accountable for his or her behavior. For example, the regulations of a police department might state, "No member of the department shall drink intoxicating liquors while on duty." Such rules make the activities of bureaucracies predictable and stable.

4. *Impartiality.* The organization's written rules and regulations apply equally to all its members. No exceptions are made because of social or psychological differences among individuals. Also, people occupy positions in the bureaucracy only because they are assigned according to formal procedures. These positions "belong to" the organization itself; they cannot become the personal property of those who occupy them. For example, a vice-president of United States Steel Corporation is usually not permitted to pass on that position to his or her children through inheritance.

5. *Employment based on technical qualifications.* People are hired because they have the ability and skills to do the job, not because they have personal contacts within the company. Advancement is based on how well a person does the job. Promotions and job security go to those who are most competent.

6. *Distinction between public and private spheres.* A clear distinction is made between the employees' personal lives and their working lives. It is unusual for employees to be expected to take business calls at home. At the same time, their family life has no place in the work setting.

Although many bureaucracies strive at the organizational level to attain the goals that Weber proposed, most do not achieve them on the practical level.

BUREAUCRACY TODAY: THE REALITY

Just as no building is ever identical with its blueprint, no bureaucratic organization fully embodies all the features of Weber's model. Studies of organizations around the world reveal that such elements as degree of hierarchical organization, adherence to rules and regulations, and job specialization vary widely — both between and within organizations (Udy, 1959; Hall, 1963–1964). One thing that most bureaucracies have in common is a structure that separates those

FIGURE 6.2

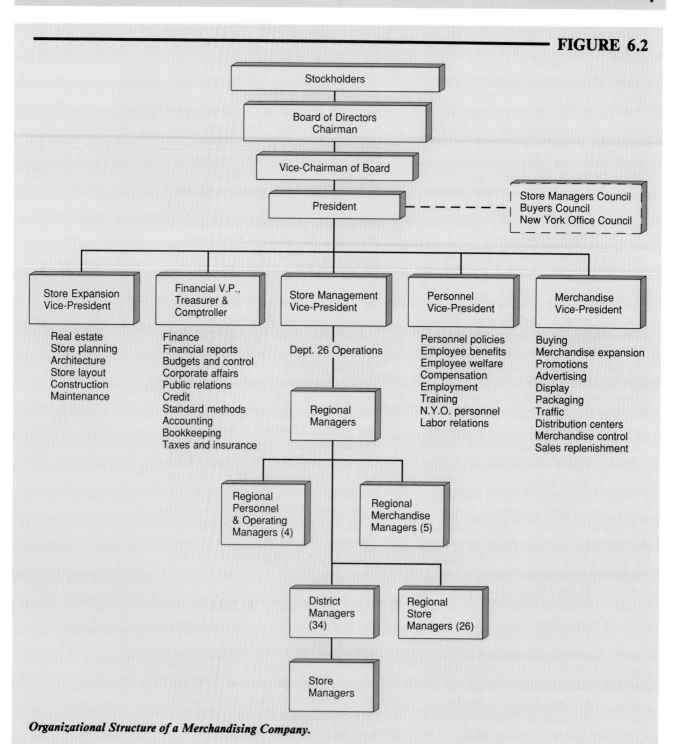

Stockholders

Board of Directors Chairman

Vice-Chairman of Board

President

Store Managers Council
Buyers Council
New York Office Council

Store Expansion Vice-President

Real estate
Store planning
Architecture
Store layout
Construction
Maintenance

Financial V.P., Treasurer & Comptroller

Finance
Financial reports
Budgets and control
Corporate affairs
Public relations
Credit
Standard methods
Accounting
Bookkeeping
Taxes and insurance

Store Management Vice-President

Dept. 26 Operations

Regional Managers

Personnel Vice-President

Personnel policies
Employee benefits
Employee welfare
Compensation
Employment
Training
N.Y.O. personnel
Labor relations

Merchandise Vice-President

Buying
Merchandise expansion
Promotions
Advertising
Display
Packaging
Traffic
Distribution centers
Merchandise control
Sales replenishment

Regional Personnel & Operating Managers (4)

Regional Merchandise Managers (5)

District Managers (34)

Regional Store Managers (26)

Store Managers

Organizational Structure of a Merchandising Company.

whose responsibilities include keeping in mind the overall needs of the entire organization from those whose responsibilities are much more narrow and task oriented. Visualize a modern industrial organization as a pyramid. Management (at the top of the pyramid) plans, organizes, hires, and fires. Workers (in the bottom section) make much smaller decisions limited to carrying out the work assigned to them. A similar division cuts through the hierarchy of the Roman Catholic church. The bishops are at the top, along with archbishops, cardinals, and the pope; the clergy are below. Only bishops can ordain new priests, and they plan the church's worldwide activities. The priests administer parishes, schools, and missions; their tasks are quite narrow and confined. Figure 6.2 illustrates the organizational structure of a large corporation.

Although employees of bureaucracies may enjoy the privileges of their position and guard them jealously, they may be adversely affected by the system in ways that they do not recognize. Alienation, adherence to unproductive ritual, and acceptance of incompetence are some of the results of a less-than-ideal bureaucracy.

Alienation

Job specialization may be efficient, but it also can have negative results. One of these is **alienation,** a term used by Karl Marx to describe the sense of loss and disconnectedness that is supposed to be present among workers in capitalistic societies. This comes about because automation and division of labor eliminate the pride and self-expression that workers would normally derive from the products of their labor (Marx, 1964). This type of alienation occurs among automobile assembly line workers who do the same task over and over again. The monotony and the lack of connection to a finished product makes it impossible for many to maintain interest in their work and in the quality of their workmanship. As a result,

Job specialization may be efficient, but the employees may lose sight of how their work contributes to the organization's or society's goals. Alienation from the work is always a real danger.

drinking or taking drugs on the job are common, and some workers even sabotage machinery and parts.

Alienation is common among the employees of bureaucracies in general. Their jobs may be so specialized that they have no real idea of how their work contributes to the organization's or society's goals. Indeed, for many employees the goals of the bureaucracy they work for (and its products) are quite unimportant; the security of having a job is all they seek. Such a lack of attachment to the work one does is likely to result in slipshod effort, and the low level of worker morale in many modern businesses seems to bear this out.

Ritualism

As Merton (1968) noted, bureaucracies may easily produce overconformity to rules—or what he calls **ritualism.** This re-

alienation A term used to describe the sense of dissociation that results from feelings of powerlessness and depersonalization, which are supposed to be present among workers in capitalistic societies.

ritualism Overconformity to rules produced by bureaucratic action.

sults from some of the basic properties of bureaucracy itself. For instance, bureaucracies demand strict adherence to rules in order to ensure reliability, but the rules may take on a symbolic meaning far beyond their original rational intent. When failure to follow rules exactly is seen as lack of loyalty to the organization, then rules may become absolute, and following them may become a required ritual. Inflexibility and inefficiency often result. For example, the receptionist who insists that certain forms be filled out before a patient can see the doctor, even though the patient is severely ill, may have lost sight of the relevance of this procedure to the case at hand.

Incompetence

In Weber's model of bureaucracy, workers are hired because they are technically competent, and it is the responsibility of supervisors to retrain, fire, or demote those workers who are incompetent. In reality, however, bureaucracies often are havens for the inept. There are a number of reasons for this, two of which occur quite often.

Laurence J. Peter and Raymond Hull (1969) popularized the notion of incompetence with what they called the "Peter Principle." In bureaucracies, they claimed, employees are promoted until they rise to their level of incompetence. In other words, because bureaucracies reward good work with advancement, employees keep rising up through the pyramid of authority until finally they reach a job for which they are not qualified. In theory, at least, this means that all positions in a bureaucracy will eventually be filled by individuals who are incompetent to perform what is required of them. This scenario rarely unfolds to its logical extreme, but the fact is that many unqualified persons manage to reach high job levels in bureaucracies, where they often try to hide their incompetence by becoming ritualistic devotees of rules and regulations (Blau and Meyer, 1971).

Protectionism

Because bureaucracies are concerned about their public images, they often are reluctant to admit to incompetence on the part of their employees. Even when inept employees do considerable damage, supervisors may hesitate to fire them for fear of looking bad themselves or of making their organization look bad to the public. Therefore bureaucracies often will protect incompetent employees in order to protect the bureaucracy from a "black eye." This results in a variety of problems: Many incompetent people are kept on in jobs they cannot handle; some are moved laterally to new jobs equally beyond their skills; and some even are promoted—sometimes with great fanfare—to a job at which they can do less harm (as a figurehead with no authority, for instance).

Bureaucracies also protect incompetent and unnecessary employees in order to maintain and increase their base of power. For example, while the number of teachers in the United States grew by 57 percent and the number of principals and supervisors by 79 percent between 1960 and 1984, the number of nonclassroom personnel skyrocketed by nearly 500 percent (*U.S. News & World Report,* April 27, 1988).

Warren Bennis (1971) also itemized the shortcomings of existing bureaucracies. These include, in somewhat modified form, the following:

1. Bureaucracy, by keeping employees in tightly defined jobs, does not adequately allow for personal growth.
2. It promotes excessive (even ritualistic) conformity and defensive avoidance (groupthink).
3. It does not build into its planned internal functioning the inevitable existence of an informal structure.
4. Its systems of control and authority are hopelessly outdated and rigid.
5. Communication is prevented, slowed, or distorted because of hierarchical divisions.

6. Innovative ideas originating from individuals who occupy low-authority positions are ignored.
7. Internal maneuverings for power distract participants in the organization from efficiently pursuing its goals.
8. Because high-level decision makers become entrenched in their positions, they prevent the organization from easily assimilating new technology or individuals with unconventional backgrounds that they do not understand.

BUREAUCRACY AND WORK IN JAPAN

In recent years it has become common to compare the situation of American and Japanese workers with respect to their positions in the typical work bureaucracy. Our attention has been drawn to the Japanese workplace because of the enormous strides the Japanese have made in the world economy. Currently, the output per hour of work in the United States is about 1 percent higher than it is in Japan and about 10 percent greater than it is in Western Europe (Stoner, 1982). However, our lead in this area has been steadily shrinking, and there has been some concern that we may soon lose out to the Japanese in this area (Capdevielle and Alverez, 1981).

The Japanese work environment is a reflection of a specific orientation toward groups and definitions of status and hierarchy within them. The Japanese view each individual as superior to, subordinate to, or (rarely) equal to another. Status within the system is established on the basis of age (older is superior), sex (male is superior), organizational status (higher rank is superior), and power and size of the organization one works for (larger and more powerful companies are superior). The concept of hierarchy pervades every aspect of the culture, even the language. It is impossible to speak with another person without recognizing his or her position over—or under—someone. This system promotes social stability and provides a frame of reference for relating to any other person.

One reason for the Japanese success in the organizational environment stems from apparent differences in the Japanese workplace. Those Japanese working for large corporations, which employ about 30 percent of the work force, operate within the concept of lifetime employment. These Japanese firms will hire young men with the expectation that they will be employed by the company until retirement. (Women are hired with the expectation that they will work for a few years, get married, and leave the company. They are expected to make the family the center of their life. Women thus do not benefit from the seniority system, get little in the way of fringe benefits, and are the first to be fired.) In effect, the Japanese male worker is pledging loyalty to the company and in return receives a permanent lifetime job, a far cry from the conflicts between American management and unions and the employment insecurity many American workers face.

In the United States the relationship between employer and employee is seen as a negotiated contract. The Japanese corporation is a miniature welfare state that offers a wide array of benefits and displays a concern for the needs of its workers. This causes the Japanese workers to identify with their employing company rather than with their profession. In contrast, the American workers identify with their profession and feel few qualms about switching from one employer to another to achieve personal advancement.

William Ouchi (1981) studied the Japanese organization and devised the "Theory Z" model of management, which many companies have attempted to apply in a modified way to the American workplace. According to Ouchi, Japanese organizations are effective because of (1) lifetime employment; (2) frequent performance reviews, which aid the worker in adjusting to the company's requirements; (3) a very high

Modern bureaucracies have an organizational structure that makes it clear to all members what rights and duties are attached to the various positions and what behavior is expected.

oligarchy Rule by a few individuals who occupy the highest positions in an organization.

level of cooperation between management and employees, as well as among the employees themselves; and (4) an interweaving of the workers' social and business lives. In effect, the Japanese corporation becomes an integral and continuing part of the workers' lives.

Many people are starting to doubt whether the Japanese system of lifetime employment will continue indefinitely. Should the Japanese economy turn sour for an extended period of time, the current system might be threatened. The Japanese corporation nonetheless offers us an example of how some of the negative aspects of bureaucracy can be avoided.

INDIVIDUAL VERSUS THE BUREAUCRACY: A MODERN DILEMMA

Modern society seems caught in a paradoxical dilemma. We need the efficiency of formal organizations and their ability to plan and organize the work of millions of individuals. Personal freedom and fulfillment, however, do not always fit easily into the realities of bureaucratized life. For one thing, the nature of bureaucratic structures is such that they tend to result in **oligarchy** —that is, rule by a few individuals who occupy the highest positions in an organization. To the extent that modern society is organized in terms of governmental and private bureaucracies, a danger exists that interlocking networks of oligarchies will run society, subject to little control by the public. Indeed, some scholars believe that this already has come to pass. C. Wright Mills, for example, argued in *The Power Elite* (1956) that in America the oligarchies that rule the nation's corporate, political, and military organizations are strongly interlinked and largely self-perpetuating. Even President Dwight D. Eisenhower, upon retiring from office in 1961, warned of the excessive and unchecked powers of the "military-industrial complex."

Another aspect of the problem of the individual and bureaucracy is how the bureaucratic social environment affects people. In essence, Weber's model tells us that bureaucracy increases in efficiency to the extent that it "depersonalizes" people and their social relationships (Bendix, 1962). Weber himself (1947) was troubled by this issue:

> It is horrible to think that the world could one day be filled with nothing but those little cogs, little men clinging to little jobs and striving towards bigger ones . . . playing an ever-increasing part in the spirit of our present administrative system. . . . This passion for bureaucracy . . . is enough to drive one to despair . . . it is such an evolution we are caught up in, and the great question is therefore not how we can promote and hasten it, but what we can oppose to this machinery in order to keep a portion of mankind free from this parcelling-out of the soul, from this supreme mastery of the bureaucratic way of life.

Robert Michels, a friend of Weber's, also was concerned about the depersonalizing effect of bureaucracy. His views, formulated at the beginning of this century, are still pertinent today.

THE IRON LAW OF OLIGARCHY

Michels (1911) came to the conclusion that the formal organization of bureaucracies inevitably leads to oligarchy, the condition discussed above, under which organizations that were originally idealistic and democratic eventually come to be dominated by a small self-serving group of people who achieved positions of power and responsibility. This can occur in large organizations because it becomes physically impossible for everyone to get together every time a decision has to be made. Consequently, a small group is given the responsibility of making decisions. Michels believed that the people in this group would become

enthralled with their elite positions and more and more inclined to make decisions that protect their power rather than represent the will of the group they are supposed to serve. In effect, Michels was saying that bureaucracy and democracy do not mix. Despite any protestations and promises that they will not become like all the rest, those placed in positions of responsibility and power often come to believe that they are indispensable to, and more knowledgeable than, those they serve. As time goes on, they become further removed from the rank and file.

This may have occurred during the Iran-contra scandal of 1987–1988 when Oliver North, John Poindexter, and other members of the National Security Council were accused of illegally selling arms to Iran and diverting the profits to the Nicaraguan contras. They were accused of doing this despite laws prohibiting such actions and without the consent of the president or Congress.

The Iron Law of Oligarchy suggests that organizations that wish to avoid oligarchy should take precautionary steps. They should make sure that the rank and file remain active in the organization and that the leaders not be granted absolute control of a centralized administration. As long as there are open lines of communication and shared decision making between the leaders and the rank and file, an oligarchy cannot easily develop.

Clearly, the problems of oligarchy, the bureaucratic depersonalization described by Weber, and personal alienation are all interrelated. If individuals are deprived of the power to make decisions that affect their lives in many or even most of the areas that are important to them, withdrawal into narrow ritualism and apathy are likely responses. Such withdrawals seem to constitute a chronic condition in some of the highly centralized socialist countries, especially those of Eastern Europe. However, there are many signs of public apathy in the United States, too. For example, in 1964

Can a Case Be Made for Bureaucracy?

Mass media depictions of bureaucracy display a surprisingly uniform picture. Writers, cartoonists, and commentators of every shade of opinion seem to share a common consensus on this "evil" worldwide phenomenon.

The bureaucrat is inevitably depicted as lazy or snarling, or both. The office occupied by this sow feeding at the public trough is bungling or inhumane, or both. The overall department is portrayed as overstaffed, inflexible, unresponsive, and power-hungry, all at once.

Here are a few examples of the excesses of bureaucracies taken from recent news reports:

- Several years ago, federal government officials put together a 700-page document outlining standards for a "rodent elimination device"—usually referred to as a mousetrap.
- A Chicago woman undergoing medical treatment applied for Medicare. She received a computer-printed letter informing her that she was ineligible because she had died the previous April.
- The Department of Energy set out to declassify millions of documents inherited from the Atomic Energy Commission. Eight of the released documents contained the basic design principles for the hydrogen bomb.
- A unit of what is now the Department of Health and Human Services sent fifteen chimpanzees to a Texas laboratory to start a chimp-breeding program. All were males.
- In New York City, fire department scuba divers were prevented from searching for survivors of a helicopter crash in the East River by police commanders in charge of the rescue missión. The reason: a bitter bureaucratic rivalry between the two uniformed forces that had little to do with public safety. One man died who might have been saved had divers found him sooner.

In each of these examples, it appears that the ultimate goal of serving the community is lost in a tangle of rules, regulations, and incompetence.

Is it possible to make any sort of case in defense of bureaucracy? Yes, says Charles T. Goodsell, an expert on bureaucracy, who has

about 70 percent of those eligible to vote for president did so. In each of the succeeding national elections this figure has dropped, and in 1988 it was 50 percent.

BUREAUCRACY AND THE FUTURE

In addition to the problems with bureaucracies already discussed, there is another difficulty that has implications for the future of bureaucratic organizations—the way that the structure prevents quick decision making. The bureaucratic gap that separates long-range planners of top-level management from short-range decision-making workers is a serious problem. Top-down decision making often becomes less and less workable.

Warren Bennis (1971) expressed this point of view clearly:

It is my premise that the bureaucratic form of organization is becoming less and less effective; that it is hopelessly out of joint with contemporary realities; that new shapes, patterns, and models are emerging which promise drastic changes in the conduct of . . . managerial practices in general.

written an entire book doing just that.

First, he points out, we should notice that most bureaucratic horror stories are usually short (we presented five here). They stress the citizen's anguish and the incident's adverse effects. Little information is given about the bureaucracy's side of the story.

Second, he says, the cases described are usually bizarre, reinforce stereotypes, and strike a responsive chord. Anyone old enough to read this has experienced incidents in which officials have acted in a baffling and frustrating way. So it is little wonder we can personally relate to bureaucratic horror stories.

But be honest. How can *all* bureaucracies be inefficient, secretive, rigid, oppressive, undemocratic, alienating, and discriminatory *all* the time?

Goodsell notes that, contrary to popular images, the majority of ordinary citizens, when asked to rate their experiences with specific bureaucracies, find them to be "satisfactory" or "acceptable."

The "bureaucrat mentality" also seems to disappear when researchers look for it. Bureaucrats tend to be just like the general population in all respects. Small wonder. Some probably live next door to you.

The low-prestige image of the bureaucrat is most common among upper-middle-class Americans. Could it be that the antibureaucracy sentiment is an elitist bias?

Critics of bureaucracies too often assume that the dissatisfaction voiced by some indicates widespread disapproval. But this is not necessarily true. Goodsell argues that most people are quite satisfied with present bureaucracies and are reluctant to press for change that may, at best, benefit a relative few.

Bureaucracy is often presented as an alien force—"us" against "them." Actually, bureaucracy is very much a part of us. It is every public institution operating in our community: the staff at our children's schools, the officials who run our towns. It is collective action on our behalf. In a very real sense, *we* are bureaucracy.

Source: Charles T. Goodsell, *The Case for Bureaucracy,* 2d ed. (Chatham, N.J.: Chatham House Publishers, Inc., 1985).

The rapid rise of new businesses at the forefront of computer technology seems to support Bennis's views. The most successful appear to be outpacing the older, more established companies by doing away with rigid hierarchical structures. They are also developing new organizational forms featuring interlocking work and planning groups that allow for flexibility in assimilating new information and planning (or changing decisions and rearranging priorities) quickly.

Rosabeth Moss Kanter (1986) agrees with Bennis. She notes that many older companies may recognize the need for innovation as a matter of corporate survival, but because they are tradition-bound do not know how to go about getting it. They have become so used to avoiding risk that they have difficulty encouraging experimentation. Top-down decision making makes it difficult for the levels below to contribute new ideas.

How will bureaucracies change to meet the challenges of the future? Much depends on how the rest of society changes, of course (a topic we shall explore in the final section of this book). One of the problems that must be addressed is the issue of individual freedom in the new organizations. Flexible, creative groupings are likely to emerge in jobs dominated by well-educated professionals. No amount of technological change, however, will alter the fact that in the foreseeable future, semiskilled individuals performing routine tasks will remain a necessary element in the organization of work. Will these people be included in the flexible planning and decision-making groups? Or will the horizontal slash through the organizational pyramid simply have been moved down-

ward a bit, which would allow greater numbers of well-educated managers at the top but cut off and isolate more than ever the less skilled workers on whose shoulders the entire structure ultimately must rest? These are some of the questions that we must face today. Sociologists are still working to find answers. After they come up with some suggested solutions, they will then have to deal with the problem of convincing bureaucrats to try them.

SUMMARY

A social group consists of two or more individuals who interact over a period of time according to some pattern of social organization and who recognize that they constitute a social unit. A social group differs from a statistical category, which consists of people classified together because they share certain characteristics. If people are merely aware of one another, it is not enough to make them a social group.

Sociologists distinguish between primary and secondary groups, in-groups and out-groups, small groups and large groups. All groups must define their boundaries, assign leadership, make decisions, set goals, assign tasks, and control their members' behavior.

A reference group sets and enforces standards of behavior and belief and provides a comparison point against which persons measure themselves and others.

Small groups are social groups such as families, peer groups, and work groups that actually meet together and contain few enough members so that all know one another. The smallest group, called a dyad, contains only two people. Adding a third member to such a group transforms it into a triad. Sociologists study small groups because such groups can have an impact on the course of history, and because they present a microcosm of society and lend

themselves to laboratory experiments. One aspect of small groups that is of interest to sociologists is the influence that group members have on one another. The cohesiveness that develops among group members can determine the success of the group as a whole. The goal of network analysis is to explain the complicated interactions people have with each other.

In contrast with small groups, associations have clearly defined goals and official ways of doing things. Jobs in associations are broken down into manageable tasks that are assigned to specific individuals.

Associations never operate entirely according to their formal organizational structure. Rather, they contain an informal structure consisting of networks of people who help out one another and take procedural shortcuts.

The most common form of large association in contemporary society is the bureaucracy. A bureaucracy is a social structure that is organized according to rules for actions; all actions are related to the purpose of the organization. Max Weber described an ideal type of bureaucracy in which there would be a clear-cut division of labor, a delegation of power and responsibility based on hierarchy, a written set of rules and regulations, an impartial system of assignment and promotion, a system of advancement based on ability and skills, and a clear distinction between employees' personal and business lives.

Although society needs the efficiency of associations in order to provide goods and services for millions of individuals, the rigidity of bureaucracy often curtails personal freedom and fulfillment. Individuals frequently suffer from alienation, tend to adhere to unproductive ritual in performing their tasks, and often are willing to accept and protect the incompetent. The nature of bureaucratic structures is such that they tend to result in oligarchy—rule by a few individuals who occupy the highest positions in an organization and make decisions without regard for, or communication with, the rank and file. When individuals are deprived of the power to make decisions that affect their lives, they tend to withdraw into ritualism and apathy.

Chapter 7

DEVIANT BEHAVIOR

The dunes of lower Cape Cod are one of the most beautiful sights in the world. Shaped by winds and tides, they tower over the white sands of the Atlantic Ocean. A pleasant area of the beach known as "Brush Hollow" is in the town of Truro. For generations this area has marked the location of a nude beach where bathers could feel free to discard their suits. Small groups of nude bathers would congregate at discrete distances from one another. When a bathing-suited wanderer strolled through the area, beach etiquette required that he or she pretend not to notice that the others were sunning themselves in the altogether.

In the 1970s the nude beach gained notoriety and an influx of nude bathers and gawkers produced a major problem for the town. A shuttle bus transported the curious between the town center and the beach, and a carnival atmosphere developed. Eventually the town of Truro put a total ban on nude bathing and Brush Hollow's unusual distinction disappeared. (Dershowitz, 1982).

Most of us would agree that appearing nude in public is an example of deviant behavior. Applying the concept of deviant behavior to the nude bathing at Brush Hollow presents some interesting issues though. Were the original visitors to this little publicized area going against the norm when they shed their bathing suits? How about the later visitors who paraded in the buff in the more boisterous atmosphere after the publicity? Would you have joined in the merri-

Sociologists believe that deviant behavior fails to conform to the norms of the group. This man has no shirt on and is lying on the sidewalk in the middle of the winter. Would this behavior conform to the standards of any group?

DEVIANT BEHAVIOR AND CULTURAL NORMS

In the United States, a mayor of a city who insures that whites and blacks have equal access to the city's beaches would be acting properly and legally. Not so in South Africa, where the mayor of Durban, Henry Klotz, found himself an outcast from President P. W. Botha's National party for not endorsing a beach segregation plan. In May 1988, Mayor Klotz's party colleagues on the city council reserved two of Durban's most attractive beaches for whites only. Mayor Klotz refused to support this segregation plan and was suspended for "acting disloyally and contrary to the interests" of the party. Declaring that he was "duty bound to act in the interests of all the citizens," the mayor resigned *(Time,* June 13, 1988).

ment? If we claim that none of this is deviant, why did the town find it necessary to ban the practice?

Every day we must make decisions about proper and improper behavior. However, if you were asked how you determine what is right and wrong, you might have to spend some time thinking about the answer. One way of addressing the question is with the law: What is legal is right; what is illegal is wrong. For example, nude sunbathing was all right until it was outlawed. Most of our behavior is not governed by law though. How do you know it is right to help a handicapped person cross a busy street? No law compels you to do it. How do you know it is wrong to be rude and discourteous? You would not get arrested for it.

We have many rules by which we live. Some are enforced by law; most are not. This chapter will explore these rules, the reasons for them, the ways in which we learn them, and the causes and effects of their violation.

DEFINING NORMAL AND DEVIANT BEHAVIOR

What makes segregated beaches wrong in America but acceptable in South Africa? Why will two men walking hand-in-hand in downtown Minneapolis cause raised eyebrows but pass unnoticed in San Francisco or in Provincetown, Massachusetts? Why do Britons who are waiting to enter a theater stand patiently in line, whereas people from the Middle East jam together at the turnstile? In other words, what makes a given action — supporting segregation, men holding hands, cutting into a line — "normal" in one case but "deviant" in another?

The answer is culture — more specifically, the norms and values of each culture (see Chapter 3). Together, norms and values make up the **moral code** of a culture — the symbolic system in terms of which behavior takes on the quality of being "good" or "bad," "right" or "wrong." Therefore, to decide whether any specific act is "normal"

moral code The symbolic system, made up of a culture's norms and values, in terms of which behavior takes on the quality of being "good" or "bad," "right" or "wrong."

IS DRUNK DRIVING DEVIANT BEHAVIOR?

Many people do not think of drunk driving as deviant behavior, let alone a serious crime. In 1986 there was one arrest for drunk driving for every 88 licensed drivers in the United States. The National Highway Traffic Safety Administration estimates that perhaps as many as a quarter of a million people were killed in alcohol-related car crashes over the last 10 years. The cost in property damage, medical costs, and other costs of drunk driving may total more than $24 billion a year.

Source: Lawrence A. Greenfeld, "Drunk Driving," *Bureau of Justice Statistics Special Report* (Washington, D.C.: U.S. Department of Justice, February 1988).

---

or "deviant," it is necessary to know more than only *what* a person did. One also must know who the person is (that is, the person's social identity) and the social and cultural context of the act.

For sociologists, then, **normal behavior** is behavior that conforms to the rules or norms of the group in which it occurs. **Deviant behavior** is behavior that fails to conform to the rules or norms of the group (Durkheim, 1960a). Therefore, when we try to assess an act as being normal or deviant, we must identify the group in whose terms the behavior is being judged. Moral codes differ widely from one society to another.

For example, there is great variation among societies in their definition of punishable sexual behavior. For that matter, even within a society there exist groups and subcultures whose moral codes differ considerably. Watching television is normal behavior for most Americans, but it would be seen as deviant behavior among the Amish of Pennsylvania.

MAKING MORAL JUDGMENTS

In earlier chapters we stated that sociologists take a culturally relative view of nor-

normal behavior Behavior that conforms to the rules or norms of the group in which it occurs.

deviant behavior Behavior that fails to conform to the rules or norms of the group in which it occurs.

What forms of dress and what types of behavior are considered deviant depends on who is doing the judging and what the context might be.

189

malcy and deviance. That is, they evaluate behavior according to the values of the culture in which it takes place. Ideally, they do not use their own values to judge the behavior of people from other cultures.

Even though social scientists recognize that there is great variation in normal and deviant behavior and that no science can determine what acts are inherently deviant, there are certain acts that are almost universally accepted as being deviant. For example, parent–child incest is severely disapproved of in nearly every society. Genocide, the willful killing of specific groups of people—as occurred in the Nazi extermination camps during World War II—also is considered to be wrong, even if it is sanctioned by the government or an entire society. The Nuremberg trials that were conducted after World War II made this point. Even though most of the accused individuals claimed they were merely following orders when they murdered or arranged for the murder of large numbers of people, many were found guilty. The reasoning was that there is a higher moral order under which certain human actions are wrong, regardless of who endorses them. Thus, de-

spite their desire to view events from a culturally relative standpoint, sociologists and others find certain actions wrong, no matter what the context.

THE FUNCTIONS OF DEVIANCE

Émile Durkheim observed that deviant behavior is "an integral part of all healthy societies" (1895, 1958). Why is this the case? The answer, Durkheim suggested, is that in the presence of deviant behavior, a social group becomes united in its response. In other words, deviant behavior creates opportunities for groups to unite, a process that is necessary to promote the cooperation essential to the survival of any group. For example, let us look at the response to a scandal in a small town as Durkheim (1895) described it:

> [People] stop each other on the street, they visit each other, they seek to come together to talk of the event and to wax indignant in common. From all the similar impressions which are exchanged, from all the temper that gets itself

In this photo from France at the end of World War II, the woman whose head has been shaven is jeered by the crowd as she is escorted out of town. She had been a Nazi collaborator during the war. Durkheim believed that deviant behavior performs an important function by focusing people's attention on the values of the group. The deviance represents a threat to the group and forces it to protect itself and preserve its existence.

expressed, there emerges a unique temper . . . which is everybody's without being anybody's in particular. That is the public temper.

When social life moves along normally, people begin to take for granted one another and the meaning of their social interdependency. A deviant act, however, reawakens their group attachments and loyalties, because it represents a threat to the moral order of the group. The deviant act focuses people's attention on the value of the group to them. Perceiving itself under pressure, the group marshals its forces to protect itself and preserve its existence.

It appears, as Kai T. Erikson (1966) found, that "unless the rhythm of group life is punctuated by occasional moments of deviant behavior . . . social organization . . . [is] impossible." For example, when crack dealers were invading the streets around northeast Washington, D.C.'s Mayfair Mansions, groups of Black Muslims stepped in to enforce the law where police had failed. In a section of Brooklyn, New York, community involvement has returned the neighborhood to the people by virtually eliminating drug dealers from the area. Deviant behavior, then, performs important social functions in promoting group unity and reinforcing group structure and organization.

Deviance also offers society's members an opportunity to rededicate themselves to their social controls. In some cases, deviant behavior actually helps teach society's rules by providing illustrations of violation. Knowing what is wrong is a step toward understanding what is right.

Deviance, then, may be functional to a group in that it (1) causes the group's members to close ranks, (2) prompts the group to organize in order to limit future deviant acts, (3) helps clarify for the group what it really does believe in, (4) teaches normal behavior by providing examples of rule violation. In addition, in some situations tolerance of deviant behavior acts as a safety valve and actually prevents more serious instances of nonconformity. For example, the Amish, a religious group that does not believe in using such "modern" examples of contemporary society as cars, radios, televisions, and fashion-oriented clothing, allow their teenagers a great deal of latitude in their behaviors before they are fully required to follow the dictates of the community. This prevents a confrontation that could result in a major battle of wills.

THE DYSFUNCTIONS OF DEVIANCE

Deviance, of course, has several dysfunctions, which is why every society attempts to restrain deviant behavior as much as possible. Included among the dysfunctions of deviant behavior are the following: (1) It is a threat to the social order, because it makes social life difficult and unpredictable. (2) In the process it causes confusion about the norms and values of that society. People become confused about what is expected, and what is right and wrong. The various social moralities compete with one another causing tension among the different segments of society. (3) Deviance also undermines trust. Social relationships are based on the premise that people will behave according to certain rules of conduct. When people's actions become unpredictable, the social order is thrown into disarray. (4) Deviance also diverts valuable resources. To control widespread deviance, society must call on vast resources and divert them from other social needs.

MECHANISMS OF SOCIAL CONTROL

In any society or social group it is necessary to have means for molding or influencing members' behavior to conform to the group's values and norms. These processes

TABLE 7.1

Severity Score and Offense

72.1 — Planting a bomb in a public building. The bomb explodes and 20 people are killed.

52.8 — A man forcibly rapes a woman. As a result of physical injuries, she dies.

43.2 — Robbing a victim at gunpoint. The victim struggles and is shot to death.

39.2 — A man stabs his wife. As a result, she dies.

39.1 — A factory knowingly gets rid of its waste in a way that pollutes the water supply of a city. As a result, 20 people die.

35.7 — Stabbing a victim to death.

33.8 — Running a narcotics ring.

27.9 — A woman stabs her husband. As a result, he dies.

26.3 — An armed person skyjacks an airplane and demands to be flown to another country.

25.9 — A man forcibly rapes a woman. No other physical injury occurs.

24.9 — Intentionally setting fire to a building causing $100,000 worth of damage.

22.9 — A parent beats his young child with his fists. The child requires hospitalization.

21.2 — Kidnapping a victim.

20.6 — Selling heroin to others for resale.

19.5 — Smuggling heroin into the country.

19.5 — Killing a victim by recklessly driving an automobile.

17.9 — Robbing a victim of $10 at gunpoint. The victim is wounded and requires hospitalization.

16.9 — A man drags a woman into an alley, tears her clothes, but flees before she is physically harmed or sexually attacked.

16.4 — Attempting to kill a victim with a gun. The gun misfires and the victim escapes unharmed.

15.9 — A teenage boy beats his mother with his fists. The mother requires hospitalization.

15.5 — Breaking into a bank at night and stealing $100,000.

14.1 — A doctor cheats on claims he makes to a federal health insurance plan for patient services.

13.9 — A legislator takes a bribe from a company to vote for a law favoring the company.

13.0 — A factory knowingly gets rid of its wastes in a way that pollutes the water supply of a city.

12.2 — Paying a witness to give false testimony in a criminal trial.

12.0 — A police officer takes a bribe not to interfere with an illegal gambling operation.

11.4 — Knowingly lying under oath during a trial.

11.2 — A company pays a bribe to a legislator to vote for a law favoring the company.

10.9 — Stealing property worth $10,000 from outside a building.

10.5 — Smuggling marijuana into the country for resale.

10.3 — Operating a store that knowingly sells stolen property.

9.6 — Breaking into a home and stealing $1,000.

8.5 — Selling marijuana to others for resale.

8.5 — Intentionally injuring a victim. The victim is treated by a doctor but is not hospitalized.

7.9 — A teenage boy beats his father with his fists. The father requires hospitalization.

7.5 — A person, armed with a lead pipe, robs a victim of $10. No physical harm occurs.

7.4 — Illegally getting monthly welfare checks.

7.2 — Signing someone else's name to a check and cashing it.

6.5 — Using heroin.

6.4 — An employer refuses to hire a qualified person because of that person's race.

6.4 — Getting customers for a prostitute.

6.2 — An employee embezzles $1,000 from his employer.

4.9 — Snatching a handbag containing $10 from a victim on the street.

4.7 — A man exposes himself in public.

4.5 — Cheating on federal income tax return.

4.4 — Picking a victim's pocket of $100.

3.8 — Turning in a false fire alarm.

2.2 — Stealing $10 worth of merchandise from the counter of a department store.

2.1 — A woman engages in prostitution.

1.9 — Making an obscene phone call.

1.6 — Being a customer in a house of prostitution.

1.6 — A male, over 16 years of age, has sexual relations with a willing female under 16.

1.4 — Smoking marijuana.

1.3 — Two persons willingly engage in a homosexual act.

1.1 — Disturbing the neighborhood with loud, noisy behavior.

0.8 — A youngster under 16 years old runs away from home.

0.8 — Being drunk in public.

0.2 — A youngster under 16 years old plays hooky from school.

Source: Marvin E. Wolfgang, Robert M. Figlio, Paul E. Tracy, Simon I. Singer, *The National Survey of Crime Severity*, U.S. Department of Justice, Bureau of Justice Statistics (Washington, D.C.: U.S. Government Printing Office, June 1985), pp. vi–x.

are referred to as **mechanisms of social control,** and sociologists distinguish between internal and external means of control.

INTERNAL MEANS OF CONTROL

As we already observed in Chapters 3 and 5, people are socialized to accept the norms and values of their culture, especially in the context of the smaller and more personally important social groups to which they belong, such as the family. The word *accept* is important here. Individuals conform to moral codes not just by *knowing* what they are but also by *experiencing* discomfort, often in the form of guilt, when they violate those codes. These guilt feelings arise from the anxiety, restlessness, tension, and self-

Even though shoplifting is a crime, most Americans do not rank it very seriously when they are asked to judge the severity of various offenses.

depreciation that are aroused in an individual who engages in behavior that violates internalized norms. In other words, a group's moral code must be internalized and become part of each individual's emotional life as well as his or her thought processes. As this occurs, individuals begin to pass judgment on their own actions. Hence, the moral code of a culture becomes an **internal means of control** — that is, it operates on the individual even in the absence of reactions by others.

For example, we can see the American moral code at work in the study presented in Table 7.1. This study, known as the National Survey of Crime Severity (NSCS), described 204 illegal events, from a 16-year-old playing hooky from school, to planting a bomb that killed twenty people in a public building. The survey used a nationwide sample and was the largest measure ever made of how the public ranks the seriousness of specific kinds of offenses.

The overall pattern of severity scores indicates that people clearly regard violent crimes as more serious than property crimes. They also view white-collar crime and drug dealing quite seriously, rating two offenses of this type higher than some forms of homicide. One of the highest scores (39.1) is awarded to a factory that causes the death of twenty people by knowingly polluting the city water supply. Running a narcotics ring is regarded more seriously (33.8) than a woman stabbing her husband to death (27.9).

In general, people tend to agree about the severity of specific crimes. A few differences appear, however, when the scores of different groups are examined. For example, blacks and members of other racial minorities in general assign lower scores than whites. The elderly found thefts of large amounts of money to be more serious than did people in younger age brackets. Men and women, however, did not differ in any significant way in their overall scoring pattern. As might be expected, victims assign higher scores than nonvictims of crime (Wolfgang, Figlio, Tracy, and Singer, 1985).

mechanisms of social control Processes used by all societies and social groups to influence or mold members' behavior to conform to group values and norms.

internal means of social control A group's moral code becomes internalized and becomes part of each individual's personal code of conduct that operates even in the absence of reactions by others.

EXTERNAL MEANS OF CONTROL: SANCTIONS

external means of social control The ways in which others respond to a person's behavior that channel his or her behavior along culturally approved lines.

External means of social control are the ways in which others respond to a person's behavior — rewarding or encouraging some kinds, punishing or discouraging others. They are social forces external to the individual that channel his or her behavior into those forms that most closely approximate the culture's norms and values.

sanctions Rewards and penalties used to regulate an individual's behavior. All external means of control use sanctions.

Sanctions are rewards and penalties by a group's members that are used to regulate an individual's behavior. Thus, all external means of control use sanctions of one kind or another. When the responses encourage the individual to continue acting in a certain way, they are called **positive sanctions.** When the responses discourage the repetition or continuation of the behavior, they are **negative sanctions.**

positive sanctions Responses by others that encourage the individual to continue acting in a certain way.

Positive and Negative Sanctions

negative sanctions Responses by others that discourage the individual from continuing or repeating the behavior.

Sanctions take many forms, which vary widely from group to group and from society to society. For example, an American audience might clap and whistle enthusiastically to show its appreciation for an excellent artistic or athletic performance, but the same whistling in Europe would be a display of strong disapproval. Or consider the *absence* of a response. In America a professor would not infer public disapproval from the absence of applause at the end of a lecture — such applause by students is the rarest of compliments. In many universities in Europe, however, students are expected to applaud after every lecture (if only in a rhythmic, stylized manner). The absence of such applause would be a horrible blow to the professor, a public criticism of the presentation.

Besides their expression in behavior, most social sanctions have a symbolic side as well. Such symbolism makes sanctions quite powerful because people's self-esteem and sense of identity are strongly affected by the symbols. Imagine the positive feelings experienced by Olympic gold medalists or those elected to Phi Beta Kappa, the national society honoring excellence in undergraduate study. Or consider the negative experience of being given the "silent treatment," such as that imposed on cadets who violate the honor code at the military academy at West Point. (To some this is so painful that they drop out.)

Sanctions often have important material qualities as well as symbolic meanings. Nobel Prize winners receive not only public acclaim but also a hefty check ($362,000 in 1988). The threat of loss of employment may accompany public disgrace when an individual's deviant behavior becomes known. In isolated, preliterate societies, social ostracism can be the equivalent of a death sentence.

Both positive and negative sanctions work only to the degree that people can be reasonably sure that they will be applied as a consequence of a given act. In other words, they work on people's expectations. Whenever such expectations are not met, sanctions lose their ability to mold social conformity.

On the other hand, it is important to recognize a crucial difference between positive and negative sanctions. When society applies a positive sanction, it is a sign that social controls are successful: The desired behavior has occurred and is being rewarded. When a negative sanction is applied, it is a result of the failure of social controls: The undesired behavior has not been prevented. Therefore, a society that frequently must punish people is failing in its attempts to promote conformity. A school that must expel large groups of students or a government that must frequently call out troops to quell protests and riots should begin to look for the weaknesses in its own system of internal means of social control to promote conformity.

Formal and Informal Sanctions

Some sanctions are applied in a public ritual, as in the awarding of a prize or an announcement of expulsion. Such responses to actions are called **formal sanctions** and usually are under the direct or indirect leadership of social authorities. Not all sanctions are formal, however. Many social responses to a person's behavior involve actions by group members that arise spontaneously with little or no formal leadership. These responses are called **informal sanctions**. Gossip is an informal sanction that is used universally. Congratulations are offered to people whose behavior is being encouraged. In teenage peer groups, ridicule is a powerful, informal, negative sanction. In contemporary American society, informal sanctions influence us while we are in our own groups. The anonymity and impersonality of urban living, however, decreases the influence of these controls when we are outside the surveillance of members of our friendship and kinship groups. We usually are not under continuous observation by those on whom we are dependent for survival.

A Typology of Sanctions

Figure 7.1 shows the four main types of social sanctions, defined by combining the two sets of sanctions we have just discussed: formal and informal, positive and negative. Although formal sanctions might appear to be stronger influences on behavior, it is actually the informal sanctions that have a greater impact on people's self-images and

informal sanctions Responses by others to an individual's behavior that arise spontaneously with little or no formal leadership.

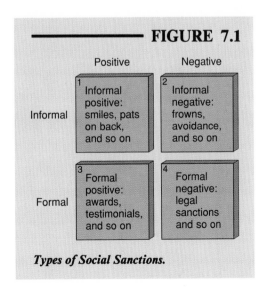

─────────── **FIGURE 7.1**

	Positive	Negative
Informal	1 Informal positive: smiles, pats on back, and so on	2 Informal negative: frowns, avoidance, and so on
Formal	3 Formal positive: awards, testimonials, and so on	4 Formal negative: legal sanctions and so on

Types of Social Sanctions.

formal sanctions Sanctions that are applied in a public ritual, usually under the direct or indirect leadership of social authorities. Examples: the award of a prize or the announcement of an expulsion.

informal positive sanctions Spontaneous actions such as smiles, pats on the back, handshakes, congratulations, and hugs through which individuals express their approval of another's behavior.

informal negative sanctions Spontaneous displays of disapproval of a person's behavior. Impolite treatment is directed toward the violator of a group norm.

formal positive sanctions Actions that express social approval of a person's behavior, such as public gatherings, rituals, or ceremonies.

formal negative sanctions Actions that express institutionalized disapproval of a person's behavior, such as expulsion, dismissal, or imprisonment. They are usually applied within the context of a society's formal organizations, including schools, corporations, and the legal system.

future behavior. This is because informal sanctions usually occur more frequently and come from close, respected associates.

1. **Informal positive sanctions** are smiles, pats on the back, handshakes, congratulations, hugs, and all other actions through which individuals spontaneously express their approval of another's behavior.
2. **Informal negative sanctions** are spontaneous displays of disapproval or displeasure, such as frowns, damaging gossip, or impolite treatment directed toward the violator of a group norm.
3. **Formal positive sanctions** are public affairs, rituals, or ceremonies that express social approval of a person's behavior. These occasions are planned and organized. In our society they include such events as tickertape parades for national heroes, the presentation of awards or degrees, and public declarations of respect or appreciation (sports banquets, for example). Awards of money are also a form of formal positive sanctions.
4. **Formal negative sanctions** are actions that express institutionalized disap-

proval of a person's behavior. They usually are applied within the context of a society's formal organizations— schools, corporations, the legal system, for example—and include expulsion, dismissal, fines, and imprisonment. They flow directly from decisions made by a person or agency of authority, and frequently there are specialized agencies or personnel (such as a board of directors, a government agency, or a police force) to enforce them.

THEORIES OF DEVIANCE

Criminal and deviant behavior has been found throughout history. It has been so troublesome and so persistent that much effort has been devoted to understanding its roots. Many dubious ideas and theories have been developed over the ages. For example, a medieval law specified that "if two persons fell under suspicion of crime the uglier or more deformed was to be regarded as more probably guilty" (Wilson and

There are two types of positive sanctions. The academy award is a formal one, while a hug or pat on the back is an informal one.

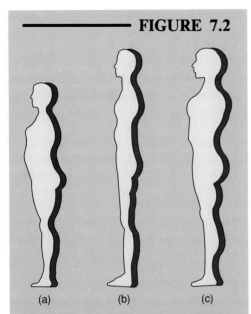

FIGURE 7.2

(a)   (b)   (c)

Sheldon's Body Types   William Sheldon identified three basic body types. (a) Endomorph: soft, round, and fat. (b) Ectomorph: skinny, fragile, and with a sensitive nervous system. (c) Mesomorph: muscular, agile, and physically strong. Sheldon believed mesomorphs were more inclined toward criminal behavior than the other two types, but subsequent research has cast considerable doubt on this conclusion.

Herrnstein, 1985). Modern-day approaches to deviant and criminal behavior can be divided into the general categories of biological, psychological, and sociological explanations.

BIOLOGICAL THEORIES OF DEVIANCE

The first attempts to provide "scientific" explanations for deviant and criminal behavior centered around the importance of inherited factors and downplayed the importance of environmental influences. From this point of view, deviant individuals are born, not made.

Cesare Lombroso (1835 – 1901) was an Italian doctor who believed that too much emphasis was being put on "free will" as an explanation for deviant behavior. While trying to discover the anatomical differences between deviant and insane men, he came upon what he believed was an important insight. As he was examining the skull of a criminal, he noticed a series of features recalling an apish past rather than a human present:

> At the sight of that skull, I seemed to see all of a sudden, lighted up as a vast plain under a flaming sky, the problem of the nature of the criminal—an atavistic being who reproduces in his person the ferocious instincts of primitive humanity and the inferior animals. (Taylor et al., 1973)

According to Lombroso, criminals were evolutionary throwbacks whose behavior is more apelike than human. They are driven by their instincts to engage in deviant behavior. These people can be identified by certain physical signs that betray their savage nature. Lombroso spent much of his life studying and dissecting dead prisoners in Italy's jails and concluded that their criminality was associated with an animal-like body type that revealed an inherited "primitiveness" (Lombroso-Ferrero, 1972). He also believed that certain criminal types could be identified by their head size, facial characteristics (size and shape of the nose, for instance), and even hair color. His writings were met with heated criticism from scholars who pointed out that perfectly normal-looking people have committed violent acts. (Modern social scientists would add that by confining his research to the study of prison inmates, Lombroso used a biased sample, thereby limiting the validity of his investigations.)

In this century, William H. Sheldon and his coworkers carried out body measurements of thousands of subjects to determine whether personality traits are associated with particular body types. They found that human shapes could be classified as three particular types (see Figure 7.2):

endomorphic (round and soft), *ectomorphic* (thin and linear), and *mesomorphic* (ruggedly muscular) (Sheldon and Tucker, 1940). They also claimed that certain psychological orientations are associated with body type. They saw endomorphs as being relaxed creatures of comfort; ectomorphs as being inhibited, secretive, and restrained; and mesomorphs as being assertive, action oriented, and uncaring of others' feelings (Sheldon and Stevens, 1942).

Sheldon did not take a firm position on whether temperamental dispositions are inherited or are the outcome of society's responses to individuals based on their body types. For example, Americans expect heavy people to be good-natured and cheerful, skinny people to be timid, and strongly muscled people to be physically active and inclined toward aggressiveness. Anticipating such behaviors, people often encourage them. In a study of delinquent boys, Sheldon and his colleagues (1949) found that mesomorphs were more likely to become delinquents than were boys with other body types. Their explanation of this finding emphasized inherited factors, although they acknowledged social variables. The mesomorph is quick to anger and lacks the ectomorph's restraint, they claimed. Therefore, in situations of stress, the mesomorph is more likely to get into trouble, especially if the individual is both poor and not very smart. Sheldon's bias toward a mainly biological explanation of delinquency was strong enough for him to have proposed a eugenic program of selective breeding to weed out those types predisposed toward criminal behavior.

In the middle 1960s, further biological explanations of deviance appeared linking a chromosomal anomaly in males, known as XYY, with violent and criminal behavior. Typically, males receive a single X chromosome from their mothers and a Y chromosome from their fathers. Occasionally, a child will receive two Y chromosomes from his father. These individuals will look like normal males; however, based on limited observations, a theory developed that these individuals were prone to commit violent crimes. The simplistic logic behind this theory is that since males are more aggressive than females and possess a Y chromosome that females lack, this Y chromosome must be the cause of aggression, and a double dose means double trouble.

Today the XYY chromosome theory has been discounted. It has been estimated (Chorover, 1979) that 96 percent of XYY males lead ordinary lives with no criminal involvement. A maximum of 1 percent of all XYY males in the United States may spend any time in a prison (Pyeritz et al., 1977). No valid theory of deviant and criminal behavior can be devised around such unconvincing data.

The biological basis for deviant behavior is still being investigated today. These investigations have yielded conflicting data and conclusions, so the existence of biologically, or at least genetically, determined deviant behavior is still far from being proven.

PSYCHOLOGICAL THEORIES OF DEVIANCE

Psychological explanations of deviance downplay biological factors and emphasize instead the role of parents and early childhood experiences, or behavioral conditioning, in producing deviant behavior. Although such explanations stress environmental influences, there is a significant distinction between psychological and sociological explanations of deviance. Psychological orientations assume that the seeds of deviance are planted in childhood and that adult behavior is a manifestation of early experiences rather than an expression of ongoing social or cultural factors. The deviant individual therefore is viewed as a psychologically "sick" person who has experienced emotional deprivation or damage during childhood.

Psychoanalytic Theory

Psychoanalytic explanations of deviance are based on the work of Sigmund Freud and his followers. Psychoanalytic theorists believe that the *unconscious,* the part of us consisting of irrational thoughts and feelings of which we are not aware, causes us to commit deviant acts.

According to Freud, our personality has three parts: the id, our irrational drives and instincts; the superego, our conscience and guide as internalized from our parents and other authority figures; and the ego, the balance among the impulsiveness of the id, the restrictions and demands of the superego, and the requirements of society. Because of the id, all of us have deviant tendencies, although through the socialization process we learn to control our behavior, driving many of these tendencies into the unconscious. In this way most of us are able to function effectively according to our society's norms and values. For some, however, the socialization process is not what it should be. As a result, the individual's behavior is not adequately controlled by either the ego or superego, and the wishes of the id take over. Consider, for example, a situation in which a man has been driving around congested city streets looking for a parking space. Finally, he spots a car that is leaving and pulls up to wait for the space. Just as he is ready to park his car, another car whips in and takes the space. Most of us would react to the situation with anger. We might even roll down the car window and direct some angry gestures and strong language at the offending driver. There have been cases, however, in which the angry driver has pulled out a gun and shot the offender. Instead of simply saying, "I'm so mad I could kill that guy," the offended party acted out the threat. Psychoanalytic theorists might hypothesize that in this case the id's aggressive drive took over, because of an inadequately developed conscience.

Psychoanalytic approaches to deviance have been strongly criticized because the concepts are very abstract and cannot easily be tested. For one thing, the unconscious can be neither seen directly nor measured. Also, there is an overemphasis on innate drives at the same time that there is an underemphasis on social and cultural factors that bring about deviant behavior.

Behavioral Theories

According to the behavioral view, people adjust and modify their behavior in response to the rewards and punishments their actions elicit. If we do something that leads to a favorable outcome, we are likely to repeat that action. If our behavior leads to unfavorable consequences, we are not eager to do the same thing again (Bandura, 1969). Those of us who live in a fairly traditional environment are likely to be rewarded for engaging in conformist behavior, such as working hard, dressing in a certain manner, or treating our friends in a certain way. We would receive negative sanctions if our friends found out that we had robbed a liquor store. For some people, however, the situation is reversed. That is, deviant behavior may elicit positive rewards. A 13-year-old who associates with a delinquent gang and is rewarded with praise for shoplifting, stealing, or vandalizing a school is being indoctrinated into a deviant life-style. The group may look with contempt at the "straight" kids who study hard, do not go out during the week, and make career plans. According to this approach, deviant behavior is learned by a series of trials and errors. One learns to be a thief in the same way that one learns to be a sociologist.

Crime as Individual Choice

James Q. Wilson and Richard Herrnstein (1985) have devised a theory of criminal behavior that is based on an analysis of individual behavior. Sociologists, almost by definition, are suspicious of explanations that emphasize individual behavior, because they believe such theories neglect the setting in which crime occurs and the broad social forces that determine levels of crime. However, Wilson and Herrnstein argue that whatever factors contribute to crime — the state of the economy, the competence of the police, the nurturance of the family, the availability of drugs, the quality of the schools—they must affect the behavior of *individuals* before they affect crime. They believe that if crime rates rise or fall, it must be due to changes that have occurred in areas that affect individual behavior.

Wilson and Herrnstein believe that individual behavior is the result of rational choice. A person will choose do to one thing as opposed to another because it appears that the consequences of doing it are more desirable than the consequences of doing something else. At any given moment, a person can choose between committing a crime and not committing it. The consequences of committing the crime consist of rewards and punishments. The consequences of not committing the crime also entail gains and losses. Crime becomes likely if the rewards for committing the crime are significantly greater than those for not committing the crime. The net rewards of crime include not only the likely material gain from the crime but also intangible benefits such as obtaining emotional gratification, receiving the approval of peers, or settling an old score against an enemy. Some of the disadvantages of crime include the pangs of conscience, the disapproval of onlookers, and the retaliation of the victim.

The benefits of not committing a crime include avoiding the risk of being caught and punished, and not suffering a loss of reputation or the sense of shame afflicting a person later discovered to have broken the law. All of the benefits of not committing a crime lie in the future, whereas many of the benefits of committing a crime are immediate. The consequences of committing a crime gradually lose their ability to control behavior in proportion to how delayed or improbable they are. For example, millions of cigarette smokers ignore the possibility of fatal consequences of smoking because they are distant and uncertain. If smoking one cigarette caused certain death tomorrow, we would expect cigarette smoking to drop dramatically.

Wilson and Herrnstein attempt to explain the higher rates of crime among black Americans by claiming they are an outgrowth of a rational decision-making process. Blacks are more likely to be arrested, convicted, and imprisoned for street crimes than their population percentage would suggest. Wilson and Herrnstein point out that blacks account for about one-half of those arrested for murder, rape, and robbery, even though they are only about 12 percent of the United States population. In the areas of burglary, larceny, auto theft, and aggravated assault, they account for between one-third and one-fourth of all those arrested. As Wilson and Herrnstein see it, "No matter how one adjusts for demographic factors such as age or urban residence, blacks tend to be overrepresented by a factor of four to one among persons arrested for violent crimes, and by a factor of nearly three to one among those arrested for property crimes."

Sociologists have provided a number of traditional explanations for the high crime rates among blacks, all of which are rejected by Wilson and Herrnstein. For example, sociologists note that blacks are typically overrepresented among "street crimes" or lower-class crimes. However, Wilson and Herrnstein note that blacks arrested for "white-collar" crimes are overrepresented to about the same extent as they are among those arrested for burglary, larceny, and auto theft. For example, one-fourth of those arrested for embezzlement and about one-third of those arrested for fraud, forgery, counterfeiting, and receiving stolen property are black.

Wilson and Herrnstein also reject the possibility that poverty and the absence of employment opportunities could also be a serious explanation for the higher crime rates. They point out that in the 1960s there was one neighborhood in San Francisco that was notable for having "the lowest income, the highest unemployment rate, the highest proportion of families with incomes under $4,000 per year, the least educational attainment, the highest tuberculosis rate, and the highest proportion of substandard housing of any area of the city." That neighborhood was Chinatown. Yet this area did not produce high crime rates. Only five persons of Chinese ancestry were committed to prison in the entire state of California in 1965.

SOCIOLOGICAL THEORIES OF DEVIANCE

Sociologists have been interested in the issue of deviant behavior since the pioneering efforts of Émile Durkheim in the late nineteenth century. Indeed, one of the major sociological approaches to understanding this problem derives directly from his work. It is called anomie theory.

Anomie Theory

Durkheim published *The Division of Labor in Society* in 1893. In it he argues that deviant behavior can be understood only in relation to the specific moral code it violates: "We must not say that an action shocks the common conscience because it is criminal, but rather that it is criminal because it shocks the common conscience" (Durkheim, 1960a).

Durkheim recognized that the common conscience, or moral code, has an extremely strong hold on the individual in small, isolated societies in which there are few social distinctions among people and everybody more or less performs the same tasks. Such *mechanically integrated* societies, he believed, are organized in terms of shared norms and values: All members are equally committed to the moral code. Therefore, deviant behavior that violates the code is felt by all members of the society to be a personal threat. As society becomes more complex — that is, as work is divided into more numerous and increasingly specialized tasks — social organization is maintained by the interdependence of individuals. In other words, as the division of labor becomes more specialized and differentiated, society becomes more *organically integrated*. It is held together less by moral

consensus than by economic interdependence. A shared moral code continues to exist, of course, but it tends to be broader and less powerful in determining individual behavior. For example, political leaders among the Cheyenne Indians led their people by persuasion and by setting a moral example (Hoebel, 1960). In contrast with the Cheyenne, few modern Americans actually expect exemplary moral behavior from their leaders, despite the public rhetoric calling for it. We expressed surprise, but not outrage during the 1988 Democratic presidential primary when Gary Hart's extramarital affairs and Joseph Biden's plagiarism were revealed. We recognize that political leadership is exercised through formal institutionalized channels, and not through model behavior.

In highly complex, rapidly changing societies such as our own, some individuals come to feel that the moral consensus has weakened. Some persons lose their sense of belonging, the feeling of participating in a meaningful social whole. For them, values and norms have little impact: The culture no longer provides adequate guides for behavior. Such individuals feel disoriented, frightened, and alone. Durkheim used the term **anomie** to refer to this condition of "normlessness." He found that it was a major cause of suicide, as we discussed in Chapter 1. Robert Merton built on this concept and developed a general theory of deviance in American society.

Strain Theory

Robert Merton (1938, 1968) believes that American society pushes individuals toward deviance by overemphasizing the importance of monetary success while failing to emphasize the importance of using legitimate means to achieve that success. Those individuals who occupy favorable positions in the social class structure have many legitimate means at their disposal to achieve success. However, those who occupy unfavorable positions lack such means. Thus, the goal of financial success

anomie The feeling of some individuals that their culture no longer provides adequate guidelines for behavior; a condition of "normlessness" in which values and norms have little impact.

innovators Individuals who accept the culturally validated goal of success but find deviant ways of reaching it.

ritualists Individuals who deemphasize or reject the importance of success once they realize they will never achieve it and instead concentrate on following and enforcing rules more precisely than ever was intended.

retreatists Individuals who have pulled back from society altogether and who do not pursue culturally legitimate goals, such as drug addicts, alcoholics, hobos, and panhandlers.

rebels Individuals who reject both the goals of what to them is an unfair social order and the institutionalized means of achieving them. They propose alternative societal goals and institutions.

combined with unequal access to important environmental resources creates deviance.

As you can see in Figure 7.3, Merton identified four types of deviance that emerge from this strain. Each type represents a mode of adaptation on the part of the deviant individual. That is, the form of deviance a person engages in depends greatly on the position she or he occupies in the social structure. Specifically, it depends on the availability to the individual of legitimate, institutionalized means for achieving success. Thus, some individuals accept the culturally validated goal of success but find deviant ways of going about reaching it. Merton calls them **innovators.** Con artists, embezzlers, bank robbers, fraudulent advertisers, drug dealers, corporate criminals, crooked politicians, cops on the take—all are trying to "get ahead" using whatever means are available.

Ritualists are deviant in a very different way. Once they realize that they will never achieve a higher level of success, they deemphasize or reject the importance of making a lot of money. However, because

they have a stable job with a predictable income, they remain within the labor force but refuse to take risks that might jeopardize their occupational security. Many ritualists are often tucked away in large institutions such as government bureaucracies. Here they "cross each *t* and dot each *i*," following and enforcing rules more precisely (and mindlessly) than ever was intended. Their deviance is in giving up the belief in being able to move beyond their present level of attainment.

Another group of people also lacks the means to attain success but does not have the institutional security of the ritualists. These **retreatists** pull back from society altogether. They are the drug and alcohol addicts who can no longer function—the hobos, panhandlers, and so-called street people who live on the fringes of society and who have ceased to pursue culturally legitimate goals.

Finally, there are the **rebels.** They reject both the goals of what to them is an unfair social order and the institutionalized means of achieving them. Rebels seek to tear down the old social order and build a new one with goals and institutions that they can support.

Merton's theory has become quite influential among sociologists. It is useful because it emphasizes external causes of deviant behavior that are within the power of society to correct. The theory's weakness is its inability to account for the presence of certain kinds of deviance that occur among all social strata and within almost all social groups in American society, for example, juvenile alcoholism and drug dependence and family violence (spouse beating and child abuse).

Control Theory

Control theory is based on the idea that social ties among people are important in determining their behavior. Instead of asking what causes deviance, control theorists ask what causes conformity. They believe that what causes deviance is the absence of

FIGURE 7.3

	Mode of adaption	Culture's goals	Institutionalized means
Conformists		Accept	Accept
Deviants	Innovators	Accept	Reject
	Ritualists	Reject	Accept
	Retreatists	Reject	Reject
	Rebels	Reject/Accept	Reject/Accept

Merton's Typology of Individual Modes of Adaptation: Conforming and Deviant. Conformists accept both (a) the goals of the culture and (b) the institutionalized means of achieving them. Deviants reject either or both. Rebels are deviants who may reject the goals or the institutions of the current social order and seek to replace them with new ones that they would then embrace.

that which causes conformity. In their view, conformity is a direct result of control over the individual. Therefore, the absence of social control causes deviance. According to this theory, people are free to violate norms if they lack intimate attachments to parents, teachers, and peers. These attachments help them establish values linked to a conventional life-style. Without these attachments and acceptance of conventional norms, the opinions of other people do not matter and the individual is free to violate norms without fear of social disapproval. This theory assumes that the disapproval of others plays a major role in preventing deviant acts and crimes.

According to Travis Hirschi (1969), one of the main proponents of control theory, we all have the potential to commit deviant acts. Most of us never commit these acts because of our strong bond to society. Hirschi believes that there are four ways in which individuals become bonded to society and conventional behavior:

1. *Attachment to others.* People form intimate attachments to parents, teachers, and peers who display conventional attitudes and behavior.
2. *A commitment to conformity.* Individuals invest their time and energies in conventional types of activities, such as getting an education, holding a job, or developing occupational skills. At the same time, people show a commitment to achievement through these activities.
3. *Involvement in conventional activities.* People spend so much time engaged in conventional activities that they have no time to commit or even think about deviant activities.
4. *A belief in the moral validity of social rules.* Individuals have a strong moral belief that they should obey the rules of conventional society.

If these four elements are strongly developed, the individual is likely to display conventional behavior. If these elements are weak, deviant behavior is likely.

Techniques of Neutralization

Most of us think we act logically and rationally most of the time. To violate the norms and moral values of society, we must go through a process that makes it possible for us to justify the illegal or deviant behavior. Gersham Sykes and David Matza (1957) have called these justifications for deviance **techniques of neutralization.** In the language of control theory, these techniques provide a mechanism by which people can break the ties to conventional society that would inhibit them from violating the rules. Techniques of neutralization are learned through the socialization process. They can take several forms:

techniques of neutralization A process that makes it possible to justify illegal or deviant behavior.

1. *Denial of responsibility.* We argue that we are not responsible for our actions. Forces beyond our control drove us to commit the act, such as a troubled family life, poverty, poor schools, or being drunk at the time of the incident. In any event, the responsibility for what we did lies elsewhere. For example, criminologist Kathleen Heide notes that 40 percent of the delinquents she studied did not see themselves as responsible for their crime. Many even blamed the victim. (*U.S. News & World Report,* August 24, 1987).
2. *Denying the injury.* We argue that the action did not really cause any harm. Who really got hurt when we illegally copied some computer software and sold it to our friends? Who is really hurt in illegal betting on a football game?
3. *Denial of the victim.* The victim is seen as someone who "deserves what he or she got." The man who made an obscene gesture to us on the highway deserved to be assaulted when we caught up with him at the next traffic light. It is all right to cheat the large utility company, because it tries to cheat the public. The angry white mob that chased

the black man Michael Griffith to his death in Howard Beach, New York, claimed he should not have been in the neighborhood in the first place.

4. *Condemnation of the authorities.* Our deviant or criminal behavior is justified because those who are in positions of power or are responsible for enforcing the rules are dishonest and corrupt themselves. Political corruption and police dishonesty leave us with little respect for these authority figures, because they are more dishonest than we are.

5. *Appealing to higher principles or authorities.* We claim our behavior is justified because we are adhering to standards that are more important than abstract laws. Acts of civil disobedience against the government are justified because of the government's misguided policy of supporting nuclear power plants. Our behavior may be technically illegal, but the way everyone does things in this business requires that we do it also.

Using these techniques of neutralization, people are able to break the rules without feeling morally unworthy. They may even be able to put themselves on a higher plain specifically because of their willingness to rebel against rules. They are basically redefining the situation in favor of their actions.

Cultural Transmission Theory

Cultural transmission theory relies strongly on the concept of learning growing out of the work of Clifford Shaw and Henry McKay, who received their training at the University of Chicago. They became interested in the patterning of delinquent behavior in that city when they observed that Chicago's high-crime areas remained the same over the decades—even though the ethnic groups living in those areas changed. Further, they found that as members of an ethnic group moved out of the high-crime areas, the rate of juvenile delinquency in

that group fell; at the same time the delinquency rate for the newly arriving ethnic group rose. Shaw and McKay (1931, 1942) discovered that delinquent behavior was taught to newcomers in the context of juvenile peer groups. And because such behavior occurred, on the whole, only in the context of peer-group activities, youngsters gave up their deviant ways when their families left the high-crime areas.

Edwin H. Sutherland and his student Donald R. Cressey (1978) built a more general theory of juvenile delinquency on the foundation laid by Shaw and McKay. It is called the **theory of differential association,** and its central notion is that criminal behavior is learned in the context of intimate groups (see Table 7.2). When criminal behavior is learned, it includes two components: (1) criminal techniques (such as how to break into houses) and (2) criminal attitudes (that is, rationalizations that justify criminal behavior). In this context, people who become criminals are thought to do so when they agree with the rationalizations for breaking the law more than with the arguments for obeying the law. They acquire these attitudes through long-standing interactions with others who hold these views. Thus, among the estimated 70,000 gang members in Los Angeles County, status is often based on criminal activity and drug use. Even arrests and imprisonment are events worthy of respect. A youngster exposed to and immersed in such a value system will conform to it, if only to survive.

In many respects, differential association theory is quite similar to the behavioral theory we discussed earlier. Both emphasize the learning or socialization aspect of deviance. Both also point out that deviant behavior emerges in the same way that conformist behavior emerges; it is merely the result of different experiences and different associations.

Labeling Theory

Labeling theory shifts the focus of attention from the deviant individual to the social

theory of differential association A theory of juvenile delinquency based on the position that criminal behavior is learned in the context of intimate groups. People become criminals as a result of associating with others who engage in criminal activities.

labeling theory A theory of deviance that assumes the social process by which an individual comes to be labeled a deviant contributes to causing more of the deviant behavior.

TABLE 7.2
Sutherland's Principles of Differential Association

1. Deviant behavior is learned.
2. Deviant behavior is learned in interaction with other persons in a process of communication.
3. The principal part of the learning of criminal behavior occurs within intimate personal groups.
4. When deviant behavior is learned, the learning includes (a) techniques of committing the act, which are sometimes very complicated or sometimes very simple, and (b) the specific direction of motives, drives, rationalizations, and attitudes.
5. The specific direction of motives and drives is learned from definitions of the legal codes as favorable or unfavorable. That is, a person learns reasons for both obeying and violating rules.
6. A person becomes deviant because of an excess of definitions favorable to violating the law over definitions unfavorable to violating the law.
7. Differential associations may vary in frequency, duration, priority, and intensity.
8. The process of learning criminal behavior by association with criminal and anticriminal patterns involves all the mechanisms used in any other learning.
9. Although criminal behavior is an expression of general needs and values, it is not explained by those general needs and values, because noncriminal behavior is an expression of the same needs and values.

Source: Adapted from Edwin H. Sutherland and Donald R. Cressey. *Criminology,* 10th ed. (Philadelphia: Lippincott, 1978), pp. 80–82.

---

process by which a person comes to be labeled as deviant and the consequences of such labeling for the individual. This view emerged in the 1950s from the writings of Edwin Lemert (1972). Since then many other sociologists have elaborated on the labeling approach.

Labeling theorists note that although we all break rules from time to time, we do not necessarily think of ourselves as deviant — nor are we so labeled by others. However, some individuals, through a series of circumstances, do come to be defined as deviant by others in society. Paradoxically, this labeling process actually helps bring about more of the deviant behavior.

Being caught and branded as deviant has important consequences for one's further social participation and self-image. The most important consequence is a drastic change in the individual's public identity. Committing an improper act and being publicly caught at it places the individual in a new status, and he or she may be revealed to be a different kind of person than they formerly were thought to be. Such people may be labeled as thieves, drug addicts, lunatics, or embezzlers and treated accordingly.

To be labeled a criminal, one need commit only a single criminal offense, and that is all the term refers to. Yet, the word carries connotations of other traits. A man who has been convicted of breaking into a house and thereby labeled a criminal is presumed to be a person likely to break into other houses. Police operate on this premise and round up known offenders for investigation after a crime has been committed. In addition, it is assumed that such an individual is likely to commit other kinds of crimes

PRISONS FOR PROFIT

The crisis in our streets has now become the crisis in our prisons. After years of rising crime rates, the public response to the growing fear of crime was to demand tougher penalties for criminals. The result—overcrowded prisons.

Today about 3.3 million Americans are under correctional supervision. This breaks down to about one out of every thirty-five white males and one out of every nine black males being on probation, on parole, or behind bars.

Without a doubt, in every area of corrections we are spending more and doing worse. The nation's 5000 prisons and jails are violent, crowded, filthy, and unproductive when it comes to rehabilitating criminals.

But a specter is haunting American corrections—the specter of capitalism.

A number of private companies are trying to convince us that the day-to-day business of imprisonment should not be left in the hands of state or federal employees.

There are approximately twenty firms that have entered the "prison market." The leader among them is Corrections Corporation of America.

Corrections Corporation of America operates a variety of facilities, including a Federal Bureau of Prisons Halfway House, two Immigration and Naturalization detention centers for illegal aliens, a maximum-security jail in Florida, and a minimum-security facility in Kentucky.

Currently, only three states have specifically enacted laws giving private firms the opportunity to operate state prisons. A dozen others are actively considering the option.

Proponents of private prisons make two assumptions. First, that there is a significant difference between private and public management styles. Private firms are believed to be more efficient, effective, and innovative than public ones.

The second assumption is that the public sector's history in managing prisons has been a disaster. Prisons have been—and continue to be—horrible places that are horribly run.

Those arguing for private prisons point out that savings of 10 to 25 percent are possible because the firms will be freed from politics, bureaucracy, and costly union contracts. The firms will have to compete with each other to maximize services while minimizing costs.

The possibility seems to make sense. So why haven't many states adopted the prisons-for-profit approach? Much of the opposition hinges on moral issues.

as well, because he or she has been shown to be a person without "respect for the law." Therefore, apprehension for one deviant act increases the likelihood that that person will be regarded as deviant or undesirable in other respects.

Even if no one else discovers the deviance or enforces the rules against it, the individual who has committed it acts as an enforcer. Such individuals may brand themselves deviant because of what they did and punish themselves in one way or another for the behavior (Becker, 1963).

There appear to be at least three factors that determine whether a person's behavior will set in motion the process by which he or she will be labeled deviant: (1) the importance of the norms that are violated, (2) the social identity of the individual who violates them, and (3) the social context of the behavior in question. Let us examine these more closely.

1. *The importance of the violated norms.* As we noted in Chapter 3, not all norms are equally important to the people who hold them. The most strongly held norms are mores, and their violation is

Opponents to private prisons question whether it is right to profit from the misfortunes of criminals and their victims. Yet the police, prison guards, and corrections officials are all making a living because these misfortunes exist. So it is hard to have too much sympathy for that argument.

The deeper moral argument rests on the view that only the state should have the authority to govern behind bars. Only the state should be able to deprive citizens of their liberty and possibly even to kill them.

The message of prisons is that "those who abuse liberty shall live without it." Prisons involve the legally sanctioned coercion of some citizens by others. In that sense, only public officials should carry out the state's duties. The patch on the prison guard's sleeve should be that of the state, not a profit-oriented company.

So where do we go from here? Do we continue to have overcrowded and ineffective public prisons, or do we allow the private sector to enter the corrections business and introduce profit-oriented management techniques? There is no simple answer here, but as states try to grapple with prison overcrowding the prisons-for-profit approach may begin to sound attractive.

Currently, three states allow private firms to operate prisons. A dozen others are considering the option.

Charles H. Logan, "Incarceration, Inc.: Competition in the Prison Business," *USA Today,* March 1986, pp. 58–61; Judith C. Hackett, Harry P. Hatry, Robert B. Levinson, Joan Allen, Keon Chi, and Edward D. Feigenbaum, "Contracting for the Operation of Prisons and Jails," U.S. Department of Justice, National Institute of Justice, Research in Brief, June 1987.

likely to cause the culprit, in short order, to be labeled deviant. The physical assault of elderly persons is an example. For less strongly held norms, however, much more nonconformity is tolerated, even if the behavior is illegal. For example, running red lights is both illegal and potentially very dangerous, but in some American cities it has become so commonplace that even the police are likely to "look the other way" rather than pursue violators.

2. *The social identity of the individual.* A rich person or an "entertainment personality" caught shoplifting or even using narcotics has a fair chance of being treated indulgently as an "eccentric" and let off with a lecture by the local chief of police. A poor person or a member of a racial or ethnic minority group is much more likely to feel the heavy hand of the law and face criminal charges. In all societies there are those whose wealth or power (or even force of personality) enable them to ward off being labeled deviant despite behavior that violates local values and norms. Such individuals are buffered against

Should Health Insurers Pay for Sex-Change Operations?

To the casual observer, Sarah Luiz appears to be an attractive 23-year-old woman with a flamboyant personality. She boasts about how attractive she is and how men like to stare at her when she walks down the street. In actual fact, though, Sarah, formerly Jeffrey Dwight Luiz, is neither male nor female. "I'm a half-and-half freak," is how she describes herself.

The problem, as Luiz sees it, is that the health insurer paid for the psychotherapy and hormone treatments that were the preparation for Jeffrey to become Sarah. But now the insurer refuses to pay for the $11,000 surgery that would complete the transformation. The decision not to pay for the surgery is based on a 1981 report by the National Center for Health Care Technology, which concluded that such an operation "is controversial in our society" and essentially experimental.

Others, however, claim that the surgery is not experimental and has been going on for over 30 years. They assert that with presurgical psychological screening and improvements in surgical techniques there are many newer and more experimental surgical procedures than sex-change operations.

Luiz suffers from gender dysphoria—a recognized medical disorder in which the patient feels that he or she is trapped in a body of the wrong sex. Luiz cannot remember a time when he/she did not want to be a female. "I never felt like a boy," she said. "All I did was dream of when I'd be a woman. I knew I wasn't gay—I was trapped in the wrong body." Luiz is attempting to solve the problem by having a sex-change operation and becoming what is commonly referred to as a transsexual.

A federal policy paper has stated that "the large majority of those who received surgery report that they are personally satisfied with the change. However, surgical complications are frequent, and a very small number of postsurgical suicides and psychotic breakdowns are reported."

To minimize such problems, most reputable gender dysphoria centers adopt a set of guidelines aimed at making as certain as possible that the patient is totally committed to the change and is capable of functioning—working, forming relationships—in the new sex. Often during the preoperative stages a patient will decide that the surgery is not necessary.

Luiz, however, does want to go through with the surgery and is suing the health insurer, arguing that they should not have paid for her preoperative treatment without informing her that they were not going to pay for the surgery. The health insurer says, "You should have asked."

As strange as the Luiz case may seem, the number of potential sex-change candidates is greater than one might think. In a 1987 article in the *Journal of Law and Medicine,* it was reported that in

Sarah Luiz, formerly Jeffrey Dwight Luiz, is seen here picketing in front of the health insurer's offices, demanding that they pay for the completion of the sex-change operation.

1983 there were an estimated 6000 transsexuals in the United States who had undergone sex-change operations. Several hundred such operations are done each year in a half-dozen specialized centers.

Source: Richard A. Knox, "Transsexual Blames Insurer for Plight," *The Boston Globe,* March 17, 1989, p. 15.

public judgment and even legal sanction. Conversely, there are those marginal or powerless individuals and groups, such as welfare recipients or the chronically unemployed, toward whom society has a "hair-trigger" response, with little tolerance for nonconformity. Such people quickly are labeled deviant when an opportunity presents itself.

3. *The social context.* The social context within which an action takes place also is important. In a certain situation an action might be considered deviant, whereas in another context it will not. Notice that we say social context, not physical location. The nature of the social context can change even when the physical location remains the same. For example, for most of the year the New Orleans police manage to control open displays of sexual behavior, even in the famous French Quarter. However, during the week of Mardi Gras, throngs of people freely engage in what at other times of the year would be called lewd and indecent behavior. During Mardi Gras the social context invokes norms for evaluating behavior that do not so quickly lead to the assignment of the label deviant.

Labeling theory has led sociologists to distinguish between primary and secondary deviance. **Primary deviance** is the original behavior that leads to the application of the label deviant to an individual. **Secondary deviance** is the behavior that people develop as a result of having been labeled deviant (Lemert, 1972). For example, a teenager who has experimented with illegal drugs for the first time and is arrested for it may be labeled a drug addict and face ostracism by peers, family, and school authorities. Such negative treatment may cause the teenager to turn more frequently to using illegal

primary deviance A term used in labeling theory to refer to the original behavior that leads to the individual's being labeled deviant.

secondary deviance A term used in labeling theory to refer to the deviant behavior that emerges as a result of having been labeled deviant.

Normally it would be considered deviant to paint your body and appear in public. During certain festivals, however, it is quite acceptable.

drugs and to associating with other drug users and pushers, and resorting to robberies and muggings to get enough money to buy the drugs. Thus, the primary deviant behavior and the labeling resulting from it lead the teenager to slip into an even more deviant life-style. This new life-style is an example of secondary deviance.

Labeling theory has proved to be quite useful. It explains why society will label certain individuals deviant but not others, even when their behavior is similar. There are, however, several drawbacks to labeling theory. For one thing, it really does not explain primary deviance. That is, even though we may understand how labeling may produce future, or secondary, acts of

deviance, we do not know why the original, or primary, act of deviance took place. In this respect, labeling theory explains only part of the deviance process. Another problem is that labeling theory ignores the instances when the labeling process may deter a person from engaging in future acts of deviance. It looks at the deviant as a misunderstood individual who really would like to be an accepted, law-abiding citizen. Clearly, this is an overoptimistic view.

It would be unrealistic to expect any single approach to explain deviant behavior fully. In all likelihood some combination of the various theories discussed is necessary for a fuller understanding of the emergence and continuation of deviant behavior.

SUMMARY

A culture's norms and values make up its moral code and help determine what is deviant behavior and what is not. Thus normal behavior is that which conforms to the rules or norms of the group in which it occurs. Deviant behavior, on the other hand, is that which fails to conform to those rules or norms.

Emile Durkheim noted that deviant behavior is a necessary part of a healthy society. This is so because deviance can cause a group's members to close ranks, prompt a group to organize to prevent future deviant acts, help the group clarify its goals, and teach normal behavior by providing examples of violation. In some situations, tolerance of deviance acts as a safety valve and actually prevents more serious instances of nonconformity.

Every society or social group must have mechanisms of social control that mold and influence members' behavior and produce conformity to the established values and norms. Internal and external means of control, positive and negative sanctions, and formal and informal sanctions are the specific means through which

social control operates. Sanctions are rewards and penalties by a group's members that are used to regulate an individual's behavior. Sanctions may be positive or negative, formal or informal.

A number of scholars have proposed theories to account for the occurrence of deviant behavior in society. Biological theories such as those proposed by Lombroso and Sheldon centered around the importance of inherited factors in producing deviance. Psychological theories emphasize the role of parents and early childhood experiences in producing deviant behavior. Wilson and Herrnstein have proposed a theory of deviance that is based on the view that such behavior is the outgrowth of a rational choice.

Sociological explanations of deviance include the anomie theory of Durkheim and strain theory of Merton, which argue that deviant behavior can be understood only in relation to the specific moral code it violates. Some people, through a condition of anomie, feel disconnected from the norms of society.

Control theory is based on the idea that

social ties among people are important in determining their behavior. Instead of asking what causes deviance, control theorists ask what causes conformity. Cultural transmission theory relies heavily on the concept of learning. Sutherland's theory of differential association is a cultural transmission theory. Sutherland argues that deviant behavior is learned in the context of intimate groups. Labeling theory shifts the focus of attention from the deviant individual to the social process by which a person comes to be labeled as deviant and the consequences of such labeling on the individual.

Part 3

SOCIAL INEQUALITY

Chapter 8

SOCIAL

STRATIFICATION

There is nothing lower-class or even middle-class about polo, the daredevil sport that pits player against player and horse against horse in quest of a goal. It is a game cultivated by the rich and played in small, exclusive polo clubs throughout America and the world — clubs like the Palm Beach Polo and Country Club, which hosts the $100,000 World Cup.

Part of the reason for the sport's upper-class appeal is that none but the wealthy can afford it. At least three horses are needed to complete each game, at a cost of between $2500 and $15,000 a horse. In addition, players must pay groom, stable, and feeding fees as well as the cost of a van to transport the horses to and from the matches. The sport can cost $40,000 or more a year to

When we think of polo we think of a sport that is played by those who are wealthy. This is essentially true, because it is an expensive sport to participate in.

social differentiation The shared perceptions of variation among individuals, social positions, or groups.

social evaluation The process of making qualitative judgments on the basis of individual characteristics or behaviors.

enjoy. There is an old adage in polo that sums up its upper-class status: Polo is an addiction that only death or poverty can cure.

Inner-city basketball is nothing like that. Unlike polo, it is a sport that takes no more than a pair of sneakers and a ball to play. It brings youths together in head-to-head competition on city courts, in school-yards, and even in the streets. These "pickup games" are an obsession for many youths who have few other outlets for their physical energy and drive. Many play day after day, game after game in the hope of achieving stardom—a basketball scholar-ship first and then an offer to play for a professional team.

Polo and basketball can be thought of as metaphors for one type of social stratifi-cation inherent in our society. Our society is stratified in other ways also, by sex, age, race, ethnicity, and religion. In this chapter we shall examine this phenomenon. Our emphasis will be on why social stratification takes place and the impact it has on the social organization of the United States. We shall try not to pass judgment, but we shall explore a variety of theories and criticisms in order to provide a basis for judgment for the reader.

THE NATURE OF SOCIAL STRATIFICATION

To understand social stratification, we must know what it includes. Social differentia-tion, social evaluation, and inequality all lead to social stratification. Let us look at each of these.

SOCIAL DIFFERENTIATION AND SOCIAL EVALUATION

The concept of **social differentiation** is fairly universal. It consists of shared perceptions of variation among individuals, social posi-tions, or groups (Vanfossen, 1979). This observation of differences is not always accompanied by qualitative judgment, however. For example, a 5-year-old child is seen as being different from an infant but is not necessarily viewed as being superior be-cause of the age difference.

When qualitative judgments are made on the basis of individual characteristics or behaviors, the process is referred to as **social evaluation.** Although a society may not value a 5-year-old more highly than an in-fant, it might place a value on old people. Compare, for example, the attitude of re-spect for the elderly in Japan with the atti-tude toward senior citizens in the United States. Values placed on physical character-istics and personality habits also vary from one society to another. For example, among Europeans and Americans, body hair on adult males is considered to be "manly" and acceptable, but it is seen by the Japa-nese as "ugly." Americans promote com-petitiveness and individualism; the !Kung San of the Kalahari Desert in southern Africa value cooperativeness and modesty (Lee, 1980). Individuals who have charac-teristics favored by their culture have an ad-vantage over those who do not. It is easier for them to win respect and prestige, to make friends, to find a mate, and to achieve positions of leadership. In all societies there are some people who are favored, who have more prestige, and who are admired; and there are others who are avoided and looked down on. In addition, all groups—even hunters and food gatherers, the most equality minded of societies—make distinctions on the basis of age and sex (see Chapter 5).

SOCIAL INEQUALITY

The outcome of social evaluation is **social inequality,** which is the uneven distribution of privileges, material rewards, opportunities, power, prestige, and influence among individuals or groups. When social inequality becomes part of the social structure and is transmitted from one generation to the next, **social stratification** exists.

Dividing a society into ranks, grades, or positions, social stratification is perpetuated by the major institutions of society, such as the economy, the family, religion, and education. For example, consider the situation in South Africa. The whites, numbering only 4.3 million, rule a country that has some 18 million blacks and a little more than 3 million people of mixed ancestry and Asian origins. The whites have ruled South Africa for over 300 years, and they own almost all of its land and industry. Although white South Africans enjoy one of the highest standards of living in the world, most blacks there live in poverty. This situation is brought about and perpetuated by a government policy known as *apartheid,* which refers to the biological, territorial, social, educational, economic, and political separation of the various racial groups that make up the country.

Yet even here in America, where no such formal policy exists, we have stratification based on wealth. The wealthy have greater access than the poor and minorities to better education, medical care, and jobs, and these advantages perpetuate their privileged position in our society. The Commission on Minority Participation in Education and American Life, for example, found that the number of blacks attending and graduating from college decreased between 1975 and 1985. During this same period the

social inequality The uneven distribution of privileges, material rewards, opportunities, power, prestige, and influence among individuals or groups.

social stratification A condition that exists when social inequality becomes part of the social structure and is transmitted from one generation to the next. Social stratification divides a society into ranks, grades, or positions and is perpetuated by society's major institutions.

In some Middle Eastern societies women are expected to cover themselves in public. Such a situation can help to perpetuate inequality between men and women.

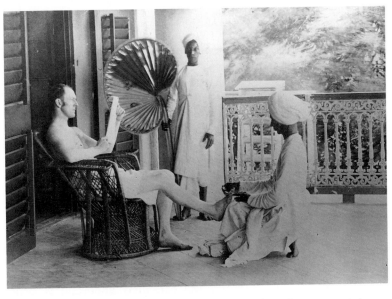

Social inequality involves the uneven distribution of privileges, material rewards, and power.

median income of blacks and Hispanics also went down (*New York Times,* May 24, 1988).

SOCIAL MOBILITY

Social mobility is the movement of an individual or a group within a stratification system that changes the individual's or group's status in society. The degree of social mobility in different societies varies. An **open society** attempts to provide equal opportunity to everyone to compete for the role and status desired, regardless of race, religion, gender, or family history. In a **closed society** the various aspects of people's lives are determined at birth and then remain fixed.

There are no purely open or completely closed societies. Even the most democratic societies make a practice of assigning some roles and statuses, and even the most closed societies have a certain amount of mobility. For example, in the United States, an open society, minorities and women continue to struggle against job discrimination. On the other hand, even in a closed society, such as the estate system of medieval Europe, a wealthy merchant whose social position was low could buy his way into the nobility and consolidate his family's new social status by marrying his children off to landed aristocracy.

Mobility may come about because of changing one's occupation, marrying into a certain family, and so on. Movement that involves a change in status (see Chapter 5) with no corresponding change in social class is known as **horizontal mobility.** For example, Adriane G. Berg started her career as an attorney. Within 15 years, she made a number of horizontal career moves, none of which appreciably changed her position in the social hierarchy. She became a financial planner, a stockbroker, an author of several successful books on financial planning, a college instructor, and finally, a radio talk show host. Although each of these career moves was extremely important to Berg, from a sociological point of view, they are perceived as involving little or no change in

prestige, power, or wealth, and hence, little mobility.

When the movement is up or down in the hierarchy, resulting in a change in social class, **vertical mobility** has taken place. The United States is filled with success stories of vertical mobility. Often this mobility is intergenerational, that is, the change in the social status occurred over two or more generations. The Kennedy family offers a prime example of this type of vertical mobility. Patrick Joseph Kennedy, the grandfather of John F. Kennedy, started life in relative poverty. He had to borrow money from family members to buy a Boston saloon. His son, Joseph P. Kennedy, became an enormously wealthy—and often unscrupulous—business tycoon. John F. Kennedy achieved the pinnacle of success and respectability in this culture by becoming president of the United States.

Vertical mobility may occur during the lifetime of an individual also. This is known as **intragenerational mobility.** There are many examples of men and women who have experienced upward intragenerational mobility. Steven P. Jobs and Stephen G. Wozniak started Apple Computer in Jobs's garage with approximately $1200. William Gates made hundreds of millions while still in his 20s as head of Microsoft Corporation. George E. Johnson, founder and president of Johnson Products Company, started his empire with $500, half of which was borrowed. Today, he is the head of a multi-million-dollar company that manufactures hair-care products and cosmetics for blacks.

Unfortunately, downward intragenerational mobility is common also. Ivan Boesky and Dennis Levine were self-made millionaires who were convicted of insider trading on Wall Street. They lost prestige, power, and wealth, as well as their freedom when they were sent to prison for their wrongdoings.

When vertical mobility occurs over two or more generations, it is known as **intergenerational mobility.** The family of two unskilled laborers who manage to send

---

vertical mobility Movement up or down in the social hierarchy that results in a change in social class.

social mobility The movement of an individual or a group from one social stratum to another.

open society A society that provides equal opportunity to everyone to compete for the role and status desired, regardless of race, religion, gender, or family history.

closed society A society in which the various aspects of people's lives are determined at birth and remain fixed.

intragenerational mobility Social changes during the lifetime of one individual.

horizontal mobility Movement that involves a change in status with no corresponding change in social class.

intergenerational mobility Changes in the social level of a family through two or more generations.

their children through college to become professionals—editors, stockbrokers, engineers, or the like—has accomplished upward intergenerational mobility.

Usually a person's social rank in the stratification hierarchy is consistent and comparatively easy to identify. However, many people do not fit neatly into one social category—their situations are examples of **status inconsistency.** A person whose great wealth is known or suspected to have been acquired illegally will probably not become part of the accepted social establishment. A black physician, despite the high prestige of the profession, may also be denied a higher social position because of racial prejudice.

Factors Affecting Social Mobility

In the United States, many people believe that if individuals work hard enough they can become upwardly mobile—that is, they will become part of the next higher social class. In fact there are several other factors that affect social mobility. For example, there may be social structural factors, such as the state of the economy, that may either help or hinder social mobility.

During periods of economic expansion the number of professional and technical jobs increases. These white-collar jobs can often be filled by upwardly mobile members of other classes. When the supply of jobs increases, one group can no longer determine who will get all the jobs. Consequently, people from lower social classes who have the necessary education, talent, and skills are able to fill some of the positions without having any inside connections. During periods of economic contraction, however, the opposite is true. Getting a job depends on factors that go beyond talent or experience, such as family ties or personal friendships.

Demographic factors also affect upward mobility. With the number of people entering the work force declining during the 1990s, it will be easier for people with the right education, skills, and experience to get a job and advance than during the 1970s when the opposite was the case.

Societies also differ in terms of how much they encourage social mobility. The values and norms of American society encourage upward mobility. In fact, Americans are expected to try to succeed and better their status in life. We often look with contempt at those who have no desire to move up the social class ladder or, worse yet, are downwardly mobile.

What is it that produces mobility? Level of education appears to be an extremely important factor. As would be expected, the greater the level of education attained by the children, the stronger the probability of their upward movement. It can even be claimed that the impact of education on occupational status is greater than that of father's occupational status. It is difficult to separate these two factors, however, because the father's occupation often has an impact on the amount of education received by his children.

The degree of social mobility in a society thus depends in great measure on the type of stratification system that exists.

STRATIFICATION SYSTEMS

There are two major ways in which stratification can occur: (1) People can be assigned to societal roles on the basis of an ascribed status—some easily identifiable characteristic, such as sex, age, family name, or skin color, over which they have no control. This will produce the caste and estate systems of stratification. (2) People's positions in the social hierarchy can be based to some degree on their achieved statuses (see Chapter 5), gained through their individual, direct efforts. This is known as the class system.

THE CASTE SYSTEM

In a **caste system** there is a rigid form of stratification based on ascribed characteris-

status inconsistency Situations in which people rank differently (higher or lower) on certain stratification characteristics than on others.

caste system A rigid form of social stratification based on ascribed characteristics that determines its members' prestige, occupation, residence, and social relationships.

In American society, the father's occupation has an important impact on the amount of education received by his children.

estate system A closed system of stratification in which social position is defined by law and membership is based primarily on inheritance. A very limited possibility of upward mobility exists.

estate A segment of a society that has legally established rights and duties.

tics such as skin color or family identity. People are born into, and spend their entire lives within, a caste, with little chance of leaving it.

Contact between castes is minimal and governed by a set of rules or laws. If interaction must take place, it is impersonal, and there is ample display of the participants' superior–inferior status. Access to valued resources is extremely unequal. A set of religious beliefs often justifies a caste system. The caste system as it existed for centuries in India before the 1950s is a prime example of how this kind of inflexible stratification works.

The Hindu caste system, in its traditional form in India, consisted of four *varnas* ("grades of being"), each of which corresponded to a body part of the mythical Purusa, whose dismemberment gave rise to the human species. Purusa's mouth issued forth priests (Brahmans), and his arms gave rise to warriors (Kshatriyas). His thighs produced artisans and merchants (Vaisyas), and his feet brought forth menial laborers (Sudras). Hindu scripture holds that each person's *varna* is inherited directly from his

or her parents and cannot change during the person's life (Gould, 1971).

Each *varna* had clearly defined rights and duties attached to it. Hindus believed in reincarnation of the soul *(karma)* and that to the extent that an individual followed the norms of behavior of his or her *varna,* the state of the soul increased in purity, and the individual could expect to be born to a higher *varna* in a subsequent life. (The opposite was also true, in that failure to act appropriately according to the *varna* resulted in a person's being born to a lower *varna* in the next life.)

This picture of India's caste system is complicated by the presence of thousands of subcastes, or *jatis.* Each of these *jatis* corresponds in name to a particular occupation (leatherworker, shoemaker, cattle herder, barber, potter, and so on). Only a minority within each *jati* actually perform the work of that subcaste; the rest find employment when and where they can.

It is important to note that the Hindus have never placidly accepted the caste system. Scholars have frequently noted continuous changes during the centuries of the caste system's development. Even today, changes in the caste system are taking place. *Varnas* are all but nonexistent, and officially the Indian caste system is outlawed, although it still exists informally.

THE ESTATE SYSTEM

The **estate system** is a closed system of stratification in which a person's social position is based on ownership of land, birth, or military strength. An **estate** is a segment of a society that has legally established rights and duties. Because the estate system is a closed system involving ascribed statuses, it is similar to a caste system, although not as extreme. Some mobility is present, but by no means as much as exists in a class system.

The estate system of medieval Europe is a good example of how this type of stratification system works. The three major estates in Europe during the Middle Ages were the nobility, the clergy, and, at the bottom of the hierarchy, the peasants. A royal landholding family at the top had authority over a group of priests and the secular nobility, who were quite powerful in their own right. The nobility were the warriors; they were expected to be brave and give military protection to the other two estates. The clergy not only ministered to the spiritual needs of all the people but were often powerful landowners as well. The peasants were legally tied to the land, which they worked to provide the nobles with food and a source of wealth. In return, the nobles were supposed to provide social order, not only with their military strength, but also as the legal authorities who held court and acted as judges in disputes concerning the peasants who belonged to their land. The peasants had little freedom or economic standing, low social status, and almost no power.

Under the estate system, the peasants were legally tied to the land, which they worked to provide the nobles with food and wealth.

Just above the peasants was a small but growing group, the merchants and craftsmen. They operated somewhat outside the estate system in that although they might achieve great wealth and political influence, they had little chance of moving into the estate of the nobility or warriors. It was this marginal group, which was less constricted by norms governing the behavior of the estates, that had the flexibility to gain power when the Industrial Revolution undermined the estate system, starting in the eighteenth century. Individuals were born into one of the estates and remained there throughout their lives. Under unusual circumstances people could change their estate, as for example when peasants — using produce or livestock saved from their own meager supply, or a promise to turn over a bit of land that by some rare fortune belonged to them outright — could buy a position in the church for a son or daughter. For most, however, social mobility was difficult and extremely limited because wealth was permanently concentrated among the landowners. The only solace for the poor was the promise of a better life in the hereafter (Vanfossen, 1979).

THE CLASS SYSTEM

Several social classes are present in a society that has a **class system** of stratification. A **social class** consists of a category of people who share similar opportunities, similar economic and vocational positions, similar life-styles, and similar attitudes and behavior. Class boundaries are maintained by limitations on social interaction, intermarriage, and mobility into that class.

Some form of class system is usually present in all industrial societies, whether they be capitalist or communist. Mobility in a class system is greater than that in either a caste or an estate system. This mobility is often the result of an occupational structure that supposedly opens up higher-level jobs to anyone with the education and experience required. A class society encourages striving and achievement. Here in the

class system A system of social stratification that contains several social classes and permits greater social mobility than a caste or estate system.

social class A category of people within a stratification system who share similar economic positions, similar life-styles, and similar attitudes and behavior.

United States, we should find this concept familiar, for ours is basically a class society.

THE DIMENSIONS OF SOCIAL STRATIFICATION

Scholars who study social stratification recognize three dimensions along which societies are stratified: economics, power, and prestige.

ECONOMICS

The total economic assets of an individual or a family are known as *wealth*. For people in the United States, wealth includes income, monetary assets, and various holdings that can be converted into money. These holdings include stocks, bonds, real estate, automobiles, precious metals and jewelry, and trusts (Jeffries and Ransford, 1980).

Information on income and wealth in the United States shows that there continues to be a high concentration of wealth in the hands of a relatively small number of people. This point is highlighted by the fact that the richest 1 percent of the American population owns about 20 percent of the nation's wealth. This figure was as high as 36 percent in 1929 and illustrates dramatically the extent to which the nation's wealth is controlled by a very few (U.S. Department of Commerce, 1987).

POWER

One of the most widely used definitions of power in sociology is a variation of one suggested by Max Weber. **Power** is the ability to attain goals, control events, and maintain influence over others—even in the face of opposition.

In the United States, ideas about power often have their origins in the struggle for

power The ability of an individual or group to attain goals, control events, and maintain influence over others—even in the face of opposition.

independence. It is a cliché of every Fourth of July speech that the colonists fought the Revolutionary War because of a desire to have a voice in how they were governed, and particularly in how they were taxed. The colonists were also making revolutionary political demands on their own political leaders as well, by insisting that special conventions be elected to frame constitutions and that the constitutions be ratified by a vote of all free white males without regard to property ownership. In the past, governments had been founded on the power of religious leaders, kings, self-appointed conventions, or parliaments. It was the middle classes' resolve for a voice in the decision-making process during the revolutionary period that succeeded in changing our thinking about political representation. The revolutionary period helped develop the doctrine that "power" in the United States should belong to "the people."

Every society has highly valued experiences and material objects. It is assumed that most people in society want to have as great a share as possible of these experiences and objects. Those who end up controlling what people want are then, by inference, the powerful (Domhoff, 1983).

In almost all societies the distribution of power is institutionalized so that some groups consistently have more power than others do. In 1956 C. Wright Mills, in his book *The Power Elite,* attacked the view that American democracy meant that simply by voting all citizens could exercise power over the major decisions that affected their lives. Mills claimed that most Americans in fact are quite powerless and that power in America is held by a relatively small segment of society from whose ranks the leaders of government, industry, and the military usually come. He further argued that it is the leaders of these three interrelated hierarchies who shape the course of events in America.

Mills took great pains to explain that America does not have a single ruling class, an aristocracy of noble families who inherit great power. But that does not mean that

THE GAP BETWEEN THE RICH AND POOR CONTINUES TO WIDEN

Between 1978 and 1987 the gap between the richest 20 percent of the population and the poorest 20 percent of the population continued to grow. In 1987, the poorest fifth of the population received 5 percent of the nation's income, while the richest fifth received 40 percent. In addition, the working poor increased by 23 percent during that time. The Census Bureau now reports that nearly 60 percent of the 20 million people who fall below the poverty line are in families with at least one working member.

What is happening to make the rich better off, while the situation of the poor continues to deteriorate? Economist Robert B. Reich believes work is being stratified in such a way that there is a wider range of earnings than at any other time in the postwar era. Reich believes the work Americans do can be divided up into three broad categories, which he calls symbolic-analytic services, routine production services, and routine personal services.

1. *Symbolic analytic services* involve the manipulation of data, words, or oral and visual symbols. Lawyers, business managers, research scientists, professors, engineers, musicians, and writers are just some of the people who fall into this category. About 40 percent of America's gross national product and about 20 percent of our jobs involve symbolic analysis.

Within the manufacturing sector, symbolic analysis jobs have been increasing three times as quickly as the total manufacturing jobs. Most routine manufacturing jobs have been either exported overseas or are being done by machines.

The large demand for these types of services on a worldwide basis has helped push these salaries up.

2. *Routine production services* involve repetitious tasks that are part of a sequence of steps in producing a finished product. These jobs take place in a centralized facility with supervisors monitoring the process. They represent about 20 percent of the gross national product and one-quarter of the jobs. Overseas competition has made it difficult for wages in these areas to rise.

3. *Routine personal services* also involve simple repetitive tasks. Instead of being a production process, however, these services are provided to another person on a one-to-one basis. Included here are cab drivers, day-care workers, restaurant workers, and security guards. Most of these workers are poorly paid.

Three-fourths of all American jobs fall into one of these categories. Most of the rest are government employees. People involved in symbolic analysis are at a competitive advantage and are seeing their salaries increase. Those who are involved in routine production services or routine personal services are seeing a corresponding increase in demand for their services but are not keeping pace with the advances made by those who are well educated and highly skilled. In this way the gap between the top and the bottom in the economy continues to widen.

Source: Robert B. Reich, "As the World Turns," *The New Republic,* May 1, 1989, pp. 23–28.

---

membership in the class called the **power elite** — the group of people who control policy making and the setting of priorities in America — is open to all:

The bulk of the very rich, the corporate executives, the political outsiders [those high-ranking planners and bureaucrats who survive in power even as different administrators come and go], the high military, derive from, at least, the upper third of the income and occupational pyramids. Their fathers were at least of the professional and business strata, and very frequently higher than that. They are native-born Americans of native parents,

power elite The group of people who control policy making and the setting of priorities.

C. Wright Mills believed there was a power elite in the United States that controlled policy making and the setting of priorities. The Rockefeller family would be part of this group.

primarily from urban areas, and, with the exceptions of the politicians among them, overwhelmingly from the East. They are mainly Protestants, especially Episcopalian or Presbyterian. In general, the higher the position, the greater the proportion of men within it who have derived from and who maintain connections with the upper classes. (Mills, 1956)

Mills showed that members of the power elite typically are graduates from a small number of prestigious colleges, belong to certain exclusive social and country clubs, and frequently marry within elite circles.

In addition, G. William Domhoff found what he called a "governing class" in America, defined in terms of economic (wealth and income) and social (education, club membership) variables. This governing class numbers about 0.5 percent of the total U.S. population. Although it is less tightly organized than the power elite suggested by Mills, its members are, nevertheless, very rich, do intermarry, spend their time in the same clubs, attend the same schools, and are extremely powerful. Despite their political party registration, the members of this governing class agree on the value of free enterprise, the profit motive, and the private ownership of property.

Domhoff suggests that even with the turmoil of the 1960s and 1970s,

> there continues to be a small upper class that owns 20 to 25 percent of all privately held wealth and 45 to 50 percent of all privately held corporate stock, sits in seats of formal power from the corporate community to the federal government, and wins much more often than it loses on issues ranging from the nature of the tax structure to the stifling of reform in such vital areas as consumer protection, environmental protection, and labor law. (Domhoff, 1983)

Some sociologists disagree with Mills's and Domhoff's view of power in America, observing that many groups compete for power. Each group is out for itself, and cooperation between them is minimal. Hence, there can be no "power elite." A major proponent of this position, Arnold Rose, presented his ideas in *The Power Structure* (1967). He believes that there are power structures within every organized area of society. Within each of these power structures there is a small elite that has unusual influence. However, there are so many power structures and so many elites that it is wrong to assume that they ordinarily have any power beyond their specific spheres. At times, however, the power of one elite segment may expand (for instance, as a result of changing political regimes, the military may gain or lose influence over government spending for defense and policy decisions).

Most likely, however, the truth is somewhere in the middle. For example, in both the military and the arts there is a small elite that exerts great influence in its particular group. However, whereas the military elite's decisions and its ability to control events affect the lives and futures of virtually all Americans, the same cannot be said of the arts. The influence of the arts elite is felt primarily in its own sphere and in fact can be overridden by other power elites — the government, for instance, which can withhold financial support for different areas of the arts, thus affecting the kinds, number, and quality of artistic presentations. Rose seems to have ignored the fact that often there is cooperation between different power structures—the political elite and large corporations, for example.

PRESTIGE

Prestige consists of the approval and respect an individual or group receives from other members of society. There are two types of prestige. To avoid confusion we can call the first type *esteem,* which is potentially open to all. It consists of the appreciation and respect a person wins in his or her daily interpersonal relationships. Thus, for example, among your friends there are some who are looked up to for their outgoing personalities, athletic abilities, reliability in times of need, and so on.

The second form of prestige is much more difficult for many people to achieve. This is the honor that is associated with specific statuses (social positions) in a society. Regardless of personality, athletic ability, or willingness to help others, individuals such as Supreme Court justices, state governors, physicians, physicists, and foreign service diplomats acquire prestige simply because they occupy these statuses. Access to prestigious statuses usually is difficult; generally speaking, the greater the prestige a status has, the more difficult it is to gain it. For example, few positions carry as much prestige as that of president of the United States —and few positions are as hard to attain.

There are, of course, times and places when stratification according to prestige groups and social classes is not fully parallel. For example, in the American South many of the existing aristocratic families were financially ruined after the Civil War, and their fall in economic position was matched by a fall from political power. Although Northern industrialists and politicians subsequently replaced them in the hierarchies of wealth and politics, the Northerners never achieved the social prominence, the local esteem, and the respect that were ac-corded the Southern aristocrats simply by virtue of their birth into "prominent" families.

OCCUPATIONAL STRATIFICATION

Occupations are perhaps the most visible statuses to which prestige is attached in industrial society. Table 8.1 shows the prestige rankings of selected occupations in the United States. These rankings, first undertaken in the 1940s by the National Opinion Research Center, have remained quite stable since then.

During the last 30 years, women have had a dramatic impact on the American labor force. As of 1986, about 52 million women were working outside the home. This is about a 200 percent increase over the number of working women at the end of World War II. During that same period, the number of men in the labor force has increased by only 50 percent.

The types of jobs held by working women have been changing, although there is still a great deal of occupational segregation. There are certain occupations that are heavily dominated by women. These include schoolteachers (74 percent female), retail salespeople (69 percent), librarians

prestige The approval and respect an individual or group receives from other members of society.

During World War II many job opportunities were created for women. After the war it became difficult for women to hold on to these jobs, but the long-term effect on the female work force was undeniable.

Occupation	Prestige	Occupation	Prestige
Physician	95.8	Insurance agent	62.5
Mayor	92.2	Private secretary	60.9
Lawyer	90.1	Floor supervisor in a hospital	60.3
College professor	90.1	Supervisor of telephone	
Architect	88.8	operators	60.3
City superintendent of schools	87.8	Plumber	58.7
Owner of a factory employing		Police officer	58.3
2000 people	81.7	Manager of a supermarket	57.1
Stockbroker	81.7	Car dealer	57.1
Advertising executive	80.8	Practical nurse	56.4
Electrical engineer	79.5	Dental assistant	54.8
Building construction		Warehouse supervisor	54.2
contractor	78.9	Assembly-line supervisor in a	
Chiropractor	75.3	manufacturing plant	53.8
Registered nurse	75.0	Carpenter	53.5
Sociologist	74.7	Locomotive engineer	52.9
Accountant	71.2	Stenographer	52.6
High school teacher	70.2	Office secretary	51.3
Manager of a factory		Inspector in a manufacturing	
employing 2000 people	69.2	plant	51.3
Office manager	68.3	Housewife	51.0
Administrative assistant	67.8	Bookkeeper	50.0
Grade school teacher	65.4	Florist	49.7
Powerhouse engineer	64.5	Tool machinist	48.4
Hotel manager	64.1	Welder	46.8
Circulation director of a		Wholesale salesperson	46.2
newspaper	63.5	Telephone operator	46.2
Social worker	63.2	Auto mechanic	44.9
Hospital lab technician	63.1	Typist	44.9
Artist	62.8	Keypunch operator	44.6
Electrician	62.5	Typesetter	42.6

This chart shows how Americans have ranked the prestige of various occupations. Generally, the more prestigious jobs are those that require the greatest number of years of formal education and those that pay the highest income.

(87 percent), nurses (96 percent), and secretaries (99 percent). In contrast, very few women are firefighters (1 percent), construction workers (2 percent), mechanics (3 percent), police officers (6 percent), or engineers (6 percent).

Even with the persistence of occupational segregation, the representation of women in several occupations is growing rapidly. These occupations include lawyers (20 percent today, compared to 5 percent in 1970), doctors (18 percent versus 10 per-

─────────── **TABLE 8.1**
Prestige Ratings of Various Occupations

Occupation	Prestige	Occupation	Prestige
Post office clerk	42.3	Person who repairs shoes	26.0
Beautician	42.4	Fruit harvester, working for own family	26.0
Piano tuner	41.0	Blacksmith	26.0
Landscape gardener	40.5		
Truck driver	40.4	Housekeeper	25.3
House painter	39.7	Flour miller	25.0
Hairdresser	49.4	Stock clerk	24.4
Pastry chef in a restaurant	39.4	Coal miner	24.0
Butcher in a shop	38.8	Boardinghouse keeper	23.7
Washing-machine repairman	38.8	Warehouse clerk	22.4
Automobile refinisher	36.9	Waitress/waiter	22.1
Someone who sells shoes in a store	35.9	Short-order cook	21.5
Cashier	35.6	Baby-sitter	18.3
File clerk	34.0	Rubber mixer	18.1
Dress cutter	33.6	Feed grinder	17.8
Cattledriver working for own family	33.0	Garbage collector	16.3
Cotton farmer	32.4	Box packer	15.1
Metal-container maker	31.4	Laundry worker	14.7
Hospital aide	29.5	Househusband	14.5
Fireman in a boiler room	29.2	Salad maker in a hotel	13.8
Floor finisher	28.8	Janitor	12.5
Assembly-line worker	28.3	Yarn washer	11.8
Book binder	28.2	Maid (F)/household day worker (M)	11.5
Textile-machine operator	27.9	Bellhop	10.6
Electric-wire winder	27.6	Hotel chambermaid (F)/hotel bedmaker (M)	10.3
Vegetable grader	27.4	Carhop	8.3
Delivery truck driver	26.9	Person living on welfare	8.2
Shirtmaker in a manufacturing plant	26.6	Parking lot attendant	8.0
		Rag picker	4.6

Source: Christine E. Bose and Peter H. Rossi, *American Sociological Review,* June, 1983 pp. 327–328.

cent), college and university professors (37 percent versus 29 percent), computer scientists (28 percent versus 14 percent), and architects (8 percent versus 4 percent). As of 1986 women made up the majority of professional employees in the United States.

One of the key issues determining labor force participation of women is the ability to combine work and family commitments. The United States has been quite slow in alleviating problems in this area. Sweden, on the other hand, has been quite innovative and has encouraged the entry of women into the labor force. Sweden has instituted a network of government-supported day-care centers designed to ease child-care responsibilities. The government has also produced legislation that makes it easier for women to work and have children. Swedish parents can receive up to 9 months maternity or paternity leave at 90 percent of full pay. They are also guaranteed a job on returning to work. The government also mandates that a worker will receive full-time pay for a shortened workday (6 hours) until a child's eighth birthday. In part, because of these measures, 66 percent of all Swedish women work. That is the highest female labor force participation rate among the industrialized nations. In the United States 55 percent of all women work (Bloom, 1986).

THEORIES OF STRATIFICATION

Social philosophers have long tried to explain the presence of social inequality — that situation in which the very wealthy and powerful coexist with the poverty-stricken and socially ineffectual. In this section we shall discuss the theories that try to explain this phenomenon.

THE FUNCTIONALIST THEORY

Functionalism is based on the assumption that the major social structures contribute to the maintenance of the social system (see Chapter 1). The existence of a specific pattern in society is explained in terms of the benefits that society receives because of that situation. In this sense the function of the family is the socialization of the young, and the function of marriage is to provide a stable family structure.

The functionalist theory of stratification as presented by Kingsley Davis and Wilber Moore (1945) holds that social stratification is a social necessity. Every society must select people to fill a wide variety of social positions (or statuses) and then motivate those people to do what is expected of them in those positions, that is, fulfill their role expectations. For example, our society needs teachers, engineers, janitors, police

Sweden has instituted a network of government-supported day-care centers that has eased child-care responsibilities considerably.

officers, managers, farmers, crop dusters, assembly-line workers, firefighters, textbook writers, construction workers, sanitation workers, chemists, inventors, artists, bank tellers, athletes, pilots, secretaries, and so on. To attract the most talented individuals to each occupation, society must set up a system of differential rewards based on the skills needed for each position.

> If the duties associated with the various positions were all equally pleasant . . . all equally important to social survival, and all equally in need of the same ability or talent, it would make no difference who got into which positions. . . . But actually it does make a great deal of difference who gets into which positions, not only because some positions are inherently more agreeable than others, but also because some require special talents or training and some are functionally more important than others. Also, it is essential that the duties of the positions be performed with the diligence that their importance requires. Inevitably, then, a society must have, first, some kind of rewards that it can use as inducements, and, second, some way of distributing these rewards differentially according to positions. The rewards and their distribution become part of the social order, and thus give rise to stratification. (Davis and Moore, 1945)

According to Davis and Moore, (1) different positions in society make different levels of contributions to the well-being and preservation of society; (2) filling the more complex and important positions in society often requires talent that is scarce and has a long period of training; and (3) providing unequal rewards ensures that the most talented and best-trained individuals will fill the roles of greatest importance. In effect, Davis and Moore imply that those people who are rich and powerful are at the top because they are the best qualified and are making the most significant contributions to the preservation of society (Zeitlin, 1981).

Many scholars, however, disagree with Davis and Moore (Tumin, 1953), and their arguments generally take two forms. The first is philosophical and questions the morality of stratification. The second is scientific and questions its functional usefulness. Both criticisms share the belief that social stratification does more harm than good, that is, it is dysfunctional.

The Immorality of Social Stratification

On what grounds, one might ask, is it morally justifiable to give widely different re-

According to functionalist explanations of stratification, providing unequal rewards for jobs ensures that the most talented and best-trained individuals will fill the roles of greatest importance to society. Conflict theorists would disagree.

STRATIFICATION BY ZIP CODE

Nutritionists may believe you are what you eat. Californians may claim you are what you drive. But Michael Weiss scoffs at all that. According to Weiss, you are where you live. Weiss can tell a great deal about you by just knowing within which one of the nation's 36,000 zip codes you live in. His information is based on clustering, a system that uses census data and consumer surveys to group the zip codes into forty life-style clusters.

Michael Weiss lives near Washington, D.C., and has never been in Somerville, Massachusetts, but he can describe the place with the accuracy of a long-term resident.

"Somerville is the poor person's bohemia," he notes. "The city is a mix of immigrants, minorities, and working-class whites, aging hippies, blue-collar laborers, and struggling artists living in ramshackle houses and funky apartments. Many are well-educated and have gone to college, but they do not have a lot of money. Typically they are making $10,000 to $20,000 per year. They join environmental organizations and like New Wave rock. They buy very few cars, but when they do, they buy the low-end compact models—Toyota Tercels, and VW Sciroccos."

How did Weiss know all this? He found out simply by typing Somerville's zip code—02143—into his computer. He can obtain a detailed profile that includes such items as residents' favorite TV shows, snack foods, and magazine and liquor choices.

The system, known as clustering, was developed by Jonathan Robbin, a social scientist who is the co-founder of Claritas, a Virginia consulting company. Robbin has been selling his information to such companies as Coca-Cola, General Motors, and American Express—as well as the Democratic National Committee and politicians. These groups use the information to target people who are likely to be receptive to their products or causes.

Weiss, a journalist, became fascinated with the system after writing a profile on Claritas for a national magazine. He set out to investigate their claims for his book *The Clustering of America* (1989). He traveled for 15 months—more than 50,000 miles—to seventy-five different communities in many different regions of the country, to see if the same cluster in New Jersey would be like the one in California. In the process he interviewed 300 politicians, reporters, shopkeepers, librarians, clergymen, and typical residents.

What he discovered was that "you can go to sleep in the Back Bay of Boston and wake up in Palo Alto, California, and except for the trees, the life-styles are really very similar. That is really one of the major points of clustering—that you can have more in common with someone 3000 miles away than you can with someone 3 miles up the road."

"The melting pot is a myth," Weiss says. "Most people have no idea how the other 95 percent live. The idea that we are all one homogenized culture and that we all grow up and move to the shopping malls is baloney. There are neighborhood types in this country where you can spend the first 25 years of your life and never see a shopping mall."

While the cluster system was originally designed for marketing purposes, other groups are finding the system useful also. The U.S. Army, for example, routinely sets up recruiting stations in places that fit a cluster called "shotguns and pickups." The cluster includes places like Zanesville, Ohio, and Jewett, West Virginia, and provides the Army with the best soldiers.

Finding a comfortable cluster can be critical to a person's well-being. Settle in the wrong one and a sense of dislocation can set in, Weiss warns.

Source: Linda Tischler, "Author Pegs People by Town," *The Boston Herald,* November 30, 1988, pp. 37, 40.

wards to different occupations, when all occupations contribute to society's ongoing functioning? How can we decide which occupations contribute "more"? After all, without assembly-line workers, mail carriers, janitors, seamstresses, auto mechanics, nurse's aides, construction laborers, truck drivers, secretaries, shelf stockers, sanitation workers, and so on, our society would grind to a halt. How can the $500,000-a-year incomes of a select few be justified when the earnings of more than 12 percent of the American population fall below the poverty level determined by the federal government and many others have trouble making ends meet? Why are the enormous resources of our society not more evenly distributed?

Many people find the moral arguments against social stratification convincing enough. But there are other grounds on which stratification has been attacked, namely, that it is destructive for individuals and the society as a whole.

The Neglect of Talent and Merit

Regardless of whether social stratification is morally "right" or "wrong," many critics contend that it undermines the very functions that its defenders claim it promotes. A society divided into social classes (with limited mobility between them) is deprived of the potential contributions of many talented individuals born into the lower classes. From this point of view it is not necessary to do away with differences in rewards for different occupations. Rather, it is crucial to put aside all the obstacles to achievement that currently handicap the children of the poor.

Barriers to Free Competition

It can also be claimed that access to important positions in society is not really open. That is, those members of society who occupy privileged positions allow only a small number of people to enter their circle. Thereby, shortages are created artificially.

This, in turn, increases the perceived worth of those who are in the important positions. For example, the American Medical Association (AMA) is a wealthy and powerful group that exercises great control over the quality and quantity of physicians available to the American public. Historically the AMA has had a direct influence on the number of medical schools in the United States and thereby the number of doctors that are produced each year, effectively creating a scarcity of physicians. A direct result of this influence is that medical care costs and physicians' salaries have increased more rapidly than the pace of inflation.

Critics of functionalist theory would ask on what grounds is it morally justifiable to give widely different rewards to different occupations when they are all important to making society work?

This situation is beginning to change, however. The allure of high earning, which attracts many new doctors, along with changing demographic characteristics will mean that by 1990 there will be a surplus of between 70,000 and 185,000 physicians (Paris, 1986). In addition, as more and more doctors fight for the same patient dollars, earnings have begun to suffer. Although physicians earn considerably more than most other professionals, the rise in their median income has started to fall short of the rate of inflation in recent years *(Statistical Abstract of the United States: 1989).* Thus, while barriers to free competition exist in our society, often the marketplace overrules them in the end.

Of course, the same market forces will probably create a shortage of doctors by the year 2010. With today's talented young people realizing that there are better (and certainly easier) ways of earning a living than medicine, medical school enrollments are bound to drop, once again creating a shortage just when the baby boom generation needs a doctor most (Schloss, 1988).

Functionally Important Jobs

When we examine the functional importance of various jobs, we become aware that the rewards attached to jobs do not necessarily reflect the essential nature of the functions. Why should a Hollywood movie star receive an enormous salary for starring in a film and a child-protection worker receive barely a living wage? It is difficult to prove empirically which positions are most important to society or what rewards are necessary to persuade people to want to fill certain positions.

CONFLICT THEORY

As we saw, the functionalist theory of stratification assumes society is a relatively stable system of interdependent parts in which conflict and change are abnormal. Functionalists maintain that stratification is necessary for the smooth functioning of society. Conflict theorists, on the other hand,

see stratification as the outcome of a struggle for dominance. Current views of the conflict theory of stratification are based on the writings of Karl Marx. Later, Max Weber developed many of his ideas in response to Marx's writings.

Karl Marx

Karl Marx believed that to understand human societies one must look at the economic conditions surrounding production of the necessities of life. Stratification emerged from the power struggles for scarce resources.

> The history of all hitherto existing society is the history of class struggles. [There always has been conflict between] freeman and slave, patrician and plebian, lord and serf, guild-master and journeyman, in a word, oppressor and oppressed. . . . (Marx and Engels, 1961)

Those groups who own or control the means of production within a society obtain the power to shape or maintain aspects of society that favor their interests. They are determined to maintain their advantage. They do this by setting up political structures and value systems that support their position. In this way the legal system, the schools, and the churches are shaped in ways that benefit the ruling class. As Marx and Engels put it, "The ruling ideas of each age have always been the ideas of its ruling class" (1961). Thus, the pharaohs of ancient Egypt ruled because they claimed to be gods. And in the first third of this century, America's capitalist class justified its position by misusing Darwin's theory of evolution. They adhered to the view—called social Darwinism (see Chapter 1)—that those who rule do so because they are the most "fit" to rule, having won the evolutionary struggles that promote the "survival of the fittest."

Marx was most interested in the social impact of the capitalist society, which was based on industrial production. In a capitalist society there are two great classes, the **bourgeoisie,** the owners of the means of pro-

bourgeoisie The label used by Karl Marx to describe the owners of the means of production and distribution in a capitalist society.

duction or capital, and the **proletariat,** or working class. The working class has no resources other than their labor, which they sell to the capitalists. In all class societies there is exploitation of one class by another.

Marx believed the moving force of history was class struggle, or class conflict. This conflict grows out of differing class interests. As capitalism develops, two conflicting trends emerge. On the one hand, the capitalists try to maintain and strengthen their position. The exploitative nature of capitalism is found in the fact that the capitalists pay the workers only a bare minimum wage, below the value of what the workers actually produce. The remainder is taken by the capitalists as profit and adds to their capital. This capital, which rightfully belongs to the workers, is then used to build more factories, machines, or anything else to produce more goods. As Marx saw it, "Capital is dead labor, that vampire-like, only lives by sucking living labor, and lives the more, the more labor it sucks" (Marx, 1906).

Eventually, in the face of continuing exploitation, the working classes find it in their interest to overthrow the dominant class and establish a social order more favorable to their interests. Marx believed that with the proletariat in power, class conflict would finally end. The proletariat would have no class below it to exploit. The final stage of advanced communism would include an industrial society of plenty where all could live in comfort.

Marx was basically a materialist. He believed that people's lives are controlled by the material world. The key issue is how wealth is distributed among the people. There are at least four ways by which wealth can be distributed:

1. *To each according to need.* In this kind of system, the basic economic needs of all the people are satisfied. These needs include food, housing, medical care, and education. Extravagant material possessions are not basic needs and have no place in this system.
2. *To each according to want.* Here wealth will be distributed according to what people desire and request. Material possessions beyond the basic needs are now included.
3. *To each according to what is earned.* People who live according to this system become themselves the source of their own wealth. If they earn a great deal of money, they can lavish extravagant possessions upon themselves. If they earn little, they must do without.
4. *To each according to what can be obtained — by whatever means.* Under this system everyone ruthlessly attempts to acquire as much wealth as possible without regard for the hardships that might be brought on others because of these actions. Those who are best at exploiting others become wealthy and powerful, and the others become the exploited and poor (Cuzzort and King, 1980).

proletariat The label used by Karl Marx to describe the mass of people in society who have no other resources to sell than their labor.

According to conflict theory, those groups who control the power structure within a society set up political structures and value systems that support their position.

In Marxist terms, the first of these four possibilities is what would happen in a socialist society. Although many readers will believe that the third possibility describes our society (according to what is earned), Marxists would say that a capitalist society is characterized by the last choice — the capitalists obtain whatever they can get in any possible way.

Max Weber

Max Weber expanded Marx's ideas about class into a multidimensional view of stratification. Weber agreed with Marx on many issues related to stratification, including the following:

1. Group conflict is a basic ingredient of society.
2. People are motivated by self-interest.
3. Those who do not have property can defend their interests less well than those who have property.
4. Economic institutions are of fundamental importance in shaping the rest of society.
5. Those in power promote ideas and values that help them maintain their dominance.
6. Only when exploitation becomes extremely obvious will the powerless object.

From those areas of agreement Weber went on to add to and modify many of Marx's basic premises. Weber's view of stratification went beyond the material or economic perspective of Marx. He included status and power as important aspects of stratification as well.

Weber was not interested in society as a whole but in the groups formed by self-interested individuals who compete with one another for power and privilege. Weber rejected the notion that conflict between the bourgeoisie and proletariat was the only, or even the most important, conflict relationship in society.

Weber believed there were three sources of stratification: economic class, so-cial status, and political power. Economic classes arise out of the unequal distribution of economic power, a point on which both Marx and Weber agreed. Weber went further, however, maintaining that social status is based on prestige or esteem — that is, status groups are shaped by life-style, which is in turn affected by income, value system, and education. People recognize others who share a similar life-style and develop social bonds with those who are most like themselves. From this inclination comes an attitude of exclusivity: Others are defined as being not as good as those who are a part of the status group. Weber did recognize that there is a relationship between economic stratification and social-status stratification. Typically, those who have a high social status also have great economic power.

Inequality in political power exists when groups are able to influence events in their favor. For example, representatives from large industries lobby at the state and federal levels of government for legislation favorable to their interests and against laws that are unfavorable. Thus, the petroleum industry has pushed for lifting restrictions on gasoline prices; the auto industry lobbied for quotas on imported cars. In exchange for "correct" votes, a politician is often promised substantial campaign contributions from wealthy corporate leaders, or endorsement and funding by a large labor union whose members' jobs will be affected by the government's decisions. The individual consumer who will pay the price for such political arrangements is powerless to exert any influence over these decisions.

Class, status, and power, although related, are not the same. One can exist without the others. To Weber they are not always connected in some predictable fashion, nor are they always tied into the economic mode of production. A southern "aristocratic" family may be in a state that is often labeled "genteel poverty," but the family name still elicits respect in the community. This kind of status is sometimes denied to the rich, powerful labor leader whose family connections and school ties

NEARLY ONE-FIFTH OF ALL AMERICANS RECEIVE WELFARE BENEFITS

A study by the United States Census Bureau showed that 18.3 percent of all Americans received welfare for at least one month during a 32-month period ending in 1986.

The study also showed that for blacks, Hispanics, single mothers and children, the rate was even higher with half of all blacks and one third of all Hispanics receiving welfare at some time during the study period. One quarter of all children were welfare recipients during the study period. The greatest welfare dependency was found among single-parent households.

About one-quarter of all children are dependent on welfare payments.

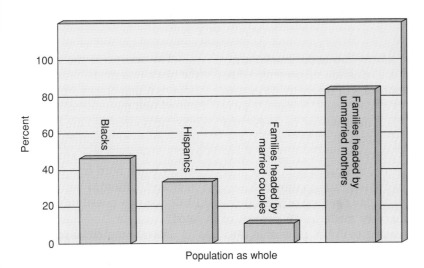

Welfare recipients. Recipients for at least one month during a 32-month period ending in 1986. In percent. Source: *Bureau of the Census, 1989.*

are not acceptable to the social elite. In addition, status and power are often accorded those who have no relationship to the mode of production. Henry Kissinger, for example, controlled no industry, nor did he have any great personal wealth; yet his influence was felt by the heads of state the world over.

Whereas Marx was somewhat of an optimist in that he believed that conflict, inequality, and exploitation could eventually be eliminated in future societies, Weber was much more pessimistic about the potential for a more just and humane society.

MODERN CONFLICT THEORY

Contemporary conflict theorists assume that people act in their own self-interest in a material world in which exploitation and power struggles are prevalent. There are five aspects of modern conflict theory:

What Is the Origin of the Black Underclass?

Information about black America is often depressing. The proportion of blacks living in poverty in 1987 was 33 percent. That is higher than it was in 1969, and three times the white rate. Forty-five percent of black children live in poverty, compared to 15 percent of white children. Even though blacks constitute 12 percent of the population, they made up 46 percent of the inmates in U.S. prisons in 1985 and 60 percent of those arrested for murder in 1987.

As bad as these figures may seem, within the black community there is an underclass, which is relatively small but growing, that has problems beyond these just cited. They can be termed "the poorest of the poor."

The source of the growth in the black underclass is not exactly clear. Is it that blacks are being absorbed into the underclass as they become poorer and are caught up in a culture of illegitimacy, drugs, and joblessness? Or are children simply being born into the underclass and failing to escape? Most likely the two possibilities are related.

How the underclass developed and what should be done about it are issues that are fiercely debated within the social sciences. There are basically three major approaches to the issue.

First, there is the "welfare school" thesis proposed by Charles Murray of the Manhattan Institute. Second, there is the "structural unemployment/social isolation" thesis proposed by William Julius Wilson of the University of Chicago. Finally, there is the "culture of poverty" thesis of Glenn Loury of Harvard University.

Charles Murray's "welfare school" approach was presented in his 1984 book *Losing Ground,* in which he argued that the liberal policies of the 1960s, such as increases in social spending, the loosening of welfare regulations, and the lowering of academic and discipline standards in public schools, are the cause of the current problems. These policies made it possible for black girls to have illegitimate babies while unemployed and to see no disadvantage to this practice. Murray claims that these

1. Social inequality emerges through the domination of one or more groups by other groups. Stratification is the outgrowth of a struggle for dominance in which people compete for scarce goods and services. Those who control these items gain power and prestige. Dominance can also result from the control of property, as others become dependent on the landowners.

2. Those who are dominated have the potential to express resistance and hostility toward those in power. Although the potential for resistance is there, it sometimes lies dormant. Opposition may not be organized because the subordinated groups may not be aware of their mutual interests. They may also be divided because of various differences.

3. Conflict will most often center on the distribution of property and political power. The ruling classes will be extremely resistant to any attempts to share their advantage in these areas. Economic and political power are the most important advantages in maintaining a position of dominance.

4. What are thought to be the common values of society are really the values of the dominant groups, who establish a value system that justifies their position. They control the systems of socialization, such as education, and impose their values on the general population. In this way the subordinate groups come to accept a negative evaluation of themselves and believe those in power have a right to that position.

policies destroyed the work ethic and made it harder for blacks to learn how to get out of poverty.

William Julius Wilson proposed the "structural unemployment/social isolation" thesis in his 1987 book *The Truly Disadvantaged.* He argued that, with the deindustrialization of the American economy and the movement of jobs to the suburbs beginning in the early 1970s, unskilled young ghetto males became increasingly unemployable and undesirable as prospects for marriage. As middle-class and working-class blacks left the ghettos, they became "communities of the underclass . . . plagued by massive joblessness, flagrant and open lawlessness, and low achieving schools . . . the

residents of these areas . . . have become increasingly socially isolated from mainstream patterns of behavior."

In his "culture of poverty" thesis, Glenn Loury notes that Murray and Wilson put too much emphasis on economic conditions, and not enough on the breakdown of values in the ghetto, and the failure of prominent blacks to help restore them. Status in the ghetto is gained from becoming a drug dealer or a mother. Loury believes black leaders need to get the message across that this is not what it means to be "cool."

Which of the three proposals are correct? Probably all of them, to some extent. Social policies have contributed to a breakdown in the

black family, industry has left the inner city, and more affluent blacks have left the ghetto.

Even though these researchers may argue over the reasons for the underclass, little is being done to address the problem. President Bush in his presidential campaign noted that he was "haunted by the lives lived by children of our inner cities." At the moment there is no concerted policy to stop the growth in the black underclass. The more this problem is ignored the worse it will get.

Source: Morton M. Kondracke, "The Two Black Americas," *The New Republic,* February 6, 1989, pp. 17–20.

5. Because those in power are engaged in exploitative relationships, they must find mechanisms of social control to keep the general population in line. The most common mechanism of social control over the masses is the threat or the actual use of force, which can include physical punishment or the deprivation of certain rights. However, more subtle approaches are preferred. By holding out the possibility of a small amount of social mobility for those who are deprived, the power elite will try to induce them to accept the system's basic assumptions. Thus, the subordinate masses will come to believe that by behaving according to the rules, they will gain a better life in the future (Vanfossen, 1979).

Conflict theorists believe the ruling classes will be extremely resistant to sharing their political power.

—————————————————————————————— **TABLE 8.2**

Functionalist and Conflict Views of Social Stratification:
A Comparison

The Functionalist View	*The Conflict View*
1. Stratification is universal, necessary, and inevitable.	1. Stratification may be universal without being necessary or inevitable.
2. Social organization (the social system) shapes the stratification system.	2. The stratification system shapes social organizations (the social system).
3. Stratification arises from the societal need for integration, coordination, and cohesion.	3. Stratification arises from group conquest, competition, and conflict.
4. Stratification facilitates the optimal functioning of society and the individual.	4. Stratification impedes the optimal functioning of society and the individual.
5. Stratification is an expression of commonly shared social values.	5. Stratification is an expression of the values of powerful groups.
6. Power is usually legitimately distributed in society.	6. Power is usually illegitimately distributed in society.
7. Tasks and rewards are equitably allocated.	7. Tasks and rewards are inequitably allocated.
8. The economic dimension is subordinate to other dimensions of society.	8. The economic dimension is paramount in society.
9. Stratification systems generally change through evolutionary processes.	9. Stratification systems often change through revolutionary processes.

Source: Arthur L. Stinchcombe, "Some Empirical Consequences of the Davis-Moore Theory of Stratification," in Jack L. Roach, Llewellyn Gross, and Orville R. Gursslin (eds.), *Social Stratification in the United States* (Englewood Cliffs, N.J.: Prentice-Hall, 1969), p. 55.

THE NEED FOR SYNTHESIS

Any empirical investigation will show that neither the functionalist nor the conflict theory of stratification is entirely accurate. This does not mean that both are useless in understanding how stratification operates in society. Ralf Dahrendorf (1959) suggests that the two theories are really complementary rather than opposed to each other. (Table 8.2 compares the two). We do not need to choose between the two but instead should see how each is qualified to explain specific situations. For example, functionalism may help explain why differential re-

wards are needed to serve as an incentive for a person to spend many years training to become a lawyer. Conflict theory would help explain why the offspring of members of the upper classes study at elite institutions and end up as members of prestigious law firms, whereas the sons and daughters of the middle and lower classes study at public institutions and become overworked district attorneys in a minority district court.

In the next chapter we will look at the issue of social stratification further by focusing specifically on social class in the United States.

SUMMARY

Social differentiation, social evaluation, and inequality all lead to social stratification, the condition that exists when social inequality becomes part of the social structure and is transmitted from one generation to the next. Social stratification divides a society into ranks, grades, or positions and is perpetuated by society's major institutions.

Social mobility is the movement of an individual or a group within a stratification system that changes the individual's or group's status in society. An open society provides equal opportunity to everyone to compete for the role and status desired, regardless of race, religion, gender, or family history. In a closed society various aspects of people's lives are determined at birth and remain fixed.

There are two major ways in which stratification can come about: (1) People can be assigned to societal roles, using as a basis for the assignment an ascribed status over which they have no control. This will produce the caste and estate systems of stratification. (2) People's positions in the social hierarchy can be based to some degree on their achieved statuses, gained through their individual, direct efforts. This is known as the class system.

In a caste system there is a rigid form of stratification according to ascribed characteristics such as skin color. People are born into, and spend their entire lives within, a caste, with little chance of leaving it.

The estate system is a closed system of stratification in which a person's social position is based on ownership of land, birth, or military strength. An estate is a segment of a society that has legally established rights and duties.

Several social classes exist in a society that has a class system of stratification. A social class is a category of people who share similar opportunities, similar economic and vocational positions, similar life-styles, and similar attitudes and behavior. Class boundaries are maintained by limiting social interaction, intermarriage, and mobility into that class. Some form of class system exists in all industrial societies, whether they be capitalist or communist. Mobility in a class system is greater than that in either a caste or an estate system.

There are three dimensions along which societies are stratified: economics, power, and prestige.

The functionalist theory of stratification as presented by Kingsley Davis and Wilber Moore holds that social stratification is a social necessity. Every society must select individual members to fill a wide variety of social positions (or statuses) and then motivate those people to do what is expected of them in those positions, that is, fulfill their role expectations. According to Davis and Moore, (1) different positions in society make different levels of contributions to the well-being and preservation of society; (2) filling the more complex and important positions in society often requires talent that is scarce and requires a long period of training; and (3) providing unequal rewards ensures that the most talented and best-trained individuals will fill the roles of greatest importance.

Many scholars disagree with Davis and Moore, and their arguments generally take two forms. The first is philosophical and questions the morality of stratification. The second is scientific and questions its functional usefulness.

Conflict theorists, on the other hand, see stratification as the outcome of a struggle for dominance. Karl Marx believed that in order to understand human societies one must look at the economic conditions centering around producing the necessities of life. Stratification emerged from the power struggles for scarce resources.

Max Weber believed there were three sources of stratification: economic class, social status, and political power. Economic classes arise out of the unequal distribution of economic power, a point on which both Marx and Weber agreed. Weber went further, however, maintaining that social status is based on prestige or esteem.

Chapter 9

SOCIAL CLASS

IN THE

UNITED STATES

The subject of class in the United States is a touchy one. As Americans, we like to think we live in a classless society. After all, we do not have inherited ranks, titles, or honors. We do not have coats of arms or rigid caste rankings. Besides, equality among all citizens is an ideal guaranteed by our Constitution and summoned forth regularly in speeches from podiums and lecterns across the land.

But are we all really equal, or are some people more equal than others? Take Donald Trump, for example. More than any other person on the scene today, he epitomizes the new upper class. By the age of 40, he was already a billionaire three times over, with real estate holdings in New York, Atlantic City, the Bahamas, and Palm Beach, among other places.

Trump's life-style leaves nothing to be desired. He owns three homes, including a 110-room mansion in Palm Beach, a spectacular triplex apartment in Trump Tower overlooking New York's Fifth Avenue, and a 45-room weekend retreat in Greenwich, Connecticut. To make transit to and from his homes and business properties easier, he also owns a Boeing 727 jet, a $2 million helicopter capable of traveling 180 miles an hour, and a $30 million yacht.

Not too many miles away in New York City lives Carol Kennedy, a 37-year-old mother of five who has seen another side of life. On and off the welfare roles for nearly 20 years, Kennedy was forced to move into a welfare hotel for 16 months when her apartment burned down. Despite her hardships, Kennedy still hopes to get a high school diploma, find a job, and be off welfare forever. What she wants more than anything from her children is that they "stay in school so they don't end up like me" (*Life*, Spring 1988).

These striking contrasts leave no doubt in anyone's mind that we live in a country characterized by extreme wealth and equally extreme poverty. Although many people are reluctant to talk about it, there are class distinctions in America based on race, education, family name, career choice, or wealth. These remain despite legislation, free public education, and political idealism. In his book *Inequality in an Age of Decline* (1980), Paul Blumberg went so far as to call the idea of class America's "forbidden thought." Although the thought may at times be forbidden, the reality of a class structure is a hallmark of our society.

objective approach The approach to measuring social stratification in which researchers decide in advance that a certain number of social classes will be used and then determine what criteria will be used for assigning people to each of the classes.

STUDYING SOCIAL STRATIFICATION

A common way of measuring social stratification in a society is to divide people into a specified number of social classes. Social classes differ in many different characteristics, and there is some disagreement among sociologists as to what is most important in determining social class. For example, if we were to define social class solely in terms of income, several problems would immediately become obvious. In many large cities a sanitation worker may receive a higher starting pay than a public-school teacher. Thus, if income were our sole criterion for determining social class, we would have to admit that the trash collector belongs to a higher social class than the public-school teacher. By the same token we would have to assign upper-class status to organized-crime figures who "earn" hundreds of thousands of dollars a year. Obviously, we must find a system of measurement that will avoid some of these problems. Sociologists have devised three approaches to measuring social class: the objective approach, the reputational approach, and the subjective approach.

OBJECTIVE APPROACH

When using the **objective approach** to measure social class, researchers determine a set number of social classes in advance and then assign people to each class according to given criteria. This method was first used by August Hollingshead (1949) in his study of the residents of New Haven, Connecticut. Using criteria that included occupation, level of education, and residence, Hollingshead grouped people into one of five categories that are similar to the social classes we will discuss.

Proponents of this method see it as an objective, relatively precise assessment tool that does not rely on subjective feelings and

The reputational approach to social class measurement relies on the opinions community members have of one another.

attitudes, and thus can be used to assign social class levels to large populations. Critics disagree. They point to the fact that researchers arbitrarily determine the number of social classes and the characteristics that put a person into each. Clearly, there may be — and often are — differences of opinion among sociologists on these classifications, making this method not as objective as its label implies.

REPUTATIONAL APPROACH

The **reputational approach** to social class relies on the opinions the community members have of one another. This approach was first used by W. Lloyd Warner and Paul Lunt (1941) in their study of a town in Massachusetts. Through personal contact with many community residents, researchers analyze the social categories into which community members place one another. For example, whereas some people are perceived as "high society," others are viewed as "trash," and still others are looked upon as "good old boys." From these judgments researchers are able to categorize community members into specific social classes. This method suffers from the need for subjective judgments from both researchers and local residents. In addition, it can be used only in a small community where most people either know, or know of one another.

SUBJECTIVE APPROACH

In the **subjective approach** to measuring social class, individuals are asked to place themselves into one of several categories. There may be as few as three — upper, middle, and lower class — or as many as ten. No matter how many categories are used, the middle category is the one most often selected — a tendency that reduces the method's accuracy and usefulness. In addition, judgments are influenced greatly by the wording of the questions and by researchers attitudes. People also tend to play down the presence and importance of social classes in their lives, and as a result, they often do not treat the issue very seriously.

subjective approach The approach to measuring social stratification in which the people being studied are asked to put themselves into one of several categories.

reputational approach The approach to measuring social stratification in which social class is determined by the opinions of other community members about an individual.

SOCIAL CLASS IN THE UNITED STATES

There is little agreement among sociologists as to how many social classes exist in the United States and what their characteristics

Social Stratification in the United States by Occupation

Class	Occupation	Education	Children's Education
Upper class	Corporate ownership; upper-echelon politics; honorific positions in government and the arts	Liberal arts education at elite schools	College and postcollege
Upper middle class	Professional and technical fields; managers; officials; proprietors	College and graduate school training	College and graduate school training
Lower middle class	Clerical and sales positions; small-business owners; semiprofessionals; farmers	High school; some college	Option of college
Working class	Skilled and semiskilled manual labor; craftspeople; foremen; nonfarm workers	Grade school; some or all of high school	High school; vocational school
Lower class	Unskilled labor and service work; private household work and farm labor	Grade school; semi-illiterate	Little interest in education; high school dropouts

Source: Adapted from U.S. Department of Commerce, Bureau of the Census, *Statistical Abstract of the United States: 1981* (Washington, D.C.: Government Printing Office, 1981).

may be. However, for our purposes here we will follow a relatively common approach of assuming that there are five social classes in the United States: upper class, upper middle class, lower middle class, working class, and lower class (Rossides, 1976; Kahl, 1960). Table 9.1 presents stratification data for each of these classes.

THE UPPER CLASS

Members of the upper class have great wealth, often going back for many generations. They recognize one another and are recognized by others by reputation and lifestyle. They usually have high prestige and a life-style that excludes those from other classes. Members of this class often have an influence on the society's basic economic and political structure. The upper class usually isolates itself from the rest of society by residential segregation, private clubs, and private schools. They are most likely to be Protestant, especially Episcopalian or Presbyterian. It is estimated that in the United States, the upper class consists of from 1 to 3 percent of the population.

During the last decade, the upper class has also come to include society's new entrepreneurs, people who have often made many millions—and sometimes billions—in business. In many respects these people do not resemble the upper class of the past. Included in this group are people like Donald Trump, mentioned earlier; David Packard, a pioneer in computers and electronics who founded Hewlett-Packard Company and is now worth some $2.56 billion; William Gates, the 34-year-old chief executive officer of the Microsoft Corporation, who has a $1.2 billion net worth; and Ted Turner, the founder of the 24-hour cable news network, whose net worth exceeds $536 million (*Newsweek*, May 30, 1988).

Not all billionaires lead such an opulent life-style, and many in the upper class would not approve of this display of wealth. More fitting of the upper-class acceptance are the Main Street billionaires like Sam Walton, who made their money in the heartland and continue to live there. Walton, the founder of Wal-Mart Stores, made his fortune through retailing geared to middle America. Another example is Leslie Wexner, founder of The Limited, a women's retailing chain, who lives and works in Columbus, Ohio. His $1.2 billion fortune has enabled him to contribute nearly $50 million to local charities, making him the city's largest benefactor (Conant, 1988).

One of the upper class's quaintest institutions is a little-known address and telephone book called the *Social Register*. It lists the names and various addresses of about 65,000 families and single adults, as well as information concerning each person's membership in clubs and ancestral societies, and colleges and universities attended and year of graduation. Social scientists can obtain a great deal of information about the upper class from this source.

The *Social Register* association does not really decide who is and who is not a member of the upper class; they merely decide who should be listed. The *Social Register* is essentially a telephone book. It should be remembered, though, that the venture has persisted since 1887. Tens of thousands of families send their forms in each year. This at least gives some small measure of proof to the fact that a self-conscious group of members of the upper class does exist in America (Domhoff, 1983).

THE UPPER MIDDLE CLASS

The upper middle class is made up of successful business and professional people and their families. They are usually just below the top in an organizational hierar-

Members of the upper class recognize one another and are recognized by others by reputation and life-style.

THE BLACK MIDDLE CLASS

For far too long, "black middle class" was a contradiction in terms. To be black meant to be poor, underprivileged, and, worse yet, stuck. Today, to be black and middle class is not only possible, it is reality for at least a third of all black families. These families earn between $25,000 and $50,000 a year. (In 1960, only 13 percent of blacks were middle class.)

Most of these families are first-generation middle class. That is, although they are professionals and corporate managers, their parents had little education, held menial jobs, and made little money. Charles H. Bowers, Jr., an obstetrician-gynecologist, fits into this group. Although he now lives in suburbia and has a Volvo, a Jeep, and a Corvette, he grew up with very little. His divorced mother held down any menial job she could get to pay the bills. Says Bowers: "In those days we were poor. But being poor in money doesn't mean poor in values or poor in the willingness to work hard" (*Business Week*, March 14, 1988).

The black middle class is growing so rapidly because blacks now have greater access to lucrative occupations than in the past. They can be lawyers, doctors, politicians, corporate executives, and three-star generals instead of laborers and domestics. And once they get their professional credentials, they can also choose to work in the white corporate culture, where the most money is to be made. Chicago lawyer Mitchell Ware advanced from handling personal injury, divorce, and bankruptcy cases "in order to survive" to specializing in commercial law for white and black corporate clients. Similarly, Curtis A. Wood and his partners moved their offices to New York's Wall Street to compete with established law firms for big corporate business. Says Wood, "We wanted to be just like any other of the major corporate law firms in New York City in terms of having highly skilled lawyers, a professional atmosphere, and a substantial client base" (Shipp, 1988).

Part of the reason black families have made such progress is the contribution of black women to family wealth. A larger percentage of black wives work than white wives, and they bring in a

chy but still command a reasonably high income. Many aspects of their lives are dominated by their careers, and continued success in this area is a long-term consideration. These people often have a college education, own property, and have a savings reserve. They live in comfortable homes in the more exclusive areas of a community, are active in civic groups, and carefully plan for the future. They are very likely to belong to a church. The most common denominations represented are Presbyterians, Episcopalians, Congregationalists, and Unitarians. Ten to fifteen percent of the United States population falls into this category.

A large percentage of the new upper middle class are two-income couples, both of whom are college educated and employed as corporate executives, high government officials, business owners, or professionals. These relatively affluent individuals are changing the face of many communities. They are gentrifying run-down city neighborhoods with their presence and their money (*New York Times*, April 29, 1988).

THE LOWER MIDDLE CLASS

The lower middle class shares many characteristics with the upper middle class, but

larger percentage of the family income. In black families where both spouses work, wives contributed almost half of the $31,549 joint income in 1986, whereas wives in white families earned only about a third of the family's joint income, which was nearly $39,000.

Ironically, at the same time these real economic gains are being made, there are fewer blacks in the educational pipeline —the best route from the lower to the middle class. In 1987, only 26 percent of blacks who graduated from high school went on to college—7 percent less than those who graduated in 1976. And with fewer in college, fewer still are attending graduate school to become corporate leaders and professionals. The reasons: a high school dropout rate that has declined, but not far enough; the poor-quality public education many blacks receive; the spiraling cost of college tuition; and the cutback in financial aid for minority college students.

Maybe because of their backgrounds, many blacks who have made the transition from lower to middle class feel financially vulnerable and insecure. "You can never feel truly comfortable," says Patricia A. Powell, an industrial and labor relations lawyer. "You could be wiped out in a second" during a recession when clients cannot pay their bills. Government statistics on the federal work force bear out the insecurity of the new black middle class. According to a survey done by the Federal Government Service Task Force, the cutbacks in federal agencies that were made during the early 1980s affected blacks and other minorities at a 50 percent greater rate than whites.

Thus, although blacks are joining the ranks of the middle class in greater numbers than ever before, they are certainly not comfortably ensconced. And as corporate America tightens its belt to compete in the world market, middle-class blacks, as well as whites, are likely to find a scarcity of good jobs—a situation that will make it harder for young blacks to achieve middle-class status.

Sources: "The Black Middle Class," Business Week, March 14, 1988, pp. 62–70; E. R. Shipp, "Black Lawyers Joining the Chase for Big Money," New York Times, May 20, 1988, p. B7; David R. Francis, "Blacks Have Made Real Economic Gains; What's Reagan's Role?" Christian Science Monitor, July 11, 1988, p. 16.

they have not been able to achieve the same kind of life-style because of economic or educational shortcomings. Usually high school graduates with modest incomes, they are the lesser professionals, clerical and sales workers, and upper-level manual laborers. They emphasize respectability and security, have some savings, and are politically and economically conservative. They are often dissatisfied with their standard of living, jobs, and family incomes. Religiously, they are likely to be represented among the Protestant denominations such as Baptist, Methodist, Lutheran, or Greek Orthodox or Catholic. They make up 25 to 30 percent of the United States population.

THE WORKING CLASS

The working class is made up of skilled and semiskilled laborers, factory employees, and other blue-collar workers. These are the people who keep the country's machinery going. They are assembly-line workers, auto mechanics, and repair personnel. They are the most likely to be buffeted by economic downturns. More than half belong to unions.

Working-class people live adequately but with little left over for luxuries. They are less likely to vote than higher classes, and feel politically powerless. Although they have little time to be involved in civic orga-

Members of the working class live adequately but have little left over for luxuries. They are likely to feel politically powerless.

finished high school. More than 50 percent of this group is likely to be Catholic. They represent 25 to 35 percent of the United States population.

THE LOWER CLASS

These are the people at the bottom of the economic ladder. They have little in the way of education or occupational skills and are consequently either unemployed or under-employed. Lower-class families often have many problems, including broken homes, illegitimacy, criminal involvement, and alcoholism. Members of the lower class have little knowledge of world events, are not involved with their communities, and do not usually identify with other poor people. They have low voting rates. Because of a variety of personal and economic problems, they often have no way of improving their lot in life. For them, life is a matter of surviving from one day to the next. They have high school dropout rates and the highest rates of illiteracy of any of the groups. The lower class is disproportionately black and Hispanic, but it is not race that defines it, or even poverty. Rather, it is a set of characteristics and conditions that are part of a broader life-style. Lower-class people often belong to fundamentalist or revivalist sects. Fifteen to twenty percent of the population falls into this class.

Money, power, and prestige are unequally distributed among these classes. However, a desire to advance and achieve success is shared by members of all five classes, which makes them believe that the system is just and that upward mobility is open to all. Therefore, they tend to blame themselves for lack of success and for material need (Vanfossen, 1979).

We tend to think of the lower class as an urban population. Yet a substantial portion of this population is rural.

nizations, they are very much involved with their extended families. The families are likely to be patriarchal with sharply segregated sex roles. They stress obedience and respect for elders. Many of them have not

INCOME DISTRIBUTION

The United States Census Bureau has published annual estimates of the distribution

TABLE 9.2
Family Income Distribution, 1987

Income Rank	Income Amount	Percent of Total Income Received by All Families
Richest 5 percent	$86,300 and above*	16.9
Fifth quintile*	52,910 and above	43.7
Fourth quintile	36,600–52,909	24.1
Third quintile	25,100–36,599	16.9
Second quintile	14,450–25,099	10.8
First quintile	14,449 or below	4.6

*Richest 5 percent is contained in fifth quintile.

Source: U.S. Department of Commerce, Bureau of the Census, *Current Population Reports,* series P-60, No. 132 and 161, *Statistical Abstract of the United States: 1989* (Washington, D.C.: Government Printing Office, 1989), p. 446.

of family income since 1947. These figures show a highly unequal distribution of wealth. In 1986, for example, the richest one-fifth of families received $9.47 of income for every $1.00 received by the poorest one-fifth.

Without further elaboration, this information allows us to imagine that the richest one-fifth of families consists of millionaire real estate moguls, Wall Street professionals, and CEOs of major companies. The image is somewhat misleading. In 1987 the richest one-fifth included all families with incomes of $52,910 or more (see Table 9.2). Keep in mind that this is a family income derived from jobs held by husbands, wives, and all other family members. Family incomes for the richest 5 percent of the population begin at $86,300 (Levy, 1987; *Statistical Abstract of the United States: 1989*).

This is not to imply, though, that there is not a significant difference in the distribution of wealth in the United States. Table 9.2 also shows that the richest 20 percent of the population receives 43.7 percent of the total income, and the poorest 20 percent receives only 4.6 percent of the total income. Income is only part of the picture. Total wealth — in the form of stocks, bonds, real estate, and other holdings — is even more unequally distributed. The richest 20 percent of American families own more than three-fourths of all the country's wealth. In fact, the richest 5 percent of all families own more than half of America's wealth.

There is also evidence to support the old adage that "the rich get richer, and the poor get poorer." The number of people in poverty grew from 24.5 million in 1978 to 32.5 million in 1987. The number of households with incomes of $35,000 and above in constant 1987 dollars grew from 24 million to over 28 million (*Statistical Abstract of the United States: 1989*).

POVERTY

On a very basic level, poverty refers to a condition in which people do not have enough money to maintain a standard of

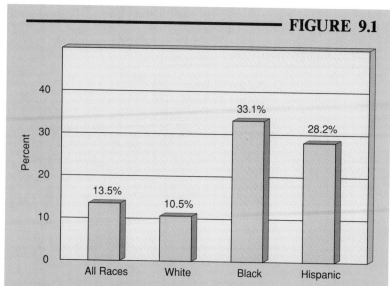

FIGURE 9.1

Persons Below Poverty Level by Race and Hispanic Origin, 1987.
Source: *U.S. Department of Commerce, Bureau of the Census,*
Statistical Abstract of the United States: 1989 *(Washington, D.C.:*
Government Printing Office, 1989), p. 454.

only on the problems of the urban poor. Even worse, the economic conditions of the rural poor are expected to deteriorate along with the decline of unskilled manufacturing jobs and changes in the mining, agriculture, and oil industries (*Newsweek*, August 8, 1988).

The problem is especially acute for those with little education or marketable job skills. For example, more than 11,000 sugar workers in southern Louisiana, almost all of whom are black and many of whom are illiterate, have lost their jobs over the past 10 years because of mechanization in the sugar industry. With nowhere to turn and with no other jobs available, many lead desperate lives of poverty (*New York Times,* June 3, 1988).

living that includes the basic necessities of life. Most official or quasi-official sources estimate that anywhere from 14 million to 45 million Americans are living in poverty. The fact is, we do not really have an unequivocal way of determining how many poor people there are in the United States.

Poverty seems to be present among certain groups much more than among others. In 1987, 13.5 percent of all Americans lived below the poverty level. While 10.5 percent of all whites were living in poverty, 33.1 percent of all blacks and 28.2 percent of all those of Hispanic origin fell into this group (see Figure 9.1). People living in the Appalachian region of the United States are much more likely to live in poverty than those living elsewhere. In Kentucky, for example, the percentage of people living below the poverty level was 17.6 percent, and in Mississippi it was 23.9 percent (*Statistical Abstract of the United States: 1989*). These figures reflect the fact that the level of poverty in rural areas is actually higher than it is in our cities. Thirty percent of the nation's poor live in rural America — a fact often overlooked by those who focus

THE FEMINIZATION OF POVERTY

Different types of families also have different earning potentials. In 1987, a family with both a husband and wife present had a median income of $34,700. For male-headed families with no wife present, the figure was $26,230, and for female-headed families, the figure was $14,620 (*Statistical Abstract of the United States: 1989*). This has caused some sociologists to speak of the "feminization of poverty," a phrase referring to the disproportionate concentration of poverty among women.

If present trends continue, 60 percent of all children born today will spend part of their childhood in a family headed by a mother who is divorced, separated, unwed, or widowed. There is substantial evidence that women in such families are often the victims of poverty. Almost half of all female-headed families with children under 18 are below the poverty line.

Not all female-headed families are the same, however. The feminization of poverty is both not as bad as, and much worse than, the above statement suggests. Families headed by divorced mothers are doing

THE POOR PAY MORE

Being poor in America means having fewer opportunities. It also means paying more for food. According to a report issued by the United States House Select Committee on hunger, most poor people are forced to rely on small, independent grocers for food. And these grocers often charge up to 30 percent more than supermarkets. The result: the poorest people in America—those who can afford it least—pay the highest percentage of their weekly budgets for food. Whereas the average consumer spends 15 percent of his or her budget on food, the poor may spend up to 61 percent, the committee found.

The following table shows how dramatic these cost differences can be. The cheapest option, food warehouses, are generally available only in the suburbs.

Source: Amy Brooke Baker, "Supermarkets Scarce in Inner Cities," *Christian Science Monitor,* May 2, 1988, pp. 3–4.

Grocery Costs Depend on Where You Shop

Item	Independent grocer	Super-market	Food warehouse
Colgate gel toothpaste 8.2-oz. tube	$3.25	$2.09	$2.12
Grade A large eggs 1 dozen	1.19	.95	.89
Green Giant green beans 16-oz. can	1.22*	.59	.47
Ground beef 75% lean, per pound	1.98	1.49	.99
Similac infant formula 32 oz.	5.76**	2.39	2.05
Wonder bread 20-oz. loaf	1.15	1.15	1.08

* Comparable brand.
** Price based on 13-oz. can.

better than the 50 percent figure, while families headed by never-married mothers are doing much worse.

What accounts for the fact that never-married mothers are so much poorer than their divorced counterparts? Seventy percent of all out-of-wedlock births occur to young women between the ages of 15 and 24. They are on average 10 years younger than divorced mothers. Never-married mothers are also, on average, much less educated. Only 53 percent have a high school diploma. Thus, inexperience and lack of education combine to give these women much poorer job prospects (Besharov and Quin, 1987).

Seventy percent of all out-of-wedlock births occur to young women between the ages of 15 and 24. Only 53 percent of them have a high school diploma. This situation has contributed to the feminization of poverty.

TABLE 9.3
Poverty Levels Based on Income for Families and Unrelated Individuals, 1987

Size of Unit	Income
1 person	$5,778
Under 65	5,909
Over 65	5,447
2 persons	7,397
Under 65	7,641
Over 65	6,872
3 persons	9,056
4 persons	11,611
5 persons	13,737
6 persons	15,509
7 persons	17,649
8 persons	19,515
9 persons	23,105

Source: U.S. Department of Commerce, Bureau of the Census, *Statistical Abstract of the United States: 1989* (Washington, D.C.: Government Printing Office, 1989), p. 420.

HOW DO WE COUNT THE POOR?

To put a dollar amount on what constitutes poverty, the federal government has devised a poverty index of specific income levels, below which people are considered to be living in poverty. Many people use this index to determine how many poor people there are in the United States. According to the index, the poverty level for a family of four in 1986 was $11,611 (see Table 9.3). See Table 9.4 for the number of people living in poverty. The poverty level income figures do not include income received in the form of noncash benefits, such as food stamps, medical care, and subsidized housing.

The official definition of poverty that we use for the poverty index was developed by the Social Security Administration in 1964. It was calculated in the following way. First, the national average dollar cost of a frugal but adequate diet was estimated. Then, because a 1955 study found that families of three or more people spent about one-third of their income on food, food costs were multiplied by three to estimate how much total cash income was needed to cover food and other necessities.

The "poverty index" was not originally intended to certify that any individual or family was in "need." In fact, the government has specifically warned against using the index for administrative use in any specific program. Despite this warning, people continue to use, or misuse, the poverty index and variations of it for a variety of purposes for which it was not intended. For example, those wanting to show that current government programs are inadequate for the poor will try to inflate the numbers of those living in poverty. Those trying to show that government policies are adequate for meeting the needs of the poor will try to show that the number of poor people is decreasing.

The poverty index has become less and less meaningful over the years. However, its continued existence over all these years has given it somewhat of a sacred character. Few people who cite it know how it is calculated and choose to assume it is a fair measure for determining the number of poor in the country.

The poverty index has never been a sufficiently precise indicator of need to make it an indisputable test of which individuals and families are poor and which are not. Regional differences in the cost of living by themselves are enough to throw the index's accuracy off substantially. The federal government uses the same poverty-level figures for every part of the country. That means the poverty threshold is the same in rural Mississippi as it is in Manhattan (O'Hare, 1988). As time went on, many other factors skewed it further.

Adding to the problem of the poverty index is the fact that food typically accounts for a considerably smaller proportion of family expenses today than it did previously. If we were to try to develop a poverty index today, we would probably have to multiply minimal food costs by a factor of five instead of three (Dukert, 1983).

When the federal government developed the poverty index in 1964, about one-quarter of federal welfare benefits were in

—————————————————————— **TABLE 9.4**
Number of Poor and Poverty Rate

Year	Number of People in Poverty	Percent Below Poverty Level
1960	39,851,000	22.2%
1965	33,185,000	17.3
1970	25,559,000	12.6
1975	25,877,000	12.3
1980	29,272,000	13.0
1985	33,272,000	14.0
1987	32,500,000	13.5

Source: U.S. Department of Commerce, Bureau of the Census, *Statistical Abstract of the United States: 1989* (Washington, D.C.: Government Printing Office, 1989), p. 452.

the form of goods and services. Today, non-cash benefits account for about two-thirds of welfare assistance (O'Hare, 1988). For example, there are now about 8 million households who receive food stamps, valued at $10 billion, which is not considered "income" under existing poverty index

Poverty statistics may not adequately count homeless families who have no permanent address.

WHEN CHILDREN WANT CHILDREN

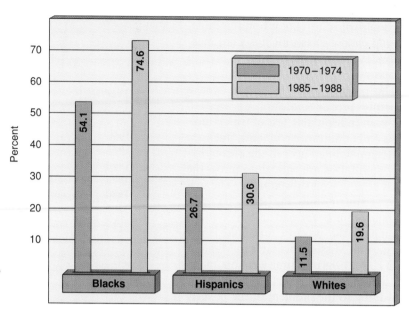

Unwed First Mothers. Source: *Bureau of the Census.*

Leon Dash is a member of the investigative news staff of The Washington Post. *When he was first assigned to investigate the phenomenon of teenage pregnancy among poor black youths, the thinking was that his story would follow traditional lines. Not at all!*

Dash lived for 18 months in one of the poorest ghettos of Washington, D.C., in order to break through the armor of distrust among these teenage parents and explain the real reasons why children want children.

O n the morning of October 30, 1984, Sherita Dreher said goodbye to her 2-year-old son, Marguis, and left to tell her story of despair to the Mayor's Blue Ribbon Panel on Teenage Pregnancy Prevention.

She began having sex, she said, at the age of 15, succumbing to the advances of her 16-year-old boyfriend. They did not use any kind of birth control because she did not believe she could get pregnant. "I laid and I paid," she declared.

The story Sherita told fit Dash's preconceptions about the issue. He assumed that the high incidence of teenage pregnancy among poor, black, urban youths

rules. Complicating the issue further, the market value of "in-kind" benefits, such as housing subsidies, school lunch programs, and health care services, among others, has jumped from $2.2 billion to more than $72.5 billion. To include noncash benefits in any measure of poverty would require that we convert these benefits into income, which would become an extremely difficult task.

The number of people living in poverty is also distorted by the fact that the Census Bureau's Current Population Survey is derived from households. It excludes all those people who do not live in traditional housing, specifically the growing numbers of the homeless, estimated at anywhere from 350,000 to 2.5 million. People in nursing homes and other types of institutions are also not included in the poverty figures because of surveying techniques (O'Hare, 1988).

This is not to downplay the number of poor people in the United States. The basic

grew out of youthful ignorance, about both birth-control methods and adolescent reproductive capabilities. He also thought the girls were falling victim to the cynical manipulation of the boys.

Seven months later, after many interviews, Dash knew that Sherita had been lying. Sherita had really wanted to get pregnant, assuming that having a baby would make her boyfriend stay with her. She knew about birth control but chose not to use it. Instead of being the victim of ignorance, Dash saw her as tough, sophisticated, and aware.

Dash realized he had been wrong on all counts. Among the adolescents he interviewed, he found that teenage boys and girls as young as 11 knew more about sex, birth control, and reproductive abilities than he knew at their age.

He found that the girls, far from being passive victims, were often equal—or greater—actors than their boyfriends in exploring sexuality and becoming pregnant. The girls were as often the leaders in their desire to have a child as the boys were. He did not find one adolescent couple where both partners were ignorant about the consequences of sexual activity without the use of contraception.

Dash discovered that for many girls in the poverty-stricken community of Washington Highlands a baby is a *tangible* achievement in an otherwise dreary and empty future. It is one way of announcing "I *am* a woman." For many of the boys, the birth of a baby represents an identical rite of passage. The boy is saying, "I *am* a man."

The desire for a child was especially acute among adolescents who were doing poorly in school. They knew they were not likely to graduate from high school. These were youths anywhere from 15 to 17 years old and still in the seventh grade, who were at the highest risk of getting pregnant or fathering a child. While the better students strove for a diploma, the poorer students achieved their own recognition with a baby.

If the crisis of black teenage pregnancy were simply a matter of ignorance, then it might be a relatively easy problem to solve. Dash, however, believes the poor academic preparation that begins in elementary school, the poverty that surrounds them, and the social isolation from mainstream American life is what really causes these youths to have children.

Source: Leon Dash, *When Children Want Children* (New York: William Morrow & Company, 1989).

fact is that trying to determine how many poor people there are depends on who you ask and what type of statistical maneuvering is involved.

MYTHS ABOUT THE POOR

We are presented with a variety of views on poverty and what should be done about it. One side argues that more government aid and the creation of jobs is needed to combat what has been produced by structural changes in the national economy (Harrington, 1984). The other side contends that government assistance programs launched with the War on Poverty in the mid-1960s have encouraged many of the poor to remain poor and should be eliminated for the able-bodied poor of working age (Murray, 1984).

Our perceptions of the poor shape our views of the various government programs available to help them. It is important that we have a clear understanding of who the poor are in order to direct public policy intelligently. There are several common myths about the poor that many Americans believe. Let us try to clear some of them up.

Myth 1: People are poor because they are too lazy to work. Most of the able-bodied poor of working age are working or looking for work. Many of the poor adults who do not work have good reasons for not working. Many of them are ill or disabled, whereas many others are going to school (mostly teenagers in high school from poor families). There are also more than 2 million poor who are retired.

Of all the families in poverty in 1987, more than half had at least one worker. However, a person working 40 hours a week, every week of the year at minimum wage, will not earn enough to lift a family of three out of poverty. The numbers of the working poor are increasing at an alarming rate. There are several reasons for this growth. First, although there are more jobs in the economy than ever before, many of these jobs are in low-paying service industries. A janitor or a cook at a fast-food restaurant earns no more than minimum wage. According to a report issued by the Joint Economic Committee, nearly six out of ten new jobs created between 1979 and 1984 pay less than $7000 a year.

Second, the better jobs the poor used to hold are no longer part of the U.S. economy. Many companies, seeking sources of cheap labor, have set up manufacturing operations overseas to increase their ability to compete in the world market. Finally, many of the working poor are women or young people with few marketable skills. Often, they are forced to settle for poorly paid, part-time work.

In many ways, the working poor are in worse straits than those on the welfare roles. For example, a mother on welfare may be eligible for public housing and a variety of services that a working-poor two-parent family may not be able to receive (*U.S. News & World Report*, January 11, 1988).

In many ways, it is easy for the government to ignore the plight of the working poor. Scattered throughout the country and with no single voice to protest with, they are relatively invisible and, therefore, easily forgotten.

Myth 2: Most poor people are black and most black people are poor. Neither of these statements is true. Most poor people are white, not black, although the poverty rate remains three times higher for blacks than whites (33.1 versus 10.5 percent in 1987) (*Statistical Abstract of the United States: 1989*).

One of the reasons that blacks are associated with the image of poverty is that they make up more than haif of the long-term poor. Another reason is that the War on Poverty was motivated in part by, and occurred simultaneously with, the civil rights movement of the 1960s (O'Hare, 1987).

Myth 3: Most poor people live in female-headed households. Although it is true that a disproportionate share of poor households are headed by women and that the poverty rate for female-headed families is extremely high, the majority of people in poverty live in male-headed families. In 1984, 11.8 million poor people lived in female-headed families, but 14.6 million lived in married-couple or male-headed families. The remainder of the poor, 7.2 million, lived by themselves or with people not related to them (O'Hare, 1987).

Myth 4: Most people in poverty live in inner-city ghettos. Nearly 36 percent of the poor live in central cities. About 26 percent of all poor families live in the suburbs, and 39 percent live in nonmetropolitan or rural areas.

Poverty is growing rapidly in areas not typically identified as poor. Many white suburbanites have been added to the list of poor, accounting for one-fourth of the growth in poverty in recent years (O'Hare, 1986).

Myth 5: The welfare roles are expanding. Contrary to popular belief, slightly fewer people were enrolled in the major welfare programs, Medicaid, Aid to Families with Dependent Children, and Supplemental Security Income programs in 1986 than 1975. The number of food stamp recipients was almost the same in 1986 as 1980. These trends in enrollment are particularly noteworthy in light of the 13 percent growth in the poverty population between 1975 and 1986.

Although government spending on social programs has grown substantially over the past 20 years, most of the growth has been in programs aiding the elderly, regardless of economic status (O'Hare, 1987).

——— GOVERNMENT ASSISTANCE PROGRAMS

The public appears to be quite frustrated and upset about perceived soaring welfare costs and growing poverty. Much of this frustration, however, stems from a misperception of what programs are behind the escalating government expenditures, a misunderstanding about who is receiving government assistance, and an exaggerated notion of the amount of assistance going to the typical person in poverty. Most government benefits go to the middle class. Many of the people reading this book would be surprised to know that they or their families may actually receive more benefits than those people typically defined as poor. The value of benefits going to the poor has fallen in recent years, while those going to the middle class have risen.

Government programs that provide benefits to families or individuals can be divided into three categories: (1) social insurance, (2) means-tested cash assistance, and (3) noncash benefits (see Table 9.5).

Social insurance benefits are not means-tested, that is, one does not have to be poor to receive them. They go primarily to the middle class. Many people receiving payments from social insurance programs, such as Social Security retirement and unemployment insurance, feel they are simply getting back the money they put into these

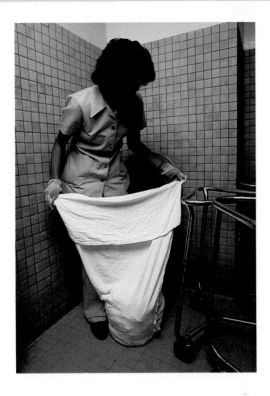

It is easy to ignore the plight of the working poor. Scattered throughout the country and with no single voice, they are relatively invisible and easily forgotten.

programs. They accuse those of receiving benefits from means-tested programs of "getting something for nothing." This is not exactly true when we recognize that many social insurance recipients get back far more than they put in, and the poor, the majority of whom work, pay taxes that contribute to their own means-tested benefits.

Social insurance programs account for the overwhelming majority of federal cash assistance expenditures, and their share has been rising rapidly. Female-headed families in poverty, often portrayed as a heavy drain on the government treasury, accounted for only 2 percent of the federal outlays for human resources. In contrast, social security for the retired elderly, the vast majority of whom are middle class, accounted for 38 percent.

Means-tested cash assistance programs go mainly to the poor and include such items as Aid to Families with Dependent Children (AFDC), and Supplemental Security Income (SSI). As social insurance cash assistance has been rising, means-tested

TABLE 9.5
Expenditures for Major Federal Government
Assistance Programs, 1987

Assistance Program	Billions of Dollars
Social Insurance (Non-Means-Tested)	
Social Security Retirement	206.0*
Established in 1935 to provide cash payments to retired workers and their dependents	
Social Security Disability Insurance	19.7*
Cash payments to disabled workers over 50 and their dependents	
Unemployment Insurance	16.1*
Provides partial wage-replacement payments to workers who lose their jobs involuntarily	
Non-Means-Tested Cash Benefits	
Medicare	80.3*
Covers most medical costs for individuals eligible for social security retirement and disability payments	
Means-Tested Cash Assistance	
Aid to Families with Dependent Children (AFDC)	10.0
Provides cash payments to needy families where one parent is absent or incapacitated	
Supplemental Security Income (SSI)	12.6
Provides cash payments to needy, aged, blind, or disabled people	
Education Aid	9.7*
Student loans, college work-study programs, Head Start, and Pell grants	
Means-Tested Noncash Benefits	
Medicaid	30.0
Covers most medical costs for individuals in AFDC families or eligible for SSI	
Housings Benefits	13.2
Provides public housing or subsidizes rent in nonpublic housing	
Food Stamps	12.5
Distributes coupons redeemable for food to individuals and families with incomes 130 percent of the poverty line	
Subsidized School Lunches	3.3
Provides free and reduced-price lunches to students from low-income families	

*Indicates recipients of benefits are predominantly middle class
  Amount going to middle-income recipients $331.8 billion
  Amount going to low-income recipients   81.6 billion

Source: U.S. Department of Commerce, Bureau of the Census, *Statistical Abstract of the United States: 1989* (Washington, D.C.: Government Printing Office, 1989), pp. 347–357.

cash assistance to the poor has been falling. Between 1975 and 1985, the average annual payment per recipient in Social Security retirement benefits, which are indexed to rise with inflation, increased by 20 percent in constant dollars. Meanwhile, the average annual federal expenditure per family in the AFDC program, which is not indexed, fell by 20 percent in constant dollars.

Noncash assistance programs include items that are both means-tested (such as Medicaid, food stamps, subsidized housing, free or reduced-price school lunch programs) and non-means-tested (such as Medicare and subsidized lunches for all students in participating schools). The middle class again wins out in federal noncash assistance. Medicare outlays are at least 50 percent more than the combined expenditures for the four above-mentioned major noncash benefit programs for the poor.

——— WORLDWIDE COMPARISONS

It appears that economic rewards are more unequally distributed in the United States than elsewhere in the Western industrialized world. In addition, the United States experiences more poverty than other capitalist countries with similar standards of living. In one international study, the poverty rates for children, working-age adults, and the elderly were tabulated for a variety of countries. The results show (see Table 9.6) that the United States has been moderately successful in holding down poverty among the elderly. Poverty afflicts the American elderly far less often than the elderly in Great Britain, approximately the same as in Norway and West Germany, and much more often than in Canada and Sweden.

The United States has been much less successful in keeping children and working-age adults out of poverty. The U.S. child poverty rate is 60 percent higher than in Great Britain, nearly 80 percent higher than in Canada, and more than double the rate in the Scandinavian countries.

How has it happened that the United States has made progress in combating poverty among the elderly, but not among other groups? Since 1960 a variety of social policies have been enacted that have improved the standard of living of the elderly relative to that of the younger population. Social

TABLE 9.6

Poverty Rates among Children, Working-Age Adults, and the Elderly in Six Nations

Country	Children	Working-Age Adults	The Elderly
United States	17.1%	10.1%	16.1%
United Kingdom	10.7	6.9	37.0
Canada	9.6	7.5	4.8
West Germany	8.2	6.5	15.4
Norway	7.6	7.1	18.7
Sweden	5.1	6.7	2.1

Source: Timothy Smeeding, Barbara Doyle Torrey, and Martin Rein, "Patterns of Income and Poverty: The Economic Status of the Young and the Old in Six Countries." Paper presented at the Conference on the Well-Being of Children and the Aged, The Urban Institute, February 1987.

security benefits were significantly increased and protected against the threat of future inflation, Medicare provided the elderly with national health insurance, SSI provided a guaranteed minimum income, special tax benefits for the elderly protected their assets during the later years, and the Older American's Act supported an array of services specifically for this age group. As a consequence of these measures, poverty among the elderly has declined substantially. Whereas 24.6 percent of those families headed by someone 65 or over lived below the poverty level in 1970, only 7.2 percent did so in 1987. By contrast, 15.4 percent of families headed by someone age 25 to 34 lived below the poverty level in 1987. (*Statistical Abstract of the United States: 1989*).

To achieve this dramatic improvement in the condition of the elderly, the federal government has had to increase greatly the amount of money spent on this age group. Currently, expenditures on the population over age 65 capture 30 percent of the annual federal budget. This is for a population that currently represents 12 percent of the country. If these arrangements are maintained, projections show about 60 percent of the federal budget going to the elderly by the year 2030. A group that has suffered particularly under this shift in expenditures to the elderly is the young. Whereas 14 percent of children lived in poverty in 1970, 20 percent do so today (Uhlenberg, 1987).

It would also surprise many people if we noted that not only are the elderly as a group not poor, they are actually better off than most Americans. They are more likely than any age group to possess money market accounts, CDs, U.S. government securities, and municipal and corporate bonds. Their median household net worth is the second highest of any age group, surpassed only by the 55- to 64-year-olds. They have the highest rate of homeownership of any age group. Seventy-seven percent of those 65 to 74 own homes, and most of those homes are fully paid for.

The elderly in the United States tend to be better off than their counterparts in Great Britain, but worse off than the elderly in Canada and Sweden.

CONSEQUENCES OF SOCIAL STRATIFICATION

Studies of stratification in the United States have shown that social class affects many factors in a person's life. Striking differences in health and life expectancy are apparent among the social classes, especially between the lower-class poor and the other social groups. As might be expected, lower-class people are sick more frequently than others. For example, in Harlem, a predominantly black ghetto of New York City, the rate of infection with tuberculosis is more than thirteen times the national average. The only other area in the Western Hemisphere to exceed this rate is Haiti (*Newsweek*, February 22, 1988).

Tuberculosis is especially common among the homeless who are forced to live in city shelters. Even if treated properly and promptly, the treatment method makes the

problem unlikely to go away. Sufferers are required to take several antibiotics daily over a period of a year—a regimen that is difficult for many of the poor and uneducated to follow. As a result, only about four in ten tuberculosis patients in New York City public hospitals get all the medication they need for a complete recovery (*Newsweek*, February 22, 1988).

Social class differences also affect the infant mortality rate. According to the Public Voice for Food and Health Policy, the 320 poorest rural counties in the country have an infant mortality rate that is 45 percent higher than the national average. Black teenagers between 15 and 19 who become pregnant are more than twice as likely as white teenagers to have a baby that dies. In addition, a black mother is three times as likely to die giving birth than a white mother (*Statistical Abstract of the United States: 1988, 1987*).

Diet and living conditions also give a distinct advantage to the upper classes because they have access to better and more sanitary housing and can afford more balanced and nutritious food. A direct consequence of this situation is seen in each social class's life-expectancy pattern. Not surprisingly, lower-class people do not live as long as those in the upper classes. White males born in 1986 have a life expectancy more than 6 years longer than that of black males, many of whom are concentrated in the lower-income brackets.

Family, childbearing, and child-rearing patterns also vary according to social class. Women in the higher-income groups who have more education tend to have fewer children than lower-class women with less schooling. Women more often head the family in the lower class than in the other groups. Middle-class women discipline their children differently from working-class mothers. The former will punish boys and girls alike for the same infraction, whereas the latter often have different standards for sons and daughters. Also, middle-class mothers will judge the misbehaving child's intention, whereas working-class

The poor tend to commit violent crimes and crimes against property. They have much less opportunity to commit white-collar crimes. Yet they are more severely punished for their crimes than the middle-class criminal.

women are more concerned with the effects of the child's action.

There is a direct relationship between a person's social class and the possibility of his or her arrest, conviction, and sentencing if accused of a crime. For the same criminal behavior, the poor are more likely to be arrested; if arrested, they are more likely to be charged; if charged, more likely to be convicted; if convicted, more likely to be sentenced to prison; and if sentenced, more likely to be given longer prison terms than members of the middle and upper classes.

The poor are singled out for harsher treatment at the very beginning of the criminal justice system. Although many surveys show that almost all people admit to having committed a crime for which they could be imprisoned, the police are prone to arrest a poor person and release, with no formal charges, a higher-class person for the same offense. A well-to-do teenager who has been accused of a criminal offense is frequently just held by the police at the station house until the youngster can be released into the

Welfare versus Workfare

Does traditional welfare under the Aid to Families with Dependent Children (AFDC) program undermine the family unit? Does it discourage welfare recipients from finding work, thereby robbing them of their self-respect? Does it encourage men to father children without worrying about child support? An increasing number of social welfare experts are seeking to redefine the basic premise of welfare from one that asks little of recipients to one that requires individuals to work for the payments they receive in jobs assigned to them by the government. Even though "workfare" as this new system is known, is already on the books in the vast majority of states and has also become law on the federal level, it is extremely controversial—especially when two basic questions are asked: Is it fair? Does it work?

Since welfare was first put into law under the Social Security Act of 1935, it has been seen as a way to help the needy, especially women without husbands, who are forced to care for young children on their own. According to Ruth Sidel, author of *Women and Children Last*, most women are forced onto welfare by a crisis that makes it impossible for them to pay their bills. A sudden illness, the birth of a child, the loss of a job, the breakup of a marriage, or even family violence can be reason enough to need public assistance. As Sidel points out, most of these women stay on welfare two years or less—just the time they need to get back on their feet. They are not malingerers, nor are they part of a "welfare culture" that encourages dependency from generation to generation. Rather, they are women in crisis who could not survive if government took away its compassionate hand.

Moreover, say supporters of the current system, the meager monthly benefits a mother receives hardly provide an incentive to stay on the dole. (Each state has a different benefit scale. In Mississippi, for example, a family of four would receive a monthly check for $144, whereas in New York the same family would get $600, which, in both cases, is just enough to survive.)

The problem with this reasoning, say proponents of workfare, is that although only 15 percent of all

---

custody of the parents; poorer teenagers who have committed the same kind of crime more often are automatically charged and referred to juvenile court.

The poor tend to commit violent crimes and crimes against property—they have less opportunity to commit such white-collar crimes as fraud, embezzlement, or large-scale tax evasion—and they are much more severely punished for their crimes than upper-class criminals. Yet white-collar crimes are far more damaging and costly to the public than poor-people crimes. It has been estimated by the government that white-collar crimes cost more than $40 billion a year—more than 10 times the total amount of all reported thefts and more than 250 times the amount taken in all bank robberies!

Even the language used to describe the same crime committed by an upper-class criminal and a poor one reflects the disparity in the treatment they receive. The poor thief who takes $2000 is accused of stealing and usually receives a stiff prison sentence. The corporate executive who embezzles $200,000 merely has "misappropriated" the funds and may receive a suspended sentence or even no arrest at all on the promise to make restitution. A corporation often can avoid criminal prosecution by signing a "consent decree," which is in essence a

welfare recipients receive payments for 8 years or longer, they alone eat up more than half the benefits the system pays out.

Moreover, a system that enables mothers to stay home with their children until they are 6 is inconsistent with a society where more than half of all women with children under the age of 1 have returned to work. Says New York Senator Daniel Patrick Moynihan, chief Senate architect of welfare reform: "A program that was designed to pay mothers to stay at home with their children cannot succeed when we now observe most mothers going to work" (*Time*, February 16, 1987).

The workfare solution requires the vast majority of welfare recipients to earn their keep or enroll in an education, training, or job-placement program. Workfare has been implemented in such states as California and Massachusetts and is now the cornerstone of a major federal welfare reform law, which took effect in 1988. To make the workfare alternative possible, the state provides subsidized day care and continues Medicaid or equivalent health insurance benefits for a given period even after the person is off the welfare roles.

How effective are these programs? Studies report real, but modest, success. They show that welfare recipients are learning job skills in these programs and that, in the end, the programs will pay for themselves.

Thus, although workfare is far from a cure-all for the problems of the current welfare system, it offers hope that the cycle of poverty can be broken. It also offers the possibility of enormous savings if long-term welfare recipients move into the work force.

Sources: William K. Stevens, "The Welfare Consensus," *New York Times,* June 2, 1988, p. Al; "Fixing Welfare," *Time,* February 16, 1987, pp. 18–21; Myron Magnet, "America's Underclass: What To Do?" *Fortune,* May 11, 1987, pp. 130–150; Barbara Ehrenreich, "A Step Back to the Workhouse?" *Ms.,* November 1987, pp. 40–42; Martin Tolchin, "Senate, 93–3, Votes Welfare Revision Mandating Work," *New York Times,* June 17, 1988, p. Al; "Welfare Reform May Finally Be in the Works," *Business Week,* November 2, 1987, pp. 108–112; Robert P. Hey, "Workfare Benefits Modest but Lasting," *Christian Science Monitor,* June 22, 1988, p. 3.

statement that it has done nothing wrong and promises never to do it again. Were this ploy available to ordinary burglars, the police would have no need to arrest them; a burglar would merely need to sign a statement promising never to burgle again and file it with the court.

Once charged, the poor are usually dependent on court-appointed lawyers or public defenders to handle their cases. The better off rely on private lawyers who have more time, resources, and personal interests for defending their cases.

If convicted of the same kind of crime as a well-to-do offender, the poor criminal is more likely to be sentenced and will generally receive a longer prison term. A study of individuals with no prior records convicted in federal courts showed that 84 percent of the nonpoor were recommended for probation, whereas only 73 percent of the poor were so treated. As for prison terms, the sentence for burglary, a crime of the poor, is generally more than twice as long as that for fraud; and a robber will draw an average sentence more than six times longer than an embezzler. The result is a prison system heavily populated by the poor (Reimann, 1979).

Another serious consequence of social stratification is mental illness. The types of mental illness suffered seem to be correlated

The mentally ill among the homeless are the least likely to reach out for help and the most likely to remain on the streets.

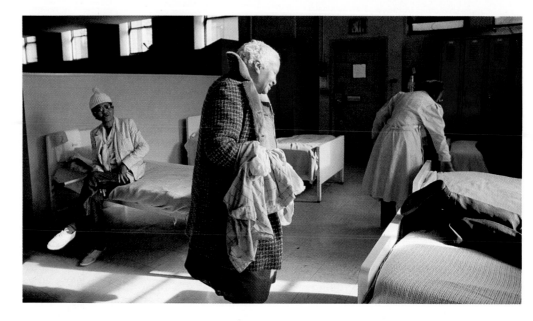

with social class, as is the likelihood of spending time in a mental hospital (Hollingshead and Redlich, 1958; Bottomore, 1966; Jencks et al., 1972). Studies have also shown that at least one-third of all homeless people suffer from schizophrenia, manic-depressive psychosis, or other mental disorders. These people are the least likely to reach out for help and most likely to remain on the streets in utter poverty and despair year after year (Torrey, 1988).

Thus, social class has very real and immediate consequences for individuals. In fact, class membership affects the quality of people's lives more than any other single variable.

SUMMARY

A society that has a class system of stratification will have several social classes defined in hierarchical terms of status or prestige present. A social class consists of a category of people who share certain distinctive attitudes, values, opportunities, similar economic and vocational positions, and similar life-styles, thus forming a subculture within the larger culture of the society as a whole.

Social classes differ in many different characteristics, and there is some disagreement among sociologists as to what is most important in determining social class.

When using the objective approach to the measurement of social class, researchers determine a set number of social classes in advance and then assign people to each class according to given criteria.

The reputational approach to social class relies on the opinions the community members have of one another.

In the subjective approach to measuring social class, individuals are asked to place themselves into one of several categories.

There is little agreement among sociologists as to how many social classes exist in the United States and what their characteristics are. Following a relatively common approach, we assume that there are five social classes in the United States: upper class, upper middle class, lower middle class, working class, and lower class.

On a very basic level, poverty refers to a condition in which people do not have enough money to maintain a standard of living that includes the basic necessities of life. Depending on which official or quasi-official approach one uses, it is possible to document that anywhere from 14 million to 45 million Americans are living in poverty. Sociologists refer to the "feminization of poverty" to describe the disproportionate concentration of poverty among women.

The official definition of poverty that we use for the poverty index was developed by the Social Security Administration in 1964.

Government programs that provide benefits to families or individuals can be divided into three categories: (1) social insurance, (2) means-tested cash assistance, and (3) noncash benefits.

Social insurance benefits are not means-tested, meaning that you do not have to be poor to receive them. They go primarily to the middle class.

Means-tested cash assistance programs go mainly to the poor and include such items as Aid to Families with Dependent Children (AFDC) and Supplemental Security Income (SSI).

Noncash assistance programs include items that are both means-tested, such as Medicaid, food stamps, subsidized housing, free or reduced-price school lunch programs, and non-means-tested, such as Medicare and subsidized lunches for all students in participating schools.

It appears that economic rewards are more unequally distributed in the United States than elsewhere in the Western industrialized world.

Studies of stratification in the United States have shown that social class affects many factors in a person's life. Striking differences in health and life expectancy are apparent among the social classes, especially between the lower-class poor and the other social groups.

Chapter 10

RACIAL AND ETHNIC MINORITIES

Paul and Philip Malone, twin brothers, wanted to join the Boston Fire Department back in 1977. The only problem was that the brothers received scores of 69 and 57, respectively, on the written portion of the test, when the passing grade was 82.

During this same period, Boston was under pressure to increase its minority population within the fire department and had separate, and lower, passing grades for non-whites.

Paul and Philip were aware of the fact that they had a great-grandmother who was black. The Malones had not given the issue of race much thought during their original application. They decided to apply again, only this time as black applicants. They took the test again and this time their scores were considered passing, because the city had imposed lower passing grades for minority applicants. The Malones were hired and were listed in the records as black.

Once on the job, the issue of race appeared to be relatively unimportant. The Malones did their job well for 10½ years and then in 1988 decided to apply for promotion. As their applications were being reviewed, questions arose about their race because they did not look black. They continued to insist that their claim to being black was legitimate and produced photos of their great-grandmother. Their protests were to no avail, however, and they were fired for misrepresenting their race on the original application (*Boston Herald,* September 26, 1988).

A similar case in which the claim of being a member of the black race was challenged took place in Stockton, California. In a close election Ralph Lee White, a black man, lost his seat on the city council to Mark Linton Stebbins, a pale-skinned, blue-eyed man with kinky reddish-brown hair. White claimed Stebbins would not represent the minority district because he was white. Stebbins claimed he was black.

Birth records showed Stebbins's parents and grandparents were white. He has five sisters and one brother, all of whom are white. Yet, when asked to declare his race, he noted: "First, I'm a human being, but I'm black."

Stebbins did not deny that he was raised as a white person. He only began to consider himself black after he moved to Stockton. "As far as a birth certificate goes, then I'm white, but I am black. There is no question about that" (*Stockton Record,* January 17, 1984).

Stebbins now belongs to a black Baptist church and to the NAACP. Most of his friends are black. He has been married three times, first to a white woman, and then to two black women. He has three children from the first two marriages; two are being raised as white, the third as black. He states he considers himself black—"culturally, socially, genetically."

Ralph Lee White remained unconvinced, especially with his former council seat having gone to Stebbins. ". . . Now, his mama's White and his daddy's White, so how can he be Black? If the mama's an elephant and the daddy's an elephant, the baby can't be a lion. He's just a White boy with a permanent" (*Stockton Record,* April 1, 1984).

Stebbins believes the issue of race is tied to identifying with a community in terms of beliefs, aspirations, and concerns. He notes that a person's racial identity depends on much more than birth records.

These two examples, which on the one hand may seem slightly humorous, are at the same time related to some very serious issues. Throughout history, people have gone to great lengths to determine what race a person belonged to. In many states laws were devised to determine your race if, like the Malones, you had mixed racial ancestry. Usually these laws existed for the purpose of discriminating against certain minority groups. Our examples also raise the question of whether you can change your race from white to black, especially if you have no black ancestors. Mark Stebbins seems to think so. In this chapter we will explore these and other issues related to race and ethnicity as we try to understand how people come to be identified with certain groups and what that membership means.

THE CONCEPT OF RACE

Although the exact origin of the word is not known, the term race has been a highly controversial concept for a long time. Many authorities suspect that it is of Semitic origin, coming from a word that some translations of the Bible render as "race," as in the "race of Abraham," but that is otherwise translated as "seed" or "generation." Other scholars trace the origin to the Czech word *raz,* meaning "artery" or "blood"; others to the Latin *generatio* or the Basque *arraca* or *arraze,* referring to a male stud animal. Some trace it to the Spanish *ras,* itself of Arabic derivation, meaning "head" or "origin." In all these possible sources, the word has a biological significance that implies descent, blood, or relationship.

We shall use the term **race** to refer to a category of people who are defined as similar because of a number of physical characteristics. Often race is based on an arbitrary set of features chosen to suit the labeler's purposes and convenience. As long ago as 1781, German physiologist Johann Blumenbach realized that racial categories did not reflect the actual divisions among human groups. As he put it, "When the matter is thoroughly considered, you see that all [human groups] do so run into one another, and that one variety of mankind does so sensibly pass into the other, that you cannot mark out the limits between them" (Montagu, 1964). Blumenbach believed racial differences were superficial and changeable, and modern scientific evidence seems to support this view.

Throughout history, races have been defined along genetic, legal, and social lines, each presenting its own set of problems.

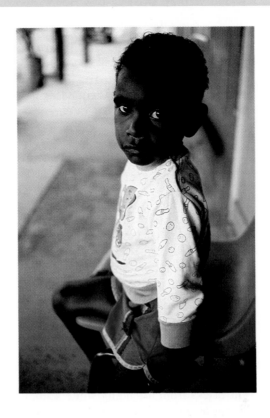

Throughout history, races have been defined along genetic, legal, and social lines, each presenting its own set of problems.

GENETIC DEFINITIONS

Geneticists define race by noting differences in gene frequencies among selected groups. The number of distinct races that can be defined by this method depends on the particular genetic trait under investigation. Differences in traits, such as hair and nose type, have proved to be of no value in making biological classifications of human beings. In fact, the physiological and mental similarities among groups of people appear to be far greater than any superficial differences in skin color and physical characteristics. Also, the various so-called racial criteria appear to be independent of one another. For example, any form of hair may occur with any skin color—a narrow nose gives no clue to an individual's skin pigmentation or hair texture. Thus, Australian aborigines have dark skins, broad noses, and an abundance of curly-to-wavy hair; Asiatic Indians also have dark skins but have narrow noses and straight hair. Like-

race A category of people who are defined as similar because of a number of physical characteristics.

wise, if head form is selected as the major criterion for sorting, an equally diverse collection of physical types will appear in each category. If people are sorted on the basis of skin color, therefore, all kinds of noses, hair, and head forms will appear in each category.

LEGAL DEFINITIONS

By and large, legal definitions of race have been devised not to determine who was black or of another race, but who was not white. The laws were to be used in instances in which separation and different treatments were to be applied to members of certain groups. Segregation laws are an excellent example. If railroad conductors had to assign someone to either the black or white cars, they needed fairly precise guidelines for knowing whom to seat where. Most legal definitions of race were devices to prevent blacks from attending white schools, serving on juries, holding certain jobs, or patronizing certain public places. The official guidelines could then be applied to individual cases. The common assumption that "anyone not white was colored," although imperfect, did minimize ambiguity.

There has been, however, very little consistency among the various legal definitions of race that have been devised. The state of Missouri, for example, made "one-eighth or more Negro blood" the criterion for nonwhite status. Georgia was even more rigid in its definition and noted:

> The term "white person" shall include only persons of the white or Caucasian race, who have no ascertainable trace of either Negro, African, West Indian, Asiatic Indian, Mongolian, Japanese, or Chinese blood in their veins. No person, any of whose ancestors [was] . . . a colored person or person of color, shall be deemed to be a white person. (Novit-Evans and Welch, 1983)

Virginia had a similar law but made exceptions for individuals with one-fourth or more Indian "blood" and less than one-sixteenth Negro "blood." These Virginians were regarded as Indians as long as they remained on an Indian reservation, but if they moved, they were regarded as blacks (Berry and Tischler, 1978).

Most of these laws are artifacts of the segregation era. However, if people think that all vestiges of them have disappeared, they are wrong. As recently as 1982, a dispute arose over Louisiana's law requiring anyone of more than one-thirty-second African descent to be classified as black. Louisiana's one-thirty-second law is actually of recent vintage, having been enacted in 1971. Before this law, racial classification depended on what was referred to as "common repute." The 1971 law was intended to eliminate racial classifications by gossip and inference. In September 1982 Mrs. Susie Guillory Phipps, having noticed that her birth certificate classified her as "colored," filed to have her classification changed to white. The state objected and produced an eleven-generation family tree tracing Mrs. Phipps's ancestry back to an early eighteenth-century black slave and a white plantation owner (Novit-Evans and Welch, 1983).

SOCIAL DEFINITIONS

The social definition of race, which is the decisive one in most interactions, pays little attention to an individual's hereditary physical features or to whether his or her percentage of "Negro blood" is one-fourth, one-eighth, or one-sixteenth. According to social definitions of race, if a person presents himself or herself as a member of a certain race and others respond to that person as a member of that race, then it makes little sense to say that he or she is not a member of that race.

In Latin American countries, having black ancestry or black features does not automatically define an individual as black. For example, in Brazil many individuals are listed in the census as white and are considered by their friends and associates to be white, even if they had a grandmother who was of pure African descent. It is much the same in Puerto Rico, where anyone who is not obviously black is classified as either mulatto or white. In the Republic of South Africa, a sharp distinction is drawn between the natives and the Cape coloured, who have mixed black and white ancestry. The latter are accorded privileges denied to blacks, and they hold a social position intermediate between that of the dominant whites and the subordinate blacks.

The U.S. census relies on a self-definition system of racial classification and does not apply any legal or genetic rules. In the 1990 census respondents are asked to place themselves within one of the fifteen possible groups listed. If a person of mixed racial parentage cannot provide a single response to the question, the race of the person's mother is used. If a single response cannot be provided for the mother, then the first race listed is used.

THE CONCEPT OF ETHNIC GROUP

An **ethnic group** has a distinct cultural tradition with which its own members identify and that may or may not be recognized by others (Glazer and Moynihan, 1975). An ethnic group need not be a numerical minority within a nation (although the term sometimes is used that way).

Many ethnic groups form subcultures (see Chapter 3): They usually possess a high degree of internal loyalty and adherence to basic customs, making for similarity in family patterns, religion, and cultural values. They often possess distinctive folkways and mores; customs of dress, art, and ornamentation; moral codes and value systems; and patterns of recreation. There is usually something to which the whole group is de-

ethnic group A group that has a distinct cultural tradition with which its own members identify and which may or may not be recognized by others.

Many ethnic groups form subcultures with a high degree of internal loyalty and adherence to basic customs.

voted, such as a monarch, a religion, a language, or a territory. Above all, there is a feeling of association. The group's members are aware of a relationship because of a shared loyalty to a cultural tradition. The folkways may change, the institutions may become radically altered, and the object of allegiance may shift from one trait to another, but loyalty to the group and the consciousness of belonging remain as long as the group exists.

An ethnic group may or may not have its own separate political unit; it may have had one in the past, it may aspire to have one in the future, or its members may be scattered through existing countries. Political unification is not an essential feature of ethnic groups. Accordingly, despite the unique cultural features that set them apart as subcultures, many ethnic groups—Arabs, French Canadians, Flemish, Scots, Jews, and Pennsylvania Dutch, for example—are part of larger political units. The Soviet Union is composed of more than a hundred ethnic groups, including polish Kazak, German, Armenian, Georgian, Tatar, and Ukrainian.

minority A group of people who, because of physical or cultural characteristics, are singled out from others in the society in which they live for different and unequal treatment, and who therefore regard themselves as objects of collective discrimination.

Prejudice against immigrant groups often centered around the competition they presented for jobs.

THE CONCEPT OF MINORITY GROUP

Whenever race and ethnicity are discussed, it is usually assumed that the object of the discussion is a minority group. Technically this is not always true, as we shall see shortly. A minority is often thought of as being small in number. The concept of minority, rather than implying a small number, should be thought of as implying differential treatment and exclusion from full social participation by the dominant group in a society. In this sense we shall use Louis Wirth's definition of a **minority** as "a group of people who, because of physical or cultural characteristics, are singled out from others in the society in which they live for differential and unequal treatment, and who therefore regard themselves as objects of collective discrimination" (Linton, 1945).

In this definition, Wirth speaks of "physical and cultural characteristics" and not of gender, age, disability, or undesirable behavioral patterns. It is obvious that he is referring to racial and ethnic groups in his definition of minorities. Some writers have suggested, however, that many other groups are in the same position as those more commonly thought of as minorities and endure the same sociological and psychological problems. In this light, women, homosexuals, adolescents, the aged, the handicapped, the radical right or left, and intellectuals can be thought of as minority groups.

PROBLEMS IN RACE AND ETHNIC RELATIONS

All too often when people with different racial and ethnic identities come together, friction develops among them. People's suspicions and fears are often aroused by those whom they feel to be "different."

PREJUDICE

There are many definitions of prejudice. Prejudice, according to one popular way of putting it, is being down on something you are not up on, the implication being that prejudice results from a lack of knowledge of, or unfamiliarity with, the subject. People, particularly those with a strong sense of identity, often have feelings of prejudice toward others who are not like themselves. Literally, prejudice means a "prejudgment." According to Louis Wirth (1944), prejudice is "an attitude with an emotional bias." But there is a problem with this definition. All of us, through the process of socialization, acquire attitudes, which may be in response not only to racial and ethnic groups but also to many things in our environment. We come to have attitudes toward cats, roses, blue eyes, chocolate cheesecake, television programs, and even ourselves. These attitudes run the gamut from love to hate, from esteem to contempt, from loyalty to indifference. How have we developed these attitudes? Has it been through the scientific evaluation of information, or by other, less logical means?

For our purposes we shall define **prejudice** as an irrationally based negative, or occasionally positive, attitude toward certain groups and their members.

What is the cause of prejudice? Although pursuing that question is beyond the scope of this book, we can list some of the uses to which prejudice is put and the social functions it serves. First, a prejudice, simply because it is shared, helps draw together those who hold it. It promotes a feeling of "we-ness," of being part of an in-group— and it helps define such group boundaries. Especially in a complex world, belonging to an in-group and consequently feeling "special" or "superior" can be an important social identity for many people.

Mexicans who live in the provinces, for example, have a we–they attitude with respect to those who live in Mexico City, the country's capital. They complain that "gauchos," as Mexico City natives are called, are a "plundering species" that, according to author José Teheran, is "contemptuous of the habits and customs of others; indifferent, impudent, infallible, and excessively cunning of tongue; underhanded, greedy, and capable of anything." (Rohter, 1988).

A second function of prejudice involves competition for limited resources. When two or more groups are competing against one another for access to scarce resources (jobs, for example), it makes it easier if one can write off his or her competitors as somehow less than human or inherently unworthy. Nations at war consistently characterize each other negatively, using terms that seem to deprive the enemy of any humanity whatsoever.

Third, psychologists suggest that prejudice allows us to project onto others those parts of ourselves that we do not like and therefore try to avoid facing. For example, most of us feel stupid at one time or another. How comforting it is to know that we belong to a group that is inherently more intelligent than another group! Who does not feel lazy sometimes? But how good it is that we do not belong to that group—the one everybody knows is lazy!

Of course, prejudice also has many negative consequences, or *dysfunctions,* to use the sociological term. For one thing, it limits our vision of the world around us, reducing social complexities and richness to a sterile and empty caricature. But aside from this affect on us as individuals, prejudice also has negative consequences for the whole of society. Most notably, it is the necessary ingredient of discrimination, a problem found in many societies—including our own.

DISCRIMINATION

Prejudice is a subjective feeling, whereas discrimination is an overt action. **Discrimination** simply means differential treatment,

prejudice An irrationally based negative, or occasionally positive, attitude toward certain groups and their members.

discrimination Differential treatment, usually unequal and injurious, accorded to individuals who are assumed to belong to a particular category or group.

ARE WE GROWING MORE OR LESS TOLERANT?

acts has decreased significantly since 1982. Whether or not this reflects what is actually happening in society remains unclear.

No one knows how many of us feel the barbs of discrimination—barbs that range from angry insults to acts of violence—simply because of our racial or ethnic identities. Data like these are impossible to collect because most of these incidents go unreported. From extremely limited information available to three separate government and private agencies, however, we see the possibility that discriminatory acts against Jews, blacks, Hispanics, and Asians are leveling off. As we can see from the graph below, the number of reported

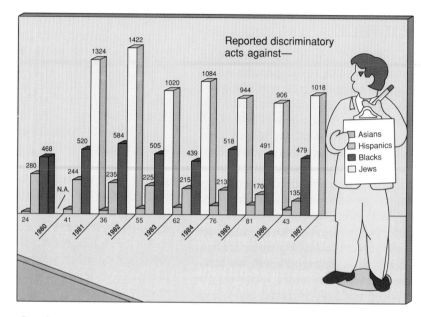

Reported discriminatory acts against—

Asians
Hispanics
Blacks
Jews

Growing Tolerance? *Source:* U.S. News & World Report, *August 29/ September 5, 1988, p. 103. Basic data: Community Relations Service, U.S. Department of Justice, B'nai B'rith International.*

usually unequal and injurious, accorded to individuals who are assumed to belong to a particular category or group. For example, in the Soviet Union some 400,000 Jews are trying to emigrate. Their reason for wanting to go: overt discrimination that prevents them from practicing their religion and limits their access to equal economic and social opportunity. Closer to home, discrimination against blacks and other minorities has occurred throughout U.S. history. At the start of World War II, for example, there were no blacks in the Marine Corps; blacks could only be admitted into the navy as mess stewards; and the army had a 10 percent quota on black enlistments. Although there are no such restric-

tions today, blacks are still underrepresented in the armed services officer corps. Although blacks make up nearly 22 percent of enlisted personnel, they make up only 6.6 percent of officers. At one time or another, most minorities in this country have been subjected to differential treatment limiting opportunity (McBride, 1988).

Prejudice does not always result in discrimination. Although our attitudes and our overt behavior are closely related, they are neither identical nor dependent on each other. We may have feelings of antipathy without expressing them overtly or even giving the slightest indication of their presence. This simple fact—namely, that attitudes and overt behavior vary independently—has been used by Robert Merton to develop the following classification of racial prejudice and discrimination. There are, he believes, four types of people.

Unprejudiced Nondiscriminators

These people are neither prejudiced against members of other racial and ethnic groups nor do they practice discrimination. They believe implicitly in the American ideals of justice, freedom, equality of opportunity, and dignity of the individual. These people are motivated to spread these ideals and values and to fight against those forms of discrimination that make a mockery of them. At the same time, unprejudiced nondiscriminators have their shortcomings. They enjoy talking to one another, engaging in mutual exhortation and thereby giving psychological support to one another. They believe their own spiritual house is in order; thus, they do not feel pangs of guilt and accordingly shrink from any collective effort to set things right.

Unprejudiced Discriminators

This type includes those who constantly think of expediency. Although they themselves may be free from prejudice, they will keep silent when bigots speak out. They will not condemn acts of discrimination but will make concessions to the intolerant and will accept discriminatory practices for fear that to do otherwise would hurt their own position.

Prejudiced Nondiscriminators

This category is for the timid bigots who do not accept the tenets of equality for all, but conform to it and give it lip service when the slightest pressure is applied. Here belong those who hesitate to express their prejudice when in the presence of those who are more tolerant. Among them are the employers who hate certain minorities but hire them rather than run afoul of affirmative action laws, and the labor leaders who suppress

In this photo from World War I, a black soldier in France is firing on the Germans. Throughout both world wars, the U.S. armed forces remained segregated.

Ku Klux Klan members are an example of what Robert Merton refers to as prejudiced discriminators.

their personal racial bias when the majority of their followers demand an end to discrimination.

Prejudiced Discriminators

These are the bigots, pure and unashamed. They do not believe in equality, nor do they hesitate to give free expression to their intolerance both in their speech and in their actions. For them there is no conflict between attitudes and behavior. They practice discrimination, believing that it is not only proper but in fact their duty to do so (Berry and Tischler, 1978).

Knowing a person's attitudes does not mean that that person's behavior always can be predicted. Attitudes and behavior are frequently inconsistent because of such factors as the nature and magnitude of the

institutionalized prejudice and discrimination Complex societal arrangements that restrict the life chances and choices of a specifically defined group.

social pressures in a particular situation. The influence of situational factors on behavior can be traced in Figure 10.1.

INSTITUTIONALIZED PREJUDICE AND DISCRIMINATION

Sociologists also tend to distinguish between individual and **institutionalized prejudice and discrimination.** When individuals display prejudicial attitudes and discriminatory behavior, it is often because they assume the out-group is inferior. By contrast, when there is institutionalized prejudice and discrimination, it is because of complex societal arrangements that restrict the life chances and choices of a specific group, as opposed to those of the dominant group. In this way, benefits are given to one group and withheld from another. Society is structured in such a way that people's values and experiences are shaped by a prejudiced social order. Discrimination is seen as a by-product of a purposive attempt to maintain social, political, and economic advantage (Davis, 1979).

An argument can be made that institutionalized prejudice and discrimination are responsible for the substandard education that many blacks receive in the United States. Schools that are predominantly black tend to be inferior at every level to schools that are predominantly white. The facilities for blacks are usually of poorer quality than those for whites. Many blacks also attend unaccredited black colleges where the teachers are less likely to hold advanced degrees and are poorly paid. The poorer education that blacks receive is one of the reasons they generally are in lower occupational categories than whites are. In this way, institutionalized prejudice and discrimination combine to maintain blacks in a disadvantaged social and economic position (Duberman, 1976).

Institutionalized prejudice and discrimination are very much factors in race relations in South Africa. In 1948, the gov-

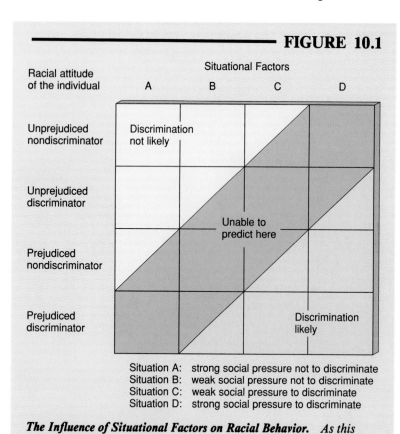

FIGURE 10.1

Situation A: strong social pressure not to discriminate
Situation B: weak social pressure not to discriminate
Situation C: weak social pressure to discriminate
Situation D: strong social pressure to discriminate

The Influence of Situational Factors on Racial Behavior. As this diagram shows, the degree of social pressure being exerted can cause individuals of inherently dissimilar attitudes to exhibit relatively similar behaviors in a given situation.

ernment formally institutionalized total segregation, and *apartheid* (separateness) has become a national policy. It extends into every aspect of life, from education to job and marriage restrictions, all the way down to separate doorways for the different "races" in public buildings. Although some *apartheid* restrictions have been relaxed recently as a result of intense international pressures, the basic policy is unlikely to be abolished in the near future.

Under the *apartheid* system, the population of South Africa is divided into four groups, rigidly defined in "racial" terms. At the top are the whites—descendants of the original Dutch (called Afrikaners) and British colonists. Below the whites are the Asians, descendants of Malaysian slaves and recent immigrants from the East. Below the Asians are the coloreds, descendants of unions among the three other groups (although official Afrikaner policy outlawed such "race mixing" until the law was changed in 1985). Finally, at the very bottom of the hierarchy, are the blacks, descendants of the original native populations and the Bantu-speaking peoples who fought the Dutch settlers for the territory. Laws have been enacted to keep these four "races," or castes, separate from one another—but most especially to ensure that economic and political power remained in the hands of the whites, who today number some 4.9 million people, out of a total population of 31 million (22.5 million of whom are blacks).

Apartheid serves the economic and political interests of the ruling white caste, and it is built into almost all the institutions of South African society—especially those controlled by Afrikaners. Until recently the Dutch Reformed church, the largest religious denomination in South Africa, endorsed segregation and declared that salvation only existed in the separation of the races (Carstens, 1978). Carstens points out that about 70 percent of all Christians in South Africa are black, suggesting that the Reformed church's concern clearly is to preserve the "racial" caste system—not Christianity.

South Africa's educational system also embodies *apartheid*. Not only are its schools fully segregated and centrally controlled, but *apartheid* also is taught as a valued norm. Support of separation of the races is instilled in every student.

The dangers of pollution through sexual contact between "racial" castes are driven home in many textbooks; the emphasis is on the plight of the children of mixed racial parentage, who, it is claimed, are rejected by blacks and whites alike.

The current policy of the South African government is to "resolve" the racial problem by relocating all 20 million blacks to ten Bantustans, or territories, that are in the process of being given token independence and that occupy 13.7 percent of South Africa's land area. But the Bantustans are located in the least desirable regions and clearly cannot be self-supporting. Thus most black males must continue to live and work in white South Africa, but are deprived of all rights as South African citizens, because they are citizens of the politically independent Bantustan nations. This "solution" perpetuates the presence in South Africa of cheap and easily exploited black workers at the same time it attempts to defuse the accusations of racism that are leveled at the South African government.

PATTERNS OF RACIAL AND ETHNIC RELATIONS

Relations among racial and ethnic groups seem to include an infinite variety of human experiences. They run the gamut of emotions and appear to be utterly unpredictable, capricious, and irrational. They range from curiosity and hospitality, at the one extreme, to bitter hostility at the other. In this section we shall show that there is a limited number of outcomes when racial and ethnic groups come into contact. These include assimilation, pluralism, subjugation, segregation, expulsion, and annihilation. In some cases, these categories overlap—for instance, segregation can be considered a form of subjugation—but each has distinct traits that make it worth examining separately.

ASSIMILATION

assimilation The process whereby groups with different cultures come to have a common culture.

Assimilation is the process whereby groups with different cultures come to have a common culture. It refers to more than just dress or language and includes less tangible items such as values, sentiments, and attitudes. We are really referring to the fusion of cultural heritages.

Assimilation is the integration of new elements with old ones. Transferring a culture from one group to another is a highly complex process, often involving the rejection of ancient ideologies, habits, customs, language, and attitudes. It also includes the elusive problem of selection. Of the many possibilities presented by the other culture, which ones will be adopted? Why did the American Indians, for example, when they were confronted with the white civilization, take avidly to guns, horses, rum, knives, and glass beads, but show no interest in certain other features to which whites themselves attached the highest value?

In the process of assimilation, one society sets the pattern, for the give-and-take of culture seems never to operate on a fifty-fifty basis. Invariably one group has a much larger role in the process than the other does, and various factors interact to make that so. Usually one of the societies enjoys greater prestige than the other, giving it an advantage in the assimilation process; or one is better suited for the environment than the other; or one has greater numerical strength than the other. Thus the pattern for the United States was set by the British colonists, and to that pattern the other groups have been asked to adjust. This process has often been referred to as **Anglo conformity** —the renunciation of the ancestral cultures

Anglo conformity A form of assimilation that involves the renunciation of the ancestral culture in favor of Anglo-American behavior and values.

in favor of Anglo-American behavior and values (Gordon, 1964; Berry and Tischler, 1978).

Sometimes assimilation is a major goal of a country, as it was in the Soviet Union immediately after the 1917 revolution. The leaders of the new socialist state believed that regional and ethnic nationalism was a holdover from feudal times and could be exploited by enemies of the new regime to divide and conquer the Soviet Union. During the 1930s and 1940s an intensive program of "Russification" was carried out through the school system, with the intention of making Russian the one true national language. Nonetheless, regional ethnic identification in the Soviet Union remains very strong both in people's sense of their own individual identity and as a form of protest against the continued political dominance by the Great Russians, who make up 53.5 percent of the entire population. Even though Russian is the official language of the entire nation, some 96 to 98 percent of the major ethnic minorities in the Soviet Union continue to use their own languages in daily life (Pipes, 1975).

Although assimilation frequently has been a professed political goal in the United States, it has seldom been fully achieved. For example, consider the case of the Native Americans (Indians). In 1924 they were granted full United States citizenship. Nevertheless, the federal government's policies regarding the integration of Native Americans into American society wavered back and forth until the Hoover Commission Report of 1946 became the guideline for all subsequent administrations. The report stated:

> A program for the Indian peoples must include progressive measures for their complete integration into the mass of the population as full, tax-paying [members of the larger society]. . . . Young employable Indians and the better cultured families should be encouraged and assisted to leave the reservations and set themselves up on the land or in business. (Shepardson, 1963)

However, to this day Native American groups remain largely unassimilated into the mainstream of American life. About 55 percent live on or near reservations, and most of the rest live in impoverished urban ghettos. In addition, many Native Americans who left the reservation for greater opportunity in America's cities are returning again. Despite the economic and life-style hardships they face on the reservation, their ethnic pride overrides any desire to assimilate (*Newsweek,* May 2, 1988).

Other groups, whether or not by choice, also have not been assimilated. The Amish, for instance, have steadfastly maintained their separate subculture in the face of Anglo conformity pressures from the larger American society.

China provides an interesting example of what might be called reverse assimilation. Usually it is the defeated minority groups who are assimilated into the culture of the politically dominant group. In the seventeenth century, however, Mongol invaders conquered China and installed themselves as rulers. The Mongols were nomadic pastoralists (see Chapter 5). They were so impressed with the advanced achievements of the Chinese civilization that they gave up their own ways and took on the trappings of Chinese culture: language, manners, dress, and philosophy. During their rule the Mongols fully assimilated the Chinese culture.

PLURALISM

Pluralism, or the development and coexistence of separate racial and ethnic group identities within a society, is a philosophical viewpoint that attempts to produce what is considered to be a desirable social situation. When people use the term *pluralism* today, they believe they are describing a condition that seems to be developing in contemporary American society. They often ignore the ideological foundation of pluralism.

The person principally responsible for the development of the theory of cultural pluralism was Horace Kallen, born in the area of Germany known as Silesia. He came to Boston at the age of 5 and was raised in an orthodox Jewish home. As he progressed through the Boston public schools, he underwent a common second-generation phenomenon. He started to reject his home environment and religion and developed an uncritical enthusiasm for the United States. As he put it, "It seemed to me that the identity of every human being with every other was the important thing, and that the term 'American' should nullify the meaning of every other term in one's personal makeup. . . ."

While Kallen was a student at Harvard, he experienced a number of shocks. Working in a nearby social settlement, he came in contact with liberal and socialist ideas and observed people expressing numerous ethnic goals and aspirations. This exposure caused him to question his definition of what it meant to be an American.

This quandary was compounded by his experiences in the American literature class of Professor Barrett Wendell, who believed that Puritan traits and ideals were at the core of the American value structure. The Puritans, in turn, had modeled themselves after the Old Testament prophets. Wendell even suggested that the early Puritans were largely of Jewish descent. These ideas led Kallen to believe that he could be an unassimilated Jew and still belong to the core of the American value system.

After discovering that he could be totally Jewish and still be American, he came to realize that the same was true for other ethnic groups as well. All ethnic groups, he felt, should preserve their own separate culture without shame or guilt. As he put it, "Democracy involves not the elimination of differences, but the perfection and conservation of differences."

Pluralism is a philosophy that not only assumes that minorities have rights but also considers the life-style of a minority group to be a legitimate and even desirable way of participating in society.

Pluralism is a reaction against assimilationism and the melting-pot idea. It is a phi-

pluralism The development and coexistence of separate racial and ethnic group identities in a society in which no single subgroup dominates.

INTERNATIONAL ADOPTION AND INTERRACIAL FAMILIES

There has been a substantial increase in international adoption in recent years. This type of adoption is an outgrowth of the frustrating obstacles families are likely to experience when trying to adopt a child through traditional channels.

The typical adopters, a white middle-class couple, have three choices. They can wait 3 to 5 years—and sometimes as long as 10 years—for a healthy, white American baby. They can at-tempt to adopt a black or special-needs child. Or they can adopt a child from abroad and wait an average of only 1 or 2 years.

The long wait is enough to discourage many couples from trying to adopt a white American infant. But what about a white couple that wishes to adopt a black child. Here there are serious problems also, even though there are thousands of black children available for adoption. The National Association of Black Social Workers issued a statement in 1985 officially noting that black children should not be placed with white families. Most adoption agencies have followed this proclamation.

The difficulties with American adoptions are producing a quiet revolution. There has been a doubling in the number of children admitted to the United States for adoption in just the last 6 years. Foreign adoptions now account for 20 percent of all unrelated adoptions in the United States.

There are usually no minimum income requirements for adopters, but they must have enough money to cover a variety of costs. They will have to pay agency fees, immigration costs, and sometimes travel costs to the child's country of origin. This usually adds up to about $5000, although in some instances it can be considerably more.

South American adoptions usually cost more than Asian adoptions because many South

Pluralism is a reaction against assimilationism and encourages minorities to celebrate their differences.

losophy that not only assumes that minorities have rights but also considers the life-style of the minority group to be a legitimate, and even desirable, way of participating in society. The theory of pluralism celebrates the differences among groups of people. The theory also implies a hostility to existing inequalities in the status and treatment of minority groups. Pluralism has provided a means for minorities to resist the pull of assimilation, by allowing them to claim that they constitute the very structure of the social order.

From the assimilationist point of view, the minority is seen as a subordinate group that should give up its identity as quickly as possible. Pluralism, on the other hand, assumes that the minority is a primary unit of society and that the unity of the whole depends on the harmony of the various parts.

American countries require one or both parents to travel to the country for a week or more while the transfer of custody takes place. Asian adoptions do not have this requirement, and the children usually are brought to the United States by escorts who bring several children at a time.

During the last decade, 74 percent of foreign adoptions have been from Asia, 21 percent from Central and South America, and 5 percent from other parts of the world. More than half the children in foreign adoptions come from South Korea. Because Korea has a strong emphasis on ancestral worship and racial purity, illegitimate children and children of mixed race have little chance of getting a good educa-tion or a good job. Married cou-ples also give up infants some-times because of lack of money or space.

South Korea cooperates with foreign adopters because of a strong concern about the chil-dren's well-being, although the country hopes to limit and even-tually end foreign adoptions.

Couples who adopt foreign-born children are generally col-lege-educated, suburban, and earn an average of $36,000 a year. They usually have no children of their own and have been married an average of 7 years.

Singles, who have usually had no chance with traditional adoptions, have also turned to foreign adoptions. Because sin-gles are excluded from adopting Korean children, they usually apply for other Asian or Central and South American children.

Singles, like other adoptive parents, are well-educated, mid-dle-income people in their mid-thirties. More likely to be women than men, they are concentrated in the helping professions.

While this adoption revolu-tion continues to grow and ap-pears to be working out well, a haunting question still remains about the need to import chil-dren, while many American mi-nority children and older and spe-cial-needs children cannot be placed in appropriate homes.

Source: Leslie Mann Smith, "Babies from Abroad," *American Demographics,* March 1988, pp. 38–41, 56.

Switzerland provides an example of balanced pluralism that so far has worked out exceptionally well (Kohn, 1956). After a short civil war between the Catholics and the Protestants in 1847, a new constitution —drafted in 1848—established a confed-eration of cantons (states), and church-state relations were left up to the individual cantons. The three major languages— German, French, and Italian—were de-clared official languages for the whole na-tion, and their respective speakers were ac-knowledged as political equals (Petersen, 1975).

Switzerland's linguistic regions are cul-turally quite distinctive. Italian-speaking Switzerland has a Mediterranean flavor; in French-speaking Switzerland one senses the culture of France; and German-speaking Switzerland is distinctly Germanic. How-ever, all three linguistic groups are fiercely pro-Swiss, and the German-Swiss especially have strong anti-German sentiments.

SUBJUGATION

One of the consequences of the interaction of racial and ethnic groups has been **subjugation**—the subordination of one group and the assumption of a position of authority, power, and domination by the other. The members of the subordinate group may for a time accept their lower status and even devise ingenious rationali-zations for it.

In theory we could assume that two groups may come together and develop an egalitarian relationship. However, there are few cases in which racial and ethnic groups have established such a relationship. For the

subjugation The subor-dination of one group and the assumption of a position of authority, power, and domination by the other.

ghetto A term originally used to refer to the segregated quarter of a city where the Jews in Europe were often forced to live. Today it is used to refer to any kind of segregated living environment.

expulsion The process of forcing a group to leave the territory in which it resides.

segregation A form of subjugation that refers to the act, process, or state of being set apart.

forced migration The expulsion of a group of people through direct action.

most part this is so because there are few instances in which group contact has been based on the complete equality of power. Differences in power will invariably lead to a situation of superior and inferior position. The greater the discrepancy in power of the groups involved, the greater the extent and scope of subjugation will be.

Why should different levels of power between two groups lead to the domination of one by the other? Gerhard Lenski (1966) proposed that it is because people have a desire to control goods and services. No matter how much they have, they are never satisfied. In addition, high status is often associated with the consumption of goods and services. Therefore, demand will exceed supply, and as Lenski claims, a struggle for rewards will be present in every human society. The outcome of this struggle thus will lead to the subjugation of one group by the other. When a racial or ethnic group is placed in an inferior position, its people are often eliminated as competitors. In addition, their subordinate position may increase the supply of goods and services available to the dominant group.

SEGREGATION

Segregation is actually a form of subjugation. It refers to the act, process, or state of being set apart. It is a situation that places limits and restrictions on the contact, communication, and social relations among groups. Many people think of segregation as a negative phenomenon — a form of ostracism imposed on a minority by a dominant group — and this is often the case. However, for some groups who wish to retain their ethnicity, such as the Amish and Chinese, segregation is voluntary.

The practice of segregating people is as old as the human race itself. There are examples of it in the Bible and in preliterate cultures. American blacks were originally segregated by the institution of slavery and later by both formal sanction and informal discrimination. Although some blacks formed groups that preached total segrega-

tion from whites as an aid to black cultural development, for most it is an involuntary and degrading experience. The word **ghetto** is derived from the segregated quarter of a city where the Jews in Europe were often forced to live. Native American tribes were often forced to choose segregation on a reservation in preference to annihilation or assimilation.

EXPULSION

Expulsion is the process of forcing a group to leave the territory in which it resides. This can be accomplished indirectly by making life increasingly unbearable for a group, as the Germans did for Jews after Adolf Hitler was appointed chancellor in 1933. Over the following 6 years, Jews were stripped of their citizenship, made ineligible to hold public office, removed from the professions, and forced out of the artistic and intellectual circles to which they had belonged. In 1938 Jewish children were barred from the public schools. At the same time the government encouraged acts of violence and vandalism against Jewish communities. These actions culminated in *Kristallnacht,* November 9, 1938, when the windows in synagogues and Jewish homes and businesses across Germany were shattered and individuals were beaten up. Under these conditions, Jews left Germany by the thousands. In 1933 there were some 500,000 Jews in Germany; by 1940, before Hitler began his "final solution," that is, the murder of all remaining Jews, only 220,000 remained (Robinson, 1976).

Expulsion can also be accomplished through direct means — that is, **forced migration.** Some estimates of the number of blacks transported from Africa to the Americas during the slave trade years range as high as 30 million. For Brazil alone, the estimates range from 3 million to 18 million.

Forced migration also was a major aspect of the United States government's policies toward Native American groups in the nineteenth century. For example, when

The Jews in this photo are arriving at the Nazi concentration camp known as Auschwitz. Most of these people were murdered and cremated within a few weeks as part of the German policy of genocide against the Jews.

the army needed to protect its lines of communication to the West Coast, Colonel "Kit" Carson was ordered to move the Navajos of Arizona and New Mexico out of the way. He was instructed to kill all the men who resisted and to take everybody else captive. He accomplished this in 1864 by destroying their cornfields and slaughtering their herds of sheep, thereby confronting the Navajos with starvation. After a last showdown in Canyon de Chelly, some 8000 Navajos were rounded up in Fort Defiance. They then were marched on foot 300 miles to Fort Sumner, where they were to be taught the ways of "civilization" (Spicer, 1962).

Although expulsion is an extreme attempt to eliminate a certain minority from an area, annihilation is the most extreme action one group can take against another.

ANNIHILATION

Annihilation refers to the deliberate practice of trying to exterminate a racial or ethnic group. In recent years it has also been referred to as *genocide,* a word coined to describe the crimes committed by the Nazis during World War II — crimes that induced the United Nations to draw up a convention on genocide. Annihilation is the denial of the right to live of an entire group of people, in the same way that homicide is the denial of the right to live of one person.

Sometimes annihilation occurs as an unintended result of new contact between two groups. For example, when the Europeans arrived in the Americas, they brought with them a disease, smallpox, new to the people they encountered. Native American groups, the Blackfeet, the Aztecs, and the Incas, among many others, who had no immunity at all against this disease, were nearly wiped out (McNeill, 1976). In most cases, however, the extermination of one group by another has been the result of deliberate action. Thus the native population of Tasmania, a large island off the coast of Australia, was exterminated by Europeans in the 250 years after the country was discovered in 1642.

The largest, most systematic program of ethnic extermination was the murder of 11 million people, close to 6 million of whom were Jews, by the Nazis before and during World War II. In each country occupied by the Germans, the majority of the Jewish people were killed. Thus, in the

annihilation The deliberate practice of trying to exterminate a racial or ethnic group; also known as genocide.

mid-1930s, before the war, there were about 3.3 million Jews in Poland, but at the end of the war in 1945 there were only 73,955 Polish Jews left (Baron, 1976). Among them, not a single known family remained intact.

Although there have been recent attempts to portray this mass murder of Jews as a secret undertaking of the Nazi elite that was not widely supported by the German people, the historical evidence suggests otherwise. During the 1930s the majority of German Protestant churches endorsed the so-called racial principles that were used by the Nazis to justify first the disenfranchisement of Jews, then their forced deportation, and finally their extermination. (Jews were blamed for a bewildering combination of "crimes," including "polluting the purity of the Aryan race" and causing the rise of communism, while at the same time manipulating capitalist economies through their "secret control" of banks.)

It would seem, then, that the majority of Germans supported the Nazi racial policies or at best were apathetic (Robinson, 1976). Although in 1943 both the Catholic church and the anti-Nazi Confessing church finally condemned the murder of innocent people and pointedly stated that race was no justification for murder, it is fair to say that even this opposition was "mild, vague, and belated" (Robinson, 1976). But the fact that such objections were raised points out that the Nazis' plan to exterminate all Jews was not a well-kept military secret. The measure of its success is that some 60 percent of all Jews in Europe — 36 percent of all Jews in the world — were slaughtered (Baron, 1976).

Another "race" also slated for extermination by the Nazis were the Gypsies, a people made up of small wandering groups who appear to be descendants of Aryan invaders of India and Central Eurasian nomads. For the previous 1000 years or so, Gypsy bands had spread throughout the continents, largely unassimilated (Ulc, 1975). In Europe they were widely disliked and constantly accused of small thefts and other criminal behavior.

The sheer magnitude and horror of the Nazi attempt to exterminate the Jews provoked outrage and attempts by the nations of the world to prevent such circumstances from arising again. On December 11, 1946, the General Assembly of the United Nations passed by unanimous vote a resolution affirming that genocide was a crime under international law that the civilized world condemned, and for the commission of which both principals and accomplices alike would be held accountable and would be punished. The assembly called for the preparation of a convention on genocide that would define the offense more precisely and provide enforcement procedures for its repression and punishment.

After 2 years of study and debate, the draft of the convention on genocide was presented to the General Assembly, and it was adopted. Article II of the convention defines genocide as

> . . . any of the following acts committed with intent to destroy, in whole or in part, a national, ethnical, racial or religious group as such:
> (a) Killing members of the group;
> (b) Causing serious bodily or mental harm to members of the group;
> (c) Deliberately inflicting on the group conditions of life calculated to bring about its physical destruction in whole or part;
> (d) Imposing measures intended to prevent births within the group;
> (e) Forcibly transferring children of the group to another group.

The convention furthermore provided that any of the contracting parties could call on the United Nations to take action under its charter for the "prevention and suppression" of acts of genocide. In addition, any of the contracting parties could bring charges before the International Court of Justice.

Here in the United States, President Harry Truman submitted the resolution to the Senate on June 16, 1949, for ratification. However, the Senate did not act on the measure, and the United States did not sign the document. In 1984 President Ronald Reagan again requested the Senate to hold hearings on the convention so that it could be signed. The United States finally signed the document in 1988.

In the more than 40 years of its existence, the Genocide Convention has never been used to bring charges of genocide against a country. Numerous examples of genocide have occurred during that period. It appears to serve more as a symbolic purpose, by asking nations to go on record that they are opposed to genocide, than as an effective means of actually dealing with actual instances of genocide (Berry and Tischler, 1978).

RACIAL AND ETHNIC IMMIGRATION TO THE UNITED STATES

Since the settlement of Jamestown in 1607, more than 45 million people have immigrated to the United States. Up until 1882, the policy of the United States was almost one of free and unrestricted admittance. The country was regarded as the land of the free, a haven for those oppressed by tyrants, and a place of opportunity. The words of Emma Lazarus, inscribed on the Statue of Liberty, were indeed appropriate:

> Give me your tired, your poor,
> Your huddled masses yearning to breathe free;
> The wretched refuse of your teeming shore.
> Send these, the homeless, tempest-tost to me,
> I lift my lamp beside the golden door!

To be sure, there were those who had misgivings about the immigrants. George Washington wrote to John Adams in 1794: "My opinion with respect to immigration is that except for useful mechanics and some particular descriptions of men or professions, there is no need for "encouragement"; and Thomas Jefferson was even more emphatic in expressing the wish that there might be "an ocean of fire between this country and Europe, so that it would be impossible for any more immigrants to come hither." Such views, however, were not widely held. There was the West to be opened, railroads to be built and canals dug; there was land for the asking. People poured across the mountains, and the young nation was eager for population.

Immigration of white ethnics to the United States can be viewed from the perspective of *old migration* and *new migration.* The *old migration* consisted of people from northern Europe who came before the 1880s. The *new migration* was much larger in numbers and consisted of people from southern and eastern Europe who came between 1880 and 1920. The ethnic groups that made up the *old migration* included the English, Dutch, French, Germans, Irish, Scandinavians, Scots, and Welsh. The *new migration* included Poles, Hungarians, Ukrainians, Russians, Italians, Greeks, Portuguese, and Armenians.

Between 1892 and 1924 some 16 million immigrants came through Ellis Island outside of New York City on the way to their new life in the United States.

FIGURE 10.2

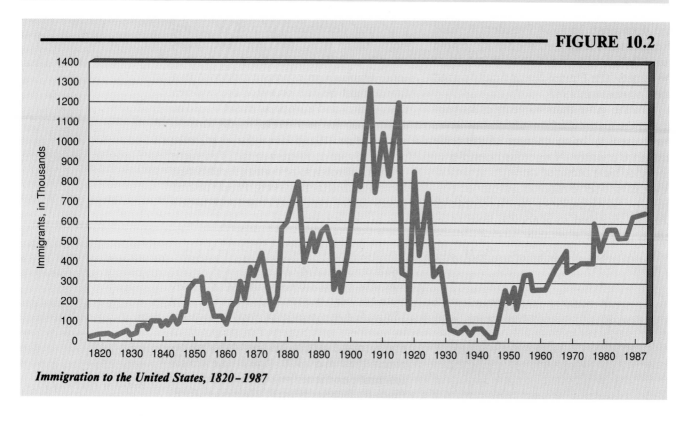

Immigration to the United States, 1820–1987

Figure 10.2 shows the number of immigrants that came to the United States each decade from 1820 and 1987. The *new migration* brought far more immigrants to the United States than the *old migration.* The earlier immigrants felt threatened by the waves of unskilled and uneducated newcomers whose appearance and culture were so different from their own. Public pressure for immigration restriction increased. After 1921 quotas were established limiting the number of people that could arrive from any particular country. The quotas were specifically designed to discriminate against potential immigrants from the southern and eastern European countries. The discriminatory immigration policy remained in effect until 1965, when a new policy was established.

In Table 10.1 you will see a listing of the people that were excluded from immigrating to the United States during each of the periods in its history. As you can see, we were much more lenient during the early days of our history. However, even with our periods of restrictive immigration, the United States has had one of the most open immigration policies in the world, and we continue to take in more legal immigrants than the rest of the world combined (Kotkin and Kishimoto, 1988).

For the past 20 years, Asian immigrants have been rising rapidly both in number and as a percentage of all immigrants to the United States. In fact, the United States's Asian immigrant population is increasing faster than the foreign-born population from Mexico, Central America, the Caribbean, and Canada combined. Forty-four percent of Asian immigrants have arrived since 1980, compared with 30 percent from Mexico, Central America, the Caribbean, and Canada. Between 1965 and 1985 the number of Asian immigrants increased an astonishing 1180 percent.

TABLE 10.1
United States Immigration Restrictions

1769–1875	No restrictions Open-door policy
1875	No convicts No prostitutes
1882	No idiots No lunatics No persons likely to need public care Start of head tax
1882–1943	No Chinese
1885	No gangs of cheap contract laborers
1891	No immigrants with dangerous contagious diseases No paupers No polygamists Start of medical inspections
1903	No epileptics No insane persons No beggars No anarchists
1907	No feeble-minded No children under 16 unaccompanied by parents No immigrants unable to support themselves because of physical or mental defects
1917	No immigrants from most of Asia or the Pacific Islands No adults unable to read and write Start of literacy tests
1921	No more than 3 percent of foreign-born of each nationality in U.S. in 1910; total about 350,000 annually
1924–1927	National Origins Quota Law; no more than 2 percent of foreign-born of each nationality already in U.S. in 1890: total about 150,000 annually
1940	Alien Registration Act; all aliens must register and be fingerprinted
1950	Exclusion and deportation of aliens dangerous to national security
1952	Codification, nationalization, and minor alterations of previous immigration laws
1965	National Origins Quota system abolished. No more than 20,000 from any one country outside Western Hemisphere: total about 170,000 annually. Start of restrictions on immigrants from other Western Hemisphere countries; no more than 120,000 annually. Preference to refugees, aliens with relatives here, and workers with skills needed in U.S.

Source: Smithsonian Institution.

Europe, on the other hand, is no longer sending many of its natives to our shores. Even with the massive immigration from Europe during our early history, only 26 percent of today's foreign-born population came from Europe, and only 13 percent of them have arrived since 1980 (Woodrow, Passel, and Warren, 1987).

Instead of the stereotype of the European immigrant arriving at Ellis Island as in previous eras, today's immigrant is likely to be from the Orient and arrive by plane.

ILLEGAL IMMIGRATION

Since 1970 the issue of illegal immigration has figured prominently in the ethnic makeup of certain regions of the United States. It is estimated that there are anywhere between 2.5 million and 4.7 million illegal immigrants in the United States, and the number is growing by 200,000 a year. It is estimated that 55 percent of the illegal immigrants are from Mexico. Latin America as a whole accounts for 77 percent. Of the remainder, about 10 percent come from Asia, 8.5 percent from Europe and Canada, and slightly more than 4 percent from the rest of the world.

The vast majority (71 percent) of the illegal immigrants are between 15 and 39. Very few are over 65. About half of all illegal immigrants live in California. Other states likely to attract illegal immigrants are New York, Texas, Illinois, and Florida.

In 1986 Congress passed the Immigration Reform and Control Act, a law designed to control the flow of illegal immigrants into the United States. The new law makes it a crime for employers, even individuals hiring household help, to knowingly employ an illegal immigrant. Stiff fines and criminal penalties can be imposed if they do so.

The law also provides legal status to illegal immigrants who entered the Untied States before 1982 and who have lived here continuously since then. This part of the law changed the legal status of more than 2 million formerly illegal U.S. residents.

What is America's racial and ethnic composition today? The United States is perhaps the most racially and ethnically diverse country in the world. (Figure 10.3 shows the major groups and their populations.) And unlike many other countries, it has no ethnic group that makes up a numerical majority of the population. In the following discussion, we shall examine the major groups in American society.

Many illegal immigrants to the United States travel across the Rio Grande River into Texas.

WHITE ANGLO-SAXON PROTESTANTS

About 63 million people claim some English, Scottish, or Welsh origin. These Americans of British origin are often grouped together as white Anglo-Saxon Protestants (WASPs). Although in numbers they are a minority within the total American population, they have been in the country the longest (aside from the Native Americans, a marginal group but growing rapidly in number). As a group, they have always had great economic and political power in the country (Mills, 1963). As a result, white Anglo-Saxon Protestants often have acted as if they were the ethnic majority in America, influencing other ethnic groups to assimilate or acculturate to their way of life, the ideal of Anglo conformity (Cole and Cole, 1954). Interestingly, although white Angle-Saxon Protestants are the economically dominant ethnic group in America, they do not have the highest per-family income. White Anglo-Saxon families have an average income only slightly higher than that of the average American family (U.S. Department of Commerce, 1983).

The Americanization of immigrant groups has been the desired goal of the dominant white Anglo-Saxon Protestants during many periods in American history. Contrary to the romantic sentiments expressed on the base of the Statue of Liberty, immigrant groups who came to America after the British Protestants had become established met with considerable hostility and suspicion.

The 1830s and 1840s saw the rise of the "native" American movement, directed against recent immigrant groups (and especially Catholics). In 1841 the American Protestant Union was founded in New York City to oppose the "subjugation of our country to control of the Pope of Rome, and his adherents" (Leonard and Parmet, 1971). On the East Coast it was the Irish Catholics who were feared, and in the Midwest it was the German "freethinkers." Protestant religious organizations across America joined forces and urged "native" Americans to organize to offset "foreign" voting blocs. They also conducted intimidation campaigns against "foreigners" and attempted to persuade Catholics to renounce their religion for Protestantism (Leonard and Parmet, 1971).

As the twentieth century dawned, American sentiments against immigrants

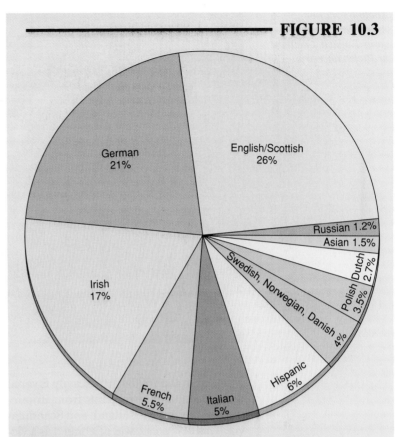

FIGURE 10.3

Ethnic Ancestry of the United States Population. Source: U.S. Department of Commerce, Bureau of the Census, Statistical Abstract of the United States: 1985 *(Washington, D.C.: Government Printing Office, 1985), p. 35.*

from southern and eastern Europe were running high. In Boston the Immigration Restriction League was formed, which directed its efforts toward keeping out "racially inferior" groups — who were depicted as inherently criminal, mentally defective, and marginally educable. The league achieved its goals in 1924 when the government adopted a new immigration policy that set quotas on the numbers of immigrants to be admitted from various nations. Because the quotas were designed to reflect (and reestablish) the ethnic composition of

About 63 million Americans proclaim some English, Scottish, or Welsh ancestry.

America in the 1890s, they heavily favored the admission of immigrants from Britain, Ireland, Germany, Holland, and Scandinavia. This new policy was celebrated as a victory for the "Nordic" race (Krause, 1966).

Another expression of Anglo conformity pressure was the Americanization Movement, which gained strength from the nationalistic passions brought on by World War I. Its stated purpose was to promote the very rapid acculturation of new immigrants. Thus, "federal agencies, state government, municipalities, and a host of private organizations joined in the effort to persuade the immigrant to learn English, take out naturalization papers, buy war bonds, forget his former origins and culture, and give himself over to patriotic hysteria" (Gordon, 1975).

From World War II until the early 1960s, Anglo conformity was pretty much an established ideal of the American way of life. In the last decades, there has been a strong organized reaction among other ethnic groups against Anglo conformity. Strong social-political movements, organized along ethnic group lines, have

formed. Blacks led the way in the later 1960s with the Black Power movement, and they were joined by Italian Americans, Mexican Americans (Chicanos), Puerto Ricans, Native Americans, and others. America once again is focusing on its ethnic diversity, and the assumptions of Anglo conformity are being challenged.

OTHER "WHITE ETHNIC" GROUPS

Sociologists often refer to the descendants of immigrants from southern and eastern Europe as "white ethnics" (Novak, 1972). Currently the term is used to refer to any whites who are not of northern European origin or Protestant. As a group, white ethnics are the largest ethnic minority in America, although the separate ethnic groups do not appear to have accepted their shared sociological label. Many of these immigrants have not been ready to discard their distinctive native cultures and embrace American ways. People from these groups often have come to the United States to better themselves economically, not to adopt a new life-style. Their goals have often been to earn enough money to send to relatives back home and eventually to return there themselves. Immigrants from the same country have tended to form their own communities—the Little Italys and the Germantowns, for instance—following their own customs and speaking their native languages. Each group has sought to preserve its own ethnic identity, and therefore explicit political cooperation among these groups has not materialized (Levine and Herman, 1974).

BLACKS

Blacks are the second-largest racial group in the country. As of 1988, there were more than 30 million blacks living in the United States, representing slightly more than 12 percent of the total population of 246 million (U.S. Bureau of the Census, *Statistical Abstract of the United States: 1989, 1988*). Of these, roughly three-quarters live in urban areas, and about 47 percent live in the North (Herbers, 1981; U.S. Bureau of the Census, 1986). This is a significant shift from the 1940s, when roughly 80 percent of American blacks lived in the South and worked in agriculture.

Black immigrants have been accounting for an increasingly greater share of all blacks in the United States in recent years. These black immigrants have come to the United States from the West Indian countries of Jamaica, Haiti, the Dominican Republic, Barbados, and Trinidad. In addition, a significant number of African blacks are also entering the United States each year. As a result of this trend, the percentage of black immigrants in the total black population is now greater than the percentage of nonblack immigrants in the total nonblack population. In some cities, such as Miami, black immigrants have become a clearly distinguishable segment of the black population. (*American Demographics,* 1984).

In 1619, when the first twenty blacks were unloaded from a Dutch man-of-war at Jamestown, Virginia, they were given the status of indentured servants. The blacks did not enjoy this status very long, however, and they began to be treated with more severity than the white European indentured servants. By the end of the seventeenth century, the status of blacks had changed to one of slavery. The underlying factor was the demand for a labor supply. Black slaves were preferable to white indentured servants for several reasons: (1) their skin color and facial features made them easy to identify should they escape; (2) because they were only slaves, the women could be put to work in the fields, contrary to the custom for indentured women; (3) as slaves, the services of blacks were available for life, whereas those of indentured servants were available only for a few years; and (4) their children, unlike servants' children, were also valuable property. Black slaves, therefore, eventually displaced white indentured servants in the cotton and tobacco colonies.

Black immigrants have been accounting for an increasingly greater share of all blacks in the United States in recent years.

Although the Civil War marked the end of slavery, it did not signal the beginning of equality for blacks. Southern states enacted laws known as Black Codes, which placed limitations on blacks' ownership and rental of property, possession of firearms, testimony in court, freedom of speech and movement, choice of occupation, and voting privileges. Heavy penalties were levied for vagrancy and breach of contract, creating what amounted to a system of forced labor. After several decades, a new pattern emerged—white southerners called it "white supremacy," while blacks referred to it as "second-class citizenship." Its features are well known. Blacks were virtually deprived of their rights of citizenship. Their economic opportunities were severely limited, with many occupations closed to them and a job ceiling established in those areas in which they were allowed to work. The educational facilities provided for them were inferior to those provided for whites. They were barred from most hotels, restaurants, theaters, barber shops, auditoriums,

In the same year that Dr. Martin Luther King made his historic "I have a dream" speech, dogs were used to break up civil rights marches.

parks, and playgrounds; the accommodations offered to them on trains, streetcars, and buses were separate but seldom equal. They were restricted and exploited as homeowners or tenants. The medical facilities available to them were limited, with the result that they suffered high mortality rates. In courts and at the hands of the law, they did not enjoy the same treatment accorded to whites.

During World War I, blacks began to break the barriers of the system as they slowly started to gain power. Their horizons expanded as some 400,000 blacks moved from the rural South to the urban North to fill the employment vacuum created by the curtailment of immigration from Europe. Nearly 350,000 entered the armed services, and 100,000 served overseas. Blacks from different parts of the country were brought together, giving them the opportunity to share new insights and goals. They began to demand their rights as citizens, with the result that during and immediately after World War I, whites reacted by initiating race riots in scores of cities and towns throughout the country. Blacks not only made demands but were prepared to fight for them. The United States Supreme Court, which had long sanctioned the white supremacy and separate-but-equal philosophies, began to render verdicts favorable to the black cause.

World War II saw an acceleration of the movement toward equality. The number of black officers in the armed services grew. President Franklin D. Roosevelt issued an executive order that forbade racial discrimination in defense industries and created the Fair Employment Practices Committee. The Supreme Court continued to hand down decisions favorable to blacks.

Change continued after World War II. The armed services were integrated. Many states adopted fair employment practices laws. In 1954 the Supreme Court handed down its historic decisions regarding the inequality of separate educational facilities.

The black demands for equality grew more insistent than ever in the 1960s and 1970s. Blacks grew impatient with the slow pace of school integration and became disillusioned when they observed how the rulings of the courts and the acts of Congress were ignored or evaded. "Freedom rides," demonstrations, marches, sit-ins, boycotts, and numerous other forms of protest became daily occurrences throughout the country. Blacks had finally become powerful enough to fight against their second-class status.

Today, however, despite decades of intensive political struggle as well as significant progress, social and economic equality still evades blacks. For example, the income of black families still averages only 59.5 percent that of whites and slightly less than 63 percent of the national average—just 2 percent above Indians, who have the lowest average income (U.S. Bureau of the Census, 1986). Most sociologists believe that this is the result of enduring prejudice directed against blacks.

Despite decades of intensive political struggle, the incomes of black families still average only 59.5 percent of those of white families.

AFRICAN DREAMS, AMERICAN REALITY

Mark Mathabane grew up in the black ghetto of Alexandra, near Johannesburg, South Africa. He parlayed his hard-won skills as a tennis player into access to the white world of Johannesburg. There he eventually met Stan Smith, a visiting white American tennis star. Mathabane dreamed of escaping to America where blacks, he heard "walked free." With the help of Smith and others, Mathabane came to the United States to enroll in college. He left a land of opportunity denied to find what he described as country of opportunity not taken. In the following selection Mark Mathabane shares with us his response to white-black relations in the United States.

When I first arrived from the South African black ghetto of Alexandra to attend college on a tennis scholarship in 1978, I was horrified by my discovery that black and white students were almost complete strangers, as if each group attended a different school. All of this was in a place, ironically, where the mutual pursuit of knowledge was supposed to engender greater communication, open-mindedness, better understanding and respect of cultural differences.

I knew from experience the dangers of this separateness. In South Africa it fueled the abomination called apartheid. Apartheid has prevented blacks and whites from knowing each other —and that is why the racism of most whites has become so ingrained that they see nothing wrong in the injustice and human degradation inherent in separate schools, churches, buses, hospitals, neighborhoods and even separate graveyards. Consequently, the lives of many blacks and whites are ruled by stereotypes, half-truths, ignorance, prejudices, unfounded fears and mistaken beliefs.

Early in my childhood I became a victim of these destructive attitudes. I was exposed only to the worst sort of whites—the soldiers who occupied the ghetto and maimed and killed blacks during peaceful protests, and the policemen, who repeatedly arrested my father for the "crime" of being unemployed and then marched my parents naked out of bed while terrorizing us children during midnight raids. Thus, I came to hate all whites.

Luckily, my mother and grandmother, though illiterate, taught me what I have come to regard as the most important lessons in race relations: There are good white people and bad white people, just as there are good

black people and bad black people. Black racism is as reprehensible and corroding to the soul as white racism. It is amazing that these women believed this after having suffered repeated indignities at the hands of whites. One time my grandmother, after I had mistakenly stepped into a whites-only bus, had to wipe the steps where I had trod to appease the irate driver who threatened to have us jailed.

In spite of my experiences at the hands of racist whites, the lessons my mother and grandmother taught me saved my life and paved the way for my eventual escape from apartheid. As a teen-ager I made some valuable white friends, some of whom helped in my quest for a decent education and tennis proficiency. An education emancipated me from mental slavery and taught me to believe in my own worth and abilities, despite the South African's government's attempt to limit my aspirations and prescribe my place in life through the inferior education system offered to blacks. Tennis became my passport to freedom in America. I continued to encounter white racists, but their bigotry failed to eradicate in me the reality that there were other whites who were different.

Given such a past, when I discovered a form of segregation among students at the colleges I attended, I felt compelled to combat it. I told myself that I hadn't escaped from apartheid bondage only to end up segregated in America.

I literally forced myself into the consciousness of white students, in ways that sought to reverse their stereotypical images of black students. First, despite my participation in collegiate sports, I put a higher premium on my education. Throughout my college career, I never allowed my grade-point average to drop below 3.0. Each time it threatened to do so, I would cut back on the hours I devoted to sports, even at the risk of incurring the coach's wrath. This startled some white students, who thought that black athletes were in college only for athletics. This stereotype is largely the result of what Arthur Ashe calls the "deep-seated cynicism of coddled, black public school athletes."

In classes where I was often the only black, I participated fully in discussions, asked incessant questions and vigorously defended my opinions. In the cafeteria I sat wherever the conversation was serious, and with whomever I wanted. While I championed the teaching of black studies as a way of enriching the college experience of white students, I valued the great books of Western civilization used in the study of the liberal arts; their contents made me better understand human society, and, by contrast, my African heritage. I volunteered to become the first black editor of the college paper—in spite of the fact that I couldn't yet type properly. I used the newspaper in part to advocate activism and idealism among black and white students, and to galvanize them around issues of common interest such as bigotry, sexism, war and peace, intolerance and defense of the liberal arts.

My attitude rankled some black students. Some felt that any black student who sat with whites in the cafeteria, worked with them on projects, shared with them black culture and socialized with them was a traitor. In their militant rage at white racism, these students apparently forgot that communicating with each other is one effective way of combatting the cancer of racism. Some white students felt uncomfortable with me because I did not fit their prejudiced view of what a black person is; those whites felt comfortable only around blacks who acted unintelligent and happy-go-lucky. Blacks like myself who were assertive, independent and stood up for their rights were called "uppity" just as similar blacks in South Africa are called "cheeky."

My college experiences have shown me how a lack of communication and interaction between the races in America forces the same attitudes that have given us legalized segregation and its attendant racism in South Africa. The irony is that in America these attitudes are flourishing 25 years after passage of landmark civil rights legislation and 35 years after the Supreme Court declared segregation education inherently unequal.

Does this mean that South African and American societies are the same? By no means. One major difference is that the United States has outlawed segregation and now equally projects the civil rights of all Americans. Black Americans enjoy a measure of freedom and opportunity undreamed of by their counterparts in South Africa.

But the similarities in the attitudes lead me to believe that racism and its harmful effects will continue to plague American society until blacks and whites begin talking to each other—rather than always about each other. Schools and colleges are one place where this process can start.

Source: Excerpted from Mark Mathabane, "Closing the Racial Communications Gap," *Los Angeles Times,* April 29, 1989.

HISPANICS

The number of Hispanics in the United States grew 30 percent between 1980 and 1987, four times faster than the U.S. population as a whole. The 18.8 million Hispanics in the United States form the nation's second-largest minority. They are not a very well understood segment of the population. First, no one knows exactly how many Hispanics have crossed the border from Mexico as illegal immigrants. Second, many Americans of Hispanic descent do not identify themselves as "Hispanic" on census forms and are not counted as such.

The Hispanic population in the United States is made up of about 12 million people of Mexican origin (63 percent of all Hispanics); 2.3 million of Puerto Rican origin (12 percent); 2.1 million of Central and South American origin (11 percent); and 1 million of Cuban origin (5 percent). The remainder come from Spain or other Spanish-speaking countries (Schwartz, 1988).

According to one set of Census Bureau projections, there should be twice as many Hispanics in the United States as there are now shortly after the year 2000. At that point, the Spanish-origin population would be growing by 1 million people per year. Continuing at this pace, the Hispanic population would be four times its present size in the year 2030. By that time, the Hispanic population would be larger than the black population (see Figure 10.4) (Exter, 1987).

The greatest concentrations of Hispanics live in Texas and California, but they are also found in large numbers in Arizona, New Mexico, Florida, and in such northern cities as Denver, Hartford, Connecticut, Union City, New Jersey, and New York City. Interestingly, although the vast majority of Hispanics come from rural areas, 90 percent settle in America's industrial cities and surrounding suburbs. Living together in tight-knit communities, they share their common language and customs. (*U.S. News & World Report,* August 10, 1987).

Today seven out of ten Hispanic students attended segregated schools, up dramatically from 55 percent 20 years ago. This increase occurred at the same time as the percentage of blacks attending predominantly minority schools dropped from 76 percent to 63 percent. In addition, the need to master English is lessened by the fact that nearly everyone in the community speaks Spanish. As a result, more than half of all

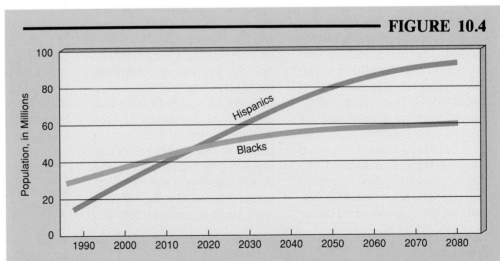

FIGURE 10.4

Population Projections for Blacks and Hispanics to the Year 2080. Source: *U. S. Bureau of the Census, "Projections of the Hispanic Population: 1983 to 2080," Current Population Reports, Series P-25, No. 995 (Washington, D.C.: Government Printing Office, 1986).*

Hispanic adults are illiterate in English. Without needed language skills and with high school drop-out rates two to three times the rate of other students, nearly 25 percent of all Hispanic families have incomes below the poverty level. In 1986 the median family income for Hispanics was $19,995; for whites it was $30,809 (Carmody, 1988).

Mexican Americans

Hispanics of Mexican descent, also known as *Chicanos,* make up the majority of the Spanish-speaking population in the United States. The main reason is proximity. The 1936-mile border we share with Mexico is the site of millions of legal and illegal crossings each year.

The term *Chicano* is somewhat controversial. It has long been used as a slang word in Mexico to refer to people of low social class. In Texas it came to be used for Mexicans who illegally crossed over the border in search of work. Recently, however, many Mexican Americans have taken to using the term themselves to suggest a tough breed of individuals of Mexican ancestry who are committed to achieving success in this country and are willing to fight for it (Madsen, 1973).

In his study of Mexican Americans in Texas, William Madsen (1973) notes that three "levels of acculturation" may be distinguished. One group has retained its Mexican peasant culture, at least in regard to values. Another group consists of persons torn between the traditional culture of their parents and grandparents on the one hand, and Anglo-American culture (learned in American schools) on the other. Many individuals in this group suffer crises of personal and ethnic identity. Finally, there are those Mexican Americans who have acculturated fully and achieved success in Anglo-American society. Some remain proud of and committed to their ethnic origins, but others would just as soon forget them and assimilate fully into the Anglo-American world.

Mexican Americans have been exploited for many years as a source of cheap agricultural labor. Others have achieved various levels of success in Anglo-American society.

Mexican Americans have been exploited for many years as a source of cheap agricultural labor. Their average family income is $19,326, two-thirds of the income for whites (U.S. Bureau of the Census, 1987). Also, because of their poverty, they have long been willing to do the "stoop labor" (literally bending over and working close to the ground, or menial labor in general) that most Anglo-Americans refuse. In addition, 19 percent of all Mexican-American families are headed by women, compared to 9 percent of all white families, and nearly a quarter of all births are out of wedlock (Chavez, 1988). Like blacks, Mexican Americans have yet to achieve true equality in the United States.

Puerto Ricans

Another group included in the Hispanic category is the Puerto Ricans. In 1898 the United States fought a brief war with Spain and as a result took over the former Spanish colonies in the Pacific (the Philippines and Guam) and the Caribbean (Cuba and Puerto Rico). Puerto Ricans were made full citizens of the United States in 1917. Although government programs improved their education and dramatically lowered the death rate, rapid population growth helped keep the Puerto Rican people poor. American business took advantage of the large supply of cheap, nonunion Puerto Rican labor and built plants there under very favorable tax laws.

Approximately 2.3 million Puerto Ricans have migrated to the American mainland seeking better economic opportunities. Most make their homes in the New York City area but return frequently to the island to visit family and friends.

Puerto Ricans living in the United States have the lowest median family income of any Hispanic group. In 1986, the median income of Puerto Ricans was $14,584 (U.S. Bureau of the Census, 1986). Ironically, the poverty of Puerto Rican families is due in part to the ease of going back and forth between their homeland and the

United States. The desire to one day return permanently to Puerto Rico interferes with a total commitment to assimilate into American culture (*Time,* July 8, 1985).

Cuban Americans

Most Cuban Americans have come to the United States relatively recently. Only in the 1970s did they begin to have a visible cultural and economic impact on the cities where they settled in sizable numbers.

Many Cubans came to the United States as a result of the 1959 revolution that catapulted Fidel Castro into power. At that time the rebel forces of Fidel Castro overthrew the Batista government. Castro, a Marxist closely aligned with the Soviet Union, began a process of restructuring the social order, including the appropriation of privately owned land and property by the state. Professionals and businesspeople who were part of the established Cuban society felt threatened by these changes and fled to the United States. More than 155,000 Cubans came to the United States between 1959 and 1962. As a whole, these immigrants have done extremely well in American society. They had the distinct advantage of coming to the United States with marketable skills and money.

The second wave of Cuban immigration occurred in 1980 when Castro allowed people to leave Cuba by way of Mariel Harbor. The result was a flotilla of boats bringing 125,000 refugees to the United States. This second wave of immigrants was poorer and less educated than the first. It also included several thousand prisoners and mental patients, many of whom were imprisoned in the United States as soon as they got off the boat. Others fled into Miami and other cities to lead a life of crime. Serious friction exists between these two waves of immigrants because of differences in background and social class.

Cubans are relatively recent immigrants, and the first-generation foreign-born predominate. They are exiles who came to the United States not so much be-

Miami, with 652,000 Cubans, has become known as "little Havana." Many shops and businesses cater to this Cuban population.

cause they preferred the U.S. way of life but because they felt compelled to leave their country. For these reasons most Cuban immigrants fiercely attempt to retain the culture and way of life they knew in Cuba. Of all the Hispanic groups, they are the most likely to speak Spanish in the home: eight out of ten families do so.

Cubans are largely found in a few major cities. Metropolitan Miami (Dade County, Florida) is the undisputed center with nearly 65 percent of all Cubans in the United States living there. Miami, with 652,000 Cubans and with Latins making up a larger percentage of the population than whites, the city has become a distinctively Cuban city. Most other Cubans live in New York City, Jersey City, Newark, Los Angeles, and Chicago, all of which are large centers for Hispanics in general.

Acculturation and assimilation have been slow in Miami, in light of the fact that the community is so self-sufficient and has such a large base. There also appears to be a lack of social and cultural integration between Cubans and other Hispanic groups in U.S. cities with sizable and differentiated Span-ish-speaking populations. Of the major Hispanic groups, only the Cubans have come as political exiles, and this has resulted in social, economic, and class differences. In the New York City area, Cubans and Puerto Ricans maintain a distinct social distance. Many Cubans feel that they have little in common with Puerto Ricans, Mexican Americans, or Dominicans.

The more than 1 million Cubans who live in the United States have fared better than any other Hispanic immigrant group. The median family income of Cubans is $26,770, a third higher than the earnings of the average Hispanic family. Between 1981 and 1986 average family income shot up 22 percent, faster than any other Hispanic group. At this rate of growth, the Cuban income could surpass the national median income within a few years.

Why have Cubans done so well? We can point to the fact that many Cubans who came to the United States were middle class, educated people. They brought money and skills with them and a determination to build a good life in the United States (Schwartz, 1988).

JEWS

There is no satisfactory answer to the question "What makes the Jews a people?" other than to say, "The fact that they see themselves—and are seen by others—as one." Judaism is a religion, of course, but many Jews are nonreligious. Some think of Jews as a "race," but their physical diversity makes this notion absurd. For more than 2000 years, Jews have been dispersed around the world. Reflecting this geographic separation, three major Jewish groups have evolved, each with its own distinctive culture: the *Ashkenazim*—the Jews of eastern and western Europe (excluding Spain); the *Sephardim*—the Jews of Turkey, Spain, and western North Africa; and the "Oriental" Jews of Egypt, Ethiopia, the Middle East, and Central Asia. Nor are Jews united linguistically. In addition to speaking the language of whatever nation they are living in, some Jews speak one or more of three Jewish languages: Hebrew, the language of ancient and modern Israel; Yiddish, a Germanic language spoken by Ashkenazi Jews; and Ladino, an ancient Romance language spoken by the Sephardim.

The first Jews came to America from Brazil in 1654, but it was not until the mid-1800s that large numbers of Jews began to arrive. These were mostly German Jews, refugees from European anti-Semitism. Then, with especially violent anti-Semitism erupting in eastern Europe in the 1880s, there was a massive increase in Jewish immigration to America. It came in two waves: in the last two decades of the nineteenth century and in the first two decades of the twentieth.

Jewish immigration was similar to that of other groups, in that it consisted overwhelmingly of young people, though the Jewish immigration also had some unique features. First, it was much more a migration of families than was that of other European immigrants, who were mostly single males. Second, Jewish immigrants were much more committed to staying here: two-thirds of all immigrants to the United States between 1908 and 1924 remained, but 94.8 percent of the Jewish immigrants settled here permanently. Third, Jewish immigrant groups contained a higher percentage of skilled and urban workers than did other groups. And fourth, especially after the turn of the century, there were many scholars and intellectuals among Jewish immigrants, which was not true of other immigrant groups (Howe, 1976).

These differences account for the fact that even though Jews encountered at least as much hostility from white Anglo-Saxon Protestants as did other immigrant groups (and also were subject to intense prejudice from Catholics), they have been relatively successful in pulling themselves up the socioeconomic ladder. Of the approximately 6 million Jews in America today, 53 percent of those working are in the professions and business (versus 25 percent for the nation as an average).

ASIAN AMERICANS

Most Asian Americans are concentrated in the major metropolitan areas. Their percentage of total population in these cities varies from 10.3 in San Francisco to 0.6 percent in St. Louis. In Honolulu 61 percent of the population is Asian or Pacific Islander (Manning and O'Hare, 1988).

The first Asians to settle in America in significant numbers were the Chinese. Some 300,000 Chinese migrated here between 1850 and 1880 to escape the famine and warfare that plagued their homeland. Initially they settled on the West Coast, where they took back-breaking jobs mining and building railroads. However, they were far from welcome and were subjected to a great amount of harassment. In 1882 the government limited further Chinese immigration for 10 years. This limitation was extended in 1892 and again in 1904, finally being repealed in 1943. The state of California set special taxes on Chinese miners, and most labor unions fought to keep them out of the mines because they took jobs from white workers. In the late 1800s and early 1900s, numerous riots and strikes were directed against the Chinese, who drew back into their "Chinatowns" for protection. The harassment had a great effect. In 1880 there were 105,465 Chinese in the United States. By 1900 the figure had dropped to 89,863 and, by 1920, to 61,729. The Chinese population in the United States began to rise again only after the 1950s (U.S. Bureau of the Census, 1976). Figures from the 1980 census show 812,000 ethnic Chinese in the United States *(Statistical Abstract of the United States: 1989, 1988),* making them the largest group of Asian origin.

Japanese immigrants began arriving in the United States shortly after the Chinese —and quickly joined them as victims of prejudice and discrimination. Feelings against the Japanese ran especially high in California, where one political movement attempted to have them expelled from the United States. In 1906 the San Francisco Board of Education decreed that all Asian children in that city had to attend a single, segregated school. The Japanese government protested, and after negotiations, the United States and Japan reached what became known as a "gentleman's agreement." The Japanese agreed to discourage emigration, and President Theodore Roosevelt agreed to prevent the passage of laws discriminating against Japanese in the United States.

Initially, Japanese immigrants were minuscule in number: In 1870 there were only 55 Japanese in America, and in 1880 a mere 148. By 1900 there were 24,326, and subsequently their numbers have grown steadily. By 1970 they had surpassed the Chinese (U.S. Bureau of the Census, 1976), but figures from the 1980 census showed that despite a sharp increase since 1970, the number of ethnic Japanese — 716,000 — was far fewer than the number of Chinese *(Statistical Abstract of the United States: 1989, 1988).*

Japanese Americans were subjected to especially vicious mistreatment during World War II. Fearing espionage and sabo-tage from among the ethnic minorities with whose home countries the United States was at war, President Franklin D. Roosevelt signed Executive Order 9066 empowering the military to "remove any and all persons" from certain regions of the country. Although before the United States entered World War II, many German Americans actively demonstrated on behalf of Germany, no general action was taken against them as a group; nor was any general action taken against Italian Americans. Nonetheless, General John L. DeWitt ordered that *all* individuals of Japanese descent be evacuated from three West Coast states and moved inland to "relocation" camps for the duration of the war. In 1942, 120,000 Japanese, including some 77,000 who were American citizens, were moved and imprisoned solely because of their national origin —even though not a single act of espionage

These Japanese Americans are about to be taken to Seattle by a special ferry, which will connect with a train to California, as part of their evacuation and internment during World War II.

The educational, occupational, and income levels attained by Japanese Americans have been far above the national average.

or sabotage against the United States ever was attributed to one of their number (Simpson and Yinger, 1972). Many lost their homes and possessions in the process. Included among those who were relocated were members of the 442nd Regimental Combat Team, a fighting group composed solely of Japanese Americans, who fought valiantly in Europe until they were interned.

In 1988, President Ronald Reagan signed legislation apologizing for this wartime action. The legislation moved to "right a great wrong" by establishing a $1.25 billion trust fund as reparation for the imprisonment. Each eligible person was to receive a $20,000 tax-free award from the government. The president noted as he signed the legislation: "Yes, the nation was then at war, struggling for its survival. And it's not for us today to pass judgment upon those who may have made mistakes when engaging in the great struggle. Yet we must recog-

nize that the internment of Japanese-Americans was just that, a mistake" (*New York Times,* August 11, 1988).

Compared to the earlier group of Asian immigrants who came primarily from China and Japan, the current wave includes many Asians from Vietnam, the Philippines, Korea, India, Laos, Cambodia, and Singapore. Approximately 250,000 new Asian immigrants are added each year to the 5 million who already call the United States their home. Within 20 years there will probably be twice as many Asians in the United States as there are today.

The vast majority of Asian immigrants are middle class and highly educated. More than a third have a college degree, twice the rate of Americans born here (immigrants from Vietnam, Cambodia, and other Indochinese countries are the exception) (*Time,* July 8, 1985).

The education, occupations, and income attainments of Asian Americans have been far above the national average. Although Asian Americans make up only 2 percent of the total U.S. population, they comprise nearly 12 percent of the freshman class at Harvard and 20 percent at the University of California at Berkeley. They have achieved stunning success in science and business. As a group they have the highest rate of business ownership of any minority group in the United States. For every one thousand Asians in the population nearly fifty-five own a business. For Hispanics the rate is 17 per thousand, and for blacks it is 12.5 per thousand (Manning and O'Hare, 1988).

NATIVE AMERICANS (INDIANS)

Early European colonists encountered Native American societies that in many ways were as advanced as their own. Especially impressive were their political institutions. For example, the League of the Iroquois, a confederacy that ensured peace among its five member nations and was remarkably successful in warfare against hostile neighbors, was the model on which Benjamin Franklin drew when he was planning the Federation of States (Kennedy, 1961).

The colonists and their descendants never really questioned the view that the land of the New World was theirs. They took land as they needed it — for agriculture, for mining, and later for industry — and drove off the native groups. Some land was purchased, some acquired through political agreements, some through trickery and deceit, and some through violence. In the end, hundreds of thousands of Native Americans were exterminated by disease, starvation, and deliberate massacre. By 1900 only some 250,000 Indians remained (perhaps one-eighth of their number in precolonial times) (McNeill, 1976). In recent years, however, their numbers have grown dramatically.

According to the 1980 United States census figures, there were 1,479,000 In-

dians in the country (up from 791,839 in 1970) *(Statistical Abstract of the United States: 1989, 1988),* about 55 percent of whom live on or near reservations administered fully or partly by the federal government's Bureau of Indian Affairs (BIA). Many of the rest are living in Indian enclaves in urban areas, where since 1952 100,000 have been relocated by the BIA (Snyder, 1971).

Interestingly, nearly 7 million Americans claimed American Indian ancestry on the 1980 census ancestry question. Yet, only somewhat more than 1 million identified themselves as American Indians. Most people who claimed American Indian ancestry did so in combination with another ancestry group, such as English or Irish.

On the whole, Native Americans are at the bottom of the American socioeconomic ladder. Their family income is only 60 per-

More than half of all Native Americans live on or near reservations administered by the government's Bureau of Indian Affairs.

The Battle over English

Which of the following statements is true?

1. English is the official language of the United States.
2. English is the official language of California, South Carolina, Georgia, and Illinois.

The first statement is false. In a recent survey, 64 percent of the population thought English was made our national language 200 years ago by the Constitution. They are wrong. The United States has no official language.

The second statement, however, is true. More than a dozen states have made English their official language, and another nineteen have legislation pending to do likewise.

Why is there such a strong movement to make English our official language today, when our founding fathers did not think it necessary to do so 200 years ago?

Some would argue it is racism. Others would say it is an outgrowth of the failure to assimilate. The debate is heated, bitter, and filled with invective.

On one side we have U.S. English, a national public-interest group that campaigns actively in support of English as our official language and has the blessing of all those who fear that the United States will become a modern-day Tower of Babel.

They point to the fact that in less than one generation, no single ethnic group will be a majority in California—the nation's most populous state. In less than four generations, about one-third of all Americans will be post-1980 immigrants and their descendants. English as a common language, they maintain, will be the only glue that can hold this diversity together.

On the other side we have opponents such as Hispanic community spokesperson Rick Mendoza who argue that the English-language bills are "clearly an act of language discrimination on an equal par with racial discrimination and in direct line with the Aryan nations' philosophy of one race, one religion, one language" (*American Demographics,* April 1987).

The debate is an outgrowth of the fact that over the past two decades the federal government has promoted bilingual education at the same time it has downplayed

cent that of whites, and their life expectancy two-thirds of the national average. One-third of all adults are illiterate; 74 percent use contaminated water; and most live in overcrowded conditions (averaging 5.4 occupants in two rooms, against the national average of 2.4 people in four rooms) *(Statistical Abstract of the United States: 1988, 1987).*

Life for those Native Americans living on reservations is particularly bad. For example, at Pine Ridge, a 5,000-square-mile reservation in southwestern South Dakota on which 18,000 Indians live, more than eight out of ten adults are unemployed and many are chronic alcoholics. As a result of these conditions, the suicide rate on the reservation is up to four times the national average (*Newsweek,* May 2, 1988). Other reservations are similarly blighted. Seven out of ten Puyallup Indians of Washington State are unemployed (*New York Times,* August 29, 1988).

PROSPECTS FOR THE FUTURE

As is evident by now, the many racial and ethnic groups in the United States present a

the importance of learning English for full participation in the political, economic, and social life of the country. This approach came at a time when immigration was at a historic high and when, for the first time in American history, a majority of immigrants spoke one particular language other than English—namely, Spanish.

In response to this perceived bilingual bias, opponents started to point out that just as it is not the government's role to promote or preserve any religion, it is not the government's role to promote or preserve ethnic or racial traditions. The government has no more business helping Mexican American children learn Spanish or appreciate mariachi music, they say, than it does telling the children of Italians that they must speak Italian and play boccie.

Bilingual education has also been promoted as a tool for producing better learning among immigrant children. Proponents claim that the goal is a speedier integration of the students into American society, not the maintenance of native cultures. It is thought that children who speak English as a second language learn more easily if they are taught in their native tongue.

Yet, there is little proof of the effectiveness of bilingual education. Most programs seem to be perpetuated for political, not educational, reasons. They give jobs and legitimacy to political opportunists in non-English-speaking communities. More often than not, these individuals wish to build a power base for reasons that have nothing to do with education.

The real political forces behind bilingual education tend to promote cultural separatism; the bilingual programs they espouse rarely are transitional and even more rarely make facility in English their primary goal. Bilingual programs hold students prisoners in their native languages and ensure students a prolonged "second-class" status.

So, who are the real racists? Those who use glib rhetoric to promote a linguistic ghetto, or those who want non-English speakers to be part of the American dream as soon as possible?

Sources: American Demographics, February 1987, p. 7; *American Demographics,* April 1987, pp. 52, 54.

---

complex and constantly changing picture. Some trends in intergroup relations can be discerned and are likely to continue—new ones may emerge as new groups gain prominence. Significant population shifts will continue to have an impact—Vietnamese, Cambodian, and mainland Chinese immigrants are examples, as are the 125,000 Cubans who were shipped to the United States by the Castro regime. The resurgence of ethnic-identity movements will probably spread and may be coupled with more collective protest movements among disaffected ethnic and racial minorities, who are demanding that they be given equal access to the opportunities and benefits of American society.

It is important to realize that the old concept of the United States as a "melting pot" is both simplistic and idealistic. Many groups have entered the United States. Most encountered prejudice, some severe discrimination, and others the pressures of Anglo conformity. Contemporary American society is the outcome of all these diverse groups coming together and trying to adjust. Indeed, if these groups can interact on the basis of mutual respect, this diversity may offer America strengths and flexibility not available in a homogeneous society.

SUMMARY

Race refers to a category of people who are defined as similar because of a number of physical characteristics. Often it is based on an arbitrary set of features chosen to serve the labeler's purposes and convenience. Race has been defined according to genetic, legal, and social criteria.

An ethnic group has a distinct cultural tradition with which it identifies and which may or may not be identified by others. Members of the group are aware of their relationship because of shared loyalty to an outside object and to one another.

The concept of minority implies a group that receives differential treatment and is excluded from full social participation by the dominant group in a society.

Prejudice is an irrationally based negative, or occasionally positive, attitude toward certain groups and their members. Although prejudice is a feeling, discrimination is an action, meaning that differential treatment is accorded to individuals who are assumed to belong to a particular category or group. In some societies, institutions are structured in such a way as to discriminate, giving benefits to one group and denying them to another. The system of apartheid, practiced in South Africa, is an example of such institutionalized discrimination.

When racial and ethnic groups come together, any one of several patterns may emerge: assimilation, pluralism, subjugation, segregation, expulsion, or annihilation.

Assimilation is the process whereby groups with different cultures come to have a common culture. Pluralism refers to the coexistence of separate racial and ethnic groups within a society. Subjugation is the subordination of one group by another. A form of subjugation, segregation is the act, process, or state of being set apart. Most often, but not always, it is a negative phenomenon imposed on a minority by a dominant group. Expulsion is the process of forcing a group to leave the territory in which it resides, and annihilation, or genocide, is the deliberate attempt to exterminate a racial or ethnic group.

Two hundred years ago America's population was mostly English and Protestant. Today, about 63 million people claim white Anglo-Saxon Protestant (WASP) ancestry. Other "white ethnic" groups—whites who are not of northern European origin or Protestant—can be thought of as the largest ethnic minority in the United States, though these groups often do not share a common identification.

In 1619 the first twenty blacks were brought to North America. Originally given the status of indentured servants, blacks were soon reduced to the status of slaves. Although slavery officially ended with the Civil War, the struggle against prejudice and institutionalized discrimination has continued to the present day. The United States' 30 million blacks are the nation's second-largest racial group.

The number of Hispanics in the United States grew 30 percent between 1980 and 1987, four times faster than the U.S. population. The greatest concentrations of Hispanics are in Texas and California. Mexican Americans make up the majority of the Spanish-speaking population in the United States.

The first Jews arrived in the United States in 1654, but they did not begin to settle here in large numbers until the mid-1800s. Today there are approximately 6 million Jews in America.

Most Asian Americans are concentrated in the major metropolitan centers, particularly Honolulu and San Francisco.

Driven from their territory and exterminated by disease, starvation, and deliberate massacre, by 1900 Native Americans (Indians) had been reduced in population to 250,000, about one-eighth of their original number. By 1980 their population had increased to more than 1.4 million.

Some future trends in intergroup relations can be discerned. New ethnic associations, resurgence of ethnic identity movements, and collective protests among disaffected ethnic and racial minorities may grow, even though there seems to be less prejudice and discrimination. In the future, American society will be pluralistic, gaining strength and flexibility from its diverse racial and ethnic subgroups.

Chapter 11

GENDER ROLES

Julie Thompson, 59, is still wistful when she thinks back on the career she abandoned 34 years ago. It was 1954, and the 25-year-old Thompson, holding a newly minted master's degree in international studies, landed a job at the National Security Agency in Washington, D.C.

A subsequent marriage to a young naval officer from Boston put an end to Thompson's fledgling career. When William Thompson said he wanted to return home after his stint in the service, his new wife never thought to protest.

The Thompsons' daughter, Margie, 26, has very different expectations. Margie, a producer in New York, is expecting her first child. She has been working since her marriage, and she plans to continue doing so after the baby is born.

The Thompsons' story is the same as that of thousands of other post–World War II mothers and their daughters born during the baby boom of that period. Julie Thompson, like her peers, gave up her career to start a family. Her daughter, whose friends are juggling motherhood and the world of work, fully expects that she, too, will have to succeed on both fronts.

Margie and her friends assume that they are breaking new ground by departing from the patterns set by their parents' generation. A closer look, however, will reveal that they are merely resuming long-standing patterns that had been in place until their parents came along and wreaked havoc with demographic trends.

Demographic data on women from 1900 to 1940 show several trends. Women were marrying at later ages. Their level of education was increasing and was nearly on a par with men's. They were having fewer children and at a later age. The divorce rate was trending up.

After World War II a remarkable turn-around took place. Women married at younger ages, were far more fertile, had their first babies at a younger age, slowed their rate of education relative to men's, and had fewer divorces.

An often overlooked fact, though, is that this was a 20-year abnormality whose major effect was a population surge known as the baby boom. It also created a false stereotype of the "traditional" American family (Tischler, 1988).

In this chapter we will examine how changes in attitudes about gender roles produce significant changes for society. We will look at some of the differences between the sexes, examine cross-cultural variations in gender roles, and try to understand how a gender identity is acquired. In the process we will begin to understand the changes that are taking place in gender roles in American society.

ARE THE SEXES SEPARATE AND UNEQUAL?

Sociology makes an important distinction between sex and gender. **Sex** refers to the physical and biological distinctions between men and women. At birth the biologically determined differences are most evident in the male and female genitalia. In

sex The physical and biological differences between men and women.

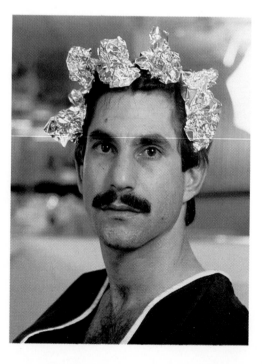

Society causes us to expect certain gender role behaviors from males and females. A changing society, however, produces changes in how these roles are carried out.

general, sex differences are made evident by physical distinctions in anatomical, chromosomal, hormonal, and physiological characteristics.

Gender refers to the social, psychological, and cultural attributes of masculinity and femininity that are based on the above-mentioned biological distinctions. Gender pertains to the socially learned patterns of behavior and the psychological or emotional expressions of attitudes that distinguish males from females. Ideas about masculinity and femininity are culturally derived and pattern the way in which males and females are treated from birth onward. Gender is an important factor in shaping people's self-images and social identities. Whereas sex refers to an ascribed status, in that a person is born either a male or female, gender is learned through the socialization process and thus is an achieved status.

Are gender-role differences innate? The dominant view in many societies is that gender identities are expressions of what is "natural." People tend to assume that acting masculine or feminine is the result of an innate, biologically determined process rather than the result of socialization and social-learning experiences. To support the view that gender-role differences are innate, people have sought evidence from religion and the biological and social sciences. Whereas most religions tend to support the biological view, both biology and the social sciences provide evidence that suggests that what is "natural" about sex roles expresses both innate and learned characteristics.

HISTORICAL VIEWS

The third-century Chinese scholar Fu Hsuan penned these lines about the status of women in his era:

> Bitter indeed it is to be born a woman,
> It is difficult to imagine anything so low!
> Boys can stand openly at the front gate,
> They are treated like gods as soon as they are born . . .
> But a girl is reared without joy or love,

> And no one in her family really cares for her,
> Grown up, she has to hide in the inner rooms,
> Cover her head, be afraid to look others in the face,
> And no one sheds a tear when she is married off . . .
> (Quoted in Bullough, 1973)

In traditional Chinese society women were subordinate to men. Chinese women were often called "Nei Ren," or "inside person." To keep women in shackles, Confucian doctrine created what was known as the three obediences and the four virtues. The three obediences were "obedience to the father when yet unmarried, obedience to the husband when married, and obedience to the sons when widowed." Thus, traditionally, Chinese women were placed under the control of the male sex from the cradle to the grave.

The four virtues were: (1) "woman's ethics," meaning a woman must know her place and act in every way in compliance with the old ethical code; (2) "woman's speech," meaning a woman must not talk too much, taking care not to bore people; (3) "woman's appearance," meaning a woman must pay attention to adorning herself with a view to pleasing men; and (4) "woman's chores," meaning a woman must willingly do all the chores in the home.

In nineteenth-century Europe, attitudes toward women had not improved appreciably. The father of modern sociology, Auguste Comte (1851), in constructing his views of the perfect society also dealt with questions about women's proper role in society. Comte saw women as the mental and physical inferiors of men. "In all kinds of force, whether physical, intellectual or practical, it is certain that man surpasses women in accordance with the general law prevailing throughout the animal kingdom." Comte did grant women a slight superiority in the realms of emotion, love, and morality.

Comte believed women should not be allowed to work outside the home, to own

gender The social, psychological, and cultural attributes of masculinity and femininity that are based on biological distinctions.

ADULTERY AS A GENDER ISSUE

Adultery is as old as marriage. Yet in some respects the words seem outdated today, at least so believes Annette Lawson, author of Adultery: An Analysis of Love and Betrayal *(1988), and a sociologist who has been studying the issue for the last decade. We interviewed Lawson to find out what gender issues are involved in our response to this practice.*

Annette Lawson points out that since the permissive revolution of the late sixties and seventies, we act as if people no longer commit adultery; they instead have "affairs," become "involved with someone," or have "a relationship."

Yet, Lawson notes, infidelity still produces devastating feelings of guilt and remorse in the adulterer, and fury and self-blame in the "victim." Interestingly, she also believes that adultery has the power to also make those involved "feel alive."

If we look closer at the way we use the words, we will notice that adultery seems to be different from an affair. An affair often implies something that is not serious.

Adultery, on the other hand, threatens the marriage in that the adulterous spouse is bringing a third person into the marriage relationship. As the dictionary notes, adultery "dilutes, poisons, pollutes or debases" the marriage.

That is why adultery and divorce seem to be tied together. Until recently, adultery had to be proved for a divorce to be granted. Today, no-fault divorce has become common, and this practice is no longer necessary, but adultery still plays a major role in the breakdown of a marriage.

Because adultery threatens the marriage, and remains strongly linked in people's minds with divorce, religion also enters the picture. To the believer, adultery is still a sin and, although rarely prosecuted, remains on the statute books as a crime in various parts of the Western world. In the Islamic world and elsewhere, it still is severely punished — even by death.

Lawson provides us with some interesting insights into adultery. She notes that throughout the ages adultery has actually been viewed as theft. Because women were seen as the property of men, adultery was then an instance of one man stealing another man's property.

But why was a woman's adultery a more serious breach of the marriage than a man's adultery? We should punish the man — that is, the thief — more than the woman who is being stolen, it would seem. The explanation in this contradiction is found in the greater privileges that men have enjoyed through the ages and in the unequal treatment of the sexes.

Lawson notes that there is another important point involved in the idea of adultery being the theft of a man's property. Not only is the man's property being stolen in the form of his wife but also in the form of inheritance.

Lawson believes that one of the reasons that the adulterous woman has always been seen as a

more serious problem than the adulterous man is that inheritance in the Western world passed through the male line. The establishment of children (especially sons) as the biological offspring of the father became critical for the passing on of property. Even if a woman is uncertain who the father of her child is, she certainly knows who the mother is. A promiscuous woman could wreak havoc with attempts to determine the rightful heirs in a family. Historically, then, it has been more important to guard against the adultery of women than the adultery of men.

In modern times, with the movement toward greater equality of the sexes, women are no longer the property of men. Previous ideas about inheritance and promiscuity have also been modified and seem to be less applicable to contemporary society. This may help to explain changes in our thinking about adultery and the fact that we no longer think of it as the theft of a man's property. It may also help to explain the more common use of the term *affair* instead of *adultery* in regard to the previously more serious but essentially same practice.

property, or to exercise political power. Their gentle nature required that they remain in the home as mothers tending to their children, and as wives tending to their husband's emotional, domestic, and sexual needs.

Comte viewed equality as a social and moral danger to women. He felt progress would result only from making the female's life "more and more domestic; to diminish as far as possible the burden of out-door labour." Women, in short, were to be the pampered slaves of men.

RELIGIOUS VIEWS

Many religions have overtly acknowledged that men are superior to women. For example, the Judeo-Christian story of creation presents a God-ordained sex-role hierarchy, with man created in the image of God and woman a subsequent and secondary act of creation. This account has been used as the theological justification that man is superior to woman, who was created to assist and help man and bear his children. This kind of legitimation of male superiority is called a **patriarchal ideology** and is displayed in the following passage.

> For a man indeed ought not to have his head veiled, forasmuch as he is the image and glory of God: but the woman is the glory of the man: for neither was the man created for the woman but the woman for the man: for this cause ought the woman to have a sign of authority on her head. (1 Cor. 11: 7–10)

In traditional India, the Hindu religion conceived of women as strongly erotic and thus a threat to male asceticism and spirituality. Women were cut off physically from the outside world. They wore veils and voluminous garments and were never seen by men who were not members of the family. Only men were allowed access to and involvement with the outside world.

Womens' precarious and inferior position in traditional India is illustrated further by the ancient Manu code, which was

Models for proper gender role behavior are widespread within society. In addition to our experiences with others, art, literature, and music play important roles in transmitting appropriate behavior to us.

drawn up between 200 B.C. and A.D. 200. The code states that if a wife had no children after 8 years of marriage, she would be banished; if all her children were dead after 10 years, she could be dismissed; and if she had produced only girls after 11 years, she could be repudiated.

Stemming from the Hindu patriarchal ideology was the practice of prohibiting women from owning and disposing of property. The prevalent practice in traditional Hindu India was that property acquired by the wife belonged to the husband. Similar restrictions on the ownership of property by women also prevailed in ancient Greece and Rome, and in Israel, China, and Japan. Such restrictions are still followed by fundamentalist Muslim states like Saudi Arabia and Iran.

Indeed, in many countries, women's role in society has deteriorated in recent years. In Iran, for example, any progress women made under the shah was reversed when the Ayatollah Khomeini took power. Khomeini and his extremist followers have

patriarchal ideology The belief that men are superior to women and should control all important aspects of society.

kept women veiled, reducing them to a subordinate — almost invisible — role.

Even in Pakistan, a relatively modern Moslem country, women have far less value than men. In a court of law, for example, the testimony of women is given half the weight of the testimony of men. According to a Moslem clergyman, this rule is necessary because of the emotional and irrational nature of women — a nature that makes women intellectually inferior. From the court's point of view, women have the same value as "the blind, handicapped, lunatics, and children" (*New York Times,* June 17, 1988).

BIOLOGICAL VIEWS

Supporters of the belief that the basic differences between males and females are biologically determined have sought evidence from two sources: studies of other animal species, including nonhuman primates — monkeys and apes — and studies of the physiological differences between men and women. We shall examine each in turn.

Animal Studies and Sociobiology

The scientific study of animal behavior is known as **ethology.** Ethologists have observed that there are sexual differences in behavior throughout much of the nonhuman animal world. Evidence indicates that these differences are biologically determined — that in a given species, members of the same sex behave in much the same way and perform the same tasks and activities. Popularized versions of these ideas, such as those of Desmond Morris in *The Human Zoo* (1970) or Lionel Tiger and Robin Fox in *The Imperial Animal* (1971), generalize from the behavior of nonhuman primates to that of humans. They maintain that in all primate species, including *Homo sapiens,* there are fundamental differences between males and females. They try to explain human male dominance and the traditional division of labor by gender in all human societies on the basis of inherent

ethology The scientific study of animal behavior.

male or female capacities. They even have extended their analysis to explain other human phenomena, such as war and territoriality, through evolutionary comparisons with other species. A more sophisticated treatment of this same theme is found in the field of sociobiology (see Chapter 1), the study of the genetic basis for social behavior (Wilson, 1975, 1978).

Sociobiologists believe that much of human social behavior has a genetic basis. Such patterns of social organization as family systems, organized aggression, male dominance, defense of territory, fear of strangers, the incest taboo, and even religion are believed to be rooted in the genetic structure of our species. The emphasis in sociobiology is on the inborn structure of social traits.

Critics note that sociobiologists overlook the important role learning plays among nonhuman primates in their acquisition of social and sexual behavior patterns (Montagu, 1973). They also observe that by generalizing from animal to human behavior, fundamental differences between human and nonhuman primates, such as the human use of a complex language system, are not taken into account. While freely acknowledging the biological basis for sex differences, these critics claim that among humans, social and cultural factors overwhelmingly account for the variety in the roles and attitudes of the two sexes. Human expressions of maleness and femaleness, they argue, although influenced by biology, are not determined by it. Rather, gender identities acquired through social learning provide the guidelines for appropriate gender-role behavior and expression.

Genetic and Physiological Differences

However, even ardent critics cannot deny that certain genetic and physiological differences exist between the sexes — differences that influence health and physi-

TABLE 11.1

Prevalence of Fatal and Nonfatal Illness among Men and Women

Women	Percent Greater*	Men	Percent Greater*
Nonfatal		*Nonfatal*	
Thyroid diseases	551	Visual impairments	49
Bladder infection, disorders	382	Hearing impairments	46
Anemias	378	Paralysis, complete or partial	25
Bunions	335	Tinnitus	21
Spastic colon	305	Hernia of abdominal cavity	18
Frequent constipation	253	Intervertebral disk disorders	14
Varicose veins	233	Hemorrhoids	5
Migraine headaches	175		
Diverticulitis of intestines	152	*Fatal*	
Chronic enteritis and colitis	111	Emphysema	59
Sciatica	85	Atherosclerosis	54
Trouble with corns, calluses	82	Ischemic heart disease	51
Neuralgia and neuritis	79	Cerebrovascular disease	32
Gallstones	64	Liver disease, including cirrhosis	23
Arthritis	59	Other selected heart diseases	3
Dermatitis	59	Ulcer of stomach, duodenum	3
Gastritis and duodenitis	54		
Heart rhythm disorders	43		
Diseases of retina	32		
Fatal			
Asthma	41		
High blood pressure**	8		

* Percentages indicate the higher prevalence of each disorder among that sex compared to the other.
** A risk factor for fatal circulatory diseases. Women's higher prevalence rates are thought to reflect earlier diagnosis and control, compared with men. For younger, premenopausal women, high blood pressure is less common than among men, and more men die from the disease because of damage done to their blood vessels at the younger age, when they do contract it in higher proportions.

Source: U.S. News & World Report, August 8, 1988, p. 53. Basic data from Lois Verbrugge of University of Michigan and unpublished data from the National Health Interview Surveys 1983–1985.

cal capacity. Accordingly, the study of gender roles must take these differences into account in such areas as size and muscle development (both usually greater in males); longevity (females, with few exceptions, live longer in nearly every part of the world, sometimes as much as 9 years longer on average); and susceptibility to disease and physical disorders (generally greater in males). As you can see from the following tables, men and women are afflicted by extremely different chronic conditions. Even though women are sick more often than men and suffer from a greater variety of problems, men are more likely to die or suffer serious disability from their illnesses than women (see Table 11.1).

The genetic and physiological differ-

Genetic and physiological differences between the sexes influence but do not determine the ease with which members of each sex can learn to perform certain tasks. NASA believes that Dr. Mae C. Jamison's abilities will complement those of the male astronauts.

ences between the sexes influence, but do not determine, the ease with which members of each sex can learn to perform certain tasks. Some researchers believe, for example, that gender differences account for the edge males appear to have in math. In one study of Scholastic Aptitude Test scores of more than 10,000 gifted junior high school students (Benbow and Stanley, 1980), it was found that the vast majority of those particularly gifted in math were boys. Benbow and Stanley speculated that the reason for this talent might be the male sex hormone, testosterone. Other studies have shown that males hold a clear advantage in determining visual-spatial relationships — an ability that emerges at around age 8 and persists throughout life.

Not everyone believes the causes of these differences are genetic though. Some sociologists suggest that there is a self-fulfilling prophecy at work, claiming boys do better in math than girls because that is what is expected of them. Girls, at the same time, are doing what is expected of them when they do not do well in math.

Responses to Stress

Gender differences also influence the way men and women react to stress, the "fight or flight" reaction that is thought to play a part in heart disease, stroke, and coronary-artery disease, among other ailments. In earlier days, when primitive man was threatened by wild animals while hunting, testosterone enabled him to react quickly to danger. This intense type of reaction is no longer important today and may be part of the reason men suffer more heart attacks than women. Women, it appears, react more slowly to stress, putting less pressure on the blood vessels and the heart. Whereas learned behavior may play a role in women's response to stress, biology is no less important (*U.S. News & World Report,* August 8, 1988).

Although many differences between males and females have a biological basis, other physical conditions may be tied to cultural influences and variations in environment and activity. Men react differently to psychological stress than women do: each sex develops severe but dissimilar symptoms. Changing cultural standards and patterns of social behavior have had a pronounced effect on other traits that formerly were thought to be sex linked. For example, the rising incidence of lung cancer among women — a disease historically associated primarily with men — can be traced directly to changes in social behavior and custom, not biology: Women now smoke as freely as men do.

In sum, different learned behaviors do contribute to the relative prevalence of certain diseases and disorders in each sex. But as has been pointed out, not all male–female differences in disease and susceptibility can be attributed to these factors. In addition to genetically linked defects, differences in some basic physiological processes, such as metabolic rates and adult secretion of gonadal hormones, may make males more vulnerable than females to certain physical problems.

SOCIOLOGICAL VIEW: CROSS-CULTURAL EVIDENCE

Most sociologists believe that the way people are socialized has a greater effect on their gender identities than biological factors. Cross-cultural and historical research offers support for this view, revealing that different societies allocate different tasks and duties to men and women and that males and females have culturally patterned conceptions of themselves and of one another.

Until the pioneering work of anthropologist Margaret Mead (1901–1978) was published in the 1930s, it was widely believed that gender identity (what then was called sex temperament) was a matter of biology alone. It never occurred to Westerners to question their culture's definitions of "male" and "female" temperament and behavior, nor did most people doubt that these were innate properties. In 1935 Mead published a refutation of this assumption in the book *Sex and Temperament,* which has become a classic. While doing research among isolated tribal groups on the island of New Guinea, she found three societies with widely different expectations of male and female behavior. The Arapesh were characterized as gentle and home loving, with a belief that men and women were of equivalent temperament. Both adult men and women subordinated their needs to those of the younger or weaker members of the society. The Mundugamor, by contrast, assumed a natural hostility between members of the same sex and only slightly less hostility between the sexes. Both sexes were expected to be tough, aggressive, and competitive. The third society, the Tchambuli, believed that the sexes were temperamentally different, but the gender roles were reversed relative to the Western pattern.

I found . . . in one, both men and women act as we expect women to act — in a mild parental responsive way; in the second, both act as we expect men to act — in a fierce initiative fashion; and in the third, the men act according to our stereotype for women — are catty, wear curls and go shopping, while the women are energetic, managerial, unadorned partners. (Mead, 1935)

Although Mead's findings are interesting and suggestive, anthropologists have cautioned against overinterpreting them. They point out that Mead's research was limited to a matter of months and that her then-husband and collaborator Reo Fortune rejected her view that the Arapesh did not distinguish between male and female temperaments. Furthermore, research (Maccoby and Jacklin, 1975) points out four areas of difference between the sexes — in girls and boys, at least:

1. Girls have greater verbal ability than boys do.
2. Boys excel in visual-spatial ability.
3. Boys excel in mathematical ability.
4. Boys are more aggressive than girls are.

Other research has shown that three elements contribute to the development of an individual's gender identity: (1) genetic factors, (2) efforts by other members of the society to mold the child into whatever the culture considers to be appropriately male or female, and (3) spontaneous imitative learning by the child (imitating the behavior of adults who themselves have been molded to their culture's norms by their socialization).

Most sociologists tend to agree that even in preliterate societies, culture is central to the patterning of gender roles. Nevertheless, biological factors may play a more prominent part in structuring gender roles in societies less technologically developed than our own. Anthropologist Clellan S. Ford (1970) believes that for preindustrial peoples, "the single most important biological fact in determining how men and women live is the differential part they play in reproduction." The woman's life is characterized by a continuing cycle of pregnancy, childbearing, and nursing for periods of up to 3 years. By the time the child is weaned, the mother is likely to be pregnant again. Not until menopause, which frequently coincides with the end of the woman's life itself, is her reproductive role over. In these circumstances it is not surprising that such activities as hunting, fighting, and forest clearing usually are defined as male tasks; gathering and preparing small game, grains, and vegetables; tending gardens; and building shelters are typically female activities, as is caring for the young.

In an early study George Murdock (1937) provided data on the division of labor by sex in 224 preliterate societies. Such activities as metalworking, making weapons, woodworking and stoneworking, hunting and trapping, building houses and boats, and clearing the land for agriculture were tasks performed by men. Women's activities included grinding grain; gathering

Weaving is tyically a female job. Among certain groups in Ghana, however, it is a male task because a high value is placed on the final product.

and cooking herbs, roots, seeds, fruits, and nuts; weaving baskets; making pottery; and making and repairing clothing. In a review of the cross-cultural literature, D'Andrade (1966) concluded that the division of labor by gender occurs in all societies. Generally, male tasks require vigorous physical activity or travel, whereas female tasks are less physically strenuous and more sedentary.

The almost universal classification of women to secondary status has had a profound effect on their work and family roles. Anthropologist Sherry Ortner (1974) observed that "everywhere, in every known culture, women are considered in some degree inferior to men." One important result of this attitude is the exclusion of women from participation in, or contact with, those areas of the particular society believed to be most powerful, whether they be religious or secular. We see these exclusionary patterns in our own society. There are no female priests in the Catholic church nor women rabbis in orthodox Judaism. No woman has ever run for president, and there are very few women chief executive officers of major U.S. corporations.

Another anthropologist, Michelle Rosaldo (1974), believes "women's status will be lowest in those societies where there is a firm differentiation between domestic and public spheres of activity and where women are isolated from one another and placed under a single man's authority in the home." She believes that the time-consuming and emotionally compelling involvement of a mother with her child is unmatched by any single involvement and commitment by a man. The result is that men are free to form broader associations in the outside world through their involvement in work, politics, and religion. The relative absence of women from these public spheres results in their lack of authority and power. Men's involvements and activities are viewed as important, and the cultural systems accord authority and value to men's activities and roles. In turn, women's work, especially when it is confined to domestic roles and activities, tends to be oppressive and lacking in value and status. Women are seen to gain power and a sense of value only when they are able to transcend the domestic sphere of activities. This differentiation is most acute in those societies that practice gender discrimination. Societies in which men value and participate in domestic activities tend to be more egalitarian.

WHAT PRODUCES GENDER INEQUALITY?

Sociologists have devoted much thought and research to understanding gender inequality. They have also tried to explain why, in most societies, males dominate. There are two theoretical approaches that have been used to explain male dominance and gender inequality: functionalism and conflict theory.

THE FUNCTIONALIST VIEWPOINT

From Chapter 1 you may recall that functionalists (or structural functionalists, to be more precise) believe that society consists of a system of interrelated parts that all work together to maintain the smooth operation of society. Functionalists argue that it was quite useful to have men and women fulfill different roles in preindustrial societies. The society was more efficient when tasks and responsibilities were allocated to particular individuals who were socialized to fulfill specific roles.

The fact that the human infant is helpless for such a long time made it necessary that someone look after the child. It is also logical that the mother who gives birth to the child and nurses it is also the one to take care of it. Because women spent their time near the home, they also then took on the duties of preparing the food, cleaning

clothes, and attending to the other necessities of daily living. To the male fell the duties of hunting, defending the family, and herding. He also became the one to make economic and other decisions important to the family's survival.

This division of labor created a situation in which the female was largely dependent on the male for protection and food, and so he became the dominant partner in the relationship. This dominance, in turn, caused his activities to be more highly regarded and rewarded. Over time, this pattern came to be seen as natural and was thought to be tied to biological sex differences.

Talcott Parsons and Robert Bales (1955) applied functionalist theory to the modern family. They argue that the division of labor and role differentiation by sex are universal principles of family organization and are functional to the modern family also. They believe the family functions best when the father assumes the *instrumental role,* which focuses on relationships between the family and the outside world. That role mainly involves supporting and protecting the family. The mother concentrates her energies on the *expressive role,* which focuses on relationships within the family and requires the mother to provide the love and support needed to sustain the family. The male is required to be dominant and competent, and the female should be passive and nurturant.

As can be imagined, there has been much criticism of the functionalist position. The view that gender roles and gender stratification are inevitable does not fit with cross-cultural evidence and the changing situation in American society (Crano and Aronoff, 1978). Critics contend that industrial society can be quite flexible in assigning tasks to males and females. Furthermore, the functionalist model was developed during the 1950s, an era of very traditional family patterns, and rather than being predictive of family arrangements, it is merely representative of the era during which it became popular.

Men increasingly are playing expressive roles as well as instrumental roles within the family.

gender-role socialization
The lifelong process whereby people learn the values, attitudes, motivations, and behavior considered appropriate to each sex by their culture.

THE CONFLICT THEORY VIEWPOINT

Although functionalist theory may explain why gender-role differences emerged, it does not explain why they persisted. According to the conflict theory, males dominate females because of their superior power and control over key resources. A major consequence of this domination is the exploitation of women by men. By subordinating women, men gain greater economic, political, and social power. According to conflict theory, as long as the dominant group benefits from the existing relationship, it has little incentive to change it. The resulting inequalities are therefore perpetuated long after they may have served any functional purpose. In this way, gender inequalities resemble race and class inequalities.

Conflict theorists believe the main source of gender inequality is the economic inequality between men and women. Economic advantage leads to power and prestige. If men have an economic advantage in society, it will produce a superior social position in both society and the family.

Friedrich Engels (1942) linked gender inequalities to capitalism, contending that primitive, noncapitalistic hunting and gathering societies without private property were egalitarian. As these societies developed capitalistic institutions of private property, power came to be concentrated in the hands of a minority of men who used their power to subordinate women and to create political institutions designed to maintain their power. Engels also believed that to free women from subordination and exploitation, society must abolish private property and other capitalistic institutions. Engels believed that socialism was the only solution to gender inequality.

Today many conflict theorists accept the view that gender inequalities may have evolved because they were initially functional. Many functionalists also agree that gender inequalities are becoming more and more dysfunctional. They believe that the origins for gender inequalities are more social than biological.

GENDER-ROLE SOCIALIZATION

Gender-role socialization is the lifelong process whereby people learn the values, attitudes, motivations, and behavior considered appropriate to each sex by their culture. In our society, as in all others, male and females are socialized differently. In addition, each culture defines gender roles differently. This process is not limited to childhood but continues through adolescence, adulthood, and into old age.

CHILDHOOD SOCIALIZATION

Even before a baby is born, its sex is a subject of speculation, and the different gender-role relationships it will form from birth on already are being decided. A scene from the early musical "Carousel" epitomizes (in somewhat caricatured form) some of the feelings that parents have about bringing up sons as opposed to daughters:

> A young man discovers he is to be a father. He rhapsodizes about what kind of son he expects to have. The boy will be tall and tough as a tree, and no one will dare to boss him around; it will be all right for his mother to teach him manners but she mustn't make a sissy out of him. He'll be good at wrestling and will be able to herd cattle, run a riverboat, drive spikes, etc. Then the prospective father realizes, with a start, that the child may be a girl. The music changes to a gentle theme. She will have ribbons in her hair; she will be sweet and petite (just like her mother) and suitors will flock around her. There's a slightly discordant note, introduced for comic relief from senti-mentality, when the expectant father brags that she'll be half again as bright as girls are meant to be; but then he returns to the main theme: she must be pro-tected, and he must find enough money to raise her in a setting where she will meet the right kind of man to marry. (Maccoby and Jacklin, 1975)

Parents carry in their minds images of what girls and boys are like, how they should behave, and what they should be in later life. Parents respond differently to girls and boys right from the beginning. After studying the behavior of parents and their infants, Michael Lewis (1972) reported that there are significant differences in the very early socialization of males and females. Thus, girls are caressed more than boys, but boys are jostled and roughhoused more. Mothers talk more to their daughters, and fathers interact more with their sons.

A variety of research studies (Lynn, 1969; Maccoby and Jacklin, 1975) reveal that there are persistent differences in the parental gender-role socialization of children. These differences are reinforced by other socializing agents—siblings, peers,

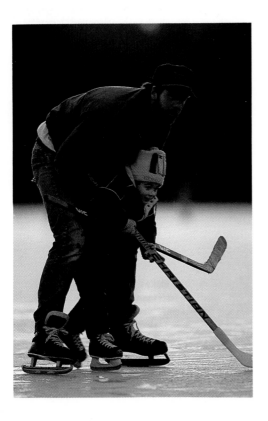

Parents, peers, and the media all play a part in shaping a gender-role identity.

Parents and grand-parents respond differently to boys and girls right from the beginning, and they carry in their minds images of what the child should be like, how it should behave, and what it should be in later life.

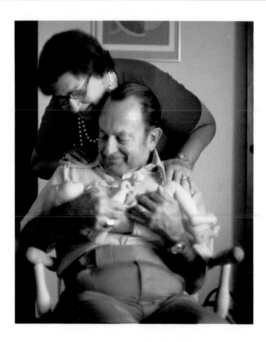

educational systems, and the mass media. Indeed, R. J. Stoller (1967), director of the UCLA Gender Research Clinic, states that "by the first two or three years of life, core gender identity—the sense of maleness or femaleness— is established as a result of the parents' conviction that their infant's assignment at birth to either the male or female sex is correct."

The pervasive manner in which the individual is socialized into the appropriate gender role can be best illustrated by cases in which an erroneous gender assignment was made at birth. For example, consider the case of Frankie, who, mistakenly classified as a male at birth, was socialized as a male. At the age of 5, "he" was brought to the hospital for examination and was diagnosed then as a female whose clitoris had been mistaken for a small penis. Lindesmith and Strauss (1956), in a report based on an unpublished document made available to them by one of the nurses assigned to the case, state that Frankie showed a decided preference for the company of little boys in the children's ward and a disdain for little girls and their "sissy" activities. After the child's real sex had been determined, the nurses were required to treat Frankie as a

little girl. One of the nurses observed that this was not easy:

> This didn't sound too difficult—until we tried it. Frankie simply didn't give the right cues. It is amazing how much your response to a child depends on that child's behavior toward you. It was extremely difficult to keep from responding to Frankie's typically little boy behavior in the same way that I responded to other boys in the ward. And to treat Frankie as a girl was jarringly out of key. It was something we all had to continually remind ourselves to do. Yet the doing of it left all of us feeling vaguely uneasy as if we had committed an error. . . . About the same time Frankie became increasingly aware of the change in our attitude toward her. She seemed to realize that behavior which had always before brought forth approval was no longer approved. It must have been far more confusing to her than it was to us and certainly it was bad enough for us. Her reaction was strong and violent. She became extremely belligerent and even less willing to accept crayons, color books and games which she simply called "sissy" and threw on the floor. (Lindesmith and Strauss, 1956)

SOCIALIZATION THROUGH CHILDREN'S BOOKS

Picture books play an important part in socializing children to gender roles in American society. The books provide children with a model of what boys and girls their own age do, say, and think. From books, children learn appropriate behavior and what is expected of them. Role models appear, which the children may emulate as they mature. In this respect, children's books are instrumental in reflecting cultural values and getting children to accept them.

In one study, sociologists Lenore J. Weitzman, Debra Eitler, Elizabeth Hokada, and Catherine Ross (1972) examined the treatment of gender roles in what were generally considered the best-illustrated children's books—the winners of the Caldecott Medal. The researchers did a statistical analysis of all Caldecott winners from the inception of the award in 1938 until 1970. In addition, to avoid bias they also examined winners of the Newberry Award (the American Library Association's prize for the best book each year for school-age children) and Little Golden Books that had sold over 3 million copies (inexpensive books that reach a more broadly based audience than the more expensive Caldecott winners), as well as children's etiquette books and others that prescribe behavior. Findings from these three supplementary samples strongly paralleled those from the Caldecott sample.

The first point noted was that in children's books, females were mentioned less often than males. The stories in these books were mostly about boys, men, or male animals and male-oriented adventures. When women did appear, they often played insignificant and inconspicuous roles.

A content analysis comparison of Caldecott winners between 1972 and 1985 with those of 1967–1971 (Williams, J. A. et al., 1987) showed some interesting trends. In the earlier books, only one in five illustrated characters was female; in the later sample the share is 42 percent. In the earlier sample, one-third of the books had no female characters at all. This was only true for 13 percent of the later sample.

Even with the improving trend, children exposed to a list of the titles of books designated as the very best children's books were bound to receive the impression that girls are not as important. The content of the books did little to dispel this impression.

In the world of picture books, boys were active, and girls were passive. Boys were presented in exciting and adventuresome pursuits that required independence. In contrast, most of the girls were passive and immobile. Some of them were restricted by their clothing, as skirts and dresses are easily soiled and prohibit more venturesome activities.

Small wonder then that many little girls might prefer to identify with the male role. These girls will face a dilemma, though, because they might be criticized by classmates and teachers for being a tomboy.

The rigidity of gender-role stereotypes was harmful to little boys in these books as well. They often felt equally constrained by the necessity to be fearless and clever. Whereas girls were allowed a great deal of emotional expression, crying or being fearful was not acceptable for boys. The only boys who cried in children's picture books were animals—dogs, frogs, or donkeys.

The image of the adult woman in children's books was also stereotyped and limited. In most stories, the adult woman was identified only as a mother or a wife.

In the Caldecott sample, not one woman had a job or profession. In a country where so many women are in the labor force and work outside the home, is seems strange that women in picture books were only mothers and wives. Moreover, the way motherhood was presented in children's books was unrealistic. Real mothers engage in a wide range of activities. The picture book mother, however, was almost always confined to the house with very little to do that was challenging or difficult. The image of the typical father or husband was no more realistic. They were never presented cleaning, shopping, or taking care of children.

From their work, the researchers concluded that pre-school children were being exposed to an extremely gender-stereotyped view of the world during a very impressionable period in their lives. The girls and women depicted were as a group dull and traditional. Little girls could only receive praise for their attractiveness. Boys, on the other hand, were admired for their accomplishments and imaginativeness.

The typical woman in children's books had status by virtue of being married to a specific man. She was the wife of a king, doctor, lawyer, or explorer, but never herself a ruler, doctor, lawyer, or explorer. The books never tell little girls that as women they can find fulfillment outside the home, through a career, or through intellectual pursuits. This is particularly strange because many of the books were written by prize-winning female authors whose own lives in no way parallel those of women in their stories.

A later study (Williams, J. A. et al., 1987) examined the twenty-four Caldecott-Award-winning children's books of 1980–1985. In this sample only one book has an adult female character who works outside the home, and she is a waitress. Only one-third of the books had any central female characters at all.

Even in the 1980s, male characters in children's books are much more likely to be independent, active, explorative, and creative. Females are colorless. Although females are no longer invisible in children's books, the study's authors conclude that "there is near unanimity in conformity to traditional gender roles."

ADOLESCENT SOCIALIZATION

Most societies have different expectations for adolescent girls than for boys. Erik Erikson (1968) believes the most important task in adolescence is the establishment of a sense of identity. He believes that during the adolescent stage, both boys and girls undergo severe emotional crises centered on questions of who they are and what they will be. If the adolescent crisis is satisfactorily resolved, a sense of identity will be developed; if not, role confusion will persist. According to Erikson, adolescent boys in our society generally are encouraged to pursue role paths that will prepare them for some occupational commitment, whereas girls generally are encouraged to develop behavior patterns designed to attract a suitable mate. Erikson observes that it is more difficult for girls than for boys to achieve a positive identity in Western society, because women are encouraged to be more passive and less achievement oriented than men are, and to pursue the development of inter-

personal skills — traits that are not highly valued in our society. Males, on the other hand, are encouraged to be competitive, to strive for achievement, and to assert autonomy and independence — characteristics that are held in high esteem in our competitive society.

The result of the adolescent gender-role socialization process becomes evident during young adulthood (ages 18 to 21). This is a period of transition from the earlier economic and psychological dependence on one's parents to the beginning of independent living. Research shows that during this period, young men experience more stress and less satisfaction with their lives than young women do (Frieze et al., 1978). Men at this age seem more burdened and concerned by the expectations and demands of their socialization process. Much of this anxiety arises from the pressure that young men face in choosing an occupation, a decision that they feel will be the prime determinant of their adult lives — affecting their future economic resources, social expectations, and friendship networks as well as defining their future work activities.

Traditionally, the pressure to choose a lifelong occupation has not been as severe for women at this age because their socialization emphasized marriage as their central adult role. Outside employment was seen as a temporary occupation subordinate to, and contingent on, marriage and future familial roles. The choice of a husband, not a job, was women's primary concern.

The predominant personality characteristics of young women during this period include a strong dependency on others for support, approval, and direction. Their sense of self is less clearly defined than that of men, and there is a tentativeness in their quest for personal identity. Many of these personality characteristics are associated with their marriage goals.

Nonetheless, female gender roles are changing rapidly, although traditional attitudes toward careers and marriage undoubtedly still remain part of the thinking

IS COGNITIVE ABILITY SEX LINKED?

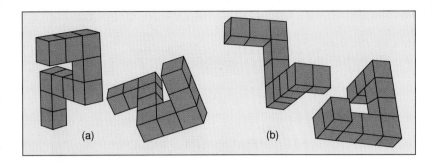

(a)   (b)

Tests of cognitive ability have long shown a male edge in mathematics and visual-spatial skills and a female advantage in work needing verbal aptitude. Take these brain-teasers to see whether your own abilities are typical.

Mathematical

A kindergarten class wants to buy a $77 tropical tree for the school. If the teacher agrees to pay twice as much as the class and the administration promises to pay four times as much as the class, how much should the teacher pay?

(a) $11.00   (d) $25.70
(b) $15.40   (e) $38.50
(c) $22.00

Answer: C

If x, y and z are three positive whole numbers and $x > y > z$, then, of the following, which is closest to the product xyz?

(a) $(x-1)yz$ (d) $x(y+1)z$
(b) $x(y-1)z$ (e) $xy(z+1)$
(c) $xy(z-1)$

Answer: A

Boys and girls do about equally well at arithmetic-problem solving. But when it comes to higher mathematics, boys have long shown a distinct advantage on average—even over girls who have taken comparable courses.

Spatial-visual

Can these pairs of three-dimensional objects be superimposed by rotation?

Answers: A yes; B yes

Males consistently outscore females in spatial-visual-abilities tests. At a young age, they are better on mazes; later, they show particular talent on exercises requiring mental manipulation of three-dimensional "objects" like those in the drawing above. The average 12-year-old boy knows that the water level remains horizontal in both glasses, but about

Verbal

Five girls are sitting side by side on a bench. Jane is in the middle, and Betty sits next to her on the right. Alice is beside Betty, and Dale is beside Ellen, who sits next to Jane. Who are sitting on the ends?

Answer: Dale and Alice

Mark the "word" that best fills the blank:

    A gelish lob relled perfully.
    I grolled the _____ meglessly.

(a) gelish (b) lob (c) relled (d) perfully

Answer: B

Assume that these glasses are half filled with water. Draw a line to indicate the top of the waterline in each.

half of college women get the answer wrong.

During early adolescence, girls begin to outperform boys on tests of verbal ability, including questions designed to measure their understanding of logical relationships. The female edge persists into adulthood.

Sources: Bias in Mental Testing, by Arthur R. Jensen (the Free Press); *The Psychology of Sex Differences,* by Eleanor Emmons Maccoby and Carol Nagy Jacklin (Stanford Univeristy Press); *Sex Differences in Cognitive Abilities,* by Diane F. Halpern (Lawrence Erlbaum Associates); College Entrance Examination Board.

325

Although female gender roles are changing rapidly, few women choose a job that is as physical and aggressive as being a jockey.

of many people in our society. Girls are being encouraged not to limit themselves to these stereotyped roles and attitudes. More and more young women expect to pursue careers before and during marriage and child rearing. Marriage is no longer considered the only desirable goal for a woman, nor is it any longer even considered necessary to a woman's success and happiness.

ADULT SOCIALIZATION

Gender-role socialization continues into adulthood. Three personality characteristics associated with adult sex differences are gender identity, self-esteem, and achievement motivation (Mandle, 1979). Because of cultural socialization, women are less likely to have an independent gender identity than men. That is, they tend to see their female identity as largely defined by, and dependent on, the characteristics of their husbands and children.

Low self-esteem, according to Mandle, the second personality trait characteristic of adult women, is associated with psychologi-

cal feelings of inadequacy and even self-hatred. One manifestation of this is that both men and women consistently devalue the attributes of women. In one study (Goldberg, 1968), a psychologist asked female college students to read professional articles from each of six fields and to rate them for persuasive impact, profundity, writing style, professional competency, and overall value. Half the women received articles purportedly written by a male author (for example, John T. McKay), and half got the identical articles supposedly written by a woman (for example, Joan T. McKay). The women gave consistently lower ratings to the identical articles when they were attributed to a female author than when they were attributed to a male author.

The third personality characteristic believed to be typical of women is low achievement motivation. Women are socialized to deemphasize qualities that are highly regarded in our society—competition, independence, intellectual achievement, and leadership. (Of course, these personality traits, like most others, are not intrinsically "good" or "bad"—the value placed on each is culturally determined.) Judith Bardwick and Elizabeth Douvan (1971) point out that the result of these factors is that "very few women have succeeded in traditionally masculine roles, not only because of disparagement and prejudice, but largely because women have not been fundamentally equipped and determined to succeed."

The job fields that women dominate are those that use skills of nurturance and empathy and that deemphasize such traits as aggressiveness and competitiveness or treat them as largely dysfunctional. These jobs include teaching, nursing, and secretarial work. It should be noted that all these occupations pay poorly compared with many male-dominated positions.

Gender-role socialization also is fostered by a society's concepts of proper public behavior—its rules of etiquette, or good manners. In traditional social behavior between the sexes in public places and in everyday life—the rules by which men are expected to open doors for women, walk on the outside of pavements (possibly to protect women from being splashed or pelted by garbage), and ask women for permission to smoke in their presence—the recurrent pattern is for men to defer to women. Underlying these deferential patterns is an imputation of women's helplessness, weakness, and frailty. Supporters of traditional rules of etiquette fail to see that these deferential patterns are in reality forms of social control that perpetuate and reinforce the power of men.

Daryl and Sandra Bem, a husband-and-wife team of psychologists, have devised two passages that expose the accepted ideological rationalization that women and men have complementary but equal positions in our society.

> Both my wife and I earned Ph.D. degrees in our respective disciplines. I turned down a superior academic post in Oregon and accepted a slightly less desirable position in New York where my wife could obtain a part-time teaching job and do research at one of the several other colleges in the area. Although I would have preferred to live in a suburb, we purchased a home near my wife's college so that she could have an office at home where she would be when the children returned from school. Because my wife earns a good salary, she can easily afford to pay a maid to do her major household chores. My wife and I share all other tasks around the house equally. For example, she cooks the meals, but I do the laundry for her and help her with many of her other household tasks. (Bem and Bem, 1976)

At first glance, the man speaking in this passage seems to express an egalitarian gender-role relationship that rejects traditional sexist ideology. But Bem and Bem point out that such a marriage may not be an instance of interpersonal equality at all. There may be hidden assumptions about the "natural" role of women that are based on traditional ideology. These unconscious assumptions become clear in the compari-

son passage in which the roles of the husband and wife are reversed:

> Both my husband and I earned Ph.D. degrees in our respective disciplines. I turned down a superior academic post in Oregon and accepted a slightly less desirable position in New York where my husband could obtain a part-time teaching job and do research at one of the several other colleges in the area. Although I would have preferred to live in a suburb, we purchased a home near my husband's college so that he could have an office at home where he would be when the children returned from school. Because my husband earns a good salary, he can easily afford to pay a maid to do his major household chores. My husband and I share all other tasks around the house equally. For example, he cooks the meals, but I do the laundry for him and help him with many of his other household tasks. (Bem and Bem, 1976)

This reversal of characters vividly illustrates that the first passage, rather than representing an egalitarian ideology, in fact perpetuates a sexist one. Why is it "her" maid, "her" laundry, "her" household tasks, and so forth? The first passage is an example of the subtlety of a nonconscious ideology. On the other hand, the second passage sounds absurd because it goes counter to the same nonconscious sexist ideology. As Sandra and Daryl Bem (1976) put it, "A truly equalitarian marriage would permit both partners to pursue careers or outside commitments which carry equal weight when all important decisions are to be made."

GENDER DIFFERENCES IN SOCIAL INTERACTION

There are some interesting differences in how men and women think about the future and solve problems. In one study researchers (Maines and Hardesty, 1987) asked undergraduates to describe what they expected would happen to them over the

SEXUAL HARASSMENT ON CAMPUS

S exual harassment is a fact of life in corporations and on college campuses. Whether you have been affected by it or not, you have probably heard stories of unwelcome advances, sexual jokes, and even requests for sexual favors—all of which may severely compromise the person being harassed. Not unexpectedly, that person is usually a woman—a fact that reflects the unequal power relationship between the harasser and the harassed. Until recently, these victims had few legal options. Today, however, thanks to a 1986 U.S. Supreme Court decision, sexual harassment is considered a form of discrimination under the Civil Rights Act.

Sexual harassment takes many forms, varying in degree from unwelcome advances and sexual jokes to touching and requests for sexual favors. Often implied in this behavior is a clear message: If the woman does not comply, she will suffer the consequences when raises, promotions, and, in the case of college students, grades are decided.

Sexual harassment pervades the workplace. According to the U.S. Merit Systems Protections Board, an independent agency that is involved in personnel actions of federal civil service workers, 42 percent of female workers say they experienced on-the-job harassment between 1985 and 1987—a figure the National Organization for Women believes reflects harassment in the private sector as well.

Study after study also shows that the problem occurs on college campuses, including the na-tion's most prestigious universities. In 1983, a survey of female graduate students at Harvard showed that 41 percent had been sexually harassed by a faculty member. And in a nationwide survey conducted in 1984, Indiana University researchers found that 25 percent of all female students were sexually harassed at some time during their college careers.

As shocking as these figures are, they tell only part of the story —a part that deals with frequency of occurrence, not the effect sexual harassment has on women. Most experts agree that young women are extremely vulnerable in these situations because they are less powerful than their male professors. When Leah Rosenberg was at Johns Hopkins University, her concern over what happened to her was typical: "It's usually very difficult for a young student to know what is profes-

next 10 years. For both male and female undergraduates today, work appears to be a universal expectation. Likewise, the kinds of jobs wanted are nearly identical. Both groups mention jobs in business, law, hospital administration, and the computer industry. Further education was anticipated by more than half of the men and women. The vast majority (94 percent) also see themselves as eventually married with a family.

Thus, at first glance there appears to be a striking similarity in men and women's future plans. They express the desire for marriage, children, and work, and the desire for higher education is equally present. However, there are significant gender dif-ferences in expectations of *how* family, work, and education will be integrated. Men and women have different assumptions and tactics for achieving the similarly desired events in their lives.

Men operate in what Maines and Hardesty call a *linear temporal world.* When they try to project what the future might hold for them they almost always define it in terms of career accomplishments— lawyer, doctor, college professor, business executive, and so on. Education is seen as something that is pursued to attain the desired career.

Men see a family as desirable and not much of an issue in terms of pursuing career goals. They see little problem in coordinat-

sional conduct—and what isn't. I've been in situations when an instructor has kissed me on the forehead. It puts you in a very untenable position."

Women who are sexually harassed feel that their future is at stake—no matter their response. Since professors determine grades and write letters of recommendation for jobs and fellowships, sexual harrassment can be perceived as an act of coercion.

Realizing this, many colleges and universities are sending clear messages to faculty members to stay away from female students, even if they are receptive to their advances. Says Karla Miller, who helped draft the University of Iowa's policy statement: A woman who enters this type of relationship "becomes uncomfortable . . . long before she is able to get out of it, mainly because she fears some sort of retaliation. She ends up feeling victimized and powerless, and not an equal at all" (FitzGerald, 1986).

Unfortunately, in the workplace and on campus female victims of sexual harassment are often given little support. In many cases, the burden of proof falls on students' shoulders. "The problem [of sexual harassment] is clearly aggravated by the fact that too many college administrators seem to be reluctant to act against it," says Dr. Bernice Sandler, director of the Project on the Status and Education of Women at the Association of American Colleges. "Their allegiance may be more with the faculty than with the students, who come and go every four years" (Dreifus, 1986).

What does a student who finds herself in this situation do? Experts suggest that young women discourage any attempts at a relationship right from the start, and if harassment continues, they should complain to the chairperson of the department. Legal action should be taken only as a last resort. These matters often take years to resolve and, all too often, victims are blamed for the crime. What is worse, women just starting out in their careers may find that their professional reputation is at stake. Says Sandler: "Most women want to be remembered as a bright young student, not as the one who did ol' Charlie in" (FitzGerald, 1986).

Sources: "Hands Off at the Office," *U.S. News & World Report,* August 1, 1988, pp. 56–58; Karen FitzGerald, "Sexual Blackmail: Schools Get Serious about Harassment, *Ms.,* October 1986, pp. 24–26; Claudia Dreifus, "Sex with Professors," *Glamour,* August 1986, p. 264; "A First on Women's Rights," *U.S. News & World Report,* June 30, 1986, p. 10; "Wide Harassment of Women Working for U.S. is Reported," *New York Times,* July 1, 1988, p. B6.

ing career and family demands. Many expect to have a traditional division of labor in their families that will provide a support system for their career pursuit. Mostly, the problems of family living are viewed as being resolved rather easily, and typically there is no mention of career adjustments to the wife's and children's needs.

Young women, on the other hand, operate in *contingent temporal worlds.* Work, education, and family are all seen as having to be balanced off against each other. Careers are seen as pursuits that may have to be suspended or halted at certain points. The vast majority of women envision problems in their career pursuits, and they see family responsibilities as a major issue that needs to be adjusted to. Nearly half say they will quit work for a few years as a solution to the conflict between family and work demands. Instead of a clear vision of steps needed to accomplish their career goals, women become much more tentative about their future, because they expect it to entail adjustments and compromises.

Young men seem to take their autonomy for granted. That is, they assume that they will be able to accomplish what they set out to do if they have the necessary education, skill, and good fortune. Women, on the other hand, feel much more limited in their control of their future, even with the necessary education and skill. The problems surrounding the integration of family and career lend an element of uncertainty to their ability to accomplish their future goals. Women plan to be flexible in order to adjust to career and family needs. This flexibility gives them only partial automony in controlling their lives.

This element of tentativeness about the future, the willingness to be flexible and adjust to the needs of others, and the realization that goals cannot easily be achieved without compromise, evidently produces a difference in how men and women approach issues. This has led Carol Gilligan (1982) to believe that men and women think differently when it comes to problem solving.

Men often think that the highest praise they can bestow on a woman is to compliment her for thinking "like a man." That usually means that the woman has been decisive, rational, firm, and clear. To think "like a woman" in our society has always had negative overtones, being characterized as fuzzy, indecisive, unpredictable, tentative, and softheaded.

Gilligan challenges the value judgments made about male versus female styles of reasoning, especially in the area of moral decision making. She argues that a woman's perspective on things is not inferior to a man's; it is just different.

To illustrate what she means, Gilligan describes the different responses that 11-year-old boys and girls made to an example used by Lawrence Kohlberg and discussed more fully in Chapter 4. In the example, Heinz, a fictional character, is caught up in a complex moral question. Heinz's wife is dying of cancer. The local pharmacist has discovered a drug that might cure her, but it is very expensive. Heinz has done all he can to raise the money necessary to buy it but can come up with only half the amount, and the druggist demands the full price. The question is: Should Heinz steal the drug?

Boys and girls differ significantly in how they answer this question. Boys often see the problem as the man's individual moral choice, stating that Heinz should steal the drug, as the right to life super-

sedes the right to property. Case closed.

The girls Gilligan questioned always seemed to get bogged down in peripheral issues. No, they maintained, Heinz should not steal the drug, because stealing is wrong. Heinz should have a long talk with the pharmacist and try to persuade him to do what is right. Besides, they point out, if Heinz steals the drug, he might be caught and go to jail. Then what would happen to his wife? What if there were children?

Instead of labeling this tentativeness as a typical example of women's inability to make firm decisions, Gilligan sees it as an attempt to deal with the consequences of actions rather than simply with "what is right." For women, moral dilemmas involving people have a greater complexity and therefore a greater ambiguity.

If your morality stresses the importance of not hurting others, as seems to be the case with most women, you will often face failure. As one of the men Gilligan interviewed said, making a moral decision is often a matter of "choosing the victim." There is "violence inherent in choice," Gilligan writes, and "the injunction not to hurt can paralyze women."

If you base your decision on an absolute principle (for example, abortion is murder; therefore it is wrong), you may then act with the decisiveness so admired by both men and women. If you base your decision on what you imagine is likely to happen (for example, if this child would be born with no father; if the fetus is likely to be seriously defective; if the mother's life would be endangered by the birth; and so on), you will often face uncertainty. Women, whose value systems are more focused on people than on principles, consequently find themselves wrestling with the problems that might result from their decisions.

Gilligan hopes that by ceasing to label a man's perspective as right and a woman's as wrong, we can begin to understand that each may be valuable, though different. For this to happen, according to Gilligan, girls and women must gain confidence in their

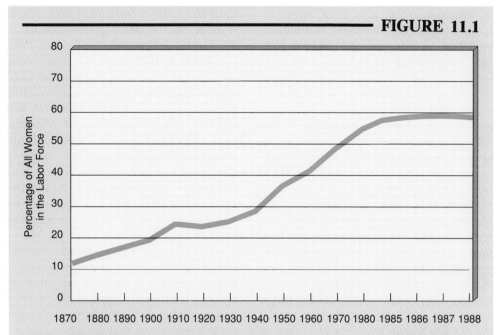

FIGURE 11.1

Women's Labor Force Participation Rates, 1870–1988. *Sources: U.S. Bureau of the Census, 1943;* Sixteenth Census of the United States: 1940; *"Population: Comparative Occupation Statistics for the United States, 1870 to 1940": Table XIV; Suzanne M. Bianchi and Daphne Spain, 1986.* American Women in Transition. *New York: Russell Sage Foundation: Table 5.2; U.S. Bureau of the Census, 1986c;* Statistical Abstract of the United States: 1987 *(107th edition): Table 639; U.S. Bureau of the Census 1987b;* Statistical Abstract of the United States: 1988 *(108th edition): Table 608;* Monthly Labor Review *III (June 1988): 77; cited in Spain, Radcliffe Conferences, December 1988.*

own ethical perspectives. Indeed, Gilligan feels, if society finally accepted women's moral view of the interconnectedness of actions and relationships, there could be enormous consequences for everything from scholarship to politics to international relations.

society. In this discussion we shall focus on economic and job-related discrimination, because these data are easily quantified and serve well to highlight the problem. It should be remembered, though, that discrimination against women in America actually is expressed in a far wider range of social contexts and institutions.

GENDER INEQUALITY AND WORK

Women's numerical superiority over men has not enabled them as yet to avoid discrimination in many spheres of American

JOB DISCRIMINATION

As of 1988, 56.5 percent of all American women were part of the paid labor force. It is projected that this percentage will reach 61.5 percent in the year 2000. Figure 11.1 shows the steady rise in women's labor force participation rates over the last century (Spain, 1988).

Presence in the labor force, however, does not mean full-time work. In 1986, 68 percent of all women were working full-time, compared to 86 percent of all men (U.S. Bureau of the Census, *Current Population Reports, 1988*).

Working women as a group consistently earn less than working men do. In 1986 the median weekly income for working men was $462, and for working women it was $290 (*Statistical Abstract of the United States: 1988, 1987*).

Women and men are concentrated in different occupational groups. Some would argue that the income and earnings differences between them result from pay differences across occupations rather than sex. An analysis of 503 occupations showed, however, that controlling for occupations makes little difference in the wage gap. Women working in the same occupations as men earn approximately 70 percent of what men earn (Bianchi and Spain, 1986). For example, male machine operators earned $20,244 in 1986, compared to $11,760 for female operators. Male accoun-

tants and auditors earned $31,959, whereas women in the same profession earned $22,006 (U.S. Bureau of the Census, 1988).

There are differences in educational attainment between men and women. Could it be that these salary differences result from educational disparities? It does not seem like that is the answer either. In 1986, male high school graduates who worked full-time year-round had an average salary of $23,759, and women had an average salary of $15,402. For college graduates the average salaries were $37,538 for men and $22,943 for women (U.S. Bureau of the Census, 1988).

A striking fact about this information is that not only are the average earnings for women lower than for men, but male high school graduates average more than female college graduates. One possible explanation for this disparity is that the less-skilled jobs men hold are typically unionized, such as construction, and therefore pay better. Women who hold less-skilled jobs, on the other hand, such as waitressing, are not unionized (Bianchi and Spain, 1986).

Job discrimination against women is a pervasive and complicated phenomenon. One study of business firms identified three ways in which women experience discrimination in the business world: (1) during the hiring process, when women are given jobs with lower occupational prestige than the jobs given men with equivalent qualifications; (2) through unequal wage policies, by which women receive less pay than men for equivalent work; and (3) in awarding promotions—women find it more difficult than men to advance up the career ladder (Staires, Quin, and Shepard, 1976).

Discrimination against women in the economic sector is often quite subtle. Women are often channeled away from participation in occupations that are socially defined as appropriate to men. For example, it cannot really be argued that women bank presidents are paid less than men; however, there are almost no women bank presidents. Women and men often do not perform equal work; therefore the

Working women as a group consistently earn less than working men do, even when employed in the same type of job.

phrase "equal pay for equal work" has little relevance. In some instances, similar work is performed by men and women, but there may be two job titles and two pay scales, for example, administrative assistant and executive secretary. The first may be a male or female; the second is usually a female and is likely to be paid less (Davidson and Gordon, 1979).

Having painted a somewhat pessimistic picture here, we should note that there has been some improvement in recent years. During the 1970s, the share of women managers and administrators grew from 16 percent to 27 percent, women accountants and auditors were up from 25 percent to 38 percent.

In 1980, men outnumbered women by 3.8 million in higher-paying managerial and professional occupations. Women outnumbered men by 9.8 million in technical, sales, and administrative support jobs. But between 1975 and 1985, the number of women managers and professionals increased 77 percent, while the number of men in these positions increased by only 26 percent (Taeuber and Valdisera, 1987).

Despite this progress women still dominate low-paying fields. Five of the top ten occupations employing women are secretaries, bookkeepers, cashiers, salespeople, and typists. The two professional positions that they dominate are relatively low-paying, namely nursing and elementary school teaching (Taeuber and Valdisera, 1987).

FUTURE TRENDS

Earlier in this chapter we alluded to certain conditions in contemporary society that have had great significance and impact on gender roles and family relations. Demographic changes, lengthened life spans, the decline in infant and child mortality and in maternal deaths during childbirth, lower birthrates, the dissociation of reproduction from sexual activities, and the shorter pe-

riod of time devoted to maternity in relation to women's total life expectancy—all have contributed to changes in attitudes and behavior in the family.

Throughout the twentieth century, women have been gaining in legal equality. Changes in women's legal status include the right of suffrage, rights of separation and divorce, and rights of equal employment and opportunity. Although equality has not been fully realized, there has been marked improvement in the power and status of women compared with their position during the nineteenth century. The result has been the growth of female independence.

CHANGES IN ATTITUDES

The Roper Organization has been asking a nationally representative sample of men and women the same questions for the last fifteen years. The results show that there has been a significant shift in the attitudes and life-styles of men and women.

When the impact of the feminist movement just began to be felt around 1970, only 38 percent of women and 40 percent of men believed women were looked on with more respect than a decade earlier. By 1985, after the feminist movement became a part of mainstream society, 60 percent of women and 61 percent of men believed women were respected more than during the previous decade.

With these changes has come the realization that gender equality benefits not only women, but men and children as well. As corporations face a shrinking work force in the 1990s, they will be forced to respond to the needs of workers with a variety of benefits, including child care, unpaid maternity leaves, flexible working hours, job sharing, and part-time work.

For the first time, the concerns of women for adequate child care and maternity leave are being shared by men. As a result, both men and women are pressing corporations and government to respond to the needs of the family. When the DuPont Corporation surveyed 3300 male em-

Should Women Receive Childbirth Benefits?

Lillian Garland's life fell apart after the birth of her baby daughter. Employed as a receptionist at the California Savings and Loan Association in West Los Angeles, Garland figured that she would take a short disability leave after the birth and then return to work. On April 20, 1982, a little more than 2 months after her baby was born, Garland called the bank's personnel office to arrange a starting date. To her dismay, instead of welcoming her back, the bank told her that her job was no longer available; they had permanently hired the person she trained. Said Garland: "I was in shock. I said, 'What am I supposed to do now?' They said, 'You can go look for a job. In the meantime if something becomes available, we'll give you a call'" (*People,* February 10, 1986).

Unable to find a job or pay her rent, Garland was forced to move in with a girl friend. Without a suitable place to live, she had no choice but to give up custody of her daughter to the girl's father. But despite her hardships, Garland was determined to right what she saw as a terrible wrong: "I think it's unfair for any woman to have to worry about not having a job because . . . she's reproducing, repopulating our society" (*People,* February 10, 1986).

Garland sued California Savings and Loan on the grounds that the bank's action violated a California law granting pregnant workers 4 months of unpaid maternity leave and a guarantee of a job when they returned. The bank stood firm, claiming the California law conflicted with a federal statute that made discrimination on the basis of sex illegal. From the bank's point of view, the California law required them to give women benefits men did not have simply because of their sex. Reasoning that since men can lose their jobs due to medical disability, the effect of the state law is to discriminate against men. Thus, in a case that would ultimately be decided by the United States Supreme Court, the sides were clearly drawn.

Ironically, siding with the bank in its attempt to overturn the California law was the National Organization for Women (NOW) and the Women's Rights Project of the American Civil Liberties Union (ACLU). Both groups feared that employers would be reluctant to hire women of childbearing age if they were forced, by law, to give them special treatment. Joan Bertin of the ACLU explains: "The question is, Should a woman with a pregnancy disability get her job back when other employees with disabilities get fired? You undermine your argument unless you say everyone is equally entitled to this

ployees in 1985, they found that only 18 percent were interested in part-time work to give them more time with their children. By 1988, the percentage had jumped to 33 percent. Similarly, in 1985 only 11 percent expressed interest in a period after the birth of a child in which they could work fewer hours. Three years later the percentage climbed to 28 percent. Clearly, in those 3 years the issue of child care evolved from a female issue into a concern of both men and women (*U.S. News & World Report,* June 20, 1988).

We should not assume that economic conditions are forcing women to go to work. When women are asked if they would continue working if they were financially secure, 70 percent of women in all age groups claim that they would. This percentage is the same as it is for men when they are asked this question. Education appears to be a deciding factor in continuing to work. Women who have dropped out of high school are most likely to not work if they do not have to, whereas those with some college education are the least likely to leave the work force if they were financially secure. The least likely of all to leave the work

benefit" (*Time,* August 18, 1986). Concerned that special treatment would eventually lead to discrimination, NOW warned of a backlash that would set women's progress back years.

Betty Friedan, Sylvia Ann Hewlett, and other feminists saw it differently. Moving away from the strict equal rights stance that had been the rallying cry of the women's movement since its inception, Friedan challenged the notion that women were "male clones." "The time has come to acknowledge that women are different from men," said Friedan. "There has to be a concept of equality that takes into account that women are the ones who have the babies." Christine Littleton, a professor of law at UCLA, agrees: "Sometimes equal treatment is what is necessary for long-term equality. Sometimes it is not" (*Time,* August 18, 1986).

In the view of this group, an acknowledgment of the pregnancy-related needs of women was critical because of the failure of the federal Pregnancy Discrimination Act of 1978 to guarantee reasonable job security to all working women. Although this act requires companies with employee disability policies to treat pregnancy like any other disability and provide equal benefits, the majority of women work for companies with no disability policy. The result: Millions of women are in job jeopardy when they take even a reasonable amount of time off to have a baby. Garland's supporters also pointed to the fact that only a handful of states have pregnancy leave laws that offer any form of additional job protection.

Five years after the birth of her daughter, Lillian Garland witnessed a landmark Supreme Court decision that upheld the California law granting women temporarily disabled by pregnancy special job protection. Writing for the majority, Justice Thurgood Marshall concluded that the California statute "promotes equal employment opportunity" by allowing "women as well as men, to have families without losing their jobs." Garland agreed: "Women should not have to choose between being a mother and having a job" (*Time,* January 26, 1987).

Sources: "Garland's Bouquet," *Time,* January 26, 1987, pp. 14–15; "Are Women 'Male Clones'?" *Time,* August 18, 1986, pp. 63–64; "A Working Mother's Fight for Job Security Goes to the Last Round—in the U.S. Supreme Court," *People,* February 10, 1986, pp. 40–41; "The Parental-Leave Debate," *Newsweek,* February 17, 1986, p. 64; "Supreme Court Gives Motherhood Its Legal Due," *U.S. News & World Report,* January 26, 1987, p. 12.

---

force are women in households with the highest incomes.

The vast majority of both men and women think that marriage is the best way to live. But the type of marriage that people want is different than the marriage of the past. In 1974, about half of all men and women thought a traditional marriage where the husband worked and the wife stayed home and took care of the house and children was ideal. By 1985, only 37 percent of women and 43 percent of men wanted this type of arrangement. The majority of men and women thought the most satisfy-ing marriage was one where husband and wife share work, housekeeping, and child care. It should also come as no surprise that younger women are the most likely to want an egalitarian life-style (Walsh, 1986).

Women's employment clearly has changed the ways in which women and men define marital and parental roles. As women become less dependent and are able to buy services, marital and parental roles may become less stressful. However, some new stresses may emerge. Employed women are likely to redefine involvement in child rearing and expect more equal participation from their husbands. This situation may produce heightened marital tensions.

It appears that nontraditional gender roles produce a gain in power and control for women. Some believe that this accounts for the lower levels of depression among working women in nontraditional marriages compared to women in traditional homemaker roles. At the same time this change may produce less control for men in such marriages and the potential for higher

levels of depression. At least in the short term, marital strain may be one of the costs for the current redefinitions of family roles (Barnett and Baruch, 1987).

Like so many other areas of American life, gender roles are undergoing rapid change. Traditional distinctions are becoming blurred and obsolete in response to new social and economic demands, but on the whole, experts expect strong family bonds to survive.

SUMMARY

Sociology distinguishes between sex—the biological differences between women and men—and gender—the social and cultural definitions of femininity and masculinity.

Two views of the nature of gender-role behavior have been proposed: either it is innate and biologically determined or it is acquired through socialization and social learning experiences.

Historically, women have been seen as inferior to men. Many religions also manifest a patriarchal ideology—the belief that men are superior to women and should control all the important aspects of a society. This ideology has been used to legitimize discrimination against women, denying them rights, power, and freedom of action.

Ethologists and sociobiologists have put forth the idea that human social and gender-role behavior, like that of other animals, is biologically and genetically determined. Critics of sociobiology maintain that social learning is the important factor.

There is evidence for both views. Many differences between men and women have a physiological or genetic basis. At the same time, other differences between males and females may be linked to cultural influences

and variations in environment and activities.

Cross-cultural and historical research offers support for the belief of most sociologists that socialization has a greater effect on gender-role behavior than biology does. Studies indicate that every culture exhibits different, culturally patterned gender-role behavior and gender identities. Other studies show that in all preindustrial societies there generally is a division of labor and activities by sex. Most scholars agree that in all societies biology may influence but does not determine differences in gender roles.

There are two theoretical approaches that have been used to explain male dominance and gender inequality: functionalism and conflict theory. Functionalists argue that it was quite useful to have men and women fulfill different roles in preindustrial societies.

According to the conflict theory, males dominate females because of their superior power and control over key resources. A major consequence of this domination is the exploitation of women by men. By subordinating women, men gain greater economic, political, and social power.

Gender-role socialization is the process by which people learn the values, attitudes, and behavior appropriate to each sex in their culture. In all cultures, males and females are socialized differently. In our society, gender identity is established by the age of 2 or 3. Different societies have different role expectations for adolescent girls than for boys. In our society, boys' roles prepare them for an occupation, and girls' roles are designed to enable them to attract a suitable mate. Boys win approval for behavior that is competitive, aggressive, and oriented toward independence and achievement (highly valued traits in our society), whereas girls are encouraged to be passive and dependent.

The three personality traits associated with adult gender roles are gender identity, self-esteem, and achievement motivation. Because women are encouraged to develop traits that are not valued highly by our society, they tend to have weaker gender identities and lower self-esteem than men.

Women experience discrimination in almost all spheres of American life, and nowhere is it more apparent than on the job. Men often are paid more or hold higher job titles than women for equivalent work and qualifications. Women also find it more difficult to climb the career ladder.

Traditionally, men participate more in public spheres of activity, which in our society carry esteem and power, whereas women generally fulfill roles in the domestic sphere, which lacks status and value. True equality between the sexes will be achieved only when both sexes take part equally in all spheres of activity, domestic and public.

Women tend to occupy a lower social status than men in every social class. The women's rights movement has helped improve this situation. Women have gained many legal rights, and their status, independence, and power have increased. A new family form has emerged—the symmetrical family—in which husbands and wives ideally share roles and responsibilities. However, the reality often falls short of this ideal.

Gender roles in our society are changing, and traditional distinctions are blurring. Although strong family bonds are expected to continue, the roles of both sexes eventually should approach true equality.

Part 4

INSTITUTIONS

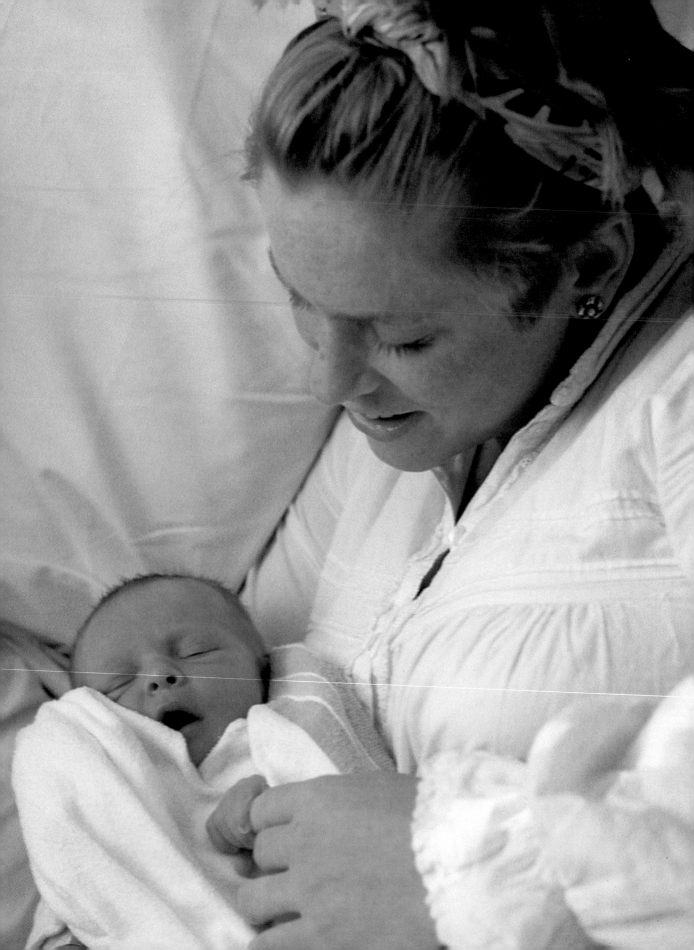

Chapter 12

MARRIAGE AND ALTERNATIVE FAMILY LIFE-STYLES

There is no single description of the American family. The family of the 1950s with a husband who worked outside the home and a wife who cared for two well-scrubbed children is gone for most Americans. In its place is a montage of family types—a diversity that adds strength to the American social landscape.

Dan Petry, 28, and his wife, Marjorie, 29, have decided to go it alone; they are a family without children. Dan explains: "This world is a crazy place to try and raise a kid. We could well blow ourselves up before the child has a chance to mature." Marjorie adds a more immediate concern: "If we wanted to take off to help world causes in Central America or South America, how could we with a child? This way nothing holds us back" (*Newsweek,* September 1, 1986).

Seventeen-year-old Vincent Sowell has not yet had a full shave. Yet he is already the father of a 3-month-old baby daughter and another child is on the way. Vincent's children have two different mothers, both teenagers themselves. "I know I've got responsibilities," says Vincent, who earns $5.50 an hour working for a landscaping firm. Most of what Vincent makes goes to pay his daughter's medical bills.

Catherine Casey did everything right —or so she thought. At 38, she is a well-established pediatrician who spent her 20s learning to be a doctor. Although she acquired impressive credentials, she had no time to date and never got married. She now feels that she may have waited too long. "I never doubted that I would get married, and I never thought education or career would have anything to do with it." Casey now feels that her biological "time clock is striking midnight" and that unless she marries soon, she will never have children (*Newsweek,* June 2, 1986).

Steve Bochco, creator of television's "LA Law" and "Hill Street Blues," and his wife, actress Barbara Bosson, have been married for 19 years. For most of that time, Bosson was a traditional homemaker, raising the couple's two children. Although she

worked occasionally, most of her time was spent at home. When she got the opportunity to play Faye Furillo, former wife of Capt. Frank Furillo on "Hill Street Blues," she jumped at it. "I needed that feeling of putting yourself on the line and succeeding or failing," said Bosson. "Those things don't happen when you're at home with a baby."

But working together with her husband created new stresses. They had to learn to relate to each other in their work roles and to separate work from marriage. Both agree that work is the place for the "rough-and-tumble exchange of ideas" but that marriage "is where you want someone to rub your toes" (*Newsweek,* August 24, 1987).

The alphabet has been undergoing close scrutiny this year in Alice Murphy's kindergarten class at the Camp Avenue School in North Merrick, Long Island. Each week, one letter is analyzed: sound and shape are discussed; word examples are given. Last week's letter: *x.*

Mrs. Murphy warned her students that finding words beginning with *x* would be difficult. Nevertheless, 6-year-old Shana Henson's hand shot up immediately.

"Do you know a word?" the surprised instructor asked.

"Sure," replied the youngster. "Exhusband" (Alexander, 1988).

These vignettes give us an idea of the diversity of family life in the United States and the many forms the family can take. The American family will continue to evolve and change even further during the next decade. By the year 2000, the United States will have 19 million more households than it does today, but the households at the turn of the century will be even less traditional than the households of today. Families will comprise only two out of three households and married couples will live in just over half of all households (U.S. Bureau of the Census, 1986).

Has the American family always been in such flux? Although information about family life during the earliest days of our country is not very precise, it does appear quite clear, beginning with the 1790 census, that the American family was quite stable. Divorce and family breakup were not common. If a marriage ended because of desertion, death, or divorce, it was seen as a personal and community tragedy.

The American family has always been quite small. There has never been a strong tradition here of the extended family, where relatives and several generations lived within the same dwelling. Even in the 1700s, the American family consisted of a husband, wife, and approximately three children. This private, inviolate enclave made it possible for the family to endure severe circumstances and to help build the American frontier.

By the 1960s, radical changes were becoming evident. The marriage rate began to fall, and the divorce rate, which had been fairly level, began its accelerating-upward trend, and fertility began to decline.

The situation today shows that this trend is continuing. In 1987 there were 2.42 million marriages, though there were also 1.16 million divorces. This information is

The American family has always been quite small; the extended family has never been a strong tradition in the U.S.

even more striking when we realize that divorce statistics do not include desertion or other forms of marital breakup, such as annulment or legal separation.

There also are other signs of change and family instability. Of all children born in 1986, 23.4 percent were born to single

In the 1960s, radical changes in marriage and family life emerged. In their effort to create a close-knit family, this computer programmer and his Radcliffe-educated wife moved into a tepee.

Even though children in the Israeli kibbutz sleep apart from their parents in "children's houses," many features typical of the family still exist.

women. Among blacks, the percentage of children born out of wedlock was 61.2 percent *(Statistical Abstract of the United States: 1989)*.

The inescapable conclusion that can be drawn from all this is that the American family is in a state of transition. But transition to what? In this chapter we shall study the institution of the family and look more closely at the current trends and what they forecast for the future.

THE NATURE OF FAMILY LIFE

For a long time, social scientists defined the family in a way that reflected "common knowledge." For example, in his classic study of social organization and the family, anthropologist George P. Murdock (1949) defined the family as

> a social group characterized by common residence, economic cooperation, and reproduction. It includes adults of both sexes, at least two of whom maintain a socially approved sexual relationship, and one or more children, own or adopted, of the sexually cohabiting adults.

This definition has proved to be too limited. For one thing, it excludes many kinds of social groups that seem, on the basis of the functions they serve, to deserve the label *family.* For example, in America single-parent families are quite common. If we expand our perspective to include other societies, we find that quite a few seem to lack the kind of group described by Murdock. For example, in 1954 Melford Spiro, an anthropologist, studied Israeli *kibbutzim* (pronounced "kee-boots-eem") — agricultural communities with communal living, collective ownership of all property, and the communal rearing of children. In some *kibbutzim,* the children sleep apart from their parents in "children's houses" and are cared for in peer groups by child-care workers assigned by the *kibbutz.* Spiro's studies at first seemed to indicate that the institution of the family did not exist within the *kibbutz,* that the psychological and social functions of the family were provided by the *kibbutz* as a whole. However, as Spiro himself later pointed out (1960), many features typical of the family exist in the *kibbutz:* couples marry and plan for children; parents call only their own children "son" and "daughter"; and parents and children together form identifiable subgroups within the *kibbutz,* even though the children live in the children's houses. Furthermore, one of the most valued times of day is the late afternoon when children of all ages return to their parents' rooms for several hours of uninterrupted socializing. So even in the *kibbutz,* the family exists as a significant social group.

Despite Murdock's restricted definition of the family, it was his 1949 study of kinship and family in 250 societies, which showed the institution of the family to be present in every one of them, that led social scientists to believe that some form of the family is found in every known human society.

Perhaps a better understanding of the concept of the family may be gained by examining the various functions it performs in society.

FUNCTIONS OF THE FAMILY

Social scientists often assign to the fundamental family unit—married parents and their offspring—several basic functions that it serves in most, if not all, societies. Although in many societies the basic family unit serves some of these functions, in no society does it serve all of them completely or exclusively. For example, among the Nayar of India, a child's biological father is socially irrelevant. Generally, another man takes on the social responsibility of parenthood (Gough, 1952). Or consider the Trobrianders, a people living on a small string of islands north of New Guinea. There, as reported by anthropologist Bronislaw Malinowski (1922), the father's role in parenthood was not recognized, and the responsibility for raising children fell to the family of their mother's brother.

Nor is the basic family always the fundamental unit of economic cooperation. Among artisans in preindustrial Europe, the essential economic unit was not the family but rather the household, typically consisting of the artisan's family plus assorted apprentices and even servants (Laslett, 1965). In some societies, members of the basic family group need not even live in the same household. Among the Ashanti of western Africa, for example, husbands and wives each live with their own mother's relatives (Fortes et al., 1947). In the United States a small but growing number of two-career families are finding it necessary to set up separate households in different communities—sometimes hundreds of miles apart. Husband and wife travel back and forth between these households to be with each other and the children on weekends and during vacations.

In all societies the family does serves the social functions discussed below.

Regulating Sexual Behavior

No society permits random sexual behavior. All societies have an **incest taboo,** which

Royal families have often engaged in first-cousin marriages, a practice that is considered incest in many societies. Such was the case with the marriage of Queen Victoria to Prince Albert, her first cousin, in 1840.

forbids sexual intercourse among closely related individuals—although *who* is considered to be closely related varies widely. Almost universally, incest rules prohibit sex between parents and their children and between brothers and sisters. But there are exceptions: The royal families of ancient Egypt, the Inca nation, and Hawaii did allow sex and marriage between brothers and sisters. In the United States, marriage between parents and children, brothers and sisters, grandparents and grandchildren, aunts and nephews, and uncles and nieces is defined as incest and is forbidden. In addition, approximately thirty states prohibit marriage between first cousins. The incest taboo usually applies to members of one's family (however the family is defined culturally) and thus promotes marriage—and consequently social ties—among members of different families.

Patterning Reproduction

Every society must replace its members. By regulating where and with whom individuals may enter into sexual relationships, society also patterns sexual reproduction. By permitting or forbidding certain forms of

incest taboo A societal prohibition that forbids sexual intercourse among closely related individuals.

marriage (multiple wives or multiple husbands, for example), a society can encourage or discourage reproduction.

Organizing Production and Consumption

In preindustrial societies the economic system often depended on each family's producing much of what it consumed. In almost all societies the family consumes food and other necessities as a social unit. Therefore, a society's economic system and family structures often are closely correlated.

Socializing Children

Not only must a society reproduce itself biologically by producing children, it must also ensure that its children are encouraged to accept the life-style it favors, to master the skills it values, and to perform the work it requires. In other words, a society must provide predictable social contexts within which its children are to be socialized (see Chapter 4). The family provides such a context almost universally, at least during the period when the infant is dependent on the constant attention of others. The family is ideally suited to this task because its mem-

bers know the child from birth and are aware of its special abilities and needs.

Providing Care and Protection

Every human being needs food and shelter. In addition, we all need to be among people who care for us emotionally, who help us with the problems that arise in daily life, and who back us up when we come into conflict with others. Although many kinds of social groups are capable of meeting one or more of these needs, the family often is the one group in a society that meets them all.

Providing Social Status

Simply by being born into a family, each individual inherits both material goods and a number of ascribed statuses (see Chapter 5). These statuses include social class or caste membership and ethnic identity. Our inherited social position, or family background, probably is the single most important social factor affecting the predictable course of our lives.

Thus, we see that Murdock's definition of the family, based primarily on structure, is indeed too restrictive. A much more productive way of defining the family would be to view it as a universal institution that generally serves the functions discussed above, although the way it does so may vary greatly from one society to another. The different ways in which various social functions are fulfilled by the institution of the family depend, in some instances, on the form the family takes.

FAMILY STRUCTURES

The most basic family form is the **nuclear family,** that is, a married couple and their children. The nuclear family is found in all societies, and it is from this form that all other (composite) family forms are derived.

There are two major composite family forms: polygamous and extended families (see Figure 12.1). **Polygamous families** are nuclear families linked together by multiple marriage bonds, with one central individual married to several spouses. When the central person is male and the multiple spouses are female, the family is **polygynous.** When the central figure is female and the multiple spouses are male, the family is **polyandrous.** Polyandry is known to exist only in a very few societies.

Extended families include other rela-tions and generations in addition to the nuclear family, so that along with married parents and their offspring there may be the parents' parents, siblings of the parents, the siblings' spouses and children, and in-laws. All the members of the extended family live in one house or in homes close to one another, forming one cooperative unit.

Families, whether nuclear or extended, trace their relationships through the generations in several different ways. Under the **patrilineal system,** the generations are tied together through the males of a family; all members trace their kinship through the father's line. Under the **matrilineal system,** just the opposite is the case: The generations are tied together through the females of a family. Under the **bilateral system,** descent passes through both females and males of a family. Although in American society descent is bilateral, the majority of the world's societies are either patrilineal or matrilineal (Murdock, 1949).

In patrilineal societies, social, economic, and political affairs usually are organized around the kinship relationships among men, and men tend to dominate the public affairs. Polygyny often is permitted, and men also tend to dominate family affairs. When men dominate their families in

nuclear family The most basic family form, made up of parents and their children, biological or adopted.

polygamous families Nuclear families linked together by multiple marriage bonds, with one central individual married to several spouses.

polygynous family A polygamous family unit in which the central person is male and the multiple spouses are female.

polyandrous family A polygamous family unit in which the central figure is female and the multiple spouses are male.

extended families Families that include, in addition to nuclear family members, other relatives, such as the parents' parents, the parents' siblings, and in-laws.

patrilineal system A descent system that traces kinship through the males of the family.

matrilineal system A descent system that traces kinship through the females of the family.

bilateral system A descent system that traces kinship through both female and male family members.

Under the patrilineal system, the generations are tied together through the males of the family.

FIGURE 12.1

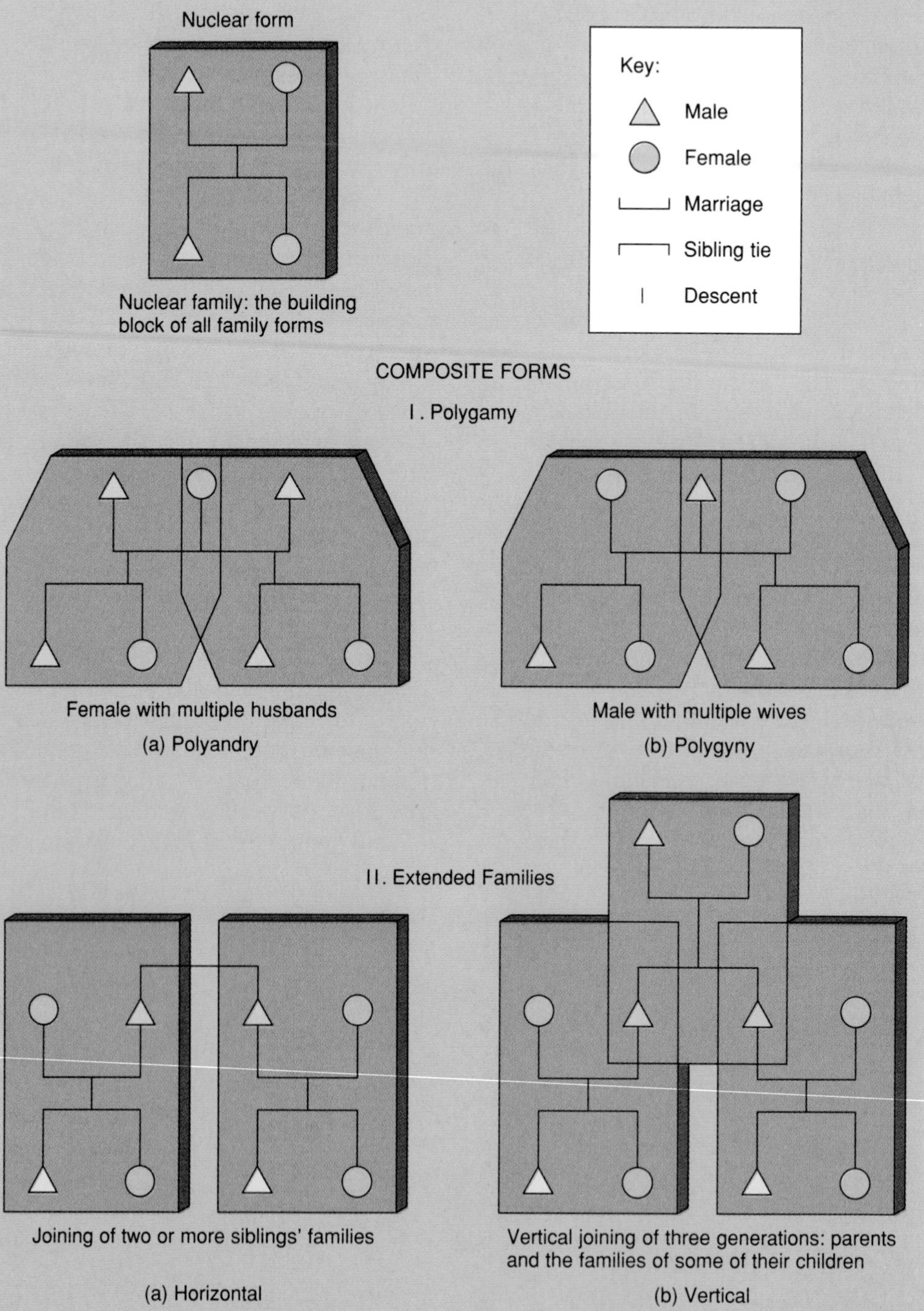

Nuclear form

Nuclear family: the building
block of all family forms

Key:

△ Male

◯ Female

⎣⎦ Marriage

⎺⎺ Sibling tie

| Descent

COMPOSITE FORMS

I. Polygamy

Female with multiple husbands

(a) Polyandry

Male with multiple wives

(b) Polygyny

II. Extended Families

Joining of two or more siblings' families

(a) Horizontal

Vertical joining of three generations: parents
and the families of some of their children

(b) Vertical

Forms of the Family. *The diagram above shows the variations that the two major composite
family forms—polygamous and extended—can assume. The basic unit within all variations,
however, is the nuclear family.*

these ways, sociologists use the term **patriarchal** to describe the family. The **matriarchal family,** in which most family affairs are dominated by women, is relatively uncommon but does exist. Typically, it emerges in matrilineal societies. The matriarchal family is becoming increasingly more common in American society, however, with the rise of single-parent families (most often headed by mothers).

Whatever form the family takes and whatever functions it serves, it generally requires a marriage in order to exist. Like the family, marriage varies from society to society in its forms.

MARRIAGE

Marriage is an institution found in all societies. It is the socially recognized, legitimized, and supported union of individuals of opposite sexes. It differs from other unions (such as friendships) in that (1) it takes place in a public (and usually formal) manner; (2) it includes sexual intercourse as an explicit element of the relationship; (3) it provides the essential condition for legitimizing offspring (that is, it provides newborns with socially accepted statuses); and (4) it is intended to be a stable and enduring relationship. Thus, although almost all societies allow for divorce—that is, the breakup of marriage—no society endorses it as an ideal norm.

ROMANTIC LOVE

Our culture is relatively unique in believing that there is a compatibility between romantic love and the institution of marriage. Not only do we believe they are compatible, but we also generally expect that they coexist. Our culture implies that without the prospect of marriage, romance is immoral and that without romance, marriage is empty. This view underlies most romantic fiction and other media presentations.

Romantic love can be defined in terms of five dimensions: (1) idealization of the loved one, (2) the notion of a one and only, (3) love at first sight, (4) love winning out over all, and (5) an indulgence of personal emotions (Lantz, 1982).

Throughout most of the world's other societies, romantic love is unknown or seen as a strange maladjustment. It may exist, but it has nothing to do with marriage. Marriage in these societies is seen as an institution that organizes or patterns the establishment of economic, social, and even political relationships among families. Three families ultimately are involved: the two families that produced the two spouses—their respective **families of origin** or **families of orientation**—and the family created by the spouses' union—their **family of procreation.** Different rules for marriage and for residence after marriage result in the creation of very different household and family forms.

MARRIAGE RULES

In every society, marriage is the binding link that makes possible the existence of the family. All societies have norms or rules governing who may marry whom and where the newlywed couples should live. These rules vary, but there are certain typical arrangements that occur in many societies around the world.

patriarchal family A family in which most family affairs are dominated by men.

matriarchal family A family in which most family affairs are dominated by women.

family of orientation The nuclear family in which one is born and raised. Also family of origin.

family of procreation The family that is created by marriage.

marriage The socially recognized, legitimized, and supported union of individuals of opposite sexes.

Throughout most of history and in most of the world's societies, romantic love is unknown or is seen as a strange maladjustment.

endogamy Societal norms that limit the social categories from which one can choose a marriage partner.

exogamy Societal norms that require an individual to marry someone outside his or her culturally defined group.

monogamous marriage The form of marriage in which each person is allowed only one spouse at a time.

multiple marriage A form of marriage in which an individual may have more than one spouse (polygamy).

Almost all societies have two kinds of marriage norms or rules: rules of **endogamy** limit the social categories from which one can choose a marriage partner. For example, many Americans still attempt to instill in their children the idea that one should marry "one's own kind," that is, someone within the ethnic, religious, or economic group of one's family of origin.

Rules of **exogamy,** on the other hand, require an individual to marry someone outside his or her culturally defined group. For example, in many tribal groups, members must marry outside their lineage. In the United States there are laws forbidding the marriage of close relatives, although the rules are variable.

These norms vary widely across cultures, but everywhere they serve basic social functions. Rules of exogamy determine the ties and boundaries between social groups, linking them through the institution of marriage and whatever social, economic, and political obligations go along with it. Rules of endogamy, by requiring people to marry within specific groups, reinforce group boundaries and perpetuate them from one generation to the next.

Marriage rules also determine how many spouses a person may have at one time. Among many groups—Europeans and Americans, for example—marriage is **monogamous,** that is, each person is allowed only one spouse at a time. However, many societies allow **multiple marriages,** in which an individual may have more than one spouse (polygamy). Polygyny, the most common form of polygamy, is found among such diverse peoples as the Swazi of Africa, the Tiwi of Australia, and, formerly, the Blackfeet Indians of the United States. Polyandry is extremely rare. Murdock (1949) lists only three societies that practice polyandry, from his sample of 250: the Toda of India, the Sherpa of Nepal, and the Marquesan Islanders of the South Pacific.

As Marvin Harris (1975) notes, "Some form of polygamy occurs in 90 percent of the world's cultures." But within each such society only a minority of people actually can afford it. In addition, the Industrial Revolution favored monogamy for reasons we shall discuss shortly. Therefore, monogamy is the most common and widespread form of marriage in the world today.

MARITAL RESIDENCE

Once two people are married, they must set up housekeeping. In most societies there are

Although their total numbers are still small, racially mixed marriages have become increasingly common in America's melting pot.

TAKING THE SOCIOLOGICAL PERSPECTIVE

GET MARRIED AND LIVE LONGER

Would you like to be happier, live longer, and stay healthier for the rest of your life? There is a simple prescription that is guaranteed to work. You will not even have to jog three times a week, cut down on cholesterol, or become a health fanatic.

Very simply, all you have to do is get married. If you are already married, give your spouse a big hug, say thank you, and make sure you stay married.

The evidence proving that married people enjoy better health than unmarried people is overwhelming and extraordinarily convincing. Compared with married men and women, the divorced, single, and separated suffer much higher rates of disease, disability, mental neurosis, and mortality. This pattern has been found for every age group (20 years and over), for both men and women, and for both whites and blacks.

The differences in death rates from cancer and heart disease between the married and unmarried is astonishing. The lung cancer rate for divorced men is twice that of married men. For some other types of cancers, it is three and four times as high. The pattern for divorced women—while not as dramatic—is similar. Among both men and women, the single and divorced die from hypertension and heart disease at rates between two and a half and three and a half times greater than those found for the married.

Just as impressive are the mental health benefits from marriage. Studies show that married people have significantly lower anxiety and depression scores than unmarried persons regardless of gender. Married individuals appear to enjoy better mental health even when they have suffered more traumatic life experiences than the unmarried.

Even the mentally ill sometimes benefit from marriage. A British study found that marriages between mentally ill people produced some improved functioning. The support from sharing mental disabilities with another in similar circumstances appears to have a positive effect.

Some feminists have agreed that marriage produces better health, but have argued that this fact is only true for men. Numerous studies, however, refute this notion. Although men do realize a somewhat greater health advantage from marriage than women, both sexes are clearly healthier if married than if unmarried.

It is not just adult men and women whose lives are affected by marriage. A study in the *New England Journal of Medicine* found that unmarried women, compared with married women, had a much greater chance of having infants with low birth weights. Birth weight is one of the best predictors of infant mortality, and babies born to unmarried mothers are at much greater risk than those born to married mothers.

What is it about marriage that accounts for such dramatic advantages to your health? Part of the answer appeared in a recently published study in the *Journal of Health and Social Behavior*. The researchers noted that married people live longer because marriage discourages a person from doing things that are hazardous to his health, such as excessive drinking, drug use, risk taking, and what they referred to as "disorderly living."

Marriage tends to impose a variety of obligations and constraints on the individual that reduce the chances of engaging in unhealthy practices. Very simply, you are less likely to spend four nights a week partying and drinking if you have family obligations that require you to be at work every morning at 8:00 A.M.

This observation may cause some readers to retort with the old joke: married people don't live longer, it just seems longer. Jokes aside, the evidence appears indisputable. Forget running, health foods, or meditation, *marriage* is the answer.

Source: Bryce J. Christensen, "The Costly Retreat from Marriage," *The Public Interest,* Spring 1988, no. 91, pp. 59–66.

marital residence rules Rules that govern where a newly married couple settles down and lives.

patrilocal residence Marital residence rules that require a newly married couple to settle down near or within the husband's father's household.

matrilocal residence Marital residence rules that require a newly married couple to settle down near or within the wife's mother's household.

bilocal residence Marital residence rules that allow a newly married couple to live with either the husband's or wife's family of origin.

neolocal residence Marital residence standards that allow a newly married couple to live virtually anywhere, even thousands of miles from their families of origin.

homogamy The tendency to choose a spouse with a similar racial, religious, ethnic, educational, age, and socioeconomic background.

strongly held norms that govern where a couple settles down. Sociologists call these norms **marital residence rules. Patrilocal residence** calls for the new couple to settle down near or within the husband's father's household—as among Greek villagers and the Swazi of Africa. **Matrilocal residence** calls for the new couple to settle down near or within the wife's mother's household—as among the Hopi Indians of the American Southwest.

The Blackfeet Indians allowed new couples to choose whether to live with the husband's or wife's family of origin; this system is called **bilocal residence.** In modern industrial society, newlyweds typically have even more freedom, and **neolocal residence** is common. With this type of residence, the couple may choose to live virtually anywhere, even thousands of miles from their families of origin. In practice, however, it is not unusual for American newlyweds to set up housekeeping near one of their respective families.

Marital residence rules play a major role in determining the composition of households. With patrilocal residence, groups of men remain in the familiar context of their father's home, and their sisters leave to join their husbands. In other words, after marriage the women leave home to live as "strangers" among their husband's kinfolk. With matrilocal residence, just the opposite is true: Women and their children remain at home, and husbands are the "outsiders." In many matrilocal societies, this situation often leads to considerable marital stress, with husbands going home to their own mothers' families when domestic conflict becomes intolerable.

Bilocal residence and neolocal residence allow greater flexibility and a wider range of household forms because young couples may move to places in which the social, economic, and political advantages may be greatest. One disadvantage of neolocal residence is that a young couple cannot count on the immediate presence of kinfolk to help out in times of need or with demanding household chores (including the raising of children). In the United States

today, a new phenomenon, the surrogate, nonkin "family," made up of neighbors, friends, and colleagues at work, may help fill this void (Wolfe, 1981). In other societies, polygynous neolocal families help overcome such difficulties, with a number of wives cooperating in the division of household work.

MATE SELECTION

As with our patterns of family life, America's rules for marriage, which are expressed through mate selection, spring from those of our society's European forebears. Because we have been nourished through songs and cinema by the notions of "love at first sight," "love is blind," and "love conquers all," most of us probably are under the impression that in the United States there are no rules for mate selection. Research shows, however, that this is not necessarily true.

If we think statistically about mate selection, we must admit that in no way is it random. Consider for a moment what would happen if it were: Given the population distribution of the United States, blacks would be more likely to marry whites than members of their race; upper-class individuals would have a greater chance of marrying a lower-class person; and various culturally unlikely but statistically probable combinations of age, education, and religion would take place. In actual fact, **homogamy**—the tendency of like to marry like—is much more the rule.

There are numerous ways in which homogamy can be achieved. One way is to let someone older and wiser, such as a parent or matchmaker, pair up appropriately suited individuals. Throughout the history of the world, this has been one of the most common ways by which marriages have taken place. The role of the couple in question can range from having no say about the matter whatsoever to having some sort of veto power. This tradition is quite strong in Islamic countries such as Pakistan. Benazir Bhutto, an outspoken political leader and daughter of a former Pakistani prime minister, agreed to an arranged marriage despite her Western education at Harvard University and feminist leanings. She submitted to Islamic cultural traditions, in which dating is not considered acceptable behavior for a woman (*New York Times,* June 17, 1988).

In the United States, most people who get married do not use the services of a matchmaker, although the result in terms of similarity of background is so highly patterned that it often seems as if a very conscious homogamous matchmaking effort were involved.

Age

In American society, people generally marry within their own age range. There are comparatively few marriages in which there is a wide gap between the ages of the two partners. In addition, only 22.1 percent of American women marry men who are younger than themselves. On the average, in a first marriage for both the man and the woman, the man tends to be 1.9 years older than the woman. This is, however, related to age at the time of marriage. For example, 20-year-old men marry women with a median age of 19 — only a 1-year difference. Twenty-five-year-old men marry women with a median age of 22. For 30-year-old men, the median age for wives is 25; for 60-year-old men, the median age for wives is 50.

The age at the time of first marriage is fairly young but has been rising steadily in recent years. The median age at the time of first marriage has fluctuated since the turn of the century. In 1890, the median age for men was 26.1 and 22.0 for women. By 1960 it had dropped to 22.8 and 20.3, respectively. Since that time it has risen again, so that in 1984 it was 25.7 for men and 23.8 for women.

For remarriages after a divorce, as might be expected, the average age of marriage is older. For men it is 38, whereas for women it is 34. For widows and widowers, the average age of remarriage is older still, 53 for women, and 61 for men.

There are also regional differences in the average age of marriage. Southern women marrying for the first time are the youngest, and brides from the East are the oldest (Wilson and London, 1987).

Age homogamy appears to hold for all groups within the population. Studies show that it is true for blacks as well as whites and for professionals as well as laborers. Clearly, the norms of our society are very effective in causing people of similar age to marry each other (Leslie, 1979; Hollingshead, 1951; Glick and Landau, 1950).

Race

Homogamy is most obvious in the area of race. As late as 1966, nineteen states sought to stop interracial marriage through legislation. The laws varied widely, and there was great confusion because of various court interpretations. In Arizona before 1967, it was illegal for a white person to marry a black, Hindu, Malay, or Asian. The same thing was true in Wyoming, and residents of that state were also prohibited from marrying mulattos.

In 1966 the state of Virginia's Supreme Court of Appeals had to decide on the legality of a marriage that had taken place in Washington, D.C., in 1958 between Richard P. Loving, a white man, and his part-Indian and part-black wife, Mildred Loving. The court unanimously upheld the state's ban on interracial marriages. The couple appealed the case to the United States Supreme Court, which agreed to decide whether state laws prohibiting racial intermarriage were constitutional. Previously, all courts had ruled that the laws were not discriminatory, because they applied to both whites and nonwhites. On June 12, 1967, the Supreme Court ruled that states could not outlaw racial intermarriage.

Since that time, the number of couples in interracial marriages has risen from 0.7 percent of all married couples in 1970 to 1.5 percent in 1987. Yet, interracial unions represent fewer than two of every one hundred married couples *(Statistical Abstract of the United States: 1989).*

The most common type of interracial marriage is one between a white husband and a wife of a race other than black. The next most common is between a white woman and a man of a race other than black. These types of interracial marriages have been increasing substantially, whereas interracial marriages between blacks and whites appear to be leveling off.

Interracial marriages are more likely to involve at least one previously married partner than are marriages between spouses of the same race. In addition, brides and grooms who marry interracially tend to be older than the national average.

The degree of education of the participants also differs in interracial marriages. White grooms in interracial marriages are more likely to have completed college than white grooms who marry within their race. In all-white couples, 18 percent of the grooms hold college degrees. In a marriage involving a white groom and a black bride, 24 percent of the men finished college. Among black men married to women of other races, only 5 percent completed college, whereas 13 percent of black men mar-

ried to white brides did so. Nine percent of black men whose spouses are also black hold college degrees.

Although the rate of interracial marriage is growing, the proportions vary widely by state. Hawaii has the distinction of having both the highest number and the greatest proportion of interracial marriages, with almost one-fourth of all marriages there being interracial, the majority of which are Asian-Caucasian unions. Florida runs a distant second, and the 1173 interracial marriages in Illinois in 1986 include 665 white brides marrying black grooms — the highest number of marriages of that combination in any state. The record for the reverse combination — black brides marrying white grooms — is held by New Jersey. Alaska comes second to Hawaii in the proportion of interracial marriages. Thirteen percent of the state's marriages are interracial. None of the other states came close to these percentages.

Even though their total numbers are still small, racially mixed marriages have become increasingly common in America's melting pot.

Religion

Unlike many European nations, none of the American states have ever had legislation restricting interreligious marriage. Religious homogamy is not nearly as widespread as racial homogamy, though most marriages still involve people of the same religion.

Attitudes toward religious intermarriage vary somewhat from one religious group to another. Almost all religious bodies try to discourage or control marriage outside the religion but vary in the extent of their opposition. Before 1970, the Roman Catholic church would not allow a priest to perform an interreligious marriage ceremony unless the non-Catholic partner promised to raise the children of the union as Catholics, and the Catholic partner promised to encourage the non-Catholic to convert. However, in the late 1960s the

Rules of endogamy encourage a person to choose a marriage partner from a certain ethnic or religious group.

Catholic church softened its policy, and since 1970 the pope has allowed local bishops to permit mixed marriages to be performed without a priest and has also eliminated the requirement that the non-Catholic partner promise to rear the children as Catholics. Nevertheless, the Catholic partner must still promise to *try* to have the children raised as Catholic.

Protestant denominations and sects also differ with regard to barriers they place on interreligious marriage of their members. At one extreme are the Mennonites, who excommunicate any member who marries outside the faith. At the other are numerous bodies that may wish their members would marry within the faith but provide no formal penalties for those who do not (Heer, 1980).

Jewish religious bodies also differ in their degree of opposition to religious intermarriage. Orthodox Jews are the most adamantly opposed to intermarriage, while Conservative and Reform Jews, although by no means endorsing it, are more tolerant of religious intermarriage when it does take place. Jewish intermarriage rates have been increasing dramatically in recent years, with nearly 40 percent of all Jews marrying someone of another religion.

Religious leaders are often concerned about religious intermarriage for a variety of reasons. Some claim that one or both intermarrying parties are lost to the religion, and others believe that the potential for marital success is decreased greatly in an intermarriage. Studies have shown that there are several complex factors in intermarriage and that simplistic and unequivocal predictions are not warranted. For example, a study in Iowa of Catholic–Protestant marriages concluded that though there was a slightly higher divorce rate among intermarried couples, the results did not justify predictions of marital problems. Moreover, the study also showed that Presbyterians, Methodists, and Baptists who married persons of other Protestant denominations had higher marital survival rates than those who married within their denomination (Burchinal and Chancellor, 1963).

Most marriages still involve those of the same religion marrying each other. There is, however, a clear trend of more religious intermarriages in the United States today.

Social Status

Level of education and type of occupation are two measures of social status. In these areas there is usually a great deal of similarity between people who marry each other. Men tend to marry women who are slightly below them in education and social status, though these differences are within a narrow range. Wide-ranging differences between the two people often contain an element of exploitation. One partner may be trying to make a major leap up the social class ladder or one may be looking for an easy way of taking advantage of the other partner because of unequal power.

The high school environment often plays a major role in maintaining social status homogamy, because in high school students have to start making plans about their future careers. Some may go to college, and others may plan on going to work directly after graduation. This process causes the students to be divided into two groups: the college-bound and the work-force-bound. Although the lines separating these two groups are by no means impenetrable, in many high schools these two groups maintain separate social activities. In this way barriers against dating and future marriage between those of unlike social status are set up. After graduation, those who attend a college are more likely to associate with other college students and choose their mates from that pool. Those who have joined the work force are more likely to choose mates from that environment. In this way, similarities in education between marriage partners really are not accidental.

As with several of the items we have discussed already, education, social class, and occupation produce a similarity of experience and values among people. Just as growing up in an Italian family may make one feel comfortable with Italian customs and traits, going to college may make one feel comfortable with those who have experienced that environment. Similarities in social status, then, are as much a result of socialization and culture as conscious choice. We most likely will marry a person we feel comfortable with—a person who has had experiences similar to our own.

Coming to terms with the constraints on our marriage choices can be a sobering experience: What we thought to be freedom of choice in selecting a mate is revealed instead by various studies to be governed by rules and patterns.

companionate marriage
Marriage based on romantic love.

THE TRANSFORMATION OF THE FAMILY

Most scholars agree that the Industrial Revolution had a strong impact on the family. In his influential study of family patterns around the world, William J. Goode (1963) showed that the modern, relatively isolated nuclear family with weak ties to an extensive kinship network is well adapted to the pressures of industrialism.

First, industrialism demands that workers be geographically mobile so that a work force is available wherever new industries are built. The modern nuclear family, by having cut many of its ties to extended family networks, is freer to move. And it was among laborers' families that extended kinship ties first were weakened. Only in the last few decades have middle- and upper-class families become similarly isolated.

Second, industrialism requires a certain degree of social mobility (see Chapter 8). This is so talented workers may be recruited to positions of greater responsibility (with greater material rewards and increased prestige). A family that is too closely tied to other families in its kinship network will find it difficult to "break free" and climb into a higher social class. On the other hand, if families in the higher social classes are too tightly linked by kinship ties, newly arriving families will find it very difficult to fit into their new social environment. Hence, the isolated nuclear family is well suited to the needed social mobility in an industrial society.

A third point is that the modern nuclear family allows for inheritance and descent through both sides of the family. Further, material resources and social opportunities are not inherited mainly by the oldest males (or females), as in some societies. This means that all children in a family will have a chance to develop their skills, which in turn means that industry will have a larger, more talented, and flexible labor force from which to hire workers.

By the early twentieth century, then, the nuclear family had evolved fully among the working classes of industrial society. It rested on (1) the child-centered family; (2) **companionate marriage** (that is, marriage based on romantic love); (3) increased equality for women; (4) decreased links with extended families or kinship networks; (5) neolocal residence and increased geographical mobility; (6) increased social mobility; and (7) the clear separation between work and leisure. In addition, most work was boring and alienating, and it was expected that the nuclear family would fulfill the function of providing emotional support for its members.

The World War II years also had a profound effect on the American family, for it was during the war that a process begun in the Depression really accelerated. The war made it necessary for hundreds of thousands of women to work outside the home to support their families. They often had to take jobs, vital to the American economy, that had been vacated when their husbands went to fight overseas. After the war, an effort was made to "defeminize" the work force. Nevertheless, many women remained on the job, and those who left now knew what it was like to work for compensation outside the home. Things were never

FAMILY PRIORITIES

A ll of us have a set of priorities in our lives. When adults in the United States, Japan, and western Europe were asked to rank the different aspects of their lives in order of importance (10 = very important; 1 = not at all important), the results showed that children's education and family life are what most Americans value most. This is not so in Japan, where health and career concerns rank high. Career is near the bottom of the U.S. list. It might surprise you that love life was a relatively low priority in the U.S., Japan, and Europe.

Source: "News You Can Use: Putting Kids First," *U.S. News & World Report,* August 1, 1988, p. 62.

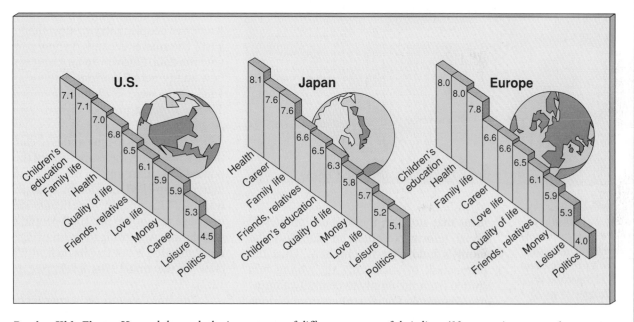

Putting Kids First. *How adults rank the importance of different aspects of their lives (10 = very important; 1 = not at all important).* Note: *Figures are average response of 1000 people interviewed in each country. The survey sample included a total of 8000 adults, with 1000 interviews carried out in each of six western European countries, in the United States, and in Japan.* Source: U.S. News & World Report, *August 1, 1988, p. 62. Basic data from Starch INRA Hooper/Roper.*

the same again for the American family, and family life began to change.

The initial changes were not all that apparent. On the contrary, by the 1950s the United States had entered the most family-oriented period in its history. This was the era of the baby boom, and couples were marrying at the youngest ages in recorded American history. During the 1950s, 96 percent of those people in the childbearing years married (Blumstein and Schwartz, 1983). The war years' experiences also paved the way for secondary groups and formal organizations (see Chapter 6) gradually to take over many of the family's traditional activities and functions. As social historian Christopher Lasch (1977) points out, this trend was supported by public policy makers who came to see the family as an obstacle to social progress. Because the family preserved separatist cultural and religious traditions and other "old-fashioned"

In 1946 (the year this photo was taken), the median family income was $2,800, television was in its infancy, and only 12.5 percent of people ages 18 to 22 went to college. In the years following World War II, a radical transformation took place in our society and in the family.

eryone working for the betterment of the whole? Or has the family structure changed throughout history in response to the economic and political changes within society? In this section we shall explore these views and attempt to clarify the current direction of family life.

CHANGES IN THE MARRIAGE RATE

Are fewer people marrying now than in the past? The answer depends on how you evaluate the data. One way to look at it is to ask how many actual marriages there are. In 1987 there were 2.42 million marriages. That is a record number of marriages in a given year (see Figure 12.2).

Another way to look at it is to calculate the marriage rate, the proportion of the total population marrying. The 2.42 million marriages in 1987, divided by total population of 243.4 million Americans, yields a marriage rate of 9.9 per 1000 people in the population. According to the marriage rate, the institution is holding its own with a rate close to the mid-1970s levels (see Figure 12.3).

The third way to get a true picture of the marriage situation in the United States is to take the marriage rate per 1000 unmarried women age 15 and older. This is the proportion of eligible women marrying. As of 1984 this rate was 59.5 per 1000 (see Figure 12.4). The rate for men was 71.7. With these rates, about 6 percent of all eligible women and 7 percent of all eligible men marry each year.

Since 1960, the number of marriages and the marriage rate has been high because the pool of eligible adults has kept expanding. Hidden in these numbers though is the fact that a rising share of eligible people are choosing not to marry. Even though the number of marriages increased from 1.5 million in 1960 to 2.42 million in 1987, the marriage rate fell from 73.5 per 1000 unmarried women in 1960 to 57.0 in 1985 *(Statistical Abstract of the United States: 1989).*

ideas that stood in the way of "progress," social reformers sought to diminish the family's hold over its children. Thus the prime task of socializing the young was shifted from the family to centrally administered schools. Social workers from various agencies intruded into the home, offering constantly expanding welfare services to families. The juvenile court system expanded in the belief that deficiencies in families of youthful offenders caused crime among children.

Thus, the modern period has seen what sociologists refer to as the *transfer of functions* from the family to other, outside institutions. This transfer has had a great effect on the family and underlies the trends that currently are troubling many people.

There are several problems in trying to assess the prevailing state of the family. Some feel that the family is deteriorating, and they cite appropriate examples of divorce rates and single-parent families to support their view. Others think of the family as an institution that is in transition but just as stable as ever. Was the family of the past a stable extended family unit with ev-

The proportion of eligible women who marry has shown a steady decline since 1970. It appears that people are less inclined to marry than they once were (Wilson and London, 1987).

CHILDLESS COUPLES

A significant trend in the last 15 years has been the growth in the number of childless couples. There are currently 6 million married women age 18 to 44 who have no children. Although the number of couples with children increased by only 8 percent between 1968 and 1985, the number of childless couples increased by 75 percent during that period (Bloom, 1986).

This trend appears to be an outgrowth of an increase in the number of women who are delaying marriage. This trend produces a substantial number of women who are well educated and have progressed in a career at the time of marriage. Many of these women decide to forego childbearing. Evidence of this is seen in the fact that the more educated the woman, the less likely she is to want children. Only 7 percent of women age 30 to 34 with less than 12 years of schooling expect to be childless, 11 percent of high school graduates expect no children, and fully 19 percent of college graduates expect to be childless. (U.S. Bureau of the Census, 1985). In addition, since fertility decreases with age, many of these women who marry later become childless involuntarily.

Religion also relates to whether women have children or not. Among married women age 35 to 44, 21 percent of those who do not practice a religion are childless, compared to 11 percent of Protestants, and just 6 percent of Catholics (Bloom and Bennett, 1986).

CHANGES IN HOUSEHOLD SIZE

Although changes in household size may be neither a positive nor a negative change, some social scientists use this point to support a negative view of the future of the family. The American household of 1790 had an average of 5.8 members. By 1988 the average number had dropped to 2.64 *(Statistical Abstract of the United States: 1989).*

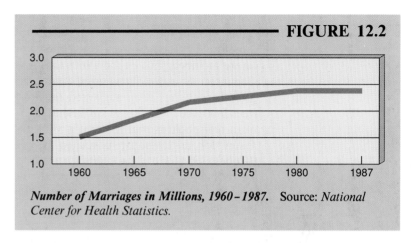

FIGURE 12.2

Number of Marriages in Millions, 1960–1987. Source: *National Center for Health Statistics.*

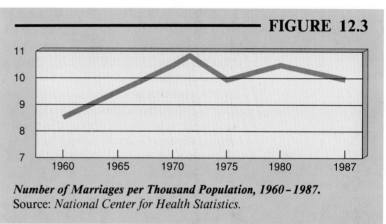

FIGURE 12.3

Number of Marriages per Thousand Population, 1960–1987. Source: *National Center for Health Statistics.*

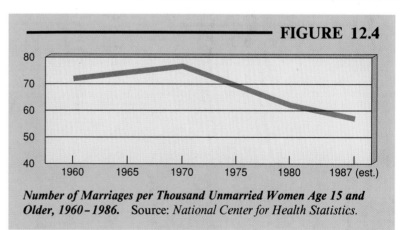

FIGURE 12.4

Number of Marriages per Thousand Unmarried Women Age 15 and Older, 1960–1986. Source: *National Center for Health Statistics.*

The same trend also has been evident in other parts of the world. The average rural household in Japan in 1660 often had 20 or more members, but by the 1960s the rural Japanese household averaged only 4.5 members. It has been suggested that one reason for the reduction in size of the American household is that today it is very unlikely for us to house unrelated people (Cohen, 1981). Until the 1940s, for a variety of reasons, it was common for people to have nonkin living with them, either as laborers in the fields or as boarders who helped with the rent payment.

The reduction in the number of nonrelatives living with the family explains only part of the continuing reduction in the average household size. Another reason that has often been cited is a rapid decrease in the number of aging parents living with grown children and their families. Some point to this as evidence of the fragmentation and loss of intimacy present in the contemporary family. At the turn of the century more than 60 percent of those 65 or older lived with one or more of their children; today this figure is less than 10 percent.

Older people prefer to remain independent and live apart from their adult children.

How can we account for so many more old people living apart from their families? We might be tempted to say that the family has become so self-centered and so unable to fulfill the needs of its members that the elderly have become the first and most obvious castoffs. However, this trend of the elderly living away from their children can also be seen as a result of the increasing wealth of the population, including the elderly. The percentage of the total population living in poverty rose from 12.6 percent in 1970 to 13.5 percent in 1987. In contrast there was a substantial drop in the number of elderly living in poverty during that same period, from 24.5 percent to 12.4 percent, indicating that their position relative to that of the general population has improved greatly *(Statistical Abstract of the United States: 1989)*.

This change in the elderly's economic position is more likely to be responsible for their living apart from their children than any supposed deterioration in family life — older people themselves are choosing to live independently. As gerontologist Gary R. Lee (1981) notes:

> While we have good evidence that the elderly *did* frequently live with their children around the turn of the century, we have no evidence that they *wanted* to do so, then or now. In our culture, unlike some others such as the Japanese, dependence on children in one's old age is no virtue, and most older people seem to prefer to avoid dependence and the appearance of dependence if they have the necessary resources. They have been increasingly likely to have these resources. Because of this, they have been increasingly able to stay in their own homes, or in homes of their own choosing, and have less often been forced to rely on the largess of children. They are not being ignored, they are being independent.

Another reason for the change in the size of the households is the increasing divorce rate. As more families separate legally and move apart physically, the number of people living under one roof has fallen.

Two other reasons for the smaller families of today are the tendency of young people to postpone marriage and the increase in the number of working women. As people marry later, they have fewer children. Many couples also are deciding to have no children; as more and more women become involved in work and careers, they tend to defer marriage and limit the number of children they bear.

All these factors point to what, according to 1980 census data, are the most significant causes of the sharp decline in the average size of the American household: the decrease in the number of children per family and the increase in the number of people living alone (Herbers, 1981). These facts will ultimately have some important consequences for the entire structure of society.

Other research indicates the enormous change in female sexual experience in that period — there was a far greater increase in premarital sex among teenage girls and women than among men (Zelnick and Kantner, 1972, 1979). Part of the reason for this increase was the widespread use of the birth-control pill as well as the legalization of abortion. Women became less fearful of becoming pregnant and of being forced into marriage because of a pregnancy.

Recent widespread concern about such sexually transmitted diseases as AIDS (Acquired Immune Deficiency Syndrome) and genital herpes may have a profound effect on reversing these trends. Even though it is reasonable to assume this should be taking place, it is still too early to find research evidence substantiating this trend.

PREMARITAL SEX

The 1970s and 1980s have seen widespread changes in attitudes toward premarital sex and a corresponding increase in the number of people who routinely have sex before marriage. The revolution in attitudes toward premarital sex was triggered by the social upheavals of the 1960s and 1970s, the accompanying changes in gender roles, and, of course, the development and accessibility of effective contraceptives. Studies (National Opinion Research Council [NORC], 1977) reflect this radical change in attitudes. In 1963, 80 percent of the people surveyed felt that premarital sex was wrong. Twenty-one years later, when 5237 students from universities in Arkansas, Louisiana, Oklahoma, and Texas were asked about premarital sex, the respondents were divided as to whether it is wrong to engage in sexual intercourse before marriage. Nearly 55 percent said they have or would engage in sexual intercourse before marriage, and 31.8 percent stated they had not or would not. Seventy-two percent indicated that it is not acceptable to experience sexual intercourse without love of one's partner (Martin and Martin, 1984).

WORKING WOMEN

The period since World War II has seen a dramatic change in the labor force participation rates of American women. Nearly 52 million women were working in 1986, representing a 200 percent increase in 40 years. The number of men in the labor force during this same period increased by only 50 percent. The change in the labor force is probably the single most important recent change that has taken place in American society.

Several factors caused this change. After World War II, many of the women who had taken jobs in record numbers to ease labor shortages during the war remained on the job. Their numbers increased the social acceptability of the working woman.

Widespread use of contraceptives was a second important factor. Effective contraception gave women the freedom of deciding whether and when to have children. As a result, many women postponed childbearing and continued their education.

Baby boomers also had different economic expectations when they entered the work force. Having two incomes became

FIGURE 12.5

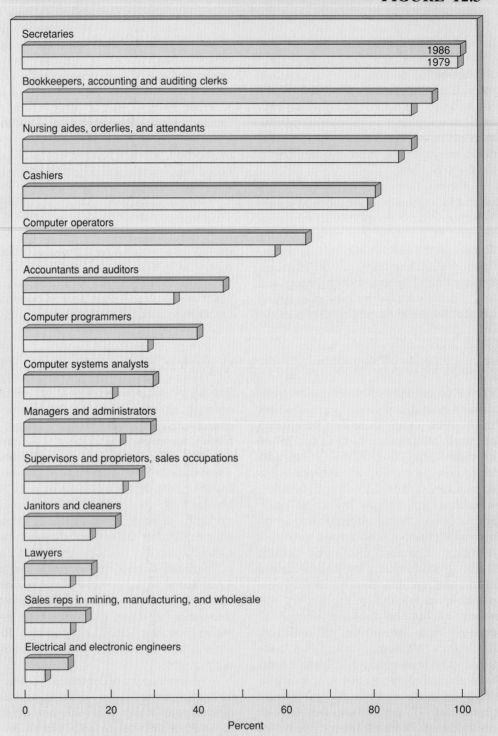

Secretaries
1986
1979

Bookkeepers, accounting and auditing clerks

Nursing aides, orderlies, and attendants

Cashiers

Computer operators

Accountants and auditors

Computer programmers

Computer systems analysts

Managers and administrators

Supervisors and proprietors, sales occupations

Janitors and cleaners

Lawyers

Sales reps in mining, manufacturing, and wholesale

Electrical and electronic engineers

0   20   40   60   80   100

Percent

Percentage of Work Force that Is Female in Selected Occupations, 1979 and 1986.   Source:
Bureau of the Census. 1980 Census and March 1987 Current Population Survey.

important to ensure the life-style and standard of living they had come to expect.

Occupational segregation is still present even though the types of jobs women are holding has been changing. Women still dominate such jobs as school-teaching (74 percent women in 1986), retail sales (69 percent), librarianship (87 percent), nursing (96 percent), and secretarial work (99 percent).

Women have been making progress in entering traditionally male occupations. Women's progress is evident among lawyers (20 percent today, up from 5 percent in 1970), doctors (18 percent, up from 10 percent), architects (8 percent, up from 4 percent), computer scientists (28 percent, up from 14 percent), and college and university professors (37 percent, up from 29 percent) (see Figure 12.5).

The entry of women into the ranks of business managers and executives has been more difficult. Only 36 percent of executives, administrators, and managers are women, even though 45 percent of American workers are women. The vast majority of the top executive positions are held by men. Katherine Graham of the Washington Post Company, is the only woman chief executive officer of a Fortune 500 company. The proportion of women who are managers is rising though. It now stands at 36 percent, up from 27 percent in 1972.

It has been noted that women who reach the executive ranks have different managerial styles. They tend to be more participatory and nurturant. The upper echelons of American companies are dominated by men, possibly making it difficult for women to initiate the management styles they would find desirable. But as women continue to enter these ranks they will add diversity to American management (Bloom, 1986).

FAMILY VIOLENCE

According to a nationwide survey (Straus, Gelles, and Steinmetz, 1980), every year some 8 million Americans are assaulted by members of their own families. Spouses attack each other, parents attack children, and even children attack and hurt both their parents and one another. Each year 16 percent of all couples who come to blows with each other, and more than a third of the time these violent confrontations include severe punching, kicking, and even biting: 3 percent of all children are punched, kicked, or bitten by parents; and more than a third of all siblings assault one another severely.

In general, research has shown the incidence of family violence to be highest among urban lower-class families. It is high among families with more than four children and in those in which the husband is unemployed. Families in which child abuse occurs tend to be socially isolated, living in crowded and otherwise inadequate housing. Research on family violence has tended to focus on lower socioeconomic groups, but scattered data from school counselors and mental health agencies suggest that family violence also is a serious problem among America's more affluent households. In fact, two sociologists found that the highest incidence of violence was in families in which both husband and wife were high school graduates. A related finding was that the children most likely to act violently toward their siblings were those whose parents had had some college education (Kenney, 1980). Other research indicates that violence often begins when couples are dating (Parke and Collmer, 1975). Some believe that the more money a woman has, the less likely she is to report abuse (*Christian Science Monitor,* July 14, 1988). In addition, in homes where the wife is battered, the children are more likely to be battered too. It is apparent from these observations that more research focused on family violence in the middle and upper classes is called for.

Sociologists have not yet been able to answer the following questions: Is family violence on the rise in American society? Or is it simply being reported and recorded more accurately than it used to be? Certainly some researchers feel that family violence is an accepted, pervasive attribute of American life (Kenney, 1980). Is family violence more prevalent in the United States than in other industrial societies or in non-industrial societies? What are the causes of family violence? These questions must be studied before it is possible to assess what can be done to help prevent the occurrence of this disturbing aspect of family life in America.

DIVORCE

Of all the changes apparent in modern American family life, the increasing incidence of divorce is one of the most prominent. The rate of divorce in America has risen fivefold since 1910. In 1970, of all American males, 2.5 percent were divorced. These figures more than doubled, to 6.6 percent, in 1986. The figures for women are higher, though roughly proportional, being 2.9 percent and 8.9 percent for 1970 and 1986, respectively. For certain age groups, the figures are considerably higher. For example, among 40- to 44-year-old males and females, the percentage divorced is 11.7 and 15.9, respectively (*Statistical Abstract of the United States: 1988, 1987*).

The likelihood of divorce varies considerably with several factors. For example, education levels seem to have a strong effect on divorce rates (see Figure 12.6). The likelihood of a first marriage ending in divorce is nearly 60 percent for those people with some college education but no bachelor's degree. Those people who have a college degree but no graduate school training have nearly a 40 percent chance of divorce and are the least divorce-prone. We could argue that those people with the personality traits and family background that lead them to achieve a college degree are also those most likely to achieve marital stability.

Women who have gone on to graduate school have a greater likelihood of divorce than some less-educated women: Approximately 53 percent of them will divorce. The problem for these women is the difficulty of combining career, marriage, and child rearing without the necessary societal supports for these often competing roles. As more and more women earn graduate degrees and as some of the barriers impeding women in combining professional and personal lives are removed, the higher rate of divorce for these women may also decline.

Divorced men are more likely to remarry than divorced women. Divorced men usually marry women who are at least 5 years younger than they are. In this way divorced men end up having a larger pool of potential partners than do divorced women, for whom the pool of potential partners decreases as they age.

For divorced women in their 30s, the likelihood of remarriage declines with increasing levels of education. Those women with no college education remarry rather quickly, whereas those with more education wait longer or remain unmarried (Norton and Moorman, 1987).

Although the divorce rate has been rising fairly steadily since 1970, it has shown signs of leveling off in recent years. In both 1986 and 1987, the divorce rate per 1000

FIGURE 12.6

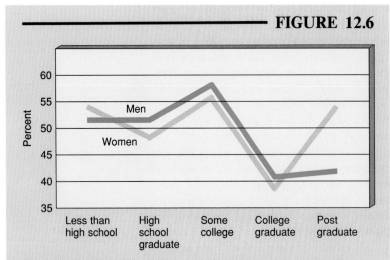

Divorce and Education: Age 25–34. Source: *Paul C. Glick. "How American Families Are Changing,"* American Demographics *6(1) (January 1984), p. 24.*

people was 4.8, the lowest it has been since 1975 (see Figure 12.7).

Even though the rate of increase in divorce rates may be leveling off, there is little evidence to suggest that the rate will decline. The United States still has the highest divorce rate in the world. Current divorce rates imply that half of all marriages will end in divorce. Many argue that society cannot tolerate such a high rate of marital disruptions. Although 30 years ago few would have believed society could tolerate even one-third of all married couples divorcing, that level has already been reached by some marriage cohorts.

The large number of divorces is itself a force that keeps the divorce rate high. These divorced people join the pool of available marriage partners, and a large majority remarry. These remarriages then have a higher overall risk of divorce and thus an impact on the overall divorce rate.

Even though divorce rates were lower in 1910, 1930, and 1950 than they are today, can we assume that family life then was happier or more stable? Divorce during those periods was expensive, legally difficult, and socially stigmatized. Many who would have otherwise considered divorce remained married because of these factors. Is it thus accurate to say that it was better for the children and society for the partners to maintain these marriages?

The higher incidence of divorce in no way implies a general disillusionment with the institution of marriage. About 75 percent of divorced women and 85 percent of divorced men remarry (Reiss, 1980). Nor are children an impediment to remarriage as 71 percent of the divorces involve children (Norton and Moorman, 1987).

As divorce becomes more common, it also becomes more visible, and such visibility can actually produce more divorces. Others become a model of how difficult marriages are handled. The model of people suffering in an unhappy marriage is being replaced by one in which people start new lives after dissolving a marriage.

Divorce also may be encouraged by the

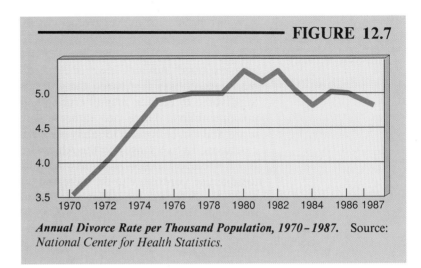

FIGURE 12.7

Annual Divorce Rate per Thousand Population, 1970–1987. Source: *National Center for Health Statistics.*

increasing tendency, mentioned earlier, for outside social institutions to assume traditional family functions that once helped hold the family together. Then again, divorce has become a viable option because people can look forward to living longer today, and they may be less willing to endure a bad marriage if they feel there is time to look for a better way of life.

Another reason for today's high divorce rate is that we have come to expect a great deal from marriage. It is no longer enough, as it might have been at the turn of the century, for the husband to be a good provider and the wife to be a good mother and family caretaker. We now look to marriage as a source of emotional support in which each spouse complements the other in a variety of social, occupational, and psychological endeavors.

Divorce rates have also increased because the possibilities for women in the work force have improved. During earlier eras, divorced women had great problems contending with the financial realities of survival, and many were discouraged from seeking a divorce because they could not envision a realistic way of supporting themselves. With their greater economic independence, many women can now consider divorce as an option.

Today's high divorce rates can also be traced to a number of legal changes that have taken place to make divorce a more realistic possibility for those couples who are experiencing difficulties. Many states have instituted "no-fault" divorce laws, and many others have liberalized the grounds for divorce to include mental cruelty and incompatibility. These are rather vague terms and can be applied to many problem marriages. Even changes by the American Bar Association, which now allow lawyers to advertise, contribute to the increased divorce rate. Advertisements that state that an uncomplicated divorce will cost only $150 put this option within the reach of many couples.

These legal changes are but a reflection of society's attitudinal changes toward divorce. We are a far cry from a generation ago when divorce was to be avoided at all costs, and when it did occur, it became a major source of embarrassment for the entire extended family. The fact that Ronald Reagan was divorced and remarried had little impact on his election to the presidency in 1980 and 1984. With so little public concern being shown, we can be sure that the role of peer-group and public opinion in preventing divorce has been greatly diminished.

Divorce Laws

In an analysis of the implications of recent changes in divorce laws, Lenore Weitzman and Ruth Dixon (1980) emphasize that the laws governing divorce reflect society's definition of marriage, provide guidelines for appropriate marriage behavior, and spell out the reciprocal rights and obligations of marriage partners. Divorce laws also define the continued obligations that the formerly married couple have to each other after they divorce. According to Weitzman and Dixon, one can generally gain an insight into how a society defines marriage by examining its provisions for divorce, for it is at the point of divorce that a society has the opportunity to reward the marital behavior it approves of, and to punish spouses who have violated its norms.

A study of changing divorce laws will reveal changes in family and gender-role patterns. We will examine no-fault divorce laws to demonstrate how "this new legislation seeks to alter the definition of marriage, the relationship between husbands and wives, and the economic and social obligations of former spouses to each other and to their children after divorce."

NO-FAULT DIVORCE The first no-fault divorce laws were introduced in California in 1970, and now are in effect in every state but South Dakota. No-fault divorce laws allow couples to dissolve their marriage without either partner having to assume blame for the failure of the marriage.

Weitzman and Dixon argue that no-fault divorce reflects changes in the traditional view of legal marriage. By eliminating the fault-based grounds for divorce and the adversary process, no-fault divorce laws recognize that frequently both parties are responsible for the breakdown of the marriage. Further, these laws recognize that previously the divorce procedure often worsened the situation by forcing potentially "amicable" individuals to become antagonists.

No-fault divorce laws advocate that the financial aspects of marital dissolution are to be based on equity, equality, and economic need rather than on fault- or gender-based role assignments. Alimony also is to be based on the respective spouses' economic circumstances and on the principle of social equality, not on the basis of guilt or innocence. No longer is alimony automatically awarded to the "injured party," regardless of that person's financial needs— no-fault divorce does not recognize an "injured party." The new laws seek to reflect the changing circumstances of women and their increased participation in the labor force. By so doing, they encourage women in their efforts to become self-supporting. Under no-fault divorce law, husbands are not automatically expected to continue to support their former wives throughout their lives.

Some see no-fault divorce legislation as a redefinition of the traditional marital responsibilities of men and women through institution of a new norm of equality between the sexes. Husbands are no longer automatically designated as the head of the household and solely responsible for support, nor are wives alone expected to assume the responsibility of domestic household activities and child rearing. Sex-neutral obligations that fall equally upon the husband and wife have been institutionalized by these new divorce laws. These changes are reflected most clearly in the new considerations for alimony allocation. In addition, property is to be divided on an equal basis. Finally, child-support expectations and the standards for child custody also reflect the new egalitarian criteria of no-fault divorce legislation. Under these new laws, both father and mother are expected to be equally responsible for the financial support of their children after divorce. Mothers are no longer to receive custody of the child automatically; rather, a sex-neutral standard instructs judges to award custody in the best interests of the child.

Weitzman (1985) spent 10 years studying the effects of no-fault divorce. She began her research assuming that no-fault divorce was a path-breaking improvement for women and families. A decade later she ended her study, disillusioned. She felt that although no-fault has worked well for some divorcing couples, it has had devastating consequences for many others. Among the problems she found were older homemakers married 35 years or more, lacking any labor-force experience or skills whatever, awarded short-term settlements, ordered to sell the family home, and instructed by the court to pursue job training. Similarly, mothers with toddlers were routinely left with virtually full responsibility for their support. Concludes Weitzman: "Divorce is a financial catastrophe for most women." The evidence she points to from her study is that men's standard of living went up 42 percent in the year following

There has been an increased recognition of fathers' rights regarding custody, reflecting the changing role of fathers.

divorce, while women's standard of living went down 73 percent—even counting child support and alimony payments.

No-fault divorce laws are based on an idealized picture of women's social, occupational, and economic gains in achieving an equality that in fact may not reflect their actual conditions and circumstances. This discrepancy between reality and the ideal can have extremely detrimental effects on women's ability to become self-sufficient after divorce.

Child-Custody Laws

Child custody is one of the areas of divorce law in which the gap between the ideal and the reality still is apparent. Although the new no-fault legislation approaches the question of child custody in a sex-neutral way, mothers still are awarded legal custody of children in about 90 percent of American divorce cases (Weiss, 1979b). Until recently, divorce laws generally discriminated against fathers in custody cases. Fathers often were advised by legal counsel of the futility of contesting custody, and the burden of proof was on the father to document the unfitness of the mother or to affirm his ability to be a better parent than the mother.

JUDITH S. WALLERSTEIN ON THE LASTING WOUNDS OF DIVORCE

Judith S. Wallerstein is the executive director of the Center for the Family in Transition in Corte Madera, California, and co-author with Sandra Blakeslee of Second Chances: Men, Women, and Children a Decade After Divorce *(1989). As a sociologist, she has been studying issues related to divorce for many years, particularly the common assumption that the scars of divorce heal within a year or two. In the following interview, Wallerstein tells us about the unexpected findings that came out of her longitudinal study of divorce.*

In 1971, I began a study of the effects of divorce on middle-class people who continue to function despite the stress of a marriage breakup. We chose families in which, despite the failing marriage, the children were doing well at school and the parents were not in clinical treatment for psychiatric disorders. This was, in other words, divorce under the best of circumstances.

Our study eventually tracked 60 families, most of them white, with a total of 131 children for 10 and, in some cases, 15 years after divorce.

We found that although some divorces work well—some adults are happier in the long run, and some children do better than they would have been expected to do in an unhappy family that remained intact—more often than not divorce is a wrenching, long-lasting experience for at least one of the former partners. Perhaps most important, we found that for virtually all the children it exerts powerful and wholly unanticipated effects.

We interviewed families at the time of separation and filing for divorce and again 12 to 18 months later, expecting to chart recoveries among both men and women and to look at how the children were mastering troubling family events.

We were stunned when, at the second series of visits, we found family after family still in crisis. An unexpectedly large number of children were on a downward course.

Dismayed, we decided to do a follow-up study in the fifth year after divorce. To our surprise, we found that although half of the men and two-thirds of the women said they were more content with their lives, only 34 percent of the children were clearly doing well. Another 37 percent were depressed, could not concentrate in school, had trouble making friends, and suffered a wide range of behavior problems. These children were not recovering as everyone thought they would.

We went back to these families again to conduct a 10-year follow-up. Many of those we had first interviewed as children were now adults. Overall, 45 percent were doing well, but another 41 percent were doing poorly. They were entering adulthood as worried, underachieving, and sometimes angry young men and women.

It was only at the 10-year point that unexpected findings became apparent. The first is something we call the sleeper effect. The sleeper effect was docu-

However, there has been an increased recognition of fathers' rights regarding custody, reflecting the changing role of American fathers and the reevaluation of the judicial practice of automatically awarding custody to the mother. In addition to giving more fathers custody of their children, the courts are now beginning to view joint custody as another legal option.

JOINT CUSTODY In 1979 only six states had statutes with express joint custody provisions. Today more than thirty states have replaced traditional sole-custody laws with

mented in 66 percent of the young women in our study between the ages of 19 and 23; half of them were seriously derailed by it.

It occurs at a time when these young women are making decisions with long-term implications for their lives. Faced with issues of commitment, love, and sex in an adult context, they are aware the game is serious. If they tie in with the wrong man, have children too soon, or choose harmful lifestyles, the effects can be tragic.

Overcome by fears and anxieties, they begin to make connections between these feelings and their parents' divorce: "I'm so afraid I'll marry someone like my dad."

Forty percent of the 19- to 23-year-old young men in our study, 10 years after divorce, still had no set goals, a limited education, and a sense of having little control over their lives.

In the decade after divorce, three in five children felt rejected by one of their parents—usually the father—whether or not it was true.

The young people told us time and again how much they needed a family structure, how much they wanted to be protected, and how much they yearned for clear guidelines for moral behavior. An alarming number of teenagers felt abandoned, physically and emotionally.

For children, divorce occurs during the formative years. What they see and experience becomes a part of their inner world, influencing their own relationships 10 and 15 years later. It is then, as these young men and women face the task of establishing love and intimacy, that they most feel the lack of a template for a loving relationship between a man and a woman. It is here their anxiety threatens their ability to create enduring families of their own.

Although our overall findings are troubling and serious, we should not point the finger of blame at divorce per se. Indeed divorce is often the only rational solution to a bad marriage. Still, we need to understand that divorce has consequences. We need to know many children will suffer for many years. As a society, we need to take steps to preserve for the children as much as possible of the social, economic and emotional security that existed while their parents' marriage was intact.

Like it or not, we are witnessing family changes that are an integral part of the wider changes in society. We are on a wholly new course, one that gives us unprecedented opportunities for creating better relationships and stronger families—but one that also brings unprecedented dangers for society, especially for our children.

Source: New York Times Syndication Sales Corporation.

---

joint custody statutes, and legislation is pending in many other jurisdictions.

In a legal sense, joint custody means that parental decision-making authority has been given equally to both parents after a divorce. It implies that neither parent's rights will be considered paramount. Both parents will have an equal voice in the children's education, upbringing, and general welfare.

Joint legal custody is not a determinant of physical custody or postdivorce living arrangements. It is, however, often confused with complicated situations in which parents share responsibility for the physical day-to-day care of the children. Such arrangements usually require children to alternate between the respective parent's residences every few days, weeks, or months.

While alternating living environments may accompany joint custody decisions, in most instances they do not. In 90 to 95 percent of joint custody awards the living arrangements are exactly the same as those under sole-custody orders, namely, the child physically resides with only one parent. However, both parents make decisions regarding the welfare of the child.

Those who believe joint legal custody is a good idea cite a variety of reasons. They note that sole-custody arrangements, which almost always involve the child living with the mother, weaken father-child relationships. They create enormous burdens for the mothers and tend to exacerbate hostilities between the custodial parent and the "visiting" parent. They continue to perpetuate outmoded sex-role stereotyping. Studies also show that sole-custody arrangements are associated with poverty, antisocial behavior in boys, depression in children, lower academic performance, and juvenile delinquency.

Such arguments assume that by giving fathers the opportunity to be available as nurturers, to be accessible, they will begin to participate more in the lives of their children — furthermore, that such participation will have beneficial effects on children.

Before we too quickly assume that joint custody alleviates problems and produces benefits, we should note that it is far from being a panacea. If couples had trouble communicating and agreeing on things before the divorce, there is no reason to assume that they will have an easier time of it afterward. Most joint-custody orders are vague and do not decide at what point the joint custodial parent's rights end and those of the parent with the day-to-day care of the child begin. What sorts of responsibilities can one parent require of the other parent? Issues such as these can easily erupt into disputes, particularly when a history of dis-agreement and distrust has preceded the joint-custody arrangement.

Joint custody does not give either parent the right to prevail over the other. To solve serious disputes the parents must return to court. In court they must engage in litigation to prove that one or the other is "unfit" — the very process that the original decision of joint custody was to have avoided.

As the number of marriages ending in divorce continues to remain at a high level and laws change in favor of joint custody, this arrangement will become more prevalent. Joint custody appears to work best with those parents who have the capacity, desire, and energy to make it work — and for the children whose characteristics and desires allow them to expend the effort necessary to make it work and to thrive under it.

ALTERNATIVE LIFE-STYLES

Several options are increasingly available to people who, for various reasons, find the traditional form of marriage impractical or incompatible with their life-styles. More young people are selecting cohabitation as a permanent alternative to marriage (although many more consider it as more of a prelude to marriage). In addition, some older men and women are opting to live together in a permanent relationship without getting married. These people choose cohabitation primarily for economic reasons — many would lose sources of income or control of their assets if they entered into a legal marriage. Several other options are discussed below.

THE GROWING SINGLE POPULATION

Americans have traditionally been the marrying kind. In 1985, about 80 percent of the

———————————————————————————————— **TABLE 12.1**

Marital Status of Population by Sex and Age, 1987

Age	*Percent Distribution*							
	Single		*Married*		*Widowed*		*Divorced*	
	M	F	M	F	M	F	M	F
18–19 years	96.8	89.8	3.1	9.9	—	—	—	0.3
20–24 years	77.7	60.8	20.7	36.0	0.1	0.1	1.5	3.2
25–29 years	42.2	28.8	52.3	63.3	—	0.3	5.4	7.6
30–34 years	23.1	14.6	68.8	73.4	0.1	0.8	8.0	11.2
35–39 years	12.4	8.4	76.6	76.7	0.2	1.3	10.9	13.6
40–44 years	6.9	6.4	81.8	76.7	0.5	2.4	10.8	14.5
45–54 years	5.9	4.5	84.1	76.6	1.2	5.8	8.8	13.1
55–64 years	5.8	4.2	84.1	70.1	2.9	16.7	7.3	9.0
65–74 years	4.8	4.8	81.5	53.0	9.0	36.7	4.8	5.5
75 years and over	4.3	6.8	68.8	23.8	23.6	67.0	3.2	2.7

Source: U.S. Department of Commerce. Bureau of the Census, *Current Population Reports.* ser.-P-20, no. 423: *Statistical Abstract of the United States: 1989* (Washington, D.C.: Government Printing Office, 1989, p. 41.

U.S. population age 20 to 54 had been married. Younger people, however, may be rejecting this tradition. In 1970, only 19 percent of the men and 11 percent of the women between the ages of 25 and 29 had never been married. In 1987, 42.2 percent of the men and 28.8 percent of the women that age had never been married (Norton and Moorman, 1987; *Statistical Abstract of the United States: 1989*).

Even though the number of people living alone nearly doubled between 1970 and 1985, this trend may mean only that more young people are postponing marriage. On the other hand, it could mean that a growing proportion of adults are staying single permanently. In fact, as we mentioned earlier in this chapter, there are studies showing that the marriage rate is declining (Rogers and Thornton, 1985).

There are numerous reasons why people are choosing not to marry. Working women do not need the financial security that a traditional marriage brings, and sex outside of marriage has become much more widespread. Moreover, many singles view marriage as merely a prelude to divorce and are unwilling to invest in a relationship that is likely to fail. As sociologist Frank Furstenburg notes: "Men who weren't married by their late 20s in the 60s were oddballs. Now they're just successful 29-year-olds."

Clearly, many singles would gladly change their marital status if the right person came along. But a large group of female baby boomers may never marry. The reality is that there are far more of them than there are available men (*Newsweek,* June 2, 1986). For the post-baby-boom group the reverse is true, and this trend may just be concentrated among a certain segment of the population.

The elderly comprise a significant proportion of the single-person households. Currently 39 percent of one-person households are maintained by persons age 65 or older, and fully 80 percent of them are elderly women. About 6.5 million women age 65 or older live alone, but fewer than 1.6 million men of that age do so. (See Table 12.1 for the percentage of single people in various age categories.)

SINGLE-PARENT FAMILIES

There has been a significant increase in the number of single-parent families in the United States. Today, only 68 percent of children live with both biological parents. Even more dramatic is the proportion of children who will live in a single-parent household sometime during their youth: 42 percent of white children and 86 percent of black children.

Most single-parent families are the result of divorce or separation and, less frequently, the death of a spouse. The increase in the divorce rate is a major reason for the increase in single-parent families. Most divorced parents now set up new households, whereas in earlier times many of them would have returned to their own parents' household.

Some single-parent families arise from illegitimate births, when the mother decides against putting her child up for adoption. In 1986, 23.4 percent of all births involved an unmarried woman. For black women the figure was 61.2 percent *(Statistical Abstract of the United States: 1989)*.

Single parents initially do not intend to change the remaining family relationship radically upon entering their new status, but they soon discover that things cannot be done as before. Single parents do not have the same resources, time, or money that once was available to the family. The children eventually become junior partners in the family and end up having to be much more responsible and independent than before. Outsiders looking at a single-parent family often interpret the behavior that accompanies this status as the result of excessive permissiveness by the single parent.

The parent–child relationship in a single-parent family is often closer than in the traditional nuclear family. A second parent is not available to establish a close relationship with the children. To the single parent, the children are what is left of the previous family. The children become extremely important emotionally to the single parent. Taking care of and raising the children properly often becomes the most important aim. In single-parent families consisting of a mother and daughter, it is common to hear their relationship described as similar to that between two sisters.

This close parent–child relationship can have some negative effects as well. For example, a single parent may become extremely dependent on the relationship. As the child matures, it may be difficult to continue the relationship at its previous level of intensity. Often the parent may begin to feel isolated, and the grown child ends up feeling guilty. However, children usually adjust reasonably well to single-parent situations, and it would be wrong to assume that they are at a marked disadvantage compared with children in two-parent families (Weiss, 1979a).

STEPFAMILIES

It should come as little surprise with the divorce and remarriage rates so high that stepfamilies are becoming a permanent part of the social landscape. Currently, one out of every six children under the age of 18 has a stepparent. By the year 2000, this figure will jump to about one in four. Stepfamilies are changing such businesses as the greeting card industry (we now have birthday wishes to stepmothers and thank-you cards to stepfathers). Schools must now ask for information on stepparents as well as biological parents.

Stepfamilies, also known as blended families, are transforming basic family relationships. Where there were once two sets of grandparents, there now may be four; an only child may obtain siblings when his mother remarries a man with children. Family trees built on stepparent relationships can be very unsettling to children as well as adults (Jarmulski, 1985).

Stepparents are taking on roles formerly held by biological parents. They are staying up nights with the spouse's sick children, attending class recitals, and having heated battles over such essential issues of childhood as curfews, television, homework, and rights to the family car. But in the minds of most children, stepparents can never take the place of their real father or mother—a fact that often leads to intrafamily problems. Studies have shown that it takes at least 4 years for children to accept a stepparent in the same way they do their biological parents. Researcher James H. Bray has noted this acceptance is harder for girls than boys: "Although divorce appears harder on elementary school-age boys, remarriage appears harder on girls" (Kutner, 1988).

At the heart of most stepfamily relationships are children who, like their parents, are casualties of divorce. In the best stepfamily relationship, all the adults work together to meet the needs of the children, realizing that all too often, no matter what they do, there will still be problems. In reality, stepfamilies are torn apart by many of the same pressures that divide intact families. Financial problems can be especially acute when parents must support children from different marriages. Resentment builds quickly when stepparents feel they have little power or authority in their own houses. The most difficult stage is the early years when stepparents want everything to go right. Once stepparents realize that relationships with stepchildren build over time and that their potential network of allies includes all the other adults in the stepfamily relationship, the adjustment for all will be faster and healthier.

COHABITATION

The increasing incidence of couples living together out of wedlock—called *cohabitation*—is a phenomenon that may well have an impact on the American family. Although we have a great deal of information on marriages, we have very little on cohabitation in the United States within the last 15 years, and almost no information about it before that time.

The Census Bureau reports that there were 2.4 million unmarried couples in the United States in 1987. This is four times as

The Census Bureau reports that there were 2.4 million unmarried couples in the U.S. in 1987.

many as there were in 1970 *(Statistical Abstract of the United States: 1989)*. It is possible that the increase in cohabitation figures represents better data collection as much as it represents an increase in couples living together. However, all signs point to a striking increase in cohabitation.

Even though the percentage of cohabiting couples in the total population is relatively small, the proportion of such couples in certain age groups is quite striking. If we look at couples in which the man is under 25, the percentage of cohabitors is 7.4. Although this figure is still considerably lower than that in some countries, such as Sweden, where the cohabitation rate is about 12 percent, it may indicate a trend (Cherlin, 1981).

Clayton and Voss (1977) found that 18 percent of American men had at one time lived with a woman for 6 months or more without being married, although only 5 percent of those men were living with a woman when they were interviewed. Cohabitation was more common among black men than among white and more prevalent among urban residents than among rural. The majority of cohabiting men had been married.

It is unlikely that the increase in cohabitation will continue indefinitely. If it did, cohabitation would start to become more common than marriage. However, now that cohabitation does not produce as much disapproval as it once did, it is likely it will become more common and more visible.

Cohabitation should not be seen as a rejection of traditional marriage. There are a number of characteristics regarding cohabiting couples that are quite different from those of traditionally married couples. First of all, cohabitation is primarily a *childless* life-style. Nearly 70 percent of cohabiting couples in 1985 did not have any children living with them. When cohabitors consider adding children to their unit, they are very reluctant to do so without marriage.

All signs also point to the fact that, for most couples, cohabitation is not a lifetime commitment. Most men in the Clayton and Voss study did *not* plan to marry their present partners and in fact did not do so (Blumstein and Schwartz, 1983).

Gay men and lesbian women form long-term relationships and have problems similar to those of heterosexual couples.

HOMOSEXUAL AND LESBIAN COUPLES

A phenomenon that is not new but one that has become more and more visible is the household consisting of a homosexual or lesbian couple. Before 1970 almost all gay people wished to avoid the risks that would come with a disclosure of their sexual preference.

Traditionally, researchers and the media have concentrated on ways in which gays and lesbians are different from heterosexuals. There has been little attention paid to the fact that gay men and lesbian women form long-term relationships and have problems similar to those of heterosexual couples.

It appears that there have been a number of historical changes in how same-sex couples have interacted. Blumstein and Schwartz (1983) believe that homosexual couples followed the family patterns that were typical of each era. During the 1950s when the traditional gender roles in marriage went unchallenged (husband as provider, wife as homemaker and nurturer), same-sex couples fell into a similar pattern of role playing. The terms *butch* and *femme,* which were part of lesbian terminology, reflected a stringent division between masculine and feminine roles. A *butch* woman was expected to perform male tasks and to be more involved in the couple's financial support, and the *femme* was expected to act along more traditionally feminine lines. Although gay men did not use the same terms, there was also an expectation that one partner would be more masculine and the other more feminine.

Traditional role playing is no longer common in same-sex couples. The women's movement and the reevaluation of gender roles in our society have affected lesbian women and gay men just as much as they have affected heterosexuals. Consequently, the same aspects of challenge and change that heterosexual couples have had to deal with have also had to be confronted by same-sex couples.

One of the primary functions of the family is the control and patterning of reproduction. This function has existed from the beginning of the family unit and continues today — despite what many consider a radically changed reproductive environment. It is no exaggeration to say that thanks to modern technology, reproduction bears a closer resemblance to a "Brave New World" than to the uncomplicated obstetrical practice of Dr. Huxtable on the Cosby Show. Infertile couples can now turn to such techniques as artificial insemination, *in vitro* fertilization, and surrogacy — mothering by contract — to bear a child.

The success of these techniques masks some serious underlying problems that call into question the role the courts should play in reproductive rights and, by extension, in the control of family size. We will focus on surrogacy contracts to see how thorny these issues have become.

On one side are childless couples like William and Elizabeth Stern who desperately want a child they cannot biologically bear. The Sterns contracted with Mary Beth Whitehead, a surrogate mother, to bear William Stern's baby. For a fee of $10,000. She also agreed to give up all parental rights to the new baby.

The Sterns believed that a valid contract was signed and that Mrs. Whitehead understood that she had no rights to the baby she would bear. They also were convinced that it was in the best interests of the baby to have just one mother (Elizabeth Stern) instead of two (Whitehead and Stern). Child psychologist Lee Salk agreed: If contact between the mother and child is not severed, said Salk, there would be "continuing turmoil in the child's life and . . . confusion, disorganization, and pain for the child" (Cadden, 1987). Neither the Sterns nor their lawyer considered surrogacy to be baby selling. Instead, they viewed the $10,000 as payment for services rendered.

Soon after giving birth to a baby, who would eventually become known to the nation as "Baby M," Mary Beth Whitehead changed her mind and refused to give up her parental rights. The case ultimately wound up in court, where the whole concept of surrogacy was placed under a legal microscope. Whitehead charged that surrogacy is nothing more than baby selling — an act already prohibited in adoption cases. She also contended that the surrogacy contract violated her parental rights — rights that were hers to keep unless she was declared unfit.

When the Sterns tried to convince the court that Whitehead was indeed unfit, class issues arose that were far broader than the individual case. Did the fact that the Sterns were a well-educated, upper-middle-class family make them better parents than Whitehead, who was from a working-class background? According to feminist Betty Friedan, this is the implication of the surrogacy agreement. "I think there is a big danger of creating a breeder class" — poor women who produce babies for the rich, said Friedan. Mrs. Whitehead may not be the best mother in the world but, if every woman were subjected to such testing, who among us would pass?" (Cadden, 1987).

In the end, the New Jersey Supreme Court sided with Whitehead, restoring her parental rights, but awarding custody of the baby, now known as Melissa Stern, to William Stern. The court also ruled that the surrogacy contract violated a prohibition against paying money for an adoption. Martha Field, a family law professor at Harvard Law School, believes a surrogate mother has the right to change her mind, just like a mother who is giving up her baby for adoption" (Lewin, 1988).

Many who agree with the court's decision also see the danger in trying to legislate what women do with their bodies. In their view, women's reproductive freedom — including the freedom to act as a surrogate for someone else — must be balanced against the need to avoid baby selling. Compromises that would enable this to happen are already taking place. In Michigan, for example, the law now permits surrogate agreements as long as they do not require the mother to give up her maternal rights.

We are moving into an age where medical technology is far outpacing any rules society may have regulating reproduction.

Sources: Vivian Cadden, "Hard Questions About the Baby M Case," *McCall's,* June 1987, pp. 58–60; Tamor Lewin, "Surrogacy: A Consensus," *New York Times,* September 22, 1988, p. A25.

The desire to form a relationship with another person appears to be quite strong among gays and lesbians. A Kinsey study in the late 1960s found that 71 percent of their sample of gay men between the ages of 36 and 45 were living with a partner. In the 1970s, Bell and Weinberg found that one-fourth of the lesbians in their study stated that being in a permanent relationship was the "most important thing in life," and another 35 percent believed that it was very important. Eighty-two percent of the women they interviewed were living with someone. By and large, gay men and lesbian women who were not in a relationship reported that they had been in one previously and believed that they would be in one again in the future. There is no doubt that "couplehood," as either a reality or an aspiration, is as strong among gay men and lesbian women as it is among heterosexuals (Blumstein and Schwartz, 1983).

THE FUTURE: BRIGHT OR DISMAL?

Given all these changes in the American family, should we be concerned that marriage and family life as we know it will one day disappear? Probably not. The divorce rate is high and will continue to be high into the 1990s. It is important, however, to keep things in perspective. Divorce is just as much a social universal as marriage. In fact, throughout human history only one society is known that did not allow for divorce — the ancient Incas of South America.

In addition, even though the divorce rate is high, the remarriage rate is also very high. The vast majority — about 75 percent — of people who divorce remarry, usually within a short time after they divorce. The high divorce rate does not necessarily mean that people are giving up on marriage. It just means there is a growing belief that marriage can be better. The high remarriage rate

indicates that people are willing to continue trying until they reach their expectations. Obtaining a divorce does not mean that the person believes that the idea of marriage is a mistake — only that a particular marriage was a mistake.

Despite claims to the contrary, there is little evidence that the family as an institution is in decline, or any weaker today than a generation ago. Nor is there any indication that people place less value on their own family relationships, or on the role of the family within society at large, than they once did.

The "traditional" family is being replaced by family arrangements that better suit today's life-styles: there are fewer full-time housewives because more women are in the work force. Nonfamily households have increased from 5 million in 1950 to more than 22 million today. The "typical family" with a working dad, housewife mom, and two or more kids accounts for only 6 percent of all households today (Schwartz, 1987).

The institutions of marriage and the family have proved to be both extremely flexible and durable and have flourished in all human societies under almost every imaginable condition. As we have seen, these institutions take on different forms in different social and economic contexts, and there is no reason to suspect that they will not continue to do so. Therefore, to make predictions about the future of the American family is equivalent to making predictions about the future of American society in particular and industrial society in general. This is extremely difficult to do, given the social, economic, political, and ecological problems facing us. However, for the foreseeable future, it seems reasonable to assume that the forces of industrialism and public policy that helped shape the current nuclear family in its one-parent and two-parent forms will persist. And therefore the contemporary nuclear family will continue to provide the basic context within which American society will reproduce itself for generations to come.

SUMMARY

Although there may be some argument about the definition of the family, most sociologists agree that some form of family is found in all societies and that it serves several basic functions: regulating sexual behavior, patterning reproduction, organizing production and consumption, socializing children, offering care and protection, and providing social status.

The basic family form is the nuclear family: a married couple and their children. There are two major composite family forms: polygamous and extended. Polygamous families are nuclear families linked together by multiple marriage bonds, with one central individual married to several spouses. Polygamous families can be polygynous or polyandrous.

Extended families are nuclear families linked by descent, by sibling ties, or by both.

Marriage is an institution found in all societies. It is the socially recognized, legitimized, and supported union of individuals of opposite sexes. Marriage takes place in a public manner; it includes sexual intercourse as an explicit element of the relationship; it provides the essential condition for legitimizing offspring; and it is intended to be a stable and enduring relationship. In many societies marriage has less to do with romantic love than with the establishment of social, economic, and political relationships among families.

Marriage rules vary from society to society. Almost all societies have two kinds of marriage rules: rules of endogamy, which limit the social categories within which one should marry; and rules of exogamy, the requirement that an individual marry outside his or her culturally defined group. Marriage rules also determine how many spouses a person may have at one time.

Most societies also have norms governing marital residence; these rules play a large role in determining the composition of households.

The modern American family assumed its current form during the Industrial Revolution, and modern American practices of mate selection reflect this new kind of family life. Although we might like to think of marriage and mate selection as being dependent on nothing other than falling in love, in reality it is tied to a variety of less-than-romantic factors: age, race, religion, and social status.

The American family has been undergoing a number of changes. Sociologists have observed a transfer of functions from the family to other, outside institutions. Other trends include changes in the marriage rate, an increase in the number of childless couples, changes in household size, the growing number of working women, a growth in family violence, and an increase in the divorce rate.

Divorce has also undergone change, with the emergence of no-fault divorce and changes in child-custody laws, including joint custody.

Sociologists have also noted the emergence of alternatives to marriage. The single population has been growing rapidly as marriage has become less universal. The number of single-parent families has also increased because of high divorce rates and the many children born out of wedlock. The incidence of cohabitation has grown, as has the number of homosexual and lesbian couples.

The institution of the family has proved to be flexible and durable and has flourished in all human societies under almost every imaginable condition. There is no reason, therefore, to think that the family will not continue to provide the basic context within which American society will carry on.

Chapter 13

RELIGION

THE NATURE OF RELIGION

The Elements of Religion

MAJOR TYPES OF RELIGION

Supernaturalism
Animism
Theism
Abstract Ideals

A SOCIOLOGICAL APPROACH TO RELIGION

The Functions of Religion
The Conflict Theory View

ORGANIZATION OF RELIGIOUS LIFE

The Universal Church
The Ecclesia
The Denomination
The Sect
Millenarian Movements
The Cult

ASPECTS OF AMERICAN RELIGION

Widespread Belief
Secularism
Ecumenism
Television Evangelism

MAJOR RELIGIONS IN THE UNITED STATES

Protestantism
Catholicism
Judaism
Social Correlates of Religious Affiliation

SUMMARY

Through his study of Mayan and Aztec calendars, José Arguelles, an art history teacher in Boulder, Colorado, concluded that during a 2-day period ending August 17, 1987, the Earth would begin to move from one epic age to another. According to Mayan lore, the year 2012 ends an epoch that lasted four centuries. During the final years of the last three epochs, the world was torn apart by a series of catastrophes. The Mayan calendar forecast a 25-year period of disaster for the modern world.

To stave off catastrophe, Arguelles recommended that 144,000 people or more gather at far-flung sites to create "a human-to-human power grid" and marshal their spiritual energies in a "harmonic convergence."

Attempting to ward off global disaster, thousands of believers assembled throughout the world. More than 2000 people crowded into one site in New York's Central Park to hold hands, hum, meditate, and sing 1960s peace songs. In Egypt, a lone figure danced near the pyramids, shouting to camel drivers and tourists alike, "I am God! I am God!" In Memphis, Tennessee, believers gathered for an all-night candlelight service atop a local hotel. Others meditated, held hands, and "resonated" by humming.

The event, however, had been criticized in advance by archaeologists, who maintained that Arguelles's interpretation of the Mayan calendar was flawed, and by astronomers, who claimed that none of the celestial conjunctions that were supposed to occur on August 16 would actually take place.

Apparently unshaken by the criticism, Arguelles that day arose before sunrise and, after extinguishing a fire that had burned all night, blew into a conch shell 144 times (Sullivan, 1987; Barron, 1987).

Such expressions of religion may be difficult to comprehend by those who do not believe or have never experienced them, but they can be studied and understood in relation to the many other ways people experience and practice religion. The important thing to realize is that although religion assumes many different forms, it is a universal human institution. To appreciate the many possible kinds of religious experiences, from the extremely emotional to the quiet meditation of believers in "harmonic convergence," requires an understanding of the nature and functions of religion in human life and society.

THE NATURE OF RELIGION

Religion is recognized as one of society's important institutions. It is a system of beliefs and practices shared by a group of people that helps them explain and function in the present world using the concepts of the supernatural and the sacred.

In his classic study *The Elementary Forms of Religious Life,* first published in 1915, Émile Durkheim observed that all religions divide the universe into two mutually exclusive categories: the profane and the sacred. He wrote, "In all the history of human thought there exists no other example of two categories of things so profoundly differentiated or so radically opposed to one another." By **profane** Durkheim meant all empirically observable things, that is, things that are knowable through common, everyday experiences. In contrast, the **sacred** consists of all things kept separate or apart from everyday experience, things that are awe-inspiring and knowable only through extraordinary experience.

The sacred may consist of almost anything: objects fashioned just for a sacred purpose (like a cross); a geographical location (Mount Sinai); a place constructed for religious observance (a temple); a word or phrase (Our Father, who art in heaven . . ."); or even an animal (the cow to Hindus, for example). To devout Muslims the sabbath, which falls on Friday, is a sacred day of the week. To Hindus the cow is holy, not to be killed or eaten. These are

---

religion A system of beliefs, practices, and philosophical values shared by a group of people that defines the sacred, helps explain life, and provides salvation from the problems of human existence.

profane All empirically observable things that are knowable through ordinary everyday experiences.

sacred Traits or objects that symbolize important values.

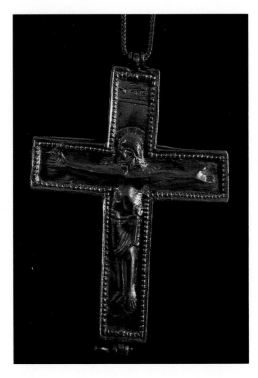

The sacred consists of all things kept separate or apart from everyday experience. Almost anything can be a sacred object.

not ideas to be debated—they simply exist as unchallengeable truths. Similarly, to Christians, Jesus of Nazareth was the Messiah; to Muslims, Jesus was a prophet; but to sociologists, the person of Jesus is a religious symbol. Religious symbols acquire their particular sacred meanings through the religious belief system of which they are a part.

Durkheim believed every society must distinguish between the sacred and the profane. This distinction is essentially between the social and nonsocial. What is considered sacred has the capacity to represent shared values, sentiments, power, or beliefs. The profane is not supported in this manner; it may have utility to one or more individuals, but it has little public relevance.

We may look at Babe Ruth's bat as an example of the transformation of the profane to the sacred. At first it was merely a profane object that had little social value in itself. Today, however, one of Babe Ruth's

bats is enshrined in baseball's Hall of Fame. It is no longer used in a profane way but instead is seen as an object that represents the values, sentiments, power, and beliefs of the baseball community. The bat has gained some of the qualities of a sacred object, thus changing from a private object to a public object.

In addition to sacred symbols and a system of beliefs, religion also includes specific **rituals.** These include patterns of behavior or practices that are related to the sacred. For example, the Christian ritual of Holy Communion is much more than eating wafers and drinking wine. To many participants these objects are the body and blood of Jesus Christ. Similarly, the Sun Dance of the Plains Indians was more than merely a group of braves dancing around a pole to which they were attached by leather thongs that pierced their skin and chest muscles. It was a religious ritual in which the participants were seeking a personal communion.

rituals Patterns of behavior or practices related to the sacred.

THE ELEMENTS OF RELIGION

All the world's religions contain certain shared elements, including ritual and prayer, emotion, belief, and organization.

Ritual and Prayer

All religions have formalized social rituals, but many also feature private rituals such as prayer. Of course, the particular events that make up rituals vary widely from culture to culture and from religion to religion.

All religions include a belief in the existence of beings or forces that are beyond the ability of human beings to experience. In other words, all religions include a belief in the supernatural. Hence, they also provide means for individuals to address or communicate with supernatural beings or forces, typically by speaking aloud while holding the body in a conventionalized posture or making stylized movements or gestures—what in our culture is called **prayer.**

prayer A religious ritual that enables individuals to communicate with supernatural beings or forces.

All religions provide a means for communicating with supernatural beings or forces.

magic Interaction with the supernatural. Magic does not involve the worship of a god or gods, but rather an attempt to coerce spirits or control supernatural forces.

In some societies, magic serves some of the functions of religion, though there are some essential differences between the two. **Magic** is a type of interaction with the supernatural. It differs from other types of religious beliefs in that there is no worship of a god or gods; instead, there is an active attempt to coerce spirits or to control supernatural forces. Magic is used to manipulate and control matters that seem to be beyond human control and that may involve danger and uncertainty. It is usually a means to an end, whereas religion is usually an end in itself, although prayer may be seen as utilitarian when a believer asks for some personal benefit. In most instances, religion serves to unify a group of believers, whereas magic is designed to help the individual who uses it. Bronislaw Malinowski (1954) notes:

> We find magic wherever the elements of chance and accident, and the emotional play between hope and fear have a wide and extensive range. We do not find magic wherever the pursuit is certain, reliable, and well under the control of rational methods.

Stark and Bainbridge (1985) note that a belief in magic has always been a major part of Christian faith. A common theme throughout the centuries has been the effort of organized religion to prohibit unorthodox practices and practitioners and to monopolize magic. Nonchurch magic was identified as "superstition." Serious efforts to root out magic once and for all emerged in the fifteenth century. Eventually, as many as 500,000 people may have been executed for witchcraft. Stark and Bainbridge write:

> In order to monopolize religion, a church must monopolize all access to the supernatural. . . . But if the church is to deny others access to the supernatural, it must remain in the magic business. The demand for magic is too great to be ignored. . . . Thus the Catholic Church remained deeply involved in dispensing magic. Immense numbers of magical rites and procedures were developed. . . . Saints and shrines that performed specialized miracles proliferated, and new procedures for seeking saintly intercession abounded. Many forms of illness, especially mental illness, were defined as cases of possession, and legions of official exorcists appeared to treat them.

Stark and Bainbridge note that magic's respectability has decreased as more scientific attitudes have proliferated. Magic, and especially magical healing, is now found mostly among sectarians and cultists. This fact makes the religious beliefs of sects and cults particularly vulnerable to criticism and refutation (Beckwith, 1986).

Emotion

One of the functions of ritual and prayer is to produce an appropriate emotional state. This may be done in many ways. In some religions, participants in rituals deliberately attempt to alter their state of consciousness through the use of drugs, fasting, sleep deprivation, and induction of physical pain. Scandinavian groups ate mushrooms that caused euphoria, as did many native Siberian tribes. Various American Indian religions feature the use of peyote, a buttonlike mushroom that contains a hallucinogenic drug. And for a while in the late 1960s, a number of countercultural groups in American relied on LSD and other drugs to induce religious experiences.

Although not every religion attempts to induce altered states of consciousness in believers, all religions do recognize that such states may happen and believe that they may be the result of divine or sacred intervention in human affairs. Prophets, of course, receive divine inspiration. Religions differ in the degree of importance they attach to such happenings.

Belief

All religions endorse a belief system that usually includes a supernatural order and often a set of values to be applied to daily life.

Belief systems can vary widely. Some religions believe that a valuable quality can flow from a sacred object—animate or inanimate, part or whole—to a lesser object. Numerous Christian sects, for instance, practice the "laying on of hands," whereby a healer channels "divine energy" into afflicted people and thus heals them. Some Christians also believe in the power of "relics" to work miracles simply because these objects once were associated physically with Jesus or one of the saints. Such beliefs are quite common among the world's religions: Native Australians have their sacred stones, and shamans from among African, Asian, and North American societies heal through sympathetic touching. In some religions the source of the valued quality is a personalized deity. In others it is a reservoir of supernatural force that is tapped.

Members of the St. John Neumann Roman Catholic Church in Lubbock, Texas, are drawn together by the belief that God's spirit is actually present in their worship. In 1988, this belief brought some

One of the functions of ritual and prayer is to produce an appropriate emotional state.

12,000 worshipers to the small church after several parishioners claimed to have received messages from the Virgin Mary. Many of those who came hoped for a miracle that would cure their ills. Others wanted to receive their own messages from Mary, to see visions of Jesus, or to strengthen their faith (Belkin, 1988).

Organization

Many religions have an organizational structure through which specialists can be recruited and trained, religious meetings conducted, and interaction facilitated between society and the members of the religion.

The organization also will promote interaction among the members of the religion in order to foster a sense of unity and group solidarity. Rituals may be performed in the presence of other members. They may be limited to certain locations, such as temples, or they may be processions from one place to another. Although some religious behavior may be carried out by individuals in private, all religions demand some public, shared participation.

MAJOR TYPES OF RELIGION

The earliest available evidence for religious practice comes from the Middle East. In Shanidar Cave in Iraq, archaeologist Ralph Solecki (1971) found remains of burials of Neanderthals — early members of our own species, *Homo sapiens,* once believed to be brutish but now recognized as fully human — dating between 60,000 and 45,000 years ago (see Chapter 3). Bodies were tied in a fetal position, buried on their sides, provided with morsels of food placed at their heads, and covered with red powder and sometimes with flower petals. These practices — the food and the ritual care with which the dead were buried — point to a belief in some kind of existence after death.

Using studies of present-day cultures as well as historical records, sociologists have devised a number of ways to classify religions. One of the simplest and most broadly inclusive schemes recognizes four types of religion: supernaturalism, animism, theism, and abstract ideals.

SUPERNATURALISM

Supernaturalism is a belief system that postulates the existence of supernatural forces that can and often do influence human events. These forces are thought to inhabit animate and inanimate objects alike — people, trees, rocks, places, even spirits or ghosts — and can come and go at will. The Melanesian and Polynesian concept of *mana* is a good example of the belief of an impersonal supernatural power.

Mana is a diffuse, nonpersonalized force that acts through anything that lives or moves, although inanimate objects such as an unusually shaped rock also may possess mana. The proof that a person or thing possesses mana lies in its observable effects. A great chief, merely by virtue of his position of power, must possess mana, as does the oddly shaped stone placed in a garden plot that then unexpectedly yields huge crops. Although it is considered dangerous because of its power, mana is neither harmful nor beneficial in itself, but it sometimes may be used by its possessors for either good or evil purposes. An analogy in our culture might be the scientific phenomenon of nuclear power, which is a natural force that intrinsically is neither good nor evil but can be turned to either end by its possessors. We must not carry the analogy too far, however, because we are able to account for nuclear power according to natural, scientific principles and can predict its effects reliably without resorting to supernatural explanations. A narrower, less comprehensive but more appropriate analogy in Western society is our idea of "luck," which can be good or bad and over which we feel we have very little control.

Although on the one hand certain objects possess mana, taboos may exist in rela-

supernaturalism A belief system that postulates the existence of impersonal forces that can influence human events.

mana A Melanesian and Polynesian concept of the supernatural that refers to a diffuse, nonpersonalized force that acts through anything that lives or moves.

Islamic pilgrims to Mecca must circle the flat-roofed kaaba seven times and, at its east corner, kiss the Black Stone. The Black Stone is said to have been received by Adam when he fell from paradise.

tion to other situations. A **taboo** is a sacred prohibition against touching, mentioning, or looking at certain objects, acts, or people, and violating a taboo results in some form of pollution. Taboos may exist in reference to foods not to be eaten, places not to be entered, objects and people not to be touched, and so on. Even a person who becomes a victim of some misfortune may be accused of having violated a taboo and may also become stigmatized.

Taboos exist in a wide variety of religions. Polynesian peoples believed that their chiefs and noble families were imbued with powerful mana that could be deadly to commoners. Hence, elaborate precautions were taken to prevent physical contact between commoners and nobles. The families of the nobility intermarried (a chief often would marry his own sister), and chiefs actually were carried everywhere to prevent them from touching the ground and thereby killing the crops. Many religions forbid the eating of selected foods. Jews and Muslims have taboos against eating pork at any time, and until fairly recently Catholics were forbidden to eat meat on Fridays. Most cultures forbid sexual relations between parents and children and between siblings (the incest taboo).

Supernatural beings fall into two broad categories: those of nonhuman origin, such as gods and spirits, and those of human origin, such as ghosts and ancestral spirits. Chief among those of nonhuman origin are the gods who are believed to have created themselves and may have created or given birth to other gods. Although gods may create, not all peoples attribute the creation of the world to them.

Many of those gods thought to have participated in creation have retired, so to speak. Having set the world in motion, they no longer take part in day-to-day activities. Other creator gods remain involved in ordinary human activities. Whether or not a society has creator gods, many other affairs are left to lesser gods. For example, the Maori of New Zealand have three important gods, a god of the sea, a god of the forest, and a god of agriculture. They call upon each god for help in the appropriate area.

Below the gods in prestige but often closer to the people are the unnamed spirits. Some of these can offer constructive assistance, and others take pleasure in deliberately working evil on people.

Ghosts and ancestor spirits represent the supernatural beings of human origin. Many cultures believe that everyone has a soul, or several souls, which survive after death. Some of these souls remain near the living and continue to be interested in the welfare of their kin (Ember and Ember, 1981).

ANIMISM

Animism is the belief in animate, personalized spirits or ghosts of ancestors that take an interest in and actively work to influence human affairs. Spirits may inhabit the bodies of people and animals as well as inanimate phenomena, such as winds, rivers, or mountains. They are discrete beings with feelings, motives, and a will of their own. Unlike mana, spirits may be intrinsically good or evil. Although they are powerful, they are not worshiped as gods, and because of their humanlike qualities, they can be manipulated—wheedled, frightened away, or appeased—by using the proper magic rituals. For example, among many Native American and South American Indian societies (as well as many other cultures in the world), sickness is thought to be caused by evil spirits. Shamans, or medicine men or women, are able to effect cures because of their special relationships with these spirits and their knowledge of magic rituals. If the shamans are good at their jobs, they are able to persuade or force the evil spirit to leave the sick person or to discontinue exerting its harmful influence. In our own culture, there are people who consult mediums, spiritualists, and Ouija boards in an effort to contact the spirits and ghosts of departed loved ones.

taboo A sacred prohibition against touching, mentioning, or looking at certain objects, acts, or people.

animism The belief in animate, personalized spirits or ghosts of ancestors that take an interest in and actively work to influence human affairs.

THEISM

People who practice **theism** believe in divine beings—gods and goddesses—who shape human affairs. Gods are powerful beings worthy of being worshiped. Most theistic societies practice **polytheism,** the belief in a number of gods. Each god or goddess usually has particular spheres of influence, such as childbirth, rain, or war, and there is generally one who is more powerful than the rest and oversees the others' activities. In the ancient religions of Mexico, Egypt, and Greece, for instance, we find a host of gods and goddesses, sometimes called a **pantheon.**

Monotheism is the belief in the existence of only one god. Only three religions are known to be monotheistic: Judaism and its two offshoots, Christianity and Islam. Yet these three religions have the greatest number of believers worldwide (see Table 13.1). Even these faiths are not purely monotheistic, however, for they include in their tenets a belief in such divine or semidivine beings as angels, a devil, saints, and the Virgin Mary. Nevertheless, because in all three religions there is such a strong belief in the supremacy of one all-powerful being, they are considered to be monotheistic.

ABSTRACT IDEALS

This type of religion focuses not on a belief in supernatural forces, spirits, or beings but on the **abstract ideals** of correct ways of thinking and behaving. The goal is not to acquire supernatural power, manipulate spirits, or worship gods but to achieve personal awareness, a higher state of being and consciousness, through religious rituals and practices and adherence to moral codes of behavior. Buddhism is an example of a religion based on abstract ideals. The Buddhist's ideal is to become "one with the universe," not through worship or magic, but by meditation and correct behavior.

Despite the profound differences in their basic assumptions, each of these types of human belief systems is recognized as religion because they all share certain basic attributes.

── A SOCIOLOGICAL APPROACH TO RELIGION

When sociologists approach the study of religion, they focus on the relationship between religion and society. The functionalist sociologists have examined the functions religion plays in social life. Conflict theorists, on the other hand, have viewed religion as a means for justifying the political status quo. In the following section we will examine each of these two approaches in detail.

THE FUNCTIONS OF RELIGION

Since at least as early as 60,000 years ago, as indicated by the Neanderthal burials at Shanidar Cave, religion has played a role in all known human societies. The question

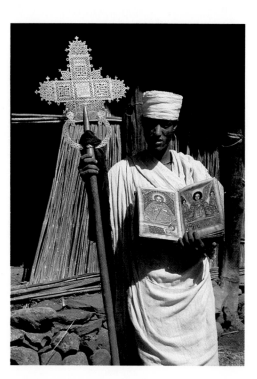

Only three religions are known to be monotheistic: Judaism, Christianity, and Islam.

TABLE 13.1

Estimated Religious Population of the World

Religions	Africa	East Asia	Europe	Latin America	Northern America	Oceania	South Asia	U.S.S.R.	World	Percent
Christians	271,035,700	78,100,000	413,920,700	399,554,500	232,048,400	21,287,100	129,076,700	103,373,400	1,644,396,500	32.9
Roman Catholic	102,522,200	9,204,000	257,155,000	371,863,600	91,209,800	7,434,000	81,694,100	5,111,900	926,194,600	18.5
Protestants	71,883,000	32,100,000	76,652,000	13,960,000	94,965,500	7,510,000	26,142,100	8,803,800	332,016,400	6.6
Orthodox	24,746,700	81,000	35,606,100	570,000	5,910,000	507,400	3,200,000	89,442,300	160,063,500	3.2
Anglicans	22,389,900	334,000	32,886,200	1,210,000	7,511,000	5,350,000	290,000	400	69,971,500	1.4
Other	49,493,900	36,381,000	11,621,400	7,950,900	32,452,100	485,700	17,750,500	15,000	156,150,500	3.1
Muslims	245,110,500	23,795,000	8,901,500	645,000	2,682,600	96,000	547,350,500	31,807,200	860,388,000	17.2
Nonreligious	1,495,000	641,756,600	50,923,940	13,237,000	21,047,700	2,884,400	20,651,100	84,332,030	836,327,770	16.7
Hindus	1,410,000	10,100	590,000	880,000	810,000	295,000	651,918,900	1,200	655,695,200	13.1
Buddhists	12,800	154,796,300	216,000	490,000	190,000	16,000	153,585,000	320,000	309,626,100	6.2
Atheists	240,000	136,886,000	17,803,000	2,538,000	1,073,000	512,000	5,300,000	60,774,500	225,126,500	4.5
Chinese folk religionists	9,500	179,103,100	49,000	60,000	110,000	16,000	8,169,400	100	187,517,100	3.7
New religionists	13,000	42,217,200	34,000	370,000	1,075,600	6,100	66,990,000	200	110,706,100	2.2
Tribal religionists	66,219,450	730,000	100	1,160,000	60,000	81,100	24,508,200	0	94,758,750	1.9
Jews	257,000	1,800	1,483,600	990,000	8,064,000	86,000	4,050,000	3,123,000	18,075,400	0.4
Sikhs	26,000	1,000	215,000	6,000	9,500	6,800	16,340,000	50	16,604,150	0.3
Shamanists	1,000	12,500,000	400	400	200	200	10,000	250,000	12,762,200	0.2
Confucians	500	5,900,000	1,000	500	10,000	200	2,000	200	5,914,400	0.2
Baha'is	1,265,000	48,400	70,500	570,000	310,000	59,000	2,300,000	5,000	4,627,900	0.1
Jains	47,500	500	9,900	2,000	2,000	900	3,400,000	20	3,462,820	0.1
Shintoists	50	3,400,000	360	800	1,000	500	200	100	3,403,010	0.1
Other religionists	65,000	62,000	310,000	6,768,800	750,000	25,000	230,000	6,000	8,216,800	0.1
World Pop.	589,206,000	1,279,308,000	494,529,000	423,053,000	268,264,000	26,372,000	1,633,882,000	283,893,000	4,997,609,000	100.0

Source: The 1988 Encyclopedia Britannica Book of the Year (Chicago: Encyclopedia Britannica, Inc., 1988), p. 303.

WOMAN OF THE CLOTH

Twelve years ago when Rev. Shirley Hoover was ordained, there were 400 women ministers in Methodist churches across the country. Today there are 4000. Even though her position within the church is becoming less unusual, she must still contend with stereotypes and preconceived ideas. The following interview with Rev. Hoover gives us an insight into what it is like to be a woman minister.

Rev. Hoover, mother of three, grandmother of two, has a down-to-earth approach to her spiritually lofty job. "There are days," says Hoover, speaking of her congregation, "I despair that either I'm not saying it right or they're not listening. But there are other days when the job has rewards like no other. Every once in a while," she says, "there's that golden moment when you realize you're the chosen instrument to transform somebody's life."

It was lonely and stressful being among the first women to break down the gender barriers in the pulpit. Hoover remembers her first pastorate. "Initially I was met with uncertainty and sometimes downright opposition," she said. "There was a time when the initial reaction to me was, 'I never saw a woman do that before.' But the world has changed." Hoover said, "And congregations are now more receptive."

Although a woman first graduated from a seminary in 1850, until the 1970s there were few studying for the ministry. However, between 1972 and 1981, the overall number of women enrolling in degree programs increased 340 percent — 13 times the percentage increase for men.

Recent studies set the share of women in professional degree programs in seminaries at 25 percent nationwide, and a full 19 percent of Master of Divinity students (the program leading to ordination) are women.

While the seminaries are increasingly opening their doors to women, society at large still is a bit uncomfortable with the idea of a woman in the pulpit. Women seeking a job in the ministry may find there is both acknowledged and unacknowledged resistance to them.

Some women thrive on the challenge, and some do not. Even when they have a congregation of their own, their battles are far from over. They must deal with stereotypes, such as one woman who had a hard time convincing a lay board that she could deal with finances.

In the Methodist church it is the responsibility of the bishop and his aides to assign pastors to churches, unlike the other denominations, where individual churches recruit candidates for the job. The Rev. Caroline Edge, district superintendent for the Methodist church's Southern New England Conference, works with the bishop to match churches with pastors. "Sometimes," she says, "when I propose a woman candidate for a pastorate, officials of the local church are skeptical. Often they ask, 'Can a woman really do it?' They never say that about a man."

Pockets of resistance do still exist, sometimes in surprising quarters. "There may be a power struggle with lay women in the congregation who have learned how to operate in a male structure and feel toppled with a female in the ministry," Edge noted.

There is also surprising support from other quarters. When she had her own church, Edge found that older women would whisper to her that she was doing what they could only dream of.

The Revs. Hoover and Edge are changing the face of the Methodist ministry, and they hope that their input will help humanize the profession.

Source: Linda Tischler, "Women of the Cloth," *Boston Herald,* March 23, 1988, pp. 33, 35.

that interests us here is, What universal functions does religion have? Sociologists have identified four categories of religious function: satisfying individual needs, promoting social cohesion, providing a world view, and acting as a form of social control.

Satisfying Individual Needs

Religion offers individuals ways to reduce anxiety and to promote emotional integration.

Although Sigmund Freud (1918, 1928) thought religion to be irrational, he saw it as helpful to the individual in coming to terms with impulses that induce guilt and anxiety. Freud argued that a belief in law-giving, powerful deities can help people reduce their anxieties by providing strong, socially reinforced inducements for controlling dangerous or "immoral" impulses.

Further, in times of stress, individuals can calm themselves by appealing to deities for guidance or even for outright help, or they can calm their fears by "trusting in God." In the face of so many things that are beyond human control and yet may drastically affect human fortunes (such as droughts, floods, or other natural disasters), life can be terrifying. It is comforting to "know" the supernatural causes of both good fortune and bad. Perhaps this is why former First Lady Nancy Reagan appealed to astrology — the belief that the position of the planets determines human fate — to plan her husband's schedule when he was president. Mrs. Reagan's belief in astrology became particularly intense following the attempted assassination of her husband in March 1981. By following the astrological charts, Mrs. Reagan was expressing concern for her husband's welfare and attempting to control the outcome of his activities (Sperling, 1988).

Another very different example occurs each year in the state of Orissa in India, where people walk barefoot through a trench filled with glowing coals. This tests their faith in the power of Kali (the mother goddess) to protect them, and their success in accomplishing this feat unharmed proves the active and protective role played by Kali in the villagers' daily lives (Freeman, 1974).

Some people attempt to control supernatural forces through magical ritual practices. Such attempts at magic should not be compared with rational thought or empirical investigation. Rather, they are two separate spheres of human thought and expression.

Social Cohesion

Émile Durkheim, one of the earliest functional theorists, noted the ability of religion to bring about group unity and cohesion. According to Durkheim, all societies have a continuing need to reaffirm and uphold their basic sentiments and values. This is accomplished when people come together and communally proclaim their acceptance of the dominant belief system. In this way people are bound to one another, and as a result, the stability of the society is strengthened.

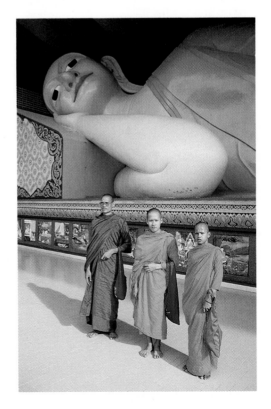

Émile Durkheim believed that when people recognize or worship supernatural entities, they are really worshipping their own society.

Not only does religion in itself bring about social cohesion, but often the hostility and prejudice directed at its members by outsiders helps strengthen their bonds. For example, during the 1820s, Joseph Smith, a young farmer from Vermont, claimed that he had received visits from heavenly beings that enabled him to produce a 600-page history of the ancient inhabitants of the Americas, known as the Book of Mormon. Shortly after the establishment of the Mormon church, Smith had a revelation that "Zion," the place where the Mormons would prepare for the millennium, was to be established in Jackson County, Missouri. Within two years, 1200 Mormons had bought land and settled in Jackson County. The other residents in this area became concerned about the influx and in 1833 published their grievances in a document that became known as the "manifesto," or secret constitution. They charged the Mormons with a variety of transgressions and pledged to remove them from Jackson County. Several episodes of conflict fol-

lowed that eventually forced the Mormons to move into an adjoining county. These encounters with a hostile environment produced a sense of collective identity at a time when it was desperately needed. Their church was less than 2 years old and included individuals from diverse religious backgrounds. There was a great deal of internal discord, and if it had not been for the unity that resulted from the conflict with the townspeople, the group might have disappeared altogether (MacMurray and Cunningham, 1973).

Durkheim's interest in the role of religion in society was aroused by his observation that religion, like the family, seemed to be a universal human institution. This universality meant that religion must serve a vital function in maintaining the social order. Durkheim felt that he could best understand the social role of religion by studying one of the simplest kinds — the totemism of the aboriginal Australian. A **totem** is an ordinary object such as a plant or animal that has become a sacred symbol to

totem An ordinary object such as a plant or animal that has become a sacred symbol to a particular group that not only reveres the totem but identifies with it.

Religious rituals fulfill a number of social functions. They bring people together physically, promoting social cohesion, and reaffirm a group's beliefs and values.

a particular group or clan, such as the aborigines, who not only revere the totem but also identify with it. Thus, reasoned Durkheim, religious symbols such as totems, as well as religion itself, arose from society itself, not outside it. When people recognize or worship supernatural entities, they are really worshiping their own society. They do not realize their religious feelings are actually the result (a crowd reaction) of the intense emotions aroused when people gather together at a clan meeting, for example. They look for an outside source of this emotional excitement and may settle on a nearby, familiar object as the symbol of both their religion and their society. Thus society — the clan — is the origin of the clan members' shared religious beliefs, which in turn help cement together their society.

Durkheim sees religious ritual as an important part of this "social cement." Religion, through its rituals, fulfills a number of social functions: It brings people together physically, promoting social cohesion; it reaffirms the group's beliefs and values; it helps maintain norms, mores, and prohibitions so that violation of a secular law — murder or incest, for instance — is also a violation of the religious code and may warrant ritual punishment or purification; it transmits a group's cultural heritage from one generation to the next; and it offers emotional support to individuals during times of stress and at important stages in their life cycle, such as puberty, marriage, and death (see Figure 13.1).

In Durkheim's view, these functions are so important that even a society that lacks the idea of the sacred must substitute some system of shared beliefs and rituals. Indeed, some theorists see communism as such a system. Soviet communism has its texts and prophets (Marx, Engels), its shrines (Lenin's tomb), its rituals (May Day parade), and its unique moral code. Durkheim thought that much of the social upheaval of his day could be attributed to the fact that religion and ritual no longer played an important part in people's lives, and without a shared belief system, the social order was breaking down.

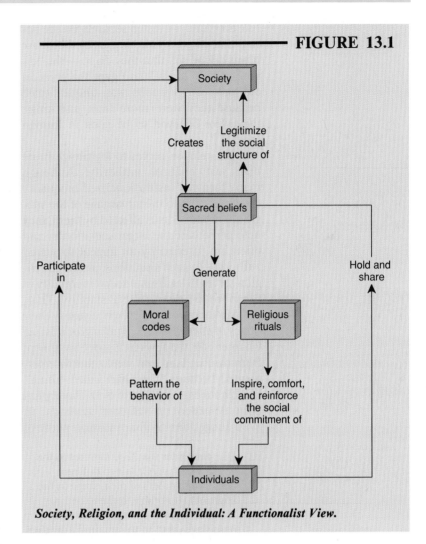

FIGURE 13.1

Society, Religion, and the Individual: A Functionalist View.

Although many sociologists today take issue with Durkheim's explanation of the origins of religion based on totemism, they nevertheless recognize the value of his functional approach in understanding the vital role of religion in society.

Secular society depends on external rewards and pressures for results, whereas religion depends on the internal acceptance of a moral value structure. Durkheim believed that because religion is effective in bringing about adherence to social norms, society usually presents these as an expression of a divine order. For example, in ancient China, as in France until the late eighteenth century, political authority — the right to rule absolutely—rested securely on the notion that emperors and kings ruled because it was divine will that they do so—the "divine right of kings." In Egypt the political authority of pharaohs was unquestioned because they were more than just kings; they were believed to be gods in human form.

But religion serves to legitimize more than just political authority. Although many forms of institutionalized inequality do not operate to the advantage of the subgroups or individuals affected by them, they help perpetuate the larger social order and often are justified by an appeal to sacred authority. In such situations, although religion serves to legitimate social inequality, it functions to sustain societal stability. Thus, the Afrikaners of South Africa justify their policy of *apartheid* on religious grounds (see Chapter 10); the Jews in Europe were kept from owning land and were otherwise persecuted because "they had killed Christ" (Trachtenberg, 1961); and even slavery has been defended on religious grounds. In 1700 Judge John Saffin of Boston wrote of

> . . . the Order that God hath set in the world, who hath Ordained different degrees and orders of men, some to the High and Honorable, some to be Low and Despicable . . . yea, some to be born slaves, and so to remain during their lives, as hath been proved. (Montagu, 1964a)

Religions do not *always* legitimize secular authority. In feudal Europe the church had its own political structure, and there often was tension between church and state. Indeed, just as the church often legitimized monarchs, it also excommunicated those who failed to take its wishes into account. However, the fact remains that religious institutions usually do dovetail quite neatly with other social institutions, legitimizing and helping sustain them. For example, though church and state in medieval Europe were separate structures and often conflicted, the church nonetheless played an important role in supporting the entire feudal system.

Establishing World Views

According to Max Weber in his classic book *The Protestant Ethic and the Spirit of Capitalism,* religion responds to the basic human need to understand the purpose of life. In doing so, religion must give meaning to the social world within which life takes place. This means creating a world view that can have social, political, and economic consequences. For instance, there is the issue of whether salvation can be achieved through active mastery (hard work, for example) or through passive contemplation (meditation). The first can be seen in Calvinism, and the second approach is evident in several of the Eastern religions. Another major issue in creating a world view is whether salvation means concentrating on a supernatural world, this world, or an inner world.

Using these ideas, Weber theorized that Calvinism fostered the Protestant ethic of hard work and asceticism and that Protestantism was an important influence on the development of capitalism. Calvinism is rooted in the concept of predestination, which holds that before they are born, certain people are selected for heaven and others for hell. Nothing anyone does in this world can change this. The Calvinists consequently were anxious to find out whether they were among those chosen for salvation. Worldly success, especially the financial success that grew out of strict discipline, hard work, and self-control, was seen as proof that a person was among the select few. Money was accumulated not to be spent but to be displayed as proof of one's chosenness. Capitalist virtues became Calvinist virtues. It was Weber's view that even though capitalism existed before Calvinist influence, it really blossomed only with the advent of Calvinism.

Weber's analysis has been criticized from many standpoints. Calvinist doctrines were not so uniform as Weber pictured them, nor was the work ethic confined to the Protestant value system. Rather, it seems to have been characteristic of the times, promoted by Catholics as well as

Protestants. Finally, one could just as well argue the reverse, that the social and economic changes leading to the rise of industrialism and capitalism stimulated the emergence of the new Protestantism—a position that Marxist analysts have taken. Today it is generally agreed that although religious beliefs did indeed affect economic behavior, the tenets of Protestantism and capitalism tended to support each other. However, the lasting value of Weber's work is his demonstration of how religion creates and legitimizes world views and how important these views are to human social and political life.

Adaptations to Society

Religion can also be seen as having adaptive consequences for the society in which it exists. For example, many would view the Hindu belief in the sacred cow, which may not be slaughtered, as a strange and not particularly adaptive belief. The cows are permitted to wander around freely and defecate along public paths.

Marvin Harris (1966) has suggested that there may be some beneficial economic consequences in India from not slaughtering cattle. The cows and their offspring provide a number of resources that could not easily be provided in other ways. For example, a team of oxen is essential to India's many small farms. Oxen could be produced with fewer cows, but food production would have to be devoted to feeding those cows. With the huge supply of sacred cows, although they are not well fed, the oxen are produced at no cost to the economy.

Cow dung is also necessary in India for cooking and as a fertilizer. It is estimated that dung equivalent to 45 million tons of coal is burned annually. Alternative sources of fuel, such as wood or oil, are scarce or costly.

Although the Hindus do not eat beef, those cattle that die naturally or are slaughtered by non-Hindus are eaten by the lower castes. Without the Hindu taboo against eating beef, these other members of the In-dian hierarchy would not have access to this food supply. Therefore, because the sacred cows do not compete with people for limited resources and because they provide a cheap source of labor, fuel, and fertilizer, the taboo against slaughtering cattle may be quite adaptive.

When societies are under great stress or attack, their members sometimes fall into a state of despair analogous, perhaps, to a person who becomes depressed. Institutions lose their meaning for people, and the society is threatened with what Durkheim called *anomie,* or "normlessness." If this continues, the social structure may break down, and the society may be absorbed by another society, unless the culture can regenerate itself. Under these conditions there sometimes emerge powerful religious movements that stress the need to return to the "good old values" of the previous, "uncorrupted" tradition. Sociologists call such developments religious **revitalization movements,** and many of them can be found in the pages of history and even are in existence today.

In the 1880s, the once free and proud Plains Indians lived in misery, crowded onto barren reservations by soldiers of the United States government. Cheated out of the pitiful rations that had been promised them, they lived in hunger—and with memories of the past. Then a Paiute by the name of Wovoka had a vision, and he traveled from tribe to tribe to spread the word and demonstrate his Ghost Dance. Give up fighting he told the people. "Give up all things of the white man. Give up guns, give up European clothing, give up alcohol, give up all trade goods. Return to the simple life of the ancestors. Live simply—and dance! Once the Indian people are pure again, the Great Spirit will come, all Indian ancestors will return, and all the game will return. A big flood will come, and after it is gone, only Indians will be left in this good time."

Wovoka's Ghost Dance spread among the defeated tribes. From the Great Plains to California, Indian communities took up the slow, trancelike dance. Some believed that the return of the ancestors would lead to the

revitalization movement Powerful religious movements that stress a return to the religious values of the past. These movements spring up when a society is under great stress or attack.

slaughter of all whites. For others, the dance just rekindled pride in their heritage. But for whatever reasons, the Ghost Dance could not be contained, despite the government soldiers' attempts to ban it.

On December 28, 1890, the people of a Sioux village camped under federal guard at Wounded Knee, South Dakota, and began to dance. They ignored orders to stop and continued to dance until suddenly someone fired a shot. The soldiers opened fire, and soon more than 200 of the original 350 men, women, and children were killed. The soldiers' losses were 29 dead and 33 wounded, mostly from their own bullets and shrapnel. This slaughter was the last battle between the Indians of the Plains and the soldiers of the dominant Anglo society (Brown, 1971).

THE CONFLICT THEORY VIEW

Karl Marx argued that "the ruling ideas of each age have always been the ideas of the ruling class" (Marx and Engels, 1961), and from this it was a small step to his claim that the dominant religion of a society is that of the dominant class, an observation that has been borne out by historical evidence. Marxist scholars emphasize religion's role in justifying the political status quo, by cloaking political authority with sacred legitimacy and thereby making opposition to it seem immoral.

The concept of alienation is an important part of Marx's thinking, especially in his ideas of the origin and functions of religion. **Alienation** is the process by which people lose control over the social institutions they themselves have invented; they then begin to believe that these institutions are separate from themselves, a part of the outside world that they are powerless to change. People begin to feel like strangers — aliens — in their own world. Marx further believed that religion is one of the most alienating influences in human society, affecting all other social institutions and contributing to a totally alienated world.

alienation The process by which people lose control over the social institutions they themselves have invented.

According to Marx, "Man makes religion, religion does not make man" (Marx, 1967). The function of God thus was invented to serve as the model of an ideal human being. People soon lost sight of this fact, however, and began to worship and fear the ideal they had created as if it were a separate, powerful supernatural entity. Thus religion, because of the fear people feel for the nonexistent god they themselves have created, serves to alienate people from the real world.

Marx saw religion as the tool that the upper classes used to maintain control of society and to dominate the lower classes. In fact, he referred to it as "the opiate of the masses," believing that through religion, the masses were kept from actions that might change their relationship with those in power. The lower classes were distracted from taking steps for social change by the promise of happiness through religion — if they followed the rules established by religion, they would receive their reward in heaven, and so they had no reason to try to change or improve their condition in this world. These religious beliefs made it easy for the ruling classes to continue to exploit the lower classes: religion served to legitimize upper-class power and authority. Although modern political and social thinkers do not accept all of Marx's ideas, they recognize his contribution to the understanding of the social functions of religion.

Although religion performs some vital functions in society — helping maintain social cohesion and control while satisfying the individual's need for emotional comfort, reassurance, and a world view — it also has negative, or dysfunctional, aspects.

Karl Marx would be quick to point out a major dysfunction of religion: through its ability to make it seem that the existing social order is the only conceivable and acceptable way of life, religion obscures the fact that people construct society and therefore can change society. Religion, by imposing the acceptance of supernatural causes of conditions and events, tends to conceal the natural and human causes of social problems in the world. In fact, in its role of justifying, or legitimizing the status quo, religion may very well hinder much-needed changes in the social structure. By diverting attention from injustices in the existing social order, religion discourages the individual from taking steps to correct these conditions.

An even more basic and subtle dysfunction of religion is its insistence that only one body of knowledge and only one way of thinking are sacred and correct, thereby limiting independent thinking and the search for further knowledge.

ORGANIZATION OF RELIGIOUS LIFE

Several forms or types of organization of religious groups are found in society.

THE UNIVERSAL CHURCH

A **universal church** includes all the members of a society within one united moral community (Yinger, 1970). It is fully a part of the social, political, and economic status quo and therefore accepts and supports (more or less) the secular culture. In preliterate society, in which religion is not really a differentiated institution but rather permeates the entire fabric of social life, a person belongs to the church simply by being a member of the society. In more complex societies, this religious form cuts across divisions of the social structure, such as social classes and ethnic groups, binding all believers into one moral community. A universal church, however, does not seek to change any conditions of social inequality created by the secular society and culture, and indeed, it may even legitimize them. (An example is the Hindu religion of India, which perpetuates a rigid caste system.)

THE ECCLESIA

Like the universal church, an **ecclesia** extends itself to all members of a society.

In the U.S., Lutheranism, Methodism, Catholicism, and Judaism each embodies the characteristics of a denomination.

However, it has so completely adjusted its ethical system to the political structure of the secular society that it has come to represent and promote the interests of the ruling classes. In this process the ecclesia loses adherents among the lower social classes, who increasingly reject it for membership in sects, be these sacred or "civil" (Yinger, 1970). The Russian Orthodox church, for example, must be seen as an ecclesia. With the rise of political and religious turmoil in Russia early in this century, the church tied itself firmly to the interests of the czar and the aristocracy. Along with them it was crushed and dispersed by the 1917 Bolshevik revolution.

THE DENOMINATION

A **denomination** tends to limit its membership to a particular class, ethnic group, or regional group, or at least to have its leadership positions dominated by members of such a group. It has no official or unofficial connection with the state, and any political

universal church A church that includes all the members of a society within one united moral community.

ecclesia A church that shares the same ethical system as the secular society and that has come to represent and promote the interests of the society at large.

denomination A religious group that tends to limit its membership to a particular "socially acceptable" class, or ethnic group, or at least to have its leadership positions dominated by members of such a group.

involvement is purely a matter of choice by the denomination's leaders, who may either support or oppose any or all of the state's actions and political positions. Denominations do not withdraw themselves from the secular society. Rather, they participate actively in secular affairs and also tend to cooperate with other religious groups. These two characteristics distinguish them from sects, which are separatist and unlikely to be tolerant of other religious persuasions (Yinger, 1970). (For that matter, universal churches, by their very nature, also typically dismiss other religions.) In America, Lutheranism, Methodism, other Protestant groups, Catholicism, and Judaism embody the characteristics of a denomination.

THE SECT

A **sect** is a rather small group that adheres quite strictly to religious doctrine that often includes unconventional beliefs or forms of worship. Sects generally represent a withdrawal from secular society and an active *rejection* of secular culture (Yinger, 1970). For example, the Dead Sea Scrolls show clearly that the beliefs of both early Christian and Jewish sects, such as the Essenes, were rooted in disgust with society's self-indulgent pursuit of worldly pleasures and rejection of the corruption perceived in the prevailing religious hierarchy (Wilson, 1969).

Early in their development, sects often are so harsh in their rejection of society that they invite persecution. Some actually thrive on martyrdom, which causes members to intensify their fervent commitment to the faith. (Consider, for example, the Christian martyrs in Rome before the conversion to Christianity of the Emperor Constantine.)

MILLENARIAN MOVEMENTS

Throughout human history in times of stress, religious leaders have emerged, fore-

telling the end of the world, the destruction of all evil people and their works, and the saving of the just, who must stop whatever they are doing to follow the bearers of the "message." Because these teachings prophesy the end of an era — often represented by the symbolic number of 1000 years — sociologists call such religious phenomena **millenarian movements.**

In the early 1950s, in the midwestern town of Lake City (a fictitious name), several people formed a group around a middle-aged woman named Mrs. Keech. This woman, who had the remarkable ability to "tune in" to communication from extraterrestrial beings, had recently received an urgent message: on December 21, 1955, the Earth would be destroyed, and only the "elect" would be taken aboard a spacecraft and saved.

Mrs. Keech and her followers were told that Earth had actually been populated by refugees from the plant Car, which had been blown to pieces when "scientists" under the leadership of Lucifer ineptly lost control of the atomic weapons they had built to fight the "people who followed the light" in the service of God under the leadership of Jesus Christ. After that cosmic disaster, Lucifer led his legions to Earth, and the "forces of light" rebuilt their civilization on other planets. Human beings, because they had lost their "cosmic knowledge," were intent on following the scientists and Lucifer — and hence were doomed to destruction.

On the night of December 21, the faithful gathered around Mrs. Keech, took off all their jewelry, ripped zippers from pants and hooks from bras (metal could not be worn on space journeys), and waited for their saviors. When the ships failed to come, Mrs. Keech received a message setting a new date for the Reckoning. But most of the followers became disheartened, and the group slowly drifted apart (Festinger, Rieken, and Schachter, 1956).

How can we understand Mrs. Keech's group? Although on television it is much in style to portray the 1950s as "happy days," this was hardly the case. Less than a decade

---

millenarian movements Religious movements that prophesy the end of the world, the destruction of all evil people and their works, and the saving of the just.

sect A small religious group that adheres strictly to religious doctrine involving unconventional beliefs or forms of worship.

DESTRUCTIVE RELIGIOUS CULTS

Some contemporary religious cults have been referred to as destructive cults because of the effect they have on their members. According to Steve Hassan, a former cult member and person who helps people leave such cults, destructive religious cults have the following characteristics:

1. The Doctrine is reality. The doctrine is the TRUTH, it is perfect and absolute. Any flaw in it is viewed as a reflection of the believer's own imperfection. The doctrine becomes a master program for all thoughts, feelings, and actions.

2. Reality is presented in simple polar terms. Cult doctrines reduce reality into two basic poles: black versus white; good versus evil; spiritual world versus physical world; us versus them. The cult recognizes no outside group as having any validity because that would threaten the cult's monopoly on the truth.

3. Elitist mentality. Members are made to feel part of an elite group. They consider themselves better, more knowledgeable, and more powerful than anyone else. This carries a heavy burden of responsibility, however, because if members are told they are not fully performing their duty, they are made to feel they are failures.

4. Group goals over individual goals. The self must be subordinated to the will of the group. Absolute obedience to superiors is a common theme in many cults. Conformity to the group is good.

5. Continued acceptance depends on good performance. One of the most attractive qualities of a cult is its sense of community. But to remain part of this community the cult member learns that he or she must meet group goals, whether they be in the area of recruitment, collecting money, allegiance to the leader, or proper behavior.

6. Manipulation through fear and guilt. The cult member lives within a narrow corridor of fear, guilt, and shame. Problems are due to the member's weakness, lack of understanding, evil spirits, and so forth. The cult member constantly feels guilty for not being "good" enough. The devil is always lurking just around the corner waiting to tempt or seduce the cult member.

7. Changes in time orientation. The past, present, and future are seen in a different light. The cult member looks back on his past life in a distorted way and sees it as totally negative. The present is marked by a sense of urgency in terms of the work that needs to be done. The future is a time when you will be either rewarded or punished for what you have done to help the cause.

8. No legitimate reason for leaving. The cult does not recognize a person's right to choose to move on. Members are made to believe that the only reason people leave is because of weakness, insanity, brainwashing (deprogramming), pride, or sin. The cult stresses that if a member leaves, terrible things will happen to themselves, their families, or the world.

Source: Steven Hassan, *Combatting Cult Mind Control* (Rochester, Vt.: Park Street Press, 1988).

---

earlier, America had dropped two atomic bombs on cities in Japan—and from then on, the world lived with the real possibility of the extermination of all human life through nuclear warfare. The 1950s brought their own age of anxiety: the Berlin blockade, the Soviet development of their own atomic bomb, and the Korean War.

THE CULT

Although a sect often develops in response to a rejection of certain religious doctrine or ritual within the larger religious organization, a **cult** usually introduces totally new religious ideas and principles. Cults generally have charismatic leaders who expect

cult A religious movement that often introduces totally new religious ideas and principles, and involves an intense sense of mission. Cults usually have charismatic leaders who expect a total commitment from the cult members.

total commitment. Members of cults, who are usually motivated by an intense sense of mission, often must give up individual autonomy and decision making. Many cults require resocialization practices so strong as to make the member seem unrecognizable in personality and behavior to former friends and relatives. Included among the best known contemporary religious cults are the Unification Church, the Church of Scientology, Church Universal and Triumphant, and The Way International.

Because the activities and excesses of some cults have taken over the headlines in recent years, we may tend to forget or even dismiss the fact that many major religions began as cults and sects. (See the "Taking the Sociological Perspective" box for a discussion of destructive religious cults.)

ASPECTS OF AMERICAN RELIGION

The Pilgrims of 1620 sought to build a sanctuary where they would be free from religious persecution, and the Puritans who followed 10 years later intended to build a community embodying all the virtues of pure Protestantism, a community that would serve as a moral guide to others. Thus religion pervaded the social and political goals of the early English-speaking settlers and played a major role in shaping the nature of colonial society. Today the three main themes that characterize religion in America are widespread belief, secularism, and ecumenism.

WIDESPREAD BELIEF

Americans generally take religion for granted. Although they differ widely in religious affiliation and degree of church attendance, almost all Americans claim to believe in God. Nine out of every ten Amer-

icans have a religious preference, even if they maintain no formal church affiliation, and four out of every ten American adults attend either church or synagogue each week.

Evidence as to whether America is experiencing a "religious revival," as some have claimed, is contradictory. When asked if they feel they have a personal relationship with God, 82 percent of Catholics, 86 percent of Protestants, and 97 percent of Evangelicals respond yes (Gallup and Castelli, 1987). Church attendance, however, has declined. In 1960, 47 percent of the people questioned said they had attended a church or synagogue during the week before they were polled. This figure dropped to 42 percent in 1985. By and large, and despite dire warnings of the erosion of religiosity because of new ways of thinking and innovative life-styles, most Americans still seem to believe in and practice various forms of religion.

More than half of all religiously affiliated individuals belong to a Protestant denomination, clearly reflecting America's colonial history (see Table 13.2). But other denominations are also well represented, especially Catholicism and Judaism. There are well over 200 formally chartered religious organizations in America today. Such pluralism is not typical of other societies and has resulted primarily from the waves of European immigrants who began to arrive in the postcolonial era. Americans' traditional tolerance of religious diversity can be seen also as a reflection of the constitutional separation of church and state, so that in theory no one religion is recognized officially as better or more acceptable than any other.

SECULARISM

Many scholars have noted that modern society is becoming increasingly **secularized,** which means that religious institutions are being confined to ever-narrowing spheres of social influence, while people turn to secu-

secularization The process by which religious institutions are confined to ever-narrowing spheres of social influence, while people turn to secular sources for moral guidance in their everyday lives.

lar sources for moral guidance in their everyday lives (Berger, 1967). This shift is reflected in the reactions of Americans, who, for the most part, are notoriously indifferent to, and ignorant of, the basic doctrines of their faiths. Stark and Glock (1968) report that a poll of Americans found that 67 percent of Protestants and 40 percent of Catholics could not correctly identify Father, Son, and Holy Spirit as constituting the Holy Trinity; 79 percent of Protestants and 86 percent of Catholics could not correctly identify a single prophet from the Old Testament; and finally, 41 percent of Protestants and 81 percent of Catholics could not identify the first book of the Bible.

Of course, social and political leaders still rely on religious symbolism to influence secular behavior. The American Pledge of Allegiance tells us that we are "one nation, under God, indivisible . . .," and our currency tells us that "In God We Trust." Since the turn of the century, however, modern society has turned increasingly to science, rather than religion, to point the way.

ECUMENISM

Partially as a response to secularism, a tendency toward **ecumenism** has been evident among many of the religions in the United States. This refers to the trend among many religions to draw together and project a sense of unity and common direction.

When asked if they feel they have a personal relationship with God, 82 percent of American Catholics responded yes.

ecumenism The trend among many religions to draw together and project a sense of unity and common direction.

TABLE 13.2
Membership of the Religious Bodies of the United States, 1986

Religious Body	Number of Members
Protestant	78,991,000
Roman Catholic	52,893,000
Jewish	5,814,000
Eastern Orthodox (Christian)	3,980,000
Old Catholic, Polish National Catholic, and Armenian Churches	829,000
Buddhist	100,000
Miscellaneous	192,000
Total	142,800,000

Source: U.S. Department of Commerce, Bureau of the Census, *Statistical Abstract of the United States: 1989* (Washington, D.C.: Government Printing Office, 1989), p. 54.

Unlike religious groups in Europe, where issues of doctrine have fostered sect-like hard-line separatism among denominations, in America most religious groups have focused on ethics, that is, how to live the good and right life. There is less likelihood of disagreement over ethics than over doctrine. Hence, American Protestant denominations typically have had rather loose boundaries, with members of congregations switching denominations rather easily and churches featuring guest appearances from ministers of other denominations. In this context, ecumenism has flourished in the United States far more than in Europe.

TELEVISION EVANGELISM

The share of Americans who attend religious services from their living rooms is now rivaling the share who go to church. A recent survey showed that 45 percent of Americans watch religious programs on television or listen to them on the radio at least monthly. Nine percent watch or listen daily.

Listenership is higher among Protestants than Catholics. When asked how often they listen or watch religious programs, 86 percent of black Protestants and 58 percent of white Protestants say they do so at least once a month. Twenty-eight percent of black Protestants, and 12 percent of white Protestants do so every day. In fact, black Protestants are more likely to watch or listen to a religious program than attend church (*American Demographics,* 1986).

The growth of the electronic church in America is truly remarkable, with four religious television networks, thirty-five religious TV stations, and an estimated 1400 religious radio stations currently in operation.

Before scandals rocked the electronic church and dealt a heavy blow to listenership, televangelists like Jerry Falwell, Jimmy Swaggart, Jim Bakker, Oral Roberts, Pat Robertson, and Robert Schuller broadcast prayers and sermons to their flock as they built empires with viewer donations. At the height of his popularity, Jimmy Swaggart drew an audience of more than 2 million households. Pat Robertson's "700 Club" program drew more than 4.4 million viewers a day. The twelve most popular ministries together collected annual sums totaling $1 billion (*Newsweek,* July 17, 1988).

Even with a number of well-publicized scandals, more people than ever are tuning in to the television ministers. In 1988 25 percent of American adults watched religious programs, up from 18 percent in 1983 (*The Gallup Report,* 1988).

Who watches these programs? The social characteristics of religious television viewers are different from those of the general population. The typical weekly viewer of religious television programs is over 50 years of age, female, Baptist, not a high school graduate, lives in the South, and has a household income below $15,000. Despite their low household income figure, these viewers are likely to donate more than $300 a year to the television ministry (*Statistical Abstract of the United States: 1989*).

Some pastors have expressed concern that the electronic church will decrease peo-

Even with a number of well-publicized scandals, more people than ever are tuning in to the television ministers.

Prayer Line (704) 543-4673

ple's involvement in local churches, or worse yet, keep prospective members from joining a church. There is also the concern that the electronic media may make religion too easy and comfortable, and encourage individualized religion. The "show business" aspect of certain religious programs also makes critics uneasy.

In their defense, we must note that religious programs reach a vast number of people who might not be reached otherwise. It is also the only way to reach the elderly, the infirm, or the handicapped. It could also be claimed that these programs raise the level of awareness of the unchurched and make them more likely to become involved in their religious communities (Gallup Organization, 1981).

MAJOR RELIGIONS IN THE UNITED STATES

Nowhere is the diversity of the American people more evident than in their religious denominations. There are more than1000 different religious groups in the United States, which vary widely in religious practices, moral views, class structure, family values, and attitudes. A recent survey found surprisingly large and persistent differences among even the major religious groups.

The national census is prohibited from asking about religion, so the U.S. government generally has little to say on the matter. However, the National Opinion Research Center has been conducting the General Social Surveys since 1972, and they do give us a way of examining American religious attitudes and practices. The center has correlated information on a variety of issues with religious affiliation. Some of its findings are summarized below.

It is useful to think of American Protestant religious denominations as ranked on a scale as to their degree of traditionalism. Conservative Protestant denominations include the fundamentalists (Pentecostals, Jehovah's Witnesses, and so on), Southern Baptists, and other Baptists. The moderates include Lutherans, Methodists, and interor nondenominationalists. Liberal Protestants are represented by Unitarians, Congregationalists, Presbyterians, and Episcopalians. This distinction among Protestants is important because the various branches often differ so markedly in their attitudes, especially toward social issues, that they resemble other religions more than the various denominations of their own.

For example, with respect to the hereafter, nearly 90 percent of the fundamentalists and Baptists believe in an afterlife. This falls to 80 percent among the moderate middle and liberal denominations. Catholics are similar to liberal Protestants in that 75 percent believe in an afterlife. Among people with no religious affiliation, 46 percent believe in an afterlife.

A strong belief in sin is typical of fundamentalists and Baptists. This situation causes them to strongly condemn extramarital and premarital sex, homosexuality, and to favor outlawing pornography. There is greater sexual permissiveness among the moderate denominations and considerably more among the liberal elite. Catholics tend to resemble the Protestant moderates. Jews tend to be more liberal than the liberal Protestant denominations in this area. Attitudes toward drugs and alcohol follow the same pattern, with smoking, drinking, and frequenting bars least common among fundamentalists and Baptists.

There are substantial social class differences among the major Protestant denominations. The average annual household income for nonblack fundamentalists and Southern Baptists is less than $15,000. For Lutherans it is $16,300, for Methodists $17,000, Presbyterians $20,500, Episcopalians $21,700, Catholics $17,400, Jews $23,300, and $17,600 for people with no religious affiliation. The pattern is the same

WHO ATTENDS RELIGIOUS SERVICES?

Although Americans talk about their faith in God, and the issue of school prayer often takes center stage in an election year, how much do we actually attend religious services? Do we follow through on our beliefs every Saturday or Sunday by going to our church or synagogue?

Since 1972, the General Social Surveys, conducted by the National Opinion Research Center, have been asking Americans this question. As you can see from recent survey results, the answer depends, in large part, on our religious affiliation:

- Fundamentalists lead the pack. Over half (51 percent) say they attend church weekly.
- More than four out of ten Catholics (42 percent) are regular churchgoers.
- Only about 22 to 24 percent of Lutherans and Methodists say they attend weekly services, and even fewer Episcopalians—a slim 18 percent—attend.
- Jews do not attend synagogue services regularly; only 8 percent say they attend each week. However, 42 percent, a significantly higher percentage, say their faith is strong. Thus, although most Jews do not actively follow rituals and attend services, they have a strong ethnic identification with Judaism.

Source: Tom Smith, "America's Religious Mosaic," *American Demographics,* June 1984, pp. 19–23.

---

for occupational prestige and education, with Jews and Episcopalians averaging 3 more years of education than fundamentalists and Baptists.

Given the wide differences in values and attitudes among religious groups, the relative proportion of the population that belongs to each group helps determine the shape of society. Protestants make up about 64 percent of the adult population, according to data from the General Social Survey. Of the five major Protestant families, the largest are the Baptists, who account for 21 percent of the adult population. Second are the Methodists with 12 percent, and next are the Lutherans with 8 percent. Roman Catholics, representing about one-quarter of the adult population, are the largest single religious denomination. Jews are 2 to 3 percent, followed by a host of religions, including Eastern Orthodox, Muslim, Hindu, Sufi, and Baha'i, which add up to a little over 1 percent.

These percentages are in a constant state of flux, however, because demographic factors such as birthrates and migration patterns may influence the numbers of people in any given religion. Religious conversion can also affect percentages. Fundamentalism, for example, is gaining among the young and winning converts.

Despite trends toward ecumenicalism, it seems that the magnitude of religious differences, the persistence of established faiths, and the continual development of new faiths will ensure that this pattern of religious diversity will continue (Smith, 1984).

PROTESTANTISM

Because American Protestantism is fragmented into so many groups, many sociologists simply have classified all non-Catholic Christian denominations in the general category "Protestant." As we just noted, however, there are differences—of greater or lesser significance—among the various denominations.

Since the 1960s there has been a 10

percent drop in the membership of the United Methodists and United Presbyterians, and the Episcopalians have seen a 15 percent decline. At the same time, the more conservative denominations have increased dramatically. In the same period of time, there has been an 18 percent increase in the number of Baptists, a 37 percent increase among the Assemblies of God, and a 34 percent increase among Seventh-Day Adventists (U.S. Department of Commerce, 1983).

At the present time the fundamentalists and evangelical Christians have become an extremely visible and vocal segment of the Protestant population, and their presence has been felt through the media and through their support of political candidates. Why are the fundamentalist and evangelical churches gaining such popularity? Some of their appeal may lie in the sense of belonging and the comfort they offer through their belief in a well-defined and self-assured religious doctrine—no ambiguities and hence few moral choices to be made.

The growth of these churches reflects religion's role as a social institution, changing over time and from place to place, partly in response to concurrent social and cultural changes and partly itself acting as an agent of social change.

CATHOLICISM

One of the most striking things about Catholics in the United States is their youth: 29 percent are under 30, 36 percent are between 30 and 49, and 35 percent are over 50. In contrast, 24 percent of Protestants are under 30, and 41 percent are over 50. The higher birth rate among Catholics in the baby boom generation, especially among Hispanic Catholics, accounts for a large part of this difference. Another part of the explanation is the difficulty mainline Protestant denominations have had in retaining young people.

American Catholics have long been an immigrant people, and that tradition is continuing today. One in five Catholics are members of a minority group. Hispanics now make up 16 percent of American Catholics. Another 3 percent are black. Another 3 percent describe themselves as "nonwhite." Since very few Hispanics identify themselves as "nonwhite," this suggests that the influx of Catholic immigrants from Southeast Asia is starting to show in national surveys. Among Protestants, 14 percent are black and 2 percent are Hispanic. This means that although the percentage of blacks among Protestants is five times greater than among Catholics, a higher percentage of Catholics overall come from minority groups.

Since the mid-1960s, Catholics have equaled Protestants in education and income levels. The overall figures for Protestants mask significant differences between denominations. When we compare Catholics with other denominations in terms of education and income, we find them still ranking behind Presbyterians and Episcopalians, about on a par with Lutherans and Methodists, and well ahead of Baptists. This comparison is striking in light of the fact that large numbers of lower-income minorities are included in the overall Catholic figures.

Catholics remain an urban people, with only one in four living in rural areas. A higher percentage of Catholics (39 percent) than of any major denomination live in central cities, and 35 percent live in suburbs. The vast majority of Catholics are concentrated in the Northeast and the Midwest.

Catholics have historically favored larger families than other Americans, but by 1985 the difference in ideal family size between Catholics and Protestants had disappeared, with both groups considering two children the ideal family size. Despite the Catholic Church's condemnation of artificial means of birth control, American Catholics have favored access to contraceptives and information about them in the same proportion as the rest of the population since the 1950s (Gallup and Castelli, 1987).

One of the most important developments in the recent history of Catholicism was the ecumenical council (Vatican II) called by Pope John XXIII, which met from 1962 to 1965 and thoroughly reexamined Catholic doctrine. This ecumenical council led to many changes, often referred to as "liberalization," including the substitution of common language for Latin in the Mass. One unintended consequence (or latent function) of Vatican II was that the centralized authority structure of the Catholic church was called into question. Laypersons and priests felt free to dispute the doctrinal pronouncements of bishops and even of the pope himself. During the same period, the percentage of Catholics using some form of birth control rose from under 60 percent to 75 percent, despite a ban on using them (Westoff and Jones, 1977).

Under the leadership of Pope John Paul II, the Catholic Church has taken a more conservative turn. It has continued to condemn all forms of birth control except the rhythm method and rejected high-technology aids to conception, such as artificial insemination, *in vitro* fertilization, or surrogate motherhood (*New York Times,* March 23, 1987). The call for a greater role for women in the church or possible ordination to priesthood has been rejected. Women have been told to seek meaning in their lives through motherhood and giving love to others (Suro, 1988).

JUDAISM

There is a strong identification among Jews on both a cultural and a religious level, and many feel that they have common ties because of their religion. This sense of connectedness is an important aspect in understanding current trends within the religion.

Jews can be divided into three groups, according to the manner in which they approach traditional religious precepts. Orthodox Jews observe traditional religious laws very closely. They maintain strict dietary laws and do not work, drive, or engage in other everyday practices on the Sabbath.

Reform Jews, on the other hand, allow for major reinterpretations of religious practices and customs, which are often in response to changes in society. Conservative Jews represent a compromise between the two extremes. They are less traditional than the Orthodox Jews but not as willing to make major modifications in religious observance, as the Reform Jews are apt to do. In addition, there is a large secularized segment of the Jewish population that still identifies itself as Jewish but refrains from formal synagogue affiliation.

Like the situation among Protestants, there are social class differences among the various Jewish groups. Reform Jews are the best educated and have the highest incomes. For Orthodox Jews, religious, not secular, education is the goal. They have the lowest incomes and the least amount of secular education. As might be expected, Conservative Jews are located between these two poles.

The state of Israel has played a major role in shaping current Jewish thinking. For many Jews, identification with Israel has come to be a secular replacement for religiosity. Support for the country is tied to many deep psychological and emotional responses. To many, Israel and its continued existence represent a way of guaranteeing that never again will millions of Jews perish in a Nazi type of Holocaust. The country is seen as a homeland that can help defend world Jewry from the unwarranted attacks that have occurred against Jews throughout history. For many Jews, identification with, and support for, the state of Israel is important to the development of their cultural and religious ties.

Recently the Jewish community has had to deal with the issue of ordination of women rabbis. Reform Jews have moved in this direction without a great deal of difficulty, and today women are the leaders of Reform congregations around the country. The issue of women rabbis produced a bitter fight among Conservative Jews. At this time, a few Conservative women rabbis have become the heads of congregations.

Orthodox Jews have not had to address the issue, as for them the existence of a woman rabbi would represent too radical a departure from tradition to be contemplated.

According to the Bible, God told the Jewish people to be fruitful and multiply. In the United States, it seems the group is doing neither. Recent estimates indicate there are 5.8 million Jews in the United States, about the same as in 1977. Demographers predict the population will decline by 5 to 17 percent by the end of the century. The American Jewish community is thus facing a crisis.

The reasons for the lack of growth in the Jewish community are varied. For one thing, Jews in the United States are not bearing enough children to replace themselves: The Jewish fertility rate has been estimated at between 1.3 to 1.7 per lifetime — well below the replacement rate of 2.1. For another, the Jewish population is quite old, with about 40 percent of the American Jewish population having a remaining life expectance of 20 years or less. Jewish immigration from the Soviet Union and Israel has helped somewhat, but is unpredictable. Finally, many young Jews are choosing to marry outside the faith, although this does not necessarily lead to a loss of Jewish identity.

Whether or not there is a population erosion, and what should be done about it is an ongoing debate in the American Jewish community. Jewish religious groups have attempted to liberalize the definition of who is a Jew and — in a radical break with tradition — to change their attitude toward and seek converts to Judaism.

A common fear is that any further decline in the number of American Jews would lessen their ability to defend their political interests. Others suggest that we would lose the contributions of Jewish scientists, artists, and performers. Even though Jews account for roughly between 2.5 and 3 percent of the U.S. population, they have constituted 20 percent of America's Nobel laureates.

Even though many of the reasons for the shrinking population are demographic in nature, the issue of how to stem the tide has been the cause of some major rifts between the various branches of the religion. Recent statistics, for example, put the rate of Jewish intermarriage at 40 percent. Strictly observant Jews blame their more liberal co-religionists for this high percentage. The liberal Reform movement is somewhat tolerant of intermarriages. Interfaith couples today have little difficulty finding Reform rabbis willing to accept them into the congregations.

A subject that has provoked even more controversy is the Reform movement's break with the tradition of matrilineal, or motherly, descent. In 1983, the Reform movement declared that a person could be considered Jewish if either the father or mother was Jewish. Before that time, Judaism could only be passed on to the child from the mother.

American Jews also differ with respect to converts to Judaism. The Reform movement's Outreach program goes against centuries of Jewish tradition in which proselytizing has been disdained. The Outreach program is quite low-key, however. There is no advertising or airwave sermonizing more common with Christian evangelical movements. Instead, Outreach sessions resemble comparative religion discussion

At the Wailing Wall in Jerusalem, thousands of Jews gather each day to pray and mourn the destruction of the second temple by the Romans in 70 A.D.

Should Christian Scientists Be Allowed to Refuse Medical Care for Their Children?

When 2-year-old Robyn Twitchell developed a high fever, his parents were worried but decided not to take him to a doctor. Instead, they turned to two Christian Science spiritual healers who came to the Twitchell house and prayed for the boy's recovery. As Robyn's condition worsened, his parents' religious faith deepened. But despite their prayers, Robyn died of a bowel obstruction five days later.

Rita and Doug Swan, also Christian Scientists, believed that faith in God could cure their 15-month-old son Matthew's high fevers. As the fevers grew worse, the Swans withheld medical care while Christian Science spiritual healers prayed for the little boy's recovery. When it became clear that Matthew was about to die, the Swans rushed him to a hospital, where they learned that he was suffering from bacterial meningitis, an illness treatable by antibiotics in its early stages. However, weeks into the illness, there was no medical cure. Matthew died within a week of his hospital admission.

Both Robyn Twitchell and Matthew Swan died because of their parents' religious faith. A basic tenet of Christian Science is the conviction that disease is rooted in the mind's blindness to God and that prayer that establishes communion with God is a treatment as real and powerful as modern medicine. As one Christian Scientist put it: "Healing happens when your sense of God becomes greater than your sense of the problem" (Gottschalk, 1988).

Thus, strict Christian Scientists will not submit to nearly any form of medical care. They refuse vaccinations, drugs, physical examinations, and surgery and turn instead to trained practitioners who charge up to $25 a day for prayer. At least 126 children have died in the United States over the last 15 years because of their parents' religious beliefs — a fact state prosecutors have been unwilling to ignore as they charge grieving parents with causing the death of their child. At issue in courts all across the country is these parents' First Amendment right to practice their religion, versus the obligation of the state to safeguard children's health.

Christian Scientists are convinced that spiritual healing is as effective as modern medicine. Citing thousands of successful "cures," they see no reason to turn to medical care. Church spokesman Nathan Talbot explains: "As with any form of treatment, Christian Science deserves to be judged on the basis of an overall assessment of its results, rather than on the a priori assumption that nothing but medical care should be acceptable by the state as a means of caring for the health of the young" (Gottschalk, 1988).

groups and introductory classes in Judaism are available to interfaith couples, as well as converts (Putka, 1984).

All religions and denominations are affected by the current mood of the country. A heightened social consciousness results in demands for reform, whereas stressful times often produce a movement toward the personalization of religion. In any event, although traditional forms and practices of religion may be changing in the United States, religion itself is likely to continue to function as a basic social institution.

SOCIAL CORRELATES OF RELIGIOUS AFFILIATION

Religious affiliation seems to be correlated strongly with many other important aspects of people's lives. Direct relationships can be traced between membership in a particular religious group and a person's politics, pro-

In the minds of church leaders, laws passed in forty-seven states protecting Christian Scientists and other religious fundamentalists from prosecution under child abuse and neglect laws, when they fail to get medical care for their sick children, are proper. Asks Talbot: "Is our society prepared to say that medicine constitutes the only valid method of care —that healing, as the New Testament teaches it, must be regarded as so suspect that those who have been practicing it for more than a century can be prosecuted when they aren't 100 percent successful?" (*U.S. News & World Report,* March 24, 1986). Christian Scientists believe that the law now recognizes the validity and effectiveness of faith healing, and when a death occurs, it is no more tragic —nor deserving of criminal prosecution—than when it occurs under the care of doctors. Said Talbot: "It isn't as though a child

dies *only* under Christian Science care" (Delaney, 1987).

State prosecutors disagree. Charging Ginger and David R. Twitchell with manslaughter after Robyn's death, the district attorney of Boston stated that medical treatment must supersede religious beliefs when a child's life is threatened. In another case, a California court stated that the law "does not sanction unorthodox substitutes for medical attendance" (*U.S. News & World Report,* March 24, 1986).

The American Academy of Pediatrics has come to the same conclusion. Said spokesman Dr. William Well: "People should be guaranteed every religious right possible. But there's no guarantee in the Constitution, and there shouldn't be at the state level, that you can act in a way that's harmful to others and excuse it due to religious beliefs. And we see case after case, from one end of the country

to the other, where children who were denied immunizations and medical care have died" (Delaney, 1987).

No matter what your viewpoint may be, the situation is heartbreaking for the parents, who often believe that their child would have lived had their faith been stronger. Said David Twitchell on ABC's "20/20": "If we were closer to God we could have stopped this from happening. In that way I blame myself" (Gottschalk, 1988).

Sources: Stephen Gottschalk, "Spiritual Healing on Trial: A Christian Scientist Reports," *The Christian Century,* June 22–29, 1988, pp. 602–605; "Boston Couple Deny Charges in Son's Death," *New York Times,* May 3, 1988, p. A20; "When a State Takes Aim at Faith Healing," *U.S. News & World Report,* March 24, 1986, p. 22; Kevin Delaney, " 'We Thought Our Faith Could Save Our Son,' " *Redbook,* January 1987, pp. 104–106; Jack Kelley, "How Could Parents Let a Child Die? *People,* May 16, 1988, pp. 136–138.

---

fessional and economic standing, educational level, family life, social mobility, and attitudes toward controversial social issues. For example, Jews, who in the 1980 census represented only 2.9 percent of the total population, are proportionally the best-educated group; they also have higher incomes than Christians in general; and a greater proportion are represented in business and the professions. Despite their high socioeconomic and educational levels,

however, Jews, like Catholics, occupy relatively few of the highest positions of power in the corporate world and politics: these fields generally are dominated by white Anglo-Saxon Protestants. Among Christian groups, there appears the same correlation among denomination, social and professional prestige, and income level. For example, Episcopalians, the smallest Protestant denomination, consistently rank highest in social prestige and income.

Other studies show equally interesting relationships between politics and religious affiliation. Studies of the major religious faiths in the United States show that about 58 percent of Jews are Democrats and only 9 percent are Republicans. A lower proportion of Catholics, but still almost 44 percent, are Democrats, and 29 percent are Republicans. Protestants have the lowest proportion of Democrats (40 percent) and the highest proportion (38 percent) of Republicans (Chi and Houseknecht, 1985).

The positions of people on controversial social questions also seem to be correlated, to some extent, with their religious affiliations. The fundamentalist and evangelical Protestant sects generally are more conservative than the major Protestant sects on key issues. According to a Gallup opinion poll (1985), when asked whether they would favor a constitutional amendment to ban abortion except for rape, incest, or threat to the mother's life, 66 percent of the Evangelicals responded yes, 59 of the Catholics agreed, as did 51 percent of the Protestants (Gallup and Castelli, 1987).

Interestingly, fundamentalists, despite their conservative views on marriage and family issues, are more likely to have unstable marriages than nonfundamentalists (Chi and Houseknecht, 1985). It appears that fundamentalists are more likely than Protestants or Catholics in general to be unhappy with their marriage if their spouses have different religious beliefs. Dissatisfaction arises from discrepancies between the "real" family life and the "ideal" family life as perceived through interpretations of the scriptures.

"Among fundamentalists, the wife is expected to submit to her husband as her 'head,' even if her husband is not a good Christian or is an unbeliever," note Chi and Houseknecht. This often creates marital problems.

Problems also arise when the wife must work outside the home. Labor-force participation is considered "a distortion of God's plan." Nevertheless, fundamentalist women are as likely to work as other Protestant or Catholic women.

Although it is clear that religious associations show definite correlations with people's political, social, and economic lives, we must be careful not to ascribe a cause-and-effect relationship to such data, which at most can be considered an indicator of an individual's attitudes and social standing.

The social and political correlates of religious affiliation continue to be important aspects of life in the United States.

SUMMARY

Religion is one of society's most important institutions. It is a system of beliefs and practices shared by a group of people that helps them to explain and function in the present world through the concept of the supernatural and the sacred. The sacred consists of all things kept separate from everyday experience, things that are knowable only through extraordinary experiences. Religion also includes rituals, patterns of behavior that are related to the sacred.

All the world's religions include ritual and prayer, emotion, belief, and organization. A simple inclusive scheme of classifying religions recognizes four major types: supernaturalism, animism, theism, and abstract ideals.

In addition, religions perform functions on both an individual and a social level, satisfying individual needs, promoting social cohesion, establishing world views, and providing social control. Religion also has its dysfunctional aspects. It tends to conceal the human causes of conditions and events and may hinder much-needed social changes, as well as independent thinking and the search for new knowledge.

There is a clear relationship between religion and other social institutions during times of social change. In times of stress, three religious phenomena typically appear: revitalization movements, millenarian movements, and sectarian splitting.

Several forms or types of organization of religious groups are found in society, including the universal church, the ecclesia, the denomination, the sect, and the cult.

Today, the three main themes that characterize religion in America are widespread belief, secularism, and ecumenism. Americans are more churchgoing than Europeans, with more than half of all religiously affiliated individuals belonging to a Protestant denomination.

Currently, the major religions and denominations in the United States are struggling with questions of doctrine and practice in response to dissatisfaction among their members. Although some practices have been liberalized, such as the language of the Catholic Mass and the acceptance of female clergy among Protestants, doctrine has often been reaffirmed more strictly. In Protestantism, fundamentalist and evangelical churches have been gaining popularity and have become both visible and vocal on the national scene.

Judaism also is undergoing changes. An important factor influencing many American Jews is identification with the state of Israel. In addition, two of the three groups, Conservative and Reform, are dealing with the issue of ordaining women as rabbis. Judaism, like other religions in America, has experienced secularization.

Chapter 14

EDUCATION

EDUCATION: A FUNCTIONALIST VIEW

Socialization
Cultural Transmission
Academic Skills
Innovation
Child Care
Postponing Job Hunting

THE CONFLICT THEORY VIEW

Social Control
Screening and Allocation: Tracking
The Credentialized Society

ISSUES IN AMERICAN EDUCATION

Unequal Access to Education
School Integration
High School Dropouts
Violence in the Schools
Standardized Testing
The Gifted

SUMMARY

In 1979, Wilson Junior High School in Rochester, New York, was plagued with many of the same problems as other inner-city schools. Instead of learning, children fought; violence was common, the building decayed, truancy was rampant, and test scores were shamefully low.

Henry Williams vowed to change all that when he took over as Wilson's principal. He demanded respect for himself and his teachers and proved that he deserved it by making the school safe once more. He turned Wilson into a magnet senior high school, designed to attract youngsters from outside the ghetto, by offering courses that would prepare them for the workplace of tomorrow. Students could choose from a dizzying array of electives, designed in part by executives from Kodak and Xerox. Robotics, electronics, and photo-optics, as well as six foreign languages, were just a few of the offerings.

Students could also depend on receiving help—on a one-to-one basis—from teachers whenever they needed it. Each teacher at Wilson took personal charge of a group of youngsters, guiding them through their high school years. By monitoring homework and academic progress, making home visits, and talking regularly with students on the phone, they set up a relationship of trust that helped sidetrack failure. At the same time this was happening, teacher pay jumped substantially. With more money came increased professionalism and self-respect for the teachers.

The results were dramatic. By 1988, 85 percent of Wilson's seniors were headed for colleges that included some of the nation's best. Twenty-one students earned State Regents Scholarships—a number higher than any other school in the city—and the dropout rate fell from 30 percent to a mere handful of students. Wilson now attracts students from all over Rochester who want the best facilities, the best teachers, and the best education. A decade ago, few would have believed this possible (*U.S. News & World Report,* June 20, 1988).

Principal Henry Williams was able to get Wilson High School to accomplish some of the goals that we expect a school to attain. But what are those goals specifically? It may sound like a simple question, but if a researcher asked you why citizens should get an education, what would you say? The

Our educational system is geared to more than job training; it does not take 12 years of schooling to prepare for most jobs. Socialization is also an important aspect of education.

Gallup Poll periodically asks people across the country just such a question, and the results may surprise you. The most common reason people give is "to get a better job," or "to get a better-paying job" (42 percent). Very few people mention things like "to acquire knowledge" (10 percent), "to learn basic skills" (3 percent), "to develop an understanding and appreciation for culture" (1 percent), or "to develop critical thinking skills" (1 percent) (*The Gallup Report,* 1986).

Clearly, our educational system is geared to more than job training. After all, it does not really take 12 years of schooling to prepare you for many jobs. You can take short courses that prepare you to be a bartender, tractor trailer driver, or hairdresser. Something else is taking place during those years as the school prepares children to become members of society. In this chapter we will examine this complex social institution. We will compare the functionalist and conflict approaches to understanding the American educational system. Functionalists stress the importance of education in socializing the young, cultural transmission, and developing skills. Conflict theorists, on the other hand, note that education preserves social class distinctions, maintains social control, and promotes inequality.

EDUCATION: A FUNCTIONALIST VIEW

What social needs does our educational system meet? What are its tasks and goals? Education has several manifest functions (see Chapter 1), that is, intended and predetermined goals, such as the socialization of the young or the teaching of academic skills. There are also some latent functions, which are unintended consequences of the educational process. These may include child care, the transmission of ethnocentric values, and respect for the American class structure.

SOCIALIZATION

In the broadest sense, all societies must have an educational system. That is, they must have a way of teaching the young the tasks that are likely to be expected of them as they develop and mature into adulthood. If we accept this definition of an educational system, then we must believe that there really is no difference between education and socialization. And as Margaret Mead (1943) observed, in many preliterate societies, no such distinction is made. Children learn most things informally, almost incidentally, simply by being included in adult activities.

Traditionally, the family has been the main arena for socialization. As societies have become more complex, the family has been unable to fulfill all aspects of its socialization function. Thus, there is a need for the formal educational system to extend the socialization process that starts in the family.

In modern industrialized societies, a distinction is made between education and socialization. In ordinary speech, we differentiate between socialization and education by talking of "bringing up" and educating children as two separate tasks. In modern society these two aspects of socialization are quite compartmentalized: whereas rearing children is an informal activity, education or schooling is formal. The role prescriptions that determine interactions between students and teachers are clearly defined, and the curriculum to be taught is explicit. Obviously, the educational process goes far beyond just formalized instruction. In addition, children also learn things in their families and among their peers. In school, children's master status (see Chapter 5) is that of student, and their primary task is to learn what is taught.

Schools, as differentiated formal institutions of education, emerged as part of the evolution of civilization. However, until

Until about 200 years ago, education was a luxury that few could afford. Schools, as we know them today, arose out of a need to create a skilled work force.

about 200 years ago, education did not help people become more productive in practical ways, and thus was a luxury that very few could afford. This changed dramatically with the industrialization of Western culture. Workers with specialized skills were required for production jobs, as were professional, well-trained managers. When the Industrial Revolution moved workers out of their homes and into factories, the labor force consisted not only of adults but also of children. Subsequently, child labor laws were passed to prohibit children from working in factories. These laws created a need for places outside the home to care for children. Schools, as we know them today, arose out of this need and the need to create a skilled work force.

CULTURAL TRANSMISSION

The most obvious goal of education is to transmit major portions of a society's knowledge from one generation to the next. Sociologists call this manifest function **cultural transmission.** In relatively small, homogeneous societies, in which almost all members share in the culture's norms, values, and perspectives, cultural transmission is a matter of consensus and needs few specialized institutions. But in a complex, pluralistic society like ours, with competition among ethnic and other minority groups for economic and political power, the decision as to what aspects of the culture will be transmitted is the outgrowth of a complicated process.

If we consider that schools are one of the major means of cultural transmission — both "vertically" (between generations) and "horizontally" (in disseminating knowledge to adults) — this lack of consensus concerning every important aspect of schooling points to a basic problem within the educational system itself. Our pluralistic American society contains many important cultural differences among its various ethnic groups and social classes. Nevertheless, for a society to hold together, there must be certain "core" values and goals — some common traits of culture — that the people share to a greater or lesser degree (see Chapter 4). In America, it seems that this "core culture" itself is in a period of rapid change.

A school's curriculum often reflects the ability of organized groups of concerned citizens to impose their views on an educational system, whether local, statewide, or nationwide. Thus, it was a political process that caused black history to be introduced into elementary, high school, and college curricula during the 1960s. Similarly, it was

cultural transmission The transmission of major portions of a society's knowledge, norms, values, and perspectives from one generation to the next. Cultural transmission is an intended function of education.

political activism that caused the creation of women's studies majors in many colleges. And even though the concept of evolution is a cornerstone of modern scientific knowledge, it is political pressure (from Christian fundamentalists) that causes textbooks to refer to it as the "theory" of evolution, prevents its being taught outright in certain states, and in other states has led to government insistence that teachers give "equal time" to other "points of view."

In recent years, bilingual education has become an educational and political issue. Proponents believe that it is critical for children whose primary language is not English to be given instruction in their native tongues. They believe that by acknowledging students' native languages, the school system is helping them make the transition into the all-English mainstream — and is also helping to preserve the diversity of American culture.

Others, such as former Secretary of Education William J. Bennett, see a danger in these programs. In Bennett's view, many bilingual education programs never make the transition into English — a fact that leaves many youngsters without the basic skills needed to earn a living and participate in our society.

How strongly a school supports bilingual education reflects the political clout of the groups involved. In the end, the debate centers on how closely our sense of who we are as a nation hinges on the language our children speak in school. For the time being, the only agreement between the two sides is that language is the cornerstone for cultural transmission (Molotsky, 1988).

Many people would agree that citizen input into school curricula is important because it ensures that what is taught reflects the cultural values. In keeping with this viewpoint, during the 1960s under President Lyndon B. Johnson, the federal government began to finance the creation of community boards to give poor people some control over local school curricula and the hiring and firing of teachers. State and local courts and legislatures followed

TAKING THE SOCIOLOGICAL PERSPECTIVE

JAPANESE MOTHERS AND SCHOOLING

The 10-year-old boy is not doing well in school. Despite his family's high expectations, he is about to flunk out. His mother, who is particularly upset with his scholastic performance, falls ill. The child blames himself for his mother's sickness and redoubles his efforts at school. His grades improve, and his mother's illness suddenly disappears.

The son in another family does no chores. "Why?" asks a researcher. "Because," his mother replies, "it would break my heart to take him away from his studies."

Strange stories from upper-middle-class suburbia, right? Wrong. In each case, the mother was actually Japanese. The Japanese mother is in the vanguard of scholastic effectiveness.

Until her child goes to school, the Japanese mother devotes herself to the rearing of the child. In verbal and nonverbal ways, she constantly reminds the child of her deep, warm feelings and that the child is the most important thing in the world to her. Then she says, "After all I've done for you, don't disappoint me." She is like the overprotective mother who says, "What do you mean you're not hungry—after I've slaved all day over a hot stove for you."

If the Japanese mother–child relationship could be summarized in a word, that word would be *amae. Amae* can be translated as love combined with a strong sense of reciprocal obligation and dependence.

The decline of education in the United States has been well documented. While politicians and educators all search for ways to remedy the situation, some researchers are looking to the Orient for answers. The Japanese, in particular, seem to be vastly outperforming their American counterparts. For example, in one study comparing fifth-graders in an American midwestern city to those in Tokyo, not one of the twenty American classrooms did as well in math as any of the Japanese classes. In other words, the average score of the highest-achieving American class was below the worst-performing Japanese class. Only one of the one hundred top-scoring fifth-grade math students was American.

Although researchers cite many reasons for this learning gap, most agree that the values instilled in the children at home are crucial. The Japanese mother is a very important influence on the education of her children. She takes it upon herself to reinforce the educational process instituted in the schools.

It is hard for us to imagine the total commitment of the Japanese mother to her child's education. She studies, she packs lunches, she waits in line for hours to register her child for exams and waits again in the hallways for hours while he takes them.

She also helps every day with homework, hires tutors and works part-time to pay for after-school tutorial classes known as *jukus. Jukus* are now a 5-billion-dollar-a-year industry with about 36,000 located throughout Japan. Sometimes the women enroll in "mother's classes" so they can be even better prepared to help with the drills at home.

So accepted is this role that it has produced its own label, *kyoiku-mama,* which translates roughly as education mother. This title is not worn openly. Many Japanese mothers are embarrassed, or modest, and simply say, "I do my best." But the best is a lot, because to Japanese women motherhood is a profession, demanding and prestigious, with education of the child the number one responsibility.

There is also considerable peer pressure on the mother. The community's perception of a woman's success as a mother depends in large part on how well her children do in school.

Some go so far as to say that a good proportion of the credit for Japan's economic miracle can be attributed to the "education mothers." Yet this miracle could not take place if the status of Japanese women were not lower than that of men. More so than in any other industrialized country, Japanese women find it difficult to advance in work or education because of very rigidly defined hierarchies that make them second-class citizens.

The price Japanese women are paying for the educational accomplishments of their male offspring is clearly much higher than most Americans would want to pay.

Source: Carol Simons, *Smithsonian,* March 1987, pp. 44–52.

this lead and in many cities mandated community-based school boards and advisory groups with significant political power. But a study commissioned by the National Institute of Education (NIE) in 1979 cast doubt on the usefulness of this approach. Investigating the impact of community boards on schools in Boston, Atlanta, and Los Angeles, the institute found that their actual impact had been minor. The research found that these groups typically are recruited from among the poor, who themselves are inadequately educated and hence lack many of the skills necessary to effect substantial changes. Also, community groups typically are controlled by city governments, and educational bureaucracies have found ways to limit their influence. Perhaps for these reasons such community groups have tended to focus on narrow and minor issues rather than on major school policies. Nor have they produced any major educational leaders who could introduce wide-ranging reforms. In fact, given the overall lack of effectiveness of community boards, the NIE study recommended eliminating federal and state program policies requiring them.

A particularly troubling aspect of American education is student performance in math and science.

ACADEMIC SKILLS

Another critical function of the schools is to equip children with the academic skills they need to function as adults — to hold down a job, to balance a checkbook, to evaluate political candidates, to read a newspaper, to analyze the importance of a scientific advance, and so on. Have the schools been successful in this area? Most experts believe they have not.

In 1983, the National Commission on Excellence in Education issued a report entitled "A Nation at Risk," which bitterly attacked the effectiveness of American education. The message of the report was clear and sobering: "The educational foundations of our society are presently being eroded by a rising tide of mediocrity that threatens our very future."

As a result of this report, reforms were instituted in all fifty states that stressed the teaching of the "three Rs" and the elimination of frivolous electives that waste valuable student and teacher time. In addition, high school graduation requirements were raised in forty states, and in nineteen states students must pass minimum competency tests, demonstrating the mastery of basic skills, to receive their high school diplomas. Forty-eight states also require new teachers to prove their competence by passing a standardized test.

Although the back-to-basics movement has worked, its success has been limited. Five years after "A Nation at Risk" appeared, a follow-up report was issued entitled "American Education: Making it Work" (1988). According to the report, "the precipitous downward slide of previous decades has been arrested and we have begun the long climb back to reasonable standards." However, despite this progress, especially among minority groups, the report condemned the performance of American schools as unacceptably low. "Too many students do not graduate from our high schools, and too many of those who do graduate have been poorly educated.... Our students know little, and their command of essential skills is too slight."

Particularly troublesome is student performance in math and science. According to a study done by the Nation's Report Card (1988), an assessment group that is part of the Educational Testing Service, the math performance of 17-year-olds is "dismal." The study found that although half the nation's 17-year-olds have no trouble with junior high school math, they flounder when asked to solve multistep high-school-level problems or those involving algebra or geometry. Fewer than one in fifteen students were able to answer these problems correctly. At fault might be the very back-to-basics movement that was supposed to rescue our educational system from failure in the early 1980s. Although rote learning helps improve the scores of the lowest-level students, it leaves others totally unprepared to analyze complex problems.

The Nation's Report Card also found American students' understanding of science "distressingly low." In a condemnation of the performance of America's schools in the area of science, the report found that most 17-year-olds did not have the skills to handle today's technologically based jobs and that only 7 percent could cope with college-level science courses.

Perhaps the most disheartening evidence of the failure of our schools to prepare Americans with essential academic skills is the astonishingly high number of functionally illiterate adults found throughout America. Some 23 million to 27 million adults, roughly 10 percent of the nation's population, cannot read and write well enough to hold down a job or otherwise function properly in society (*U.S. News & World Report,* June 20, 1988).

This failure will become even more critical as businesses place greater demands on workers. Studies predict that by the year 2000 almost all new jobs will require more than a high school education and literacy skills to match. Right now millions of workers are unable to meet these basic literacy standards. Some 14 million workers

Between 23 and 27 million adults in the United States are functionally illiterate and cannot read these signs.

read at a fourth-grade level and an additional 23 million at an eighth-grade level. They continue to be employed even though 70 percent of all work-related documents are written at the ninth-grade level or above. This type of functional illiteracy costs businesses millions of dollars each year in poor productivity, low product quality, on-the-job accidents, and absenteeism (Daniels, 1988).

INNOVATION

A primary task of educational institutions is to transmit society's knowledge, and part of that knowledge consists of the means by which new knowledge is to be sought. Learning how to think independently and creatively is probably one of the most valuable tools the educational institution can transmit. This is especially true in the scientific fields in institutions of higher education. Until well into this century, scientific research was undertaken more as a hobby than as a vocation. This was because science was not seen as a socially useful pursuit. Gregor Mendel (1822–1884), who discovered, by breeding peas, the principles of genetic inheritance, worked alone in the gardens of the monastery where he lived. And Albert Einstein supported himself between

It was only in this century that scientific research was seen as a socially useful pursuit.

breakthroughs—without the training provided by these schools. In the United States alone, 11,405 doctorates were awarded in 1986 in the biological and physical sciences, mathematics, computer science, and engineering. During 1985 the combined fields of science and engineering employed 396,000 scientists in institutions of higher education *(Statistical Abstract of the United States: 1989)*. Second, the universities of the highest caliber continue to serve as the point of origin for some of the most significant research currently undertaken in both the biological and the physical sciences.

In addition to their manifest or intended functions, the schools in America have come to fulfill a number of functions that they were not originally designed to serve.

1905 and 1907 as a patent office employee while making several trail-blazing discoveries in physics, the most widely known of which is the "special theory of relativity."

Today, science obviously is no longer the province of part-timers. Modern scientific research typically is undertaken by highly trained professionals, many of whom frequently work as teams; and the technology needed for exploration of this type has become so expensive that most research is possible only under the aegis of extensive government or corporate funding. In 1987 the federal government spent $117.9 billion on research and development funding *(Statistical Abstract of the United States: 1989)*. Research and development in the areas of national defense, space exploration, and health research receive by far the greatest amount of support. In research alone, the leading three areas are life sciences (biological sciences and agriculture), engineering, and the physical sciences.

The achievements of government and industrial research and development notwithstanding, the importance of the contributions to science by top academic institutions cannot be overestimated. First, there could be no scientific innovations—no

CHILD CARE

One latent function of many public schools is to provide child care outside the nuclear family. This has become increasingly important since World War II, when women began to enter the labor force in large numbers. As of 1988, 72.5 percent of married females with school-age children (age 6 to 17), were in the labor force, as well as 83.9 percent of divorced women with children that age *(Statistical Abstract of the United States: 1989)*.

A related service of schools is to provide children with at least one nutritious meal a day. In 1975 the number of public-school pupils in the United States participating in federally funded school lunch programs was 25,289,000, at a cost of $1.28 billion. By 1987 the number of pupils in the school lunch program had dropped to 11,600,000, at a cost of $3.28 billion *(Statistical Abstract of the United States: 1989)*. Recent across-the-board federal reductions have established new and stringent criteria of eligibility for the program and in addition have appreciably reduced the monetary amount of government subsidization.

However, despite this, a move is on to make free or reduced-cost breakfasts available to a larger number of students. Proponents of this program claim a positive relationship between early-morning nutrition and improved learning and performance. Many children are forced to fend for themselves early in the morning and, all to often, they leave home without breakfast. Currently, only 37,000 schools across the country serve breakfasts, compared to 90,000 who serve subsidized lunches. *(New York Times,* June 22, 1988).

POSTPONING JOB HUNTING

More and more young American adults are choosing to continue their education after graduating from high school. In 1986, 36.2 percent of male and 36.9 percent of female high school graduates age 18 to 21 were enrolled in college *(Statistical Abstract of the United States: 1989).* Even though some of these individuals also work at part-time and even full-time jobs, an important latent function of the American educational system is to slow down the entry of young adults into the labor market. This helps keep down unemployment, as well as competition for low-paying unskilled jobs.

Originally, two factors pointed to the possibility that college enrollments would not continue to increase. Because of low birth rates, the number of high school graduates peaked at 3.2 million in 1977 and began a 15-year decline. There were 16 percent fewer high school graduates in 1987 than 1977, and the number will drop another 11 percent by 1992. Another concern and possible cause of decreased enrollments may be the rigor that is now being applied to the government subsidization of student loans. Strict new criteria for loan eligibility are being enforced, and in addition, higher interest rates and shorter repayment periods may mean that thousands fewer students from all socioeconomic levels will be able to afford a college education or graduate studies.

Colleges and universities, in anticipa-

tion of the potential enrollment problems, have embarked on concerted efforts to ward off disaster. Through hard work and luck they have succeeded. Despite the loss of half a million high school graduates in the last decade, total enrollment in two- and four-year colleges rose from 11.5 million in 1977 to 12.4 million in 1986.

Colleges have also benefited from the fact that the U.S. economic base has shifted from manufacturing jobs to service jobs. This has caused the demand for professionals and technicians to grow. The salaries for these types of positions are considerably higher than manufacturing jobs. In one study of the average annual incomes of men 25 to 34 years old, those with college degrees earned 40 percent more than high school graduates and 93 percent more than high school dropouts (Edmondson, 1987). Small wonder that the most common reason given today for going to college is "to get a better job."

Colleges have also benefited from two other trends. The first is the increase in the number of women going to college, and the second is the increase in the number of older students. Beginning in 1980, the majority of college students were women. In

A noneducational service of many schools is to provide children with at least one nutritious meal a day.

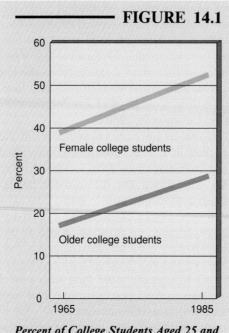

FIGURE 14.1

Percent of College Students Aged 25 and Over and Percent Female, 1965 and 1985. *Women are now a majority of college students, while older students account for more than one-fourth of college enrollment.* Source: *U.S. Bureau of the Census:* Current Population Reports; *"School Enrollment, Social and Economic Characteristics of Students: October 1985," ser. P-20, no. 409.*

changing gender-role expectations (see Figure 14.1).

THE CONFLICT THEORY VIEW

To the conflict theorist, society is an arena for conflict, not cooperation. In any society, certain groups come to dominate others, and social institutions become the instruments by which those in power are able to control the less powerful. The conflict theorist thus sees the educational system as a means for maintaining the status quo, which it is able to do in a variety of ways. The educational system socializes students in values dictated by the powerful majority. Schools are seen as systems that stifle individualism and creativity in the name of maintaining order. To the conflict theorist the function of school "is to produce the kind of people the system needs, to train people for the jobs the corporations require and to instill in them the proper attitudes and values necessary for the proper fulfillment of one's social role" (Szymanski and Goertzel, 1979).

1985 the figures were 52 percent female and 48 percent male. This trend is an outgrowth of changing attitudes about the status of women in our society, and the breakdown in gender-role stereotypes (see Chapter 11).

Older students (age 25 and over) represent the most rapidly growing group of college students, accounting for 45 percent of all undergraduate and graduate students (*Newsweek,* June 6, 1988). Women are again overrepresented in this group, as are part-time students. Many of these returning women students are also responding to

SOCIAL CONTROL

In the United States, schools have been assigned the function of developing personal control and social skills in children. Although the explicit, formally defined school curriculum emphasizes basic skills such as reading and writing, much of what is taught is in fact oriented away from practical concerns. Many critics point out that much of the curriculum (other than in special professional training programs) has little direct, practical application to everyday life. This has led conflict theorists and others to conclude that the most important lessons learned in school are not those listed in the formal curriculum but, rather, are the social *attitudes and values* that schools drum into children explicitly and implicitly. This **hidden curriculum** is what prepares children to accept the requirements of adult life and to "fit into" the social, political, and economic statuses the society provides.

To succeed in school, a student must learn both the official (academic) curriculum and the hidden (social) curriculum. The hidden curriculum is often an outgrowth of the structure within which the student is asked to learn. Within the framework of mass education, it would be impossible to provide instruction on a one-to-one basis or even in very small groups. Consequently, students are usually grouped into relatively large classes. Because this system obviously demands a great deal of social conformity by the children, those who divert attention and make it difficult for the teacher to proceed are punished. In many respects the hidden curriculum is a lesson in being docile. For example, an article in *Today's Education,* the journal of the National Education Association, gives an experienced teacher's advice to new teachers: "During the first week or two of teaching in an inner-city school, I concentrate on establishing simple routines, such as the procedure for walking downstairs. I line up the children, and . . . have them practice walking up and down the stairs. Each time the group is allowed to move only when quiet and orderly."

Social skills are highly valued in American society, and a mastery of them is widely accepted as an indication of a child's maturity. The school is a "miniature society," and many individuals fail in school because they are either unable or unwilling to learn or use the values, attitudes, and skills contained in the hidden curriculum. We do a great disservice to these students when we make them feel that they have failed in education, when they have in fact only failed to conform to the school's socialization standards.

SCREENING AND ALLOCATION: TRACKING

From its beginning, the American school system *in principle* has been opposed to **tracking**—the stratification of students by ability, social class, and other categories. Legislators saw in compulsory public education a way to allow each individual to rise to what was believed to be the level of his or her "innate" ability. This approach had several goals. First, it was intended to diminish the grip of inherited social stratification by providing the means for individuals to rise as high as their achieved skills would allow. In the words of Horace Mann, an influential American educator of the late nineteenth century, public education was to be "the great equalizer of the conditions of men." The second goal of mass education, closely related to the first, was the desired "Anglo conformity" of the crowds of immigrants whose ethnic and cultural diversity was seen by many as a dangerous source of potential social chaos (see Chapter 10). The third aim of universal public education was to give workers a wide range of skills to match the requirements of an increasingly complex industrial economy.

hidden curriculum The social attitudes and values learned in school that prepare children to accept the requirements of adult life and to "fit into" the social, political, and economic statuses of adult life.

tracking The stratification of students by ability, social class, and various other categories.

To succeed in school, a student must learn both the official academic curriculum and the hidden curriculum.

Despite the principles on which it is based, the American educational system does utilize tracking. Although tracking in American education is not as formally structured or as irreversible as in most other industrial societies, it is influenced by many factors, including socioeconomic status, ethnicity, and place of residence. It is also consistently expressed in the differences between public and private schools, as well as in the differences among public schools. (In New York City, for example, there are highly competitive math- and science-oriented and arts-oriented high schools, neighborhood high schools, and vocational high schools.) And of course, tracking occurs in higher education in the selection of students by private colleges and universities, state colleges, and junior colleges.

Tracking begins with stratifying students into "fast," "average," and "slow" groups, from first grade through high school. It can be difficult for a student to break out of an assigned category because teachers come to expect a certain level of performance from that individual. In turn, the student, sensing this expectation, will often give the level of performance that is expected. In this way, tracking becomes a self-fulfilling prophecy.

In one study of this phenomenon, Rosenthal and Jacobson (1966) gave IQ tests to 650 lower-class elementary school pupils. Their teachers were told that the test would predict which of the students were the "bloomers" or "spurters." In other words, the tests would identify the superior students in the class. This approach was in fact not the one employed. Twenty percent of the students were randomly selected to be designated as "superior," even though there was no measured difference between them and the other 80 percent of the school population. The point of the study was to determine whether the teacher's expectations would have any effect on the "superior" students. At the end of the first year, all the students were tested again. There was a significant difference in the gain in IQ scores between the "superior" group and the control group. This gain was most pronounced among those students in the first and second grades. Yet the following year, when these students were promoted to another class and assigned to teachers who had not been told that they were "superior," they no longer made the sorts of gains they had during the previous year. Nonetheless, the "superior" students in the upper grades did continue to gain during their second year, showing that there had been long-term advantages from positive teacher expectations for them. Apparently, the younger students needed continuous input to benefit from the teacher's expectations, whereas the older students needed less.

Some authors (Bowles and Gintis, 1976) go so far as to assert that the idea that educational success is determined by merit or intelligence is an illusion fostered by the schools. Educational success, they claim, is much more likely to be determined by the possession of appropriate personality traits, and by conformity to school norms. These traits are acquired in the family and home environments of the students. The educational system, while claiming to reward those who demonstrate objective displays of merit, in fact is rewarding behavioral characteristics already possessed by individuals from specific social class backgrounds, that is, the middle class.

THE CREDENTIALIZED SOCIETY

Conflict theorists would also argue that we have become a "credentialized society" (Collins, 1979) in the last 30 years. A degree or certificate has become necessary to perform a vast variety of jobs. This credential may not necessarily cause the recipient to perform the job better. Even in professions such as medicine, engineering, and law, most knowledge is acquired by performing tasks on the job. However, credentials have become a rite of passage, and a sign that a certain process of indoctrination and social-ization has taken place. It is recognized that the individual has gone through the educa-tional socialization that constitutes ade-quate preparation to hold the occupational status. Therefore, colleges and universities act as gatekeepers, allowing those who are willing to play by the rules to succeed, and barring those who may disrupt the existing social order.

At the same time, advanced degrees are undergoing constant change and becoming less specialized. Obtaining a law degree from Harvard, Yale, or Columbia is less an indication of the quality of the training of a particular candidate, but rather provides a basis upon which leading corporations, major public agencies, and important law firms can recruit those who will maintain the status quo. The degree signifies that the candidate has forged links with the estab-lished networks and achieved a grade neces-sary to obtain a degree.

Colleges and universities are miniature societies more than centers of technical and scientific education. In these environments students learn how to operate within the established order and to accept traditional social hierarchies. In this sense they provide the power structure with a constantly re-plenishing army of defenders of the estab-lished order. At the same time those who could disrupt the status quo are not permit-ted to enter positions of power and responsi-bility.

ISSUES IN AMERICAN EDUCATION

How well have American schools done in educating the population? The answer to this question depends on the standards one applies. Americans take it for granted that everyone has a basic right to an education and that the state should provide free ele-

mentary and high school classes. The United States pioneered this concept long before similar systems were introduced in Europe.

As we have attempted to provide for-mal education to everyone, we have also had to contend with a wide variety of prob-lems stemming from the diverse popula-tion. In this section we will examine some of the concerns in contemporary American education.

UNEQUAL ACCESS TO EDUCATION

American blacks have sought equal access to public schools for two centuries. Tracing these efforts over the generations reveals a pattern of dissatisfaction with both inte-grated and segregated schools.

Black parents attributed the ineffective instruction at the schools attended by their children to one of two causes. If the schools were all-black, failure was attributed to the

Schools act as gate-keepers, allowing those who are willing to play by the rules to succeed and barring those who may disrupt the existing social order.

racially segregated character of those schools. If whites were attending those schools, black parents concluded, conditions would be better. This has been the predominant theme both in the nineteenth and twentieth centuries.

Discontent has also occurred when black children have attended predominantly white schools. In those instances, the racially integrated character of the school was seen as a problem because white students were favored by the teachers.

In 1954 the Supreme Court ruled that school segregation was illegal. The Court held that "in the field of public education, the doctrine of separate but equal has no place. Separate educational facilities are inherently unequal." Segregating black schoolchildren from white schoolchildren was a violation of the equal protection clause of the Constitution.

Ten years later, the federal government attempted to document the degree to which equality of education among all groups had been achieved. It financed a cross-sectional study of 645,000 children in grades one, three, six, nine, and twelve attending some 4000 different schools across the country. The results, appearing in James S. Coleman's now-famous report *Equality of Educational Opportunity* (1966), supported unequivocally the conclusion that "American education remains largely unequal in most parts of the country, including those where Negroes form any significant proportion of the population." Coleman noted further that on all tests measuring pupils' skills in areas critical to job performance and career advancement, not only did Native Americans, Mexican Americans, Puerto Ricans, and blacks score significantly below whites but the gaps widened in the higher grades. Now for a subtle but extremely important point: although there are acknowledged wide inequalities of educational opportunity throughout the United States, the discrepancies between the skills of minorities and those of their white counterparts could not be accounted for in terms of how much

money was spent on education per pupil, quality of school buildings, number of labs or libraries, or even class sizes. In spite of good intentions, a school presumably cannot usually outweigh the influence of the family backgrounds of its individual students and of the family background of its student population as a whole. The Coleman study thus provided evidence that schools per se do not play as important a role in student achievement as was once thought. It appears that the home environment, the quality of the neighborhood, and the types of friends and associates one has are much more influential in school *achievement* than the quality of the school facilities or the skills of teachers. In effect, then, the areas that schools have least control over — the areas of social influence and development — are the most important in determining how well an individual will do in school.

Colleges and universities have had mixed results in increasing minority enrollment. Between 1980 and 1985, the number of blacks enrolled as undergraduates was on a steady decline before rising again slightly in 1986. Many qualified students do not apply because their families cannot afford tuition, despite the fact that complete aid packages are available. To overcome this problem, many schools have taken an aggressive recruitment stance, believing that once they find qualified candidates, they can convince them to attend. For example, at Guilford College in Greensboro, North Carolina, the tuition and living expenses of needy minority students are covered in full. At Harvard University, where 214 blacks were accepted to the freshman class in 1988 — the largest number in the school's history — no student is turned away because of financial need.

Still, thousands of qualified minority students never attend college, and many who do attend fail to graduate. The reasons for low graduation rates include financial problems, poor preparation, and the feeling that they are not really welcome. Many cannot afford the loss of income that comes with being a full-time student. For many, family survival depends on the money they contribute. Others are victims of inadequate schools. They simply do not have the skills needed to complete college. Still others drop out because they feel out of place in the predominantly white world of higher education.

SCHOOL INTEGRATION

There are two types of segregation. The first, **de jure segregation,** is an outgrowth of local laws that prohibit one racial group from attending school with another. This is the form of segregation the Supreme Court declared illegal in 1954. The second type, **de facto segregation,** is much more common today. De facto segregation results from residential patterns in which minority groups often live in areas of a city where there are few whites or none at all. Consequently, when children attend neighborhood schools, they are usually taught in an environment that is racially segregated.

The Coleman report pointed out that lower-class nonwhite students showed better school achievement when they went to school with middle-class whites. Racial segregation, therefore, hindered the educational attainments of nonwhites.

A direct outgrowth of the Coleman report pointing to the harm of de facto segregation was the busing of children from one neighborhood to another to achieve racial integration in the schools. The fundamental assumption underlying school busing was that it would bring about improved academic achievement among minority groups. Nationwide, many parents, both black and white, responded negatively to the idea that their school-age children must leave their home neighborhoods. For all practical purposes, busing is no longer a major issue today. Those schools that needed to desegregate have done so, and other less disruptive approaches to desegregation are attempted.

One factor that has increased the difficulty of integrating public schools is so-called white flight, the continuing exodus of white Americans by the hundreds of thousands from the cities to the suburbs. White flight has been prompted partly by the migration of blacks from the South to the inner cities of the North and Midwest during the past two decades, but some authorities strongly maintain that it is also closely related to school desegregation efforts in the large cities.

In a later view of desegregation attempts (1977), James Coleman vastly revised his position in his 1966 report, stating that urban desegregation has in some instances had the self-defeating effect of emptying the cities of white pupils. Some authorities (Pettigrew and Green, 1975), however, took exception to the Coleman thesis, and others believe that what may appear to be flight is more directly related to the characteristic tendency of the American middle class to be "upwardly mobile" and constantly to seek a better life-style. Even though there is some evidence of a counter-trend in which middle-class whites are beginning to "regentrify" inner cities, there seems to be no abating of this migration. Nor have most established communities relinquished the ideal of self-determination as embodied in the right to maintain "neighborhood" schools.

Since the Coleman report was issued, the integration of our schools has continued to be a critical problem, especially in urban areas where the vast majority of minority group members live. According to a study by the National School Boards Association, there has been "no significant progress on the desegregation of black students in urban districts since the mid-1970s," and some areas have shown "severe increases in racial isolation" (Fiske, 1988). Schools in Atlanta and Detroit, for example, are more segregated now than they were a decade ago.

Only about 3 percent of the nation's white students attend one of the central city schools. As a result, these schools "have be-

de jure segregation Segregation that is an outgrowth of local laws that prohibit one racial group from attending school with another.

de facto segregation Segregation of community or neighborhood schools that results from residential patterns in which minority groups often live in areas of a city where there are few whites or none at all.

TABLE 14.1
Percentage Change of Student Populations, 1968–1986

District	White	Black	Hispanic	Asian
Baltimore	−16	15	0	0
Broward County, Fla.	−10	2	5	1
Chicago	−24	5	17	2
Dade County, Fla.	−34	9	25	1
Dallas	−40	19	20	2
Detroit	−30	31	1	0
Houston	−36	10	24	3
Los Angeles	−36	−4	36	4
Memphis	−22	24	0	1
New York	−22	8	11	5
Philadelphia	−14	5	7	3
San Diego	−32	7	9	15

Source: New York Times, June 23, 1988, p. A16. Reprinted by permission.

come almost irrelevant to the nation's white population." There are currently many more minority and far fewer white students in our public schools than in the past (Fiske, 1988).

As whites are leaving the inner city schools, they are being replaced by blacks, Hispanics, and Asian Americans. However, these groups tend to be isolated from one another, and often their relationships are characterized by as much friction as the relationship between blacks and whites. Table 14.1 shows the shifting student population in twelve of our nation's largest school districts. The task ahead is to successfully reconcile the differences among these various minority groups in order to meet the needs of all the children in inner-city schools.

HIGH SCHOOL DROPOUTS

Dropping out of high school has long been viewed as a serious educational and social problem. By leaving high school before graduation, dropouts risk serious educational deficiencies that severely limit their economic and social well-being.

Over the last 75 years, the proportion of people in the adult population who have failed to finish high school has decreased substantially. In 1910 the proportion of the adult population (age 25 and over) that had completed at least 4 years of high school was 13.5 percent. It stood at 24.5 percent in 1940; at 55.2 percent in 1970; and at 74.7 percent in 1986. Among young people (age 25 to 29) the drop is even more striking, with 86.2 percent having completed high school in 1986.

Despite these long-term declines in dropout rates, interest in the dropout issue among educators and policy makers has increased substantially in recent years. Legislators and education officials are devoting ever more time and resources to dealing with the issue. For example, the "Dropout Prevention and Re-entry Act," which was passed in 1986, authorizes $50 million a year in federal funds for dropout-plagued school systems. In New York City, $38 million a year goes into dropout prevention programs (Finn, 1987).

If the long-term trend is that dropout rates are declining, why has the concern for this problem increased lately? First, although the long-term trend of dropping out has declined, the short-term trend has remained steady and even increased for some groups.

A second reason is that minority populations, who have always had higher dropout rates than whites, are increasing as a proportion of the public high school population. Racial and ethnic minorities now represent the majority of students enrolled in most large U.S. cities and more than 90 percent of all students in some cities, such as Newark, Atlanta, and San Antonio (Plisko and Stern, 1985).

Dropout rates are higher for members of racial, ethnic, and language minorities; higher for males than females; and higher for persons from the lower socioeconomic classes. Hispanics have the highest dropout rates — 19.1 percent, compared to 17.2 percent for blacks, and 13.0 percent for whites. Among Hispanics, Puerto Ricans have the highest dropout rates, followed by Mexican Americans and Cubans. Dropout rates are also particularly high among American Indians.

Factors associated with dropping out include low educational and occupational attainment levels of parents, low family income, speaking a language other than English in the home, single-parent families, and poor academic achievement.

The influence of peers is also important, but has not received much attention in previous research. Many dropouts have friends who are also dropouts, but it is not clear to what extent and in what ways a student's friends and peers influence the decision to leave school (Rumberger, 1987).

Dropping out of high school affects not only those who leave school, but also society at large. In addition, the social consequences go beyond the economic and psychological impact on the dropout. In a comprehensive study of the dropout problem, Levin (1972) identified seven social consequences of dropping out of high school:

1. A loss of national income because dropouts earn less than graduates
2. A loss of tax revenues because of the lower earnings of dropouts
3. Increased demand for social services, including welfare, medical assistance, and unemployment compensation
4. Increased crime
5. Reduced political participation
6. Reduced intergenerational mobility
7. Poorer levels of health

Levin estimates that every dollar invested in dropout programs would produce $6 in national income and almost $2 in tax revenues. A more recent study estimated that the costs of dropout prevention programs in Chicago are only 1 percent of the benefits derived from increased tax revenues, reduced welfare payments, and reduced crime (Hess and Lauber, 1985).

Peer influence is an important factor in a student's decision to drop out of high school.

HAVE SCHOOLS LOST THEIR INNOCENCE?

W hen people talk longingly of the "good old days," it is usually a good idea to question whether yesteryear was really that good. (Things often appear better as time passes.)

However, fond memories for days-gone-by in our nation's schools may be well deserved. When it comes to school discipline, we have left behind a more innocent age and substituted in its stead an age of violence.

Source: Time, February 1, 1988, p. 54. Reprinted by permission.

THE GOOD OLD DAYS
Leading school discipline problems: a California study compares today with a more innocent age

1940s	1980s
Talking	Drug abuse
Chewing gum	Alcohol abuse
Making noise	Pregnancy
Running in the hallways	Suicide
Getting out of place in line	Rape
Wearing improper clothing	Robbery
Not putting paper in wastebaskets	Assault
	Burglary
	Arson
	Bombings

Study was conducted by the Fullerton, Calif., police department and the California department of education. The results were published in *Junior League Review.*

TIME Charts by Cynthia Davis

Given these facts, it is small wonder that the U.S. Department of Education has focused an increasing amount of attention on how to improve high school completion rates.

VIOLENCE IN THE SCHOOLS

Nothing undermines the effectiveness of our educational system more than unsafe schools. Throughout the country students carry to school drugs, guns, knives, and other paraphernalia of destruction. Gone are books, pencils, and paper—the tools of learning that must be present for education to take place. In some high schools, metal detectors are used to reduce the number of weapons brought into the schools. In New York City, there were about 1400 incidents involving weapons in the schools in 1987. In some Chicago schools, where gangs freely sell drugs to students within school buildings, principals chain doors to keep dealers out and students in. Philadelphia has schools where students are afraid to use filthy school bathrooms because of the gang members who hang out there.

The violence that fills America's inner-city schools came to the public's attention when Joe Clark, principal of Eastside High in Paterson, New Jersey, graced the cover of *Time* magazine. When Clark took over Eastside in 1982, he found deplorable conditions that he was determined to change. In response,

Clark chained doors against pushers and threatened any strays that might leak through with a baseball bat. . . . Bellowing through the bullhorn and the school's p.a. system, he banned loitering, mandated keep-to-the-right and keep-moving rules for the corridors, and set up a dress code forbidding hats and any gangish . . . clothing. Students who got to school late or cut class could expect latrine or graffiti-scrubbing duty. (*Time,* February 1, 1988)

Although Clark's methods have been severely criticized by many educators and government officials throughout the country, and praised by others, including former President Reagan, his actions showed the desperate conditions of inner-city schools and the measures some are willing to take to improve them. Inner-city schools are made up primarily of minority students, have high dropout rates, high assault rates, and a staff that expects failure and violence (see Table 14.2).

STANDARDIZED TESTING

In American schools, the standardized test is the most frequently used means of evaluating students' aptitudes and abilities. Every year more than 100 million standardized tests are administered, ranking the mental talents of individuals from nursery school to graduate school.

Children encounter standardized tests almost from the first day they come to school. Usually their first experience with testing takes the form of an intelligence test. These are given to more than two million youngsters each year. Students are also required to take a number of achievement tests, beginning in elementary school. High school and college seniors take college admissions tests that decide whether they will be accepted at universities and graduate schools.

Much criticism has been leveled against standardized tests. The testing services claim their tests merely try to chart,

TABLE 14.2

City (Number of students in thousands)	**Minorities** % of students that are black and Hispanic	**Dropouts** % who enter ninth grade but left before 4 years*	**Assaults** Number of cases reported last year	**Counselors** Ratio to high school students
Boston (56)	63%	46%	410	1/313
Chicago (431)	83%	45%	698	1/398
Houston (192)	81%	41%	128**	1/500
Los Angeles (592)	75%	45%	493	1/298
Miami (255)	75%	NA	909 ('86)	1/420
New York (939)	72%	34%	1,606	1/623
St. Louis (47)	76%	30%	NA	1/390

*Cities compute rate in different ways; figures include students who moved   NA — Not available   **Arrests

Source: Time, February 1, 1988, p. 55. Reprinted by permission.

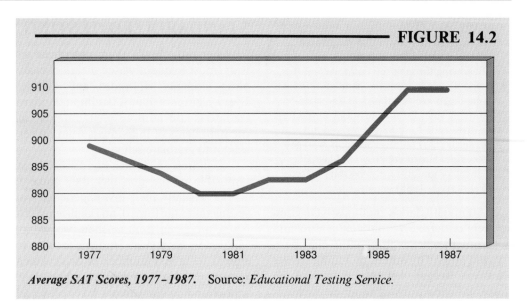

FIGURE 14.2

Average SAT Scores, 1977–1987. Source: *Educational Testing Service.*

scientifically and objectively, different levels of mental achievement and aptitude. The critics charge that the tests are academically invalid and biased against minorities.

The Educational Testing Service's (ETS) Scholastic Aptitude Test (SAT) is the best-known college admissions test and is required by about 1200 colleges and universities. Another 2800 American colleges require or recommend the American College Test (ACT). Students wishing to go to graduate school are required to take other exams that are tailored to measure the ability and skills used in the field that they wish to enter.

The ETS claims to be meticulous in its test construction. It hires college students, teachers, and professors to assist its staff in writing questions. Each of the approximately 3000 questions that are created each year are reviewed by about fifteen people for style, content, or racial bias.

The criticism of standardized tests, however, continues to grow. Many claim that all standardized tests are biased against minorities. The average black or Hispanic youngster encounters references and vocabulary on a test that is likely to be more familiar to white middle-class students. Many others oppose the secrecy surrounding the test companies. Groups have pushed for "truth in testing," meaning that the test makers must divulge all exam questions and answers shortly after the tests are given. This would enable people to evaluate the tests more closely for cultural bias and possible scoring errors. The testing industry is opposed to such measures, because it would be forced to create totally new tests for each administration, without the possibility of reusing valid and reliable questions.

No one would claim that standardized tests are perfect measuring instruments. At best they can provide an objective measure to be used in conjunction with teachers' grades and opinions. At worst, they may discriminate against minorities or not validly measure potential ability. Yet, college admissions officers insist that results from standardized college admissions tests give them a significant tool to use in evaluating students from a variety of backgrounds and many different parts of the country.

As you can see from Figure 14.2, more students are taking the SAT than ever before, a fact that might be expected to result in lowered scores. Instead, average combined SAT scores have risen sixteen points since 1980, reversing a trend that saw scores drop ninety points from 1963 to 1980. In part, these increased scores can be attributed to the more rigorous standards of the back-to-basics movement—a movement that has brought about modest gains among poor performers.

THE GIFTED

The very term *gifted* is emotionally loaded. The word may evoke feelings that range from admiration to resentment and hostility. Throughout history, people have displayed a marked ambivalence toward the gifted. It was not unusual to view giftedness as either divinely or diabolically inspired. Genius was often seen as one aspect of insanity. Aristotle's observation "There was never a great genius without a tincture of madness" continues to be believed as common folklore.

People also tend to believe that intellectualism and practicality are incompatible. It is expressed in such sayings as "He (or she) is too smart for his (her) own good," or "It's not smart to be too smart." High intelligence is often assumed to be incompatible with happiness.

There is little agreement on what constitutes giftedness. The most common measure is performance on a standardized test. All those who score above a certain level are defined as gifted, though there are serious problems when this criterion alone is used. Arbitrary approaches to measuring giftedness tend to ignore the likelihood that active intervention could increase the number of candidates among females, the disabled, and selected minorities, groups that are often underrepresented among the gifted.

Females tend to be underrepresented among the gifted because popular culture deems that high intelligence is incompatible with femininity; thus some girls quickly learn to deny, disguise, or repress their abilities. Minorities are hindered by the fact that commonly used assessment tools discriminate against ethnic groups whose members have had different cultural experiences or use English as a second language. The intellectual ability of disabled youngsters is often overlooked. Their physical handicaps may mask or divert attention from their mental potential, particularly when communica-

Schools spend much more money on programs for the learning disabled than they do on programs for the gifted.

Does Television Make Kids Stupid?

Critics of television claim that instead of reading and doing homework, today's kids settle in front of the tube with vacant minds, mesmerized and numbed by constant movement and visual change. The evils of television are said to be reduced attention span, hyperactivity, loss of creativity and imagination, poor reading ability, and even deterioration of the left half of the brain. Can it really be that bad?

After examining more than 165 studies on the topic from the time of television's inception to the present, researchers Daniel R. Anderson and Patricia A. Collins can find almost no scientific evidence that television has a negative effect on the intellectual ability of children.

Some of the questions they asked were:

1. Are children mesmerized by TV? Not really. Children between 5 and 11 years old actually only look at the TV about two-thirds of the time. They are usually doing something else while they are watching and look away from the set over one hundred times an hour.

2. Do children have blank minds when they watch TV? Not likely. Studies show that children actively try to comprehend what they are watching, make judgments about it, and try to anticipate the outcome. This is very similar to what a child does when reading or listening to the radio.

3. Does TV replace other valuable intellectual activities? Not really. The studies note that television replaces other entertainment media, such as movies, radio, and comic books. There is virtually no reduction in the reading of books or magazines due to television.

tion is impaired, because this is a key factor in assessment procedures.

Teachers often confuse intelligence with unrelated school behaviors. Children who are neat, clean, and well mannered, have good handwriting, or manifest other desirable but irrelevant classroom traits may often be thought to be very bright.

Teachers often associate giftedness with children who come from prominent families, have traveled widely, or have had extensive cultural advantages. Teachers are likely to discount high intelligence when it might be present in combination with poor grammar, truancy, aggressiveness, or learning disabilities.

The first attempt to deal with the gifted in public education took place in the St. Louis schools in 1868. The program involved a system of flexible promotions enabling high-achieving students not to have to remain in any grade for a fixed amount of time. By the early 1900s, special schools for the gifted began to appear.

There has never been a consistent, cohesive national policy or consensus on how to educate the gifted. Those special programs that have been instituted have reached only a small fraction of those who conceivably could benefit from them. A serious problem with the education of the gifted arises from philosophical considerations. Many teachers are reluctant to single out the gifted for special treatment, because they think the children are already naturally privileged. Sometimes, attention given to gifted children is seen as antidemocratic.

No matter how inadequate it may seem, the effort to provide for the educational needs of learning-disabled children has far exceeded that expended for the gifted. Similarly, the time and money spent

This should not be surprising. The typical American child did very little reading outside of school before television arrived and the situation is no different today.

4. Does TV reduce attention span? Educational programs such as "Sesame Street" and "Mister Rogers" appear to have positive effects, while violent action programs appear to have negative effects.

5. Does TV watching impair reading ability? Poor readers spend more time watching TV than reading, but that does not mean that TV produces poor reading. Most studies have shown there is no effect.

6. Does television have any positive effects on intellectual development? Preschool children learn some vocabulary from television and educational programs can educate. On the whole, however, there is little evidence that television either enhances or detracts from development of the intellect.

Anderson and Collins go on to point out that this does not mean that television is good for children. It does shape their thinking about the world. If society is depicted as violent and people are depicted as motivated by greed, children will learn these messages. Thus while the medium may be neither good nor bad, the messages may have an undesirable effect.

Source: Daniel R. Anderson and Patricia A. Collins, "Does TV Make Kids Stupid?," *The Boston Globe,* January 15, 1989, p. A21, A23.

on research for educating slower children far outstrip that set aside for research on materials, methodology for teaching, and so on, for the gifted.

When schools do have enrichment programs, they are rarely monitored as to their effectiveness. Enrichment programs are often provided by teachers totally untrained in dealing with the gifted, for it is assumed that anyone qualified to teach is presumably capable of teaching the gifted. Yet, most basic teacher certification programs do not require even one hour's exposure to information on the theory, identification, or methodology of teaching such children in the classroom. Most administrators do not have the theoretical background or practical experience necessary to establish and promote successful programs for the gifted.

There is some evidence that the nation's population of gifted children—and possibly, prodigies—is growing. Researchers who test large numbers of children have detected a startling proportion in the 170 to 180 IQ range.

But while psychologists would agree that early exceptional ability should be nurtured in order to thrive, they do not necessarily think that the current movement to produce "superbabies" by force-feeding a diet of mathematics and vocabulary to infants is a good idea. Pediatricians have begun seeing children with backlash symptoms—headaches, tummyaches, hair-tearing, anxiety, depression—as a result of this pressure to perform.

History has shown that being an authentic child prodigy creates problems enough of its own. The fine line between nurturing genius and trying to force a bright but not brilliant child to be something he is not is clearly one that must be walked with care.

It appears that there are more than 2.5 million schoolchildren in the United States that can be described as gifted, or about 3 percent of the school population. Giftedness is essentially *potential*. Whether these children will achieve their potential intellectual growth will depend on many factors, not the least of which is the level of educational instruction they receive. We must question why we continue to show such ambivalence toward the gifted and why we are willing to tolerate incompetence and waste in regard to such a valuable resource (Baskin and Harris, 1980).

SUMMARY

All societies must have an educational system. There must be a way of teaching the young what is expected and required by the culture. As we grow from childhood into adulthood, we acquire the knowledge and skills that will prepare us to fulfill our own needs and those of society. Much of a child's learning occurs through socialization (being reared or "brought up"), and much also results from schooling (education). So-called primitive cultures tend not to compartmentalize socialization and education, whereas in modern Western societies socialization is distinguished as an informal activity and education as a formal one.

In America, from the late nineteenth century onward, public education has been heralded as the great equalizer of the "conditions of men," offering every individual the opportunity for intellectual, social, and material advancement to the limits of his or her innate abilities. Although many modern educators concur as to the educational system's overall responsibilities, the conflicting values of our pluralistic society have produced a lack of consensus regarding which curricula should be taught, which teaching techniques are best, and who should determine what students will be expected to learn.

The functions that the educational system serves can be divided into manifest (intended) ones and latent (incidental, or unintended) ones. The manifest functions include socialization and cultural transmission, the passing on to successive generations the norms and values of the society or group to which one belongs. Teaching academic and social skills and innovation are other manifest functions. Latent functions include child care and the postponement of job hunting by young adults.

Conflict theorists view the educational system as a means for maintaining the status quo, which has caused them to conclude that the most important lessons learned in school are the social values and attitudes that schools teach children explicitly and implicitly. This is sometimes known as the hidden curriculum. Conflict theorists also see the schools as maintaining the status quo through screening and tracking.

The United States has one of the lowest illiteracy rates in the world, though American education still has a number of problems, including unequal access to education. Although the U.S. Supreme Court in 1954 outlawed racial segregation in the schools, the ethnic makeup of thousands of American communities, particularly in the inner cities, sustains existing patterns of all-white and all-minority schools. Court-ordered busing, initiated as a means of desegregating schools and thereby promoting better academic performance among minorities, has generally been resisted by white and black parents and in some instances has caused large numbers of whites to migrate from the cities to the suburbs.

Two other current and related problems in American education are high school dropouts and violence in schools. Deficiencies in school curricula and poor teaching methods have led to many of the disciplinary problems in city and suburban schools alike. These problems include violence, theft, and alcohol and drug abuse in both elementary and high schools. Although many schools have been forced to adopt "police tactics" to maintain order and safety, these measures alarmingly contradict the motives and ideals of education.

Teaching the gifted and the continued importance of standardized testing to our society are major concerns today.

Our schools reflect society as a whole. If education is in a state of upheaval because of crime, social inequality, and racial unrest, it is because these problems also confront the rest of our culture. Society produces the schools, and the schools produce the individuals who will make up society. In this way, cultural values—currently in flux throughout the United States—directly influence education, and vice versa.

Chapter 15

LAW AND

SOCIAL CONTROL

The law had been followed, yet everything went wrong—at least, that is how Charles L. Koster saw it. Koster, 67 years old and a former New York policeman and bank security guard, spent the last 7 years helping his daughter, Carolee Koster, press a sexual harassment and discrimination suit against Chase Manhattan Bank, her former employer. Charging that she had been denied promotion and subsequently dismissed by the bank after she ended a love affair with her boss, Ms. Koster instituted a $2.5 million lawsuit against the bank.

Between 1981 and 1988 both father and daughter were consumed with the litigation. They spent much of their life savings on court costs but felt that in the end the court would award Ms. Koster the financial damage settlement she sought. Before the suit came to trial, Chase offered to settle the case out of court, but Ms. Koster refused; the settlement would be large, but not the $2.5 million she wanted. As is every citizen's right, Koster decided to let a judge decide the merits of her case.

All through this ordeal—through years of motions and delays—Charles Koster was by his daughter's side, emotionally and financially.

On May 19, 1988, Judge Daronco dis-

One of the questions sociologists ask is "When do we reach the point where norms are no longer voluntary and need to be codified and given the power of authority for enforcement?"

legal code The formal body of rules adopted by a society's political authority.

laws Elements of a society's formal body of rules.

missed all of Ms. Koster's claims against Chase and her former boss, stating that there was no evidence to show sexual harassment or discrimination. The judge wrote that Ms. Koster was "responsible for her own termination" because she "overstated her experience and potential, refused to accept management's contrary assessment and declined the only position at the time for which she was qualified."

The world fell apart for the Koster family. Despite their 7-year crusade, the judge ruled that they did not have a case. The verdict was too much for Charles Koster to handle. Broke, and angry at the judge who made the decision, he took the law into his own hands. Two days after the verdict, Koster shot Judge Daronco to death at the judge's home and then killed himself. (McFadden, *New York Times,* May 23, 1988).

For 7 years Charles Koster tried to get the judgment he felt his daughter deserved through the legal system. When that did not happen Koster broke the law himself to obtain the justice he thought his daughter was entitled to. Societies cannot tolerate this type of behavior. If everyone took the law into their own hands we would have chaos. A system of laws and control is needed in every society.

THE IMPORTANCE OF LAW

There are some interests that are so important to a society that folkways and mores are not adequate enough to insure orderly social interaction. Therefore laws are passed to give the state the power of enforcement. These laws become a formal system of social control that is exercised when other informal forms of control are not effective.

Laws influence virtually every area of social interaction. They are used to protect us; to define ownership; to regulate business; and to raise taxes.

The law is also used to uphold certain institutions such as the family, or the educational system. Laws regulate marriage and divorce, and require school attendance for children.

It is important not to confuse a society's moral code with its legal code. Some legal theorists have argued that the legal code is an expression of the moral code, but this is not necessarily the case. For example, although 41 states and at least 300 municipalities have enacted some sort of antismoking law, smoking is not an offense against morals. Conversely, it is possible to violate American "moral" sensibilities without breaking the law.

What, then, is the legal code? The **legal code** consists of the formal rules, called **laws,** adopted by a society's political authority. The code is enforced through the use of formal negative sanctions when rules are broken. Ideally, laws are passed to promote conformity to those rules of conduct that the authority believes are necessary for the society to function and that will not be followed if left solely to people's internal controls or the use of informal sanctions. Others argue that laws are passed to benefit or protect specific interest groups with political power, rather than society at large (Quinney, 1974).

THE EMERGENCE OF LAWS

How is it that laws come into society? How do we reach the point where norms are no longer voluntary and need to be codified and given the power of authority for enforcement? Two major explanatory approaches have been proposed, the consensus approach and the conflict approach.

The **consensus approach** assumes that laws are merely a formal version of the norms and values of the people. There is a general consensus among the people on these norms and values and the laws reflect this consensus. For example, people will generally agree that it is wrong to steal from another person. Therefore, laws emerge formally stating this fact and provide penalties for those violating the law.

The consensus approach is basically a functionalist model for explaining a society's legal system. It assumes that social cohesion will produce an orderly adjustment in the laws. As the norms and values in society change, so will the laws. Therefore, *"blue laws,"* which were enacted in many states 100 to 200 years ago, and which prohibited people from working or opening shops on Sunday, have been changed, and now vast shopping malls do an enormous amount of business on that day of the week.

The **conflict approach** to explaining the emergence of laws sees dissension and conflict between various groups as a basic aspect of society. The conflict is resolved when the groups in power achieve control. The conflict approach to law assumes that the elite use their power to enact and enforce laws that support their own economic interests against the interests of the lower classes. As Chambliss (1973) notes:

> Conventional myths notwithstanding, the history of criminal law is *not* a history of public opinion or public interest. . . . On the contrary, the history of the criminal law is everywhere the history of legislation and appellate-court decisions which in effect (if not in intent) reflect the interests of the economic elites who control the production and distribution of the major resources of the society.

The conflict approach to law is supported by Richard Quinney (1974) when he notes, "Law serves the powerful over the weak; . . . Moreover, law is used by the state . . . to promote and protect itself."

Chambliss used the development of vagrancy laws as an example of how the conflict approach to law works. He believes the emergence of such laws paralleled the need of landowners for cheap labor in England during a time when the system of serfdom was breaking down. Later, when cheap labor was no longer needed, vagrancy laws were not enforced. Then in the sixteenth century, the laws were modified to focus on those who were suspected of being involved in criminal activities and interfering with those engaged in the transportation of goods. Chambliss (1973) notes, "Shifts and changes in the law of vagrancy show a clear pattern of reflecting the interests and needs of the groups who control the economic institutions of the society. The laws change as these institutions change."

There are two types of law, criminal law and civil law. **Criminal law** deals with violations against the interests of society, whereas **civil law** deals with violations against the individual. The distinction is not as clear as it sounds. Many actions that are punishable under criminal law because

consensus approach An explanation of how laws come into being which assumes that laws are merely a formal version of the norms and values of the people.

conflict approach An explanation of how laws come into being that sees dissension and conflict between various groups as a basic aspect of society. The conflict is resolved when the groups in power achieve control. Laws support the economic interests of the elite.

criminal law Laws that deal with violations against the interests of society.

civil law Laws that deal with violations against the individual.

It is difficult to know with certainty how many crimes are committed each year.

they are a threat to society are also directed against individuals. For example, rape is an action against a specific individual but is also a threat to general safety. In the next section we will examine those actions punishable under criminal law.

CRIME IN THE UNITED STATES

crime Behavior that violates a society's criminal code.

Crime is behavior that violates a society's criminal code. In the United States what is criminal is specified in written law, primarily state statutes. Federal, state, and local jurisdictions often vary in their definitions of crimes, though they seldom disagree in their definitions of serious crimes. (See Table 15.1 for the characteristics of the most common serious crimes.)

A distinction is often made between violent crimes and property crimes. A *violent crime* is an unlawful event such as homicide, rape, or assault that may result in injury to a person. *Robbery* is also a violent crime because it involves the use or threat of force against the person.

A property crime is an unlawful act that is committed with the intent of gaining property but that does not involve the use or threat of force against an individual. Larceny, burglary, and motor vehicle theft are examples of property crimes.

Criminal offenses are also classified according to how they are handled by the criminal justice system. In this respect, most jurisdictions recognize two classes of offenses: felonies and misdemeanors. Felonies are not distinguished from misdemeanors in the same way in all areas, but most states define felonies as offenses punishable by a year or more in a state prison. Although the same act may be classified as a felony in one jurisdiction and as a misdemeanor in another, the most serious crimes are never misdemeanors, and the most minor offenses are never felonies.

UNIFORM CRIME REPORTS

It is very difficult to know with any certainty how many crimes are committed in America each year. The *Uniform Crime Reports* program has been developing national statistics on crime from local police records since 1930. But sociologists and critics in other fields note that for a variety of reasons these statistics are not always reliable. For example, each police department compiles its own figures, and so definitions of the same crime vary from place to place.

There are eight crimes that make up the *Reports.* They are murder and nonnegligent manslaughter, forcible rape, robbery, aggravated assault, burglary, larceny-theft, motor vehicle theft, and arson. Not included are federal offenses — political corruption, tax evasion, bribery, or violation of environmental protection laws, among others (Bureau of Justice Statistics, Bulletin, 1981).

Other factors affect the accuracy of the crime figures and rates published in the *Reports* — for example, a law enforcement agency or a local government may change its method of reporting crimes, so that the new statistics reflect a false increase or decrease in the occurrence of certain crimes. These changes may even be deliberate: The government or agency may want to stress its achievements or gain some other benefit (Reid, 1979).

NATIONAL CRIME SURVEY

You have probably heard or seen media presentations on the victims of crime in the United States. This information comes directly from the victims themselves and provides another way of looking at crime and its consequences. To learn more about crimes and the victims of crime, in 1973 the compilers of the *National Crime Survey* began to collect victimization data from households across the country.

The *Survey* measures six crimes, both reported and unreported: rape, robbery, assault, household burglary, personal and household larceny, and motor vehicle theft.

The similarity between these crimes and the *Reports* is obvious and intentional. Two crimes are missing from the *Survey* that appear in the *Reports*. Murder cannot be measured through victim surveys because obviously the victim is dead. Arson cannot be measured well through such surveys because the victim may in fact have been the criminal. A professional is often needed to determine whether a fire was actually arson (Bureau of Justice Statistics, Bulletin, 1981).

Whereas the *Reports* depends on police departments' records of reported crimes, the *Survey* attempts to assess the total number of crimes committed. The *Survey* obtains its information by asking a national sample of 60,000 households, representing 135,000 people over the age of 12, about their experiences as victims of crime during a specified period of time.

Of the 34,100,000 crimes that took place in 1986, the *Survey* estimated that only about 37 percent were reported to the police. The specific crimes most likely to be reported were motor vehicle theft (69 percent) and aggravated assault (58 percent). The specific crimes least likely to be reported were pickpocketing (29 percent) and household larceny (25 percent).

The particular reason most frequently mentioned for *not* reporting a crime was that it was not important enough. For violent crimes the reason most often given for not reporting was that it was a private or personal matter. For an example of the reporting rates for a variety of crimes, see Figure 15.1.

The *Reports* and the *Survey* produce different results because they serve different purposes and are based on different sources of information. The *Reports* counts only crimes coming to the attention of the police, whereas the *Survey* obtains information on both reported and unreported crimes. The *Reports* counts crimes committed against individuals, businesses, and government agencies as well as any other victims. The *Survey* counts only crimes committed against persons over 12 within a household. The two surveys may also, in some in-

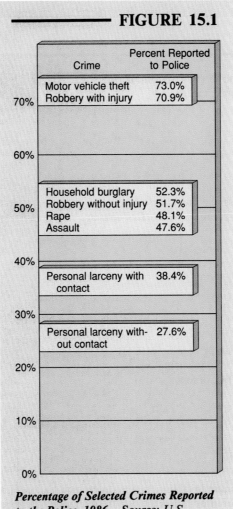

FIGURE 15.1

Percentage of Selected Crimes Reported to the Police, 1986. Source: *U.S. Department of Commerce, Bureau of the Census,* Statistical Abstract of the United States: 1989 *(Washington, D.C.: Government Printing Office, 1989), p. 164.*

stances, count crimes differently. For example, a situation in which a criminal robs a victim and steals someone else's car for the getaway will be recorded in the *Reports* as robbery, the more serious crime; but it may be recorded in the *Survey* as two crimes.

Each survey is subject to the kinds of errors and problems typical to its method of data collection. Despite their respective drawbacks, they both are valuable sources of data on nationwide crime.

Crime	Definition	Facts
Homicide	Causing the death of another person without legal justification or excuse.	Homicide was the least frequent violent crime. Ninety-three percent of the victims were slain in single-victim situations. At least 55 percent of the murderers were relatives or acquaintances of the victim. Twenty-four percent of all murders occurred or were suspected to have occurred as the result of some felonious activity.
Rape	Unlawful sexual intercourse with a person, by force or without legal or factual consent.	Among rape and attempted rape victims, close to three-quarters were unmarried women about half were from low-income families four-fifths were white, but compared to their proportion in the general population black women were significantly more likely than white women to be victims Only about 61 per cent of all rape and attempted rapes were reported to the police.
Robbery	Unlawful taking or attempted taking of property that is in the immediate possession of another, by force or threat of force.	Robbery is the violent crime that typically involves more than one offender (in about half of all cases). Slightly less than half of all robberies involved the use of a weapon. The robbers were male in 90 percent of the offenses and black in about half. Less than 2 percent of the robberies reported to the police were bank robberies.
Assault	Unlawful intentional inflicting, or attempted inflicting, of injury upon the person of another. *Aggravated assault* is the unlawful intentional inflicting of serious bodily injury or unlawful threat or attempt to inflict bodily injury or death by means of a deadly or dangerous weapon with or without actual infliction of injury. *Simple*	Simple assault occurred more frequently than aggravated assault. Assault was the most common type of violent crime.

KINDS OF CRIME IN THE UNITED STATES

It should be obvious that the crime committed can vary considerably in terms of the impact it has on the victim and on the self-definition of the perpetrator of the crime. White-collar crime is as different from street crime as organized crime is from juvenile crime. In the next section we shall examine these differences.

TABLE 15.1
Characteristics of the Most Common Serious Crimes

Crime	Definition	Facts
Assault	*assault* is the unlawful intentional inflicting of less than serious bodily injury without a deadly or dangerous weapon or an attempt or threat to inflict bodily injury without a deadly or dangerous weapon.	
Burglary	Unlawful entry of any fixed structure, vehicle, or vessel used for regular residence, industry, or business, with or without force, with the intent to commit a felony or larceny.	Forty-five percent of all household burglaries occurred without *forced* entry. Someone was at home during 13 percent of all burglaries, and 30 percent of such incidents end in a violent crime. Burglary occurred more often in warmer months than in colder months.
Larceny (theft)	Unlawful taking or atempted taking of property other than a motor vehicle from the possession of another, by stealth, without force and without deceit, with intent to permanently deprive the owner of the property.	Pocket picking and purse snatching most frequently occurred inside nonresidential buildings or on street locations. Unlike most other crimes, pocket picking and purse snatching affected the elderly as much as other age groups. Most personal larcenies with contact occurred during the daytime, but most household larcenies occurred at night.
Motor vehicle theft	Unlawful taking or attempted taking of a self-propelled road vehicle owned by another, with the intent of depriving the owner of it permanently or temporarily.	Motor vehicle theft is relatively well reported to the police because reporting is required for insurance claims and vehicles are more likely than other stolen property to be recovered. About three-fifths of all motor vehicle thefts occurred at night.
Arson	Intentional damaging or destruction or attempted damaging or destruction by means of fire or explosion of the property without the consent of the owner, or of one's own property or that of another by fire or explosives with or without the intent to defraud.	Single-family residences were the most frequent targets of arson. More than 17 percent of all structures where arson occurred were not in use.

Source: Bureau of Justice Statistics, *Dictionary of Criminal Justice Data Terminology, 1981; FBI Uniform Crime Reports, 1981;* Bureau of Justice Statistics, *National Crime Survey, 1981;* as reported in *Report to the Nation on Crime and Justice* (Washington, D.C.: Government Printing Office, 1983); Bureau of Justice Statistics, Data Report, 1987, 1988.

Juvenile Crime

Juvenile crime refers to the breaking of criminal laws by individuals under the age of 18. Regardless of the specific statistic's reliability, one thing is clear: Serious crime among our nation's youth is a matter of great concern. Hard-core youthful offenders—perhaps 10 percent of all juvenile criminals—are responsible, by some estimates, for two-thirds of all serious crimes. Although the vast majority of juvenile de-

juvenile crime The breaking of criminal laws by individuals under the age of 18.

443

MOTOR VEHICLE THEFT

According to the National Crime Survey (NCS), nearly 1 million cars are stolen each year. There are another 550,000 attempted thefts each year also. This comes down to seven completed and four attempted thefts each year for every 1000 registered motor vehicles. Here are some other facts:

- Sixty-two percent of all stolen cars are recovered.
- Losses from motor vehicle theft after recoveries and reimbursements by insurance companies amount to $1.2 billion annually.
- Motor vehicle thefts, whether completed or attempted, most often take place at night near the victim's home.
- Attempted thefts are more likely to result in property damage than completed thefts.
- Blacks, Hispanics, central city residents, and the poor are most likely to be the victims of motor vehicle theft.
- Those over 55 and rural residents are the least likely to be victimized.

Source: Caroline Wolf Harlow, "Motor Vehicle Theft," U.S. Department of Justice, *Bureau of Justice Statistics, Special Report,* March 1988.

---

linquents commit only minor violations, the juvenile justice system is overwhelmed by these hard-core criminals (*U.S. News & World Report,* August 24, 1987).

Serious juvenile offenders are predominantly male, are disproportionately minority group members—compared with their proportion in the population—and are typically disadvantaged economically. They are likely to exhibit interpersonal difficulties and behavioral problems both in school and on the job. They are also likely to come from one-parent families or families with a high degree of conflict, instability, and inadequate supervision.

Arrest records for 1987 show that youths under age 18 accounted for 16.5 percent of all arrests *(Statistical Abstract of the United States: 1989).* Arrests, however, are only a general indicator of criminal activity. The greater number of arrests among young people may be due partly to their lack of experience in committing crimes and partly to their involvement in the types of crimes for which apprehension is more likely, for example, theft versus fraud. In addition, because youths often commit crimes in groups, the resolution of a single crime may lead to several arrests. (See Table 15.2 for arrest rates by age.)

Indeed, the major differences between juvenile and adult offenders are the importance of gang membership and the tendency of youths to engage in group criminal activities. Gang members are more likely than other young criminals to engage in violent crimes, particularly robbery, rape, assault, and weapons violations. Gangs that deal in the sale of crack have become especially violent in the last few years.

There is conflicting evidence on whether juveniles tend to progress from less to more serious crimes. The evidence suggests that violent adult offenders began their careers with violent juvenile crimes; thus they began as and remained serious offenders. However, minor offenses of youths are often dealt with informally and may not be recorded in crime statistics (U.S. Department of Justice, 1983).

The juvenile courts—traditionally meant to treat, not punish—have had limited success in coping with such juvenile offenders (Reid, 1979). Strict rules of confidentiality, aimed at protecting juvenile offenders from being labeled as criminals make it difficult for the police and judges to know the full extent of a youth's criminal record. The result is that violent youthful offenders who have committed numerous crimes often receive little or no punishment.

Defenders of the juvenile courts contend, nonetheless, that there would be even more juvenile crime without them. Others, arguing from learning and labeling perspectives, charge that the system has such a negative impact on children that it actually encourages **recidivism,** or repeated criminal behavior after punishment (Paulsen, 1967). All who are concerned with this issue agree that the juvenile courts are less than efficient, especially in the treatment of repeat offenders. One reason for this is that perhaps two-thirds of juvenile court time is devoted to processing children guilty of what are called **status offenses,** behavior that is criminal only because the person involved is a minor (examples are truancy and running away from home).

Recognizing that status offenders clog the courts and add greatly to the terrible overcrowding of juvenile detention homes, states have sought ways to deinstitutionalize status offenders. One approach, known as **diversion**—steering youthful offenders away from the juvenile justice system to nonofficial social agencies—has been suggested by Edwin M. Lemert (1981).

Diversion is a process in which individuals who have been involved in delinquent acts and would normally be dealt with by police or court action are instead handled by other community agencies. In the area of juvenile justice, diversion achieves several ends: (1) it avoids the labeling of young people as juvenile delinquents; (2) it helps overcome the clogging of juvenile courts with a backlog of minor cases; (3) it keeps young people in the community and out of detention; and (4) it encourages community involvement in and responsibility for dealing with youthful offenders.

Under traditional juvenile justice approaches, once labeled a youthful offender, a young person might have difficulty living

TABLE 15.2

Age Distribution of Arrests, 1986

Age Group	Percentage of U.S. Population	Percentage of Persons Arrested
12 years or younger	18.7	1.7%
13 to 15	4.4	6.7
16 to 18	4.6	13.2
19 to 21	4.8	14.0
22 to 24	5.3	13.2
25 to 29	9.2	17.9
30 to 34	8.6	12.4
35 to 39	7.8	8.1
40 to 44	6.0	4.7
45 to 49	4.9	2.9
50 to 54	4.5	2.0
55 to 59	4.7	1.4
60 to 64	4.5	0.9
65 and older	12.1	0.9

Source: Timothy J. Flanagan and Edmund F. McGarrell, eds., *Sourcebook of Criminal Justice Statistics—1987.* U.S. Department of Justice, Bureau of Justice Statistics (Washington, D.C.: U.S. Government Printing Office, 1988), p. 371.

down this "record." The community may view and react to a youth so labeled as a juvenile delinquent. With diversion, a youth can be helped without being branded with a negative label.

At least half the cases finally brought before juvenile courts are dismissed. Many others result in only minor charges and the release of the offender. Diversion keeps many of these cases out of the courts, allowing the courts to concentrate on the more serious cases.

Diversion is also beneficial in that any period of detention for a young person can mean valuable time out of school, time that may be lost forever, forcing the youth to drop back a year in school or even to drop out. Diversion avoids this problem by keeping the youth in the community.

Finally, by encouraging the community to be actively involved in helping youthful offenders, diversion compels the

recidivism Repeated criminal behavior after punishment.

status offenses Behavior that is criminal only because the person involved is a minor.

diversion Steering youthful offenders away from the juvenile justice system to nonofficial social agencies.

Arrest records show that youths under age 18 account for 16.5 percent of all arrests. Juvenile crime has turned some schools into fortresses patrolled by the police.

community to recognize its responsibility in preventing conditions leading to youthful revolt.

To deal with really difficult juvenile crime problems, several states are instituting treatment programs that combine punishment with psychological counseling and coping skills for real-life problems that teenagers are likely to face when they are released. In South Carolina, where 210 delinquents who committed serious crimes received remedial education and vocational skills, only 7 percent later returned to an institution, compared with 20 percent of those youths who did not receive the education.

As juvenile justice officials try to cope with issues of treatment and recidivism, they must also deal with alcohol and drug problems. These problems require additional intervention programs (*U.S. News & World Report,* August 24, 1987).

Violent Crimes

In 1987 there were 2,545,000 violent crimes reported in Detroit, 1,910,000 in Los Angeles, and 2,036,000 in New York City. If we keep in mind that only about 48 percent of all violent crimes are reported to the po-

lice, we can see how high the incidence of violent crime really is *(Statistical Abstract of the United States: 1989).*

Whereas by far the majority of violent crimes used to occur among people who knew one another—in families, among relatives and social acquaintances—violence committed against strangers has risen in the last few years. This has added greatly to a growing "terror of the night," because people feel that violence may strike them anonymously and unpredictably.

The United States' violent crime rate also includes the highest homicide rate in the industrialized world. There are more murders in any one of the cities of New York, Detroit, Los Angeles, or Chicago each year than in all of England and Wales combined.

The U.S. homicide rate averages 8 per 100,000 people in the population. In some cities this rate is significantly higher. For example, Detroit has a homicide rate of 62.8 per 100,000 population, for Dallas it is 32.0, and for Baltimore it is 29.5 *(Statistical Abstract of the United States: 1989).*

In contrast, the average homicide rate in Australia is 1.9 homicides per 100,000 people; in Israel, 1.8; in Japan, 1.0; and in England and Wales, 0.4) (Barlow, 1987).

In addition to homicide, other violent crimes that have an impact on American households are rape, aggravated assault, and robbery. In 1987, 108,000 households reported a rape, 1,258,000 reported an aggravated assault, and 884,000 reported a robbery (Bureau of Justice Statistics, Bulletin. (See Figure 15.2 for the yearly percentage of households experiencing a rape, aggravated assault, or robbery.)

Nonviolent Crimes

Ninety percent of all crime in the United States is what is referred to as crime against property, as opposed to crime against the person, which we just discussed. In all instances of crime against property the victim is not present and is not confronted by the criminal.

FIGURE 15.2

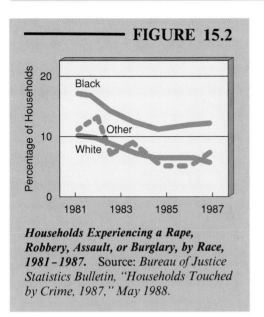

Households Experiencing a Rape, Robbery, Assault, or Burglary, by Race, 1981–1987. Source: *Bureau of Justice Statistics Bulletin, "Households Touched by Crime, 1987," May 1988.*

A white-collar computer criminal can transfer vast sums of money into unauthorized accounts, stealing far more money than a daring bank robber ever could.

The most significant nonviolent crimes are burglary, auto theft, and larceny-theft. In 1987, 4,717,000 households reported a burglary, 1,379,000 reported an auto theft, and 9,745,000 reported a household theft (Bureau of Justice Statistics, Bulletin, 1988). Keep in mind that only about 27 percent of all household thefts are reported *(Statistical Abstract of the United States: 1988, 1987).*

White-Collar Crime

The term **white-collar crime** was coined by Edwin H. Sutherland (1940) to refer to individuals who, while occupying positions of social responsibility or high prestige, break the law in the course of their work, for the purpose of illegal personal or organizational gain. Another term often used to refer to what typically are nonviolent crimes by "respectable" individuals is *upper-world crime.* White-collar crimes include such illegalities as embezzlement, bribery, fraud, theft of services, kickback schemes, and others in which the violator's position of trust, power, or influence has provided the opportunity to use lawful institutions for unlawful purposes. White-collar offenses frequently involve deception.

Although white-collar offenses are less visible than crimes such as burglary and robbery, their overall economic impact may be considerably greater. A white-collar embezzler can transfer millions of dollars into unauthorized accounts and cover his tracks by way of the computer. Compare this to the take of a daring bank robber, who, on a good day, might steal $10,000 or $20,000. Among the white-collar cases filed by U.S. attorneys in 1985, more than 140 persons were charged with offenses estimated to involve more than $1 million each, and sixty-four were charged with offenses valued at greater than $10 million each. In comparison, losses from all bank robberies reported to the police in that year were under $19 million, and losses from all robberies reported to the police totaled $313 million (Bureau of Justice Statistics).

Not only is white-collar crime very expensive, it is a threat to the fabric of society. Sutherland (1961) has argued that because white-collar crimes involve a violation of public trust, it contributes to a disintegration of social morale and threatens the social structure. This problem is compounded by the fact that in those cases in which white-collar criminals actually are prosecuted and convicted, punishment usually is

white-collar crime Crime committed by individuals who occupy positions of social responsibility or high prestige and who break the law in the course of their work for the purpose of illegal personal or organizational gain.

relatively light. For example, only about 40 percent of convicted white-collar criminals are given prison terms, compared to 54 percent of non-white-collar offenders. In addition, those who do receive prison terms receive shorter average sentences (29 months) than other federal offenders (50 months) (Bureau of Justice Statistics, 1987).

New forms of white-collar crime involving political and corporate institutions have emerged in the past decade. For example, the dramatic growth in high technology has brought with it sensational accounts of computerized "heists" by sophisticated criminals seated safely behind computer terminals. The possibility of electronic crime has spurred widespread interest in computer security, by business and government alike.

Organized Crime

organized crime Structured associations of individuals or groups who come together for the purpose of obtaining gain mostly from illegal activities.

Organized crime refers to structured associations of individuals or groups who come together for the purpose of obtaining gain mostly from illegal activities. Organized

The distribution and sale of drugs used to be a major organized crime activity. In the last decade, other groups have taken over this lucrative criminal activity.

crime groups possess some of the following characteristics:

They conduct their activities in a methodical, systematic, or highly disciplined and secret fashion.

In at least some of their activities they commit or threaten to commit acts of violence or other acts that are likely to intimidate.

They insulate their leadership from direct involvement in illegal activities by their intricate organizational structure.

They attempt to gain influence in government, politics, and commerce through corruption, graft, and legitimate means (U.S. Department of Justice, 1983).

Organized crime has its roots in the decaying neighborhoods of ethnic minorities. It is organized nationally through a governing structure of twenty-four "families" or "syndicates" dominated by men of Sicilian descent (Cressey, 1969). Figure 15.3 shows the organizational structure of a typical organized crime family.

Organized crime makes most of its money through providing illegal goods and services. It was Prohibition that gave it the ability to organize nationwide, because for the first time there was a uniform national demand for illegal goods: alcoholic beverages. Today organized crime profits from illegal activities that include illegal gambling, the smuggling and sale of illicit drugs, the production and distribution of pornography, prostitution, and loan sharking. To be able to account for and spend their wealth, the families of organized crime have bought controlling interests in innumerable "legitimate" businesses in which their funds can be "laundered" and additional, legitimate profits can be made (Wickman, Whitten, and Levey, 1980). For example, profits from an illegal gambling operation can show up on the books of a legitimate, cash-oriented business such as a restaurant or vending-machine enterprise. Virtually all major figures in organized crime insist they are nothing but businesspeople. Al Capone, the head of Chicago's organized crime syndicate in the 1920s, protested vigorously when newspapers called him a racketeer. "I call myself a businessman," he explained. "I make my money by supplying a public demand. If I break the law, my customers, who number hundreds of the best people in Chicago, are as guilty as I am. The only difference is that I sell and they buy" (Silberman, 1978). Although Capone's logic clearly was self-serving, his observation is accurate: Organized crime exists only because it is supported actively and tolerated passively by most Americans. Without customers, organized crime would die.

Organized crime was dominated by Irish Americans in the early part of the twentieth century, and by Jewish Americans in the 1920s. From the 1930s organized crime has been dominated by those of Italian ancestry. This has changed within the last decade and other ethnic groups are gaining a significant foothold. The power of these groups varies from city to city. In Miami, Cubans control illegal gambling and Canadians dominate loan sharking and money laundering. In Detroit, organized crime members are Lebanese or black. In New York, Koreans run illegal massage parlors and Russian immigrants are involved in extortion and contract murder. Police call this trend the "internationalization of crime" in the United States (*U.S. News & World Report,* January 1, 1988).

Victimless Crimes

Usually we think of crimes as involving culprits and victims—that is, individuals who suffer some loss or injury as a result of a criminal act. But there are some crimes that do not produce victims in any obvious way, and so some scholars have coined the term *victimless crime* to refer to them.

Basically, **victimless crimes** are acts that violate those laws meant to enforce the moral code. Usually they involve the use of narcotics, illegal gambling, public drunkenness, the sale of sexual services, or status offenses by minors. If heroin and crack ad-

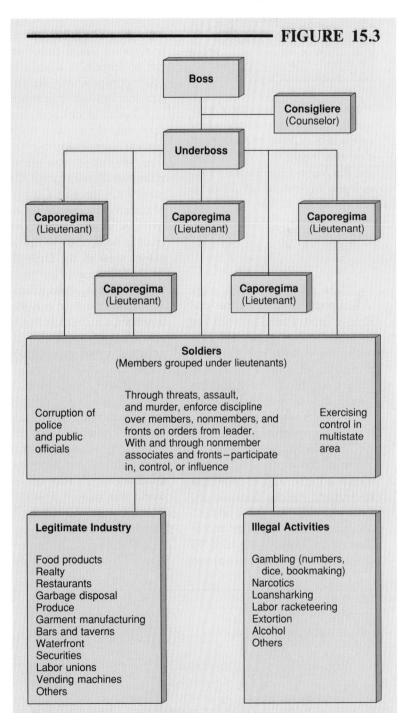

FIGURE 15.3

An Organized Crime Family. The structure of a "successful" crime syndicate is often that of an efficient business hierarchy.

victimless crimes Acts that violate those laws meant to enforce the moral code.

BRING BACK THE MAFIA

It seems strange to compare organized crime with disorganized crime and to come to the conclusion that organized crime is better. But that is exactly what criminologist Richard Moran decides is the case after looking at the violence produced by today's drug traffickers.

As I read more and more about gang violence and drug-related crime, I'm beginning to long for the "good" old days when the Mafia ran the drug trade. For when the Mafia ran the drug trade there was a lot less crime and violence. And even fewer dangerous drugs.

The mob still controls heroin, but heroin is no longer the name of the game. In the early 1980s cocaine and its powerful derivative, crack, became the drug of choice for street addicts, Yuppies, and Wall Street executives. The Mafia, weakened by federal prosecutions and saddled with aging crime bosses, was slow to respond to the changing market to imported drugs. And so other groups seized the opportunity to enter the drug business.

Today blacks and Hispanics dominate the cocaine trade. The blacks are either Jamaicans or native Americans who are mainly members of street gangs. The Hispanics are mostly Colombians, Mexicans, Dominicans, or Cubans. A small piece of the drug trade is controlled by motorcycle gangs, such as the Hells Angels, whose members are predominantly working-class whites.

The failure of the Mafia to maintain a monopoly has created a violent free-for-all. Upstart criminal syndicates—Mafias in embryo—are killing one another over market share. Like the airline and banking industries, the drug trade has become deregulated. Without the Mafia to maintain peace, arbitrate disputes, set rules and enforce discipline, violence reigns. It's a dog-eat-pit-bull world out there, survival of the fittest, vulture capitalism, Adam Smith gone mad.

The Jamaican "posses," or gangs, are among the most dangerous and powerful of the new drug-trafficking organizations. Most reports show that approximately 10,000 Jamaicans are involved in the drug trade in this country. They are believed to have been responsible for more than 1,400 drug-related homicides. Indeed, the Jamaicans' reputation for violence is so great that most drug cartels prefer not to deal with them. Even the Mafia has been known to back down, conceding turf rather than facing a bloody war with the posses.

In the "good" old days, Mafia hits were selective. Most of the people who got hurt were directly involved in illegal activities. If the mob killed a rival gang member, it usually provided for the financial well-being of his family. Today's criminal organizations often kill the entire family and anyone else who happens to be standing around. No peculiar blend of compassion and brutality for these modern-day gangsters.

The new criminal organizations are more violent because the stakes are higher and the people involved younger and more desperate. For many ghetto dwellers dicts can support their illegal addiction legitimately, then who is the victim? If prostitutes provide sexual gratification for a fee, who is the victim? If a person bets $10 or $20 per week with the local bookmaker, who is the victim? If someone staggers drunk through the streets, who is the victim? If a teenager runs away from home because conditions there are intolerable, who is the victim?

Some legal scholars argue that the perpetrators themselves are victims: Their be-

and recent immigrants (both legal and illegal) the American Dream has become a nightmare. They have grown up in a violent atmosphere in which both drugs and life are cheap. Gang members use automatic weapons like the Uzi and AK-47 that spray bullets almost indiscriminately. Devoid of familial or communal ties, the drug traffickers kill with little provocation.

Historically, ethnic minorities have often been drawn to organized illegal activities. First, the Irish and European Jews, and then the Italians, used the rackets as the fastest (in not the safest) route to wealth and power. But the recent explosion in crack use in the United States has opened up opportunities that were unimaginable a few decades ago. You don't have to be a ghetto youth with little hope for a secure financial future to be lured by the promise of big money. Five thousand dollars a week looks pretty good even to a tenured college professor earning a moderately comfortable living.

Virtually none of what I have described would have happened if the Mafia were still in control.

The Mafia was a mature business. Their scores were already settled. They had the drug territory all mapped out. The mob had standards, a code of honor. And, most of all, it understood that undisciplined violence only brought increased public pressure and police crackdowns. During Al Capone's entire 6-year reign over organized crime in Chicago, only 80 gangsters were killed. And that was when Capone was in the process of consolidating his power, the most violent period in the mob's history. Last year gang-related violence in Los Angeles alone killed 257 people, many of them innocent bystanders.

Although things will probably get worse before they get better, they *will* get better. Already many of the fledgling criminal organizations have begun to pattern themselves after the Mafia, most notably the Mexican-based Herrera family and the California prisons-based La Nuestra Familia. As these new criminal organizations mature, they will move from uncontrolled to disciplined violence. There will be fewer public shoot-outs and fewer innocent victims killed. Increased pressure

by law enforcement should help speed along the maturation process as the weaker drug-trafficking gangs fall not only to increased competition but to criminal prosecution as well. In the next 10 to 20 years the "shakeout" that is occurring will be completed and the drug trade will become reregulated.

Where does all this leave us? A pragmatist might argue that law enforcement would do well to assist the Mafia in regaining control of the drug business. I know that this suggestion is too horrible for most Americans to contemplate. Believe me, as someone who has spent his adult life studying crime, I could never bring myself to advocate it. But, nonetheless, if we're going to have crime then there are certain advantages to having organized crime. And if we're going to have a drug trade — and I see no way around it — then we might be better off with an organized drug trade.

Source: Reprinted from Richard Moran, "Bring Back the Mafia," *Newsweek*, August 7, 1989, p 8.

havior damages their own lives. This is, of course, a value judgment, but then the concept of deviance depends on the existence of values and norms (Schur and Bedau, 1974). Others note that such offenses against the public order do in fact contribute to the creation of victims, if only indirectly: Heroin addicts rarely can hold jobs and eventually are forced to steal to support themselves; prostitutes are used to blackmail people and to rob them; chronic gamblers impoverish themselves and bring ruin on their families;

drunks drive and get into accidents and may be violent at home; and so on.

Clearly the problems raised by the existence of victimless crimes are complex. In recent years American society has begun to recognize that at least some crimes truly are victimless and that they should therefore be decriminalized. Two major activities that have been decriminalized in many states and municipalities are the smoking of marijuana (though not its sale) and sex between unmarried, consenting adults of the same gender.

VICTIMS OF CRIME

We have been discussing crime statistics, the types of crimes committed, and who commits them. But what about the victims of crime? Is there a pattern? Are some people more apt than others to become crime victims? It seems that this is true; victims of crime are not spread evenly across society. Although the available crime data are not always reliable, a pattern of victimization can be seen in the reported statistics. A person's race, sex, age, and socioeconomic status have a great deal to do with whether

Despite the concern about crimes against the elderly, it is young people between ages 16 and 24 who are most likely to be victims of serious crime, and this rate decreases steadily with age.

that individual will become a victim of a serious crime.

Statistics show that, overall, males are much more likely than females to be victims of serious crimes. When we look at crimes of violence and theft separately, however, a more complex picture emerges. Victims of crime are more often men than women. Younger people are much more likely than the elderly to be victims of crime. Blacks are more likely to be victims of violent crime than are whites or members of other racial groups. People with low incomes have the highest violent-crime victimization rates. Theft rates are the highest for people with low incomes (less than $5,000 per year) and for those with high incomes (more than $30,000 per year). Students and the unemployed are more likely than housewives, retirees, or the employed to be victims of crime. Rural residents are less often crime victims than people living in cities (U.S. Department of Justice, 1988).

Despite the growing and well-founded concern about crimes against the elderly, figures show that it is young people between the ages of 16 and 24 who are most likely to be victims of serious crimes and that this rate decreases steadily with age. (See the *Taking the Sociological Perspective* box for the probability of your being the victim of a crime.)

VICTIM INJURY

Information gathered from the National Crime Survey (NCS) noted that using physical force, trying to attract attention, and doing nothing to protect oneself resulted in the highest proportions of seriously injured victims (16, 14, and 12 percent respectively). On the other hand, those who tried to talk themselves out of their predicament, or took nonviolent evasive action were less likely to incur serious injury (both 6 percent).

The pattern of serious injury associated with a variety of self-protective measures was consistent for all NCS-measured violent crimes except robbery and simple as-

WHAT ARE YOUR CHANCES OF BEING A VICTIM OF CRIME?

I am sure none of you awoke this morning wondering what your chances were of sometime during your lifetime being the victim of a robbery, a rape, or an assault. But just in case you wish to scare yourself with precise answers to such questions, there are people at the Bureau of Justice laboring long and hard with your tax dollars to come up with the information.

The information is not going to make you feel very safe, however, and you may be sorry to get answers to questions you did not ask. So as a final warning, do not read on if you wish to avoid spending money on security systems and bulletproof vests.

Annual victimization rates are occasionally mentioned in stories on crime in America. They refer to the number of people per 100,000 who end up being the victims of a particular type of crime.

Upon hearing that the homicide rate is about 8 to 10 per 100,000 people in the population, one may feel reasonably safe. After all, this translates to 1 chance in 10,000 of being murdered and does not produce fear, particularly if you believe that murders occur mainly in ghetto areas among minority groups.

In fact, however, at current homicide rates about 1 of every 133 Americans will become a murder victim. For black males the chances are 1 in 30 that they will be murdered (Bureau of Justice Statistics, 1987).

The information on rape is similarly unsettling. Whereas 16 out of 10,000 women are rape victims annually, the lifetime chances of suffering a rape are much greater. Nearly 1 in 12 white females and 1 out of 9 black females will be a rape victim at some point in their lives.

We used to say that the only things certain in life were death and taxes. Add to that now that nearly everyone will be the victim of a personal theft at least once in their lives. In fact the vast majority of us (7 out of 8) will be victimized three or more times.

The chances are also very good that we will be the victim of an assault. Only 1 in 5 males and only 2 in 5 females will escape this experience.

It would be wrong to just paint a picture of doom and gloom here without offering any bright points. The one optimistic thing we can say is that as you age your chances of being a victim of crime continue to decrease.

It is not that you just have fewer years to still be victimized. The elderly are less likely than younger people to be victims of crime. Teenagers and young adults under age 25 have the highest victimization rates.

A 60-year-old has only half the chance of being the victim of a violent crime that a 30-year-old has. Similarly, those who are 30 are five times more likely than those who are 60 to be injured during a robbery or assault.

The reason the elderly are less likely to be the victims of violent crime than the young is related in part to differences in lifestyle and income. Younger people may more often be in situations that place them at risk. They may frequent neighborhood hangouts, bars, or events that are likely places for an assault to take place.

The elderly still do experience high rates of victimization for crimes of larceny. Criminals may believe that the elderly are more likely to have large amounts of cash and are less likely to defend themselves. As a result, the elderly are still quite vulnerable to crimes such as robbery, purse snatching, or pocket picking.

There is a bright spot for those who live in the suburbs. Their chances of being victimized are less than those for city dwellers, and victimization is even less likely in rural areas.

Crime continues to be a very real fact of life and very few escape being touched by it.

Source: Bureau of Justice Statistics, Technical Report, "Lifetime Likelihood of Victimization," March 1987.

sault. Victims of these crimes were less likely than victims of other violent crimes to be injured seriously if they did nothing to protect themselves. This finding is important, since each type of violent crime tends to provoke different responses by victims. For example, rape victims are particularly likely to use physical force to repel rapists. This may be an automatic reaction to being grabbed.

Each incident of violent crime has unique features that may affect how victims are able to protect themselves, but the NCS data suggest that the responses of physical force, attracting attention, or deliberate inaction are related to a higher likelihood of injury. Nonviolent evasive action or trying to talk yourself out of the predicament appears to be the safest response to a violent crime (U.S. Department of Justice, 1983).

CRIMINAL JUSTICE IN THE UNITED STATES

Every society that has established a legal code has also set up a **criminal justice system** — personnel and procedures for arrest, trial, and punishment — to deal with violations of the law. The three main categories of our criminal justice system are the police, the courts, and the prisons.

THE POLICE

The police system in the United States is a highly decentralized one. It exists on three levels: federal, state, and local. On the federal level, the United States does not have a national police system. There are, however, federal laws enacted by Congress. These laws govern the District of Columbia and all states when a "federal" offense has been committed, such as kidnapping, assassination of a president, mail fraud, bank robbery, and so on. The Federal Bureau of Investigation (FBI) enforces these laws and

criminal justice system Personnel and procedures for the arrest, trial, and punishment of those who violate the law.

also assists local and state law enforcement authorities in solving local crimes. If a non-federal crime has been committed, the FBI must be asked by local or state authorities to aid in the investigation. If a particular crime is a violation of both state and federal law, state and local police often cooperate with the FBI to avoid unnecessary duplication of effort.

The state police patrol the highways, regulate traffic, and have primary responsibility for the enforcement of some state laws. They provide a variety of other services also, such as a system of criminal identification, police training programs, and computer-based records systems to assist local police departments.

The jurisdiction of police officers at the local level is limited to the state, town, or municipality in which the person is a sworn officer of the law. Some problems inevitably result from such a highly decentralized system. Jurisdictional boundaries sometimes result in overlapping, communication problems, and difficulty in obtaining assistance from another law enforcement agency.

August Vollmer, a recognized authority on police administration, dramatized the high expectations society has of the police by noting that we expect the police officer

> . . . to have the wisdom of Solomon, the courage of David, the patience of Job and the leadership of Moses, the kindness of the Good Samaritan, the strategy of Alexander, the faith of Daniel, the diplomacy of Lincoln, the tolerance of the Carpenter of Nazareth, and, finally, an intimate knowledge of every branch of the natural, biological and social sciences. (Quoted in Pray, 1987).

Such expectations are, of course, unrealistic. Historically police in the United States have been young white males with a high school education or less. Most still come from working-class backgrounds. In recent years attempts have been made to raise the educational levels of the police, as well as produce a more heterogeneous distribution including women and minorities.

THE COURTS

The United States has a dual court system consisting of state and federal courts, with state and federal crimes being prosecuted in the respective courts. Some crimes may violate both state and federal statues. About 85 percent of all criminal cases are tried in the state courts.

The state court system varies from one state to the other. Lower trial courts exist for the most part to try misdemeanors and petty offenses. Higher trial courts can try felonies and serious misdemeanors. All states have appeal courts. Many have only one court of appeal, which is often known as the state supreme court. Some states have intermediate appeal courts also.

The federal court system consists of three basic levels, excluding such special courts as the United States Court of Military Appeals. The United States *district courts* are the trial courts. Appeals may be brought from these courts to the *appellate courts.* There are eleven courts at this level, referred to as *circuit courts.* Finally, the highest court is the *Supreme Court,* which is basically an appeal court, although it has original jurisdiction in some cases.

The lower federal courts and the state courts are separate systems. Cases are not appealed from a state court to a lower federal court. A state court is not bound by the decisions of the lower federal court in its district, but it is bound by decisions of the United States Supreme Court (Reid, 1979).

PRISONS

Prisons are a fact of life in the United States. As much as we may wish to conceal them, and no matter how unsatisfactory we think they are, we cannot imagine doing without them. They represent such a fundamental defense against crime and criminals that we now keep a larger portion of our population in prisons than any other nation with the exception of the Soviet Union and South Africa, and for terms that are longer than in many countries. Small wonder that we Americans invented the prison.

Before prisons serious crimes were redressed by corporal or capital punishment. Jails existed, but mainly for pretrial detention. The closest thing to the modern prison was the workhouse. This was a place of hard labor designed almost exclusively for minor offenders, derelicts, and vagrants. The typical convicted felon was either physically punished or fined, but not incarcerated. Today's system of imprisonment for a felony is a historical newcomer.

The colonists were required to follow the British criminal code, which depended on corporal and capital punishment. Many of the punishments were designed to terrorize offenders and hold them up to ridicule. Common punishments included the ducking stool, the stocks and the pillory, branding the hand or forehead, and public flogging.

The death penalty was very common and execution could be prescribed for such crimes as high treason, petty treason, murder, burglary, rape, sodomy, malicious maiming, manslaughter by stabbing, witchcraft by conjuration, and arson.

Toward the end of the 1700s people began to realize that cruel and harsh punishment did not curb crime. The old penal

Today's police use sophisticated devices to track criminals, such as this finger matrix machine, which speeds up the process of analyzing fingerprints.

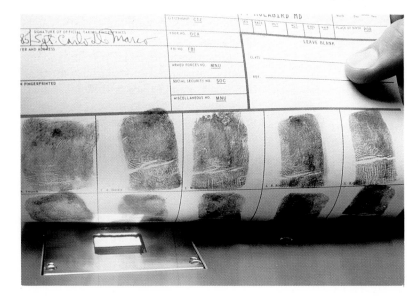

code and its punishments were perceived as not only obsolete and barbaric, but also a foreign intrusion from the hated British. A more American solution was sought.

The largest groundswell of support for reform came from the Quakers, who played a crucial role in inventing the prison. The first prison appeared in Philadelphia in 1790 and spread from there to other cities in the United States and Europe. The same questions that we ask today about how prisons can and should work—what they can achieve and how they might fail—began to be asked then also. The history of prisons is the history of a search for solutions to one of society's most basic problems (Pray, 1987).

A Shortage of Prisons

Today's criminal justice system is in a state of crisis over prison crowding. Even though our national prison capacity has expanded, it has not kept up with demands. The National Institute of Justice estimates we must add 1000 prison spaces a week just to keep up with the growth in the criminal population.

Compounding the problem is the fact that many states have mandated prison terms for drunk drivers and for those who commit gun crimes. Yet, nearly every community will have an angry uprising if the legislature suggests building a new prison in their town.

Given state financial pressures, community resistance, and soaring construction costs, people face a difficult choice. They must either build more prisons or let most convicted offenders go back to the community.

Letting them go back to the community has been a common choice lately. Our reluctance to send people to prison is highlighted by the fact that there were 11.5 million people arrested in 1984, but only 180,418 of these actually ended up in prison.

A key consideration in sending a person to prison is money. The custodial cost of incarceration in a medium-security prison is $15,000 a year. The cost is closer to $25,000 once you add to this the cost of actually building the prison and additional payments to dependent families. You can see why judges are quick to use probation as an alternative to imprisonment, particularly when the prisons are already overcrowded.

The other side of the question, however, is how much does it cost us *not* to send these people to prison? Although it is easy to calculate the cost of an offender's year in prison, it is considerably more difficult to figure the cost to society of letting that individual roam the streets.

A recent study suggests that it is more expensive to release an offender than to incarcerate him when you weigh the value of crime prevented through imprisonment.

Hardened, habitual criminals can be one-person crime waves. When inmates were studied in California, Michigan, and Texas, it was found that each inmate averaged between 187 and 287 crimes per year, exclusive of drug deals. Ten percent of the inmates *each* committed more than 600 crimes per year. That's almost two crimes per day. Can there be any doubt in anybody's mind that it is cheaper to incarcerate these individuals than to let them pursue their trade on society? (Bureau of Justice Statistics, 1988)

Just in case anyone still needs to be convinced, let us see how much each crime costs the public. The National Institute of Justice has come up with a figure of $2300 per crime. This number undoubtedly overestimates the value of petty larcenies, and underestimates the value of rapes, murders, and serious assaults. It is an average, however, and it does give us some way of comparing the costs of incarceration with the costs of freedom.

Using this number, we find that a typical inmate committing 187 crimes (the low estimate) is responsible for $430,000 in crime costs per year. Sending 1000 additional offenders to prison, instead of putting them on probation, would cost an additional $25 million per year. The crimes averted, however, by taking these individuals out of the community would save society $430 million (Bureau of Justice Statistics, 1988).

This approach merely gives us a dollars-and-cents way of making a comparison. It does not in any way account for the personal anguish and trauma to the victim of crime that would be averted.

Looking at the issue from this perspective overwhelmingly supports the case for more prison space. It costs communities more in real losses, social damages, and security measures than it does to incarcerate offenders who are crowded out by today's space limitations.

Women in Prison

As prison reform began in this country, the practice was to segregate women into sections of the existing institutions. There were few women inmates, a fact that was used to "justify" not providing them with a matron. Vocational training and educational programs were not even considered. In 1873 the first separate prison for women, the Indiana Women's Prison, was opened, with its emphasis on rehabilitation, obedience, and religious education.

Most women's prisons were originally located in rural areas or small towns. In some cases, towns have grown up around them so that many are now at least fairly close to additional facilities and resources. Still, many women offenders are in prisons quite a distance removed from family and friends and not accessible by public transportation.

In contrast with institutions for adult males, institutions for adult women are generally more esthetic and less secure. Women inmates are usually not considered high security risks, nor have they proved to be as violent as male inmates are. There are some exceptions, but on the whole, women's institutions are built and maintained with the view that their occupants are not great risks to themselves or to others.

Women inmates also usually have more privacy than men do while incarcerated, and they usually have individual rooms. With the relatively smaller number of women in prison, there is a greater opportunity for the inmates to have contact with the staff, and there is also a greater chance for innovation in programming (Reid, 1981).

Female inmates appear to have greater difficulty than males adjusting to the absence of their families, especially to the absence of their children. According to one study, the majority of female offenders had dependent children living at home at the time of their incarceration. In those cases, only 10 percent had husbands who made arrangements for child care. For 85 percent of the women, their families took care of the children. The average number of children per inmate mother was 2.48. It is estimated that there are some 30,000 children in this country whose mothers are in prison.

Men commit more crimes and are arrested for more serious crimes than women are. Women are more likely to commit property crimes such as larceny, forgery, fraud, and embezzlement, and drug offenses. They are less likely to be involved in robbery or burglary (U.S. Department of Justice, 1983).

The National Institute of Justice estimates we must add 1000 prison spaces a week just to keep up with the growth in the criminal population.

Goals of Imprisonment

Prisons exist to accomplish at least four goals: (1) separation of criminals from society, (2) punishment of criminal behavior, (3) deterrence of criminal behavior, and (4) rehabilitation of criminals.

1. *Separation of criminal from society.* Prisons accomplish this purpose once convicted felons reach the prison gates. Inasmuch as it is important to protect society from individuals who seem bent on repeating destructive behavior, prisons are one logical choice among several others, such as exile and capital punishment (execution). The American criminal justice system relies principally on prisons to segregate convicts from society, and in this regard they are quite efficient.

2. *Punishment of criminal behavior.* There can be no doubt that prisons are extremely unpleasant places in which to spend time. They are crowded, degrading, boring, and dangerous. Not infrequently prisoners are victims of one another's violence. Inmates also are constantly supervised, sometimes harassed by guards, and deprived of normal means of social, emotional, intellectual, and sexual expression. Prison undoubtedly is a severe form of punishment.

3. *Deterrence of criminal behavior.* The rising crime figures cited earlier suggest that prisons have failed to achieve the goal of deterring criminal behavior. There are some good reasons for this. First, by their very nature prisons are closed to the public. Few people know much about prison life, nor do they often think about it. Inmates who return to society frequently brag to their peers about their prison experiences to recover their self-esteem. To use the prison experience as a deterrent, the very unpleasant aspects of prison life would have to be constantly brought to the attention of the population at large. To promote this approach, some prisons have allowed inmates to develop programs introducing high school students to the horrors of prison life. From the scanty evidence available to date, it is unclear whether such programs really deter people from committing crimes. Another reason that prisons fail to deter crime is the funnel effect, which we will discuss later in this chapter. No punishment can deter undesired behavior if the likelihood of being punished is minimal. Thus, the argument regarding the relative merit of different types of punishment is pointless until there is a high probability that whatever forms are used will be applied to all (or most) offenders.

4. *Rehabilitation of criminals.* Many Americans believe that rehabilitation—the resocialization of criminals to conform to society's values and norms and the teaching of usable work habits and skills—should be prisons' most important goal. It is also the stated goal of almost all corrections officials. Yet, there can be no doubt that prisons do not come close to achieving this aim. According to the FBI, about 70 percent of all inmates released from prison are arrested again for criminal behavior (Bureau of Justice, 1988).

Sociological theory provides ample explanations for the high recidivism rate. For example, Sutherland's ideas on cultural transmission and differential association point to the fact that inside prisons, the society of inmates has a culture of its own, in which obeying the law is not highly valued. New inmates are quickly socialized to this peer culture and adopt its negative attitudes toward the law. Further, labeling theory tells us that once somebody has been designated as deviant, his or her subsequent behavior often conforms to that label. Prison inmates who are released find it difficult to be accepted in the society at large and to find legitimate work. Hence, former inmates quickly take up with their old acquaintances, many of whom are active criminals. It thus becomes only a matter of time before they are once more engaged in criminal activities.

This does not mean that prisons should be torn down and all prisoners set free. As we have indicated, prisons do accomplish important goals, though certain changes are needed. Certainly it is clear that the entire criminal justice system needs to be made more efficient and that prison terms, as well as other forms of punishment, must follow predictably the commission of a crime. Another idea, which gained some approval in the late 1960s but seems of late to have declined in popularity, is to create "halfway" houses and other institutions in which the inmate population is not so completely locked away from society. This way, they are less likely to be socialized to the prison's criminal subculture. Labeling theory suggests that if the process of delabeling former prisoners were made open, formal, and explicit, released inmates might find it easier to win reentry into society. Just as new prisoners are quickly socialized into a prison's inmate culture, released prisoners must be resocialized into society's culture. This can be accomplished only if means are found to bring former inmates into frequent, supportive, and structured contact with stable members of the wider society (again, perhaps, through halfway houses). The simple separation of prisoners from society undermines this goal.

THE "FUNNEL" EFFECT

One complaint voiced by many of those concerned with our criminal justice system is that although many crimes are committed, few people ever seem to be punished. The **funnel effect** begins with the fact that of all the crimes committed, the *National Crime Survey* reports that in 1986 only 37 percent were reported to the police (Bureau of Justice Data report, 1987). Only about 26 percent led to an arrest. Next, false arrests, lack of evidence, and plea bargaining (negotiations in which individuals arrested for a crime are allowed to plead guilty to a lesser charge of the same crime, thereby saving the criminal justice system the time and money spent in a trial) considerably reduce the number of complaints that actually are brought to trial.

In one Bureau of Justice study of 532,000 felony arrests in eleven states, 84 percent of those adults arrested were prosecuted; 62 percent were convicted; 36 percent were sentenced to incarceration; and 13 percent were imprisoned for more than 1 year (Bureau of Justice Statistics, January 1988). (See Figure 15.4 for the typical outcome of one hundred felony arrests.)

Ernest van den Haag and others contend from such figures that crime goes unchecked because streetwise criminals know that their chance of being caught and punished is very small indeed; therefore, punishment has lost its force as a negative sanction.

funnel effect The condition in our criminal justice system where many crimes are committed but few people ever seem to be punished.

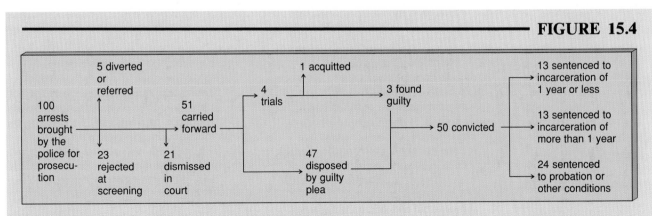

FIGURE 15.4

Typical Outcome of 100 Felony Arrests Brought by Police for Prosecution in 37 Jurisdictions. Source: *Bureau of Justice Statistics,* BJS Data Report, 1987, *January 1988, p. 42.*

The Continuing Debate over Capital Punishment: Does It Deter Murderers?

Capital punishment has been opposed for many years and for many reasons. In this country, the Quakers were the first to oppose the death penalty and to provide prison sentences instead.

According to Amnesty International, U.S.A., capital punishment is a "horrifying lottery" where the penalty is death and the odds of escaping it are determined more by politics, money, race, and geography than by the crime committed.

They base their impression on the fact that black men are more likely to be executed than white men; southern states, especially Texas, Florida, Louisiana, Georgia, and Virginia, account for the vast majority of executions that have taken place since the Supreme Court reinstituted the death penalty in 1977.

Yet the arguments for capital punishment continue to mount, centering mainly around the issue of deterrence. As Professor Ernest Van Den Haag notes: "If by executing convicted murderers there is any chance, even a mere possibility, of deterring future murderers, I think we should execute them. The life even of a few victims who may be spared seems infinitely precious to me. The life of the convicted murderer has negative value. His crime has forfeited it" (Van Den Haag, 1986).

Which brings us back to the age-old question, Does the death penalty deter homicide? Until the 1970s, social scientists continued to argue that they could find no evidence that it did. In 1975, however, Isaac Erlich presented information based on sophisticated statistical techniques showing that the death penalty had an enormous deterrent effect on murder. In fact, he concluded that eight additional homicides were prevented by every execution. That is, eight people escape being the homicide victims of future murderers every time an execution takes place.

A more recent study by economist Stephen K. Layson concludes that every execution of a convicted murderer prevents eighteen future murders. Therefore, putting a murderer to death saves many additional lives (Layson, 1985).

There may be more involved in deterrence than we think. Plato believed we were deterred from committing crimes by seeing others punished. He was referring to punishments administered in public, where everyone could see the gory details of torture and execution.

Fortunately, today executions

[In New York City] police and city officials have tacitly agreed to allow certain kinds of criminal behavior to go on without harassment or punishment. The authorities have enlarged the scope of unchallenged criminal behavior to include not only quality-of-life offenses such as aggressive panhandling, smoking in the subway, drunkenness, brawling, urinating on sidewalks and in the subways, but also certain muggings, burglaries, narcotics transactions, purse snatchings, car thefts, and larcenies.

There is neither the manpower nor the courtroom space available for police to make the kinds of disorderly-conduct arrests they routinely made in the past. If outraged citizens complain strenuously enough, a patrolman will try to move the violators along or issue a summons. These summonses are not really supposed to be a deterrent to the offender so much as a pacifier for the angry citizen. (Pileggi, 1981)

To be fair, the situation is not quite as bad as it appears. In regard to serious

Currently, there are some 2000 inmates on death row across the country.

are not held in public and only a small number of people witness them. In place of actually seeing the execution we now have mass media reports that become our "eyes."

Therefore, deterrence should be related to how much an execution is publicized (Stark, 1987).

Using this approach, one researcher (Phillips, 1980) argued that deterrence does not depend on how many executions there actually are, but rather on how much publicity they generate. One well-publicized execution has a far greater deterrent effect than several little-known executions. Indeed it was shown that the greater the number of inches a newspaper devoted to an execution, the greater the drop in the homicide rate during that week.

Even so, the deterrent effect of an execution is short-lived. The drop in the homicide rate only lasts for about two weeks. At that point homicides climb back to the pre-execution level (Phillips, 1980).

If by some chance we could arrange to hold and publicize an execution every two weeks, the deterrent effect would probably wear off also. We would then become so used to hearing about executions that they would have little impact on potential murderers.

Currently, there are some 2000 inmates on death row across the country. With public support for the death penalty increasing, and with no broad legal challenges to capital punishment being waged, we can expect many more executions to take place.

Source: David P. Phillips, "The Deterrent Effect of Capital Punishment: New Evidence on an Old Controversy," *American Journal of Sociology* 86, pp. 139–148. Isaac Ehrlich, "The Deterrent Effect of Capital Punishment: A Question of Life and Death," *American Economic Review* (1975), pp. 397–417.

---

crimes, the number of arrests is considerably more than it is for crimes in general.

What about punishment? Those who criticize the system in terms of its "funnel" effect seem to regard only a term in prison as an effective punishment. Yet the usual practice is to send to prison only those criminals whose terms of confinement are set at more than one year. The number of American prisoners, after declining through the 1960s, rose sharply through the 1970s and 1980s (see Figure 15.5). Many thousands of other criminals receive shorter sentences and serve them in municipal and county jails. Thus, if the number of people sent to local jails as well as to prison are counted, the funnel effect is less severe than it often is portrayed. The question then becomes one of philosophy: Is a jail term of less than one year an adequate measure for the deterrence of crime? Or should all convicted criminals have to serve longer sentences in federal or state prisons, with jails used primarily for pretrial detention?

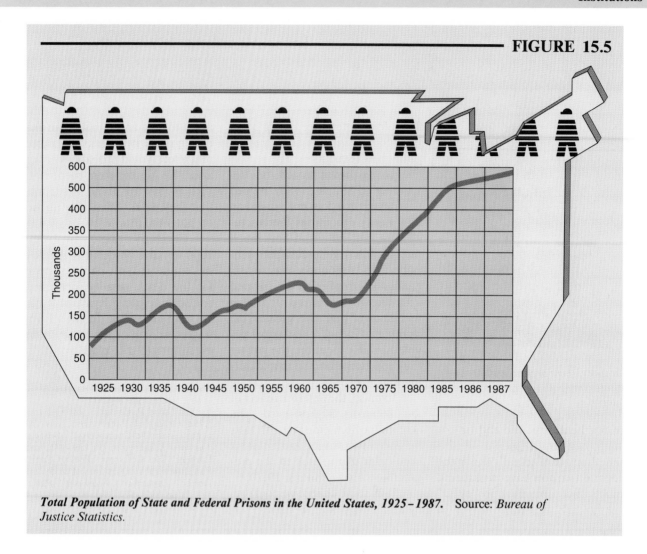

FIGURE 15.5

Total Population of State and Federal Prisons in the United States, 1925–1987. Source: *Bureau of Justice Statistics.*

To date, no society has been able to come up with an ideal way of confronting, accommodating, or preventing criminal behavior. Although much attention has been focused on the causes of and remedies for criminal behavior, no theory, law, or social-control mechanism has yet provided a fully satisfying solution to the problem.

SUMMARY

There are some interests that are so important to a society that folkways and mores are not adequate enough to insure orderly social interaction. Therefore, laws are passed to give the state the power of enforcement. These laws become a formal system of social control that is exercised when other informal forms of control are not effective.

Laws influence virtually every area of social interaction. They are used to protect us; to define ownership; to regulate business; and to raise taxes.

The legal code consists of the formal rules, called laws, adopted by a society's political authority. The code is enforced through the use of formal negative sanctions when rules are broken.

How is it that laws come into society? The consensus approach assumes that laws are merely a formal version of the norms and values of the people. The conflict approach to explaining the emergence of laws sees dissension and conflict between various groups as a basic aspect of society. The conflict is resolved when the groups in power achieve control. The conflict approach to law assumes that the elite use their power to enact and enforce laws that support their own economic interests against the interests of the lower classes.

There are two types of law, criminal law and civil law. Criminal law deals with violations against the interests of society, whereas civil law deals with violations against the individual.

Crime is behavior that violates a society's criminal code. In the United States what is criminal is specified in written law, primarily state statutes.

The *Uniform Crime Reports* program has been developing national statistics on crime from local police records since 1930. These statistics are not always reliable. For example, each police department compiles its own figures, and so definitions of the same crime vary from place to place. To learn more about crimes and the victims of crime, in 1973 the *National Crime Survey* began to collect victimization data from households across the country. The *Survey* measures both reported and unreported crimes.

Juvenile crime refers to the breaking of criminal laws by individuals under the age of 18. Arrest records for 1986 show that youths under age 18 accounted for 16.8 percent of all arrests.

In addition to homicide, other violent crimes that have an impact on American households are rape, aggravated assault, and robbery. Ninety percent of all crime in the United States is nonviolent crime and is what is referred to as crime against property, as opposed to crime against the person.

The term *white-collar crime* was coined by Edwin H. Sutherland to refer to individuals who, while occupying positions of social responsibility or high prestige, break the law in the course of their work for the purpose of illegal personal or organization gain.

Organized crime refers to structured associations of individuals or groups who come together for the purpose of obtaining gain mostly from illegal activities.

There are some crimes that do not produce victims in any obvious way, and so some scholars have coined the term *victimless crime* to refer to them. Basically, victimless crimes are acts that violate those laws meant to enforce the moral code.

Victims of crime are more often men than women. Younger people are much more likely than the elderly to be victims of crime. Blacks are more likely to be victims of violent crime than are whites or members of other racial groups. People with low incomes have the highest violent-crime victimization rates.

Every society that has established a legal code has also set up a criminal justice system — personnel and procedures for arrest, trial, and punishment — to deal with violations of the law. The three main categories of our criminal justice system are the police, the courts, and the prisons.

Prisons exist to accomplish at least four goals: (1) separation of criminals from society, (2) punishment of criminal behavior, (3) deterrence of criminal behavior, and (4) rehabilitation of criminals.

Chapter 16

THE ECONOMY

Americans save far less than almost any other industrial nation. In 1987, Portuguese families saved, on average, 25.4 percent of their household income; the Japanese, 16.6 percent; and the West Germans, 12.2 percent; the U.S. savings rate was a dismal 3.9 percent.

What would account for this difference? Is it a buy now, pay later mentality among Americans, or does the explanation exist at another level? Let us see how German and Japanese citizens think of savings.

Saving, says Martin Hufner, an executive at the Deutsche Bank AG in Frankfurt, is part of the "German mentality." With most of West Germany destroyed after World War II, "we were forced to save since there was no money." This attitude has stayed on, with the result that borrowing is out of character for most Germans.

Saving is even more fundamental to the Japanese. Its origin, says Hideo Karino of Nikko Securities, can be found in the Buddhist tradition. People who spend a great deal of money are not well respected. On a more practical level, the Japanese equivalent of our social security system pays very little, forcing people to build their own retirement nest egg.

Americans do not feel driven to save in the same manner as the Germans and Japanese. Many in our society are consuming instead of saving. We are buying homes, cars, electronic equipment, and the latest skis instead of stashing money away for the future. In fact, our economy depends on consumption.

Some of our reasons for saving less are economic ones. Unlike the Japanese, we cannot deduct the interest earned on the money we save. Instead, it is taxed as regular income and whatever is left is depleted even more by the effects of inflation. At the same time, the government gives us an incentive to borrow, by allowing us to deduct the interest we pay on our home mortgages. Our political leaders in Washington are sending a loud and clear message that it is smarter to borrow than to save. In West Germany the opposite is true.

How much we save then, tells us a great deal about ourselves and our society. At one and the same time, our economy mirrors our culture and determines what we do. It is difficult for us to step back and look objectively at our own economic system. After all, we have grown up as a part of it and interacted with it every day. We tend to take it for granted that whenever we want to buy something, such as a book, a bar of soap, or a car, we will be able to do so, without considering that a complicated economic system is required to make these items available to us. The economy affects more than our pocketbooks. Our sense of well-being, our social interactions, and our political decisions are inextricably linked to the economy.

economy An institution whose primary function is to determine the manner in which society produces, distributes, and consumes goods and services.

How is the economic system that we know so well in the United States different from that in other countries? What role does the government play in determining the economic system? What impact does the economic system have on the total structure of society? These are just some of the questions we will address in this chapter.

ECONOMIC SYSTEMS

In its simplest terms, the **economy** is a social institution whose function is to determine the manner in which society produces, distributes, and consumes goods and services. Money, goods, and services do not flow of their own accord. People work at particular jobs, manufacture particular products, distribute the fruits of their labor, purchase basic necessities and luxury items, and decide to save or spend their money.

A very simple society may only produce and distribute food, water, and shelter. As a society becomes more complex and productive, the products produced and distributed become increasingly more elaborate. To be useful, all these goods and services must be distributed throughout the society. We depend on impersonal distribution systems to bring us such essential items as food, water, housing, clothing, health care, transportation, and communication systems, all of which we consume according to our ability to pay for them.

The problem for any society is to decide how much to be involved in the production and distribution of goods and services. In most economies, *markets* play the major role in determining what gets produced, how, and for whom. Which means, is there a demand for something? Who is willing to produce it? How much are people willing to pay for it? Economies that do not allow markets to function are known as command economies.

Capitalism is an economic system based on private ownership of the means of production in which resource allocation depends largely on markets.

CAPITALISM

In its classic form, **capitalism** is an economic system based on private ownership of the means of production, and in which resource allocation depends largely on market forces. The government plays only a minor role in the marketplace, which works out its own problems through the forces of supply and demand.

There are two basic premises behind capitalism. The first, as Max Weber noted, is production "for the pursuit of profit and ever renewed profit." Capitalism notes that people are entitled to pursue their own self-interest, and this activity is desirable and eventually benefits society through what is known as the "invisible hand" of capitalism. For example, pharmaceutical companies may have no other goal in mind than profit when they develop new drugs. The fact that their products eventually benefit society is an indirect benefit brought about by this invisible hand.

The second basic premise behind capitalism is that the free market will determine what is produced and at what price.

Adam Smith is regarded as the father of modern capitalism. He set forth his ideas in his book *The Wealth of Nations* (1776), which is still used today as a yardstick for analyzing economic systems in the Western world. According to Smith, capitalism has four features: private property, freedom of choice, freedom of competition, and freedom from government interference.

capitalism An economic system based on private ownership of the means of production in which resource allocation depends largely on market forces.

The "invisible hand" of capitalism allows for the development of new products that eventually benefit society.

Private Property

Smith believed that the ability to own private property acts as an incentive for people to be thrifty and industrious. These motivations, although selfish, will benefit society, because those who own property will respect the property rights of others.

Freedom of Choice

Along with the right to own property is the right to do with it what one pleases as long as it does not harm society. Consequently, people are free to sell, rent, trade, give away, or retain whatever they possess.

mixed economy An economy that combines free-enterprise capitalism with government regulation of business, industry, and social-welfare programs.

Freedom of Competition

Smith believed society would benefit most from a free market in which there is unregulated competition for profits. Supply and demand would be the main factors determining the course of the economy.

Freedom from Government Interference

Adam Smith believed that government should promote competition and free trade and keep order in society; it should not regulate business or commerce.

Smith believed government should promote competition and free trade and keep order in society. It should not regulate business or commerce. The best thing the government can do for business is leave it alone. This view that government should stay out of business is often referred to as *laissez-faire capitalism.* (The French expression *laissez faire* is translated as "allow to act.")

Laissez-faire capitalism and command economies are completely opposite ways for societies to deal with the distribution of goods and services. In the United States the government does play a vital role in the economy. Therefore, the U.S. system cannot be seen as an example of pure capitalism. Rather, many have referred to our system as modified capitalism, also known as a mixed economy (Rachman, 1985).

A **mixed economy** combines free-enterprise capitalism with governmental regulation of business, industry, and social-welfare programs. Although private property rights are protected, the forces of supply and demand are not allowed to operate with total freedom. The distribution of resources takes place through a combination of market and governmental forces. Because there are few nationalized industries in this country (the Tennessee Valley Authority and Amtrak are two exceptions), the government uses its regulatory power to guard against private-industry abuse. Our government is also involved in such areas as antitrust violations, the environment, and minority employment. Ironically, this involvement may be even greater than it is in some of the more socialistic European countries.

Most countries have a mixed economy. Some countries, such as the United States and Hong Kong, are closer to the free-market end of the continuum, whereas Soviet bloc countries are closer to the command-economy end. The absolute extremes of a complete command economy or complete capitalism do not exist, whether it be in Soviet bloc countries or the United States. The Soviet bloc countries let consumers choose some of the goods they buy and allow private agricultural markets to some extent. In the United States, the government regulates economic activity not only by setting minimum wage levels,

requiring safety standards for the workplace, and instituting antitrust laws and farm price supports but also by assuming partial or total control of privately owned businesses when their potential collapse might have a significant impact on the people. Two examples include the government involvement in Amtrak and, for a time, the Chrysler Corporation.

THE MARXIST RESPONSE TO CAPITALISM

Adam Smith believed that ordinary people would thrive under capitalism, that not only would their needs for goods and services be met, but that they would also benefit by being part of the marketplace. In contrast, Karl Marx was convinced that capitalism produces a small group of well-to-do individuals, while the masses suffer under the tyranny of those who exploit them for their own profit.

Karl Marx argued that capitalism causes people to be alienated from their labor and from themselves. Under capitalism, the worker is not paid for part of the value of the goods produced. Instead, this "surplus value" is taken by the capitalist as profit at the expense of the worker.

Workers are also alienated by doing very small specific jobs, as on an assembly line, and not feeling connected to the final product produced. The worker feels no relationship or pride in the product being produced and merely works to obtain a paycheck and survive—a far cry from work being the joyous fulfillment of self that Marx believed it should be.

Karl Marx believed nineteenth-century capitalism contained several contradictions that were the seeds of its own destruction. The main problem with capitalism, he contended, is that profits will decline as production expands. This in turn will force the industrialist to exploit the laborers and pay them less in order to continue to make a profit. As the workers are paid less or are fired, they are less able to buy the goods being produced. This then causes profits to fall even further, leading to bankruptcies, greater unemployment, and even a full-scale depression. After an increasingly severe series of depressions, the workers will rise up and take control of the state. They then will create a socialist form of government in which private property is abolished and turned over to the state. The workers now will control the means of production and the exploitation of workers will end.

The reality of capitalism has not matched Marxist expectations. As we mentioned earlier, capitalist economies have become much more mixed economies than the capitalist model developed by Adam Smith. This has avoided some of Marx's prophesied outcomes. The level of impoverishment that Marx predicted for the workers has not taken place, as labor unions have been able to obtain higher wages and better working conditions for the labor force. Marx thought these changes could only come about through revolution. Labor-saving machinery has also led to higher profits without the predicted unemployment, and the production of goods to meet consumer demands has increased accordingly.

Marxists have offered a number of explanations for capitalism's continued success. Some have suggested that capitalism has been able to survive because Western societies have been able to sell their excess goods to developing countries and that these sales have enabled the capitalists to maintain high prices and profits. However, Marxists see this as only a temporary solution to the inevitable decline of capitalism. Eventually the whole world will be industrialized, and the contradictions in capitalism will be revealed. They believe the movement toward socialism has not been avoided, but only postponed.

COMMAND ECONOMIES

In a **command economy** the government makes all the decisions about production and consumption. A government planning

command economy An economy in which the government makes all the decisions about production and consumption.

Whereas capitalism views profit as the ultimate goal of economic activity, socialism is based on the belief that economic activity should be guided by public need rather than private profit. This Soviet wheat farm receives much greater governmental attention than would an American farm.

socialism An economic system in which the government owns the sources of production, including factories, raw materials, and transportation systems. Centralized planning is used to set production and distribution goals, and the rich and middle class are heavily taxed to support a wide range of social-welfare programs.

office decides what will be produced, how, and for whom and instructs workers and firms about what they are to produce.

Such planning is an incredibly complicated task, and there are no complete command economies where all allocation is done by others. There is, however, a large dose of central direction and planning in communist countries, where the state owns factories and land and makes many of the decisions about what people should consume and how much they should work.

To appreciate the immensity of the task of central planning, try to imagine what it would be like if the economy of the city you live in were run by command. Think of the food, clothing, and housing allocations you would have to make to everyone. Then consider how you would know who should get what and how to produce it. These decisions are currently being made by the market.

Often, this planning fails to deliver the goods and services needed by the population. Although, for example, the Soviet Union has more farmers than all Western nations and Japan combined, its farm output is dismal; Soviet farmers produce only one quarter as much food and fiber as their Western counterparts. As a result, grocery store shelves are poorly stocked, and consumers are issued rationing coupons to control demand. Even these are ineffective in controlling food shortages, though. In Leningrad, for example, milk, sour cream, sugar, sausage, and other staples of the Soviet diet are often absent from store shelves (Keller, 1988a).

In addition, rigidity often blocks efficiency. Afraid to try new technologies, command-economy bureaucrats stick with the old tried-and-true methods for much too long. For example, while the open-hearth method of steel production had been all but abandoned in the West by 1985, 40 percent of the steel produced in the Eastern bloc countries still used this method (Keller, 1988b).

Total command economies then, are not realistic ways of distributing goods and services. In the next section we will examine how distribution functions are performed by capitalistic and socialistic economic systems.

SOCIALISM

Socialism is one type of command economy that is an alternative to and a reaction against capitalism. Whereas capitalism views profit as the ultimate goal of economic activity, socialism is based on the belief that economic activity should be guided by public needs rather than private profit. **Socialism** is an economic system in which the government owns the sources of production, including factories, raw materials, and transportation and communication systems. Much greater centralized planning is present than in capitalist societies. This planning is oriented toward output rather than profit. It ensures that key industries run smoothly and that the public "good" is met. Individuals are heavily taxed in order to support a wide range of social-welfare programs that benefit every member of the society. Many socialist countries are described as having a "cradle-to-grave" welfare system.

Instead of relying on the marketplace to determine prices, under socialism prices for major goods and services are set by government agencies. Socialists believe that major economic, social, and political decisions should be made by elected representatives of the people in conjunction with the broader plans of the state. The aim is to influence the economic system so that wealth and income are distributed as equally as possible. The belief is that everyone should have such essentials as food, housing, medical care, and education before some people can have luxury items, such as cars and jewelry. Accordingly, in socialist societies consumer items are very expensive, whereas the basic necessities are inexpensive by Western standards.

THE CAPITALIST VIEW OF SOCIALISM

Capitalists view the centrally planned economies of the socialist societies as inefficient and concentrating power in the hands of one group whose authority is based on party position. Any worker disagreement with the policies of this group, such as advocating strikes or organized efforts to change policies, is seen as disloyalty to the state. The workers thus are controlled both economically and politically, having very little opportunity to improve their life-styles or participate in political decisions.

Capitalists also raise such questions as, If essential goods and services are subsidized by the state and the consumers do not pay their full cost, what will prevent them from using more than they are entitled to and taking advantage of the system? If the producers of goods and services are immune from competition and have few incentives, what will encourage them to produce high-quality products?

The critics of socialism believe the workers actually have very little freedom and that the centrally planned economy is ineffective, compared with a system based on market forces and individual incentives.

DEMOCRATIC SOCIALISM

In western Europe, **democratic socialism** has evolved as a political and economic system that attempts to preserve individual freedom in the context of social equality and a centrally planned economy.

With the parliamentary system of government present in many European countries, social democratic political parties have been able to win representation in the government. They have been able to enact their economic programs by being elected to office, as opposed to producing a worker's uprising against capitalism. The social democrats have also attempted to appeal to middle-class workers and highly trained technicians, as well as to industrial workers.

Under democratic socialism the state assumes ownership of only strategic industries and services, such as airlines, railways, banks, television and radio stations, medical services, colleges, and important manufacturing enterprises. Certain enterprises can remain in private hands as long as government policies can ensure that they are responsive to the nation's common welfare. High tax rates prevent excessive profits and the concentration of wealth. In return the population receives extensive welfare bene-

democratic socialism A convergence of the capitalist and socialist economic theories in which the state assumes ownership of strategic industries and services, but other enterprises remain in private hands.

Under socialism, any worker disagreement with the policies of the state, such as advocating strikes and organizing efforts to change policies, is seen as disloyal.

fits, such as free medical care, free college education, or subsidized housing.

The social democratic movement is an example of the convergence of the capitalist and socialist economic theories, a trend that has been evident for some time now. Capitalist systems have seen an ever-greater introduction of state planning and government programs, and socialist systems have seen the introduction of market forces and the profit motive. The growing economic interdependence of the world's nations will help continue this trend toward convergence.

corporation The most important form of business ownership in the United States, the corporation is considered a legal entity with all the rights of an actual person. A corporation has the major advantage of protecting its owners from personal responsibility for business liabilities.

THE UNITED STATES ECONOMY

Although considered a mixed economy, our economic system is still based on the concept of private ownership of the means of production and distribution. There may be hundreds of thousands of businesses in the United States, but the health of the U.S. economy is still determined by the giants of American business (for example, General Motors, IBM, and Exxon). The 500 largest commercial and industrial concerns exert enormous political and economic influence on our society.

Big business, as we know it today, is a twentieth-century phenomenon. Before the turn of the century, the country's largest companies, including Du Pont, Swift, Armour, and Ford, were family owned and family controlled. Men like John D. Rockefeller, Andrew Carnegie, and J. P. Morgan built industrial empires on a scale never to be duplicated. Their companies grew at such speed that by the early 1900s family ownership and control became impractical. It was at this time that the control of the principal American corporations passed from their owners to salaried managers who decided production, marketing, and pricing policies. In addition, legal ownership was placed in the hands of thousands and sometimes millions of anonymous stockholders. By 1963 not one of the nation's 200 largest corporations was privately owned, and in nearly 85 percent of the cases no single stockholder or even group of stockholders owned even 10 percent of a corporation (Samuelson, 1976).

To understand America's private production and distribution systems, we will look at the private corporation.

PRIVATE CORPORATIONS

The most important form of business ownership in the United States, the **corporation** is considered a legal entity with rights similar to those of an individual. Even though a corporation has the legal rights of an individual, it is owned by thousands or even hundreds of thousands of stockholders. A corporation has the major advantage of protecting its owners from personal responsibility for business liabilities. As of 1985, the most recent year for which information is available, there were nearly 3.3 million privately owned corporations in America, with combined receipts of $8398 billion *(Statistical Abstract of the United States: 1989)*. The power of today's corporations has evolved over the years, and one of the most important stimuli to its growth was the separation of corporate ownership and control.

It would thus appear that present-day corporate ownership and control are firmly divided between company stockholders and managers, respectively. However, some financial analysts maintain that this separation is illusory; they point out that although the small group of directors of a corporation together may own as little as 5 percent of the stock, such an amount is sufficient to ensure control of the company, because the rest of the stock often is spread among so many stockholders that none owns even a fraction of that percent. As a result, the control of the typical large corporation effectively resides in one small group of top managers and directors.

OLIGOPOLY

Expansion and growth are key elements of American business. It is the goal of all corporations to capture increasingly larger shares of the market and thus to diminish the effectiveness of their competition. The result of corporate expansion is corporate **oligopoly,** the domination of industries and markets by a handful of monolithic corporations.

The automobile industry is a good example of how oligopoly works. In 1904, when the auto industry was still in its infancy, thirty-five separate manufacturers competed with one another in the marketplace. This began to change in 1908, when General Motors was founded. By the late 1940s, General Motors and Ford had acquired most of their smaller competitors, with the result that today only four major automakers remain in the American market.

The power of America's largest companies is expressed in the performances of "the Fortune 500." In 1986 the sales of these 500 companies totaled $1.7 trillion, which was 61 percent of the nation's **gross national product (GNP),** or the total dollar value of all goods and services produced in a given year in the United States. Together they held $1560.8 billion in assets, earned $65 billion in profits, and employed 13.4 million workers, which represented 15 percent of the nation's entire labor force (*Fortune,* April 27, 1987).

Critics of corporate oligopoly charge that corporate power of this magnitude undermines the capitalistic principle of free competition among many manufacturers. With only a few firms controlling the market, corporations no longer need to strive to provide consumers with the best products at the lowest prices. Furthermore, they can engage in such practices as parallel pricing, in which similar products from various conglomerates all are priced at approximately the same level and are essentially indistinguishable in quality from one another.

CONGLOMERATES

A **conglomerate** is formed when firms that produce goods in greatly diversified fields come together under one corporate head. International Telephone and Telegraph (ITT), one of the nation's largest conglomerates, includes such unrelated firms as a hotel chain, a rental car company, a bakery products manufacturer, an insurance company, a publisher, a glass company, and many others. In total, ITT operates more than 150 affiliated companies.

Conglomerate mergers first became popular during the late 1960s when companies began purchasing (merging with) other companies. Conglomerate activity declined during the early 1970s but picked up with a vengeance in the 1980s. Recently such giant companies as Gulf Oil, Kraft, RCA, Beatrice Foods, General Foods, Burroughs, and Sperry were swallowed up by other Fortune 500 companies. Unchecked, conglomerate mergers can pose serious problems to businesses and consumers alike. A sales leader can gain even more power at the expense of its competitors after becoming part of a powerful conglomerate. Mergers can also create a favorable environment for corporate secrecy and monopolization.

conglomerate The result of firms that produce goods in greatly diversified fields coming together under one corporate head.

oligopoly The domination of industries and markets by a handful of monolithic corporations.

Control of the typical large corporation resides in one small group of top managers and directors.

WORKING FOR A JAPANESE BOSS

With Japanese corporations investing more and more in the United States every year, the likelihood that you might one day work for a Japanese boss is increasing. Currently, some 250,000 Americans employed by the Japanese are building motorcycles in Marysville, Ohio, welding Sony TVs in San Diego, assembling Nissan cars and pickup trucks in Smyrna, Tennessee, manufacturing Toshiba microwave ovens in Lebanon, Tennessee, and so on. In the state of Tennessee alone, the Japanese employ 10,000 workers in 35 manufacturing and 25 sales or distribution facilities.

As you might expect, some of the ground rules are different if your boss is Japanese:

Company loyalty. The Japanese want all employees to feel part of the company. As one worker put it, "they want you to feel that this is your company, not theirs, so that you're working for yourself, too" (*U.S. News & World Report,* May 9, 1988).

Cooperation. Cooperation is the cornerstone of Japanese management. Workers are asked for their opinions and their ideas are valued. As a result, productivity is usually higher than it is at American-owned firms, and union membership is lower. Instead of having an "us" against "them" relationship with their bosses, workers recognize that the cooperative spirit that pervades the company is in their best interest, as are the higher wages and job security Japanese firms offer.

An assembly line that moves at a killing pace. Although the Japanese give a lot to their employees, they also expect a lot in return. Factories are highly automated, with robots working alongside humans. And, according to workers, the pace of the assembly line is brutal and production quotas high.

Culture-based sexism. Although the Japanese are forced by

MULTINATIONALS

multinational corporation A corporation that does business in more than one nation.

Companies that do business in more than one country are considered **multinational corporations.** About 300 of the 500 largest multinational companies are based in the United States and export their products abroad. Many of the other large multinationals are based in Japan. Of the ten largest multinationals, five are American and five are Japanese. (See Table 16.1).

Increasingly, the United States is becoming a prime market for foreign multinationals seeking to tap the vast American market. British companies have the highest direct investment in the United States, followed by the Dutch, Japanese, Canadians, West Germans, and Swiss.

Although they are only in third place, Japanese multinationals have received a great deal of publicity in recent years as they have moved onto American shores. By 1987, Japanese multinationals had made their presence known in some dramatic ways. Between 1983 and 1987, Japanese-owned factories in the United States increased from 190 to 640, and the number of workers employed at these plants climbed from 45,500 to 160,000. Japanese invest-

TABLE 16.1
The World's Ten Largest Multinational Corporations

Based in U.S.	Rank	Based in Japan	Rank
IBM	1	Tokyo Electric	4
Exxon	2	Sumitomo Bank	6
General Electric	3	Toyota Motor	7
AT&T	5	Dai-Ichi Kangyo Bank	9
General Motors	8	Nomura Securities	10

Source: Wall Street Journal, 1986.

American law to hire women—and, indeed, many factories have more female than male workers—female managers are few and far between.

Sexism is also implicit in the language the Japanese use to address one another. The version of the language spoken by women is deferential to men, whereas the version used by men is condescending to women. (Men and women use two distinct versions of colloquial Japanese.) Japanese bosses "order you around all the time," said a Japanese woman who worked for a Japanese securities firm on Wall Street. "Before being asked, you're supposed to know all his requests. You must be careful to select the right word,

the right level of politeness, not to hurt his ego" (Breslin, 1988). Although American women do not communicate with their bosses in Japanese, the culture-based condescension is present nonetheless.

Never an easy decision. The Japanese deliberate over every decision they make. Unlike Americans, who make decisions quickly, the Japanese analyze every aspect of a problem, build a consensus as to how to solve it, and then, after what seems to Americans an interminable amount of time, make a decision. "It can absolutely drive you crazy," said one worker. "But once a decision is reached, execution comes quickly and screw-ups are minimized. With American

companies, it's often the other way around" (*U.S. News & World Report,* May 9, 1988).

After a period of adjustment, most Americans find that they can adapt to the unique management style of the Japanese and even grow to like it. However, they feel like a foreigner in their homeland at the start. It takes work on both sides to form a comfortable, productive working relationship.

Sources: "How Japan is Winning Dixie," *U.S. News & World Report,* May 9, 1988, pp. 43–59; Catherine Breslin, "Working for the Japanese," *Ms.,* February 1988, pp. 27–32; "The Difference Japanese Management Makes," *Business Week,* July 14, 1986, pp. 47–50.

---

ments in the United States increased from $18.5 billion to $30.9 billion between 1985 and 1987 (see Figure 16.1) (*U.S. News & World Report,* May 9, 1988).

Corporations expand their activities abroad for several reasons. Often, they find cheaper sources of labor and raw materials, a ready market for their goods, less stringent regulations, and effective tax credits for business done abroad. Unfortunately, when unchecked by government regulations, multinational corporations have sometimes abused their power in foreign markets by taking unfair profit margins and using exploitative employment, investment, and marketing practices. In one of the most extreme cases of this abuse, ITT worked with the United States Central Intelligence Agency to overthrow Salvadore Allende, the democratically elected president of Chile, who had begun to nationalize the commercial holdings of ITT as well as those of other U.S. corporations.

Companies that do business in more than one country are considered multinational corporations. About 300 of the 500 largest multinationals are based in the United States and export their products abroad.

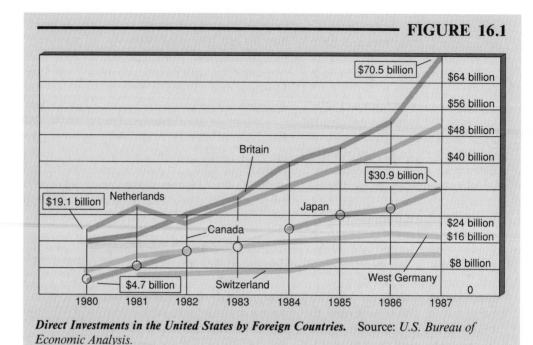

FIGURE 16.1

$70.5 billion

$64 billion

$56 billion

$48 billion

$40 billion

Britain

$30.9 billion

$19.1 billion   Netherlands

Japan

$24 billion

$16 billion

Canada

$8 billion

$4.7 billion   Switzerland   West Germany

0

1980   1981   1982   1983   1984   1985   1986   1987

Direct Investments in the United States by Foreign Countries.   Source: *U.S. Bureau of Economic Analysis.*

CORPORATE BUREAUCRACY

corporate bureaucracy A formally structured business organization with an explicit hierarchy, definite procedural rules, and a well-maintained division of labor.

Huge corporations control people as well as money. Formally organized **corporate bureaucracies** have an explicit hierarchy, definite procedural rules, and a well-maintained division of labor, employing millions of workers who are viewed as members of the organization rather than as individuals. The result, critics charge, is a dehumanized working environment in which individuals lose their sense of self-worth and pride in a job well done.

Although corporate bureaucracies have serious flaws, they are also necessary to the smooth functioning of industrial production. Without clear lines of authority, an explicit division of labor, and a formal system of rules and regulations, corporations would not be able to achieve their production goals or earn profits for their shareholders. A major reason for this is the sheer size of today's corporations. (With 741,000 employees, General Motors could not operate without a highly structured bureaucracy.)

Although recognized by our legal system as an entity separate and apart from the individuals who run it, a corporation is also made up of a collection of people — a labor force — who have come together to produce goods and services. In an attempt to humanize working conditions and create greater involvement in the production process, many U.S. firms are using *quality circles* to bring employees at all levels together to analyze and solve work-related problems.

Originally a Japanese concept, quality circles have been shown to increase productivity and improve quality while at the same time reducing costs. They are able to do this for two reasons: First, participation by all workers at all levels of production brings new approaches to old problems. Someone on the assembly line may have a more practical solution to a problem than a manager who never worked on the line. Second, greater employee participation improves the quality of work life, which, in turn, increases productivity and product quality while reducing costs. Some of America's largest companies are using quality circles, including Chrysler, Lockheed Aircraft, and Honeywell.

Corporations may have a great deal of power in society, but ultimately, it is the role of government to limit that power and make sure the corporations function in a way that is in keeping with the larger economy.

THE ROLE OF GOVERNMENT IN THE ECONOMY

About one-third of all the money earned in the United States ends up as taxes collected by the federal, state, and local governments. This is a smaller share than that of the governments in most industrialized countries. However, it does give enormous power to the governments to regulate economic activity and bring about desired economic goals.

Of the money that governments take in taxes, about 60 percent is spent on goods and services, and the remaining 40 percent is spent on transfer payments. Federal government defense spending and state and local government spending on education and fire-fighting services are examples of spending on goods and services. Unemployment benefits, welfare payments, and social security payments are examples of transfer payments.

Like it or not, government is an essential ingredient in our capitalistic economy. By issuing money and credit, it makes economic activity possible; by settling cases in its judicial system, it makes contracts binding and private property inviolate; by regulating business activity, it protects businesses, workers, and consumers from illegal competitive practices; by buying products, it employs workers throughout the economy and stimulates economic growth; and by taxing or not taxing profits, it influences nearly every aspect of economic activity. Let us examine some of the ways in which the government plays a role in the economy.

REGULATION AND CONTROL OF INDUSTRY AND TRADE

Federal intervention in the economy began during the 1800s, when at the initiation of business, government began to build roads, railroads, and canals to facilitate the transport of goods and workers throughout the country and also began regulating banks, credit, and the circulation of money to establish security in the economic system. It was at this time, too, that Americans began to feel the need for governmental protection against unscrupulous business leaders. Left unchecked, many of these large firms expanded and formed oligopolies, practiced discriminatory employment, exploited workers, wasted valuable natural resources, and bribed and pressured high government officials in order to attain their goals. As a result, the first protective regulations regarding industry and trade were passed. (As early as 1906, government regulations protected consumers from contaminated foods and dangerous drugs.)

Today, governmental regulations extend into nearly every aspect of our nation's economic life. Fifty-four regulatory agencies set rules in such diverse areas as radio and television station licensing, fuel efficiency and safety standards for cars and trucks, licensing and control of nuclear power plants, and the protection of employees against on-the-job accidents in some 3.5 million work situations. The economy spends billions each year on government rules and regulations, a cost that usually must be passed along to the consumer.

Government regulations affect nearly every aspect of our nation's economic life, including such diverse areas as radio and television licensing, fuel efficiency and safety standards for cars, and nuclear power plant regulation.

monetary policy The controls set forth by the Federal Reserve system to control the supply of money and credit in the economy.

reserve requirements One of the three primary monetary policies of the Federal Reserve, reserve requirements determine the amount in a bank's checking and savings accounts that must be kept as security for deposits.

open-market operation One of the three primary monetary policies of the Federal Reserve, the open-market operation buys and sells government securities.

discount rate One of the three primary monetary policies of the Federal Reserve, the discount rate is the interest charged by the Fed to banks making loans.

fiscal policy Government policy that attempts to influence economic activity by raising and lowering levels of government spending, borrowing, and taxation.

When, for example, General Motors spends billions of dollars to improve the crash resistance of its car bumpers, that cost is passed along to consumers in the form of higher automobile prices. And the money spent by industries to meet government clean air requirements translates into higher utility bills, more expensive washing machines, and so on.

CONTROL OF MONEY FLOW

The ebb and flow of economic activity that causes recession or boom does not simply happen but is manipulated in certain important ways by the government's monetary and fiscal policies.

Monetary Policy

Early in the century, when bank failures were rampant and the resulting personal and business bankruptcies ruinous, the federal government passed the Federal Reserve Act to control the availability and flow of money in the economy. As a result of this act, the Federal Reserve System was established to regulate the U.S. banking system and control the country's supply of money and credit to ensure economic growth and a stable dollar. The Federal Reserve, which is also known as "the Fed," attempts to control economic cycles through three distinct **monetary policies.**

Through its **reserve requirements,** the Federal Reserve determines the amount in a bank's checking and saving accounts that must be retained as security for the deposits it accepts from customers. By increasing the reserve requirement, the Fed decreases the amount banks have available for consumer and business loans. By decreasing this requirement, it makes money more available.

The Fed also uses an **open-market operation,** which buys and sells government securities, to control the money supply. When it buys U.S. Treasury obligations on the open market, it increases the money supply available to banks, thereby making consumer and business loans more readily available. When it sells U.S. Treasury securities, it decreases the money supply.

Finally, the Fed manipulates the national money supply through its **discount rate**—the rate of interest charged to banks making loans. When the Fed's member banks need money, they come to the Fed, which acts as their central source of funds. When faced with a high discount rate, which makes the money they borrow more expensive, banks are discouraged from issuing new consumer and business loans. A low rate, on the other hand, makes the cost of money cheaper and encourages greater loan activity.

Fiscal Policy

Government **fiscal policy** attempts to influence economic activity by raising and lowering levels of government spending, borrowing, and taxing. The government can stimulate the economy by spending more money than it collects. The extra money the government puts into the economy increases consumer and business demands for products and services. To slow economic activity, the government takes the opposite tack, tightening its budget purse strings and increasing taxes.

Our system of progressive income taxes, which levies higher taxes on higher incomes, also influences economic activity. In prosperous times, when business activity and consumer spending are higher, federal taxes take a large share of earned income, which helps dampen inflationary pressures. When, on the other hand, business and consumer activity are slow, less tax money is collected, which in turn encourages consumer and business spending. This result can also be achieved by lowering the tax rate.

SPECIAL-INTEREST GROUPS

The government does not make its spending and policy decisions in a vacuum. It is subject to interest-group pressure from major corporations, labor unions, professional organizations, and civil rights organizations, among others, all of which try to maintain or increase programs that are favorable to them. The American Council of Life Insurance, for example, attempts to influence government leaders on behalf of the country's life insurance companies. The AFL-CIO works on behalf of the millions of union members. And the American Bar Association attempts to enhance the interest of lawyers.

Much of the pressure that interest groups exert on government occurs during political campaigns. Interest groups such as the American Medical Association and the AFL-CIO contribute millions of dollars to congressional candidates who they feel will champion their interests once they are in office. These contributions are intended to create a feeling of indebtedness in government leaders who believe—rightly or wrongly—that they could not have been elected without interest-group support.

The monetary and fiscal policies chosen by an administration to improve the nation's economy benefit some groups more than others. These policies, which are a reflection of the administration's political philosophy, may favor business, the working class, or the poor in need of government assistance, for example.

THE UNITED STATES LABOR FORCE

The United States Bureau of Labor Statistics has issued labor force projections to the year 2000. These projections show some interesting trends.

Overall, the labor force will grow only 1.2 percent a year between 1986 and 2000.

The government is subject to interest-group pressure from a variety of sources. This woman teamed up with environmentalists after inadequate toxic waste storage poisoned her water supply.

A significant shift in the labor force of the future will be an increase in minority workers.

blue-collar occupations
Occupations that require either specific skills or physical effort to produce goods and services.

white-collar occupations
Occupations that include professional, managerial, sales, and clerical jobs.

This is down from an average growth rate of 2.2 percent between 1972 and 1986. This is the slowest rate of labor force growth since the 1930s and may cause labor shortages in selected areas.

The slower labor force growth is partly due to slower population growth and a maturing of the baby boom generation. The baby boom generation is already part of the labor force, and the baby bust group that followed them is now entering the labor force and will supply the nation's workers until the year 2000.

This trend will cause the labor force to be older. The maturing of the baby boom will raise the median age in the labor force from 35.3 years in 1986 to 38.9 years in 2000. An aging work force may affect productivity because older workers traditionally have been less willing to retrain or to move to a different part of the country for a new job.

The future work force is also going to contain more females. The Bureau of Labor Statistics projects an annual increase in women's labor force participation double the rate for the labor force as a whole for the rest of this century. By the year 2000, 81 percent of women in the prime working years should be in the labor force, up from 71 percent in 1986. Women will account for

nearly two-thirds of all new workers and represent fully 47 percent of all workers by the year 2000, up from 39 percent in 1972.

A third significant shift in the labor force will be the increase in minority workers. Hispanics will account for 29 percent of all new workers as the number of Hispanic workers grows by 4.1 percent a year for the rest of the century. Asians and "other" racial groups will account for 11 percent of all new workers, growing by 3.9 percent a year. If immigration rates continue to be high, Asians will become an important source of new workers. As it is, immigrants will represent the largest share of new workers at any time since World War I.

THE WHITE-COLLAR SOCIETY

The American work force is also being transformed by another trend. Blue-collar jobs—long the mainstay of our economy—are growing at a slower rate than white-collar jobs. **Blue-collar occupations** require either specific skills or physical effort to produce goods and services. **White-collar occupations** include professionals, managers, and sales and clerical workers. In 1970, white-collar workers represented 48.3 percent of the labor force, and blue-collar workers represented 35.3 percent of the labor force. In 1985, white-collar workers had increased their share of the labor force to 53.3, and blue-collar workers represented only 28.8 percent of the labor force (U.S. Bureau of Census, 1987). Table 16.2 shows the degree to which this shift to a white-collar society is taking place.

To a large extent, this change is due to the explosion of technology that has transformed the workplace in recent years. Job opportunities in many old-line manufacturing industries have all but disappeared, while the same innovations have created high-technology, white-collar jobs. Despite these changes, blue-collar occupations still account for more than 30 million jobs.

In addition to traditional white- and blue-collar jobs, service occupations are

TABLE 16.2
Changing Job Patterns in the United States, 1958–1986

	Total Employed		% Increase (Decrease) 1958–1986	% Increase (Decrease) 1986–2000
	1958	1986		
White-collar workers	26,827,000	60,304,000	125	
Professional, technical	6,961,000	17,264,000	148	29.0
Managers, administrators	6,785,000	10,583,000	56	28.7
Sales workers	3,977,000	12,606,000	217	29.6
Clerical workers	9,104,000	19,851,000	118	11.4
Blue-collar workers	23,356,000	30,224,000	29	
Crafts and other skilled workers	8,469,000	13,924,000	64	12.0
Operators, fabricators and laborers	14,888,000	16,300,000	13	2.6
Service workers	7,515,000	16,555,000	120	32.7
Farming, forestry, and fishing workers	5,338,000	3,556,000	(33)	(4.6)

Source: Bureau of Labor Statistics, 1987.

filled by another 14.4 million workers. **Service occupations** encompass a range of jobs that center on providing a service rather than on producing a tangible product. (Hotel and restaurant workers, nurses, police officers, barbers, government workers, and flight attendants are examples of people in service positions.) Between 1958 and 1986 the number of people in service jobs went up 92 percent, and it is projected they will increase another 32.7 between 1986 and the year 2000.

The Bureau of Labor Statistics predicts that nearly all new jobs created in the United States between now and the year 2000 will be in service-producing industries. On the face of it, this seems dramatic, but in reality almost all industries outside manufacturing and agriculture are service industries. These include low-paying retail trades, but also education, health care, government, and finance, all of which offer large numbers of high-paying jobs.

The major increase in jobs in the service sector will produce a great deal of diversity in this sector of the economy. Between now and the year 2000, for the first time in history, a majority of all new jobs will require postsecondary education. At the same time there will be a stable trend in those low-paying service jobs that require the least education. Consequently, there will be wide income disparities among people working in the service sector.

The service-occupation sector is a stabilizing force in the U.S. economy. Although goods-producing industries are sensitive to economic change, service industries tend to fluctuate less than others in employment, wages, and production (Arenson, 1982). Part of the reason for this is the nature of service commodities. When

service occupations Occupations that provide services rather than tangible products.

TABLE 16.3
Labor Force Participation Rate of Women in Selected Countries, 1987

Country	Labor Force Participation Rate (%)	Women as Percent of Total Labor Force
United States	66.5	43.8
Canada	64.3	42.9
France	57.2	42.7
Germany, F.R.	51.4	39.0
Italy	42.0	35.8
Japan	57.4	39.8
Sweden	80.5	47.3
United Kingdom	63.5	42.0

Source: U.S. Department of Commerce, Bureau of the Census, *Statistical Abstract of the United States, 1988* (Washington, D.C., 1987), p. 812.

With 66.5 percent of all women over age 15 working outside the home, women now constitute 43.8 percent of the labor force.

times are difficult economically, people continue using the same automobiles, stoves, cameras, and other goods that they purchased years before. In contrast, although they may cut down on some service purchases, such as travel and dining out, most people continue to use essentially the same level of services in periods of economic stress. In addition, the movement of women in the labor force has resulted in an increased demand for such services as child care, restaurant meals, and cleaning (Arenson, 1982).

WOMEN IN THE LABOR FORCE

In the last 30 years, the number of women holding jobs outside the home has more than doubled, from less than 22 million in 1960 to nearly 52 million in 1986. With 66.5 percent of all women over the age of 15 working, women now constitute 43.8 percent of the labor force. (See Table 16.3 for a comparison of women's labor force participation rates in selected countries around the world.) This rise reflects such factors as a change in attitude toward the role of women in society, high divorce rates, women's search for professional satisfaction, the later average age of marriage, and the need for two incomes instead of one.

It seems that there has been a massive influx of women into the labor force. A significant proportion of this growth is primarily due to a drop in the exit rate of women from the work force. In the past women would work for a certain period of time and then devote themselves to family matters. Now more women tend to remain in their jobs for the reasons stated above.

Unfortunately, despite their numbers, women have shown little success in equalizing entrenched discriminatory pay patterns. Women's pay scales continue to be considerably lower than those for men. Part of the reason for this is the concentration of women in low-paying clerical and service jobs. But women must also contend with the discriminatory practices that pay them less than men, even when they have the same educational and work experience.

COMPARABLE WORTH

You have probably noticed that there are wide discrepancies in pay for jobs that seem to require similar levels of skill and training, a fact that has caused some people to call for a system of comparable worth. The idea of

STRESSES ON THE JOB

Y ou know that awful feeling in the pit of your stomach right before you are going to take an exam. Well, the feeling does not go away when you start work. True, there are no more exams, but there are a whole host of other stresses that go along with holding a job. Figure 16.2 lists some of the events that managers consider stressful.

Source: U.S. News & World Report, July 25, 1988, p. 66.

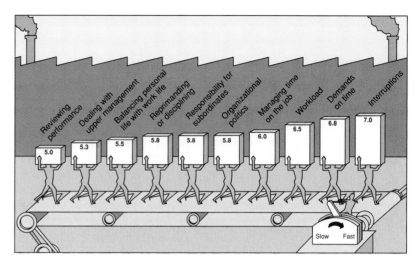

Rough Day at the Office. 1 = Never stressful. 10 = Always stressful. Source: U.S. News & World Report, *July 25, 1988, p. 66.*

comparable worth, or pay equity as it is sometimes called, rests on three propositions. First, that it is possible to compare jobs, even if they are totally dissimilar, and establish some appropriate pay relationship between them. Second, pay relationships that have been established by supply and demand are frequently inequitable and discriminatory, particularly with respect to women's pay. Third, the government must intervene to ensure that pay relationships are correct. The comparable worth idea is an extension of the federal Equal Pay Act of 1963, which required employers to pay men and women equally when they do the same job. Proponents of the comparable worth idea wish to extend this proposition to dissimilar jobs that are nevertheless deemed to be comparable in value.

To establish which jobs are comparable, the employer would hire one of the many consulting firms that specialize in job evaluation studies. The consultant would rank the jobs according to a variety of criteria, such as knowledge and skill required to do the work, the accountability of the person doing the job, and any hazards or

unpleasantness associated with the work.

These aspects would then lead to a total point score for each job, and the points would determine the range for the job's base pay. If after the evaluation, jobs thought to be comparable had different pay scales, it would be assumed that an inequity existed. For example, if jobs predominantly held by men paid more than comparable jobs held by women, it could be an example of sex discrimination.

Studies have shown that women's work has been underpaid. When a comparison was made between job categories that were either predominantly (70 percent or more) male or predominantly female, it was found that male jobs paid about 20 percent more on the average after adjustment for point scores.

Among the problems with the comparable worth system is the inherent subjectivity in job evaluations. Job evaluation consultants inevitably differ among themselves on what factors to measure and what weights to assign to different factors. Another problem with job evaluation scores is that they do not take into account labor

Should We Have a Higher Minimum Wage?

Currently, a worker earning the minimum wage makes less than $8,000 a year—an amount below the poverty level for a family of three. So why not raise the minimum wage? In the view of organized labor, a minimum wage increase is not much to ask. But business disagrees, and, as you will see, there are convincing arguments on both sides.

At the heart of organized labor's position is the belief that the minimum wage should function to keep the nation's working poor out of poverty. When he introduced a bill in Congress in 1987 to "make the minimum wage a living wage," Senator Edward M. Kennedy implored his fellow congressmen to see the inequities of a wage on which workers cannot live. Said Kennedy: "A minimum wage that does not permit full-time workers to provide the bare necessities for their families is unacceptable: It permits unscrupulous firms with significant market power to exploit their lowest-paid workers. It violates the work ethic by condemning to lives of hardship and deprivation millions of citizens who are ready, willing, and able to work. A full-time job in the workplace should never mean a lifetime of poverty or welfare dependency" (*Congressional Digest,* August – September 1987).

Lane Kirkland, president of the AFL-CIO, agrees: "Today's minimum wage will not hold even one person and one child above the poverty threshold. Workers in poverty must depend on other forms of income, such as public assistance, and to the extent that they do, the U.S. taxpayers are subsidizing low-wage employers" (*Congressional Digest,* August – September 1987).

Currently, there are some 8 million workers earning at or below the minimum wage, most of whom are adults and about 2 million of whom are household heads. Proponents of a bolstered minimum wage argue that these workers should not be treated as sacrificial lambs to keep the economy on track. Although they acknowledge the possibility that unemployment might rise slightly following a wage increase, they point to the shrinking youth population, which in their view will cause shortages of first-time workers. Thus, employers facing a shortage of workers will not be likely to let existing workers go

market issues. What if two jobs turned out to be of comparable worth, but one was hard to fill and the other had an endless supply of applicants? A third problem with the comparable worth proposal is that, to be completely fair, such a system should attempt to adjust pay levels in all jobs; that is, there should also be reductions in pay for certain kinds of jobs. At the moment, proponents of this plan are mostly concerned with raising the pay level of jobs held by women.

It appears unlikely that a comprehensive system of comparable worth will be instituted in the near future, but it is likely that we shall see special "equity" raises for certain kinds of jobs that have been traditionally held by women (Seligman, 1984).

YOUTH IN THE LABOR FORCE

There are two distinctly different faces of youth in the American work force today. The first, born in the 1960s and 1970s and now attending college, graduate school, or already in the work force, is better educated than any previous generation our country has known. The second, consisting of youths who have dropped out of high school, is unemployed and largely unemployable. These two groups have little else in common except youth.

A positive picture of youth in the work force emerges if we analyze adults in the population bulge between 25 and 44 years of age. In 1960, the median years of school

even if they are forced to pay them more.

The risk of increased unemployment, especially among youth and minority group members, is what concerns opponents most. Business leaders predict that as many as 300,000 jobs could be lost following a minimum wage increase, with the hardest hit being teenage workers. The reason: Millions of small businesses across the country cannot afford to employ workers at higher wages without raising the prices they charge consumers. Those who choose this route face the possibility of creating an upward inflationary spiral, which all agree is incompatible with prosperity. Realizing this, most employers choose instead to eliminate jobs or reduce employee hours.

If the minimum wage is increased, economists predict that the lowest-paid workers — those closest to the current minimum — would be the first to go, and those making close to the new minimum would have a far better chance of keeping their jobs. Clifford J. Ehrlich, manager of human resources for the Marriott corporation and the Roy Rogers restaurants, a Marriott subsidiary, put these economic facts in perspective when he said: "The newest, least-skilled, least-productive people will be the most expendable" (*Business Week,* July 27, 1987).

Opponents also fear the "ripple" effect a minimum wage increase would have on earnings for higher-paid workers. Studies of past wage increases have found that as wages at the lowest levels rise, so do wages for higher-paid skilled and experienced employees. The result: a wage-driven inflationary spiral.

In a way, both sides make the same argument. They want to improve the plight of America's working poor. Their disagreement lies in the effect a minimum wage increase would have on this goal.

Sources: "The Real Costs of a Higher Minimum Wage," *Business Week,* July 27, 1987, pp. 64–65; "Minimum wage myths," *Nation's Business,* June 1987, pp. 35–38; "Should the 'Minimum Wage Restoration Act of 1987' Be Approved?" *Congressional Digest,* pp. 200–223; David R. Francis, "Sorting Out the Economics of a Higher Minimum Wage," *The Christian Science Monitor,* October 4, 1988, p. 19.

completed by whites over 25 years old was 10.9 and by blacks, 8.0. By 1987 the number of years of schooling completed by each group had jumped to 12.7 and 12.4, respectively. Today, most Americans finish or nearly finish high school, a trend that has unquestionably affected youth of every socioeconomic class. With more years of better education behind them, young people are expecting to get more satisfying, higher-paying jobs than their parents *(Statistical Abstract of the United States: 1989).*

The problem of unemployment is particularly acute for teenagers. In 1987, the unemployment rate for males 16 to 19 averaged 17.8 percent. The situation was far worse for black males than for whites: The rate of unemployment among black teen-

Unemployment rates are particularly high among teenagers. In 1987, 17.8 percent of white males and 34.5 percent of black males ages 16 to 19 were unemployed.

age males was 34.5 percent—more than twice that for all teenagers *(Statistical Abstract of the United States: 1989).*

This picture is likely to continue in the years ahead, as the demand for unskilled labor in manufacturing industries continues to decline and as increasing numbers of teenagers leave school functionally illiterate and with no employable skills.

LABOR UNIONS

As the size and power of corporations in the United States grew, workers needed a means to protect themselves against the sometimes unfair, unequal, and inhuman treatment they received at the hands of their employers. Realizing that power was possible only if they united, the workers formed **labor unions** to bargain collectively for higher wages, better working conditions, job security, fringe benefits, and grievance procedures.

As of 1988, 17,002,000 workers throughout the country, representing approximately 16.8 percent of the labor force, were members of unions. These figures are down from 22,366,000 workers and 22.5 percent of the labor force in 1980. The greatest concentration of union membership and power is held by the nation's eight largest unions *(Statistical Abstract of the United States: 1989).*

Contract negotiations between unions and corporate management are a give-and-take process. Neither side gets—or expects—exactly what is asked for when the talks begin, but most often settlements are reached, and labor-management peace is assured for the term of the contract. When talks break down, unions have the ultimate weapon of a strike, or work cessation, at their disposal. Used as a last resort to pressure management to come to terms, strikes can cause extreme difficulties on both sides. Companies can no longer produce the goods and services that keep them in business, and workers are left with no means to earn a living.

Although its impact in the economy remains substantial, the union movement

labor union An organization of workers who have united in order to bargain collectively for higher wages, better working conditions, job security, fringe benefits, and grievance procedures.

professional organization A formal organization that attempts to further the interests of its members, who are professionals.

has fallen on hard times in recent years. During the past two decades, unions have experienced either no growth or a loss of growth, and they now represent the smallest share of the U.S. labor force since World War II. Blue-collar unions, such as the United Steel Workers of America, have sustained the harshest effects. Plant closings in the auto, steel, rubber, and trucking industries, for example, have caused widespread unemployment, with a decline in union membership. Moreover, as such plants reopen and as other plants modernize, automation will take a further toll on blue-collar union membership. In addition, the "right to work" laws found in twenty-one states forbid requiring workers to join a union as a condition of employment.

Many of the growth industries in the white-collar, technological fields of computers and electronics have long been outside organized labor's domain. As these industries continue to expand, unions will have an increasingly difficult time maintaining their slice of the work force pie. Their only ray of hope lies in the expansion of such service-industry unions as the American Federation of State, County, and Municipal Employees (AFSCME).

These trends have caused unions to rethink many of their long-held goals. Instead of pushing for big wage and benefit packages, unions are now focusing on job security as their key bargaining element. Some unions, such as the United Auto Workers and the Teamsters, have actually given back some of their earlier gains in order to keep plants open and jobs secure.

Professional Organizations

Most professionals in the U.S. work force are not unionized. Rather, they form such **professional organizations** as the American Medical Association, the American Bar Association, and the National Education Association to further their common interests. Such organizations may endorse political candidates who share their views and may lobby for or against legislation that affects their membership.

SUMMARY

The economy is a social institution whose function is to determine the manner in which society produces, distributes, and consumes goods and services. These functions are performed in different ways by the capitalist and socialist economic systems. In its classic form, capitalism is an economic system based on private ownership of the means of production and in which resource allocation depends largely on market forces. The government plays only a minor role in the marketplace, which works out its own problems through the forces of supply and demand. Adam Smith is regarded as the father of modern capitalism.

Many have referred to the system of capitalism that exists in the United States as a mixed economy, which combines free-enterprise capitalism with governmental regulation of business, industry, and social-welfare programs.

In a command economy the government makes all the decisions about production and consumption. Socialism is one type of command economy that is an alternative to and a reaction against capitalism.

Socialism is an economic system in which the government owns the sources of production, including factories, raw materials, and transportation and communication systems. Socialists believe major economic, social, and political decisions should be made by elected representatives of the people in conjunction with the broader plans of the state.

In western Europe, democratic socialism has evolved as an alternative to socialism. European social democratic parties have chosen to work within the democratic system. They have been able to enact their economic programs by getting elected to office, as opposed to the violence and expropriation of property that Marx endorsed.

The most important form of business ownership in the United States, the corporation is considered a legal entity with rights similar to those of an individual. If corporations expand too far, the result is oligopoly, the domination of industries and markets by a handful of monolithic corporations.

A conglomerate is formed when firms that produce goods in greatly diversified fields come together under one corporate head. Companies that do business in more than one country are called multinational corporations.

The government exerts enormous power over the economic activities of corporations and individual workers, regulating nearly every aspect of the nation's economic life and also controlling the nation's flow of money through federal monetary and fiscal policies. The Federal Reserve attempts to maintain a healthy economy through its reserve requirements, open-market operation, and discount rate. The government's fiscal policy attempts to influence economic activity by raising and lowering taxes and the level of government spending and borrowing. Government spending decisions are subject to interest-group pressure from a variety of sources.

In recent years, the American labor force has changed as a result of improved agricultural technology and increases in the number of white-collar and service employees. The American people now have more affluence and leisure and better health.

In just 22 years, the number of women holding jobs outside the home has more than doubled. The idea of comparable worth has been presented, in reaction to the fact that pay relationships established by supply and demand are frequently inequitable and discriminatory, particularly with respect to women's pay.

Labor unions exist to bargain collectively for higher wages, better working conditions, and job security. Most professionals are not unionized; rather, they form professional organizations.

Chapter 17

THE

POLITICAL SYSTEM

In 1975, Willie Horton was sentenced to life imprisonment without parole for the murder of a service-station attendant. After serving 10 years of his sentence, he was allowed to take part in a special weekend furlough program designed to help inmates reenter the community.

At the end of his weekend away, he failed to return to prison. Instead, he fled to the Washington, D.C., area, where he raped a woman and slashed her boyfriend. Ten months after his weekend furlough, he was finally caught and arrested.

The story of Willie Horton became an important issue in the 1988 presidential election. Willie Horton had been fur-

politics The process that determines which groups or individuals exercise power over others.

loughed from a prison in Massachusetts while presidential candidate Michael Dukakis had been governor; George Bush noted that this situation showed that Dukakis was soft on crime. Bush also hammered away at the idea that the Willie Horton case was an example of Dukakis's liberalism and permissiveness.

The Bush forces used the Willie Horton case in a very effective media campaign. The television advertisements, showing a revolving door of justice through which convicted criminals moved at will, fed the concerns that most Americans have about crime. The message was clear: Elect Dukakis president and there will be many more Willie Hortons walking the streets.

In fact, though, the concerns raised by the Bush campaign were not really presidential issues. First of all, the vast majority of prison furloughs take place at the state level, and the legislation involving them is a state matter. Second, the federal prison system also has a furlough program that includes murderers, and sixty-four of them received furloughs in 1987 alone.

power The ability to carry out one person's or one group's will even in the presence of resistance or opposition from others.

The Willie Horton incident gives us an insight into American politics. Presidential elections are won and lost on the basis of advertising campaigns more than on the merits of the case presented. It seems that American people tend to respond more to harsh rhetoric than to carefully reasoned facts.

Yet, although the Willie Horton incident may show us some of the worst aspects of the American political process, other aspects of it are quite good. There are more than 800 candidates for the House of Representatives every other year. Americans also get to vote for senators, governors, and a host of other officials on a regular basis. Candidates ring our doorbells, shake our hands, stuff our mailboxes, and exhort us through our television sets. They make promises they often cannot keep. This is politics, American style. Small wonder that it has been said that politics, like baseball, is the great American pastime. This chapter will help clarify what is unique about our

authority Power that is regarded as legitimate by those over whom it is exercised, who also accept the authority's legitimacy in imposing sanctions or even in using force if necessary.

two-party system and where the American political system fits into the whole spectrum of political institutions.

POLITICS, POWER, AND AUTHORITY

What *is* politics? **Politics** is the process that determines which groups or individuals exercise power over others. Hence, running for president of the United States is a political activity. So is enacting legislation. So is taxing property owners to subsidize the digging of sewers. So is going to war. The study of the political process, then, is the study of power.

POWER

Max Weber (1958a) referred to **power** as the ability to carry out one person's or group's will, even in the presence of resistance or opposition from others. In this sense, power is the capability of making others comply with one's decisions, often exacting compliance through the threat or actual use of sanctions, penalties, or force.

In some relationships the division of power is spelled out clearly and defined formally. Employers have specific powers over employees, as do army officers over enlisted personnel, ship captains over their crews, professors over their students. In other relationships, the question of power is less clearly defined and may even shift back and forth, depending on individual personalities and the particular situation: between wife and husband, among sisters and brothers, or among friends in a social clique.

Power is an element of many types of relationships, and it is a complex phenomenon that covers a broad spectrum of interactions. At one pole is **authority**—power that is regarded as legitimate by those over whom it is exercised, who also accept the authority's legitimacy in imposing sanctions or even in using force if necessary. For example, here in the United States few people are eager to pay income taxes; yet most do so regularly. Most taxpayers accept the authority of the government not only to demand payment but also to impose penalties for nonpayment.

At the other extreme is **coercion**—power that the people or groups over whom it is exerted regard as illegitimate. Their compliance is based on fear of reprisals that are not recognized as falling within the range of accepted norms.

Power based on authority is quite stable, and obedience to it is accepted as a social norm. Power based on coercion, on the other hand, is unstable. People will obey only out of fear, and any opportunity to test this power will be taken. Power based on coercion will fail in the long run.

The American Revolution, for example, was preceded by the erosion of the legitimacy of the existing system. The authority of the king of England was questioned and his power, based increasingly on coercion rather than on acceptance as a social norm, inevitably crumbled.

POLITICAL AUTHORITY

An individual's authority often will apply only to certain people in certain situations. For example, a professor has the authority to require students to write term papers in a course but no authority to demand the students' votes should he or she run for public office.

In the same sense, Max Weber pointed out that the most powerful states do not impose their will by the use of physical force alone, but by insuring that their authority is seen as *legitimate.* In such a state people accept the idea that the allocation of power is as it should be and that those who hold power do so legitimately.

Max Weber (1957) identified three kinds of authority: rational-legal authority, traditional authority, and charismatic authority.

Legal-Rational Authority

Found in most modern corporations and organizations, **legal-rational authority** emphasizes rationally purposeful action. The authority of individuals derives from the fact that they are officials with clearly defined rights and duties who uphold and implement rules and procedures impersonally. Indeed, that is the key: Power is vested not in individuals but in particular positions or offices. There usually are rules and procedures designed to achieve a broad purpose. Rulers acquire political power through meeting requirements for office, and they hold power only as long as they themselves obey the laws that legitimize their rule.

Traditional Authority

Traditional authority, on the other hand, is rooted in the assumption that the customs of the past legitimate the present—that things are as they always have been and basically should remain that way. Usually both rulers and ruled recognize and support the tradition that legitimizes the rulers' political authority. Typically, traditional authority is hereditary, although this is not always the case. For example, throughout most of English history the English crown

legal-rational authority
Authority that derives from the fact that specific individuals have clearly defined rights and duties to uphold and implement rules and procedures.

coercion Power that the people or groups over whom it is exerted regard as illegitimate.

traditional authority
Power that is rooted in the assumption that the customs of the past legitimize the present.

Legal-rational authority found in most modern corporations and organizations emphasizes rationally purposeful action.

was the property of various families. As long as tradition is followed, the authority is accepted.

Charismatic Authority

charismatic authority
The power that derives from a ruler's force of personality. It is the ability to inspire passion and devotion among followers.

The power that derives from a ruler's force of personality is called **charismatic authority.** It is the ability to inspire passion and devotion among followers. Weber noted that a charismatic leader—who is most likely to emerge during a period of crisis—will emerge when followers (1) perceive a leader as somehow supernatural; (2) blindly believe the leader's statements; (3) unconditionally comply with the leader's directives; and (4) give the leader unqualified emotional commitment. Others have added that charismatic leaders must also perform seemingly extraordinary feats and have outstanding speaking ability (Willner, 1984).

Sitting Bull and Red Cloud, for example, were charismatic leaders of the Sioux Indians. Their people followed them because they led by example and inspired per-

sonal loyalty. However, individuals were free to disagree, to refuse to participate in planned undertakings, and even to leave and look for a group led by people with whom they were more likely to agree (Brown, 1974). This was not true in Rome under Julius Caesar, in Russia under Lenin, in Germany under Hitler, or in Iran under the Ayatollah Khomeini. These men all were charismatic rulers but also had the political authority necessary to enforce obedience or conformity to their demands.

Charismatic authorities and rulers emerge when people lose faith in their social institutions. Lenin led the Russian Revolution in the chaos left in the wake of World War I. Hitler rose to power in a Germany that had been defeated and humiliated in World War I and whose economy was shattered: inflation was so bad that money was almost worthless. Khomeini rose to power in a country in which rapid modernization had undercut traditional Islamic norms and values, in which great poverty and great wealth existed side by side, and in which fear of the Shah's secret police left the populace constantly anxious for its personal safety. The great challenge facing all charismatic rulers is to sustain their leadership after the crisis subsides and to create political institutions that will survive their death or retirement. Weber pointed out that if the program that the leader has implemented is to be sustained, the leader's charisma will have to be "routinized" in some form. For example, after Christ's death—and after it became apparent that his return to earth was not imminent—the apostles began to set up the rudiments of a religious organization with priestly offices.

The power of a charismatic leader derives from the ruler's force of personality and his ability to inspire passion and devotion among his followers. President John F. Kennedy was the closest the United States has come to having a charismatic leader.

GOVERNMENT AND THE STATE

Governments vary according to the relationship that exists between the rulers and the ruled. In some societies, political power is shared among most or all adults. This is true of the Mbuti pygmies and the ¡Kung San of Africa, for instance, for whom the group is its own authority and decisions are made by a consensus among adults. Among such societies the concept of government is meaningless. But in modern societies, government does exist.

In complex societies the **state** is the institutionalized way of organizing power within territorial limits. Just as a true government is nonexistent in some societies, so too is the state limited to certain societies. Its presence indicates a high level of social and political development.

Modern thought regarding the nature of government and its forms is derived directly from the ideas of three Greek philosophers: Socrates, his student Plato, and Plato's student Aristotle. In the *Republic,* written around 365 B.C., Plato was concerned with the form of government that would be most just. It is important to know that when Plato was writing, Athens had been through a period of political upheaval. For that reason Plato was concerned with the problem of maintaining social order. Hence, he rejected democracy, or rule by the majority, because he believed that this form of government would lead to chaos. He also rejected **autocracy,** or rule by one person, because he thought that no single person could be wise or competent enough to make decisions for a whole society. Rather, he favored what he called **aristocracy,** a form of **oligarchy,** or rule by a select few.

Plato called his proposed ruling class the guardians of society. The guardians, he argued, should be bred from the most exemplary parents but then separated from them at birth. They should live in poverty for 30 years while being trained in mind and body, and then they should fill positions of government in which they would execute their responsibilities wisely and without favoritism. (It is important not to confound Plato's use of the term aristocracy with the modern usage. Plato explicitly rejected the ideal of inherited political power, which he believed inevitably results in power falling to unqualified individuals — leading to an unjust society.)

Aristotle (384 – 322 B.C.) was the tutor of Alexander the Great and a political scholar. Unlike Plato, he recognized that even in just societies, social class interests produce class conflicts, which are the business of the state to control. Aristotle favored centering political power in the middle class (consisting of merchants, artisans, and farmers), but he insisted on defining the rights and duties of the state in a legal constitution (Laslett and Cummings, 1967).

FUNCTIONS OF THE STATE

Although a preindustrial society can exist without an organized government, no modern industrial society can thrive without those functions that the state performs: establishing laws and norms, providing social control, ensuring economic stability, setting goals, and protecting against outside threats.

Establishing Laws and Norms

The state is the focus for the establishment of laws that formally specify what is expected and what is prohibited in the society. The laws often represent a codification of specific norms; for example, one should not steal or commit violent crimes against others. The establishment of laws also brings about the enactment of penalties for violating the laws.

Providing Social Control

In addition to establishing laws, the state also has the power to enforce them. The police, courts, and various government agencies make sure that the violation of laws is punished. In the United States, the Internal Revenue Service seeks out tax evaders, the courts sentence criminals to prison, and the police attempt to maintain order.

state The institutionalized way of organizing power within territorial limits.

autocracy A political system in which the ultimate authority rests with a single person.

aristocracy The rule by a select few; a form of oligarchy.

oligarchy Rule by a select few, as in an aristocracy.

Ensuring Economic Stability

In the modern world, no individual can provide entirely for his or her own needs. Large work forces must be mobilized to build roads, dig canals, and erect dams. Money must be minted, and standards of weights and measures must be set and checked; and merchants must be protected from thieves, and consumers from fraud. The state tries to ensure that a stable system of distribution and allocation of resources exists within the society.

Setting Goals

The state sets goals and provides a direction for the society. If a society is to curtail its use of oil, for instance, the government must promote this as a goal. It must encourage conservation and the search for alternative energy sources and must discourage (perhaps through taxation or rationing) the use of oil. But how is the government able to accomplish these tasks? How can it bring about individual and organizational compliance? Obviously, it would be best if the government could rely on persuasion alone, but this course seldom is enough. In the end the government usually needs the power to compel compliance.

One of the tasks a state must perform is to protect itself from outside threats, especially those of a military nature.

Protecting Against Outside Threats

Historic data leave little doubt that the rise of the state was accompanied almost everywhere by the intensification of warfare (Otterbein, 1970, 1973). As early as the fourteenth century, Ibn Khaldun (1958), a brilliant Islamic scholar of the time, noted this connection and even attributed the rise of the state to the needs of sedentary farmers to protect themselves from raids by fierce nomads. His views were echoed by Ludwig Gumplowicz (1899): "States have never arisen except through the subjugation of one stock by another, or by several in alliance." In any event, it is clear that one of the tasks of maintaining a society is to protect it from outside threats, especially those of a military nature. Hence, governments build and maintain armies. Although the lack of military preparedness may invite an expansionist attack from a neighboring society, it does not follow that such preparedness necessarily will prevent attack.

Although there is widespread agreement that the functions just described are tasks that the state should and usually does perform, not all social scientists agree that the state emerged because of the need for these functions.

TYPES OF STATES

Different types of states exist side by side and must deal with one another constantly in today's shrinking world. To comprehend their interrelationships, one needs to understand the structure of each main form of government—autocracy, totalitarianism, democracy, and socialism.

Autocracy

In an autocracy the ultimate authority and rule of the government rest with one person, who is the chief source of laws and the major agent of social control. For example, the pharaohs of ancient Egypt were autocrats. More recently, the reigns of Ferdinand

Marcos of the Philippines and the Perons of Argentina have been autocratic.

In an autocracy the loyalty and devotion of the people are required. To ensure that this requirement is met, dissent and criticism of the government and the person in power are prohibited. The media may be controlled by the government, and terror may be used to prevent or suppress dissent. For the most part, however, no great attempt is made to control the personal lives of the people. A strict boundary is set up between people's private lives and their public behavior. Individuals have a wide range of freedom in pursuing such private aspects of their lives as religion, the family, and many other traditional elements of life. However, virtually all present-day autocracies have witnessed exploitation of the poor by the rich and powerful — a situation supported by the respective governments.

Totalitarianism

In a **totalitarian government,** one group has virtually total control of the nation's social institutions. Any other group is prevented from attaining power. Religious institutions, educational institutions, political institutions, and economic institutions all are managed directly or indirectly by the state. Typically, under totalitarian rule six major elements interact to concentrate political power.

1. *A single political party* controls the state apparatus. It is the only legal political party in the state. The party organization is itself controlled by one person or by a ruling clique.
2. *The use of terror* is implemented by an elaborate internal security system that intimidates the populace into conformity. It defines dissenters as enemies of the state and often chooses, arbitrarily, whole groups of people against whom it directs especially harsh oppression (for instance, the Jews in Nazi Germany or minority tribal groups in several of the recently created African states).
3. *The control of the media* (television, radio, newspapers, and journals) is in the hands of the state. Different opinions are denied a forum. The media communicate only the official line of thinking to the people.
4. *Control over the military apparatus.* The military and the use of weapons are monopolized by those who control the political power of the totalitarian state.
5. *Control of the economy* is wielded by the government, which sets goals for the various industrial and economic sectors and determines both the prices and the supplies of goods.
6. *An elaborate ideology,* which rejects previous sociopolitical conditions and legitimizes the current state, provides more or less explicit instructions to citizens on how to conduct their daily lives. This ideology offers explanations for nearly every aspect of life, often in a simplistic and distorted way (Friedrich and Brzezinski, 1965).

Two distinct types of totalitarianism are found in the modern world. Although they share the same basic political features described above, they differ widely in their economic systems. Under **totalitarian socialism,** in addition to almost total regulation of all social institutions, the government controls and owns all major means of production and distribution: there is little private ownership or free enterprise. This political-economic system is usually labeled **communism** and is typified by the government of the Soviet Union. **Totalitarian capitalism,** on the other hand, denotes a system in which the government, while retaining control of social institutions, allows the means of production and distribution to be owned and managed by private groups and individuals. However, production goals usually are dictated by the government, especially in heavy industry. Hitler's Germany is a good example of totalitarian capitalism. The mammoth Krupp industrial complex was owned and managed by the family of that name, but the government

totalitarian government A government in which one group has virtually total control of the nation's social institutions.

totalitarian socialism In addition to almost total regulation of all social institutions, the government controls and owns all major means of production and distribution.

communism The name commonly given to totalitarian socialist forms of government.

totalitarian capitalism A political-economic system in which the government retains control of the social institutions, but allows the means of production and distribution to be owned and managed by private groups and individuals.

constitutionalism The rule of the government is limited. The various agencies of government can act only in specified legal ways.

fascism A political-economic system characterized by totalitarian capitalism.

representative government The authority to govern is achieved through, and legitimized by, popular elections.

electorate Those citizens eligible to vote.

had the company gear its efforts toward producing munitions and heavy equipment to further the nation's political and militaristic aims. We know this form of totalitarianism as **fascism.**

One of the problems faced by totalitarian governments is that because their total control over their citizenry allows no organized independent opposition, they are never sure whether the populace's conformity to the laws is based on its acceptance of the government's legitimate authority or is motivated primarily by fear of coercion by a ruling power it considers illegitimate. This inability to judge accurately its citizens' perceptions of its legitimacy is considered by many observers to be a source of great anxiety to the Soviet government and explains some of its oppressive actions, such as imprisoning artists and intellectuals.

Democracy

Democracy has not always been regarded as the best form of government. People often approved of the aims of democracy, yet argued that democracy was impossible to attain. Others argued that it was logically unsound. Today, however, there is hardly a government anywhere in the world that does not claim to have some sort of democratic authority. In the United States we regard our political system as democratic, and the same claim is made by leaders in communist countries. The word *democracy* seems to have so many different meanings today that we face the problem of distinguishing democracy from other political systems.

Democracy comes from the Greek words—*demos,* meaning people, and *kratia,* meaning authority. By *democracy,* then, the Greeks were referring to a system in which the rule was by the people rather than a few selected individuals. Because of the growth in population, industrialization, and specialization, it has become impossible for citizens to participate in politics today as they did in ancient Athens. Today, **democracy** refers to a political system operating under the principles of constitutionalism, representative government, majority rule, civilian rule, and minority rights.

Constitutionalism means that government is limited. It is assumed that there is a "higher" law superior to all other laws. The various agencies of government can act only in specified legal ways. Individuals possess rights, such as freedom of speech, press, assembly, and religion, which the government cannot take away.

A basic feature of democracy is that it is rooted in **representative government,** which means that the authority to govern is achieved through, and legitimized by, popular elections. Every government officeholder has sought, in one way or another, the support of the **electorate** (those citizens eligible to vote) and has persuaded a large enough portion of that group to grant its support (through voting). The elected official is entitled to hold office for a specified term and generally will be reelected as long as that body of voters is satisfied that the officeholder is adequately representing its interests.

Representative institutions can operate freely only if certain other conditions prevail. First, there must be what sociologist Edward Shils (1968) calls civilian rule. That is, every qualified citizen has the legal right to run for and hold an office of government. Such rights do not belong to any one class (say, highly trained scholars, as in ancient China), caste, set, religious group, ethnic group, or "race." These rights belong to every citizen. Further, there must be public confidence in the fact that such organized agencies as the police and the military will not intervene in, or change the outcome of, elections (as happened in Panama under General Noriega in 1989, in Chile with the overthrow of President Salvadore Allende in 1973, and in Pakistan with the overthrow and eventual execution of President Ali Bhutto in 1979).

In addition, **majority rule** must be maintained. Because of the complexity of a modern democracy it is not possible for "the people" to rule. One of the most im-

majority rule The right of people to assemble to express their views and seek to persuade others, to engage in political organizing, and to vote for whomever they wish.

democracy A political system operating under the principles of constitutionalism, representative government, majority rule, civilian rule, and minority rights.

portant ways for people to participate in the political life of the country is to vote. For this to happen, people must be free to assemble, to express their views and seek to persuade others, to engage in political organizing, and to vote for whomever they wish.

Democracy also assumes that **minority rights** must be protected. The majority may not always act wisely and it may be unjust. The minority abides by the laws as determined by the majority, but the minority must be free to try to change these laws.

Democratic societies contrast markedly with totalitarian societies. Ideally, they are open and culturally diverse; dissent is not viewed as disloyalty; there are two or more political parties; and terror and intimidation are not an overt part of the political scene.

The economic base of democratic societies can vary considerably. Democracy can be found in a capitalistic country like the United States and in a more socialistic one like Sweden. However, it appears necessary for the country to have reached an advanced level of economic development before democracy can evolve. Such societies are most likely to have the sophisticated population and stability necessary for democracy (Lipset, 1960).

Democracy and Socialism

Critics of capitalism argue that "true" democracy is an impossible dream in capitalist society. They claim that although in theory all members of a capitalist society have the same political rights, in fact capitalist society is inherently stratified, and therefore wealth, social esteem, and even political power of necessity are unequally distributed (see Chapter 8). Because of this, some critics contend, "true" democracy can be achieved only under **socialism** — an economic system in which the government owns and controls the major means of production and distribution (thus avoiding inequality of ownership among its members) and in which there is no social stratification (Schumpeter, 1950).

As we have noted, there is no obvious reason that socialist societies cannot be democratic. In fact, though, many societies whose economies are socialist tend to be communist states. One reason is that, historically, socialist societies often have been born in revolution. Political revolutions by definition mean a redistribution of power (see discussion of political change later in this chapter). One group seizes power from another and then tries to prevent the old group from retaking it. Lenin argued that in order to consolidate power the new group must use strong repressive measures against the old — in fact, build a dictatorship. A **dictatorship** is a totalitarian government in which all power rests ultimately in one person, who generally heads the only recognized political party, at least until all the economic resources of the old group are

minority rights The minority has the right to try to change the laws of the majority.

dictatorship A totalitarian government in which all power rests ultimately in one person.

The socialist revolution in Cuba resulted in the dictatorship of Fidel Castro. He has been in power since 1959, and his rule has not been "temporary," nor has the state "withered away."

socialism An economic system in which the government owns and controls the major means of production and distribution and in which social stratification is limited.

seized, its links to all political agencies are broken, and its claims to political legitimacy are wiped out. Lenin (1949) quoted Marx on this point:

> Between capitalist and communist society lies the period of the revolutionary transformation of the one into the other. Corresponding to this is also a political transition period in which the state can be nothing but *the revolutionary dictatorships of the proletariat* [the working class].

Lenin (1949) put it more graphically himself:

> The proletariat needs state power, a centralised organisation of force, and organisation of violence, both to crush the resistance of the exploiters and to *lead* the enormous mass of the population . . . in the work of organising a socialist economy.

In the Soviet Union, eastern Europe, China, Cuba, and more recently in African and Southeast Asian countries, socialist revolutions all have resulted in dictatorships. Families of the previous ruling classes have been executed, jailed, "reeducated," or exiled, and their properties have been seized and redistributed. In none of these societies has the dictatorship proved to be temporary, nor has the state gradually "withered away," as Marx and Engels predicted it would after socialism was firmly established. Many Marxists claim that this will happen in the future, especially once capitalism has been defeated all around the globe and socialist states no longer need to protect themselves against "counterrevolutionary" subversion and even direct military threats by capitalist nations. However, it is fair to observe that even the ancient Greeks knew that power corrupts and that those groups who have power are unlikely ever to give it up voluntarily. So we may expect that at least in the foreseeable future, socialist states that have emerged through revolution will—despite their disclaimers—remain totalitarian communist dictatorships.

By contrast, in those societies in which socialist reforms of capitalist abuses have been introduced, democracy appears to be firmly rooted and is likely to survive. **Democratic socialism** (see Chapter 16) as a political system often exhibits the dominant features of a democracy, but control of the economy is vested in the government to a greater extent than under capitalism. Democratic socialism flourishes to various degrees in the Scandinavian countries, in Great Britain, and in Israel. These countries all have a strong private (that is, capitalist) sector in their economies, but they also have extensive government programs to ensure the people's well-being. These programs pertain to such things as national health service, government ownership of key industries, and the systematic tying of workers' pay to increases in the rate of inflation. Many observers believe that the American political economy has been moving in this direction.

democratic socialism A political system in which control of the economy is vested in the government to a greater extent than in capitalism.

Under the democratic socialist type of government present in most of Scandinavia, there are extensive government programs to ensure the people's well-being.

FUNCTIONALIST AND CONFLICT THEORY VIEWS OF THE STATE

Functionalists and conflict theorists hold very different ideas about the function of the state. As our discussion of social stratification in Chapter 8 revealed, functionalist theorists view social stratification — and the state that maintains it — as necessary devices that provide for the recruitment of workers to perform the tasks necessary to sustain society. Individual talents must be matched to jobs that need doing, and those with specialized talents must be given sufficiently satisfying rewards. Functionalists therefore maintain that the state emerged because society began to get so large and complex that only a specialized, central institution (that is, the state) could manage society's increasingly complicated and intertwined institutions (Davis, 1949; Service, 1975).

Marxists and other conflict theorists take a different view. They argue that technological changes resulting in surplus production brought about the production of commodities for trade (as opposed to products for immediate use). Meanwhile, certain groups were able to seize control of the means of production and distribution of commodities, thereby succeeding in establishing themselves as powerful ruling classes that dominated and exploited workers and serfs. Finally, the state emerged as a means of coordinating the use of force, by means of which the ruling classes could protect their institutionalized supremacy from the resentful and potentially rebellious lower classes. As Lenin (1949) explained, "The state is a special organisation of force: it is an organisation of violence for the suppression of some class."

There is evidence to support this view of the state's origins. The earliest legal codes of ancient states featured laws protecting the persons and properties of rulers, nobles, landholders, and wealthy merchants. The Code of Hammurabi of Babylon, dating back to about 1750 B.C., prescribed the death penalty for burglars and for anybody who harbored a fugitive slave. The code regulated wages, prices, and fees to be charged for services. It provided that a commoner be fined six times as much for striking a noble or a landholder as for striking another commoner. And it condemned to death housewives who were proved by their husbands to be uneconomical in managing household resources (Durant, 1954).

Nevertheless, the functionalist view also has value. The state provides crucial organizational functions, such as carrying out large-scale projects and undertaking long-range planning, without which complex society probably could not exist. Because it provides a sophisticated organizational structure, the state can — and does — fulfill many other important functions. In most modern societies, the state supports a public school system to provide a basic, uniform education for its members. The health and well-being of its citizens also have become the concern of the state. In our own country, as in many others, the government provides some level of medical and financial support for its young, old, and disabled, and at the same time it sponsors scientific and medical research for the ongoing welfare of its people. Regulating industry and trade to some degree also has become a function of the modern state, and it has devised ways (different for each kind of state) of establishing, controlling, and even safeguarding the civil rights and liberties of its citizens. And certainly one of the most important functions of any state is the protection of its people. Long gone are the days when cave dwellers, lords of the manor, or frontiersmen themselves defended their territories and other members of their groups from attack or encroachment; the state now provides such protection through specialized agencies: armies, militias, and police forces.

When groups in a society develop sufficient dissatisfaction with their present system of government and achieve the strength

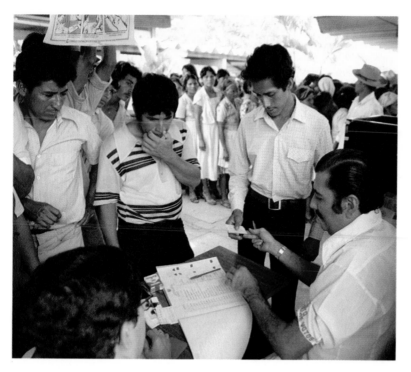

The laws and traditions of a democracy ensure the orderly changeover of politicians. In a dictatorship or a totalitarian society, a change can only come about through violent or illegal means.

rebellions Attempts— typically through armed force—to achieve rapid political change that is not possible within existing institutions.

to influence the direction of that system, changes in government can take place. After such changes the state may perform the same functions, but it may do so in a different way and under different leadership.

──── POLITICAL CHANGE

Political change can occur when there is a shift in the distribution of power among groups in a society. It is one facet of the wider process of social change, the topic of the last part of this book. Political change can take place in a variety of different ways depending on the type of political structure the state has and the desire for change present among the people. People may attempt to produce change through established channels within the government, or they may rise up against the political power structure with rebellion and revolution. Here we shall consider briefly three forms of

political change: institutionalized change, rebellion, and revolution.

INSTITUTIONALIZED POLITICAL CHANGE

In democracies the institutional provision for the changing of leaders is implemented through elections. Usually, candidates representing different parties and interest groups must compete for a particular office at formally designated periods of time. There may also be laws that prevent a person from holding the same office for more than a given number of terms. If a plurality or a majority of the electorate is dissatisfied with a given officeholder, they are given the opportunity to vote the incumbent out of office. Thus, the laws and traditions of a democracy ensure the orderly changeover of politicians and, usually, of parties in office.

In dictatorships and totalitarian societies, if a leader unexpectedly dies, is debilitated, or is deposed, a crisis of authority may occur. In dictatorships, illegal, violent means must often be used by an opposition to overthrow a leader or the government because there is no democratic means by which legally to vote a person or group out of power. Thus, we should not be surprised that revolutions and assassinations are most likely to occur in developing nations that have dictatorships. Established totalitarian societies, such as the Soviet Union and China, are more likely than dictatorships to offer normatively prescribed means by which a ruling committee decides who should fill a vacated position of leadership.

REBELLIONS

Rebellions are attempts—typically involving armed force—to achieve rapid political change that is not possible within existing institutions. But rebellions do not change the society's political and class structure. In other words, rebellions typically do not call into question the legitimacy of power, but rather its uses. For example, consider Shays's Rebellion. Shortly after the American colonies won their independence from Britain, they were hit by an economic depression followed by raging inflation. Soon, in several states, paper money lost almost all its value. As the states began to pay off their war debts (which had been bought up by speculators), they were forced to increase the taxation of farmers, many of whom could not afford to pay these new taxes and consequently lost their land. Farmers began to band together to prevent courts from hearing debt cases, and state militias were called out to protect court hearings. Desperate, farmers in the Connecticut valley region armed themselves under Daniel Shays, a former officer of the Continental Army (Blum et al., 1981). This armed band was defeated by the Massachusetts militia, but its members eventually were pardoned and the debt laws were loosened somewhat (Parkes, 1968). Shays's Rebellion did not intend to overthrow the courts or the legislature; rather, it was aimed at effecting changes in their operation. Hence, it was a typical rebellion.

REVOLUTIONS

Revolutions, if they are successful, result in far greater changes than do rebellions, because they change the society's previously existing power structure. Sociologists further distinguish between political and social revolutions.

Political Revolutions

Relatively rapid transformations of state or government structures that are not accompanied by changes in social structure or stratification are known as **political revolutions** (Skocpol, 1979). The American War of Independence is a good example of a political revolution. The colonists were not seeking to change the structure of society nor even necessarily to overthrow the ruling order. Their goal was to put a stop to the abuse of power by the British. After the war, they created a new form of government, but they did not attempt to change the fact that landowners and wealthy merchants held the reins of political power, just as they had

revolutions Relatively rapid transformations that produce change in a society's previously existing power structure.

political revolutions Relatively rapid transformations of state or government structures that are not accompanied by changes in social structure or stratification.

In 1989, students in China tried to bring about major changes in their government. This banner reads "Democracy—Our Common Goal." Despite widespread support, Chinese troops crushed the movement and imprisoned and executed many people.

Under the dictatorship of Porfirio Diaz, poverty was widespread. This discontent produced a revolution in 1910 that brought about a change in the government.

social revolutions Rapid and basic transformations of a society's state and class structures.

class struggle provided both the context and the driving force. The old ruling classes were stripped of political power and economic resources; wealth and property were redistributed; and state institutions were thoroughly reconstructed (Wolf, 1969).

Although the American Revolution did not arise from class struggle and did not result immediately in changes in the social structure, it did mark the beginning of a form of government that eventually modified the social stratification of eighteenth-century America.

THE AMERICAN POLITICAL SYSTEM

The United States political system is unique in a number of ways growing out of a strong commitment to a democratic political process and the influence of a capitalist economy. It has many distinctive features that are of particular interest to sociologists. In this section we will examine the role of the electorate and how influence is exerted on the political process.

before the shooting started. In the American Revolution, then, a lower class did not rise up against a ruling class. Rather, it was the American ruling class going to war to shake loose from inconvenient interference by the British ruling class. The initial result, therefore, was political, but not social, change.

Social Revolutions

Social revolutions, by contrast, are rapid and basic transformations of a society's state and class structures; and they are accompanied and in part carried out through "class-based revolts" (Skocpol, 1979). Hence, they involve two simultaneous and interrelated processes: (1) the transformation of a society's system of social stratification brought about by upheaval in the lower class(es); and (2) changes in the form of the state. Both processes must reinforce each other for a revolution to succeed. The French Revolution of the 1790s was a true social revolution. So were the Mexican Revolution of 1910, the Russian Revolution of 1917, the Chinese Revolution of 1949, and the Cuban Revolution of 1959—to name some of the most prominent social revolutions of our century. In all these revolutions,

THE TWO-PARTY SYSTEM

Few democracies have only two main political parties. Besides the United States, there are Canada, Australia, New Zealand, and Austria. The other democracies all have more than two major parties, thus providing proportional representation for a wide spectrum of divergent political views and interests. In most European democracies, if a political party receives 12 percent of the vote in an election, it is allocated 12 percent of the seats in the national legislature. Such a system insures that minority parties are represented.

The American two-party political system, however, operates on a "winner-take-all" basis. Therefore, groups with different political interests must face not being represented if their candidates lose. Conversely, candidates must attempt to gain the support of a broad spectrum of political-interest groups, because a candidate representing a narrow range of voters cannot win. This system forces accommodations between interest groups on the one hand and candidates and parties on the other.

Few, if any, individual interest groups (like the National Organization for Women, the National Rifle Association, or the Sierra Club), represent the views of a majority of an electorate, be it local, state, or national. Hence, it is necessary for interest groups to ally with political parties in which other interest groups are involved as well, hoping thereby to become part of a majority that can succeed in electing one or more candidates. Each interest group then hopes that the candidate(s) it has helped elect will represent its point of view. But for most interest groups to achieve their ends more effectively, they must find a common ground with their allies in the party they have chosen to support. And in doing so they often have to compromise some strongly held principles. Hence, party platforms often tend to be composed of mild and uncontroversial issues, and party principles tend to adhere as closely as possible to the center of the American political spectrum.

When either party attempts to move away from the center to accommodate a very strong interest group with left- or right-wing views, the result generally is disaster at the polls. This happened to the Republican party in 1964, when the politically conservative (or right-wing) Goldwater forces gained control of its organizational structure and led it to a landslide defeat: in that year's presidential election the Democrats captured 61.1 percent of the national vote. Eight years later the Democratic party made the same "mistake." It nominated George McGovern, a distinctly liberal (or left-wing) candidate who, among other things, advocated a federally subsidized minimum income. The predictable landslide brought the Republicans and Richard Nixon 60.7 percent of the vote. In 1984, when the Democrats put a woman, Geral-dine Ferraro, on the ticket as the vice-presidential nominee, the Republicans won 58.8 percent of the vote and swept every state except Minnesota, the home state of the presidential nominee, Walter Mondale *(Statistical Abstract of the United States: 1987, 1986)*. So, in winner-take-all two-party systems, political-interest groups must compromise, and political parties usually stay close to the political center.

The candidates themselves have other problems. To gain support within their parties, they must somehow distinguish themselves from the other candidates. In other words, they must stake out identifiable positions. Yet, to win state and national elections, they must appeal to a broad political spectrum. To do this, they must soften the positions that first won them party support. Candidates thus often find themselves justly accused of "double-talking" and vagueness as they try to finesse their way through this built-in dilemma. This is most true of presidential candidates. It is no accident that once they have their party's nomination, some candidates may express themselves differently and far more cautiously than they did before.

THE DISTRIBUTION OF POWER

The assumption behind a democratic form of government is that power is vested with the people. Sociologist Gaetano Mosca (1939) believed that every society contains a group that rules and a group that is ruled. The group that rules is invariably a minority. If a small group ends up ruling a country, whose interests are they likely to represent? In the United States, there are two decidedly different views of how political and economic power are held, and by whom.

The Pluralist Theory

As we have already noted, our society's political and economic sectors contain groups representing many interests, based on class, race, ethnicity, religion, demography, and occupation. Such interest groups use money, organization, lobbying, campaigns, and votes to have their political candidates elected. In return, those candidates are expected to reward their supporters by promoting all manner of legislation favorable to the interest groups with which they are aligned. In the United States the two major political parties are viewed as the principal means through which special-interest groups advance their respective causes.

Most interest groups are also in either direct or indirect competition with one another. (For example, management and labor bargain collectively in the private sector and use the Republican and Democratic parties to achieve their political ends.) The **pluralist theory of power** maintains that power is distributed among many different interest groups that compete with one another in the private sector of the economy and in the government (Rose, 1967). When these rival interest groups are relatively equal in strength, then an equilibrium or balance of power exists.

The main problem with the pluralist model of democracy is that all interest groups are not adequately represented in the American political process. The poor, for instance, tend to register and vote in smaller numbers than do other socioeconomic groups. Furthermore, they control neither large resources of money nor well-organized blocs of votes. Therefore, they may be ignored with relative impunity by both the Republican and Democratic parties. The Democratic party, for instance, is much more responsive to the demands of organized labor than to the needs of the lower class, because the major unions control large sums of money and influence the votes of millions of workers. Similarly, Republican politicians tend to be more closely aligned with the demands of industrial lobbyists and well-funded professional associations than with the lower middle class or with supporters over the age of 50.

David Riesman (1950) does not believe that there is an organized elite that dominates society; instead, he sees two

pluralist theory of power A theory maintaining that power is distributed among many different interest groups that compete in the private sector of the economy and in the government.

power-elite theory A theory maintaining that those who control the largest private corporations and the highest political and military positions are the leaders who control the nation.

levels of power in the United States. One level consists of veto groups that try to protect themselves from proposals that might encroach on their interests. These veto groups unite with or separate from other groups, depending on the issues involved. On the second level is the unorganized public, which is often sought as an ally of the veto groups. Those who seek power must respond to public opinion to be successful.

The Power-Elite Theory

The American sociologist C. Wright Mills (1959) wrote that those who control the largest private corporations and the highest political and military positions are the leaders who control the nation. According to this **power-elite theory,** these leaders share similar upper-class origins and social values, are white, Anglo-Saxon, and Protestant. They also share a common world view as to what the goals of the nation should be and work together closely to shape national policy.

What is the evidence for Mills's analysis of power? G. William Domhoff (1967) pointed out that the upper class of American society (about one-half of 1 percent) dominates the boards of directors of the top fifteen banks, the top fifteen insurance corporations, and the top twenty industrial corporations. More recent research (Useem, 1984) found that in both the United States and England high-level business executives play a significant role in shaping the political scene. Another study concluded (Freitag, 1975) that between 1897 and 1973, 87.8 percent of presidential cabinet officials had been associated with corporations, either as directors and officers or as corporate attorneys. Other American presidential administrations have had just this type of interlock: 85.7 percent of the cabinets of the Eisenhower and Johnson administrations and 95.7 percent of the cabinet in the Nixon administration came from the private sector.

Among the major criticisms of the

A GENDER GAP AT THE POLLS

There is a gender gap at the polls and the Republicans are losing. If you look at the results of presidential elections since 1972, you will see that the Republicans have generally received more votes from men than women.

In 1988, the gender gap was a serious problem for George Bush. At the final tally, 7 percent more men voted for him than women —a gap he was probably grateful for because early in the campaign his male supporters outnumbered his female supporters by 15 percentage points.

		Men	Women
1988	Dukakis	41%	49%
	Bush	57%	50%
1984	Mondale	38%	42%
	Reagan	62%	58%
1980	Carter	36%	45%
	Reagan	57%	47%
	Anderson	7%	9%
1976	Carter	51%	51%
	Ford	49%	49%
1972	McGovern	37%	39%
	Nixon	63%	61%

Basic data: Roper Center for Public Opinion Research

Source: U.S. News & World Report, June 6, 1988, p. 12; "Portrait of the Electorate" (*New York Times*/CBS News Poll), *New York Times,* November 10, 1988, p. B6.

---

power-elite theory are the following (Weissberg, 1981):

1. Public officials may have corporate affiliations or be from the upper class without uniformly being committed to advancing corporate interests. (Franklin D. Roosevelt was just such an individual.)
2. It cannot be categorically maintained that the power elite always works toward a common goal, because there is obviously intense competition within and across the various industries. (For instance, most agricultural industries support free trade, whereas many manufacturers demand protection against the incursions of the foreign-import market.)
3. Over the past 20 years, the government has exerted considerably more power over the private sector than vice versa, forcing corporations to accept many policies that had been vigorously opposed. (Examples are stringent pollution regulations, strengthened consumer-protection laws, prohibitions against discrimination in housing, and increased emphasis on employee safety in industry.)

FIGURE 17.1

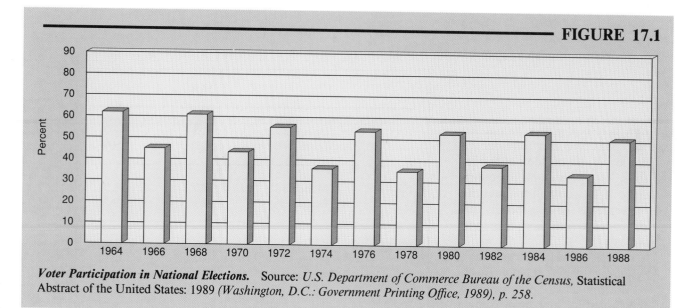

Voter Participation in National Elections. Source: *U.S. Department of Commerce Bureau of the Census,* Statistical Abstract of the United States: 1989 *(Washington, D.C.: Government Printing Office, 1989), p. 258.*

In conclusion, it should be noted that the proponents of both the power-elite and the pluralist theories of power agree that it is a small segment of the population that makes the decisions that affect people in the cities, towns, and in society itself. And those citizens who are not represented by an active, well-organized, and well-funded interest group are likely to have their welfare and concerns ignored.

VOTING BEHAVIOR

In totalitarian societies, strong pressure is put on people to vote. Usually there is no contest between the candidates, because there is no alternative to voting for the party slate. Dissent is not tolerated, and nearly everyone votes.

In the United States there is a constant progression of contests for political office, and in comparison with many other countries, the voter turnout is quite low. Since the 1920s the turnout for presidential elections has ranged from about 50 percent to nearly 70 percent of the potential voters. (See Figure 17.1 for a summary of voter participation rates in national elections.)

Considering the emphasis that Americans place on living in a democratic society, it is interesting that participation in national elections is declining steadily, a cause of grave concern to social scientists and political observers alike.

Voting rates vary with the characteristics of the people. For example, those over 45 years old and with a college education and a white-collar job have high rates of voter participation. Hispanics, the young, and the unemployed have some of the lowest voter participation rates. (See Table 17.1 for voter participation by selected characteristics.)

The Democratic party has tended to be the means through which the less privileged and the unprivileged have voted for politicians whom they hoped would advance their interests. Since 1932 the Democratic party has tended to receive most of its votes from the lower class, the working class, blacks, southern and eastern Europeans, Hispanics, Catholics, and Jews (Cummings and Wise, 1981). Thus, almost all the legislation that has been passed to aid these groups has been promoted by the Democrats and opposed by the Republicans: prounion, social security, unemployment compensation, disability insurance, antipoverty legislation, Medicare and Medicaid, civil rights, and consumer protection.

The Republican party has tended to receive most of its votes from the upper middle and lower middle classes, Protestants, and farmers. Americans under 30 tend to vote the Democratic ticket; and those over 49 tend to vote for the Republican party, even though the Democratic party has been responsible for almost all the legislation to benefit older citizens.

These voting patterns are, of course, generalizations and may change during any

The democratic party has been the means through which the less privileged and the underprivileged have voted for politicians whom they hoped would advance their interests.

TABLE 17.1
Voter Participation by
Selected Characteristics, 1986

Characteristic	Percent Voting
Male	45.8
Female	46.1
White	47.0
Black	43.2
Hispanic	24.2
18–20 years old	18.6
21–24 years old	24.2
25–34 years old	35.1
35–44 years old	49.3
45–64 years old	58.7
65 and over	60.9
Less than eight years of education	32.7
High school graduate	44.1
College graduate	62.5
Unemployed	31.2
Employed	45.7

Source: U.S. Department of Commerce, Bureau of the Census, *Statistical Abstract of the United States: 1989* (Washington, D.C.: Government Printing Office, 1989), p. 257.

specific election. For example, during the 1988 presidential election, Democrat Michael Dukakis won the black, Hispanic, Jewish, union and blue-collar vote. He also won the votes of people earning less than twenty-five thousand dollars a year, full-time students, teachers, and the unemployed.

Republican George Bush won both the male and female vote, the white vote, as well as the white Protestant, Catholic, and fundamentalist vote. He also won the majority of votes of those earning more than $50,000 a year, professionals and managers, the retired, and the traditionally Democratic young (Dionne, 1988).

The politicians of both parties tend to be most responsive to the needs of the best-organized groups with the largest sources of funds or blocs of votes. Thus, we would expect the Republicans to represent best the interests of large corporations and well-funded professional groups (such as the

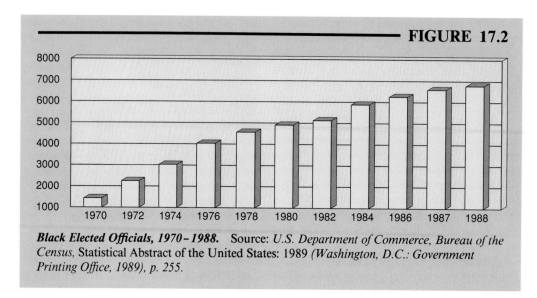

FIGURE 17.2

Black Elected Officials, 1970 – 1988. Source: *U.S. Department of Commerce, Bureau of the Census,* Statistical Abstract of the United States: 1989 *(Washington, D.C.: Government Printing Office, 1989), p. 255.*

American Medical Association). The Democrats, on the other hand, would be more closely aligned with the demands of unions.

Factors other than the social characteristics of voters and the traditional platforms of parties may affect the way people vote (Cummings and Wise, 1981). Indeed, the physical attributes, social characteristics, and personality of a candidate may prompt some voters to vote against the candidate of the party they usually support. More important, the issues of the period may cause voters to vote against the party with which they usually identify. When people are frustrated by factors such as war, recession, inflation, and other national or international events, they often blame the incumbent president and the party he or she represents.

Recently there have been efforts to increase the number of minority members who register to vote and to improve their voting rate. The greater prominence of minority candidates, such as Jesse Jackson, has helped with this effort, because minority groups are more likely to vote if they think that the elections are relevant to their lives. As minority group members increase their voting rates, they also become successful in electing members of their groups. Fig-

ure 17.2 shows the consistent rise, from 1970 to 1988, in the number of black elected officials. There were more than four times as many blacks in office in 1988 as in 1970.

Women have also been successful in increasing their representation in state legislatures. Figure 17.3 shows that the number of women holding such offices nearly doubled between 1975 and 1988.

Despite these advances, the members of Congress are still overwhelmingly white males over 40 years of age. In 1989 the Senate had only two women members and no blacks; the other ninety-eight members were white males. The lack of women and blacks in the House of Representatives was also striking (see Table 17.2 for a description of selected characteristics of members of Congress).

It would be wrong to conclude from the figures cited that Americans are politically inactive. There is more to political activity than voting. A study of American political behavior identified four different modes of participation (Verba, 1972):

1. Some 21 percent of Americans eligible to vote do so more or less regularly in municipal, state, and national elections

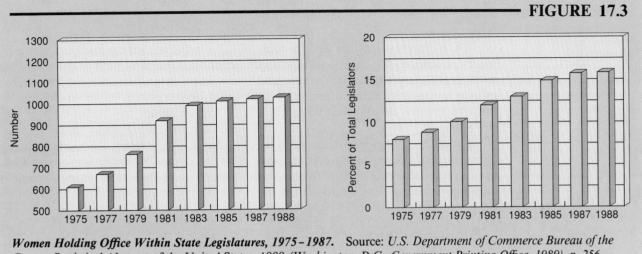

FIGURE 17.3

Women Holding Office Within State Legislatures, 1975–1987. Source: *U.S. Department of Commerce Bureau of the Census,* Statistical Abstract of the United States: 1989 *(Washington, D.C.: Government Printing Office, 1989), p. 256.*

but do not engage in other forms of political behavior.

2. Roughly 4 percent of the American electorate not only vote but also make the effort to communicate their concerns directly to government officials in an attempt to influence the officials' actions.

3. Some 15 percent of the electorate vote and also periodically take part in political campaigns. However, they do not involve themselves in ongoing local political affairs.

4. About 20 percent of eligible voters are relatively active in ongoing community politics. They vote but do not get involved in political campaigns.

BLACKS AS A POLITICAL FORCE

Black Americans always seem to receive attention before major political campaigns, as each candidate attempts to convince them that his or her campaign takes their interests to heart. Black voters have often been skeptical of those preelection promises, sensing that once the election is won, their concerns will once again be given low priority.

Indeed, the statistics on black progress in economic areas are still grim. Although progress has occurred in a variety of areas in

TABLE 17.2

Selected Characteristics of Members of Congress, 1989

	Senators	*Representatives*
Male	98	412
Female	2	23
White	100	412
Black	0	23
Married	90	371
Unmarried	10	64
Under 40	5	63
40–49 years old	30	153
50–59 years old	36	137
60–69 years old	22	56
70–79 years old	5	24
Over 80 years old	2	2

Source: U.S. Department of Commerce, Bureau of the Census, *Statistical Abstract of the United States, 1989* (Washington, D.C.: Government Printing Office, 1989), p. 252.

recent years, the economic gap between whites and blacks continues to remain large.

The picture is somewhat more promising for education, but when one considers such areas as fertility, mortality rates, and income, the movement of American blacks into mainstream middle-class America is still a long way off.

Statistics show an improvement in income levels of black married-couple families, and in educational attainment and home ownership among blacks during the last decade. There have been setbacks also, demonstrated by high black unemployment, sharply increased divorce and separation rates, and a rise in family households maintained by black females.

A cursory look at income statistics makes blacks appear better off than they are. Black married couples have closed the income gap with whites, but the proportion of black married couples in the total black population is smaller than a decade ago. There are more blacks in poverty today

than a decade ago. In 1985, 11.4 percent of whites had incomes below the poverty level, but fully 31.3 percent of blacks did.

Part of the reason for this figure is the continued fragmentation of the black family. The Census Bureau found that the median income of black married couples rose in the last decade, but the number of married couples among blacks has declined significantly. As a result, the median income for all types of black families — single-parent combined with married-couple — fell during the decade, and black families, on the average, fell farther behind whites.

Blacks have also fallen farther behind whites in the accumulation of wealth, partly because they were less likely to own property and therefore were not able to take advantage of rapidly rising real estate values over the last decade. No matter what income level you look at, blacks tend to have less wealth than whites do. Even blacks who already own a home or eventually manage to purchase a home must contend with the fact that most blacks' homes are in central cities, areas where property values are less likely to appreciate than in the suburbs.

In the political arena blacks are not just another interest group. Blacks experience deep-seated economic differences that make them skeptical of political promises. These differences have made blacks leery of white Democrats, no matter how liberal their voting records are (Robey, 1984).

HISPANICS AS A POLITICAL FORCE

Hispanics make up less than 4 percent of all registered voters in the population, yet their votes are critical in many presidential elections. The main reason is the geographical distribution of the voters. Approximately 8 million Hispanic voters are registered in six major states — New York, New Jersey, Florida, Illinois, Texas, and California — which together can give a presidential candidate most of the electoral votes he needs to win the election.

With the Hispanic population expected to grow rapidly over the next few decades, we will see more Hispanic politicians such as Miami mayor Xavier Suarez.

CONSERVATIVES ON CAMPUS

It was not that long ago that political conservatism had absolutely no place on college campuses. Certainly in the 1960s the college years were years of protest —against the Vietnam War and the draft, against the oppression of women and blacks, against restrictive campus policies. The liberalism that formed the foundation for these attitudes began to fade in the 1970s and a new era of conservatism took its place. For many, it was a conservatism born of economic worry.

Author Paul Loeb notes: "Compared with students 20 years ago, today's college undergraduates take on greater debt, more of them work part time and they enter a significantly shakier job market when they leave school. It is not surprising, then, that colleges continue to experience massive shifts away from the liberal arts—whose students traditionally spearheaded campus-based movements—and toward presumably more realistic majors such as business and, to a lesser degree, engineering" (Loeb, 1988).

Ronald Reagan also played a critical role in this swing to the right. His politics of conservatism captured the imaginations of many students as he steamrolled over his Democratic challengers, Jimmy Carter and Walter Mondale. In 1984, Reagan captured 56 percent of the student vote—a shift few expected considering the traditional liberal outlook of most college students. What attracted many college students to Reagan was his optimism about the future and conviction that individual efforts can make a difference.

In large measure because of Reagan, by 1988 far more 18-year-olds considered themselves Republicans than Democrats, yet another indication of the conservative mood on campus. Only 20 percent of men and 30 percent of women in this age group labeled themselves Democrats, compared to 41 percent of men and 33 percent of women who called themselves Republicans.

For many college students, political conservatism leaves little room for trying to undo injustice. As one engineering student explained, although he sympathized with the peace movement, "he had to learn 'too many Omega Three frequencies' to study issues such as Central America or the arms race. Engineers were pushed, he stressed, to deal 'simply with the problems at hand'" (Loeb, 1988).

Although this premature pragmatism is pervasive, there are pockets of liberalism on most college campuses. In 1985, thousands of students on some seventy college campuses across the country held a National Anti-Apartheid Protest Day, complete with sit-ins, rallies, marches, and teach-ins, to protest the treatment of blacks in South Africa and to demand that their universities stop investing in companies that do business there.

There are many other examples we could point to, yet despite them, most students still take a straight and narrow view of their future—one that involves getting the best grades they can and finding the highest-paying job they can. Kaye Howe, vice chancellor for academic services at the University of Colorado in Boulder is philosophical about this new era of conservative values: "Most of us [who went to college in the 1960s] see these things as cyclical. We used to joke in college that our kids would all be FBI agents or IBM executives—and indeed they are. That cyclical nature leads to a certain calm that this isn't a change for all time" (*U.S. News & World Report,* January 13, 1986).

Sources: "Campus Conservatives on the Offensive," *U.S. News & World Report,* January 13, 1986, pp. 20–21; Paul Loeb, "Willful Unconcern," *Psychology Today,* June 1988, pp. 59–62; "Days of Rage, '80s Style," *Newsweek,* May 6, 1985, p. 26; "A Generation of Young Fogies?" *U.S. News & World Report,* September 26, 1988, p. 79.

The importance of the Hispanic vote to presidential candidates was clearly demonstrated in 1988. Michael Dukakis addressed crowds in the Mexican-American barrios of East Los Angeles in fluent Spanish. George Bush's son Jeb, who is married to a Mexican woman and is also fluent in Spanish, pleaded his father's cause throughout the campaign.

Hispanic voters are overwhelmingly Democratic. Sixty-nine percent voted for Dukakis in 1988, and 61 percent voted for Mondale in 1984. Hispanics tend to support Democratic candidates because of the support these candidates give to social programs that help the poor. The fact that Hispanics, like blacks, have a harder time climbing the socioeconomic ladder keeps them in the Democratic camp.

With the Hispanic population expected to grow rapidly over the next few decades, both Democrats and Republicans will be paying more attention to the needs of this group. It is also likely that Hispanics will be electing greater numbers of Hispanic candidates to political office (Franchi, 1988).

A GROWING CONSERVATISM

In 1984 the Republicans captured the largest electoral margin in history, yet most Americans still call themselves Democrats. Have the voters become more conservative or are we seeing a temporary swing-voting behavior?

Public opinion tends to change as the age composition of the population changes. Older people are typically more conservative than younger people. Because the average age of the population of the United States has been going up, we can expect conservatism to increase. In addition, if the younger population is also growing more conservative in its own right, as many have claimed, the swing toward conservatism will accelerate.

Data to help us decide whether these assumptions are correct exist in the General Social Survey (GSS) from the National Opinion Research Center (NORC). Ten years of GSS results leave little doubt that a conservative mood has pervaded the country. All age groups participated in the shift toward conservatism. Overall, self-described liberals dropped from 30 percent of Americans in 1975 to 25 percent in 1985, while self-described conservatives increased from 30 percent to 36 percent.

The results also confirm that people become more conservative as they age. People who were 20 to 29 in 1975 grew more conservative about welfare spending as they got older. For example, 41 percent of them were against it in 1975, whereas 48 percent of this age group were against it in 1985.

The leading edge of the baby boomers consisted of people who were 30 to 39 in 1985. They were more conservative on capital punishment, the courts, welfare spending, gun control, pornography, and spending on blacks, the cities, and space exploration than they were in 1975 when they were age 20 to 29. There was only one issue on which they became more liberal as they aged: spending for foreign aid (see Table 17.3). This same group when asked to categorize themselves as conservative, moderate or liberal grew decidedly more conservative. In 1985 only 29 percent of them called themselves liberal compared to 46 percent in 1975 (Exter and Barber, 1986).

The Democratic party has undergone a good deal of soul-searching in recent years. Some have criticized the party for moving to the right in response to perceived shifts in public opinion. If the Democratic party is to continue as a viable political force, it must contend with the changing political climate. Labor unions, long a bastion of Democratic support, are in decline, and the new college-educated service workers are more likely to be Republican. The ranks of those who call themselves Republicans or Independents are growing, while the number of people who call themselves Democrats is declining. The next 5 years should present us with a major turning point in American politics.

————————————————————————— TABLE 17.3
Percent of People with a Conservative Response by Age*

Percent who think . . .	TOTAL		20–29		30–39		40–49		50–59		60–69	
	1985	1975	1985	1975	1985	1975	1985	1975	1985	1975	1985	1975
Courts are too lenient	87%	85%	83%	78%	86%	83%	89%	87%	91%	88%	90%	93%
Capital punishment is needed	79	64	79	57	82	66	79	65	79	68	83	69
Foreign aid spending is excessive	68	77	56	74	66	82	77	78	69	85	71	75
Crime spending is inadequate	66	70	69	66	67	69	61	65	66	75	63	75
Welfare spending is excessive	47	45	43	41	48	49	56	49	43	49	44	44
Public school prayer should be allowed	45	37	58	49	50	37	42	30	36	34	31	25
Pornography should be illegal for all**	41	41	22	21	30	33	40	43	58	48	64	61
Gun control legislation is unnecessary	27	25	26	20	25	26	34	29	26	23	28	24
Spending on blacks is excessive	22	26	21	10	23	18	21	25	24	31	13	29
Spending on cities is excessive	19	14	15	8	15	17	23	15	19	15	16	15
Defense spending is inadequate	15	18	17	13	13	18	10	21	16	22	17	20
Space spending is inadequate	12	8	11	9	16	10	18	14	11	6	4	3
Spending on environment is excessive	8	10	8	4	6	12	7	12	11	10	6	17
Spending on education is excessive	5	12	4	6	4	9	3	12	8	13	5	19

* "Don't know" responses not included in percentage base.
** Responses from 1984 and 1975.

Source: General Social Survey, National Opinion Research Center.

THE ROLE OF THE MEDIA IN ELECTIONS

No sooner had George Bush announced that Dan Quayle would be his running mate than the mass media focused on facts that diverted all attention from the issues Mr. Bush wanted to address in his campaign.

Instead of having to do battle with Dukakis and Bentsen, Bush had to fend off the media, which had launched an intensive investigation of Quayle's tour of duty in the National Guard and his lackluster previous career.

This situation is an example of how the mass media have contributed to a radical transformation of election campaigns in the United States. This transformation involves changes in how political candidates communicate with the voters and in the information journalists provide about election campaigns.

On one side we have candidates who are trying to present self-serving and strategically designed images of themselves and their campaigns. On the other side are television and print journalists who believe that they should be detached, objective observers motivated primarily by a desire to inform the U.S. public accurate'y.

Although this norm is often violated, there is no doubt that the journalistic perspective is markedly different from that of the candidate. Campaign coverage is far more apt to be critical and unfavorable toward a candidate than favorable. Journalists strive to reveal a candidate's flaws and weaknesses and to uncover tasty tidbits of hushed-up information.

Journalists exercise considerable political power in four important ways. The first and most obvious way they exert power involves deciding how much coverage to give a campaign and the candidate involved.

A candidate who is ignored by the media has a difficult time becoming known to the public and acquiring important political resources, such as money and volunteers. Such candidates have little chance of winning.

In the beginning stages of presidential nomination campaigns, for example, a candidate's goal is typically to do something that will result in news coverage and stimulate campaign contributions. These contributions can then be used for further campaigning, helping to convince the press and the public that the candidate is both credible and newsworthy.

Second, the media decide which of

Doonesbury

TELEVISION NEWS AND ELECTION CAMPAIGNS

Television news coverage of presidential election campaigns has become a major issue in recent years. The effects of sound bites, media polls, and the quality of news reporting have all been criticized. We asked Cheryl Gould, senior producer of the "NBC Nightly News with Tom Brokaw," about the role of television news in the 1988 presidential election and about the relationship between the medium and the candidates.

"Many critics blame television news when candidates refuse to talk about the issues. This is not justified. In many instances we analyze issues even when the candidates refuse to talk about them. Even before television, candidates have always tried to steer clear of issues that made them uncomfortable.

"Even though the handlers are very savvy, the networks know when something is being staged just for media coverage. Although we try to avoid doing just what the candidates want us to do, to some extent our hands are tied. We are forced to talk about what that candidate has done that day, and show him or her in the contexts they have created. To counter this, our correspondents point out to viewers that they are watching staged events and that reporters were not allowed to ask certain questions.

"At campaign stops our reporters ask the candidates hard questions on the issues. All they get in return are the same canned answers, which the reporters boil down to shorter and shorter sound bites. In essence, a sound bite is the reporter's way of giving a brief synopsis of the tone and content of what the candidate had to say. Prepared statements are not news. Our reporters would rather use the precious air time analyzing and debating the issues in their own words rather than resorting to the candidate's canned responses.

"We are all growing up together. On the one hand, I think that public figures — both candidates and elected officials — are under far more scrutiny than ever before because of telvision. On the other hand, they are also becoming more comfortable with the camera and more skilled at setting the agenda.

"We in television broadcasting have to stay ever more vigilant as they become more adept. We have to stay one step ahead so that we can remain the critical factor in the equation. There is a more mature, critical, and sophisticated press today than many critics want to acknowledge. That can only work for the good in our democratic society.

many possible interpretations to give to campaign events. Because an election is a complex and ambiguous phenomenon, there are different conclusions that can be drawn about its meaning. Here the journalists help us to form specific impressions of the candidates.

For example, presidential candidates are always concerned with how the results of presidential primaries are interpreted. Candidates want to be seen as winners who are gaining momentum. But at the same time, to be seen as the frontrunner too early leaves you open for being shot down later.

The media also exercise discretion in how favorably candidates are presented in the news. Although norms of objectivity and balance prevent most campaign coverage from including biased assertions, a more subtle and pervasive "slant" or "theme" to campaign coverage is possible and can be significant.

It is in this way that Quayle benefited in his House and Senate races from his family's ownership of newspapers and their willingness to shape the news in his favor.

Finally, journalists also may officially endorse a candidate. This can be particularly important to the candidate if the newspaper is one of the major national publications (Joslyn, 1984).

Politicians need the mass media to get the coverage they need to win. At the same time they can very easily fall victim to the intense scrutiny that is likely to result.

Although a great deal has been written about the "power of the press," little is known about the upper echelons of the newspaper hierarchy—the top decision makers or the boards of directors of newspaper-owning corporations. Much of what is known about these individuals comes from official and unofficial biographies of publishers, histories of particular newspapers, and journalistic accounts. Although these studies suggest that publishers and board members can have an influence on the general tone of a paper as well as on specific stories, there has been little systematic research on the characteristics of these people and how (or if) they are connected to other sectors of the U.S. power structure.

One sociologist did examine the media elites' position in the U.S. power structure. Dreier (1982) defined the U.S. power structure as the top institutions in society, including the nation's elite corporations, business policy groups, universities, and social clubs.

The newspaper elite is defined as the directors of the twenty-four largest newspaper companies in the United States. After checking several sources, a list of 290 directors was drawn up.

Dreier found that the nation's major newspaper firms are, in fact, closely linked to the nation's power structure. The study found that the twenty-four major newspaper companies had "447 ties with elite organizations, including 196 with *Fortune*'s 1,300 largest corporations, 97 with the 15 major business policy groups, 24 with the 12 major private universities, and 130 with the 47 elite social clubs."

The power elite is able to influence government policy not only through lobbying but also through campaign contributions, policy statements, and by placing representatives in high-level appointed positions in government, and the newspaper industry is no exception. Dreier was able to show that thirty-six newspaper directors had been appointed to at least one (past or present) high-level federal government position, including cabinet posts, presidential advisory commissions, advisory committees to federal agencies, and regional boards of the Federal Reserve Bank.

One of the mass media's major roles in society is to shape public opinion on crucial issues, to socialize individuals to social roles and behavior, and to legitimate or undermine powerful institutions, individuals, and ideas. In so doing, they exert a great deal of political influence, the extent of which is underscored by the close ties among newspaper directors and the country's power structure.

MASS POLITICAL MOVEMENTS

There is another important form of political activism in America that takes place outside conventional political agencies and institutions. Political and social protest movements, such as the civil rights movement of the 1950s and 1960s, the antiwar movement of the 1960s and early 1970s, and the women's rights movements of the 1970s and 1980s, often have profound effects on American politics. Although the government may attempt to discourage, disrupt, and dissipate these movements through overt and covert means, it is clear that such movements have made critical contributions to the emergence of new social and political climates in this country that have resulted in an impressive list of political changes. For example, the legal basis for "racial" segregation was eliminated; election reforms were instituted, making it far easier for ethnic minorities and women to take part in party politics; affirmative action programs were adopted; a president (Lyndon Johnson) was discouraged from seeking a second term in office; the massive American involvement in the Vietnam War was ended; and women not only have become more accepted and visible in traditionally male spheres of activity, they also have succeeded in focusing attention on their need to achieve equal treatment before the law and in job and salary opportunities. In a sense, then, mass political protest movements have become legitimate elements of the American political system.

One reason for the success of mass political protest movements in effecting change in American society is that they generally have not had revolutionary goals. Never have they posed a realistic threat to state institutions or to the established social order. The American government could afford to allow itself (eventually) to be influenced by these movements because its inherent legitimacy was not being called into question, nor was its continued existence at stake. In Europe, however, mass political movements traditionally have been more revolutionary in nature. Therefore, governments have taken more repressive stances against them. Hence, the American political system is almost unique in the degree to which it allows mass social movements to effect limited political changes, even though at times their tactics involve breaking the law.

SPECIAL-INTEREST GROUPS

With the government spending so much money and engaged in so much regulation, special-interest groups constantly attempt to persuade the government to support them financially or through favorable regulatory practices. These attempts at influencing government policy are known as **lobbying.** Farmers lobby for agricultural subsidies, labor unions for higher minimum wages and laws favorable to union organizing and strike actions, corporate and big business interests for favorable legislation and less government control of their practices and power, the National Rifle Association to prevent passage of legislation

requiring the registration or licensing of firearms, consumer-protection groups for increased monitoring of corporate practices and product quality, the steel industry for legislation taxing or limiting imported steel, and so on.

Lobbyists

Of all the pressures on Congress, none has received more publicity than the role of the Washington-based lobbyists and the groups they represent. The popular image of a lobbyist is an individual with unlimited funds trying to use devious methods to obtain favorable legislation. The role of today's lobbyist is far more complicated than that.

The federal government now has tremendous power in many fields, and changes in federal policy can spell success or failure for special-interest groups. With the expansion of federal authority into new areas and the huge increase in federal spending, the corps of Washington lobbyists has grown markedly. As of 1986 there were 8200 registered lobbyists, more than twice as many as in 1976. There also may be as many as 20,000 unregistered lobbyists (Thomas, 1986).

Lobbyists usually are personable and extremely knowledgeable about every aspect of their interest group's concerns. They cultivate personal friendships with officials and representatives in all branches of government, and they frequently have conversations with these government people, often in a semisocial atmosphere, such as over drinks or dinner.

The pressure brought by lobbyists usually has self-interest aims, that is, to win special privileges or financial benefits for the groups they represent. On some occasions the goal may be somewhat more objective, as when the lobbyist is trying to further an ideological goal or to put forth a group's particular interpretation of what is in the national interest.

There are certain liabilities associated with lobbyists. The key problem is that they may lead Congress to make decisions that

lobbying Attempts by special-interest groups to influence government policy.

Should Political Action Committees Be Limited?

F ew people can remain neutral about political action committees — better known as PACs. To know something about them — indeed, anything about them — is to have an opinion about the way they influence political campaigns and elections.

To understand why PACs arouse so much controversy, let us look at why they were created and how they operate. PACs came into existence in 1972 as a direct result of the reforms brought about by the Watergate scandal. They were designed to curb the corruption — or the appearance of corruption — that goes hand in hand with large political contributions. (Contributions of $100,000 and more were not unusual.) PACs limited large contributions and provided a mechanism through which they could be made. Under the current law, no individual PAC can give a candidate more than $5000 for an election — a far cry from the system it replaced.

Supporters applaud the current system for a variety of reasons. First, it brings millions of ordinary citizens into the political process by encouraging small contributions. (The average contribution is about $50.) People who believe in the positions set forth by such special-interest groups as labor unions and professional organizations (the National Association of Realtors and the National Education Association are two examples), contribute to these organizations' political action committees, which, in turn, support candidates responsive to their causes. The money PACs contribute is easily traceable back to the PAC itself. There is nothing under the table, nothing illegal that could exert undo pressure on the candidate.

Today, there are thousands of PACs in operation, with the number growing every year. This diversity adds to the debate, for on any given issue PACs compete with one another to make their point heard. This diversity, says Senator Durenberger, "reflects the pluralism of our democracy" (*Congressional Digest,* February 1987).

So what is wrong with this system? Critics claim that PAC dollars have created more problems than solutions:

- PACs favor congressional incumbents to such a degree that Congress has become a private club open to challengers only when an incumbent dies or retires. The vast war chests collected by incumbents from PACs makes the following statistic possible: In

benefit the pressure group but may not serve the interests of the public at large. A group's influence may stem less from the merits of their position than from the size of their membership, the amount of their financial resources, or the number of lobbyists and their astuteness.

Lobbyists may focus their attention not only on key members of a committee but also on the committee's professional staff. Such staffs can be extremely influential, particularly when the legislation involves highly technical matters about which members of Congress may not be that knowledgeable. Lobbyists also exert influence through testimony at congressional hearings. These hearings may give the lobbyist a propaganda forum and also access to key Congress members who could not have been contacted in any other way. The lobbyists may rehearse their statements before the hearing, ensure a large turnout from their constituency for the hearing, and may even give leading questions to friendly committee members so that certain points can be made at the hearing.

Lobbyists do perform some important and indispensable functions, including

1986, 98.5 percent of the representatives running for reelection won. (The Soviet Central Committee of the Communist party has a higher turnover rate.) By mid-1988, incumbents running for reelection had raised $102 million in PAC money, whereas their challengers had raised only $38 million.

• Many special interest PACs, exerting influence in Washington, do not reflect the sentiments of most Americans. Thus, the voice our elected representatives hear is a voice motivated by the self-concern of a privileged few.

• PACs encourage single-issue politics and single-issue thinking. Oklahoma Senator David L. Boren explains: PACs cause us to become fragmented and "to think of ourselves in our own self-centered identities with our own economic self-interests instead of . . . as Americans seeking a consensus as to what is right in the national interest" (*Congressional Digest,* February 1987).

• PAC money is pumped into political campaigns, driving the cost of campaigning into the millions. Incumbents, seeking reelection, spend much of the time they are in office raising funds for their next election. West Virginia Senator Robert C. Byrd explains: "Senators are having to go out and spend time when they ought to be here, voting; here, working in committees; here, looking after the mail from their constituents; here meeting with their constituents. Instead, they are forced to go out and spend hours and days and weekends traveling all over this country in order to raise money for their next campaign" (*Congressional Digest,* February 1987).

Considering the cost of an election campaign, PAC money is rarely turned down. Whether changes should be imposed on PACs or on the candidates receiving their money is still being debated in Congress. Ironically, the people who are in the position to change the system are those who benefit from it most.

Source: "Limiting Political Action Committees: Pro & Con," *Congressional Digest,* February 1987, pp. 33–64; "For Members Only," *Newsweek,* November 14, 1988, pp. 22–23; Richard L. Berke, "PAC's Discard Ideology and Bet on Incumbency," *New York Times,* October 20, 1988, p. B10; M. S. Forbes, Jr., "Be Careful of PAC-Bashing," *Forbes,* February 24, 1986, p. 23; "A Case of Legal Corruption," *U.S. News & World Report,* November 7, 1988, pp. 20–23.

---

helping inform both Congress and the public about specific problems and issues that normally may not get much attention, stimulating public debate, and making known to Congress who would benefit and who would be hurt by specific pieces of legislation (*Congressional Quarterly,* 1980). Many lobbyists believe that their most important and useful role, both to the groups they represent and to the government itself, is the research and detailed information they supply. And, in fact, many members of the government find the data and suggestions they receive from lobbyists valuable in studying issues, making decisions, and even in voting on legislation.

Political Action Committees

According to the Federal Election Commission, campaign contributions to House and Senate candidates more than doubled in the last decade. Contributions from individuals, which were 83 percent of the total in 1977–1978, are now less than 70 percent. Hidden in these figures is the growing influence of an extremely influential form of special-interest group, the **political action**

political action committee (PAC) A special-interest group often concerned with a single issue and usually representing corporate, trade, or labor interests.

committee **(PAC).** These groups are characterized by two important features: they often represent single-issue groups, and most of their actions and political contributions represent corporate, trade, or labor interests. There are thousands of PACs in operation, and between 1985 and 1986, PACs contributed $107 million to congressional campaigns (U.S. Department of Commerce, 1987). Local candidates also are supported by PACs.

With their rapid growth and abundant resources, PACs have had a significant influence on politics and policy. The lobbying group Common Cause estimates that in 1985 the twenty-seven incumbent senators who were running for reelection spent $15.9 million on their campaigns, with 62 percent of the money coming from PACs. For the 399 House incumbents, 73 percent of their money came from PACs (Edmondson, 1986).

Several criticisms have been leveled at these special-interest groups. Among the most prominent is that they represent neither the majority of the American people nor all social classes. Most PACs represent groups of affluent and well-educated individuals or big organizations. Only about 10 percent of the population is in a position to exert this kind of pressure on the government. Disadvantaged groups — those who most need the ear of the government — have no access to this type of political action (Cummings and Wise, 1981).

PACs also tend to favor incumbents. Two-thirds of all PAC committee contributions in recent elections have gone to incumbents. Challengers therefore end up being much more dependent on the small donations from individuals or from the Democratic and Republican national committees. PACs may ultimately diminish the role of the individual voter.

SUMMARY

Politics is the institutionalized process through which decisions that affect a community, a municipality, a state, or a society are made and enforced. Through politics people acquire and use power.

Power is the ability to carry out one's will even in the presence of resistance or opposition from others. Authority is power that is accepted as legitimate by those over whom it is exercised. There are three principal kinds of authority: charismatic, traditional, and legal-rational.

Our modern concept of government — those individuals and groups who control the political power at any given time — comes from the ancient Greeks. Their ideas have evolved into a variety of forms of government in the world today. These include autocracy, totalitarianism, and democracy.

No matter what form of government exists in a particular society, it is expected to perform certain functions: to establish laws and norms, to enforce social control, to provide economic stability, to get goals, and to protect against outside threats.

In an autocracy the ultimate authority and rule of the government rests with one person. In a totalitarian government, one group has virtually total control over the nation's social institutions. Democracy refers to a system in which rule is by the people rather than a few selected individuals. Some contend that democracy can only exist under socialism. Democratic socialism is a political system that exhibits the dominant features of a democracy, but the control of the economy is vested in the government to a greater extent than under capitalism.

Political change is the shift in the distribution of power among groups in a society. In a democracy such change is usually institutionalized; that is, it comes about through accepted legitimate channels such as elections. Political change can also emerge from rebellions and revolutions.

Rebellions are attempts to achieve rapid political change that is not possible within the existing institutions. They do not change the society's political and class structure. Revolutions, on the other hand, result in changes in the previously existing power structure of a society. Sociologists distinguish between political and social revolutions.

The American political system has certain distinctive characteristics that are of great interest to sociologists: (1) a winner-take-all two-party system, (2) a democracy in which voter participation is declining steadily, (3) a trend toward voting against, not for, a candidate or issue, (4) a tolerance for political and social protest movements, and (5) well-financed lobbies and political action committees that work to influence elections as well as government spending and legislation.

Marin 33

POPULATION AND DEMOGRAPHY

wan, xi, shao. These Chinese words mean later, longer, fewer. Later marriage, longer periods of time between pregnancies, and fewer children.

Just a few years ago that slogan launched a birth control campaign — unprecedented in scale in all of history — in the People's Republic of China. Posters proclaiming the message appeared virtually everywhere, even in the smallest village outposts.

At first the goal was not specified, but a three-child family was considered an acceptable limit. Then, two. Now the emphasis is on the last word: *shao,* "fewer": as few as possible, as fast as possible.

And *shao* has been reinterpreted downward three times from the original "fewer" to "one is best" and finally to "one is enough."

In the 1970s, the average Chinese woman of childbearing age was giving birth to six children. The Chinese government decided to take drastic action to ensure future survival.

A goal of a population of no more than 1.2 billion people by the year 2000 was set. To accomplish this goal, China instituted a nationwide campaign to convince couples to follow the government's guidelines.

To promote acceptance of the one-child limit, the government devised a reward-punishment system that makes daily life easier and richer for those who comply and burdensome for those who do not. A nationwide campaign to promote the one-child family features the Glorious One Child Certificate, under which couples sign an agreement to limit their family to a single child in exchange for extensive benefits.

As long as they only have one child, an urban couple receives a monthly bonus of $5 (Chinese dollars, equal to $3.50 American). Because the average working family income is only $30 to $35 (Chinese dollars) a month, the bonus amounts to an extra 15 percent in income.

In China, under the Glorious One Child Certificate plan, a couple may also choose between two other types of preferential treatment. They can opt for child care at no cost at nursery schools until the child is 7 years old or for free medical care for the child until age 14. They also receive preferential treatment in living accommodations, food allowances, and work assignments.

Couples who have two children — spaced over a long period of time — are neither punished nor rewarded. They receive no extra money, no extra work points, and no free education or medical benefits for a second child. They must assume the extra cost of raising the second child themselves, with no help from the state.

Penalties are harsh for those who have a third child. Ten percent of their pay or work points will be deducted from the time of the fourth month of pregnancy until the third child is 14 years old. The same penalties are imposed on couples who have their second child in fewer than 4 years and on women who have a child out of wedlock (McLaughlin, 1980).

An additional punishment for the three-or-more-child couple is denial of any job promotion and loss of all work bonuses for at least 3 years. This is to make sure that couples who exceed the state limit for children do so at the price of personal sacrifice. They cannot prosper by doing extra work.

Are these policies working? By 1984, the fertility rate for women of childbearing age had dropped to 1.94. This is just below the number required for the population to remain stable. By 1986, the fertility rate had started to move up again, owing to a less stringent interpretation of the one couple, one child rule.

POPULATION DYNAMICS

Chinese leaders have given the one-child policy top priority, ahead of competing social goals, because population growth overshadows all other issues in that country. An estimated 1 billion people live in China, one-fifth of the world's habitants. The dramatic impact the one-child policy can have on population growth can be seen if we compare population projections based on a three-child family and a one-child family. If for the next 100 years couples were to have an average of only three children, China's population would reach 4.2 billion by the year 2080.

If, on the other hand, the planned one-child family were to prevail over that period of time, China by 2080 could bring its population way down to a socially and economically manageable 370 million, still 125 million more people than in the United States today in a land area virtually the same size.

China is responding to a basic demographic fact, namely, that population problems become progressively more pressing because of what is referred to as *exponential growth*. The yearly increase in population is determined by a continuously expanding base. Each successive addition of one million people to the population requires less time than the previous addition required even if the birth rate does not increase. The best way to demonstrate the effects of exponential growth is to use a simple example. Let us assume that you have a job that requires you to work 8 hours a day, every day, for 30 days. At the end of that time, your job is over. Your boss offers you a choice of two different methods of payment. The first choice is to paid $100 a day for a total of $3000 dollars. The second choice is somewhat different. The employer will pay you one cent for the first day, two cents for the second day, four cents for the third, eight cents for the fourth, and so on. Each day you will receive double what you received the day before. Which form of payment will you choose? The second form of payment will yield a significantly higher total payment, in fact so high that no employer could realistically pay that amount. Through this process of successive doubling, you would be paid $5.12 for your labor on the tenth day. Only on the fifteenth day would you receive more than the flat $100 a day you could have received from the first day under the alternative payment plan: the amount that day would be $163.84. However, from that day on, the daily pay increase is quite dramatic. On the twentieth day you would receive $5,242.88, and on the twenty-fifth day your daily pay would be $167,772.16. Finally on the thirtieth day, you would be paid $5,368,708.80, bringing your total pay for the month to more than $10 million.

This example demonstrates how the continual doubling in the world's population produces enormous problems. The annual growth rate in the world's population has declined from a peak of 2.04 percent in the late 1960s to 1.7 percent today. This difference between global birthrates and death rates means that the world's population now doubles every 42 years instead of every 35. Although this is an improvement for the world as a whole, many countries have not seen any improvement in their growth rates; in fact the reverse may be true. In some countries in Africa, the national fertility rates have actually increased in the past decade, and Africa is now the area of the world with the most rapid population growth. For the continent as a whole, the yearly increase in population is 3 percent, which means that the population of the entire continent will double in 23 years and will be ten times the number it is today within 77 years.

In some parts of the world, the growth rate is even beyond what we just described. In Kenya, for example, the average woman now has eight children. When this fact is combined with the declining infant mortality rate, the country's population could balloon from 22 million today to 160 million in the year 2050. Rwanda, Zambia, and

In China, to promote acceptance on the one-child policy, the government has devised a reward-punishment system that makes daily life easier and richer for those who comply and burdensome for those who do not.

Tanzania are three other countries for which enormous growth has been projected. (See Table 18.1 for projected yearly population growth percentages for selected countries.)

Most of the world's growth in population in the next few decades will take place in the developing countries. The population of the richer countries will increase by 200 million by the year 2050, whereas the developing areas will have added about 6 billion (see Figure 18.1).

Symbolizing the shift in population from the developed to the less-developed world is São Paulo, Brazil. In 1950, this city was smaller than Manchester, England, but by 2000 São Paulo could have a population of 25.8 million and be one of the largest cities in the world. London, which was the second largest city in the world in 1950, will not be in the top twenty-five largest cities in 2000 if current growth trends continue.

Demography, the study of the dynamics of human populations, is influenced by three major factors: *fertility, mortality, and migration.*

FERTILITY

Fertility refers to the actual number of births in the population. One common way of measuring fertility is by means of the **crude birthrate,** a statement of the number of annual births per 1000 people in the population. The crude birthrate for the United States fell from 24.1 in 1950 to 16.0 in 1985 (World Bank, 1987).

Another indicator of reproductive behavior is the **fertility rate,** the number of annual births per 1000 women of childbearing age, usually defined as age 15 to 44.

As you will see later in this chapter, the fertility rate is linked to industrialization. Fertility declines with modernization, but not immediately. This lag is a source of tremendous population pressure in developing nations that have benefited from the introduction of modern medical technology, which immediately lowers mortality rates.

demography The study of the dynamics of human populations.

fertility The actual number of births in the population.

crude birthrate The number of annual births per 1000 population.

fertility rate The number of annual births per 1000 women of childbearing age in a population.

mortality The frequency of actual deaths in a population.

crude death rate The annual number of deaths per 1000 population.

age-specific death rates The annual number of deaths per 1000 population at specific ages.

infant mortality rate The number of children who die within the first year of life per 1000 live births.

──────────────── **TABLE 18.1**
Annual Population Projections for Selected Countries, 1985–2000

Country	Percent Increase
Kenya	4.0
Saudi Arabia	3.8
Tanzania	3.5
Zambia	3.5
Malawi	3.3
Mozambique	3.1
Ethiopia	2.9
Guatemala	2.5
Philippines	2.2
El Salvador	2.0
Brazil	1.8
Israel	1.4
Argentina	1.2
Hong Kong	1.0
Ireland	0.8
Poland	0.6
United States	0.6
Greece	0.3
Japan	0.4
Italy	0.1
United Kingdom	0.1
Denmark	−0.1
Germany, Federal Republic of	−0.2

Source: World Development Report, 1987 (Washington, D.C.: The World Bank, 1987), pp. 254–255.

Note: A 4 percent yearly increase means population doubles every 18 years. A 3 percent yearly increase means population doubles every 23 years. A 2 percent yearly increase means population doubles every 35 years.

MORTALITY

Mortality is the frequency of actual deaths in a population. The most commonly used measure of this is the **crude death rate,** that is, the annual number of deaths per 1000 population. Demographers also look at **age-specific death rates,** which measure the annual number of deaths per 1000 population at specific ages. For example, one measure used is the **infant mortality rate,** which is the number of children who die within the first year of life per 1000 live births. Some countries have extremely high infant mortality rates. In Mali, for example, 174 out of every 1000 infants die before age one. In Ethiopia, the figure is 168 (World Bank, 1987).

In the United States the infant mortality rate dropped from 47.0 in 1940 to 10.6 in 1985. This rates does not apply to all infants, however. In 1940 whites had an infant mortality rate of 43.2 (below the national average), and nonwhites had an infant mortality rate of 73.8. In 1985 the rates were 9.3 for whites and 15.8 for nonwhites *(Statistical Abstract of the United States: 1989).* These figures suggest that good infant medical care is not equally available to all Americans. Different cultural patterns of child rearing may also affect infant mortality.

Although the infant mortality rate in

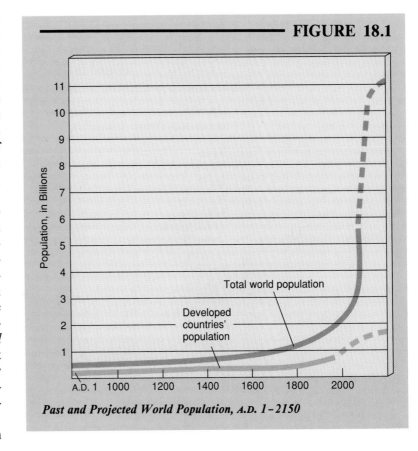

FIGURE 18.1

Past and Projected World Population, A.D. 1–2150

Most of the world's population growth in the next few decades will occur in the developing countries.

TABLE 18.2
Life Expectancy for Children Born in 1985

Country	Male	Female
Japan	75	80
Australia	75	80
Spain	74	80
Italy	74	79
Israel	73	77
United States	72	80
Denmark	72	78
Hungary	67	74
Mexico	64	69
Chile	63	67
Jordan	63	66
Saudi Arabia	60	64
Peru	57	60
Morocco	57	61
India	57	56
Indonesia	53	57
Bolivia	51	54
Zambia	50	54
Nigeria	48	52
Nepal	47	46
Bhutan	44	43
Guinea	39	41
Sierra Leone	39	40

Source: World Development Report, 1987 (Washington, D.C.: The World Bank, 1987), pp. 258–259.

life expectancy The average number of years that a person born in a particular year can expect to live.

the United States is considerably lower than the rates in developing countries, it is higher than that of twenty-seven nations, including such Asian countries as Japan and Hong Kong, as well as most of northern Europe. The lowest infant mortality rates in the world are found in Japan and Switzerland, where 6 infants out of every 1000 die before their first birthday (*U.S. News & World Report,* August 8, 1988).

Mortality is reflected in people's **life expectancy,** the average number of years that a person born in a particular year can expect to live (see Table 18.2 for life expectancies in selected countries). Life expect-

ancy is usually determined more by infant than adult mortality. Once an individual survives infancy, his or her life expectancy improves dramatically. In the United States, for example, only when individuals reach their 60s do their chances of dying approximate those of their infancy (Bureau of the Census, 1987).

It is often overlooked that the rapid increase in population growth in the Third World countries is caused by sharp improvements in life expectancy, *not* by a rise in the birthrate. Disease took a dramatic toll on life expectancy in the United States also in the not too distant past. For example, Abraham Lincoln's mother died when she was 35 and he was 9. Before her death she had three children: Abraham's brother died in infancy and his sister died in her early 20s. Of the four sons born to Abraham and Mary Todd Lincoln, only one survived to maturity.

In developing countries, the proportion of infant and child deaths is quite high, resulting in a significantly lower life expectancy than that in developed countries. In Bangladesh, infant deaths account for more than one-third of all deaths. In the United States, that figure is about 1 percent. The high proportion of deaths can be attributed to impure drinking water and unsanitary conditions. In addition, the diet of pregnant women and nursing mothers often lacks proper nutrients, and babies and children are not fed a healthy diet. Flu, diarrhea, and pneumonia are common, as are typhoid, cholera, malaria, and tuberculosis. Many children are not immunized against common childhood diseases such as polio, measles, diphtheria, and whooping cough, and the parents' income is often so low that when the children do fall ill, they cannot provide medical care (World Bank, 1984).

The world became aware of the tragedy of children dying in developing countries during the disastrous famine that devastated Africa in the mid-1980s. Millions died in countries like Ethiopia, Chad, the Sudan, Angola, Botswana, and Mozambique, and most of them were children. In Chad, infants die at the rate of 240 per thousand, some twenty-two times the rate in the United States. In the Sudan, somewhere between 350,000 and 700,000 children died at the height of the famine from diseases like diarrhea and measles (*Newsweek,* June 3, 1985; *U.S. News & World Report,* January 20, 1986).

Life expectancies in the developing nations vary greatly. They range from an average regional low of about 51 years in Africa to 66 years in Latin America. A major contributor to the overall death rate is infant mortality. A rapid decrease in infant mortality in a developing nation will result in a significant rise in the overall rate of population growth.

A good example of a country that has experienced a decline in mortality, but no decrease in fertility, is Kenya. Kenya has experienced an incredible population growth rate of 4 percent a year. If this rate of increase continues, Kenya's population of 22 million people will double in 18 years (Haub, 1987).

MIGRATION

Migration is the movement of populations from one geographical area to another. When a population leaves an area, it is said to be *emigrating;* when it enters an area, it is *immigrating.* All migrations, therefore, are both emigrations and immigrations.

Of the three components of population change — fertility, mortality, and migration, migration historically exerts the least impact on population growth or decline.

Most countries of the world do not encourage immigration. When it is permitted, it is often viewed as a way to provide needed skilled labor or to provide unskilled labor for jobs the resident population no longer wishes to do. Exceptions to this trend are the traditional receiver countries, such as the United States, Australia, and Canada. These countries owe much of their growth to immigrant populations.

Where migration is a significant factor, it is necessary to take into account the age and sex of the migrants as well as their number. These characteristics tell us the number

of potential workers among the migrants, the number of women of childbearing age, the number of school-age children, the number of elderly, and other factors that will affect society. In recent years, the United States has experienced an influx of illegal immigrants from Mexico. See this chapter's Controversial Issue, "Dealing with the Problem of Illegal Immigrants," for an examination of how these immigrants are changing our society.

Sometimes it is important to distinguish between those movements of populations that cross national boundary lines from those that are entirely within a country. To make this distinction, sociologists use the term **internal migration** for movement within a nation's boundary lines — in contrast to **immigration,** in which boundary lines are crossed.

Since 1970, population growth in the United States has been greatest in the Sun Belt states, reflecting continued migration patterns toward the South and West. California, Texas, and Florida are growing significantly faster than the United States as a whole because they attract many northeastern and midwestern residents. There is some indication, however, that internal mi-

Life expectancy in many Scandinavian countries is longer than it is in the U.S.

migration The movement of populations from one geographical area to another.

internal migration The movement of a population within a nation's boundary lines.

immigration The movement of a population into an area.

gration patterns may be starting to change. Typically, northern and midwestern migrants moved to the three major sunbelt states and then distributed themselves to the surrounding states. It now appears that future migration patterns in the United States could resemble an enormous cyclone, with a long westward flow to California from the Northeast and Midwest, and a series of shorter eastward flows through the South beginning in California and continuing to Florida and back up the Atlantic coast (Sanders and Long, 1987).

THEORIES OF POPULATION

The study of population is a relatively new scholarly undertaking; it was not until the eighteenth century that populations as such were carefully examined. The first person to do so, and perhaps the most influential, was Thomas Malthus.

MALTHUS'S THEORY OF POPULATION GROWTH

Thomas Robert Malthus (1776–1834) was a British clergyman, philosopher, and economist who believed that population growth is linked to certain natural laws. The core of the population problem, according to Malthus, is that populations will always grow faster than the available food supply. With a fixed amount of land, farm animals, fish, and other food resources, agricultural production can be increased only by cultivating new acres, catching more fish, and so on—an additive process that Malthus believed would increase the food supply in an arithmetic progression (1, 2, 3, 4, 5, and so on). Population growth, on the other hand, increases at a geometric rate (1, 2, 4, 8, 16, and so on), because couples have 3, 4, 5, and more children. (A stable population requires that two individuals produce no more than 2.1 children: 2 to reproduce themselves and 0.1 to make up for those people who remain childless.) Thus, if left

Thomas Malthus believed that increases in the available food supply cannot keep up with population growth.

unchecked, human populations are destined to outgrow their food supplies and suffer poverty and a never-ending "struggle for existence" (a term coined by Malthus that later became a cornerstone of Darwinian and evolutionary thought).

Malthus recognized the presence of certain forces that limit population growth, grouping these into two categories: preventive checks and positive checks. **Preventive checks** are practices that limit reproduction. These include celibacy, the delay of marriage, and such practices as contraception within marriage, extramarital sexual relations, and prostitution (if the latter two are linked with abortion and contraception). **Positive checks** are events that limit reproduction either by causing the deaths of individuals before they reach reproductive age or by causing the deaths of large numbers of people, thereby lowering the overall population. Positive checks include famines, wars, and epidemics. Malthus's thinking was assuredly influenced by the plague that wiped out so much of Europe's population during the fourteenth and fifteenth centuries.

Malthus refuted the theories of the *utopian socialists,* who advocated a reorganization of society in order to eliminate poverty and other social evils. Regardless of any planning, Malthus argued, misery and suffering are inevitable for most people. On the one hand, there is the constant threat that population will outstrip the available food supplies; on the other, there are the unpleasant and often devastating checks on this growth, which result in death, destruction, and suffering.

History proved Malthus wrong, at least for the developed countries. Technological breakthroughs in the nineteenth century enabled Europe to avoid many of Malthus's predictions. The newly invented steam engine used energy more efficiently; labor production was increased through the factory system. An expanded trade system provided raw materials for growing industries and food for workers. Fertility declined and emigration eased Europe's population pres-

sures. By the end of the nineteenth century, Malthus and his concerns had been all but forgotten.

MARX'S THEORY OF POPULATION GROWTH

Karl Marx and other socialists rejected Malthus's view that population pressures and their attendant miseries are inevitable. Marxists argue that the sheer number of people in a population is not the problem. Rather, it is industrialism (and in particular, capitalism) that creates the social and economic problems associated with population growth. Industrialists need large populations to keep the labor force adequate, available, flexible, and inexpensive. In addition, the capitalistic system requires constantly expanding markets, which can be assured only by an ever-increasing population. As the population grows, large numbers of unemployed and underemployed people compete for the few available jobs, which they are willing to take at lower and lower wages. Therefore, according to Marxists, the norms and values of a society that encourages population growth are rooted in its economic and political systems. Only by reorganizing the political economy of industrial society in the direction of socialism, they contend, is there any hope of eliminating poverty and the miseries of overcrowding and scarce resources for the masses.

DEMOGRAPHIC TRANSITION THEORY

Sweden has been keeping records of births and deaths longer than any other country. Throughout the centuries, Sweden's rate of births and deaths fluctuated widely. There were periods of rapid population growth, followed by periods of slow growth, and even population declines during famines. In the late 1800s Sweden's death rate began a sustained decline while the birthrate remained high. Eventually Sweden's birthrate also declined, so that today its births and deaths are virtually in balance.

The shift in Sweden's population can

preventive checks Practices described by Thomas Robert Malthus that limit reproduction. Examples: contraception, prostitution, and other "vices."

positive checks Events described by Thomas Robert Malthus that limit reproduction either by causing the deaths of individuals before they reach reproductive age or by causing the deaths of large numbers of people, thereby lowering the overall population. Examples: famines, wars, and epidemics.

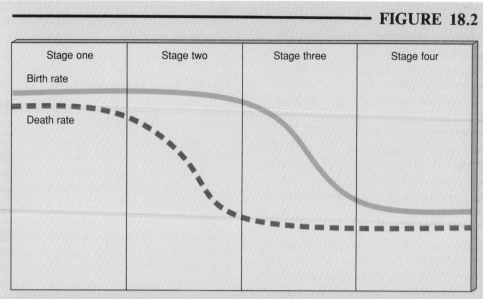

FIGURE 18.2

The Demographic Transition. *The demographic transition theory states that societies pass through four stages of population change. Stage 1 is marked by high birth rates and high death rates. In stage 2, populations rapidly increase as death rates fall, but birth rates stay high. In stage 3, birth rates begin to fall. Finally, in stage 4, both fertility and mortality rates are relatively low.*

demographic transition theory A theory that explains population dynamics in terms of four distinct stages, from high fertility and high mortality to relatively low fertility and mortality.

be explained by a theory of population dynamics developed by Warren Thompson (1929). According to the **demographic transition theory,** societies pass through four stages of population change. During stage 1, a high fertility rate is counterbalanced by a high death rate due to disease, starvation, and natural disaster. The population tends to be very young, and there is little or no population growth. During stage 2, populations rapidly increase as a result of a continued high fertility that is linked to the increased food supply, development of modern medicine, and public health care. Slowly, however, the traditional institutions and religious beliefs that support a high birthrate are undermined and replaced by values stressing individualism and upward mobility. Family planning is introduced, and the birthrate begins to fall. This is stage 3, during which population growth begins to decline. Finally, in stage 4 both

fertility and mortality are relatively low, and population growth once again is stabilized (see Figure 18.2).

Applications to Industrial Society

The first wave of declines in the world's death rate came in countries experiencing real economic progress. These declines gradually gained momentum as the Industrial Revolution proceeded. Advances in agriculture, transportation, and commerce made it possible for people to have a better diet, and advances in manufacturing made adequate clothing and housing more widely available. A rise in people's real income facilitated improved public sanitation, medical science, and public education.

Although the preceding explanation applies well to Western society, it does not explain the population trends in the underdeveloped areas of today's world. Since 1920 these areas have experienced a much faster drop in death rates than Western societies without a comparable rate of increase in economic development. The rapid rate of decline in the death rate in these countries has been due primarily to the application of medical discoveries made and financed in the industrial nations. For example, the most important cause of death being eliminated is infectious disease. These diseases have been controlled through the introduction of vaccines, antibiotics, and other medical advances developed in the industrial nations. Those of us who are used to paying high costs for private medical care will find it hard to believe that preventive public health measures in underdeveloped countries can save millions of lives at costs ranging from a few cents to a few dollars per person.

Because the mortality rates in underdeveloped countries have been significantly reduced, the birthrate, which has not fallen as fast or as consistently, has become an increasingly serious problem. Often this problem persists and worsens despite monumental government efforts at disseminating birth-control information and contraceptive devices. In India, for example, despite the government's commitment to controlling population size through birth control and sterilization, the population is expected to increase from 717 million in 1982 to 994 million in 2000 (World Bank, 1984).

These failures have shown that the birthrate can be brought down only when attention is paid to the complex interrelationships of biological, social, economic, political, and cultural factors. For example, a mother in India may reject sterilization because four of her five children may be girls. With no social security, private pension plans, or other forms of social insurance for the elderly, parents know that they will need at least one son to take care of them in old age. India's high infant mortality rate creates the belief that parents should have two or three sons to insure that at least one will survive (Freed and Freed, 1985).

A SECOND DEMOGRAPHIC TRANSITION

The original demographic transition theory ends with the final stage involving an equal distribution of births and deaths and a stable population. Some people (van de Kaa, 1987) have suggested that Europe has gone beyond the original theory and entered a second demographic transition. The start of this second demographic transition is arbitrarily set at 1965. The principal feature of this transition is the decline in fertility to a level well below replacement.

If fertility stabilizes below replacement, as seems likely in most of Europe, and barring major changes in immigration, the population of these countries will decline. As of 1985, this second demographic transition was already taking place in four countries, namely, Austria, Denmark, Germany, and Hungary.

The United States is not expected to experience a population decline in the near future. United Nations population projections to the year 2025 indicate that the United States will continue to grow modestly, even with continued low fertility and reduced immigration levels (Teitelbaum and Winter, 1985).

The reasons for the second demographic transition center around a strong desire for individual advancement and improvement. In European societies, as in American society, this advancement is dependent on education and a commitment to develop and use one's talents. This holds for both men and women. Getting married and having children presents a number of trade-offs, especially for women. A child may interrupt career plans, as well as add to the financial costs of the family. In European societies, children are no longer either expected or required to support their parents in old age or help with the family finances. Therefore, the emotional satisfaction of parenthood can usually be satisfied

A BIRTH DEARTH?

In 1987 Ben J. Wattenberg wrote The Birth Dearth, *a book that presented his view that people in Western countries are having too few children to reproduce themselves and continue population growth. Some have criticized this position and pointed out that more babies were born in the United States in 1988 than any year since the end of the baby boom. The Census Bureau now projects that even if American women continue to reproduce at their present modest rate, the population will not start to decline for over half a century. We interviewed Ben Wattenberg and asked him to elaborate on his controversial position.*

Since World War II we have become so used to thinking only in terms of population growth that we can hardly conceive of a decline. In the late 1950s, in America, we had a fertility rate of 3.7 children per woman, a rate you see today only in the Third World. In the last 15 to 20 years, our fertility rate has declined dramatically to 1.8—a number well below the 2.1 replacement figure.

The reality of the birth dearth has been masked because so many baby boomers are having children of their own. With this great multitude reaching their reproductive years at about the same time, the population level has not fallen, even though the number of children born per woman has declined radically. What we are seeing is a decline in population growth, which is different than a decline in population.

As this birth dearth continues into the 1990s, we are going to see the western European nations actually losing population and American growth rates declining even more. We will also see the absolute number of young adults in this country dropping by 18 percent.

People tend to understand this phenomenon and notice it only when it is actually happening to them. People in midwestern farm towns are aware of it today. However, you get a very different response in Phoenix, Tampa, Houston, or Los Angeles—cities that are still growing by leaps and bounds.

I believe we should have some pronatal policies to make it easier for people who want to have children to be able to have them. I am in favor of federal help of some sort for day care. I am in favor of maternal leave. I am in favor of anything that is pronatal.

Another way to encourage families is to provide tax bonus money—in effect, a children's allowance—to parents of children. If a woman wants or needs to work, she can use the money for day care. If she wants to stay home while her children are young, she can use the money to make it easier to leave her job.

We know that many women never have children or have only one child. This means that some women must have three or four children to maintain the population growth. If having a large family remains very difficult, we will see a continuation of fertility rates below replacement level. We should make it easy for people who want to have large families to be able to do so. I am not talking about any kind of population coercion. I just want to take the negative bias out of the system.

I know that a society operating at a substantially negative fertility rate is an aging society. The great French demographer, Alfred Sauvy, described this below-replacement-level society as "old people living in old houses with old ideas." That is not the kind of vigorous society that will lead the world.

by having either one or perhaps two children. Multiplied on a large scale, this trend produces births per woman that are below replacement level.

Pronatalist Policies

In most of this chapter we are presenting information about population growth rates that appear to be out of control. Yet the second demographic transition in Europe is producing government policies in some countries that are designed to encourage people to have children.

Some countries have adopted measures that make it difficult to obtain contraceptives or to resort to abortion. In 1966, Romania instituted an abrupt cutoff of legal abortion and imported contraceptives. Initially the birthrate soared, but declined again in subsequent years, and today stands exactly where it was in 1966. Hungary adopted a similar measure in the 1970s with no increase in the birthrate.

A second set of pronatalist measures adopted by European countries attempt to make children a more attractive proposition and ease the financial burdens. Since 1964 in Czechoslovakia, women with five or more children are entitled to their old-age pension at 53, those with three or four children at 54, those with two at 55, those with one at 56, and the childless at 57. Also in Czechoslovakia, newlywed couples receive low-interest loans that do not have to be paid back if they have enough children (Pavlik, 1986).

Other pronatalist incentives include full-paid maternity leave of up to twenty-six weeks and subsidized leave thereafter (until the child's third birthday in Hungary), subsidized nurseries and kindergartens, educational and transportation grants, tax rebates, and free medical care during pregnancy and delivery.

Studies of pronatalist policies have shown that they hardly ever lead to spectacular long-term effects on the birthrate. They may, however, contribute toward slowing down the fertility decline and improving the living conditions of the parents and their children.

Sometimes pronatalist and antinatalist policies can exist in the same country, as is the case in the Soviet Union. In 1987 Tass reported that benefits available to large families elsewhere in the Soviet Union would be withdrawn in the predominantly Muslim Soviet Republic of Tadzhikistan to reduce

the fertility rate there, which was three times that in the rest of the country (van de Kaa, 1987).

CURRENT POPULATION TRENDS: A TICKING BOMB?

Matej Gaspar was born at 8:25 A.M. on July 11, 1987, in Zagreb, Yugoslavia. A few minutes later, United Nations Secretary-General Javier Perez de Cuellar took tiny Matej in his arms and proclaimed him the 5 billionth person on the planet.

That evening in the stadium where the Day of the Five Billion was observed, a large chorus sang "Ode to Joy" and the challenge to humanity symbolized by Matej's birth was surely on the mind of many.

Every minute, 150 babies are born in the world. That means about 220,000 new human beings a day—80 million a year who need to be fed, clothed, sheltered, educated, and employed. At this rate the 6 billionth person will arrive before the year 2000 (*U.N. Chronicle,* 1987).

Along with the prediction of the 6 billionth person are some of the following troublesome predictions:

FIGURE 18.3

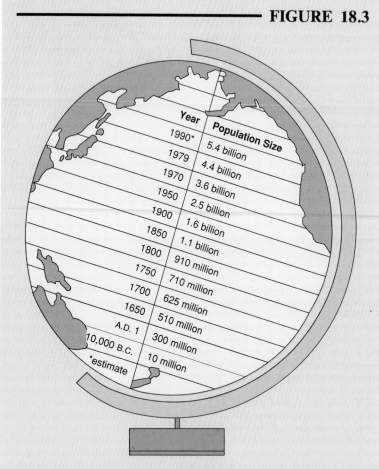

Year	Population Size
1990*	5.4 billion
1979	4.4 billion
1970	3.6 billion
1950	2.5 billion
1900	1.6 billion
1850	1.1 billion
1800	910 million
1750	710 million
1700	625 million
1650	510 million
A.D. 1	300 million
10,000 B.C.	10 million
*estimate	

The Population Explosion. Source: *Data through 1970,* The World Almanac *(New York: Newspaper Enterprises, Inc., 1980), p. 734. Data for 1979, U.S. Department of Commerce, Bureau of the Census,* Statistical Abstract of the United States, 1984 *(Washington, D.C.: Government Printing Office, 1983).*

- In the year 2000 at least nineteen of the poorest nations will be unable to grow enough food to feed their people even if they use new technology.
- By 2000 poor countries will have half the water per person that they had in 1975, and the availability of water will be halved again by 2035.
- Six hundred million new jobs will be needed in developing countries by 2000 just to employ persons already born and soon to enter the work force.

- Many cities in poor countries face a doubling in population by the year 2000 (Population Reference Bureau, 1986).

"Short of nuclear war itself, population growth is the gravest issue that the world faces over the decade ahead. . . . Both can and will have catastrophic consequences. If we do not act, the problem will be solved by famine, riot, insurrection, war."

This view was put forth by Robert S. McNamara, a former secretary of defense and president of the World Bank. Like many other specialists in this field, he believes that overpopulation is now threatening the basic fabric of world order.

The problem is underscored by the increasing speed with which the world's population is multiplying. In 1650 there were an estimated 510 million people in the entire world. One hundred years later there were 710 million, an increase of some 39 percent. By 1900 there were 1.6 billion. Only 87 years later the world population had spiraled to 5 billion. The World Bank estimates that in the year 2025, the global population will be 8.3 billion. Of that total, approximately 7 billion will be residents of the poorest and least-developed nations. As you can see in Figure 18.3, the world population has been rising at an ever-increasing rate.

Right now, the world population is doubling about every 42 years. If it were to continue to expand in this way, by the year 2150 there would be 37.4 billion people crowded onto this planet—a situation in which widespread poverty and famine seem almost assured. In recent years, however, there has been a small but significant slowing in the rate of world population growth: Between 1965 and 1970 the annual rate of growth was 2.1 percent, but between 1975 and 1985 it had dropped to 1.7 percent (U.S. Bureau of the Census, 1986). If this slowing trend continues, by the year 2100 the world population will be twice its present size, some 8.4 billion people—a staggering number in and of itself but far smaller than the 37.4 billion previously predicted. This more hopeful pattern is contingent on the average family size being limited to two children.

We have already seen a significant trend throughout the world toward smaller families. The developing countries that are cutting their population growth most quickly are Costa Rica, Colombia, India, Mauritius, and Tunisia. Others include Thailand, Malaysia, Peru, and the Dominican Republic. Young women in these nations have, on the average, about two fewer children than their mothers and grandmothers had. In Costa Rica, for example, women between the ages of 45 and 49 had an average of 7.3 children. When 15-year-old to 44-year-old women were added to this group, the average number of children dropped to 3.8. Researchers credit increased education, government propaganda, the rapid spread of contraceptive devices, mass communications (legitimizing new norms for families in previously isolated, tradition-dominated societies), and the diminishing necessity to have large numbers of children to ensure adequate labor for family agriculture for this development (The World Bank, 1987).

DETERMINANTS OF FERTILITY

How many children a family has will have an impact on that family's life-style in both developed and undeveloped countries. There are a substantial number of factors that enter into determining the typical family size in a country. In this section we will examine some of these in an attempt to gain an insight into the variety of economic, social, and psychological issues that have to be addressed when trying to limit population growth. (See Table 18.3 for a summary of some of the determinants of fertility.)

Average Age of Marriage

Early marriage provides more years during which conception can take place. It also de-

creases the years of schooling and limits employment opportunities.

In South Asia and sub-Saharan Africa, about half of all women between 15 and 19 are, or have been, married. In Bangladesh, the mean age for women at marriage is 16, and thus the fertility rates in these areas are extremely high. By way of contrast, the average age of marriage in Sri Lanka is 25. If we compare the births per woman, we find that in Bangladesh the average woman has 6 children, whereas in Sri Lanka she has 3.7 children (Merrick, 1986).

Some countries have tried to establish a minimum age for marriage in order to limit fertility. In 1950, China legislated the minimum age for marriage at 18 for women and 20 for men. It also recognized the effect that social controls can have on the marriage age and so increased institutional and community pressures for later marriage. In 1980, China again raised the legal minimum ages to 20 for women and 22 for men, and it is one of the few countries that has been successful in raising the average age of marriage.

TABLE 18.3
Determinants of Fertility

Number of children
  1. Women's average age at first marriage
  2. Breast-feeding
  3. Infant mortality
Demand for children
  1. Gender preferences
  2. Value of children
    a. Children as insurance against divorce
    b. Children as securers of women's position in family
    c. Children's value for economic gain
    d. Children's value for old-age support
  3. Cost of children
Fertility control
  1. Use of contraception
  2. Factors influencing fertility decisions
    a. Income level
    b. Education of women
    c. Urban or rural residence

Breast-Feeding

Breast-feeding delays the resumption of menstruation and therefore offers limited protection against conception. It also avoids some of the considerable health risks connected with bottle feeding, particularly when the powdered milk may be improperly prepared; adequate sterilization is not possible; and families cannot afford an adequate supply of milk powder. These risks have produced an outcry against certain large companies that produce powdered milk and that have been trying to encourage bottle-feeding in Third World countries.

In Bangladesh, Pakistan, Nepal, and most of sub-Saharan Africa, where very few women use contraception, breast-feeding is one of the few controls on fertility rates.

In the United States, breast-feeding was relatively unpopular until the late 1960s. As the advantages of breast-feeding became known, better-educated women began to use it more. Today, college-educated women are the most likely to start breast-feeding and continue it for the longest period.

Infant and Child Mortality

High infant mortality promotes high fertility. Parents who assume some of their children will die may give birth to more babies than they really want as a way of ensuring a family of a certain size. This sets in motion a pattern of many children born close together, weakening both the mother and babies and producing more infant mortality.

In the short term, the prevention of ten infant deaths may produce only one to five fewer births. Initially, lower infant and child mortality will lead to somewhat larger families and faster rates of population growth than before. However, the long-term effects are the most important. With improved chances of survival, parents give greater attention to their children and are willing to spend more on their children's health and education. Eventually, the lower mortality rates help parents achieve the desired family size with fewer births and lead them to want a smaller family as well.

Gender Preferences

The issue of gender preference on fertility is actually more complicated than it might appear at first glance. In most countries throughout the world there is a strong preference for male children. Logically this does not make that much sense. In most of the underdeveloped countries, daughters typically help their mothers with household chores. One would think that this would increase their worth to the family. Clearly, there must be countervailing factors to reduce the desire for daughters. For example, during the drought in Somalia, mothers brought their sons to feeding centers for emergency rations, but not their daughters (*Newsweek,* June 3, 1985). It has been suggested that it may be tied in with the expense of a dowry or the early loss of the daughter's help through marriage (Mason, 1987). The Philippines is one of the few countries in the world where daughters are preferred over sons (Williamson, 1983).

The preference for sons, however, may not be all that important in countries with high fertility rates. In Bangladesh, for example, the preference for sons is extremely strong, but the fact that couples desire large families, combined with little practice of contraception, probably has more of an impact on fertility than gender preference (Ahmed, 1981).

In countries with declining fertility rates the preference for sons may cause the fertility rate to level off above replacement level. Couples may continue to have children until they have the desired son.

Benefits and Costs of Children

In underdeveloped countries the benefits of having children have generally been greater for an individual family than the costs. The costs and benefits change with the second, third, fourth, and fifth children.

For a rural sample in the Philippines, three-quarters of the costs involved in rearing a third child come from buying goods and services; the other quarter comes from costs in time (or lost wages). But receipts from child earnings, work at home, and old-age support offset 46 percent of the total. The remaining 54 percent, the net cost of a child, is equivalent to about 6 percent of a husband's annual earnings.

By contrast, a study of urban areas of the United States showed that almost half the costs of a third child are time costs. Receipts from the child offset only 4 percent of all costs.

Only economic costs and benefits are taken into account in these calculations. To investigate social and psychological costs, other researchers have examined how individuals perceive children. Economic contributions from children are clearly more important in the Philippines, where fertility is higher than in Korea or the United States; concern with the restrictions children impose on parents, on the other hand, is clearly greatest in the United States.

In all three countries, however, couples demonstrate a progression in the values they emphasize as their families grow. The first child is important to cement the marriage and bring the spouses closer together, as well as to have someone to carry on the family name. Thinking of the first child, couples also stress the desire to have someone to love and care for and the child bringing play and fun into their lives.

In considering a second child, parents emphasize more the desire for a companion for the first child. They also place weight on the desire to have a child of the opposite sex from the first. Similar values are prominent in relation to third, fourth, and fifth children; emphasis is also given to the pleasure derived from watching children grow.

Beyond the fifth child, economic considerations predominate. Parents speak of the sixth or later children in terms of their helping around the house, contributing to the support of the household, and providing security in old age. For first to third chil-

dren, the time taken away from work or other pursuits is the main drawback; for fourth and later children, the direct financial burden is more prominent than the time cost (The World Bank, 1984).

Contraception

Apart from the factors already mentioned, fertility rates are eventually tied to the increasing use of contraception. Use of contraception is partly a function of a couple's wish to avoid or delay having children and partly related to its costs. People have regulated family size for centuries, through abortion, abstinence, and even infanticide. However, the costs, whether economic, social, or psychological, in preventing a birth may be greater than the risk of having another child.

Use of contraception varies widely, with rates of 10 percent or fewer for married women in almost all of sub-Saharan Africa, to usage rates between 70 and 80 percent for women in Europe and the United States (*Population Reports,* 1985).

Contraception is most likely to be effective when such programs are publicly subsidized. Not only do such programs ad-

In underdeveloped countries, the benefits of having children have generally been greater than the costs for the individual family.

The support given to family planning programs differs dramatically from country to country. The government of India is active in providing birth-control information devices, while Roman Catholic countries follow anti-birth-control policies.

dress the economic costs in spreading contraception, but they also help communicate the idea that birth control is possible. These programs also offer information about the private and social benefits of smaller families, which also helps reduce the desired family size.

The support given to family planning programs differs dramatically from country to country. At one end of the family planning spectrum are the governments of India and China, which provide birth-control information and devices and actively support the termination of pregnancy through abortion. At the other end are countries such as Bolivia and the Philippines whose large Roman Catholic populations follow the anti-birth-control and antiabortion teachings of the church (Helmore, 1988).

Income Level

It is a well-established fact that people with higher incomes want fewer children. Alternative uses of time, such as earning money, developing or using skills, and pursuing leisure activities, become more attractive, particularly to women. The children's economic contributions become less important

to the family welfare, because the family no longer needs to think of children as a form of social security in old age. It is not the higher income itself, but rather the life changes it brings about that lowers fertility.

This relationship between income and fertility holds true only for those with an income above a certain minimum level. If people are extremely poor, increases in income will actually increase fertility. In the poorest countries in Africa and Asia, families are often below this threshold. Above the threshold, though, the greatest fertility reduction with rising income will take place among low-income groups.

Education of Women

One of the strongest factors in reducing fertility is the education of women. The number of children that women have declines quite substantially as their level of education increases. The differences can sometimes be quite large; for example, in Colombia, women in the lowest educational group have, on the average, four more children than do women in the highest educational group.

Studies also show that women's level of education has a greater impact on fertility than that of men. There are a number of reasons for this. In most instances, children have a greater impact on women, in terms of time and energy, than they do on men. The more educated a woman is, the more opportunities she may encounter that conflict with having children. Education also appears to delay marriage, which in itself lowers fertility. In ten out of fourteen developing countries, women with 7 or more years of education marry at least 3.5 years later than do women with no education. Educated women are also more likely to know about and adopt birth-control methods. In Mexico, 72 percent of those women with 9 or more years of education are likely to use contraception, whereas only 31 percent of those with 5 or fewer years of education are likely to do so.

MONEY AND CHILDREN

F amilies who get a taste of the good life are reluctant to give it up to care for large families. According to the Census Bureau, there is an inverse relationship between money and children: The more money you have, the fewer children you are likely to bear. Statistics show that fertility rates in the United States decrease dramatically by income level:

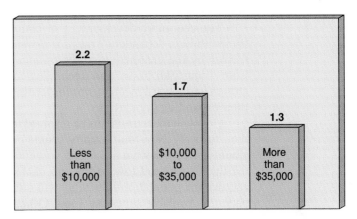

Rich and Poor. *Note: Income levels are annual figures. Basic Data: U.S. Census Bureau.*

Urban or Rural Residence

Urban fertility in developing countries tends to be lower than rural fertility, although it still is at least twice as high as fertility in developed countries (Salas, 1987). Urban dwellers usually have access to better education and health services, a wider range of jobs, and more avenues for self-improvement and social mobility than their rural counterparts. They are exposed to new consumer goods and are encouraged to delay or limit their childbearing in order to increase their incomes. They also face higher costs in raising children. As a result, urban fertility rates are usually one to two children lower than rural fertility rates.

The urban woman marries on the average at least 1½ years later than the rural woman does. She is more likely to accept the view that fertility should be controlled, and the means for doing so are more likely to be at her disposal.

Population officials in China are hoping that the dramatic increase in the number of people moving into cities will help slow the country's growth. Between 1983 and 1988, the Chinese population has changed from predominantly rural to a population split between urban and rural areas (Gargan, 1988).

PROBLEMS OF OVERPOPULATION

As long as many of the developing nations remain in stage 2 of demographic transition (high fertility but falling mortality), they will continue to be burdened by overpopulation, which slows economic development and creates widespread severe hunger.

The **dependency ratio** is the number of people of nonworking age in a society for every hundred people of working age. Overpopulation undermines economic growth by raising this ratio disproportionately. Because populations at stage 2 have a high proportion of children, compared with adults, they have fewer able-bodied workers than they need. For example, 51 percent of Kenya's population is below the age of 15,

dependency ratio The number of people of nonworking age in a society, for every hundred people of working age.

compared with 22.9 percent in the United States (The World Bank, 1984).

The economic development of countries with high dependency ratios is slowed further by the channeling of capital away from industrialization and technological growth and toward mechanisms for feeding their expanding populations.

How will these problems be resolved in the future? Neo-Malthusians paint a gloomy picture of what lies ahead, contending that as we head toward the end of this century the population inevitably will outpace the available supply of food. Others

believe that we have the technological means to provide all the world's people with food. They speak of a "Green Revolution" in which new breeds of grain and improved fertilizers will raise harvest yields and eliminate the threat of a food shortage. The only thing holding back the revolution is international cooperation in planning the production and distribution of food. However, the Green Revolution, widely proclaimed in the 1970s, has failed to materialize, owing to a number of serious limitations (Brown, 1974; Brown and Eckholm, 1974; Crossen, 1975).

For one thing, there are inherent limits to the land, water, fertilizer, and energy available for food production. The total availability of land, for example, is declining as the climatic drying trend we have seen in recent decades reduces millions of acres of previously arable land to desert. (Hundreds of thousands of people in northern Africa face starvation because of this problem.) In addition, an unhappy paradox links today's increased agricultural production to the possibility of a smaller food production capacity tomorrow. Overfarming and the indiscriminate destruction of forests have increased erosion, and excess fertilization has polluted rivers and lakes, killing fish and threatening the entire food chain. These factors indicate that the problem of widespread hunger is more complicated than the sole fact of a rising world population.

There are inherent limits to the land, water, fertilizer, and energy available for food production. Overfarming and the indiscriminate destruction of forests has produced deserts. Proper use of the land, as seen in this example of terrace farming, can save many people from starvation.

PREDICTIONS OF ECOLOGICAL DISASTER

A group of some one hundred scientists, businesspeople, and academics known as the Club of Rome created great controversy with their predictions of worldwide economic and ecological collapse due to continuing population growth (Meadows et al., 1972). Using elaborate computer models developed at the Massachusetts Institute of Technology, they concluded that the current worldwide trends in population, production, and pollution were on a direct collision course with the production limits imposed by natural resources and the environment's pollution-absorbing capacity.

This "doomsday model" of the future asserts that modern technology is inevitably headed toward the exhaustion of the earth's natural resources. It assumes that we will eventually run out of oil, coal, copper, silver, arable land, and other items vital to production. Further, this model argues that modern technology also is heavily dependent on the environment for waste disposal. Eventually the increased waste from the increased production will go beyond the environment's absorbent capacity. At this point we will not be able to live with our own pollution.

The Club of Rome concluded that if current trends continue, the limits of growth on this planet will be reached within the next 100 years. The result will be a sudden and uncontrollable decline in population and production capacity:

> We have tried in every doubtful case to make the most optimistic estimate of unknown qualities, and we have also ignored discontinuous events such as wars or epidemics, which might act to bring an end to growth even sooner than our model would indicate. In other words, the model is biased to allow growth to continue longer than it probably can continue in the real world. We can thus say with some confidence that under the assumption of no major change in the present system, population and industrial growth will certainly stop within the next century, at the latest. (Meadows et al., 1972)

SOURCES OF OPTIMISM

The gloomy predictions presented by the Club of Rome have sparked a great deal of controversy and criticism. Critics point to a number of logical fallacies in its reasoning. Julian Simon and Herman Kahn (1984) argue that these dire predictions ignore the role of the marketplace in helping to produce adjustments that bring population, re-

sources, and the environment back in balance. They cited evidence that the prices of goods have fallen rather than risen over the long run, and listed the inventions that human ingenuity has produced in response to population growth.

In their optimistic view, population growth is a stimulus, not a deterrent, to economic advance. If imbalances exist, it is because markets are not allowed to operate freely to permit innovators, investors, and entrepreneurs to provide solutions.

Others have questioned the basic assumptions of the "doomsday model," namely, exponential growth in population and production, and absolute limits on natural resources and technological capabilities. The following (McConnell, 1977) are some of these counterarguments:

1. *Wider application of existing technology.* Greater efficiency and wider application of technology on a worldwide basis could continue to supply the world's needs far into the future. For example, it is estimated that greater efficiency in land cultivation would result in increased capacity to feed the world's population for many years. Many poorer countries that now find their agricultural output limited by pest infestation would see rapid improvement if modern technology were applied.

2. *Discovery of new resources.* Some critics also argue that the supply of natural resources is not really as fixed as the doomsday predictors claim. These critics maintain that technological advances can create new uses for formerly worthless substances. In this way new resources come into play that were not previously anticipated. Therefore, technology will stay ahead of resource use, and the doomsday scenario will never be enacted.

3. *Exponential increase in knowledge.* It is further argued that just as the doomsday predictors claim there will be an exponential growth in population and

production, there will also be an exponential growth in knowledge that will enable societies to solve the problems associated with growth. New technological information and discoveries, furthermore, will alleviate new problems as they arise.

Population issues will continue to have an impact on the developed and developing areas of the world. There is a strong trend toward an improving situation. In the next decade we will see whether this trend is developing fast enough to prevent further outbreaks of famine and misery for millions of people.

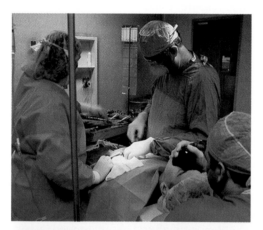

HEALTH CARE IN THE UNITED STATES

In this overview of the traits and processes of human populations, we have examined the ways in which populations interact with their environment. Now it is time to take a closer look at one particular demographic factor — health. Specifically, we shall focus on health care in the United States and consider the fact that such care is not equally distributed throughout the American population.

The United States has the most advanced health-care resources in the world. The average medical bill per person came to $1837 in 1986. That is up from $205 per person in 1965. In 1986 we had 6954 hospitals, 594,700 highly trained physicians, and 1,593,000 nurses, and we are prepared to treat illness and injury with the most modern techniques available *(Statistical Abstract of the United States: 1989).* We can scan a brain for tumors, reconnect nerve tissues and reattach severed limbs through microsurgery, and eliminate diseases like poliomyelitis that crippled a president only

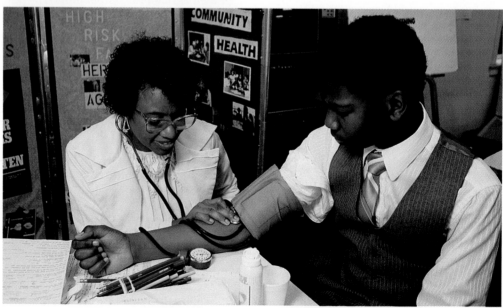

The U.S. has the most advanced health-care resources in the world, yet Americans are not the healthiest people.

———————————————— **TABLE 18.4**
Changes in United States Mortality Rate, 1920–1985

Mortality Data	*1920*	*1950*	*1980*	*1985*
Death rates (per 1000 population)	13.0	9.6	8.8	8.5
Life expectancy	54.1	68.2	73.7	74.9
Infant mortality (per 1000 live births)	*	29.2	12.6	10.6
Maternal mortality (per 1000 live births)	*	83.3	9.2	7.8

* Data not available.

Sources: Mortality Statistics, 1950, Department of Health, Education and Welfare, National Center for Health Statistics; *Monthly Vital Statistics Report,* 22 (13) (June 27, 1974); *U.S. National Health Survey,* Series B-10 and Series 10, No. 95. U.S. Department of Commerce, Bureau of the Census, *Current Population Reports,* and *Statistical Abstract of the United States: 1989* (Washington, D.C.: Government Printing Office, 1989).

a little more than four decades ago. (See Table 18.4 for some major medical advances, as reflected by increased life expectancies and drastically reduced death rates.) We can do all this and much more; yet many would consider our health-care system wholly inadequate to meet the needs of *all* Americans. These critics maintain that the current U.S. health-care system is one that pays off only when the patient can pay.

Even with our large investment in health care, Americans are not the healthiest people in the world. The high death rate among blacks causes the United States to rank twentieth in infant mortality out of twenty-two members of the Organization for Economic Cooperation and Development. United States life expectancy ranks in the lower half of the scale.

POVERTY AND HEALTH

Poverty contributes to disease and a shortened life span both directly and indirectly. It is estimated that some 25 million Americans do not have enough money to feed themselves adequately and as a result suffer from serious nutritional deficiencies that lead to illness and death.

Poverty also produces living conditions that encourage illness. Pneumonia, influenza, tuberculosis, whooping cough, and even rat bites are much more common in poor minority populations than among white, middle-class ones. Inadequate housing, heating, and sanitation all contribute to these acute medical problems.

Health Insurance

Most people pay for their health services through some form of health insurance. In 1986 Americans paid almost $141 billion in insurance premiums *(Statistical Abstract of the United States: 1989).* Poor people, however, cannot afford these premiums or the out-of-pocket expenses required before insurance coverage begins. They receive coverage through the government-sponsored Medicare and Medicaid programs. Medicare covers many of the medical expenses of those over 65, and Medicaid is designed to pay for medical care for those who are below or near the poverty level.

Even with these forms of government insurance, the care that the poor receive is inferior to that received by the more affluent. Many doctors will not accept Medicare or Medicaid assignments, requiring patients to reimburse them for the difference between the insurance coverage and their bill. Moreover, most doctors will not practice in poor neighborhoods, with the result that the poor are relegated to overcrowded, demeaning clinics. Under conditions like these it is no surprise that the poor generally wait longer before seeking medical care than more affluent patients, and many seek medical advice only when they are seriously ill and intervention is already too late.

AGE AND HEALTH

As advances in medical science prolong the life span of most Americans, the problem of medical care for the aged is becoming more acute. Since the turn of the century, the median age of Americans has risen from 22.9 to 31.8. In 1900 there were only 3.1 million Americans age 65 or older, a group that constituted a mere 4 percent of the total population. But by 1986 there were 29.2 million Americans age 65 or older—fully 11.6 percent of the total population. This change in the age structure of the American population has had important consequences for health and health care in the United States.

At the turn of the twentieth century, more Americans were killed by pneumonia, influenza, tuberculosis, infections of the digestive tract, and other diseases caused by microorganisms than by anything else. By comparison, only 8 percent of the population died of heart disease and 4 percent of cancer. Today, this situation is completely reversed. Heart disease, cancer, stroke, and related disorders are now the three most common causes of death. These diseases are tied to the bodily deterioration that is a natural part of the aging process.

The result of these changes in health patterns is increased hospitalization for those over 65. Only 1 percent of all Americans are institutionalized in medical facilities. But of those 65 and older, 5 percent are institutionalized in convalescent homes, homes for the aged, hospitals, and mental hospitals. The elderly are thirty times as likely as people under 65 to be in nursing homes, and, unfortunately, their care is often wholly inadequate.

AIDS

AIDS (Acquired Immune Deficiency Syndrome), a disease now known virtually everywhere, was only identified in 1981, and the retrovirus that causes it was only discovered in 1983. Yet this disease could transform the global future in ways no one imagined even a few years ago. It appears that the impact of this disease in the 1990s could be as great as a major war unless a vaccine or cure can be developed soon.

The vast majority of those infected are young adults who do not realize they are infected, and the numbers are doubling nearly every year. In 6 to 10 years, half those infected will have developed AIDS. Death follows a year or so after the disease emerges. Almost all those infected will be contagious to others for the rest of their lives and will eventually die of AIDS-related diseases.

The transmission of AIDS is also puzzling. It is transmitted sexually but not as easily as is commonly assumed, perhaps because carriers are only intermittently infectious. It takes as long as 2 years before half of the spouses or regular sex partners of infected persons become infected. Half the babies born to infected mothers also become infected and die very young (Platt, 1987).

Up until now, the majority of U.S. victims of AIDS have been male homosexuals. AIDS, however, is not a gay disease; it can be transmitted between any two people of any sex by the exchange of infected blood or semen. AIDS may simply have gotten started most visibly in the gay community because of earlier widespread promiscuity.

AIDS can also be transmitted nonsexually, for example, through the sharing of

WE ALL BEAR THE BURDEN OF AIDS

Population statistics have a way of depersonalizing death. Your response to the fact that by 1991 AIDS will probably be the leading killer of 25- to 44-year-olds may be, "But what does that have to do with me." In short, everything—even if you or a member of your family are never victims of this dread disease. AIDS is burdening every one of us right now, for we all are paying higher costs for hospital care, life insurance, and group health insurance protection.

Hospital care. Going to the hospital will cost us a lot more because of AIDS. Experts predict that the cost of hospital care will rise 20 percent a year over the next few years—an increase brought about by the gap between private and public insurance coverage and the actual cost to care for AIDS patients. The financial burden AIDS is placing on hospitals is causing many of them to cut back on staffing and services in other areas. Family planning programs have suffered, and often there are longer lines in the emergency room and longer waits for elective surgery admissions.

Insurance. By the year 2000, AIDS-related deaths could cost life insurance companies up to $50 billion. These costs will be passed along to every one of us with a life insurance policy—especially in states that restrict the use of blood tests to detect the presence of the AIDS virus.

Employee benefits. Most working people get their health insurance coverage through their employers. With AIDS-related claims skyrocketing over the next few years, it will cost all of us more in the form of larger health insurance premiums and bigger deductibles.

As we confront the reality of these costs, we must also look at what we as a society owe those suffering from AIDS and AIDS-related complex (ARC). (Victims of ARC include the approximately 1.5 million Americans whose blood indicates that they have been infected with the AIDS virus but who have not come down with the actual illness.) These people, who may never get sick or who may not show signs of illness for years, are losing their jobs, being denied housing, and being forced out of school despite the presence of nondiscrimination laws.

Much of the discrimination AIDS victims experience is caused by the fear people have of catching the disease—a fear that has been greatly exaggerated, because AIDS cannot be transmitted through casual contact. Often, our fear is so extreme that we abuse victims' right to privacy. Only the presence of laws insuring confidentiality protects the lives of those afflicted with ARC from being destroyed even before they are sick.

Dollars and cents and issues of nondiscrimination cloud the real tragedy of AIDS—the loss of people at the prime of life.

Sources: Diane Harris, "We'll All Pay," *Money,* November 1987, pp. 109–134; "Fighting AIDS Discrimination," *Time,* September 5, 1988, p. 38; "A Burden Too Heavy to Bear," *Time,* August 31, 1987, p. 39; Bernard M. Dickens, "Legal Rights and Duties in the AIDS Epidemic," *Science,* February 5, 1988, pp. 580–585.

---

infected needles among drug users and accidental contact with infected blood. The spread of AIDS among intravenous drug users is now becoming a major cause of concern in many communities. The mayor of Boston attempted to have a needle exchange program instituted to stop the sharing of needles among drug users as a way of stopping the spread of AIDS.

On a national scale, the spread of AIDS is still small, but there are certain "hot spots." In 1987, the Centers for Disease Control of the U.S. Public Health Service estimated that there were about 1.5 million

Dealing with the Problem of Illegal Immigrants

In May 1988, the United States officially closed the door on illegal immigrants according to the provisions of the new immigration reform bill. The new bill offered illegal immigrants who had been in this country for more than 5 years amnesty and the opportunity to become U.S. citizens. Strict laws were imposed to prevent others from obtaining employment. But legislation alone could not seal the borders, especially the 1936-mile stretch separating the United States from Mexico. During the first 4 months of 1988, some 400,000 illegals were caught trying to cross over from Mexico, a 13 percent increase over the same period a year earlier. Although estimates of the number of illegal aliens residing in the United States are just guesses, numbers range from 4.5 million to 7 million, the vast majority of whom did not apply for amnesty.

That means that millions of people were left untouched by the immigration reform bill and hundred of thousands more will enter our country illegally each year. Like all immigrants before them, they come for the opportunity that America promises — an opportunity that for many is a mixed blessing. Because of their illegal status, they are forced to live in the shadows. They are a frightened underclass, most of whom do not speak English, exploited by unscrupulous employers who know they have no place to turn.

Do illegal aliens have any positive effect on our society? Do they contribute anything of value or do they drain off precious resources from our own poor? The answer is more complex than it might seem.

The debate centers on jobs and wages. Without a doubt, illegal immigrants have taken jobs away from U.S. citizens, but the question must be asked whether these are jobs Americans want. In general, illegal immigrants are unskilled and are forced to find work at the bottom of the economic barrel. They take jobs the natives do not want.

Moreover, many economists and businesspeople argue that illegals help keep jobs in the United States. Says Warren Henderson, a Florida Department of Commerce official: "Without an abundant pool of willing workers at a relatively low cost, many industries will be forced to shut down entirely or move offshore" (*Time*, July 5, 1985). This pattern of employing illegal immigrants at minimum wage, or below, is likely to

infected people in the United States. This amounts to one in thirty men age 30 to 50 carrying the infection. In New York City, however, which has 30 percent of all cases and deaths from the disease, the rates are ten times higher. In that city it is assumed that about one in three men under 50 may be infected. AIDS has become the leading cause of death in New York City for both men and women in their 30s (Platt, 1987).

Infection through drug abuse has made the disease a severe problem in the black and Hispanic communities, as well as in prisons. In some prisons the death rate from AIDS is one hundred times that of the general population (Platt, 1987).

As the death rate from AIDS increases it could have an impact on life expectancy figures. The total deaths of young men already infected could reach 1 million within the next decade, which would be greater than the deaths from all our wars.

The Institute of Medicine of the National Academy of Sciences projects a total of about 270,000 AIDS cases by 1991. If the current situation of thirty to fifty infections being present per diagnosed AIDS case holds, this number of cases would imply

continue despite the harsh penalties imposed on employers by the new immigration reform law. Seeing the benefit in a cheap pool of labor, unscrupulous employers are already devising methods to avoid government detection. Others are simply willing to factor these penalties into the cost of doing business.

Illegals also create new jobs across the economic spectrum. In Los Angeles alone, an estimated 52,000 new jobs have been created for American citizens and legal immigrants to serve the needs of the illegal population. Government services have been forced to expand, offering job opportunities for doctors, nurses, teachers, sanitation workers, and policemen. Ironically, this burgeoning population of illegals has helped create opportunity for blacks to take their rightful place in America's middle class.

Immigrants, both legal and illegal, have another value few recognize. With the U.S. fertility rate stuck at 1.8 births per woman, below the level needed to replace the population, immigrants are essential to maintain population growth. If all immigration ceased immediately, the U.S. population would dwindle from its present 243 million to less than 100 million within 200 years.

The other side of the coin is far less hopeful. Illegals pay limited taxes, and the social services required to meet their needs increase the tax burden of all U.S. citizens, especially those in border states. In addition, many who cross the border illegally are in poor health and often require public medical care. Moreover, a significant percentage of illegal aliens have enough skill to qualify for jobs Americans want and need.

Illegal immigration is a fact of American life that will not go away. With six out of every ten Mexican workers unemployed or underemployed, the thrust across the border is unstoppable despite the severity of our laws. As a nation, we must decide how to handle this critical population problem instead of wishing it would go away.

Sources: "The Unstoppable Surge of Illegal Aliens," *U.S. News & World Report,* June 6, 1988, pp. 36–37; Howard La Franchi, "Aliens without Amnesty Face Life in the Shadows," *Christian Science Monitor,* May 6, 1988, p. 3; "A Most Debated Issue," *Time,* July 8, 1985, p. 75; "Profile of Tomorrow's New U.S." *U.S. News & World Report,* November 24, 1986, p. 32.

some 10 million infections by that time. If only half of those infected get AIDS and die with 10 years, we could have half a million deaths per year in the 1990s. If it reached 1 million per year, the U.S. population would begin to decline.

AIDS is not just a U.S. problem, though. The World Health Organization (WHO) has reports on AIDS from 113 countries. From these reports, it estimates that there will be 100 million infected people worldwide by 1991.

With a projection of about 100 million people infected by 1991, the total worldwide deaths from AIDS in the 1990s could be 50 million. The number infected could double several more times after that, particularly in the poorer countries, before vaccines or drugs could be developed.

The Black Death swept through Europe along the trade routes from Italy to Sweden in 1347–1350, killing some 30 million people out of a population of 75 million in 4 years. Some believe AIDS has the potential to do the same. The main difference with AIDS is that its long period of incubation could cause it to be the Black Death in slow motion (Platt, 1987).

AIDS can be transmitted from parents to children. This child acquired the disease from his mother.

The question of when the AIDS epidemic will level off is the crucial issue in the total impact of AIDS. If AIDS continues its present course, most of humanity will still survive, but by then we will see the development of new social structures and new behaviors.

FAILINGS IN THE U.S. HEALTH-CARE DELIVERY SYSTEM

Are many of the shortcomings of the U.S. health-care system due to the way health care is delivered? Many critics who believe this to be true point to the fact that the United States is the only leading industrial nation that does not have an organized, centrally planned health-care delivery system. In addition, despite attempts to enact some form of comprehensive national health insurance that would guarantee all Americans access to medical care, no plan as yet exists.

The American Medical Association has been a leading opponent of national health insurance and has failed to deal with such other health-care delivery problems as the very uneven geographic distribution of doctors and the overabundance of specialists. In 1986 for example, only 12.1 percent

of the nation's physicians were in general practice, even though many more general practitioners are needed to treat the total population, especially the poor and the elderly. This is partially due to the fact that general practitioners earn less than specialists. In 1986 the average gross earnings for a general practitioner were $181,000, whereas for an obstetrician they were $271,800 and for a plastic surgeon they were $357,200 (*Statistical Abstract of the United States: 1989*).

In essence, because of pressures from the American Medical Association and other sectors of the medical establishment, the United States' health-care system focuses primarily on benefits received by doctors. The fee-for-service system of remuneration gives doctors a vested interest in pathology rather than in good health. Instead of emphasizing preventive medical care, the American health care system emphasizes cure (Friedman and Friedman, 1980). A change in direction is needed to make the health system work for all Americans, no matter what their ages or socioeconomic status.

Our cultural values cause us to approach health and medicine from a particular vantage point. We are conditioned to distrust nature and assume that aggressive medical procedures work better than other approaches. This situation has caused about one quarter of all births in the United States to be by caesarean section. The rate of hysterectomy is twice that in England and three times that in France. Sixty percent of these hysterectomies are performed on women under 44. Our rate of coronary bypass operations is five times that of England.

We tend to be a "can do" society in which doctors emphasize the risk of doing nothing, and minimize the risk doing something. This approach is then coupled with the fact that Americans want to be in perfect health. The result is far more surgery being performed than in any other country. We tend to think that if something is removed, then our health will return (Payer, 1988).

SUMMARY

Demography is the study of the dynamics of human populations. There are three processes that influence populations: fertility, mortality, and migration. Fertility refers to the actual number of births in the population and is measured by the crude birthrate and the fertility rate. Mortality refers to the frequency of actual deaths in a population and is measured by the crude death rate and age-specific death rates. Migration is the movement of populations from one geographic area to another.

Theories of population growth include the Malthusian theory, proposed by Thomas Robert Malthus, which states that populations will always grow faster than the available food supply will; the Marxist theory, which links industrialism and capitalism to population growth; and demographic transition theory, which states that societies have four distinct stages of population change.

The population of the world is doubling every 42 years. However, a slowing trend is now being seen as increased education, government propaganda, contraception, and changing societal norms influence families to have fewer children. Overpopulation channels the capital of underdeveloped nations away from industrialization and technological growth into mechanisms for feeding expanding populations. Despite huge government efforts to feed the masses, between one and two billion people are currently undernourished. Citing these staggering statistics, neo-Malthusians argue that as we head toward the year 2000, the population inevitably will outpace the available food supply. Others see a "Green Revolution" in which new and improved agricultural techniques will eliminate the threat of a food shortage.

According to the demographic transition theory, societies pass through four stages of population change. During stage 1, high fertility rates are counterbalanced by a high death rate due to disease, starvation, and natural disaster. The population tends to be very young, and there is little or no population growth. During stage 2, populations rapidly increase as a result of a continued high fertility that is linked to the increased food supply, development of modern medicine, and public health care. Slowly, however, the traditional institutions and religious beliefs that support a high birthrate are undermined and replaced by values stressing individualism and upward mobility. Family planning is introduced, and the birthrate begins to fall. This is stage 3, during which population growth begins to decline. Finally, in stage 4 both fertility and mortality are relatively low, and population growth once again is stabilized.

There are a substantial number of factors that enter into determining the typical family size in a country. They include the average age of marriage, breast-feeding, infant and child mortality, gender preferences, benefits and costs of children, contraception, income level, the education of women, and whether people live in urban or rural environments.

The U.S. health-care system does not serve all people equally. Even though the United States has the most advanced health-care system in the world, the poor and the elderly are underserved and often receive inferior care. Critics charge that a health-care system that is oriented toward care rather than health maintenance serves the needs of the nation's doctors rather than its citizens.

Chapter 19

URBAN SOCIETY

They tell me you are wicked and I believe
   them, for I have seen your painted women
   under the gas lamps luring farm boys.
And they tell me you are crooked and I
   answer: Yes, it is true I have seen the
   gunman kill and go free to kill again.
And they tell me you are brutal and my reply
   is: On the faces of women and children I
   have seen the marks of wanton hunger.

And having answered so I turn once more to
   those who sneer at this my city, and I give
   them back the sneer and say to them:
Come and show me another city with lifted
   head singing so proud to be alive and
   coarse and strong and cunning . . .

Carl Sandburg, *Chicago Poems,* 1916

Stand in your window and scan the sights,
On Broadway with its bright white lights.
Its dashing cabs and cabarets,
Its painted women and fast cafés.
That's when you really see New York.
Vulgar of manner, overfed,
Overdressed and underbred.
Heartless and Godless, Hell's delight,
Rude by day and lewd by night.

Anonymous, 1916, cited in Palen, 1987

The two poems that you have just read display the range of responses to the city. At one and the same time we are fascinated by cities, as well as terrified and revolted by them. Most of us now live in urban environments, and we have found ways of adjusting to city life. In this chapter we will attempt to gain a better understanding of our urban society and the impact it has on people.

THE DEVELOPMENT OF CITIES

According to archeologists, people have been on the earth for a couple of million years. During the vast majority of that time human beings lived without cities. In spite of the fact that today we accept cities as a fundamental and basic part of human life, cities are a relatively recent addition to the story of human evolution, appearing only within the last 7000 to 9000 years.

The city's dominance in social, economic, and cultural affairs is even more recent. Nonetheless, what we label "civilization" only emerged during the time span that coincides with the city. The whole history of human triumphs and tragedies is encompassed within this period. The very terms "civilization" and "civilized" come from the Latin *civis,* which means a person living in a city.

The cities of the past were still very unusual in an overwhelmingly rural world of small villages. In the year 1800, 97 percent of the world lived in rural areas of fewer than 5000 people. By the year 1900, 86 percent of the world still lived in rural areas (Palen, 1987).

England was the first country to undergo an urban transformation. One hundred years ago it was the only predominantly urban country. It was not until 1920 that the United States held the same distinction.

Today we are on the threshold of living in a world that will for the first time be more urban than rural. Currently, some 45 percent of the world's population is urban. By the year 2000 it will increase to more than half (Hauser and Gardner, 1982).

Not all of the world is urbanizing at the same pace though. In the more industrialized areas of the world — North America, Europe, and the Soviet Union — urban growth has either stopped or slowed considerably (Spates and Macionis, 1987). For example, in 1970, 73.5 percent of the U.S. population lived in urban areas, whereas in 1980 it had increased to only 73.7 percent *(Statistical Abstract of the United States: 1989).*

The area of greatest urban growth is now in the nonindustrial world, such as Latin America, Africa, the Middle East, and Asia. In fact, the ten countries with the highest urban growth rates are all in these four areas, and the ten with the *lowest* are all, with one exception (Uruguay in South America), in western Europe (Kurian, 1984).

Already there are 118 cities of more than 1 million people in the less developed countries. Most of us have never heard the names of more than a few of these cities. The United Nations projects that by the year 2000 there will be 284 such cities. By that year the population projections for Mexico City are 26.3 million, for São Paulo,

Brazil, 24 million, and 16.6 million for Calcutta (Palen, 1987).

The rapid transformation from a basically rural to a heavily urbanized world, along with the urban life-styles that accompany this shift are having a dramatic impact on the world's peoples. In this chapter we will examine the historical development of cities and urbanization trends.

THE EARLIEST CITIES

Two requirements had to be met for cities to emerge. The first was that there had to be a surplus of food and other necessities. Farmers had to be able to produce more food than their immediate families needed to survive. This surplus made it possible for some people to live in places where they could not produce their own food and had to depend on others to supply their needs. These settlements could become relatively large, densely populated, and permanent.

The second requirement was that there had to be some form of social organization that went beyond the family. Even though there might be a surplus of food, there was no guarantee that it would be distributed to those in need of it. Consequently, a form of social organization adapted to these kinds of living environments had to emerge.

The world's first fully developed cities arose in the Middle Eastern area, mostly in what is now Iraq, which was the site of the Sumerian civilization. The land is watered by the giant Tigris and Euphrates rivers, and it yielded an abundant food surplus for the people who farmed there. In addition, this area (called Mesopotamia) lay at the crossroads of the trade networks that already, 6000 years ago, tied together East and West. Not only material goods but also the knowledge of technological and social innovations traveled along these routes.

Sumerian cities were clustered around temple compounds that were raised high up on brick-sheathed mounds called *ziggurats*. The cities and their surrounding farmlands were believed to belong to the city god, who

Artists' conceptions of the early cities were often not very flattering. Pieter Bruegel painted this "Tower of Babel" scene to depict the fifth-century B.C. ziggurat of Babylon.

lived inside the temple and ruled through a class of priests who organized trade caravans and controlled all aspects of the economy. In fact, these priests invented the world's first system of writing as well as numerical notation late in the fourth millennium B.C. in order to keep track of their commercial transactions. Because warfare both among cities and against marauders from the deserts was chronic, many of these early cities were walled and fortified, and they maintained standing armies. In time the generals who were elected to lead these armies were kept permanently in place, and their positions evolved into that of a hereditary kingship (Frankfort, 1956).

These early Sumerian cities had populations that ranged between 7000 and 20,000. However, one Sumerian city, Uruk, extended over 1100 acres and contained as many as 50,000 people (Gist and Fava, 1974). By today's standards the populations of these early cities seem rather small. They do, however, present a marked contrast with the small nomadic and seminomadic bands of individuals that existed prior to the emergence of these cities.

Within the next 1500 years, cities arose across all of the ancient world. Memphis was built around 3200 B.C. as the capital of Egypt, and between 2500 and 2000 B.C. major cities were built in what is now Pakistan. The two largest, Harappa and Mohenjo-Daro, were the most advanced cities of their day. They were carefully planned in a modern grid pattern with central grain warehouses and elaborate water systems, including wells and underground drainage. The houses of the wealthy were large and multistoried, built of fired brick in neighborhoods that were separated from the humble dried-mud dwellings of the common laborers. Like the Sumerian cities, they were supported by a surplus-producing agricultural peasantry and were organized around central temple complexes.

By 2400 B.C. cities were established in Europe, and by 1850 B.C. in China. No fully developed cities were erected in the Americas until some 1500 years later during the so-called Late Preclassic times (300 B.C. to 300 A.D.). In Africa, cities of prosperous traders appeared around 1000 A.D. in Ghana and Zimbabwe (formerly Rhodesia).

PREINDUSTRIAL CITIES

preindustrial cities Cities established before the Industrial Revolution. These cities were usually walled for protection, and power was typically shared between feudal lords and religious leaders.

Preindustrial cities — so named to indicate their establishment before the Industrial Revolution — housed only 5 to 10 percent of a country's population. In fact, most preindustrial cities had populations of less than 10,000. They often were walled for protection and densely packed with residents whose occupations, religion, and social class were clearly evident from symbols of dress, heraldic imagery, and manners. Power typically was shared between the feudal lords and religious leaders.

These cities often served as the seats of political power and as commercial, religious, and educational centers. Their populations were usually stratified into a broad-based pyramid of social classes: A small ruling elite sat at the top; a small middle class of entrepreneurs rested just beneath;

and a very large, impoverished class of manual laborers (artisans and peasants) was at the bottom. Religious institutions were strong, well established, and usually tightly interconnected with political institutions, the rule of which they supported and justified in theological terms. Art and education flowered (at least among the upper classes), but these activities were strongly oriented toward expressing or exploring religious ideologies.

Gideon Sjoberg (1965) has noted that three things were necessary for the rise of preindustrial cities. First, it was necessary that there be a favorable physical environment. Second, some advanced technology in either agricultural or nonagricultural areas had to have developed in order to provide a means of shaping the physical environment — if only to produce the enormous food surplus necessary to feed city dwellers. Finally, a well-developed system of social structures had to emerge so that the more complex needs of society could be met: an economic system, a system of social control, and a political system were needed.

INDUSTRIAL CITIES

We use the term *Industrial Revolution* to refer to the application of scientific methods to production and distribution, wherein machines were used to perform work that had formerly been done by humans or farm animals. Food, clothing, and other necessities could be produced and distributed quickly and efficiently, freeing some people — the social elite — to engage in other activities.

The Industrial Revolution of the nineteenth century forever changed the face of the world. It created new forms of work, new institutions, and new social classes and multiplied many times over the speed with which humans could exploit the resources of their environment. In England, where the Industrial Revolution began about 1750, the introduction of the steam engine was a major stimulus for such changes. This engine required large amounts of coal, which

England had, and made it possible for cities to be established in areas other than ports and trade centers through its use for transportation vehicles. Work could take place wherever there were coal deposits; industries grew; and workers streamed in to fill the resulting jobs. Thus, industrial cities arose, cities with populations that were much larger than those of preindustrial times.

Nineteenth-century urban industrialization produced industrial slums which were seen as some of the worst results of capitalism. Fredrich Engels (1973), a close associate of Karl Marx, described the horrors of one of these areas.

> The view from this bridge—mercifully concealed from smaller mortals by a parapet as high as a man—is quite characteristic of the entire district. At the bottom the Irk flows, or rather stagnates. It is a narrow, coal-black stinking river full of filth and garbage which it deposits on the lower-lying bank. In dry weather, an extended series of the most revolting blackish green pools of slime remain standing on this bank, out of whose depths bubbles of miasmatic gases constantly rise and give forth a stench that is unbearable even on the bridge forty or fifty feet above the level of the water.

Modern-day **industrial cities** are large and expansive, often with no clear physical boundary that separates them from surrounding towns and suburbs. They house a relatively high percentage of the society's population, which works primarily in industrial or service-related jobs. Like the preindustrial cities before them, industrial cities are divided into neighborhoods that reflect differences in social class and ethnicity. (See Table 19.1 for a comparison of the preindustrial and industrial city.)

The industrial cities of today have become centers for banking and manufacturing. Their streets are designed for autos and trucks as well as for pedestrians, and they feature mass transportation systems. They are stratified, but class lines often become

The Industrial Revolution created new forms of work. In this photo, taken in 1911, a young woman is seen taking home piecework.

blurred. The elite class is large and consists of business and financial leaders as well as some professionals and scientists. There is a large middle class consisting of white-collar salaried workers and professionals, such as sales personnel, technicians, teachers, and social workers.

Formal, political bureaucracies with elected political officeholders at the top govern the industrial city. Religious institutions no longer are tightly intertwined with the political system, and the arts and education are secular with a strong technological orientation. Mass media disseminate news and pattern the consumption of material goods as well as most aesthetic experiences. Subcultures proliferate, and ethnic diversity often is great. As the industrial city grows, it spreads out, creating a phenomenon known as *urbanization.*

industrial cities Cities established during or after the Industrial Revolution, characterized by large populations that work primarily in industrial or service-related jobs.

URBANIZATION

The vast majority of the people in the United States live in urban areas. We should not confuse urban areas with cities. In fact, there are several terms that often are

——————————————————————— **TABLE 19.1**
Comparison of the Preindustrial City and the Industrial City

	Preindustrial City	*Industrial City*
Physical characteristics	A small, walled, fortified, densely populated settlement, containing only a small part of the population in the society	A large, expansive settlement with no clear physical boundaries, containing a large proportion of the population in the society
Transportation	Narrow streets, made for travel by foot or horseback	Wide streets, designed for motorized vehicles
Functions	Seat of political power; commercial, religious, and educational center	Manufacturing and business center of an industrial society
Political structure	Governed by a small, ruling elite, determined by heredity	Governed by a larger elite made up of business and financial leaders and some professionals
Social structure	A rigid class structure	Less rigidly stratified but still containing clear class distinctions
Religious institutions	Strong, well established, tightly connected with political and economic institutions	Weaker, with fewer formal ties to other social institutions
Communication	Primarily oral, with little emphasis on record keeping beyond mercantile data; all records handwritten	Primarily written, with extensive record keeping; use of mechanized print media
Education	Religious and secular education for upper-class males	Secular education for all classes but with differences related to social class

city An area that typically has been incorporated according to the laws of the state within which it is located.

used inappropriately when cities or urban areas are discussed that must be clarified. Thus, when we discuss cities, we are referring to something that has a legal definition. A **city** is a unit that typically has been incorporated according to the laws of the state within which it is located. Legal and political boundaries may be quite arbitrary, however, and a "city-type," or urban, environment may exist in an area that is not

officially known as a city. For example, in New England there are places known as towns—such as Framingham, Massachusetts, with a population of nearly 70,000— that for all practical purposes should be known as cities. Yet, they do not adopt the city form of government, with a mayor, a city council, and so on because of an attachment to the town council form of government.

WILLIAM H. WHYTE ON THE IMPACT OF THE CITY ON THE INDIVIDUAL

Thirty-three years ago William H. Whyte wrote the classic book The Organization Man. *Since that time his interests have moved into the area of urban environments and the impact they have on people. For the past 16 years William Whyte has been walking the streets of the city, with a camera and notebook in hand. For this interview we asked him about his pioneering work on pedestrian behavior and city dynamics.*

*Q*uestion: What do you think of the older cities?

Answer: I grew up in the northeast. It is amazing how well the older cities work. They started with a very tight grid system and more or less stuck to it. Boston has a fascinating center city, as does New York City and Philadelphia. The good cities are all walking cities. They do not spill out into a dribble drabble of parking and freeways.

Q: What about the newer cities?

A: The really new cities, particularly in the southwest, like Phoenix, put all their bets on the car. Half the city is given over to parking. There are better uses for space in the city than a bunch of cars. I am in favor of less parking.

It is good I am not running for office.

Q: What about gentrification?

A: The damage was done before the middle class showed up. Gentrification is not the fault of young couples fixing up townhouses. There has been no affordable housing built in this country for the last 10 years. Now there is a shortage of housing. We should try to get more affordable units.

Q: What do you think of the large office parks springing up in the suburbs?

A: A more dismal thing you are not likely to see. They are not real communities. I talked to people in office parks. They pointed out the parking and the convenience, and then they said, "I hate it."

Q: What do you think of the trend of many businesses leaving the city?

A: I looked at the exodus of companies from New York City. I followed their investment performance for the years after their move. The companies did markedly less well than those that stayed in the city. If you move from the city you lose something. It may be tranquil, but it is not where the core is.

Q: What about suburban malls?

A: Suburban malls are a very successful institution. They are an excellent distribution method for a middle range of goods. But they have hurt cities a great deal. Their hallmark is that they are hermetically sealed. You cannot see in or out. There is a real conflict between malls and downtown busi-

nesses. The worst mistake is to copy them and move them into the city. Look at the Renaissance Center in Detroit. It did not do well. Planners thought that to draw people back into the city you had to give them safety. But people do not go to the city for safety.

Q: What do people want in public spaces?

A: They are likely to say they want lots of greenery and peace and quiet, but they don't really. There is a tendency for them to cluster. They tend to seek out other people.

Q: What do people do that contradicts common sense?

A: A lot of business conferences on rather touchy matters take place on the streets. You will see three people — it's two o'clock and the others have gone back to work — but they are not quite finished yet. One says, "Hey, Charlie, we forgot the deal." Why, of all places, do they do this on a busy street corner? Because both sides are there on equal footing. Nobody is the host. They do not want to be on the other person's turf.

The legal boundaries of a city seldom encompass all the people and businesses that depend on the city or have an impact on it. The U.S. Bureau of the Census has realized that it is necessary to consider the entire population in and around the city.

urban population The inhabitants of an urbanized area and the inhabitants of incorporated or unincorporated areas with a population of 2500 or more.

metropolitan area An area that has a large population nucleus, together with the adjacent communities that are economically and socially integrated into that nucleus.

metropolitan statistical area (MSA) An area that has either one or more central cities, each with a population of at least 50,000, or a single urbanized area that has at least 50,000 people and that is part of an MSA with a total population of 100,000.

urbanized area An area that contains a central city and the continuously built-up and closely settled surrounding territory that together have a population of 50,000 or more.

urbanization A process whereby a population becomes concentrated in a specific area because of migration patterns.

CLASSIFICATION OF URBAN ENVIRONMENTS

The legal boundaries of a city seldom encompass all the people and businesses that have an impact on that city. The U.S. Bureau of the Census has realized that for many purposes it is necessary to consider the entire population in and around the city that may be affected by the social and economic aspects of an urban environment. As a result, the bureau recognized the need for a complex set of terms to describe and classify urban environments. As of 1982 the terms the Bureau of the Census applies to urban data included urbanized area, urban population, metropolitan statistical area, primary metropolitan statistical area, and consolidated metropolitan statistical area (Federal Committee on Standard Metropolitan Statistical Areas, 1979).

An **urbanized area** contains a central city and the continuously built-up, closely settled surrounding territory that together have a population of 50,000 or more. The term thus refers to the actual urban population of an area regardless of the political boundaries, such as county or state lines. This term is often confused with **urbanization,** which refers to the process whereby a population becomes concentrated in a spe-

cific area because of migration patterns. More simply, *urbanized area* refers to a certain place, and *urbanization* refers to a set of events that are taking place.

Urban population refers to the inhabitants of an urbanized area and the inhabitants of incorporated or unincorporated areas with a population of 2500 or more.

A **metropolitan area** is an area that has a large population nucleus, together with the adjacent communities that are economically and socially integrated into that nucleus (U.S. Department of Commerce, 1983). A metropolitan area emerges as an industrial city expands ever outward, incorporating towns and villages in its systems of highways, mass transportation, industry, and government.

A **metropolitan statistical area (MSA)** has either one or more central cities, each with a population of at least 50,000, or a single urbanized area that has at least 50,000 people and that is part of an MSA with a total population of 100,000. Each MSA also contains at least one central county; more than half the population of an MSA resides in these central counties. There also may be outlying counties that are more rural but have close economic and social ties to the central counties, cities, and urbanized areas in the MSA.

An MSA with more than 1 million people may contain one or more **primary metropolitan statistical areas (PMSAs),** which consist of a large, urbanized county or cluster of counties.

Expanding metropolitan areas draw on surrounding areas for their labor pool and other resources to such an extent that all levels of planning—from the building of airports, sports complexes, and highway and railroad systems to the production of electric power and the zoning of land for industrial use—must increasingly be undertaken with their possible effects on entire regions kept in mind. In America the most dramatic examples of this trend are the Los Angeles metropolitan area, the Dallas-Fort Worth area, and the so-called "Boswash," a 500-mile northeast corridor from Washington, D.C., to Boston, Massachusetts, that includes 60 million people and is forming one enormous metropolis—sometimes called a megalopolis—with New York City as its hub. A **megalopolis** is a metropolitan area with a population of 1 million or more that consists of two or more smaller metropolitan areas. To the federal government, these are known as **consolidated metropolitan statistical areas (CMSAs).**

Despite the much-heralded flow of population to nonmetropolitan areas, more than one-third of all Americans live in the country's twenty-three megalopolises, or CMSAs. New York-northern New Jersey-Long Island ranks first among the megalopolises/CMSAs in population size, and it will continue to be number one well into the future. However, the Houston-Galveston-Brazoria area in Texas should experience the most rapid rate of population growth of any CMSA (see Table 19.2).

Basically, then, the United States can be seen as a three-tiered system of metropolitan areas: 257 freestanding MSAs; 78 larger PMSAs; and 23 very large CMSAs.

Before a city grows outward to form a metropolitan area or become part of a megalopolis, it has gone through certain internal developments that establish the placement of various types of industrial, commercial, and residential areas.

THE STRUCTURE OF CITIES

The community and the city have been two of the primary areas of study ever since the beginning of American sociology. In the 1920s classical *human ecology* blossomed under the leadership of Robert Park and Ernest Burgess at the University of Chicago. The early human ecologists were attempting to systematically apply the basic theoretical scheme of plant and animal ecology to human communities.

Theories of human communities were developed that were analogous to theories explaining plant and animal development. For example, if you were to drive from the mountains to the desert, you would find that different soil, water, and climate conditions produce entirely different types of vegetation. By analogy, driving from a city's business district to its suburbs, you will also notice different types of communities based on a competition for specific types of land use.

In fact, the human ecologists believed human communities could be understood from a Darwinian perspective. Communities and cities have evolved and changed as a consequence of competition for prime space and of invasion, succession, and segregation of new groups.

Park and Burgess and other members of the Chicago school of sociologists studied

The 500-mile northeast corridor from Washington, D.C., to Boston includes 60 million people. Shuttle flights between the cities make it possible for distances to seem insignificant.

primary metropolitan statistical area (PMSA) A large urbanized county or cluster of counties that is part of a metropolitan statistical area with one million people or more.

megalopolis Another term for consolidated metropolitan statistical area. See CMSA for definition.

consolidated metropolitan statistical area (CMSA) A metropolitan area with a population of one million or more that consists of two or more smaller metropolitan areas.

TABLE 19.2

CMSAs Ranked by 1987 Population and Rate of Population Growth, 1980–1990

CMSAs Ranked by 1987 Population		CMSAs Ranked by Projected Rate of Population Growth, 1980–1990	
1. New York-Northern New Jersey-Long Island, NY-NJ-CT*	18,054,000	1. Houston-Galveston-Brazoria, TX	31.8%
2. Los Angeles-Anaheim-Riverside, CA	13,471,000	2. Miami-Fort Lauderdale, FL	19.2
3. Chicago-Gary-Lake County, IL-IN-WI	8,147,000	3. Denver-Boulder, CO	18.6
4. San Francisco-Oakland-San Jose, CA	5,953,000	4. Dallas-Fort Worth, TX	16.6
5. Philadelphia-Wilmington-Trenton, PA-NJ-DE-MD	5,891,000	5. Seattle-Tacoma, WA	14.3
6. Detroit-Ann Arbor, MI	4,629,000	6. Portland-Vancouver, OR-WA	13.9
7. Boston-Lawrence-Salem-Lowell-Brockton, MA-NH*	4,093,000	7. Providence-Pawtucket-Woonsocket, RI*	13.6
8. Dallas-Fort Worth, TX	3,725,000	8. San Francisco-Oakland-San Jose, CA	12.6
9. Houston-Galveston-Brazoria, TX	3,626,000	9. Los Angeles-Anaheim-Riverside, CA	11.8
10. Miami-Fort Lauderdale, FL	2,954,000	10. Cincinnati-Hamilton, OH-KY-IN	5.9
11. Cleveland-Akron-Lorain, OH	2,767,000	11. Kansas City, MO-KS	5.7
12. St. Louis-East St. Louis-Alton, MO-IL	2,458,000	12. Chicago-Gary-Lake County, IL-IN-WI	5.6
13. Seattle-Tacoma, WA	2,341,000	13. Detroit-Ann Arbor, MI	5.2
14. Pittsburgh-Beaver Valley, PA	2,296,000	14. Milwaukee-Racine, WI	4.5
15. Denver-Boulder, CO	1,861,000	15. Boston-Lawrence-Salem-Lowell-Brockton, MA-NH*	4.5
16. Cincinnati-Hamilton, OH-KY-IN	1,715,000	16. Hartford-New Britain-Middletown-Bristol, CT*	4.0
17. Milwaukee-Racine, WI	1,562,000	17. St. Louis-East St. Louis, Alton, MO-IL	3.5
18. Kansas City, MO-KS	1,546,000	18. Philadelpia-Wilmington-Trenton, PA-NJ-DE-MD	3.0
19. Portland-Vancouver, OR-WA	1,383,000	19. New York-Northern New Jersey-Long Island, NY-NJ-CT*	2.6
20. Buffalo-Niagara Falls, NY	1,175,000	20. Cleveland-Akron-Lorain, OH	2.4
21. Providence-Pawtucket-Woonsocket, RI*	1,118,000	21. Pittsburgh-Beaver Valley, PA	2.0
22. Hartford-New Britain-Middletown-Bristol, CT*	1,057,000	22. Buffalo-Niagara Falls, NY	−0.1

* New England County Metropolitan Areas

Source: U.S. Department of Commerce, Bureau of the Census, *Statistical Abstract of the United States: 1989* (Wasington, D.C.: Government Printing Office, 1989), pp. 29–31.

the internal structure of cities as revealed by what they called the ecological patterning (or spatial distribution) of urban groups. In investigating the ways in which cities are patterned by their social and economic systems and by the availability of land, these sociologists proposed a theory based on concentric circles of development.

Concentric Zone Model

The **concentric zone model,** sometimes irreverently called the bull's-eye model, is illustrated in Figure 19.1 (Park, Burgess, and McKenzie, 1925). According to this perspective, the typical city has at its center a business district made up of various kinds of office buildings and shops. Radiating out from the business district is a series of adjacent zones: (1) a transitional zone of low-income, crowded but unstable, residential housing with high crime rates, prostitution, gambling, and other vices; (2) a working-class residential zone; (3) a middle-class residential zone; and (4) an upper-class residential zone in what we would now think of as the suburbs. These zones reflect the fact that urban groups are in competition for limited space and that not all space is equally desirable in terms of its location and resources.

concentric zone model A theory of city development in which the central city is made up of a business district and, radiating from this district are zones of low-income, working-class, middle-class, and upper-class residential housing.

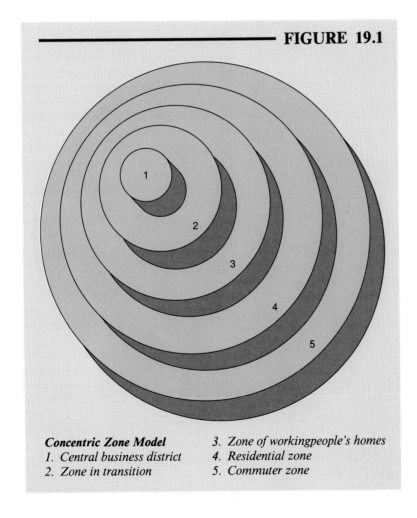

FIGURE 19.1

Concentric Zone Model
1. *Central business district*
2. *Zone in transition*
3. *Zone of workingpeople's homes*
4. *Residential zone*
5. *Commuter zone*

The concentric zone model initially was quite influential in that it did reflect the structure of certain cities, especially those like Chicago that developed quickly early in the Industrial Revolution, before the development of mass transportation and the automobile introduced the complicating factor of increased mobility. It did not, however, describe many other cities satisfactorily, and other models were needed.

Sector Model

In the 1930s Homer Hoyt (1943) developed a modified version of the concentric zone model that attempted to take into account the influence of urban transportation systems. He agreed with the notion that a business center lies at the heart of a city but abandoned the tight geometrical symmetry of the concentric zones. Hoyt suggested that the structure of the city could be better represented by a **sector model,** in which urban groups establish themselves along major transportation arteries (railroad lines, waterways, and highways). Then, as the city becomes more crowded and desirable land is even farther from its heart, each sector remains associated with an identifiable group but extends its boundaries toward the city's edge (see Figure 19.2).

sector model A modified version of the concentric zone model in which urban groups establish themselves along major transportation arteries around the central business district.

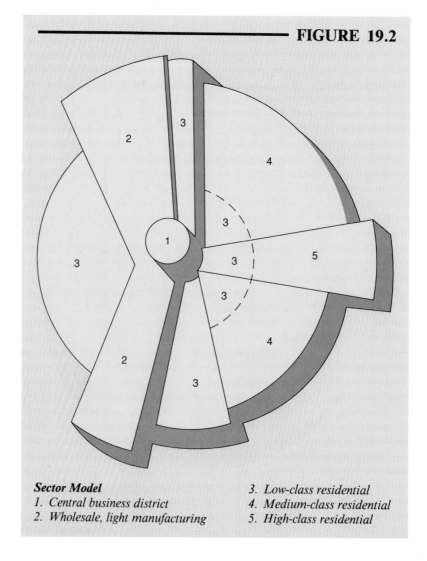

FIGURE 19.2

Sector Model
1. *Central business district*
2. *Wholesale, light manufacturing*
3. *Low-class residential*
4. *Medium-class residential*
5. *High-class residential*

Multiple Nuclei Model

A third ecological model, developed at roughly the same time as the sector model, stresses the impact of land costs, interest-rate schedules, and land-use patterns in determining the structure of cities. This **multiple nuclei model** (Harris and Ullman, 1945) emphasizes the fact that different industries have different land-use and financial re-

quirements, which determine where they establish themselves (see Figure 19.3). Some industries, such as scrap metal yards, need to be near railroad lines. Others, such as plants manufacturing airplanes or automobiles, need a great deal of space. Still others, such as dressmaking factories, can be squeezed into several floors of central business district buildings. Thus, similar industries tend to be established near one another, and the immediate neighborhood is

multiple nuclei model A theory of city development that emphasizes the fact that different industries have different land-use and financial requirements, which determine where they establish themselves. As similar industries are established close to one another, the immediate neighborhood is strongly shaped by the nature of its typical industry, becoming one of a number of separate nuclei that together constitute the city.

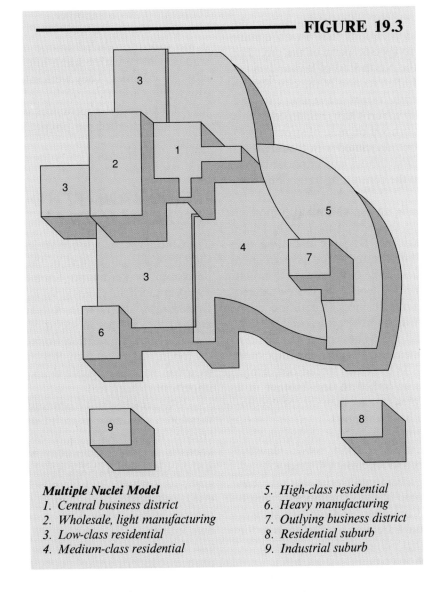

FIGURE 19.3

Multiple Nuclei Model
1. *Central business district*
2. *Wholesale, light manufacturing*
3. *Low-class residential*
4. *Medium-class residential*
5. *High-class residential*
6. *Heavy manufacturing*
7. *Outlying business district*
8. *Residential suburb*
9. *Industrial suburb*

strongly shaped by the nature of its typical industry, becoming one of a number of separate nuclei that together constitute the city. In this model, a city's growth is marked by an increase in the number and kinds of nuclei that compose it.

The limitations of the ecological approach to studying urban structure is that it downplays variables that often strongly influence urban residential and land-use patterns. For instance, the ethnic composition of a city may be a powerful influence on its structure: A city with but one or two resident ethnic groups will look very different from a city with many. Another important variable is the local culture—the history and traditions that attach certain meanings to specific parts of the city. For example, the North End of Boston has become the Italian section of the city. People who normally might leave the city and move to the suburbs have remained in this city neighborhood because of strong ties to the traditions associated with that area. Indeed, cultural factors are important contributors to the continuing trend of urbanization.

The early ecologists could not predict some of the trends that have taken place since World War II. Since that time our eastern and midwestern cities have declined in population while the sprawling Sun Belt cities of the South and West have gained population and business. In addition, cities everywhere are more decentralized because of the automobile. The central business districts of cities have become less important over time. As the cities spread out, urban areas become linked to one another in a more complex manner than the early ecologists could have imagined.

Contemporary urban ecologists (Exline, Peters, and Larkin, 1982; Hawley, 1981; Berry and Kasarda, 1977) have developed more advanced theories that take into account some of the contemporary developments. Computers and modern statistical techniques are now used to analyze the variables that influence the growth and development of a city.

Gemeinschaft A community in which relationships are intimate, cooperative, and personal.

Gesellschaft A society in which relationships are impersonal and independent.

THE NATURE OF URBAN LIFE

Ever since sociologists began writing about communities, they have been concerned with differences between rural and urban societies and with changes that take place as society moves away from small homogeneous settlements to modern-day urban centers. These changes have been accompanied by a shift in the way people interact and cooperate with one another.

The "Chicago school" of sociology, as it was called, produced a large number of studies dealing with human interaction in city communities. They were interested in discovering how the sociological, psychological, and moral experiences of city life were a reflection of the physical environment.

GEMEINSCHAFT TO *GESELLSCHAFT*

The Chicago sociologists in their studies of the city were using some of the concepts developed by Ferdinand Tönnies (1865–1936), a German sociologist. In his book *Gemeinschaft und Gesellschaft,* Tönnies examined the changes in social relations attributable to the transition from rural society (organized around small communities) to urban society (organized around large impersonal structures).

In a **Gemeinschaft** (community), Tönnies noted, relationships are intimate, cooperative, and personal. The exchange of goods is based on reciprocity and barter, and people look out for the well-being of the group as a whole. In a **Gesellschaft** (society), relationships are impersonal and independent—people look out for their own interests, goods are bought and sold, and formal contracts govern economic exchanges. Modern urban society is, in Tön-

A small town is likely to produce a Gemein-schaft, in which relationships are intimate, cooperative, and personal; a city is likely to produce a Gesell-schaft, in which relationships are impersonal and people look out for their own interests.

nies's terms, typically a *Gesellschaft,* whereas rural areas retain the more intimate qualities of a *Gemeinschaft.*

For example, among the Amish there is such a strong community spirit that should a barn burn down, members of the community will quickly come together to rebuild it. In just a matter of days a new barn will be standing—the work of community members who feel a strong tie and responsibility to another community member who has encountered some misfortune.

In a *Gesellschaft* everyone is seen as an individual who may be in competition with others who happen to share a living space. Tönnies saw *Gesellschaft* as the end product of mid-nineteenth-century social changes that grew out of industrialization, in which people no longer automatically want to help one another or to share freely what they have. There is little sense of identification with others in a *Gesellschaft,* in which each individual strives for advantages and regards the accumulation of goods and possessions as more important than the quality of personal ties.

In small rural communities and preliterate societies the family provided the context in which people lived, worked, were socialized, were cared for when ill or infirm, and practiced their religion. In contrast, modern urban society has produced many secondary groups in which these needs are

met. It also offers far more options and choices than did the society of Tönnies's *Gemeinschaft:* educational options, career options, life-style options, choice of marriage partner, choice of whether or not to have children, and choice of where to live. In this sense the person living in today's urban *Gesellschaft* is freer.

MECHANICAL TO ORGANIC SOLIDARITY

Tönnies wrote about communities and cities from the standpoint of what we described in Chapter 6 as an "ideal type," in that no community or city actually could conform to the definitions he presented. They are basically concepts that help us understand the differences between the two. In the same sense Émile Durkheim devised ideas about mechanical and organic solidarity.

According to Durkheim, every society has a **collective conscience**—a system of fundamental beliefs and values. These beliefs and values define for its members the characteristics of the "good society," which is one that meets needs for individuality, for security, for superiority over others, and for any of a host of other values that could become important to the people in that society. **Social solidarity** emerges from the peo-

collective conscience A society's system of fundamental beliefs and values.

social solidarity People's commitment and conformity to a society's collective conscience.

mechanically integrated society A type of society in which members have common goals and values and a deep and personal involvement with the community.

organically integrated society A type of society in which social solidarity depends on the cooperation of individuals in many different positions who perform specialized tasks.

An organically integrated society depends on the cooperation of individuals in many different positions who perform specialized tasks. When one group does not do its job, as in a garbage strike, many others suffer.

ple's commitment and conformity to the society's collective conscience.

When a society's collective conscience is strong and there is a great commitment to that collective conscience, we have what is known as a **mechanically integrated society.** In this type of society, members have common goals and values and a deep and personal involvement with the community. A modern-day example of such a society is that of the Tasaday, a food-gathering community in the Philippines. Theirs is a relatively small, simple society, with little division of labor, no separate social classes, and no permanent leadership or power structure.

In contrast, in an **organically integrated society,** social solidarity depends on the cooperation of individuals in many different positions who perform specialized tasks. The society can survive only if all the tasks are performed.

With organic integration, which is found in the United States, social relationships are more formal and functionally determined than are the close, personal relationships of mechanically integrated societies.

Although we may take the movement from *Gemeinschaft* to *Gesellschaft,* or me-

chanically integrated to organically integrated societies for granted, it is only relatively recently in the course of human history that these changes have taken place.

SOCIAL INTERACTION IN URBAN AREAS

The anonymity of social relations and the cultural heterogeneity of urban areas give the individual a far greater range of personal choices and opportunities than typically are found in rural communities. People are less likely to inherit their occupations and social positions. Rather, they can pick and choose and even improve their social position through education, career choice, or marriage. Urbanism makes for a complicated and multidimensional society with people involved in many different types of jobs and roles.

Louis Wirth, in his classic essay "Urbanism as a Way of Life" (1938), defined the city as "a relatively large, dense, and permanent settlement of socially heterogeneous individuals." For years urban sociologists tended to accept Wirth's view of the city as an alienating place where, because of population density, people hurry by one another without personal contact. However, in *The Urban Villagers* (1962) Herbert Gans helped refocus the way sociologists see urban life. Gans showed that urbanites can and do participate in strong and vital community cultures, and a number of subsequent studies have supported this view. For example, researchers in Britain found that people who live in cities actually have a greater number of social relationships than rural folk (Kasarda and Janowitz, 1974). Other investigators have discovered that the high population density typical of city neighborhoods need not be a deterrent to the formation of friendships; under certain circumstances, city crowding may even enhance the likelihood that such relationships will occur. And Gerald Suttles (1968) showed that in one of the oldest slum areas of Chicago, ethnic communities flourish with their own cultures—with norms and values that are well adapted to the poverty in which these people live.

Of course, increased population size can lead to increased superficiality and impersonality in social relations. People interact with one another because they have practical rather than social goals in mind. For example, adults will patronize neighborhood shops primarily to purchase specific items rather than to chat and share information. As a result, urbanites rarely know a significant number of their neighbors. As Georg Simmel (1955) noted, in rural society people's social relationships are rich because they interact with one another in terms of several role relationships at once (a neighbor may be a fellow farmer, the local baker, and a member of the town council). In urban areas, by contrast, people's relationships tend to be confined to one role set at a time (see Chapter 5).

With increasing numbers of people it also becomes possible for segments or subgroups of the population to establish themselves—each with their own norms, values, and life-styles—as separate from the rest of the community. Consequently, the city becomes culturally heterogeneous and increasingly complex. As people in an urban environment come into contact with so many different types of people, typically they also become more tolerant of diversity than rural people.

Although urban areas may be described as alienating places in which lonely people live in crowded, interdependent, social isolation, there is another side to the coin, one that points to the existence of vital community life in the harshest urban landscapes. Further, urban areas still provide the most fertile soil for the arts in modern society. The close association of large numbers of people, wealth, communications media, and cultural heterogeneity are an ideal context for aesthetic exploration, production, and consumption.

URBAN NEIGHBORHOODS

People sometimes talk of city neighborhoods as if they were all single, united communities, such as Spanish Harlem or Little Italy in New York City, or Chinatown in San Francisco. These communities do display a strong sense of identity, but to some extent this notion is rooted in a romantic wish for "the good old days" when most people still lived in small towns and villages that were in fact communities and that gave their residents a sense of belonging. Yet, although the sense of community that does develop in urban neighborhoods is not exactly like that in small, closely knit rural communities, it is very much present in many sections throughout a city. Urban dwellers have a mental map of what different parts of their city are like and who lives in them.

Gerald Suttles (1972) found that people living in the city draw arbitrary (in terms of physical location) but socially meaningful boundary lines between local neighborhoods, even though these lines do not always reflect ethnic group composition, socioeconomic status, or other demographic variables (see Chapter 18). In Suttles's view, urban neighborhoods attain such symbolic importance in the local culture because they provide a structure according to which city residents organize their expectations and their behavior. For example, in New York

With large numbers of people, a city becomes culturally heterogeneous and can support many types of activities, such as this outdoor jazz festival in Chicago.

City the neighborhood of Harlem (once among the most fashionable places to live) "begins" east of Central Park on the north side of Ninety-sixth Street and is a place that has symbolic significance for all New Yorkers. Whites tend to think of it as a place where they are not welcome and which is inhabited by black and Spanish-speaking people. For many blacks and Hispanics, on the other hand, Harlem represents the "real" New York City and is the place where most of their daily encounters take place.

Even those urban neighborhoods that are well known, that have boundaries clearly drawn by very distinctive landmarks, and that have local and even national meaning are not necessarily homogeneous communities. For example, Boston's Beacon Hill neighborhood is divided into four (or possibly five) subdistricts (Lynch, 1960), and New York's Greenwich Village consists of several communities defined in terms of ethnicity, life-style (artists), and subculture (especially homosexual).

On the whole, Jane Jacobs's observations in *The Death and Life of American Cities* (1961) seem to hold true. She argues that the social control of public behavior and the patterning of social interactions in terms of what might be called community life are to be found on the level of local blocks rather than entire neighborhoods. Once city dwellers venture beyond their own block, they tend to lose their feeling of identification. In fact, one of the typical features of urban life is the degree to which people move through many neighborhoods in their daily comings and goings — rushing here and there without much attention or attachment to their surroundings. Occasionally a city as a whole may have meaning to all or most or its residents and may, for this reason, assume some communitylike qualities. Consider, for example, the community spirit expressed in spontaneous celebrations for homecoming World Series or Super Bowl winners.

Although urban blocks and neighborhoods may offer a rich context for commu-

nity living, there are some inescapably unpleasant facts about urban America that make many people decide to live elsewhere. Cities and urban areas in general can be crowded, noisy, and polluted; they can be dangerous; and they may have poorer schools than those in the suburbs. Consequently, many families, especially those with children, choose the suburbs as an alternative to urban life. Other city dwellers, such as the elderly living on fixed incomes, may be forced to remain despite their wish to move.

URBAN DECLINE

A grim circle of problems threatens to strangle urban areas. Since World War II there has been a migration of both white and black middle-class families out of the cities and into the suburbs. The number of black middle-class families moving to the suburbs increased sharply in the aftermath of the civil rights movement of the 1960s. This migration pattern has led to a greater concentration of poor people in the central cities, which is reflected in the loss of revenues that many large cities have experienced. As the more affluent families leave urban areas, so do their tax dollars and the money they spend in local businesses. In fact, many businesses have followed the middle class to the suburbs, taking with them both their tax revenues and the jobs that are crucial to the survival of urban neighborhoods. This has meant a shrinking of the central cities' tax base, while at the same time creating conditions (such as the loss of jobs) that force people to rely on government assistance.

It is not easy to entice suburbanites to move back into cities, even though the U.S. Department of Housing and Urban Development has created several financial incentive programs designed to make it attractive. Because most United States suburbs were created in the last 40 years, their facilities and physical plants (schools and hospitals) are still relatively new, clean, and attractive. So are the shopping centers that

As the more affluent residents leave the urban areas, so do their tax dollars and the money they spend on local businesses.

process known as **gentrification.** Critics contend that gentrification depletes the housing supply for the poor. Others counter that it improves neighborhoods and increases a city's tax base. So far, however, this trend has been limited to a handful of cities. The trend may be short-lived, because these young adults may once again abandon the city once they start having children and find city life unsuitable for child rearing. If it continues and grows, however, it clearly will have a major impact on the future of urban life and could serve as a convincing argument against doomsday predictions about the city.

HOMELESSNESS

The movement to the suburbs of post–World War II America emphasized the suburban ideal of a single-family home. The city was where one worked during the day, and once nightfall came one left for the safety of the suburban community.

If the movement to the suburbs required abandoning the downtown streets at nightfall, there were many people who did not leave the central city. There are, of course, the working-class neighborhoods of the older cities where family life goes on in close proximity to the central business district, under somewhat less private and more crowded conditions than in the suburbs.

There are also the marginal people for whom downtown provided alternatives not available elsewhere. Commercial and industrial areas, as well as fringe areas in decaying working-class districts, have tended to provide the housing stock vital to poor persons not living in conventional families. Single-room-occupancy hotels, rooming houses, and even skid row flophouses all have provided low-cost single accommodations for those who might not be able to come by them elsewhere.

Downtowns in many older cities have also traditionally contained the cities' skid rows and red-light districts, which provided shelter and a degree of tolerance for deviant individuals and activities. Being close to

gentrification A trend that involves young, middle-class people moving to marginal urban areas, upgrading the neighborhood, and displacing some of the poor residents who become priced out of the available housing.

continue to mushroom across the country and that offer their suburban patrons local outlets of prestigious "downtown" stores as well as supermarkets, discount warehouses, specialty shops, and even entertainment centers. In the central cities many buildings are old, and apartment dwellers must pay higher rents for accommodations that are inferior to those of their suburban counterparts.

Gans (1977) suggests that if we are to save the central cities, we can do so only by mobilizing resources at the national level and raising central-city residents themselves to middle-class economic status. He believes this is more likely to succeed than trying to convince suburbanites to move back into urban areas. Many people believe, however, that the vicious circle outlined really is a sinking spiral and that some of our cities have already spun downward and out of control. They see no way of resurrecting them and forecast their gradual demise as the population spreads itself out across the country, particularly into the Sun Belt of the South and Southwest.

A small countertrend has been noticed. Many middle-class young adults have begun to find urban life attractive again. Most of these people are single or are married with no children. This trend has produced an upgrading of previously marginal urban areas and the replacement of some poor residents with middle-class ones, a

NOT IN MY BACKYARD, YOU DON'T

Call it the NIMBY syndrome. It is happening in New York City, where middle-class home-owners are on trial on charges of setting fire to a foster home for infants. In tiny Louisa, Ky., it is the battle cry against a proposed hazardous-waste incinerator. It has cropped up in Berkeley, where residents banded together to keep out a drop-in center for the emotionally disturbed. The acronym stands for "not in my backyard," and it symbolizes a perverse form of antisocial activism, "Everybody says, 'Take care of the homeless, take care of the boarder babies,'" says New York City Mayor Edward Koch. "But when you need a facility, they say, 'Not in my backyard.'"

Such problems are growing because there are more homeless, more AIDS victims, more drug addicts, more prisoners, more garbage, more toxic waste. The result is budget-busting pressure for more services that many people do not want in their vicinity. But beyond the fiscal debate, there is a painful ethical dilemma for many communities: Who should bear the burden of the common good? As often as not, neighborhoods are rising up to resist responsibility, and in some cases are turning to violence. "Too often we assume that the human being can achieve a good life without attending to the collective good," says Dr. Willard Gaylin, head of the Hastings Center for ethics in Briarcliff, N.Y.

In April 1987 the tranquility of Gladwin Avenue, in the Queens section of New York City, was shattered when a fire erupted in a two-story house that the city had rented to use as a foster home. Today five respected citizens who live on the block each face up to 25 years in prison if they are convicted of arson. "These are nice middle-class people, not hoodlums," says Defense Lawyer Jacob Evseroff. . . .

"We're paralyzed," says Frank Popper, chairman of urban studies at Rutgers University. "Nationwide, no one has been able to place a major hazardous-waste dump since 1980. No large metropolitan airport has been sited since 1961. The lack of locations for new prisons has caused such overcrowding that some cities have had to release convicted prisoners." . . .

In searching for remedies for the NIMBY syndrome, some innovative approaches have been tried. The New Jersey Supreme Court broke new ground in 1975 when it ruled that wealthy suburbs must share the burden of low-cost housing. In Arkansas officials have proposed that any county that refuses a prison should pay the state to house its criminals. In each instance, the principle of community responsibility for the greater good was paramount. "One of the few things we deprive our middle class of is the opportunity to serve," says Ethicist Gaylin. Whether the problem is a waste dump, a shelter for the homeless or an AIDS hospice, an equitable and beneficial solution, however imperfect, is likely to be one that the community has had a strong hand in shaping.

Source: Excerpted from Margot Hornblower, "Not in My Backyard, You Don't," *Time*, June 27, 1988, pp. 44–45.

transportation and requiring little initial outlay (often renting by the week), single-room housing has traditionally been utilized by the elderly poor, the seasonally employed, the addicted, and the mentally handicapped.

In the United States there are more than 150 skid rows, but the number and size of such areas has been decreasing. There are two principal reasons for the decrease. First, the economy no longer requires large numbers of unskilled migratory workers; second, the land occupied by skid rows is being converted by real estate developers to other uses (Palen, 1987).

As the old skid rows decrease in size or disappear, the traditional skid row inhabitants, older single men, are being supplemented with large numbers of people of both sexes, many of whom were released from mental hospitals during the 1970s. The process of deinstitutionalization caused many of those who previously would have been committed to institutions to become homeless street people. They are not necessarily physically dangerous, but rather are disturbed or marginally competent individuals without supportive families.

According to one study (Sosin, 1986), three factors differentiate the homeless from the poor in general: extreme poverty, fewer years of schooling, and less family support.

These trends, coming at a time when competition for inner-city space has been intensified because of gentrification, have been sharply reflected in shelter populations and on the streets. It is estimated that there are 27,000 men and 9000 women living on the streets of New York City alone (Palen, 1987).

In recent years, the downtown sections of many American cities have undergone extensive renovation and revitalization. This "back to the city" or "gentrification" movement has been both hailed as an urban renaissance and condemned for disrupting urban neighborhoods and displacing inner-city residents.

As city land becomes more desirable, it has an effect on what is usually considered to be the nation's least desirable housing stock, namely single-room occupancy hotels, rooming houses, and shelters. Although these places have long been seen as the very symbols of urban decay, they serve the vital needs of people with few resources or alternatives. Gentrification has placed these powerless people in direct competition for inner-city space. The results may be at least a partial explanation for the growing ranks of the homeless on the streets of many cities.

The deinstitutionalized, the former offender, the addicted, the poor, the sick, and the elderly all bring to the central city a lifestyle incompatible with that of the new urban middle class. Yet these people will not go away simply because their housing is eliminated. They remain on our streets and tax the strained resources of the remaining shelters. Unlike the suburb, the newly gentrified inner city cannot close its gates to marginal members of society. It therefore becomes imperative that new alternatives be provided.

FUTURE URBAN GROWTH IN THE UNITED STATES

What will metropolitan areas look like in the year 2000? Which cities will grow the most? Which cities will lose the most population?

One way to answer such questions would be simply to extend into the future the trends of the 1970s and 1980s. A forecast of this sort would show only modest growth for the economy, with decreased reliance on manufacturing and increased service and energy-producing activities.

Regionally, such a forecast would indicate that metropolitan areas in the industrial Northeast and Midwest would stagnate. The economic vitality that those cities once had would continue to be drained as population and jobs were lost. The migration pattern of American families in the previous two decades to the rapidly growing cities in the West and South would suggest that the manufacturing centers of the country would no longer lead economic recoveries as they had in the not-so-distant past.

Historically, the United States population has become increasingly more urban as people moved from rural areas to find employment in industrial centers. The growth in the population of urban areas at the expense of population in the surrounding rural areas has long been considered a trademark of advancing societies. However, during the 1970s and 1980s the percentage of Americans living in metropolitan areas did not grow, moving from 76.0 percent in 1970 to 76.9 percent in 1987 *(Statistical Abstract of the United States: 1989)*. Hidden in these figures is the fact that rural areas not classified as metropolitan in 1970 were included, because of revised definitions, in the figures in 1980. Therefore, we could argue that there has actually been a decline in the population of metropolitan areas.

The percentage of people living in metropolitan areas is also expected to decline in the future. By the year 2000 it is expected to be 74.8 percent. This slowdown in the growth of metropolitan areas relative to the surrounding countryside is new to the United States. The last time that such a slowdown in urban growth occurred was early in the nineteenth century, when the country's land area expanded rapidly (Holdrich, 1984).

Although many of the cities in the South and West have grown rapidly, constraints on their continued expansion are beginning to appear.

The decline in the urban population is due to the fact that employment opportunities in all metropolitan areas together are expected to remain stable throughout the end of the century. Approximately 78 percent of all U.S. jobs will be located in urban areas, though the types of jobs available in the metropolitan areas are changing. By 2000, metropolitan areas are expected to support only 77 percent of all manufacturing jobs (Holdrich, 1984).

Manufacturing jobs for the nation as a whole have been growing less rapidly in recent years because of international competition and increased productivity, which reduce the amount of labor required to produce goods. In fact, manufacturing has been supplanted by the service sector as the largest employer of American workers, indicating a major shift in the economy.

Metropolitan trends vary widely according to region. Some metropolitan areas are expected to maintain high growth rates over the next two decades. These are primarily in the South and the West. Ninety percent of the nation's population growth since 1980 can be accounted for by the rapid growth rate in these regions. Between 1980 and 1985, the population of the South grew by 6.7 million, while that of the West grew by 4.7 million. The Northeast increased by 724,000 and the Midwest by only 331,000. The South in particular has experienced substantial growth. "Between 1970 and 1980, overall net migration to the South was twice that to the West. Spurred by a substantial increase in migration from the Midwest, net migration to the South between 1980 and 1985 increased to nearly three times that to the West" (Kasarda, Irwin, and Hughes, 1986). (See Figure 19.4 for a comparison of growth rates for the various regions of the United States.)

Although many of the cities in the South and West have grown rapidly, constraints to this expansion are appearing. The rate of growth for Houston and other southern and western metropolitan areas should slow somewhat, as well as in most other Sun Belt areas.

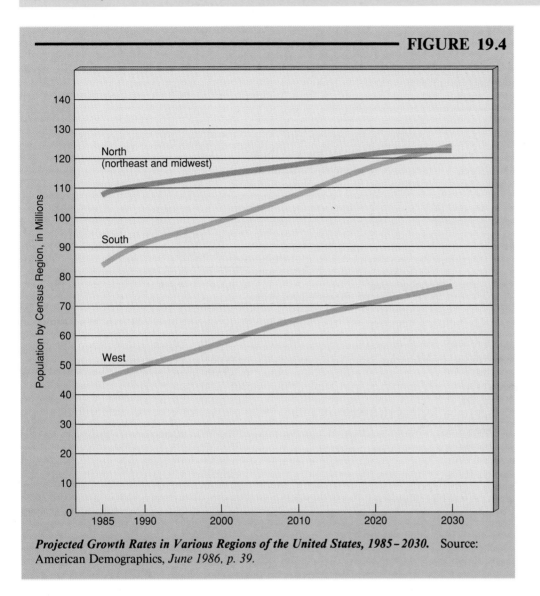

FIGURE 19.4

Projected Growth Rates in Various Regions of the United States, 1985–2030. Source: American Demographics, *June 1986, p. 39.*

SUBURBAN LIVING

Suburbs consist of those territories that are part of a metropolitan statistical area but outside the central city. According to this definition, 60 million people lived in the suburbs in 1960, 74 million in 1970, and about 98 million in 1986 (U.S. Bureau of the Census, 1987). In fact, most people now living in metropolitan areas live in suburbs rather than in the central cities.

Originally the small-scale agriculture of suburban gardeners was mocked by farmers. City newspaper editors derided the lack of cultural facilities in the suburbs. Suburbanites inhabited a territory that did not fit any traditional definition of city or country.

In many respects, at least until recently, suburbs have served as a dramatic contrast to city life. Suburbs generally are cleaner than cities, less crowded, less noisy, and less crime-ridden. Often their school systems are newer and better. Many characteristics of urban life, however, have followed people to the suburbs.

We accept the sprawling landscape of single-family houses on small lots without

suburbs Those territories that are part of a metropolitan statistical area but outside the central city.

WHERE THE JOBS WILL BE IN 2010

I n which metropolitan areas are you most likely to find employment in the years ahead? The job outlook will vary considerably from city to city. Here is a comparison of the top thirty metropolitan areas ranked according to their prospects for job growth between 1987 and 2010.

Metropolitan Statistical Area	Jobs Added 1987–2010	
	Number	Rank
Los Angeles-Long Beach, CA	1,045,000	1
Anaheim-Santa Ana, CA	352,000	2
Washington, DC-MD-VA	762,000	3
Houston, TX	729,000	4
Dallas, TX	657,000	5
Atlanta, GA	633,000	6
Boston-Lawrence-Salem-Lowell-Brockton, MA	579,000	7
San Diego, CA	491,000	8
Phoenix, AZ	484,000	9
San Jose, CA	465,000	10
Chicago, IL	438,000	11
Denver, CO	413,000	12
Minneapolis-St. Paul, MN-WI	412,000	13
Philadelphia, PA-NJ	408,000	14
Tampa-St. Petersburg-Clearwater, FL	404,000	15
Seattle, WA	391,000	16
Nassau-Suffolk, NY	374,000	17
San Francisco, CA	322,000	18
Fort Lauderdale-Hollywood-Pompano Beach, FL	303,000	19
Orlando, FL	301,000	20
Oakland, CA	286,000	21
Riverside-San Bernardino, CA	278,000	22
Baltimore, MD	273,000	23
Miami-Hialeah, FL	272,000	24
Sacramento, CA	272,000	25
New York, NY	261,000	26
Detroit, MI	244,000	27
West Palm Beach-Boca Raton-Delray Beach, FL	240,000	28
St. Louis, MO-IL	233,000	29
Fort Worth-Arlington, TX	232,000	30

Source: NPA Data Services, Inc., 1988.

question today and assume that suburbs have always been with us. We give little thought to the suburbs' origin.

Suburbs, as we know them, developed relatively recently and largely without any planning. They were a direct response to changes that made commuting easier. Well-surfaced roads and hundreds of new bridges began to appear in the early nineteenth century. The steamship also changed matters dramatically in the New York City region. Individuals discovered a new lifestyle that included steaming down the Hudson in the early morning and cruising slowly upstream in early evening.

Railroads were also instrumental in the development of the suburbs. Trains made it possible to travel in all kinds of weather, prompting thousands of upper-class Americans to use them. Originally, the railroad companies discouraged short-haul commuting, but eventually demand created the commuter train.

Suburbs began to blossom all along the railroad routes that led to the city. Thousands of middle-income families settled in these suburbs, which offered the advantages of both rural and urban living.

The typical suburban house was part farmhouse and part urban residence and reflected a desire for open space, sanitation, and security. It usually had many large closets, a large cellar, an attic, a pantry, a back hall—even guest rooms.

Suburbanites also started to copy the front lawn that was typical of estates and English country houses. The lawn mower began to appear in the 1880s, and magazines explained the use of the new machines. By the 1920s the idea of a smooth, green lawn became widely accepted. Lawn mower manufacturers determined that grass height should be about 1½ inches, and suburbanites were quick to follow the recommendation.

Suburban growth slowed during the Depression and the subsequent war years when gasoline rationing took place. Once the war ended, however, suburban growth resumed. By the mid-1950s, the automobile made it possible for suburbs to exist far beyond the range of railroads and trolleys.

Popular television shows such as "I Love Lucy" and "Leave It to Beaver" responded to the public sentiment, which was turning against the city, and shifted their locales to the suburbs.

The way in which homes were purchased also influenced the growth of the suburbs. Before the 1920s, a home buyer borrowed 30 to 40 percent of the cost of the property. Mortgage interest payments of 5 or 6 percent were made semiannually. At the end of anywhere from 3 to 8 years, the principal was repaid in one lump sum or the mortgage was renegotiated. After the 1920s, savings and loan associations replaced the informal, individual lender. After World War II the government guaranteed mortgages to veterans. Former GIs needed only the smallest of down payments to purchase a home, and a building boom emerged.

For the children of these families, the suburbs represented the world, a world ruled by women more than men. Men went to work in the city and returned every evening to the suburban landscape. As commuting time increased, the fathers looked for jobs in the suburbs and began deserting the city altogether. When white-collar workers started to appear in the suburbs in large numbers, suburbs entered their present stage.

The suburbs of today are markedly different from those three decades ago. A declining birthrate changed the nature of many residential neighborhoods and forced the closing of many schools. The vast increase in the number of women working outside the home caused many suburban areas to appear uninhabited during the weekday. Many suburban areas now really are urban areas that have grown horizontally rather than vertically and experience many of the same concerns and problems as large cities do (Stulgoe, 1984). (For an example of the diversity in today's suburbs, see Table 19.3 showing the 10 richest and 10 poorest American suburbs.)

Suburbs increasingly are suffering

TABLE 19.3
The Ten Wealthiest and Ten Poorest Suburbs, 1987

	Per Capita Income	Population	Metropolitan Area
Wealthiest Suburbs			
Kenilworth, IL	$61,950	3,530	Chicago
Bloomfield Hills, MI	$59,830	3,755	Detroit
Hewlett-Woodsburgh, NY	$59,300	3,270	New York
Ladue, MO	$55,962	9,450	St. Louis
Mission Hills, KS	$55,136	4,170	Kansas City, Mo.
Sands Point, NY	$54,393	2,590	New York
North Hills-Roslyn Estates, NY	$52,150	2,750	New York
Harding Township, NJ	$52,067	3,520	New York
Oyster Bay Cove-Mill Neck, NY	$51,650	2,780	New York
Cherry Hills, CO	$50,016	6,150	Denver
Poorest Suburbs			
Ford Heights, IL	$4,943	5,240	Chicago
Cudahy, CA	$5,170	21,020	Los Angeles
Bell Gardens, CA	$5,337	37,030	Los Angeles
Alorton, IL	$5,795	2,720	St. Louis
East St.Louis, IL	$5,973	49,250	St. Louis
Coachella, CA	$6,185	13,350	Riverside, Calif.
Huntington Park, CA	$6,298	55,050	Los Angeles
Camden, NJ	$6,304	82,440	Philadelphia
Centreville, IL	$6,341	4,400	St. Louis
Florida City, FL	$6,490	6,510	Miami

Sources: U.S. Department of Commerce, Bureau of the Census, and Roosevelt University, Chicago.

from some of the serious problems that used to be thought of as exclusively urban in nature. Perhaps the most dramatic of these is the sharp rise in juvenile alcoholism, drug addiction, and delinquency. At least one reason for this seems to be that suburban areas typically have few resources that address the needs of youths. There is little for teenagers to do, few places for them to go. Consequently, they often are bored. Furthermore, many suburban populations are less willing to spend tax money on social services to address these problems, and even the public buildings and common areas of

many suburbs are beginning to show signs of "urban" decay.

One characteristic that still separates suburban from city neighborhoods is that suburbs tend to be homogeneous with regard to the stage of development of families in their natural life cycle. For example, in the suburbs, retired couples rarely live among young couples who are just starting to have children. Aside from the rather dulling "sameness" of many suburban tracts that results from this, it also creates problems in the planning of public works. For example, a young suburb might well invest money in school buildings, which, some 20 years later, are likely to stand empty when the children have left home.

Gradually the suburban "dream life" is showing signs of strain. Although many wealthy suburbs are not experiencing these problems, less affluent suburbs—with diminishing resources, obsolete structures resulting from poor planning, and a seeming inability to solve such problems as adolescent boredom and the provision of services for the elderly—appear to be heading for a period of reassessment by those seeking a better life.

THE EXURBS

For the last 20 years a new trend has been noticed throughout the country. The fastest-growing areas appear to be located in a newer, second ring beyond the old suburbs. These areas, often called **exurbs,** have been designated as the "new heartland" by some authors. This "heartland" is a mixture of urban, rural, and suburban living (Herbers, 1986).

The exurb is taking shape largely within metropolitan boundaries, but it differs sharply from the traditional suburb. For one thing, development in the exurbs is much less dense, emerging near farms and rural land in the remotest fringes of metropolitan areas. (See Table 19.4 for a comparison of growth rates in cities of various sizes.)

Suburbs traditionally are dependent on the city for jobs and services. Not so in the exurb, which creates its own economic base in its shopping malls, office complexes, and decentralized manufacturing plants. Whereas the earlier wave of fringe development may have been an expansion of the city, the new areas may be anticity (Townsend, 1987). By and large, the people moving there are white, relatively wealthy, highly educated, and professional.

Why are so many people moving still farther out from the central city? Recent research suggests a variety of reasons, but, on the whole, reasons that are not very sur-

One characteristic of suburbs is that they tend to be homogeneous with respect to the stage of development of families in their natural life cycle. While children will be well represented, there will be few older families.

prising when we consider the suburban exodus of the early postwar era. When people are asked why they moved to the exurbs, typical responses are "retirement," "be-

exurbs The fast-growing areas located in a newer, second ring beyond the old suburbs.

——————————————— **TABLE 19.4**

Number of U.S. Cities by Population Size, 1960–1986

	Number of Cities			
Population Size	*1960*	*1970*	*1980*	*1986*
1,000,000 or more	5	6	6	8
500,000–1,000,000	16	20	16	15
250,000–500,000	30	30	34	37
100,000–250,000	79	97	116	122
50,000–100,000	180	232	254	286
25,000–50,000	366	455	529	563
10,000–25,000	978	1127	1278	1302

Source: U.S. Department of Commerce, Bureau of the Census, *Statistical Abstract of the United States: 1989* (Washington, D.C.: Government Printing Office, 1989), p. 33.

FIGURE 19.5

The Rancher in Levittown

$59 A MONTH
No Down Payment for Veterans!

▶ The famous Rancher of Levittown is now being built in two more sections of Levittown. When these are sold there will be no more Ranchers; we haven't any more room for them.

▶ It's a beauty of a house that's priced unbelievably low at $8990. Carrying charges are only $59 monthly, and veterans need absolutely no down payment. Non-veterans need only a total of $450 down. Can you think of anything much easier than that?

▶ The house at $8990 comes with two bedrooms, but you can have a third bedroom for only $250 more. If you're a veteran you still don't need any money down, and a non-veteran needs only $100 more. We think that's a bargain, don't you?

▶ Of course, you're not buying just a house. You own the ground—60 x 100—beautifully landscaped. You have ac-

cess to the community-owned swimming pools, recreational areas, etc.

▶ Your house itself is charming, cheerful, and convenient. Such things as a four-foot medicine chest completely mirrored, picture windows from floor to ceiling, an outside garden storage room, a Bendix washer, an oil-fired radiant heating system, complete rock-wool insulation—all add to your comfort and enjoyment.

▶ Get your application in as soon as possible. Occupancy may be any time from January thru May. You pick the month. You'll need a good-faith deposit of $100, but you'll get it back at settlement if you're a veteran; credited against your down payment if you're a non-veteran.

▶ O, yes, we almost forgot! Total settlement charges are just $10! See you soon, folks!

Furnished Exhibit Homes open every day until 9 P. M.

TO LEVITTOWN

By car from Philadelphia: Drive out Roosevelt Boulevard continuing on Route 1 for about 5 miles. Turn right at Levittown sign to Route 13. Turn left on Route 13 about 4 miles to the Exhibit Center.

By bus from Philadelphia: Take Levittown Express—Bus at Bridge Street station of Elevated direct to Exhibit Center.

By car from Camden: Drive out Route 130–Burlington Pike to Burlington. Turn left and cross bridge into Bristol. Turn right on Route 13 four miles to Exhibit Center.

By car from Trenton: Cross the bridge into Pennsylvania, turn left to Route 13 Bristol Pike. Continue on Route 13 four miles past Morrisville.

Levitt and Sons
INCORPORATED
U. S. ROUTE 13 • LEVITTOWN, PA. • Telephone WINDSOR 6-1100

Philadelphia Inquirer—November 14, 1954
Philadelphia Bulletin—November 12, 1954
Camden Courier-Post—November 12, 1954
Trenton Times—November 12, 1954

Buying a Home in the Suburbs. Note the no-money-down pitch and small monthly payments in this 1954 Levittown, Pennsylvania, advertisement (Levitt Homes).

cause my job is there (or nearby)," "because I like to live in the country and have some open space around me," "because I have friends or family in the area," and "because I wanted to get out of the city" (Fuguitt, 1984).

Herbers (1986) suggests that the state of North Carolina could be the prototype for America's future. North Carolina offers scenic beauty alongside economic vitality, thanks in part to a conscious policy of dispersed development. To avoid the problems of large urban areas, the state decentralized the university system over sixteen campuses, improved roads even in the remotest areas, and encouraged scattered industrial development. As a result, North Carolina is a leading manufacturing state but has no city larger than Charlotte, with 350,000 people.

In short, the exurb, like the suburb before it, is seemingly another step in the quest for the American dream.

Urbanism has become an American way of life. Although the shape and form of metropolitan areas continue to change, their influence continues to dominate the manner in which we interact with our environment.

In the last 20 years the fastest-growing areas have been the exurbs, an area where development is much less dense, located in a newer, second ring beyond the old suburbs.

SUMMARY

Two requirements had to be met in order for cities to emerge. The first was that there had to be a surplus of food and other necessities. Farmers had to be able to produce more food than their immediate families needed to survive. This surplus made it possible for some people to live in places where they could not produce their own food and had to depend on others to supply their needs.

The second requirement was that there had to be some form of social organization that went beyond the family. The world's first fully developed cities arose in the Middle Eastern area, mostly in what is now Iraq, which was the site of the Sumerian civilization.

Preindustrial cities—so named in order to indicate their establishment prior to the Industrial Revolution—housed only 5 to 10 percent of a country's population. In fact, most preindustrial cities had populations of less than 10,000. They often were walled for protection and densely packed with residents whose occupations, religion, and social class were clearly evident from symbols of dress, heraldic imagery, and manners.

The industrial city was a product of the Industrial Revolution—the application of scientific methods to production and distribution. Modern-day industrial cities are large and expansive, often with no clear physical boundary that separates them from surrounding towns and suburbs. They house a relatively high percentage of the society's population, which works primarily in industrial or service-related jobs. As the industrial city grows, it spreads out, creating a phenomenon known as urbanization.

The internal structure of cities may follow a pattern of concentric circles (the con-

How Many Homeless Are There?

A decade ago every city had its "skid row" with "bums," "derelicts," and "vagrants." Aside from the occasional story about the executive who became an alcoholic and ended up sleeping in "flop houses," little interest or sympathy was expressed for the denizens of these marginal areas of the city.

Today, not only have the words that we use to describe these people changed, but so has our thinking and attitudes about them. The "bum" or "hobo" of the past has become today's "homeless person." The sense of personal responsibility for their fate attributed to them before has now been replaced with a view that the homeless are the victims of a selfish, even ruthless, society.

What has really changed? Has society become more heartless and created more victims, or have we become more compassionate and become more aware of the problem? Have the numbers of homeless gone up so much that we are forced to recognize the issue? Have the advocates for the homeless become more adept at manipulating the media? A case could be made for all of these statements.

Advocates for the homeless often claim that these people are out on the streets because of a lost job, a low minimum wage, or a lack of affordable housing—all things outside the control of the homeless. Certainly there are many situations where that is the case, particularly among those homeless for a short spell. However, for the broader category of the homeless, we will find very few autoworkers laid off from well-paying jobs. Most homeless will have histories of chronic unemployment, poverty, family dis-organization, illiteracy, crime, mental illness, and welfare dependency, problems that cannot be corrected by quick or simple economic measures.

Although advocates for the homeless will deny this fact, the largest single category of homeless people is made up of the mentally ill. Estimates from neutral sources claim that this number is anywhere from 30 to 40 percent or more of the total. Many of today's homeless were dumped onto the streets as a result of the deinstitutionalization process that began in the sixties. Others who have reached adulthood since then have never been institutionalized, but would have been during previous decades.

Homelessness was not the intended result of this process. The original idea was to free the patients from the wretched and abu-

centric zone model), a pattern based on major transportation arteries (the sector model), or a pattern of land-use and financial requirements (the multiple nuclei model).

A city is a unit that typically has been incorporated according to the laws of the state within which it is located. As of 1982, the terms the Bureau of the Census applies to urban data include urbanized area, urban population, metropolitan statistical area, primary metropolitan statistical area, and consolidated metropolitan statistical area.

Tönnies examined the changes in so-cial relations attributable to the transition from rural society (organized around small communities) to urban society (organized around large impersonal structures).

In a *Gemeinschaft* (community), Tönnies noted, relationships are intimate, cooperative, and personal. In a *Gesellschaft* (society), relationships are impersonal and independent—people look out for their own interests, goods are bought and sold, and formal contracts govern economic exchanges.

According to Durkheim, every society has a collective conscience—a system of

sive conditions in mental hospitals and allow them instead to be treated in the community. However, community treatment never materialized and many ended up on the streets uncared for and unable to care for themselves.

It is also unclear how many homeless there are. Because the homeless are so difficult to find and to count, estimates range widely. Advocates claim the population ranges from 2 million to 3 million and will rise to 18 million by the end of the century. The media often use the 2- to 3-million figure, which represents about 1 percent of the population, even though no study has ever supported this contention. A little thought would show that it is ridiculous to claim that 1 percent of the U.S. population is homeless.

At the other end, the Department of Housing and Urban Development (HUD) did a study that estimated the homeless population at a drastically lower 250,000 to 350,000. Both estimates are probably wrong. The HUD figure because it was a poorly done study, and the advocates' figure because of the lack of any study.

Advocates for the homeless justify their inflated numbers by referring to the "hidden homeless," who cannot be located, and the "borderline homeless," who live with relatives because they cannot afford suitable housing. But sociologist Peter Rossi of the University of Massachusetts, himself an advocate for more public spending on the homeless, says, "we have never been able to locate any data from which these numbers were derived. There is no evidence that they are anything but guesses."

Whatever the numbers may be, the issue of homelessness defies easy explanation or understanding. Why are we seeing this problem when unemployment is at a 10-year low, when more than 16 million jobs have been created since 1983, when housing vacancy rates nationally are at a 20-year high? Yet, the ranks of the homeless seem to have expanded most since 1983. No sociologist has offered an adequate explanation of why this problem has emerged to such an extent in recent years.

Source: "Homelessness in America: Myth vs. Reality, Handout vs. Hand Up," *Insight*, May 16, 1988, pp. 8–19.

---

fundamental beliefs and values. Social solidarity emerges from the people's commitment and conformity to the society's collective conscience. When a society's collective conscience is strong and there is a great commitment to that collective conscience, we have what is known as a mechanically integrated society. In an organically integrated society, social solidarity depends on the cooperation of individuals in many different positions who perform specialized tasks.

The majority of people in the United States live in cities, even though living conditions may be difficult and costs may be high. A migration to the suburbs has taken place because of the promise of less noise and pollution, a lower crime rate, and better education. In recent years, however, young people who are single or married with no children have been returning to some cities.

Although cities may be viewed as agents of depersonalization and alienation, a spirit of community often exists within blocks or neighborhoods.

Chapter 20

COLLECTIVE BEHAVIOR AND SOCIAL MOVEMENTS

It was a beautiful day in May of 1988 when the Cincinnati Reds were playing the New York Mets. The baseball game was proceeding normally until manager Pete Rose became incensed by a call by umpire Dave Pillone. Rose yelled, jumped around, kicked the dirt, and finally shoved the umpire. The crowd of 41,032 took over from there. Receiving encouragement from the radio broadcasters covering the game, the crowd started throwing garbage, portable radios, and anything else they could get their hands on, onto the field.

Reds owner Marge Schott tried to calm the crowd by instructing the scoreboard operator to display her personal plea for order. Nothing worked until the umpire left the field. This was the first time in memory an umpire was forced to take cover for fear of what an angry crowd might do.

In 1987 the United States and Cuba agreed to an immigration pact that called for Cuba to take back more than 2000 "undesirables" who had traveled to the United States in the 1980 Mariel boatlift.

News of the pact sparked riots among Cuban inmates in two detention centers. The Cubans took over the facilities and claimed they would not end their siege until they received assurances that they would not be sent back to Cuba. After extensive negotiation, the riot was quelled.

To draw attention to the plight of the homeless, a number of well-known Americans, including actor Martin Sheen, Mayor Marion Barry, Jr., and former House Majority Whip Tony Coelho took part in an event billed as the "Grate American Sleep-Out," sleeping out on heating grates on a Washington, D.C., street corner.

At a rock concert in Cincinnati, thousands of fans rushed forward as the doors were opened to obtain good seats. In the crush, eleven people were trampled to death, and countless others were knocked down and injured.

In New York City, Reverend Sun Myung Moon of the Unification church held a mass wedding ceremony for 2074 couples, many of whom had been paired up only a few days before.

By this time in your reading of this book you have probably noticed that sociol-

ogy makes us aware of the fact that most social behavior is patterned and follows agreed-upon rules. We may interact with each other according to specific social statuses and roles, or participate in rituals of social solidarity. At other times, however, it appears that people act in ways that seem to escape the control of common expectations and their behavior strikes us as bizarre and unpredictable. How can we begin to explain the violence and hysteria of a prison riot? Or the willingness of people to participate in a mass wedding ceremony to spouses they hardly know? These actions fall under the general category of collective behavior.

Collective behavior is the term we use to refer to relatively spontaneous social actions that occur when people respond to unstructured and ambiguous situations. Collective behavior has the potential for causing the unpredictable, and even the improbable, to happen. Collective actions are capable of unleashing surprisingly powerful social forces that catch us off guard and change our lives, at times temporarily, but at other times even permanently. It is the more dramatic forms of collective behavior that we tend to remember: riots, mass hysterias, lynchings, or panics. Fads, fashion, and rumor, however, are also forms of collective behavior.

THEORIES OF COLLECTIVE BEHAVIOR

There are two ways of approaching the topic of collective behavior. We can think of such collective behavior as riots, demonstrations, and religious revivals as the means for improving society. These actions provide the needed push to overcome the inertia of established institutions in dealing with human problems. Social reform comes about when the system is pushed by the pressure of large groups of people. Thus, it can be argued that the civil rights legislation

collective behavior Relatively spontaneous social actions that occur when people respond to unstructured and ambiguous situations.

of the 1960s occurred only because legislators were pushed by the protest demonstrations of that period.

On the other hand, we can argue that collective behavior is pathological and destructive to the fabric of society. Gustav Le Bon espoused this view when he viewed "the crowd" as something of a reversion to the bestial tendency in human nature. People are swept away in the contagious excitement of the crowd. Civilized members of society who would never engage in antisocial acts as individuals engage in just such acts under the cloak of anonymity provided by the crowd.

In the next section we will examine several theories that have been devised to account for crowd behavior. These include the contagion (or "mentalist") theory, the emergent norm theory, the convergence theory, and the value-added theory.

CONTAGION ("MENTALIST") THEORY

Gustave Le Bon (1841–1931) was a French sociologist whose major interest was the role played by collective behavior in shaping historical events such as the storming of the Bastille in 1789, a turning point in the launching of the French Revolution. In 1895 Le Bon published his classic *The Psychology of Crowds* (1960), in which he argued that once individuals experience the sense of anonymity in a crowd, they are transformed. Hence, they think, feel, and act quite differently than they would alone. They acquire a crowd mentality, lose their characteristic inhibitions, and become highly receptive to group sentiments. Concerns for proper behavior or norms disappear, and individuals give up their personal moral responsibilities to the will of the crowd. When this happens, the crowd becomes a social entity greater than the sum of its individual parts.

Herbert Blumer (1946) explains the contagion that sweeps through a crowd in terms of what he calls a "circular reaction" that typifies crowd behavior. In his view, a crowd begins as a collectivity of people more or less waiting for something to happen. Sooner or later an "exciting event" stirs them, and people react to it without the

According to Herbert Blumer, a crowd is a collectivity of people more or less waiting for something to happen. Eventually something stirs them, and they react without the kind of caution and critical judgment they would normally use.

kind of caution and critical judgment they would ordinarily use if they were experiencing the event alone. Individuals become excited, the excitement spreads, the original event is invested with even greater emotional significance, and people give in to the "engulfing mood, impulse, or form of conduct." In this manner a crowd can spiral out of control, as when a casual crowd of onlookers observing the arrest of a drunken driver is transformed into an acting crowd of rioters.

There are several problems with the contagion theory. Le Bon did not specify under what conditions contagion would sweep through a crowd. In addition, the theory does not account for events that could limit the spread of contagion or for the fact that contagion may affect only one portion of a crowd. Finally, research has not borne out Le Bon's basic premise that the average person can be transformed through crowd dynamics from a civilized being into an irrational and violent person.

EMERGENT NORM THEORY

Rather than viewing the formation of crowd sentiments and behavior as inherently irrational, as Le Bon and Blumer did, Ralph H. Turner (1964), as well as other sociologists,

espouse the emergent norm theory of collective behavior. This theory implies that crowd members have different motives for participating in collective behavior. They acquire common standards by observing and listening to one another. In this respect, contagion does play a role in establishing the crowd's norms. A few leaders may help in the emergence of these norms by presenting the crowd with a particular interpretation of events. However, even without leaders, the crowd still can develop shared expectations about what behavior is appropriate.

The emergent norm theory provides the basis for analyzing the factors that push a crowd in one direction or another. If people bring with them into a crowd situation a set of expectations about the norms that are likely to be established, then the emergence of such norms will not be just a matter of the collective processes of the moment (Lang and Lang, 1961). Thus, many hockey fans attending the Boston Bruins games in Boston Garden expect to vent hostile feelings against opposing players, expect that members of the crowd will throw beer cans and other debris, and expect that management will encourage this fanaticism by playing "Charge!" music on the public address system, by flashing violence-oriented slogans on the scoreboard, and by selling alcoholic beverages. In other words, the fans expect to become frenzied. Predictably, fights often occur in the stands, sportswriters from out of town are subjected to abuse, and players from opposing teams are harassed. As one journalist put it, "A sense of hostility . . . pervades the arena . . ." (Fischler, 1980)

CONVERGENCE THEORY

Whereas contagion theory assumes that a crowd mentality arises when people are gathered in a specific area and interact in ways that produce common perceptions and common behavior, **convergence theory** views collective behavior as the outcome of situations in which people with similar

convergence theory Collective behavior is the outcome of situations in which people with similar characteristics, attitudes, and needs are drawn together.

characteristics, attitudes, and needs are drawn together. In contrast with contagion theory, it is not the crowd situation that produces unusual behavior, but rather the bringing together of certain kinds of people who are predisposed to certain kinds of actions. Consequently, if violent or unusual collective behavior takes place during and after a rap music concert, it is because people who are predisposed to this type of behavior have been drawn to the event.

Convergence theory is helpful because it stresses the role of the individual and points out that no matter how powerful a group's influence may be, not everyone will respond to it. Therefore, it is unlikely that a group of conservative bankers who are in attendance at the above-mentioned rap music event will be part of any unusual collective action.

The problem with convergence theory is that it cannot explain why crowds often pass through stages, from disorganized milling to organized action against specific targets. If the participant's characteristics do not change, what does produce the changes in the crowd behavior? Convergence theory also does not tell us which events will ignite a crowd with common characteristics into action and which will thwart collective behavior.

VALUE-ADDED THEORY

Of all the attempts to understand collective behavior, the value-added theory of sociologist Neil Smelser (1962) is in many ways the most comprehensive. It attempts to explain whether collective behavior will occur and what direction it will take. Smelser suggests that, when combined, the following six conditions shape the outcome of collective behavior.

1. *Structural conduciveness.* **Structural conduciveness** refers to the conditions that may promote or encourage collective behavior and is tied to the arrangement of the existing social order. For instance, in the example at the beginning of the chapter of

Convergence theory notes that it is not the crowd situation but the type of people brought together that produces unusual behavior.

the Cuban inmates rioting in two detention centers, the social isolation, free time, and crowding that are common in prison all provide a fertile ground for collective action.

2. *Structural strain.* When a group's ideals conflict with its everyday realities, **structural strain** occurs. For the Cuban inmates, the disparity between their dream of gaining freedom in the United States, and the reality of their lives if they were returned to Cuba, produced unbearable structural strain.

3. *Growth and spread of a generalized belief.* People develop explanations for the structural strains under which they must struggle to exist. When these explanations are clearly expressed and widely shared, collective behavior may take the shape of well-organized social movements, such as the civil rights and labor movements. The less clearly these explanations are expressed or the more competing explanations there are, the more likely it is that collective behavior will emerge in an unstructured form, a riot, for example. In the Atlanta and Oakdale detention centers, the widely shared beliefs included a strong resentment of the guards, a hope that their release was imminent, and a strong desire not to return to Cuba. The hope that they would one day be free to live in the United States made it pos-

structural strain One of sociologist Neil Smelser's six conditions that shape the outcome of collective behavior, structural strain refers to the tension that develops when a group's ideals conflict with its everyday realities.

structural conduciveness One of sociologist Neil Smelser's six conditions that shape the outcome of collective behavior, structural conduciveness refers to the conditions within society that may promote or encourage collective behavior.

SAVING BABY JESSICA

Some of the collective behavior we have talked about in this chapter has been negative. We have seen crowds explode into violence, mass hysteria, and destruction. But when people come together, they are also capable of a great deal of good. This occurred in October of 1987, when hundreds of people joined forces to rescue 18-month-old Jessica McClure, who had fallen down a well while playing in her aunt's backyard in Midland, Texas. Jessica remained trapped 22 feet below ground for 58 grueling hours while a dedicated team tried to save her. People came together to help and in so doing brought out the best in each other.

Workers drilled a 26-foot-long shaft right next to the one that imprisoned Jessica and inserted a 5-foot-long horizontal tube to connect the two. The team was forced to drill through solid bedrock and their progress was agonizingly slow. As one volunteer described the work: "It would be as if someone gave you a hammer and chisel and told you to cut through a 3-foot wall. . . . It was like hitting a piece of steel."

All through the rescue effort, the workers had no way of knowing whether they would get Jessica out alive. As the first day moved into the second, the effort to save the little girl would have worn down a weaker team — but these people were stronger than that. Adversity had made them so. They, along with everyone else in Texas, had suffered hard times in recent years as they rode the oil-powered economic roller coaster from good times to bad.

As a result, there was an immeasurable amount of moral support and civic pride in the air. It was as if the people of Midland had to prove to themselves and the world that they were down, but not out, and that they still knew how to drill a well better than anyone.

When the team finally pulled little Jessica out, injured but not critically hurt, grown men cried and millions across the country who had been watching the rescue on television celebrated. In Midland, the mood was euphoric. People lined the streets, cheering as an ambulance rushed little Jessica to the hospital. Horns blared, firecrackers blasted, and church bells chimed. A baby was saved — and, in many ways, a town was reborn, all through the efforts of a collectivity who rose to the occasion.

Sources: Peter Applebome, "Toddler Is Rescued After 2½ Days in Texas Well," *New York Times,* October 17, 1987, p. 1; Peter Applebome, "Girl's Rescue Bolsters Texas City's Pride," *New York Times,* October 19, 1987, p. A16; "The Epic Rescue of Jessica McClure," *People,* November 2, 1987, pp. 42–46; "The Girl in the Well Outpolls the Men in the Race," *New York Times,* November 19, 1987, p. D.30; "A Brave Little Girl," *Newsweek,* October 26, 1987, p. 42.

---

sible for them to tolerate the structural strain. Once that hope was shattered and no other type of structured collective behavior was possible, conditions leading to the riot followed.

4. *Precipitating factors.* In all cases of collective behavior there is an event, or a related set of events, that triggers a collective response. In the prison riots it was the news of the pact between the United States and Cuba that would cause the "undesirables" to be sent back to Cuba. For a group of California mothers who organized a campaign against drunk drivers, it was the loss or maiming of their children and other relatives by alcohol-impaired drivers that caused them to unite and take action.

5. *Mobilization for action.* A group of people must be mobilized or organized into taking action. When there are no previously recognized leaders to take charge, a group is easily swayed by its more boisterous members. In the Cuban community there was no immediately available organized mecha-

nism for politically channeled social action on behalf of the prisoners. Hence, the signing of the pact mobilized the inmates into unplanned, expressive acts that included scattered fires and destruction of the facilities. By the time community leaders attempted to intervene, the riot had escalated out of control.

6. *Mechanisms of social control.* At this point the course that collective behavior follows depends on the various ways those in power respond to the action in order to reestablish order. In the prison riots example, Edwin Meese, who was attorney general at the time, promised to declare a moratorium on the return of Cubans to their homeland pending a review of each case, if the uprisings ended, and the hostages received fair and humane treatment. Shortly thereafter, the inmates called a halt to the riots.

According to Smelser, the final outcome of collective behavior depends on how each of the six determinants has built on the previous one. Each becomes a necessary condition and an important part of the next determinant.

CROWDS: CONCENTRATED COLLECTIVITIES

A **crowd** is a temporary concentration of people who focus on some thing or event but who also are attuned to one another's behavior. There is a magnetic quality to a crowd: it attracts passersby who often will interrupt whatever they are doing to join. Think, for example, of the crowds that gather "out of nowhere" at fires or accidents. Crowds also fascinate social scientists, because crowds always have within them the potential for unpredictable behavior and group action that erupts quickly and often seems to lack structure or direction — either from leaders or from institutionalized norms of behavior.

ATTRIBUTES OF CROWDS

In his study *Crowds and Power* (1978), social psychologist Elias Canetti attributed to crowds the following traits.

1. *Crowds are self-generating.* Crowds have no natural boundaries. When boundaries are imposed artificially — for example, by police barricades intended to isolate a street demonstration — there is an ever-present danger that the crowd will erupt and spill over the boundaries, thereby creating chaos. So, in effect, crowds always contain threats of chaos, serious disorder, and uncontrollable force.

2. *Crowds are characterized by equality.* Social distinctions lose their importance within crowds. Indeed, Canetti believes that people join crowds specifically to achieve the condition of equality with one another, a condition that carries with it a charged and exciting atmosphere.

3. *Crowds love density.* The circles of private space that usually surround each person in the normal course of events shrink to nothing in crowds. People pack together shoulder to shoulder, front to back, touching each other in ways normally reserved for intimates. Everyone included

In all cases of collective behavior, there is an event (or series of events) that triggers a collective response.

crowd A temporary concentration of people who focus on some thing or event but who also are attuned to one another's behavior.

within the body of the crowd must relinquish a bit of his or her personal identity in order to experience the crowd's fervor. With a "we're all in this together" attitude, the crowd discourages isolated factions and detached onlookers.

4. *Crowds need direction.* Many crowds are in motion. They may physically move from place to place as they do in a marching demonstration or psychologically as at a rock concert. The direction of movement is set by the crowd's goals, which become so important to crowd members that individual and social differences lessen or disappear. This constant need for direction contains the seeds of danger: Having achieved or abandoned one goal, the crowd may easily seize on another, perhaps destructive one. The direction that a crowd will take depends on the type of crowd involved.

TYPES OF CROWDS

In his essay on collective behavior, Herbert Blumer (1946) classified crowds into four types: acting, expressive, conventional, and casual.

Acting Crowd

acting crowd A group of people whose passions and tempers have been aroused by some focal event, who come to share a purpose, who feed off one another's arousal, and who often erupt into spontaneous acts of violence.

threatened crowd A crowd that is in a state of alarm, believing itself to be in some kind of danger.

An **acting crowd** is a crowd in its most frightening form. It is a *mob*—a group of people whose passions and tempers have been aroused by some focal event, who come to share a purpose, and who feed off one another's arousal and often erupt into spontaneous acts of violence. When members of the studio audience of the "Geraldo" show saw black activist Roy Innis get so angry at a neo-Nazi for calling him an Uncle Tom that he began choking him on camera, they stormed the set and joined in the violence by hurling punches and epithets and throwing chairs.

Acting crowds can become violent and destructive, as 400 million worldwide television viewers discovered in the summer of

An acting crowd is made up of people whose passions and tempers have been aroused by some focal event.

1985. Sixty thousand soccer fans had assembled in Brussels to watch the European Cup finals between Italy and Great Britain. Verbal taunts quickly turned into rock and bottle throwing. Suddenly, British fans stormed the fence and surged toward the Italian fans, trampling hundreds of helpless spectators. Before the horror could be stopped, thirty-eight people were dead and another four hundred injured.

Threatened Crowd

A **threatened crowd** is a special form of acting crowd. It is a crowd that is in a state of alarm, believing there to be some kind of danger present. Such a crowd is in a state of panic, as when a crowded nightclub catches fire and everybody tries to get out, jamming exits and trampling one another in their rush to escape. A threatened crowd created havoc when a busboy accidentally ignited an artificial palm at the Coconut Grove Night Club in Boston on November 28, 1942, spreading fire instantaneously through the rooms of the club. The fire lasted only 20 minutes, but 488 people died. Most died needlessly when panic gripped the crowd. Fire investigators found that the club's main entrance—a revolving door—

was jammed by hundreds of terrified patrons. With their escape route blocked, these people died of burns and smoke inhalation only feet away from possible safety (Veltfort and Lee, 1943). In this as well as other threatened crowds, there is a lack of communication.

Expressive Crowd

An **expressive crowd** is drawn together by the promise of personal gratification for its members through active participation in activities and events. For example, many rock concert audiences are not content simply to listen to the music and watch the show. In a very real sense they want to be part of the show. Many dress in clothing calculated to draw attention to themselves, take drugs during the performance, dance in the aisles and in packed masses up against the stage, scream and chant, sometimes in unison, and delight in giving problems to security personnel.

Conventional Crowd

A **conventional crowd** is a gathering in which people's behavior conforms to some well-established set of cultural norms and in which people's gratification results from a more passive appreciation of an event than it does in an expressive crowd. Such crowds include the audiences attending lectures, the theater, and classical music concerts, where it is expected that everybody will follow traditional norms of etiquette.

Casual Crowd

A **casual crowd** is the inevitable outgrowth of modern society, in which large numbers of people live, work, and travel closely together. Any collection of people who just happen, in the course of their private activities, to be in one place at the same time and focus their attention on a common object or event is called a casual crowd. On Fifth Avenue in New York City at noon, many casual crowds gather to watch the construction of a new building, an accident, a purse snatcher, or a theatrical performer. A casual crowd has the potential of becoming an acting crowd or an expressive crowd; the nature of a crowd can change if events change.

THE CHANGEABLE NATURE OF CROWDS

Although the typology presented is useful for distinguishing among kinds of crowds, it is important to recognize that any particular crowd can shift from one type to another. For example, if a sidewalk musician starts playing a violin on Fifth Avenue, part of the aggregate walking by will quickly consolidate into a casual crowd of onlookers. Or an expressive crowd at a rock concert will become a threatened crowd if a fire breaks out.

Changing times may also affect the nature of crowds. For example, until the 1970s, British soccer matches generally attracted conventional crowds who occasionally would turn into expressive crowds chanting team songs. In the last decade or so, however, British soccer fans have become active crowds: Fighting in the stands is epidemic, charging onto the field to assault players and officials has become common, and near rioting has taken place. In 1988 when British fans traveled to West Germany to watch their national team take part in the European championships, four nights of street fighting followed between the English and West German fans that resulted in 500 arrests (Raines, 1988).

Because they are relatively concentrated in place and time, crowds present rich materials for sociological study (even if much of the data must be tracked down after the dust has settled). Fads, fashions, rumors, public opinion, panics, and mass hysteria are also examples of collective behavior. They are, however, widely dispersed among large numbers of people whose connection with one another is minimal or elusive.

expressive crowd A crowd that is drawn together by the promise of personal gratification for its members through active participation in activities and events.

conventional crowd A crowd in which people's behavior conforms to some well-established set of cultural norms and in which people's gratification results from a passive appreciation of an event.

casual crowd A crowd that is made up of a collection of people who, in the course of their private activities, just happen to be in one place at the same time.

fad A transitory social change that has a very short life span marked by a rapid spread and an abrupt drop from popularity.

fashion A transitory change in the standards of dress or manners in a given society.

mass A collection of people who, although physically dispersed, participate in some event either physically or with a common concern or interest.

DISPERSED COLLECTIVE BEHAVIOR

In this age of mass media, with television and other systems of communication spreading information instantaneously throughout the entire population, collective behavior shared by large numbers of people who have no direct knowledge of one another has become commonplace. Sociologists use the term **mass** for such a collection of people who, although physically dispersed, participate in some event either physically or with a common concern or interest.

A nationwide television audience watching a presidential address or a super-bowl game is a mass. So are those individuals who rush out to buy the latest best-selling record and the fashion conscious whose hemlines, lapel widths, and designer jeans always reflect the "in" look.

FADS AND FASHIONS

Fads and **fashions** are transitory social changes (Vago, 1980), patterns of behavior that are widely dispersed among a mass but that do not last long enough to become fixed or institutionalized. Yet it would be foolish to dismiss fads and fashions as unimportant just because they fade relatively quickly. In modern society, fortunes are won and lost trying to predict fashions and fads—in clothing, in entertainment preferences, in eating habits, in choices of investments.

Probably the easiest way to distinguish between fads and fashions is to look at their typical patterns of diffusion through society. Fads have a very short life span marked by a rapid spread and an abrupt drop from popularity. This was the fate of the Hula-Hoop in the 1950s and the dance known as the "twist" in the 1960s. The roller-skating fad that emerged in 1979 rolled off into the pages of history sometime in the 1980s, as did Rubik's Cube, and Coleco, the company that made cabbage-patch dolls, went bankrupt in 1988. A fad that is especially

Fashions relate to standards of dress and manners during a particular time. They spread more slowly and last longer than fads.

short-lived may be called a **craze.** The mohawk hairstyle among both young males and females was a relatively short-lived craze, as was streaking, or running naked down a street or through a public gathering, in 1974.

At the peak of their popularity, fads and crazes may become competitive activities. For example, when streaking was a craze, individual streaking was followed by group streaking, streaking on horseback, and parachuting naked from a plane.

Fashions relate to the standards of dress or manners in a given society at a certain time. They spread more slowly and last longer than fads. In his study of fashions in European clothing from the eighteenth to the present century, Alfred A. Kroeber (1963) noted that although minor decorative features come and go rapidly (that is, are faddish), basic silhouettes move through surprisingly predictable cycles. Kroeber correlates these cycles with degrees of social and political stability. In times of great stress, fashions change erratically, but in peaceful times they seem to oscillate slowly in cycles lasting about 100 years.

Georg Simmel (1957) believed that changes in fashion (such as dress or manners) are introduced or adopted by the upper classes, who seek in this way to keep themselves visibly distinct from the lower classes. Of course, those immediately below them observe these fashions and also adopt them in an attempt to identify themselves as "upper crust." This process repeats itself again and again, with the fashion slowly moving down the class ladder, rung by rung. When the upper classes see that their fashions have become commonplace, they take up new ones, and the process starts all over again.

Blue jeans have shown that this pattern may no longer be true today. Jeans started out as sturdy work pants worn by those engaged in physical labor. Young people then started to wear them for play and everyday activities. College students wore them to class. Eventually fashion designers started to make fancier, higher-priced versions, known as designer jeans, worn by the middle and upper classes. In this way the introduction of blue jeans into the fashion scene represents movement in the opposite direction from what Simmel noted.

Of course, the power of the fashion business to shape consumer taste cannot be ignored. Fashion designers, manufacturers, wholesalers, and retailers earn money only when people tire of their old clothes and purchase new ones. Thus, they shift hemlines up and down and widen and narrow lapels to create new looks, which consumers purchase.

This backfired in 1987 when the fashion industry decided that American women were once again ready for the short skirt, even though most women buy skirts to wear at work. Women said no, leaving manufacturers with inventory they could not sell (*New York Times,* July 17, 1988).

Indeed, the study of fads and fashions provides sociologists with recurrent social events through which to study the processes of change. Because they so often use concrete and quantifiable objects, such as consumer goods, fads and fashions are much easier to study and count than are rumors, another common form of dispersed collective behavior.

RUMORS

A **rumor** is information that is shared informally and spreads quickly through a mass or a crowd. It arises in situations that, for whatever reasons, create ambiguity with regard to their truth or their meaning. Rumors may be true, false, or partially true, but characteristically they are difficult or impossible to verify.

Rumors are generally passed from one person to another through face-to-face contact, but they can be started through television, radio, and newspaper reports as well. However, when the rumor source is the mass media, the rumor still needs people-to-people contact to enable it to escalate to the point of causing widespread concern (or even panic).

craze A fad that is especially short-lived.

rumor Information that is shared informally and spreads quickly through a mass or a crowd.

DO ADVERTISING SCARE TACTICS WORK?

Advertisers often think that we can get people to stop undesirable behavior through a scare campaign. They are wrong.

A scare campaign is more likely to get people to deny that the problem exists and in fact actually promote the undesirable behavior. Scare campaigns appear to be particularly ineffective in getting people to stop smoking, drinking, or using drugs.

People who hear that smoking will kill them are likely to believe they have already destroyed their lungs, and there is no reason to stop smoking now. When it comes to drinking and driving, people are more afraid of losing their license than they are of getting killed in an accident.

Source: R. F. Soames Job, "Effective and Ineffective Use of Fear in Health Promotion Campaigns," *American Journal of Public Health* 78(2) (Summer 1988).

Sociologists see rumors as one means through which collectivities try to bring definition and order to situations of uncertainty and confusion. In other words, rumors are "improvised news" (Shibutani, 1966). Recognizing this, sociologists have been able to help prevent riots in some potentially inflammable situations. For example, a national motorcycle race was planned for the Labor Day weekend at Upper Marlboro, Maryland, in the summer of 1965. But earlier that summer, after the national championship motorcycle races in Laconia, New Hampshire, on July 4, the nearby resort town of Weir Beach had erupted into riot. Planners for the Labor Day races were worried that it might happen again—a fear that was strengthened when three Hells Angels motorcyclists (who had been arrested and jailed for disorderly conduct) threatened to "tear up the county." Two sociologists offered their services to law-enforcement officials planning crowd control. Among other things, they set up a system for investigating all rumors and quickly disseminating correct information. In their analysis of the "riot that didn't happen" the sociologists credited the continuous flow of accurate information as being one of the major factors in keeping the crowds—which at times were quite unstable—from erupting into serious violence (Shellow and Roemer, 1965).

Some rumors die more easily than others. Hard-to-believe rumors usually disappear first, but this is not always the case. For 103 years, Procter & Gamble has used the symbol of the moon and thirteen stars as a company logo on its products. Around 1979 a rumor started to circulate that this symbol indicated a connection between the giant corporation and satanic religion. There was no evidence to substantiate this rumor, yet unable to dispel the rumor, the company finally decided to remove the logo from its products in 1985 (Koenig, 1985).

PUBLIC OPINION

The term *public* refers to a dispersed collectivity of individuals concerned with or engaged in a common problem, interest, focus, or activity. An *opinion* is a strongly held belief. Thus, **public opinion** refers to the beliefs held by a dispersed collectivity of individuals about a common problem, interest, focus, or activity. It is important to

public opinion The beliefs held by a dispersed collectivity of individuals about a common problem, interest, focus, or activity.

recognize that a public that forms around a common concern is not necessarily united in its opinions regarding this concern. For example, Americans concerned with the issue of abortion are sharply divided into pro and con camps.

Whenever a public forms, it is a potential source of support for, or opposition to, whatever its focus is. Hence, it is extremely important for politicians, market analysts, public relations experts, and others who depend on public support to know the range of public opinion on many different topics. These individuals often are not willing to leave opinions to chance, however. They seek to mold or influence public opinion, usually through the mass media. Advertisements are attempts to mold public opinion, primarily in the area of consumption. They may create a "need" where there was none, as they did with fabric softeners, or they may try to convince consumers that one product is better than another when there is actually no difference at all. Advertisements of a political nature, seeking to mobilize public support behind one specific party, candidate, or point of view, technically are called **propaganda** (but usually by only those lay persons in disagreement). For example, radio broadcasts from the Soviet Union are habitually called "propaganda blasts" in the American press, but similar "Voice of America" programs are called "news" or "informational broadcasts."

Opinion leaders are socially acknowledged experts to whom the public turns for advice. The more conflicting sources of information there are on an issue of public concern, the more powerful the position of opinion leaders becomes. They weigh various news sources and then provide an interpretation in what has been called the two-step flow of communication. These opinion leaders can have a great influence on collective behavior, including voting (Lazarsfeld et al., 1968), patterns of consumption, and the acceptance of new ideas and inventions. Typically, each social stratum has its own opinion leaders (Katz, 1957). Jesse Jackson, for example, is an

Opinion leaders are socially acknowledged experts to whom the public turns for advice. Jesse Jackson is an opinion leader within the black community.

propaganda Advertisements of a political nature seeking to mobilize public support behind one specific party, candidate, or point of view.

opinion leaders Socially acknowledged experts to whom the public turns for advice.

opinion leader in the black community. The mass media have made news anchor people like Dan Rather, Tom Brokaw, and Peter Jennings accepted opinion leaders for a broad portion of the American public.

When rumor and public opinion grip the public imagination so strongly that "facts" no longer seem to matter, terrifying forces may be unleashed. Mass hysteria may reign, and panic set in.

MASS HYSTERIAS AND PANICS

On a Wednesday in June 1962 reports began emerging from a small southern town of a mysterious illness that had stricken workers in a local clothing plant. According to the 6 P.M. news, at least ten female employees were hospitalized after complaining of feeling nauseated. Although no hard evidence was available, the broadcast blamed the outbreak on some kind of "bug" that may have found its way into the country on a shipment of cloth from England. By the time the 11 P.M. news aired, the stricken workers had narrowed the cause of their illness to the bite of a small insect. They quickly labeled this insect the "June Bug."

Two days later, experts from the U.S. Public Health Service Communicable Disease Center in Atlanta arrived at the plant to investigate the cause of the mysterious outbreak. They set up a task force of community and health-service officials to search the plant for the small black bug most employees believed was responsible for the outbreak. Their efforts were fruitless. The only bugs they found in the entire plant were a housefly, a black ant, a mite, and several entirely innocent gnats and beetles. Even though the investigators reported that they could not find the cause of the illness (indeed, no cause was ever found), the outbreak continued. By the time it ended, sixty-two people were stricken in what sociologists believe was a case of mass hysteria (Kerckhoff and Back, 1968).

When large numbers of people are overwhelmed with emotion and frenzied activity or become convinced that they have experienced something for which investigators can find no discernible evidence, they are suffering from a case of **mass hysteria.** A **panic** is an uncoordinated group flight from a perceived danger, as in the public reaction to the 1938 Orson Welles radio broadcast of H. G. Wells's *War of the Worlds.*

According to Irving Janis and his colleagues (1964), people generally do not panic unless four conditions are met. First, they must feel that they are trapped in a life-threatening situation. Second, they must perceive a threat to their safety that is so large that they can do little else but try to escape. Third, they must realize that their escape routes are limited or inaccessible. Fourth, there must be a breakdown in communication between the front and rear of the crowd. Driven into a frenzy by fear, people at the rear of the crowd make desperate attempts to reach the exit doors, their actions often completely closing off the possibility of escape.

California state officials are working to devise a plan to minimize widespread panic should a major earthquake hit the Los Angeles or San Francisco areas. Despite their

best efforts, though, the major problem officials face is public apathy. Unwilling to accept the inevitability of a major earthquake, Californians refuse to take heed, thus increasing the likelihood that when the quake hits, panic will prevail (Reinhold, 1988).

The perception of danger that causes a panic may come from rational as well as irrational sources. A fire in a crowded theater, for example, can cause people to lose control and trample one another in their attempt to escape. This happened when fire broke out in the Beverly Hills Supper Club on May 28, 1977. In their attempt to escape the overcrowded, smoke-filled room, people blocked the exit doors and 164 died.

Such bizarre events are not very common, but they do occur often enough to present a challenge to social scientists, some of whom believe there is a rational core behind what at first glance appears to be wholly irrational behavior (Rosen, 1968). For example, sociologist Kai Erikson (1966) looked for the rational core behind the wave of witchcraft trials and hangings that raged through the Massachusetts Bay Colony beginning in 1692, when a group of mostly adolescent girls first pointed their accusing fingers at three "witches": a slave-woman from Barbados, an old and decidedly odd spinster, and a lady of rather high social standing whose chastity had been suspect and the subject of much gossip. Erikson joins most other scholars in viewing this troublesome episode in American history as an instance of mass hysteria (Brown, 1954). He accounts for it as one of a series of symptoms, suggesting that the colony was in the grip of a serious identity crisis and needed to create real and present evil figures who stood for what the colony was not—thus enabling the colony to define its identity in contrast and build a viable self-image.

Mass hysterias account for some of the more unpleasant episodes in history. Of all social phenomena, they are among the least understood—a serious gap in our knowledge of human behavior.

mass hysteria A condition in which large numbers of people are overwhelmed with emotion and frenzied activity or become convinced that they have experienced something for which investigators can find no discernible evidence.

panic An uncoordinated group flight from a perceived danger.

SOCIAL MOVEMENTS

A **social movement** is an important form of collective behavior in which large numbers of people are organized or alerted to support and bring about, or to resist, social change. By their very nature, social movements are an expression of dissatisfaction with the way things are, or with changes that are about to take place.

Participation in a social movement is for most people only informal and indirect. Usually large numbers of sympathizers identify with and support the movement and its program without joining any formal organizations associated with the movement. For people to join a social movement, they must think that their own values, needs, goals, or beliefs are being stifled or challenged by the social structure or specific individuals. The people feel that this situation is in fact undesirable and something must be done to "set things right." Some catalyst, however, is needed to actually mobilize the discontent that people feel. There are two major theories, relative deprivation theory and resource mobilization theory, that attempt to explain how social movements emerge.

RELATIVE DEPRIVATION THEORY

Relative deprivation is a term that was first used by Samuel A. Stouffer (1950). It refers to the situation where deprivation or disadvantage is measured not by objective standards, but by comparison to the condition of others with whom one identifies or thinks of as a reference group.

A social movement can result from the feeling of relative deprivation when large numbers of people believe they lack the income, living conditions, working conditions, political rights, or social dignity that they feel they are entitled to.

From the standpoint of relative deprivation theory, the actual degree of deprivation people suffer is not automatically related to whether they will feel deprived and therefore join a social movement to correct the situation. Rather, deprivation is considered unjust when others with whom the people identify do not suffer the deprivation (Gurr, 1970).

Karl Marx (1968) expressed this view when he noted:

> A house may be large or small; as long as the surrounding houses are equally small it satisfies all social demands for a dwelling. But let a palace arise beside the little house, and it shrinks from a little house to a hut. . . . Our desires and pleasures spring from society; we measure them, therefore, by society and not by the objects which serve for their satisfaction. Because they are of a social nature, they are of a relative nature.

social movement A form of collective behavior in which large numbers of people are organized or alerted to support and bring about, or to resist, social change.

relative deprivation theory A theory that assumes social movements are the outgrowth of the feeling of relative deprivation among large numbers of people who believe they lack certain things they are entitled to.

For people to join a social movement, they must think that their own values, needs, goals, or beliefs are being stifled or challenged by the social structure or by specific individuals.

There is a flaw in the theory of relative deprivation in that often the people who protest a situation or condition may not be deprived themselves. Sometimes people protest because a situation violates their learned standards of justice. The white civil rights marchers in the 1960s were not personally the victims of antiblack discrimination. We could, however, argue that they were experiencing deprivation in the sense that the reality was not judged to be what it ought to be. They were experiencing a moral as opposed to a material or personal social deprivation (Rose, 1982).

RESOURCE MOBILIZATION THEORY

resource mobilization theory A theory that assumes that social movements arise at certain times and not at others because some people know how to mobilize and channel popular discontent.

The **resource mobilization theory** assumes that discontent exists virtually everywhere. Social movements arise at certain times and not at others because some people know how to mobilize and channel the popular discontent.

A social movement will not emerge until specific individuals actually mobilize resources available to a group, by persuading people to contribute time, money, information, or anything else that might be valuable to the movement. An organizational format must also be developed for allocating these resources. Leadership, therefore, becomes a crucial ingredient for the emergence of a social movement.

The hope is that the leadership will be able to formulate the ideology in such an attractive fashion that many others will join the movement. It is not enough to make speeches and distribute fliers, the messages have to strike a respondent chord in others (Ferree and Hess, 1985).

One of the most successful people in terms of resource mobilization was Saul Alinsky. Alinsky was an activist who devoted his life to developing "people's organizations" at the neighborhood level to combat exploitation and poor living conditions.

Alinsky was not the sort of man people were impartial about. He was abrasive, forceful, witty, antagonistic, irreverent, and not above shocking or lying to people. Some saw him as a menace. Corporations hired detectives to follow him. What people were really responding to was not Alinsky the person, but the method of community organizing that came to be associated with him.

To accomplish his goals, he followed a few guidelines. First, he believed the professional organizer was the key catalyst for social change. Community organizing is difficult and requires crucial and correct decisions. He believed democracy was important, but the organizer was even more so.

Second, the goal was to win and use any tactics necessary. The end justified the means, Alinsky counseled. For example, Alinsky described the tactics used by one of his organizations in the following way:

> When [they have] a bunch of housing complaints they don't forward them to the building inspector. They drive forty or fifty members—the blackest ones they can find—to the nice suburb where the slumlord lives and they picket his home. Now we know the picket line isn't going to convert the slumlord. But we also know what happens when his white neighbors get after him and say, "We don't care what you do for a living—all we're telling you is to get those niggers out of here or you get out." That's the kind of jujitsu operation that forces the slumlord to surrender and gets repairs made in the slum. (Quoted in Fisher, 1984)

Alinsky throughout his life was involved in countless organizing efforts, and his methods were adopted by a vast array of groups. He was a clear example of a leader who knew how to mobilize and channel the deprivation and dissatisfaction that existed among the poor.

Today, Jesse Jackson also has these skills. During his 1988 race for the presidency, Jackson's vision and extremely effective rhetorical style mobilized millions of voters who felt left out of the economic recovery that marked the Reagan years. Blue-collar workers, union members, the poor, the unemployed, and those who simply believed in his message rallied to his cause. Perhaps his biggest single achievement during the campaign was to convince millions of people across the nation to register and vote. Jackson also gave blacks and other minorities hope that change was possible through the political process (*New York Times,* July 19, 1988).

TYPES OF SOCIAL MOVEMENTS

In the previous chapter we discussed rebellions and revolutions, which certainly qualify as social movements; but there are other kinds of social movements as well. Scholars differ as to how they classify social movements, but some general characteristics are well recognized. We shall discuss these characteristics according to William Bruce Cameron's (1966) four social movement classifications: reactionary, conservative, revisionary, and revolutionary. In addition, we shall examine the concept of expressive social movements first developed by Herbert Blumer (1946).

Although this classification is useful to sociologists in their studies of social movements, in practice it is sometimes difficult to place a social movement in only one category. This is because any social movement may possess a complex set of ideological positions in regard to the many different features of the society, its institutions, the class structure, and the different categories of people within that society.

Reactionary Social Movements

Reactionary social movements embrace the aims of the past and seek to return the general society to yesterday's values. Using slogans like "the good old days" and our "grand and glorious heritage," reactionaries abhor the changes that have transformed

Reactionary social movements are committed to creating a set of social conditions that are believed to have existed at an earlier time.

society and are committed to recreating a set of valued social conditions that they believe existed at an earlier time. Reactionary groups, such as the neo-Nazis and the Ku Klux Klan, hold a set of racial, ethnic, and religious values that are more characteristic of a previous historic period. The Klan has sought to uphold white dominance and traditional morality. To do this, it has threatened, flogged, mutilated, and, on occasion, murdered. The main purpose of the Klansmen has been to defend and restore what they conceive as traditional cultural values. Their values legitimize prejudice and discrimination on the basis of race, ethnicity, and religion, patterns that are now neither culturally legitimate nor legal (Chalmers, 1980).

Recently, this kind of reactionary fanaticism has been displayed by organized groups of teenagers who are part of a neo-Nazi political movement. The teens, known as skinheads, are white supremacists who are committing a variety of hate crimes against blacks, immigrants, and Jews across the country. According to the Anti-Defa-

reactionary social movement A social movement that embraces the aims of the past and seeks to return the general society to yesterday's values.

mation League of B'nai B'rith, there are approximately 2000 neo-Nazi skinheads nationwide, including many who now have ties to the California-based White Aryan Movement, an organization of young racists run by the son of a former Ku Klux Klansman (Bishop, 1988).

Conservative Social Movements

conservative social movement A social movement that seeks to maintain society's current values.

Conservative social movements seek to maintain society's current values. Reacting to change or threats of change that they believe will undermine the status quo, conservative movements are organized to prevent these changes from happening. Many of the evangelical religious groups hold conservative views. For example, they often are opposed to the forces that promulgate equal rights for women. To preserve what they consider traditional values of the family and religion, these groups have threatened to boycott advertisers that sponsor television programs containing sex and violence and have mounted successful campaigns to defeat political candidates who oppose their views.

revolutionary social movement A social movement that seeks to overthrow all (or nearly all) of the existing social order and replace it with an order it considers to be more suitable.

Conservative movements are most likely to arise when traditional-minded people perceive the threat of change that might alter the status quo. Reacting to what might happen if another movement achieves its goals, members of conservative movements mobilize an "anti" movement crusade. Thus, the conservative forces that opposed the equal rights amendment set up a highly successful anti-ERA campaign, and anti-gun control groups have waged political war against any group seeking to restrict the public's access to handguns. Although reactive in nature, conservative movements such as these are far different from true reactionary movements, which attempt to restore values that have already been changed.

expressive social movement A social movement that stresses personal feelings of satisfaction or well-being and that typically arises to fill some void or to distract people from some great dissatisfaction in their lives.

Revisionary Social Movements

revisionary social movement A social movement that seeks partial or slight changes within the existing order but does not threaten the order itself.

Revisionary social movements accept certain societal values but not others. They seek partial or slight changes within the existing order but do not threaten the order itself. The women's movement, for example, seeks to change the institutions and practices that have imposed prejudice and discrimination on women. The civil rights movement, the antinuclear movement, and the ecology movement are all examples of revisionary social movements.

Revolutionary Social Movements

Revolutionary social movements seek to overthrow all or nearly all of the existing social order and replace it with an order they consider to be more suitable. For example, the black guerrilla movement in Zimbabwe (formerly Rhodesia) was a revolutionary movement. Through the use of arms and political agitation, the guerrillas were successful in forcing the white minority to turn over political power to the black majority and in creating a new form of government that guaranteed that eighty of the one hundred seats in the country's legislative body would be held by blacks.

Although both revolutionary and revisionary social movements seek change in society, they differ in the degree of change they seek. The American Revolution, for example, which sought to overthrow British colonial rule and led to the formation of our own government, differed significantly from the women's movement, which seeks change within the existing judicial and legislative structures.

Expressive Social Movements

Expressive social movements typically arise to fill some void or to distract people from some great dissatisfaction in their lives. Although other types of movements tend to focus on changing the social structure in some way, expressive social movements stress personal feelings of satisfaction or well-being. Movements such as the "Hare Krishnas" and the "Moonies" of the Unification church are religious movements of this type.

Expressive social movements typically arise to fill some void or to distract people from some dissatisfaction with their lives.

THE LIFE CYCLE OF SOCIAL MOVEMENTS

Social movements, by their nature, do not last forever. They rise, consolidate, and eventually succeed, fail, or change. Armand L. Mauss (1975) suggested that social movements typically pass through a series of five stages: (1) incipiency, (2) coalescence, (3) institutionalization, (4) fragmentation, and (5) demise. However, these stages are by no means common to all social movements.

Incipiency

The first stage, **incipiency,** begins when large numbers of people become frustrated about a problem and do not perceive any solution to it through existing institutions. This occurred in the nineteenth century when American workers, desperate over their worsening working conditions, formed the U.S. labor movement. It is a time of some disorder, when people feel the need for something to give their lives direction and meaning or to channel their behavior toward achieving necessary change. Disruption and violence may mark a social movement's incipiency. In 1886 and 1887, for example, as the labor movement grew,

workers battled private Pinkerton agents and state militiamen and called nationwide strikes. Although physically beaten, the workers continued to organize.

It is also a time when leaders emerge. Various individuals offer competing solutions to the perceived societal problem, and some are more persuasive than others. According to Max Weber (see Chapter 17), many of the more successful leaders have charismatic qualities derived from exceptional personal characteristics. Samuel Gompers, who launched the American Federation of Labor (AFL) in 1881, was such a leader, as was Martin Luther King.

Coalescence

In the stage of **coalescence,** groups begin to form around leaders, to promote policies, and to promulgate programs. Some groups join forces; others are defeated in the competition for new members. Gradually a dominant group or coalition of groups emerges that is able to establish itself in a position of leadership. Its goals become the goals of many; its actions command wide participation; and its policies gain influence. This occurred in the labor movement when in 1905 William D. Haywood orga-

incipiency The first stage in the life cycle of a social movement, when large numbers of people perceive a problem without an existing solution.

coalescence The second stage in the life cycle of a social movement, when groups begin to form around leaders, promote policies, and promulgate programs.

Are We Encouraging Americans to Gamble?

Thomas Jefferson called gambling on the lottery "a wonderful thing; it lays taxation only on the willing."

It would appear that Americans like to be taxed, if their involvement in gambling is any indication, so much so that they spend more money on gambling than they give to their churches or to higher education.

In fact, last year the amount Americans wagered was fifteen times what they donated to churches, twice what they spent on higher education, and more than half what they spent for food.

Jefferson would not be happy to note, however, that of the roughly $19 billion that was wagered last year, nearly a third of it went to illegal gambling and therefore escaped taxation.

Of the remaining two-thirds that was spent on legalized gambling, 28 percent went to casinos, 22 percent to lotteries, and 16 percent to race tracks.

As Jefferson's quote might suggest, lotteries in particular are an American tradition. Their revenues supported the revolutionary war and helped build Harvard, Princeton, and Yale. Scandals led Congress and the states to outlaw them in the nineteenth century.

New Hampshire legalized the first modern state lottery in 1964. By 1981, legal lotteries in densely populated Massachusetts and New York were offering multimillion dollar jackpots.

Today legalized gambling is increasingly popular with voters and legislators because it promises revenues without raising taxes. There are approximately thirty state lotteries. In addition, eight bills have been filed in Congress for a national lottery. It is estimated that a national lottery could cut $5 billion from the federal deficit.

Despite its political popularity, gambling is still not for everyone. Lottery opponents say that lotteries amount to a regressive tax because minorities, those with low incomes, and older people are the heaviest ticket buyers.

Not everyone is likely to gamble, either. The likelihood of gambling, favorite games, and the amount people are willing to risk are all strongly influenced by a person's age, sex, income, education, and religion.

Four out of five lottery players are age 35 and over. Most players are men with annual incomes between $18,000 and $35,000. Nonplayers are overwhelmingly white with higher incomes and more education than the players.

Overall, Catholics are the most likely to gamble; 80 percent are bettors. Fundamentalist Christians and, surprisingly, atheists, are the least likely to gamble, 33 percent and 40 percent respectively.

There is a special group of heavy players that adds a great deal to the lottery coffers. The frequent lottery players, those who buy more than twenty tickets a month, purchase more than 70 percent of the tickets. Heavy players are more likely to be black, Hispanic, or Asian than average players. They are also poorer and less educated.

It seems strange that those who can least afford it spend the most on gambling, whereas those who would not miss the few extra dollars each week are the least likely to gamble.

Part of the explanation for the discrepancy is the general attitude toward the potential prizes. To a person making $15,000 a year, a $50 prize is a lot of money. To the middle-class breadwinner, it does not even pay for groceries.

Once the potential prize reaches a large amount, though, the higher-income people join the game. A $5- or $10-million prize brings out the lighter players who decide to take a chance buying five or ten dollars worth of tickets. This explains why ticket sales really start to climb when the lottery prize reaches a potential multimillion-dollar jackpot after a few weeks without winners.

We are now at a point where many states would have serious fiscal problems if the revenues from legalized gambling were eliminated. We are rapidly encouraging a practice we used to outlaw.

Source: Brad Edmundson, "The Demographics of Gambling," *American Demographics,* July 1986, pp. 39–41, 50–53.

nized the Industrial Workers of the World (IWW), which led its increasingly dissatisfied members in a number of violent strikes. Labor coalescence continued in 1935, when such militant industrial union leaders as John L. Lewis of the United Mine Workers and David Dubinsky of the International Ladies' Garment Workers founded the Committee for Industrial Organization (CIO), which rapidly organized the steel, automobile, and other basic industries. Thus, through coalescence, the labor movement gradually created several large, increasingly powerful organizations.

Institutionalization

During the stage of **institutionalization,** social movements reach the peak of their strength and influence. Their leadership no longer depends on the elusive quality of charisma to motivate followers. Rather, it has become firmly established in formal, rational organizations (see Chapter 6) that have the power to effect lasting changes in the social order. At this point, the organizations themselves become part of the normal pattern of everyday life.

When the institutionalization of the U.S. labor movement became formalized with the legalization of unions in the 1930s, union leaders no longer used the revolutionary rhetoric that was necessary when unions were neither legitimate nor legal. Instead, they talked in pragmatic terms, worked within the political power structure, and sought reforms within the structure of the existing democratic, capitalistic system.

Not all social movements become institutionalized. In fact, social movements fail and disappear more often than they reach this stage. Institutionalization depends, to a great degree, on how the members feel about the movement — whether it reflects their goals and has been successful in achieving them — and on the extent to which the movement is accepted or rejected by the larger society.

Ironically, the acceptance of a social movement may also mark its end. Many members drop out or lose interest once a movement's goals have been reached. It can be argued that a certain amount of opposition from those in power reminds the members that they still must work to accomplish their goals. Movement leaders often hope for a confrontation that will clarify the identity of the opposition and show the members against what and whom they must fight. Movements that evoke an apathetic or disinterested response from the institutions controlling the power structure have little around which to unite their membership.

Fragmentation

Having achieved their goals, social movements undergo **fragmentation** and gradually begin to fall apart. Their organizational structures no longer seem necessary because the changes they sought to bring about have been institutionalized or the changes they sought to block have been prevented. Disputes over doctrine may drive dissident members out, as when the United Auto Workers (UAW) and the Teamsters left the AFL-CIO. Also, demographic changes may transform a once strong social movement into a far less powerful force. Economic changes have been largely responsible for the fragmentation of the American labor movement. As was pointed out in Chapter 16, unions now represent the smallest share of the labor force since World War II, even though the work force continues to expand. Their lost power is due, in part, to a sharp decrease in the percentage of more easily unionized blue-collar workers in the labor force and a dramatic increase in the percentage of white-collar employees, who are largely resistant to unionization.

Demise

Eventually many social movements experience a **demise** and cease to exist. The organizations they created and the institutions they introduced may well survive — indeed, their goals may become official state policy

institutionalization The third stage in the life cycle of a social movement, when the movement reaches its peak of strength and influence and becomes firmly established.

fragmentation The fourth stage in the life cycle of a social movement, when the movement gradually begins to fall apart.

demise The last stage in the life cycle of a social movement, when the movement comes to an end.

—however, they are no longer set apart from the mainstream of society. Transformed from social movements into institutions, they leave behind well-entrenched organizations that guarantee their members the goals they sought. This pattern of social-movement demise has occurred in parts of the American labor movement. The United Auto Workers, for example, is no longer a social movement fighting for the rights of its members from the outskirts of the power structure. Rather, it is now an institutional-ized part of society. But all unions have not followed this course. Labor is still very much a social movement, for it is trying to organize such previously unorganized groups as farm workers, nonunionized clerical and professional workers, and all workers in the traditionally nonunion South. The American Federation of State, County, and Municipal Employees, which tripled in size between 1968 and 1980, is a recent example of the labor movement's continued organizational efforts.

SUMMARY

Collective behavior refers to spontaneous actions by a number of people drawn together for a limited time in relatively unstructured patterns of behavior. There are several theories that have emerged to account for crowd behavior. These include the contagion (or "mentalist") theory, the emergent norm theory, the convergence theory, and the value-added theory.

Neil Smelser devised the value-added theory, suggesting that the following six conditions shape the outcome of collective behavior: structural conduciveness, structural strain, growth and spread of a generalized belief, precipitating factors, mobilization for action, and mechanisms of social control.

A crowd is a temporary concentration of people who are focused on some thing or event but who are also attuned to one another's behavior. The behavior of crowds consists of group action that erupts quickly and often seems to lack structure or direction. Canetti (1978) attributed the following traits to crowds: (1) crowds are self-generating; (2) equality exists within the crowd; (3) density is important; and (4) direction is needed.

An acting crowd, often called a mob, frequently erupts into spontaneous acts of violence. A threatened crowd is an acting crowd in a state of alarm, believing itself to be in some kind of danger. An expressive crowd is drawn together by the promise of personal gratification for its members through active participation in activities and events. A conventional crowd is a gathering in which people's behavior conforms to some well-established set of cultural norms, whose gratification results from passive appreciation. A casual crowd is any collectivity of people who just happen to be in one place at the same time. The nature of a crowd does not necessarily remain stable and can change if events change.

Because today's systems of communication spread information quickly among millions of people, collective behavior is often shared by large numbers of people who have no direct knowledge of or contact with one another. Such a collectivity is called a mass. Fads and fashions are patterns of behavior that are widely dispersed among a mass. Rumor is a form of information that spreads quickly and informally through a mass or a crowd. The mass can often be influenced by public opinion: advertisements, propaganda, and opinion leaders. When rumor and public opinion catch the mass imagination so strongly that facts no longer seem to matter, mass hysteria and panic may set in.

A social movement is a conscious, collective, organized attempt to bring about or resist large-scale change in the social order by noninstitutionalized means. Some catalyst is needed to actually mobilize the discontent that people feel. According to relative deprivation theory, the catalyst occurs when large numbers of people believe they lack the income, living conditions, working conditions, political rights, or social dignity they feel they are entitled to. According to resource mobilization theory, social movements arise because some people know how to mobilize and channel popular discontent.

There are several types of social movements. Reactionary social movements embrace the aims of the past and seek to return the general society to yesterday's values. Conservative social movements seek to maintain society's current values. Revisionary social movements seek partial or slight changes within the existing order but do not threaten the order itself. Revolutionary social movements seek to overthrow all or nearly all of the existing social order and replace it with an order they consider to be more suitable. Expressive social movements stress personal feelings of satisfaction and well-being and arise to fill some void or to distract people from their problems.

Social movements typically pass through a series of five stages: (1) incipiency, (2) coalescence, (3) institutionalization, (4) fragmentation, and (5) demise.

Chapter 21

SOCIAL CHANGE

On November 13, 1987, Baby "J" was born 15 weeks prematurely. From the beginning, her prognosis was grim as she struggled for life. During her 4-month stay at the intensive care nursery at Georgetown University Hospital in Washington, D.C., she suffered from serious brain hemorrhaging and badly damaged and immature lungs that may leave her permanently brain damaged and with cerebral palsy. The same doctors who used heroic efforts to save the baby now question whether she will ever be able to swallow or suck.

Baby "J" 's parents are emotionally shattered by what has happened and conflicted about their daughter's future. "There was a time when we were afraid she would die," the baby's father said. "Now there are times when we're afraid she'll live. Without this technology, she would have died naturally, and we wouldn't have had to ask ourselves these questions. Maybe that would have been better."

All over the country, parents of premature babies with serious medical problems are asking themselves these same questions as they watch the world of modern medicine struggle to save their babies' lives. These babies are as young as 24 weeks (a full-term gestation is 40 weeks) and as little as 500 grams (a little more than a pound). Five years ago, doctors would not have even tried to save these tiny lives. But advances in the care of newborns have been dramatic. Babies so small that they can fit in the palm of an adult's hand are now being treated successfully for the lung disease, hemorrhaging, and infection that once killed them.

But there are costs:

Costs in terms of dollars and cents. A baby born 4 months premature may run up a staggering hospital bill that can top $350,000.

Costs in terms of the toll on families. No one can guarantee survival or normalcy as the baby deals with one life-threatening problem after another. Families must contend with this as well as with the constant probability of death and the fear of raising a seriously ill child.

Costs in terms of a never-ending medical debate. Doctors have a legal obligation to treat premature infants—even when there is no hope for life as we know it. Federal regulations force a doctor to try to keep the baby alive. Said one doctor looking at a hopelessly ill baby who would certainly die within 6 months, "Here's a case where technology has overtaken rational thought."

Costs in terms of society's priorities. Modern technology has forced on us questions we cannot answer: Who among us can decide what is an acceptable quality of life? Should so much money and technological resources and manpower be devoted to so few patients, many of whom have little chance of living or leading a normal life? Should the money be directed instead toward preventing premature births? Here we see technology giving some families great joy as they take healthy, thriving babies home from the hospital and forcing others to live with great hardship. We see

money being spent in one area and not another, and we see society changing because of it. (Kanner, 1988; Pryor, 1988; Newsweek, May 16, 1988)

As you will see in this chapter, technology is one of the primary sources of social change—and it is also one of the primary sources of social stress. The beliefs, norms, and values that regulate our lives are all being tested by the pace of change.

Twenty-five centuries ago the Greek philosopher Heraclitus lectured on the inevitability of change. "You cannot step into the same river twice," he said, "for . . . waters are continually flowing on." Indeed, "he observed," . . . everything gives way and nothing stays fixed" (Wheelright, 1959). Social and technological change is an important topic for sociological study. The last decade has seen impressive technological changes, and the social changes growing out of them are still evolving. In this chapter we will examine how, why, and in what specific directions societies are likely to change.

SOCIETY AND SOCIAL CHANGE

What, exactly, is social change? The best way to analyze how sociologists define social change is through example. The invention of the steam locomotive was not in itself a social change, but the acceptance of the invention and the spread of railroad transportation were. Martin Luther's indictments of the Catholic church nailed to the door of Wittenberg Cathedral in 1517 were not in themselves social change, but they helped give rise to one of the major social changes of all time, the Protestant Reformation. Adam Smith's great work *An Inquiry into the Nature and Causes of the Wealth of Nations* (first published in 1776) was not in itself social change, but it helped initiate a social change that altered the world, the Industrial Revolution. Thus, individual discoveries, actions, or works do not themselves constitute social change, but they may lead to alterations in shared values or patterns of social behavior or even to the reorganization of social relationships and institutions. When this happens, sociologists speak of social change. Hans Gerth and C. Wright Mills (1953) define social change "as whatever happens in the course of time to the roles, the institutions, or the orders comprising a social structure, their emergence, growth and decline." To put it simply, using terms we defined in Chapter 5, **social change** consists of any modification in the social organization of a society in any of its social institutions or social roles.

Some social changes are violent and dramatic, like the French Revolution of 1789 or the 1917 Russian Revolution. However, not all cases of violent social or collective behavior are instances of social change. Thus, the United States' race riots of the late 1960s and early 1970s were not in themselves examples of social change. For that matter, not all social change need be violent. For example, the transformation of the family into its modern forms over the last 200 years represents an enormous social change that has profoundly affected the general nature of society as well as each person's childhood and adult experiences. Similarly, the rise of computer technology and developments in telecommunications over the last few decades have resulted in the emergence of what sociologist Edward Shils (1971) described as "mass society," in which vast numbers of individuals share collectively in the community and in a common language.

It would be a mistake to think of social change only in terms of the social structure. Morris Ginsberg (1958) observed that "the term social change must also include changes in attitudes and beliefs, in so far as they sustain institutions and change with them." In addition, individual motivation always plays a real but immeasurable role in social change.

SOURCES OF SOCIAL CHANGE

What causes social change? Sociologists have linked several factors to social change. These factors, which we shall consider here,

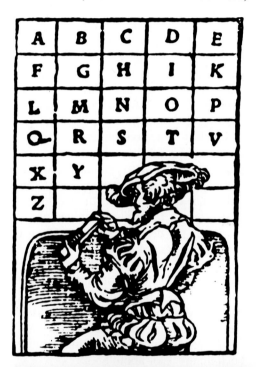

social change Any modification in the social organization of a society in any of its social institutions or social roles.

Technology is one of the primary sources of social change. The printing press had a dramatic impact on society, as did the personal computer.

TAKING THE SOCIOLOGICAL PERSPECTIVE

WHAT IS IT LIKE TO WORK AT HOME?

Millions of Americans work at home in what Alvin Toffler described as wired-up "electronic cottages." About 13 million people earn their primary income from home-based businesses, another 10 million take work home from the office, and another 3 million have full-time office jobs but run small businesses on the side. As everyone who works at home quickly learns, rolling out of bed and into the office may not be as easy as it sounds. Adjusting to a noncorporate office environment can be stressful, especially if there are children around.

For many, the biggest problem is isolation. Out of touch with their coworkers and away from the camaraderie of the corporation, they feel like they have been sent to the outer reaches of Siberia. At home, coffee breaks are solitary and there is no such thing as bouncing an idea off a colleague at the next desk. Many home-based workers cope by making frequent visits to the office and arranging lunch dates with friends.

Maintaining a professional stance can also be difficult if family and friends equate being at home with not working. Home-based workers often get phone calls from friends who just want to chat and requests from neighbors to carpool children to and from activities.

Modern technology makes this life-style possible. Home office computers are connected to corporate headquarters by way of ordinary phone lines. And documents can be sent anywhere throughout the world by way of facsimile machines or overnight delivery services. Over the last decade, this technology has become affordable even to the smallest businessperson. A computer and telephone hookup can be purchased for about $1500, a fax machine for less than $1000, and a professional-quality copier for about $500.

Moreover, many companies now accept the fact that home-based workers can also be productive workers. At San Francisco-based Pacific Bell, for example, between 500 and 1000 workers work at home up to four days a week. And J. C. Penney routinely hires telephone workers to accept phone orders that are diverted to employees' homes.

Certainly, the adjustment to this life-style is great, but the rewards are also substantial. Lunch breaks with the kids, no commute, and no dressing up every day are benefits that make working at home the answer to many people's prayers. Of course, with no boss looking over your shoulder, the responsibility to get things done is all up to you. Clearly, if you are not self-disciplined, working at home would be a mistake.

Sources: "Your Home, the Office," *U.S. News & World Report,* September 26, 1988, pp. 64–66; Robin Micheli, "Home Is Where the Office Is," *Money,* July 1988, pp. 68–78; Laura Van Tuyl, "Clocking in at Home," *Christian Science Monitor,* November 8, 1988, p. 23.

---

are categorized as internal and external sources of change.

INTERNAL SOURCES OF SOCIAL CHANGE

Internal sources of social change include those factors that originate within a specific society and that singly or in combination produce significant alterations in its social organization and structure. The most important internal sources of social change are technological innovation, ideology, cultural conflicts, and institutionalized structural inequality.

Technological Innovation

Technological change in industrial society is advancing at a dizzying pace, carrying so-

internal sources of social change Those factors that originate within a specific society and that singly or in combination produce significant alterations in its social organization and structure.

cial organizations and institutions along with it. Computer and communications-based electronic information technology has already transformed American life as we know it in the home, family, workplace, and school.

Homes have already been transformed into what Alvin Toffler (1970) called "electronic cottages" in which people both work and live. Receiving and sending information through computer terminals, workers are no longer limited to working in a specific office.

Already, signs of these trends are plentiful. We can deposit funds and pay bills through electronic banking centers without ever handling money. Home computers are already in millions of American homes. Even crime patterns have been changed by the computer. Clever thieves have diverted funds using computer codes in banks. In fact, so much about society is changing so quickly as a result of advanced computer technology that scholars are beginning to worry whether humans have the psychological resilience to adapt to the social changes that must follow.

Ideology

The term **ideology** is used in many ways. Most often it refers to a set of interrelated religious or secular beliefs, values, and norms that justify the pursuit of a given set of goals through a given set of means. Throughout history, ideologies have played a major role in shaping the direction of social changes.

Conservative (or traditional) **ideologies** try to preserve things as they are and indeed may slow down social changes that technological advances are promoting.

Liberal ideologies seek limited reforms that do not involve fundamental changes in the social structure of society. Affirmative action programs, for example, are intended to redress historical patterns of discrimination that have kept women and minority groups from competing on an equal footing with white males for jobs. Although far-

President Roosevelt's New Deal policies, which included the Civilian Conservation Corps, were attacked by both conservatives and radicals. Conservatives saw it as "creeping socialism," while radicals saw it as a desperate attempt to save capitalism.

reaching, these liberal ideological programs do not attempt to change the economic system that more radical critics believe is at the heart of job discrimination.

Radical (or revolutionary) **ideologies** reject liberal reforms as mere tinkerings that simply make the structural inequities of the system more bearable and therefore more likely to be maintained. Like the socialist political movement described in Chapter 17, radical ideologists seek major structural changes in society. Interestingly, radicals sometimes share the objectives of conservatives in their opposition to liberal reforms that would lessen the severity of a problem, because they make it less likely for structural changes to occur. For example, conservative as well as many radical groups bitterly attacked President Franklin D. Roosevelt's New Deal policies, in which federal funds were used to create jobs and bring the country out of the Depression. Conservatives attacked the New Deal as "creeping socialism," while radicals saw it as a desperate (and successful) attempt to save the faltering capitalist system and stave off a socialist revolution.

radical ideologies Ideologies that seek major structural changes in society.

ideology A set of interrelated religious or secular beliefs, values, and norms justifying the pursuit of a given set of goals through a given set of means.

conservative ideologies Ideologies that try to preserve things as they are.

liberal ideologies Ideologies that seek limited reforms that do not involve fundamental changes in the structure of society.

external sources of social change Changes within a society produced by events external to that society.

Cultural Conflicts and Institutionalized Structural Inequality

Cultural conflicts and institutionalized structural inequality promote social change, because society must accommodate to demands for social, economic, political, or cultural reforms.

Cultural conflict exists in America in a variety of forms. Blacks, Hispanics, and other minorities, for example, are often the victims of institutionalized inequality. As these groups have asserted their right to equality, the institutions have been forced to change. (Federal, state, and local laws have been passed to make it illegal to discriminate against minorities in voting, in the schools, in the labor force, in housing, and in other sectors of American life.) The labor and civil rights movements arose because of structural inequalities in American society.

EXTERNAL SOURCES OF SOCIAL CHANGE

As we described in Chapter 3, diffusion is the transmission of traits from one culture to another. It is what we would call an **external source of social change.** It occurs when groups with different cultures come into contact and exchange items and ideas with one another. It does not take the diffusion of many culture traits to result in profound social changes, as the anthropologist Lauriston Sharp (1952) demonstrated with regard to the introduction of steel axes to the Yir Yoront, a Stone Age tribe inhabiting southeastern Australia. Before European missionaries brought steel axes to the Yir Yoront, these tools were made by chipping and grinding stone, a long, laborious process. Axes were very valuable, had religious importance, and also were the status symbol of tribal leaders. Women and young men had to ask permission from a leader to use an ax, which reinforced the patriarchal authority structure. However, anybody could earn a steel ax from the missionaries simply by impressing them as being "deserving." With women and young men thus having direct access to superior tools, the symbols representing status relations between male and female as well as young and old were devalued, and the norms governing these traditional relationships themselves were upset. In addition, introducing into the tribe valuable tools that did not have religious sanctions governing their use led to a drastic rise in the incidence of theft. In fact, the entire moral order of the Yir Yoront was undermined because their myths explained the origins of all important things in the world—but did not account for the arrival of steel axes. This, as Sharp observed, caused conditions fertile for the introduction of a new religion, a happy circumstance for the missionaries.

Diffusion occurs wherever and whenever different cultures come into contact with one another, though contact is not essential for traits to diffuse from one culture to another. For example, Native American groups below the Arctic smoked tobacco long before the arrival of the Europeans. But in Alaska the Inuit (Eskimos) knew nothing of its pleasures. European settlers

After World War II ended, the departing American troops left empty steel supply drums behind. The native population converted these drums into musical instruments, which are now basic to their musical culture. This is an example of an external source of social change.

In general, diffusion takes place from the more technologically advanced societies to those less so.

brought tobacco back to Europe, where it immediately became popular and diffused eastward across central Europe and Eurasia, up into Siberia, and eventually across the Bering Strait to the Inuit.

Today, of course, when so many of the world's peoples increasingly are in contact with one another through all forms of mass communication, cultural traits spread easily from one society to another. But the *direction* of diffusion rarely is random or balanced among societies. In general, traits diffuse from more powerful to weaker peoples, from the more technologically advanced to the less so. When social change is imposed by might or conquest on weaker peoples, sociologists speak of **forced acculturation.**

Why do these internal and external social changes occur? Different theories offer some important insights into the process of social change.

THEORIES OF SOCIAL CHANGE

The complexity of social change makes it impossible for a single theory to explain all its ramifications. Because each theory views social change from an entirely different perspective, contradictions are common. For example, functionalist and conflict theories are diametrically opposed, but this does not make one theory "right" and the other "wrong." Rather, they are complementary views that must be analyzed together in order to understand the total theoretical framework of social change.

EVOLUTIONARY THEORY

By the middle of the nineteenth century, the concept of **evolution**—the continuous change from a simpler condition to a more complex state—was the dominant concern of European scholars in a variety of disciplines. The most influential evolutionary theorist was Charles Darwin, who in his 1859 volume *On the Origin of Species* described what he believed to be the biological evolutionary process that moved populations of organisms toward increasing levels of biological complexity.

Darwin's evolutionary theory influenced the work of sociologist Herbert Spencer, who used terms like "survival of the fittest" and "struggle for existence" to explain the superiority of Western cultures over non-Western ones. In Spencer's view, Western cultures had reached higher levels of cultural achievement because they were better adapted to compete for scarce resources and to meet other difficult challenges of life.

Late-nineteenth-century and early-twentieth-century philosophers continued to be influenced by what has come to be known as social-evolutionary thought. Although given different names, the theories they developed proposed similar stages through which societies progress. Two of the more influential social-evolutionary theorist, Émile Durkheim and Ferdinand Tönnies, were discussed in Chapter 19.

Durkheim argued that evolutionary changes affect the way society is organized, particularly with regard to work. Small,

evolution The continuous change from a simpler condition to a more complex state.

forced acculturation The situation that occurs when social change is imposed by might or conquest on weaker peoples.

As the first female leader of a major Islamic nation, Harvard-educated Benazir Bhutto is bringing about change in that area of the world.

primitive societies whose members share a set of common social characteristics, norms, and values come together in a bond of solidarity Durkheim called *mechanical solidarity.* These people tend to be of the same ethnicity and religion and share similar economic roles. As society grows larger, it develops a more complex division of labor. People play different economic roles; a more complex class structure develops; and members of the society increasingly do not share the same beliefs, values, and norms. However, they must still depend on one another's efforts in order that all may survive. Durkheim called the new advanced form of cohesion *organic solidarity.*

Ferdinand Tönnies's views of social evolution parallel those of Durkheim. In his view societies shift from the intimate, cooperative relationships of small societies, characterized by Gemeinschaft to Gesellschaft —the specialized impersonal relationships typical of large societies. Tönnies did not believe that these changes always brought progress (a feeling shared by Durkheim).

Rather, he saw social fragmentation, individual isolation, and a general weakening of societal bonds as the direct results of the movement toward individualization and the struggle for power that characterize urban society.

Much of the early evolutionary theory has been harshly criticized by contemporary sociologists, who charge that it uses the norms and values of one culture as absolute standards for all cultures. In response to these problems, modern evolutionists propose sequences of evolutionary stages that are much more flexible in allowing for actual historical variation among societies. Anthropologist Julian H. Steward (1955) proposes that social evolution is "multilineal," by which he means that the evolution of each society or cultural tradition must be studied independently and must not be forced into broad, arbitrary, "universal" stages. Marshall D. Sahlins and Elman R. Service (1960) distinguish between "general" evolution (the trend toward increasing differentiation) and "specific" evolution (social changes in each specific society that may move either in the direction of greater simplicity or greater complexity).

Sociologists today realize that change occurs in many different ways and does not necessarily follow a specific course. Nor does change necessarily mean progress (Lenski and Lenski, 1982). All evolutionary theories suffer to a greater or lesser degree from an inability to give a convincing answer to the question, Why do societies change? One approach that attempts to deal with this question is conflict theory (Lenski and Lenski, 1982).

CONFLICT THEORY

According to conflict theory, conflicts rooted in the class struggle between unequal groups lead to social change. This, in turn, creates conditions that lead to new conflicts.

Modern conflict theory is rooted in the writings of Karl Marx, whose theory of society and social conflict was introduced in

Chapter 1. In *Das Kapital,* first published in 1867, Marx argued that social class conflict is the most basic and influential source of all social change. The classes are in conflict because of the unequal allocation of goods and services. Those with money may purchase these; those without cannot. To Marx, it is a division between the exploiting and exploited classes.

Europe's transition from a feudal to a capitalistic society gave Marx the source of this model for social change: "Without conflict no progress: this is the law which civilization has followed to the present day" (Marx, 1959).

Several modern conflict theorist have modified Marx's theories of class conflict in light of recent historical events. Ralf Dahrendorf (1959), one of the foremost contemporary conflict theorists, sees as too simplistic the view that all social change is the outgrowth of class conflict. He believes that conflict and dissension are present in nearly every part of society. For example, non–social-class conflict may involve religious groups, political groups, or even nations. Dahrendorf does accept, however, the basic principle of conflict theory that social conflict and social change are built-in structural features of society.

Marx believed that social change within capitalist society would occur through a violent revolution of the workers against the capitalists. However, Marx did not foresee that those who controlled the means of production would tolerate the legalization of unions, collective bargaining, strikes, and integration of the less privileged into legal, reform-oriented parties of the Left. Marx also did not foresee that those who controlled the means of production would accept government regulation of corporations, welfare legislation, civil rights legislation, and other laws aimed at protecting employees and consumers.

FUNCTIONALIST THEORY

Functionalists view society as a **homeostatic system,** that is, an assemblage of interrelated parts that seeks to achieve and maintain a settled or stable state (Davis, 1949). A system that maintains a stable state is said to be in equilibrium. Because society is inherently an open system subject to influence from its natural and social environments, complete equilibrium never can be achieved. Rather, functionalists describe society as normally being in a condition of *dynamic* or *near equilibrium,* constantly making small adjustments in response to shifts or changes in its internal elements or parts (Homans, 1950).

Probably the best-known spokesman for functionalist theory in America was Talcott Parsons (1951, 1954, 1966), who saw society as a homeostatic "action system" (see Chapter 3) that seeks to "integrate" its elements and whose patterns of actions are "maintained" by its culture. According to Parsons, it is the role of society to fulfill six basic needs: (1) member replacement, (2) member socialization, (3) production of goods and services, (4) preservation of internal order, (5) provision and maintenance of a sense of purpose, and (6) protection from external attack. These needs are in a constant state of equilibrium with one another, and when one changes, the others must accommodate. For example, when industrialization shifted the burden of socializing young people from the family to the school, schools enlarged their educational function to include the education of the whole child. Parent–teacher associations were established, and guidance counselors were hired to coordinate the function of the school with those of the family and other institutions. Thus, when the family became more specialized, the schools stepped in to fill the vacuum. In this case, as in all others, argued Parsons (1951, 1971), change promotes adaptation, equilibrium, and eventual social stability.

As functionalist theory developed, it began to trace the cause of social change to people's dissatisfactions with social conditions that personally affect them. Consider the area of medicine. Technological advances in medical science have made the

homeostatic system An assemblage of interrelated parts that seeks to achieve and maintain a settled or stable state.

practice of general medicine all but impossible and encouraged the development of medical subspecialties. Patients, who were forced to see a different specialist for almost every one of their health-care needs, quickly became dissatisfied, even though the technical ability of each subspecialist was greater than that of the general practitioner. Responding to this dissatisfaction and to patients' convictions that their all-around health care was suffering as a result of the system of medical subspecializations, the medical profession created the "new" specialty of family medicine. Thus, the needs met by the old "family doctor" are once again being addressed by the "new family medicine specialist."

Another example of the functionalist view of social change is the American civil rights movement of the 1960s, which gained strength outside the normal channels of political action. Hundreds of thousands of individuals joined in street protests, and many thousands were arrested. Occurring against the backdrop of race riots in Watts and other inner-city neighborhoods (see Chapter 20), the civil rights movement threatened the society with widespread rebellion and chaos. In response, political and social leaders launched a series of important adjustments that functioned to reform the society's institutional structure. These structural changes included the passage of the Civil Rights Act of 1964, which was intended to eliminate discrimination in public accommodations and in the labor force. Affirmative action programs were established to integrate blacks into the labor force and provide equal access to higher education. The Voting Rights Act of 1965 was passed to attack discrimination in voting, particularly in the registration procedures in the South. In 1968 Congress passed the first laws to attack discrimination in housing. Institutions that did not comply with these new federal rulings faced the possible withdrawal of all federal funds. Hence, though American society was pushed toward disequilibrium in the 1960s and early 1970s, greater equilibrium was reestablished through selected institutional adjustments that diminished organized expressions of discontent.

Functionalist theory successfully explains moderate degrees of social change, such as the adjustments that diffused the civil rights movement in America. The concepts of equilibrium and homeostasis are not very helpful, however, in explaining major structural changes (Bertalanffy, 1968). This criticism was summed up by Gnessous (1967) when he said that an equilibrium theory like that of Parsons's can neither explain the occurrence of radical changes in society nor account for the phenomena that accompany them; it says nothing about what happens when a social system is in disequilibrium . . . it is tied to the image of a society whose historical development holds no surprises."

William F. Ogburn's (1964) concept of *cultural lag,* discussed in Chapter 3, attempts to deal with these criticisms and explain social change in functionalist terms. Although all elements of a society are interrelated, Ogburn asserted, some elements may change rapidly and others "lag" behind. According to Ogburn, technological change typically is faster than change in the nonmaterial culture, that is, the beliefs,

William Ogburn has suggested that technological change is typically faster than change in values, beliefs, and norms that regulate society. This may produce cultural lag.

norms, and values that regulate people's day-to-day lives in friendship and kinship groups and in religion. Therefore, he argued, technological change often results in culture lag. New patterns of behavior may emerge, even though they conflict with traditional values. When the birth-control pill (a product of our material culture) was developed, for example, orthodox religious norms forbade its use. Catholic women who wanted to limit their family size thus were on the horns of a dilemma. If they took the pill, they would violate the dictum of the church. If they did not, they would face additional pregnancies and the concomitant economic and family stress. Thus, even though Ogburn adopts a functionalist approach to social change, his theories incorporate the idea that stresses and strains or "lack of fit" among the parts of the social order are inevitable.

Popular during the 1940s and 1950s, the functionalist theory of social change has been criticized widely in recent times. Aside from the criticisms that we have mentioned, critics argue further that functionalism is a conservative theory that overestimates the amount of consensus in society and underestimates the effects of social conflict.

CYCLICAL ("RISE AND FALL") THEORY

Inherent in cyclical theories of social change is the assumption that the rise and fall of civilizations is inevitable and the notion that social change may not be for the good. Shocked by the devastation of World War I, people began to see social progress as the decline of society rather than as its enhancement. These feelings were crystallized in the works of Oswald Spengler, Arnold Toynbee, and Pitirim Sorokin.

In his controversial work *The Decline of the West* (1932), German historian Oswald Spengler theorized that every society moves through four stages of development: childhood, youth, mature adulthood, and old age. Spengler felt that Western society had reached the "golden age" of maturity

during the Enlightenment of the eighteenth century, and from then had begun the inevitable crumbling and decline that go along with old age. Nothing, he believed, could stop this process. Just as the great civilizations of Babylon, Egypt, Greece, and Rome had declined and died, so too would the West.

British historian Arnold Toynbee (1946) theorized that the rise and fall of civilizations were explicable through the interrelated concepts of societal *challenge* and *response*. Every society, he observed, faces both natural and social challenges from its environments. Are its natural resources plentiful or limited? Are its boundaries easy or difficult to defend? Are important trade routes readily accessible or difficult to reach? Are its neighbors warlike or peaceful? When a society is able to fashion adequate responses to these challenges, it survives and grows. When it cannot, it falls into a spiral of decline. According to Toynbee, as each challenge is met, new challenges arise, placing the society in a constant give-and-take interaction with its environments.

Pitirim A. Sorokin (1889–1968) theorized that cultures are divided into two groups: **ideational cultures,** which emphasize spiritual values; and **sensate cultures,**

Oswald Spengler believed that the disappearance of the Egyptian civilization was part of the inevitable crumbling and decline that is part of the life cycle of any society.

ideational culture A term developed by Pitirim A. Sorokin to describe a culture in which the spiritual has the greatest value.

sensate culture A term developed by Pitirim A. Sorokin to describe a culture in which people are dedicated to self-expression and the gratification of their immediate physical needs.

which are based on what is immediately apparent through the senses. In an ideational culture, progress is achieved through self-control and adherence to a strong moral code. In a sensate culture, people are dedicated to self-expression and the gratification of their immediate physical needs.

Sorokin believed societies are constantly moving between the two extremes of sensate and ideational cultures. The main reason for this back and forth movement is that neither sensate nor ideational culture provides the basis for a perfect society. As one culture begins to deteriorate, its weaknesses and excesses become apparent, and there is a movement in the opposite direction. Occasionally, however, a culture may reach an intermediate place between these extremes. Sorokin called this the **idealistic point,** at which sensate and ideational values coexist in a harmonious mix.

Although cyclical, or "rise and fall," theories offer an interesting perspective on social change, they assume social change cannot be truly controlled by those who experience it. There is a supposedly inevitable cycle that all societies follow. The actions of people are part of an elaborate, predetermined cyclical progression of events that has a life of its own.

Most social change involves modernization, a process that includes both social and interpersonal dynamics.

idealistic point A term developed by Pitirim A. Sorokin to refer to the situation where sensate and ideational values coexist in a harmonious mix.

— MODERNIZATION: GLOBAL SOCIAL CHANGE

modernization The complex set of changes that take place as a traditional society becomes an industrial one.

Modernization refers to a complex set of changes that take place as a traditional society undergoes industrialization. Modernization as we know it today is a phenomenon that first began with the Industrial Revolution some two centuries ago. Whereas the modernization of Western society evolved steadily over that time, the modernization

of the Third World developing nations is proceeding at a much more rapid pace.

MODERNIZATION: AN OVERVIEW

As modernization progresses from the first stages onward, many different changes occur. In the first stages of modernization, farmers move beyond subsistence farming to produce surplus food, which they sell in the market for money instead of bartering them for goods and services. In addition, a few limited cash crops and natural resources are exploited, bringing a steady flow of money into the economy. Simple tools and traditional crafts are replaced by industrialized technology and applied scientific knowledge. And whenever possible, human physical power is replaced by machines.

As a society modernizes, work becomes increasingly specialized. New jobs—often requiring special training—are created, and people work for wages rather than living from the products of their labor. The economic system is freed from the traditional restraints and obligations rooted in kinship relations, and money becomes the medium of exchange. Educational institutions become differentiated from family life, and the population becomes increasingly literate. Cities rise as industrial and commercial centers and attract migrants from rural areas. Thanks to modern medicine, the death rate of the population falls, but the birthrate stays the same (at least in the early stages of modernization), creating excessive overcrowding.

Modernization reduces the role of the family to the socialization of young children. Nuclear families are cut off from extended kinship networks, and many traditional constraints on behavior, such as notions of family pride and religious beliefs, lose their potency. Frequently, social equality between men and women increases as new social statuses and roles allow for changes in institutionalized behavior. Wealth is unequally distributed between the upper and lower classes (Dalton, 1971;

Moore, 1965; Smelser, 1971). As you may have noted, many of these developments are separate facets of the overall pattern of increasing differentiation, which is a key trait of modernizing societies.

MODERNIZATION IN THE THIRD WORLD

Whereas modernization was indigenous to most of Europe, it was forced on Third World nations by conquering armies, missionaries, plantation managers, colonial administrators, colonist groups, and industrial enterprises. Colonial administrators did not hesitate to destroy existing political structures whenever they seemed to endanger their rule. Missionaries used the threat of military force, bribery, and even good deeds (such as the construction of hospitals and schools) to draw people away from their traditions. They stamped out practices they did not approve of (such as polygamy) and arbitrarily imposed European customs. Occasionally these missionary activities had comic consequences, as when women unaccustomed to covering their breasts simply cut holes in the fronts of their missionary-issued T-shirts. Other results were less humorous: People in tropical climates suffered skin infections after missionaries convinced them to dress in Western clothes but neglected to introduce soap.

Until recently, modernization and Westernization were thought of as more or less the same thing. A developing country that wanted to adopt Western technology had to accept its cultural elements at the same time. However, as Third World nations have gained some measure of economic control over their resources, many have asserted political independence and insisted that modernization be guided by their own traditional values. One need only think of the oil-rich Islamic countries to realize the different directions that the modernization of developing countries is now taking.

The goals and methods of modernization in the Third World vary widely from region to region and even from one nation to another. Nevertheless, because of the extreme abruptness and pervasiveness of the social changes created by modernization, certain common problems confront many of the developing nations.

Technological innovation takes hold only when there is some need and social acceptance for it.

MODERNIZATION AND THE INDIVIDUAL

Modernization has given people in developed countries improved health, increased longevity, more leisure time and affluence. Poverty, malnutrition, and disease, which were problems of Western nations as recently as 1890, have been reduced dramatically for the bulk of the population. Life expectancy at birth increased from 47.6 years in 1900 to 73.8 years, and the workweek has been reduced from about 62 hours in 1890 to about 37 hours today. Indeed, modernization has given many in Western society the "luxury" of turning their attention to the problems of affluence, including anxiety, obesity, degenerative diseases, divorce, high taxes, inflation, and pollution.

The positive psychological effects of modernization were demonstrated by sociologists Alex Inkeles and David H. Smith (1974), who interviewed factory workers in Argentina, Bangladesh, Chile, India, Israel, and Nigeria. There researchers found that attending school and going to work in a factory had been a valued, liberating experience for many of these workers. They had improved their standard of living, overcome their fear of new things and foreign people, become more flexible about trying new ways of doing things, and adopted a more positive and action-oriented attitude toward their own lives.

Despite these benefits, modernization is not without its costs. Max Weber, who valued modernization as a means for making society more rational and efficient, nevertheless was painfully aware of its emotional costs, of its damaging impact on the spirit of the individual:

> . . . [If] the performance of each individual worker is mathematically measured, each man becomes a little cog in the machine and, aware of this, his one preoccupation is whether he can become a bigger cog (Weber, 1956).

Anthropologists and others have documented the severe psychological dislocation suffered by many peoples around the world as a result of modernization. The collapse of traditional cultures under the pressures of modernization has left individuals emotionally adrift in a world they do not understand and cannot control. Probably the most horrifying story is Colin Turnbull's (1972) account of the Ik, a hunting and food-gathering people of Uganda who were relocated and forced to become farmers. Within 5 years their society, including its basic family unit, had disintegrated. Unable to feed themselves or their families in their traditional way, individuals starved, became demoralized, and lost their ability to empathize with one another.

Thus, it is clear that modernization has a profound psychological effect on people's lives. The *degree* of personal stress and dislocation that individuals experience as their society modernizes depends on many things, including the historical traditions of the culture, the conditions under which modernization is introduced, and the degree to which the masses are allowed to share in the material benefits of the change.

——— SOCIAL CHANGE IN THE UNITED STATES

There is virtually no area of life in the United States that has not changed in some respect since the relatively simple days of the 1950s. In addition, the pace of change will quicken even more as the turn of the century approaches. The following are a few of the major forces that are shaping future life in the United States.

TECHNOLOGICAL CHANGE

In the past dozen years the personal computer has transformed the workplace and our lives; videocassette recorders, which are now present in 66 percent of all households (*American Demographics,* 1988), and compact discs have added dramatically to home entertainment activities; and biotechnology has helped us discover genetically engineered vaccines and a host of other benefits to society. What could possibly top what has already happened and the changes that have been produced?

The answer is the technological innovations about to take place will be part of a new era that one author (Bylinsky, 1988) has called "The Age of Insight," in which advances will help us understand how things work and how to make them work better. The immediate future will produce not just more and more data but also some startling new discoveries. The computer is being transformed from a number cruncher into a machine for insight and discovery.

The Age of Insight will help us understand the workings of the human body in a way never before attainable. If we can decipher the body's own healing substances and the underlying causes of disease, it will allow researchers to develop new drugs and novel methods of treatment. Researchers will increasingly tap the body itself as a new source of medications that genetic engineers can copy and improve on. New insights into human diseases should essentially make it possible to prevent such autoimmune diseases as rheumatoid arthritis, multiple sclerosis, and insulin-dependent diabetes, in which the body mistakenly attacks its own tissue (Bylinsky, 1988).

Many changes have already taken place in the area of telecommunications. Telecommunications experts see a world linked by vast computerized networks that process voice, data, and video with equal ease. Desktop workstations will have the power of what we now know as supercomputers.

Even the individual scientist can now conduct research impossible just a short time ago. With a personal computer and newly developed compact computer disks that hold enormous amounts of information, huge databases can be tapped (Crispell, 1987). Additional databases can be accessed via the telephone lines, making hard-to-find information available in minutes.

Supercomputers themselves are expected to advance to the point where they will enable scientists to "see" objects on a

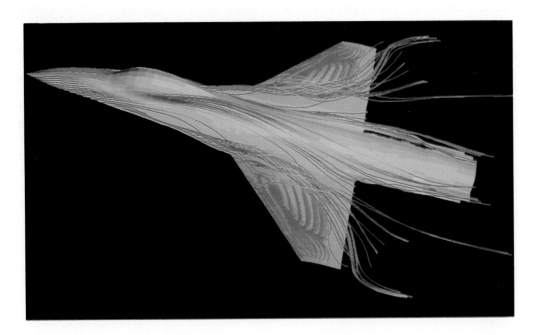

Many believe we are on the brink of "The Age of Insight," a period in which advances will help us understand how things work and how to make them work better. This is a computer image of the air flow below a vertical-takeoff-and-landing jet aircraft. This sophisticated technology makes it possible to design high-speed aircraft.

smaller scale than microscopes can. This should make a vital contribution to chemistry, chemical engineering, molecular biology, and other fields. Supercomputers will also be able to describe complex events, such as the chemistry involved in photosynthesis, in greater detail than is possible with today's instruments.

"Visual computing" in effect reproduces the world around us mathematically within a computer. The objects can then be both seen and manipulated in all sorts of ways. A researcher can then describe the nature and behavior of an object or phenomenon with equations and present it visually. The objects simulated can include anything from the wing of an airplane to the interior of the sun. This kind of computing will create new areas of scientific inquiry and the development of new consumer products (Bylinsky, 1988; Crispell, 1987).

When sociologists examine technological change, they often refer to **technological determinism.** This is a view that technological change has an important effect on a society and affects its culture, social structure, and even its history. For example, the printing press, the automobile, the jet engine, and nuclear weapons have all had a phenomenal social impact.

We must be careful to realize that technology *influences* rather than determines social change. Technological innovation always occurs in the context of other forces —political, economic, or historical— which themselves help shape the technology and its uses. Technological innovation only takes hold when there is some need for it and social acceptance for it. Technology itself is neutral; people decide whether and how to use it (Rybczynski, 1983).

THE WORK FORCE OF THE FUTURE

Technological change will also produce changes in the work force. According to projections from the Bureau of Labor Sta-

technological determinism
The view that technological change has an important effect on a society and has an impact on its culture, social structure, and even its history.

tistics, the United States will have 21 million more workers in the year 2000 than in 1986. This represents an 18 percent increase in absolute numbers but a slowing down in the rate of growth achieved in the period from 1972 to 1986, when the labor force increased by almost 31 million, or 35 percent.

The rapid growth during the past 15 years was the result of the entrance into the labor force of the baby boom generation and the rapid increase in the number of women entering the labor force. The effects of these two trends will be less marked in the future as the number of young people ready to enter the labor force declines and the entry of women into the labor force slows.

The labor force in the year 2000 will have more minority and female workers and fewer young workers than it does today. Although the number of white men in the labor force will grow by 5 million, this is an increase of only 8.8 percent. Other groups will grow at much faster rates. Black labor force participation, for example, is expected to increase 23 percent, adding 3.6 million members to the labor force. The number of women in the labor force is projected to rise 25 percent, up more than 13 million. Asians, American Indians, and members of other racial groups will add 2.4 million workers (Kutscher, 1988).

Hispanics represent one of the fastest-growing segments of the labor force today. They are expected to increase by 74 percent, or 6 million, by the year 2000. In fact, women and blacks, Asians, Hispanics, and other races will account for more than 90 percent of all labor force growth. In addition, as many as 23 percent of the new workers will be immigrants (U.S. Bureau of Labor Statistics, 1987).

Service-producing industries will account for nearly all of the projected growth. The finance, insurance, and real estate industries are projected to add more than 1.6 million jobs. This number, however, represents a considerable slowing in this sector when compared with the nearly 2.4 million jobs added over the previous 14 years. The service industries themselves will expand by more than 10 million jobs. Health-care services and business services will be important contributors as they continue to produce new services that greatly add to their overall demand and employment growth (U.S. Bureau of Labor Statistics, 1987).

There will be a number of effects from the expected changes in the growth and composition of the labor force. For example, as the number of job seekers ages 16 to 19 declines, the unemployment rate for this group, which has been historically high, should also decline. There will also be a much smaller market for goods and services primarily targeted at 16- to 24-year-olds (Kutscher, 1988).

Five occupational groups are projected to grow faster than average between now and the year 2000. These include technicians, service workers, professional workers, sales workers, and executive and managerial employees. Two groups—agriculture, forestry, and fishing workers and private household workers—are expected to decline. (See Tables 21.1 and 21.2 for the fastest-growing and fastest-declining occupations.)

In certain parts of the country the shape of future employment is already quite clear. On the West Coast and in New England a great concentration of high-tech industries has produced a demand for a large work force in science, engineering, and technical occupations. In fact, in California, Massachusetts, Washington, Connecticut, New Hampshire, and New Jersey, at least 13.5 percent of the work force now works in those areas (Giese and Testa, 1988).

The occupational projections are significant where education is concerned. For the most part, occupations that require the most education will grow the most rapidly. There will still be plenty of jobs available for those with only a high school degree. However, the prospects for someone with less than a high school education will be dim (Kutscher, 1988).

TABLE 21.1
Projections for Fastest Growing Occupations, 1986–2000

	Percent Gain 1986–2000
Paralegal personnel	103.7
Medical assistants	90.4
Physical therapists	87.5
Data-processing equipment repairers	80.4
Home health aides	80.1
Podiatrists	77.2
Computer systems analysts	75.6
Medical record technicians	75.0
Employment interviewers	71.2
Computer programmers	69.9

Many of the jobs that will be increasing the most rapidly between 1986 and 2000 will require at least a college degree.

TABLE 21.2
Projections for Fastest Declining Occupations, 1986–2000

	Percent Decline 1986–2000
Electrical and electronic assemblers	−53.7
Railroad conductors and yardmasters	−40.9
Gas and petroleum plant and system occupations	−34.3
Industrial truck and tractor operators	−33.6
Shoe sewing machine operators and tenders	−32.1
Telephone installers and repairers	−31.8
Chemical equipment workers	−29.7
Stenographers	−28.2
Farmers	−28.1
Statistical clerks	−26.4

Changing technology and cheap labor in other countries will require fewer workers for these jobs.

Source: Occupational Outlook Quarterly (Spring 1988); Bureau of Labor Statistics, 1987.

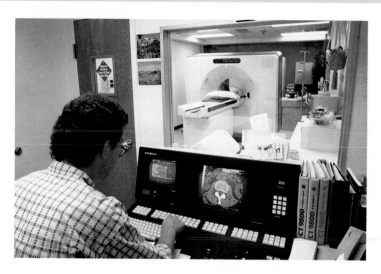

A major increase in the elderly population in the United States will increase the demand for medical services.

AN AGING SOCIETY

For the first time in our history, there are more people age 65 and over in the population than there are teenagers, and it is expected that as of 1990 the number of older citizens will surpass 31 million, whereas the teenaged population will have dropped to 23 million.

Relatively stagnant birthrates and big jumps in life expectancy have been the

causes for this trend. In addition, the enormous baby boom generation, born between 1946 and 1964, which now represents about one-third of the population, is moving into middle age. By 1990, the number of people between the ages of 30 and 44 is expected to surge by 20 percent and total 60 million. Some people worry about the potential for conflict between the generations, as the elderly and young battle over spending priorities (U.S. Bureau of the Census).

As the baby boom population ages, its large numbers will cause cycles of relative growth and decline at each stage of life. The aging of the baby boom generation will push the median age, now at 31 years, to over 38 years by 2010, and to almost 42 years by 2050.

The years from 1985 through 2020 cover the most economically productive years for the baby boom generation. In 2010 the oldest members of the baby boom will be nearing 65, while the youngest will have just passed 45. As the baby boom cohorts begin to reach age 65 starting in 2011, the number of elderly persons will rise dramatically.

In about 2030, the final phase of the elderly explosion caused by the baby boom will begin. At that point the population age 85 and over will be the only older age group still growing and will have increased from 2.7 million now to 8.6 million in 2030, to more than 16 million by 2050 (U.S. Bureau of the Census) (see Table 21.3).

To put it another way, today one in one hundred people is 85 years old or older; in 2050, one in twenty persons could be so old. Persons 85 and older could constitute close to one quarter of the older population by then.

Concerns associated with problems of the older population are exacerbated by the large excess of women over men in the older ages. Among the aged, women outnumber men 3 to 2. That imbalance increases to more than 2 to 1 for persons 85 and over.

Increased longevity and the aging of the baby boom generation will mean that many people will find themselves caring for

TABLE 21.3
Growth Rate Among Age Cohorts, 1980–2010 and 2010–2030

	Average Annual Percent of Growth 1980–2010	Average Annual Percent of Growth 2010–2030
Preschool (under 5)	+0.3	*
School age (5–17)	*	+0.1
Young adult (18–34)	−0.2	−0.1
Adult (35–44)	+1.4	+0.5
Middle age (45–64)	+2.5	−0.4
Young old (65–74)	+1.0	+3.5
Old old (75+)	+2.9	+3.0

Source: U.S. Bureau of the Census, *Statistical Brief,* December 1986.

WHO WILL FUND SOCIAL SECURITY?

A s our society grows older, there will be fewer people paying into the social security system and more beneficiaries. As you can see in the following table, this worker-beneficiary ratio will drop from 5.1 workers to 1 beneficiary in 1960 to an expected 1.9 to 1 in 2035. This demographic trend threatens the retirement benefits of the baby boom generation and the viability of the entire social security system. In the years ahead a solution to this problem will have to be found.

Source: Peter T. Kilborn, "The Temptations of the Social Security Surplus," *New York Times,* November 27, 1988, p. E5.

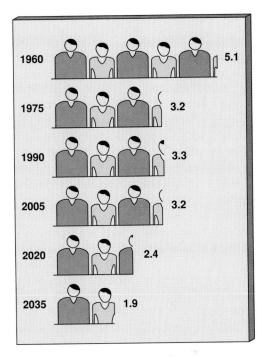

Number of Workers per Beneficiary, with Projections for Years 1990 and Beyond.

very old persons after they themselves have reached retirement age. Assuming that generations are separated by about 25 years, persons 85, 90, or 95 would have children who are anywhere between 60 and 70 years old. It is estimated that every third person 60 to 74 years old will have a living elderly parent by 2010.

Now there are more than twice as many children as there are elderly persons. By 2030, the proportion of children will have shrunk and the proportion of elderly will have grown until these two groups are approximately equal, at just over one-fifth of the population each (U.S. Bureau of the Census).

For the first time in our history, there are more people age 65 and over in the population than there are teenagers.

Should Sex-Selection Abortions Be Permitted?

Should a woman be allowed to have an abortion because the baby is not going to be the sex the parents had in mind? Increasingly, this is an issue that doctors and the general public must face as advancing medical technology makes sex selection possible.

In 1973, the year that the Supreme Court made abortions legal, only 1 percent of medical geneticists approved of sex selection as a reason for an abortion. Today that figure has jumped to 20 percent.

There are two ways of looking at this issue. On the one hand, because abortion on demand is the law of the land, we have no legal grounds to withhold test results that could result in a sex-selection abortion. How can we make an argument against such abortions when you can have an abortion for any reason?

On the other hand, it seems to be one of the most frivolous uses of abortion yet, and one wonders how doctors can go along with it. But they do, and sex selection appears to be covered by the Supreme Court's view that abortion is a private matter.

Yet, what is legal is not always moral. The search for the perfect baby has caused some women to abort fetuses that would be born only marginally disabled. It seems to be only a small step then to abort a fetus for being the wrong sex.

If sex-selection abortions become widespread, they could have a significant impact on the male-to-female ratio. Studies in the early 1970s suggested such abortions could produce a 7 percent increase in males. It could be that this figure is too low, however.

In Seoul, Korea, in 1983, obstetricians reported that 109 male babies were born for every 100 girls. In 1984, the number was 110 boys for every 100 girls. By 1985 it climbed to 117 boys to 100 girls. At that point South Korea banned testing the sex of fetuses as a result of this trend. The parents responsible for this trend were not backward peasants, but rather members of the well-educated urban elite.

On a worldwide basis, sex-selection abortions are the natural successors to female infanticide as a method for increasing the ratio of males to females. Throughout history countless female babies have been killed because a male baby was desired. Even today we see this practice taking place as China's one-child policy has produced a reemergence of this phenomenon.

Surveys show that two-thirds of American couples would like their first child to be a boy. It is also a well-documented fact that first-born children have significant advantages over those born later. Would we also be producing significantly different levels of achievement if most firstborns are

male? What are the implications for the family of the future where the typical pattern is a favored older son and the not-so-favored younger daughter?

Sex-selection abortions have also produced a problem for feminists, who have steadfastly supported abortions. Having for so long defended a woman's right to choose to have an abortion for any reason, they are now confronted with the fact that female fetuses are the most likely ones to be aborted for gender reasons.

Feminists must consider the implications for women's equality if instead of being 51 percent of the population, as they now are, women's numbers dropped to 45 percent of the population? What if the numbers approached the Korean example? A long-term trend that produced a 15 to 20 percent change in the sex ratio would be a social disaster and would have enormous implications for the future of that society.

When medical technology reaches the point where we can determine future intelligence or ultimate height or physical ability, will we abort for those reasons also? If we do, what kind of society will we become?

Source: John Leo, "Baby Boys, To Order," *U.S. News & World Report,* January 9, 1989, p. 59.

There are few certainties about the future, but the demographic outlook seems relatively clear, at least for persons already born. Careful consideration of the impact of our aging population can be an important tool in planning for the future.

What will the future really be like, and what social changes are we in store for? Although we have tried to offer you some insights about future trends here, we cannot be totally accurate in our predictions, and the ultimate outcome depends on crucial choices made by our government and individuals. The sociological perspective that this book has tried to convey should give you the tools necessary to see how you shape the world you are a part of, as well as how you are shaped by it. We hope your understanding of society has increased because of this text. Thank you for reading this far.

SUMMARY

Social change consists of alterations in a society's social organization, statuses, and social structure. Social change is caused by such internal factors as technological innovation, ideology (which may be conservative, liberal, or radical), and cultural conflicts and institutionalized structural inequality. Diffusion — the transmission of traits from one culture to another — is the primary external source of social change.

No one theory of social change explains all its ramifications, as each theory views social change from an entirely different perspective. The evolutionary theory of social change is based on the assumption that Western cultures have reached higher levels of cultural achievement because they are better adapted to compete for scarce resources and to meet other difficult challenges. Conflict theory is rooted in the assumption that the class struggle between unequal groups leads to social change, which in turn creates conditions that lead to new conflicts. Functionalist theory describes society as being in a condition of near equilibrium, constantly making small adjustments in response to shifts or changes in its elements or parts.

Modernization is the complex set of changes that take place as a traditional society experiences the processes of industrialization. Modernization first occurred in Western society after the Industrial Revolution. It was forced on Third World nations by conquering armies, missionaries, and other representatives of Western societies who believed that modernization and Westernization were the same thing. Modernization has been a mixed blessing to both developed and developing nations. On the one hand, it has provided improved health, increased longevity, leisure time, and affluence. On the other, it has generated many strains as people have had to cope with industrialization, urbanization, secularization, and rapid social changes.

There is virtually no area of life in the United States that has not undergone considerable change since the 1950s. There are many forces that will shape life in the United States in the future. These include technological changes, changes in the work force, and the aging of our society.

REFERENCES

ABERLE, D. F., A. K. COHEN, A. K. DAVIS, M. J. LEVEY, JR., and F. X. SUTTON. 1950. "The functional prerequisites of a society." *Ethics,* **60,** pp. 100–111.

ANTHONY, JAMES E., and THERESE BENEDEK (eds.). 1970. *Parenthood: Its Psychology and Psychopathology.* Boston: Little, Brown.

ARENSON, KAREN W. 1982. "Services: Bucking the slump." *New York Times,* May 18, p. D1.

ASCH, SOLOMON. 1955. "Opinions and social pressure." *Scientific American,* **193,** November, pp. 18, 31–35.

———. 1951. "Effects of group pressure upon the modification and distortion of judgments." In H. Guptzkow (ed.), *Groups, Leadership and Men.* Pittsburgh: Carnegie Press.

BALES, R. F. 1958. "Task roles and social roles in problem-solving groups." In E. E. Maccoby, T. M. Newcomb, and E. L. Hartley (eds.), *Readings in Social Psychology.* 3rd ed. New York: Holt, Rinehart and Winston.

———, and F. L. STRODTBECK. 1951. "Phases in group problem solving." *Journal of Abnormal and Social Psychology,* **46,** pp. 485–495.

BANDURA, A. 1969. *Principles of Behavior Modification.* New York: Holt, Rinehart and Winston.

BARDWICK, JUDITH W., and ELIZABETH DOUVAN. 1971. "Ambivalence: The socialization of women." In Vivian Gornick and Barbara K. Moran (eds.), *Woman in Sexist Society: Studies in Power and Powerlessness.* New York: Basic Books.

BARLOW, HUGH D. 1987. *Introduction to Criminology.* 4th ed. Boston: Little, Brown.

BARNETT, ROSALIND C, and GRACE K. BARUCH. 1987. "Social roles, gender, and psychological distress." In Rosalind C. Barnett, Lois Biener, and Grace K. Baruch (eds.), *Gender and Stress.* New York: Free Press.

BARON, SALO W. 1976. "European Jewry before and after Hitler." In Yisrael Gutman and Livia Rothkirchen (eds.), *The Catastrophe of European Jewry.* Jerusalem: Yad Veshem.

BASKIN, BARBARA H., and KAREN HARRIS. 1980. *Books for the Gifted Child.* New York: R. R. Bowker.

BAUMRIND, DIANE. 1975. "Early socialization and adolescent competence." In Sigmund E. Dragastin and Glen H. Elder, Jr. (eds.), *Ado-lescence in the Life Cycle.* New York: Halsted Press.

BECK, MELINDA et al. 1988. "A nation still at risk." *Newsweek,* May 2, pp. 54–55.

BECKER, HOWARD. 1963. *Outsiders: Studies in the Sociology of Deviance.* New York: Free Press.

BECKWITH, BURNHAM P. 1986. "Religion: A growing or dying institution?" *Futurist,* **20,** July/August, pp. 24–25.

BELL, ALAN P., MARTIN S. WEINBERG, and SUE KIEFER HAMMERSMITH. 1981. *Sexual Preference: Its Development in Men and Women.* Bloomington, Ind.: Indiana University Press.

BELL, D. 1973. *The Coming of the Postindustrial Society: A Venture in Social Forecasting.* New York: Basic Books.

BEM, SANDRA L., and DARYL J. BEM. 1976. "Case study of a nonconscious ideology: Training the woman to know her place." In Sue Cox (ed.), *Female Psychology: The Emerging Self.* Chicago: Science Research Associates (SRA).

BENDIX, R. 1962. *Max Weber: An Intellectual Portrait.* Garden City, N. Y.: Doubleday/Anchor.

BENEDICT, RUTH. 1961 (1934). *Patterns of Culture.* Boston: Houghton Mifflin.

———. 1938. "Continuities and discontinuities in cultural conditioning." *Psychiatry,* **1,** pp. 161–167.

BENNIS, W. 1971. "Beyond bureaucracy." In S. G. McNall (ed.), *The Sociological Perspective.* 2nd ed. Boston: Little, Brown.

BEQUAI, AUGUST. 1977. "Wanted: The white-collar ring." *Student Lawyer,* May 5, p. 45.

BERGER, PETER. 1967. *The Sacred Canopy.* New York: Doubleday.

———. 1963. *Invitation to Sociology: A Humanistic Perspective.* New York: Doubleday.

BERNARD, L. L. 1924. *Instinct.* New York: Holt, Rinehart and Winston.

BERRY, BREWTON, and HENRY L. TISCHLER. 1978. *Race and Ethnic Relations.* 4th ed. Boston: Houghton Mifflin.

BERRY, BRIAN J., and JOHN D. KASARDA. 1977. *Contemporary Urban Ecology.* New York: Macmillan.

BERTALANFFY, LUDWIG VON. 1968. *General System Theory.* New York: George Braziller.

BESHAROV, DOUGLAS J., and ALISON J. QUIN. 1987. "Not all female-headed families are created equal." *Public Interest,* Fall, pp. 48–56.

BETTELHEIM, B. 1967. *The Empty Fortress.* New York: Free Press.

BIANCHI, SUZANNE M., and DAPHNE SPAIN. 1986. *American Women in Transition.* New York: Russell Sage Foundation.

BIERSTADT, ROBERT. 1974. *The Social Order.* 4th ed. New York: McGraw-Hill.

BISHOP, KATHERINE. 1988. "Neo-Nazi activity is arising among U.S. youth." *New York Times,* June 13, p. A12.

BLAU, PETER M. 1964. *Exchange and Power in Social Life.* New York: John Wiley.

———, and M. W. MEYER. 1971. *Bureaucracy in Modern Society.* 2nd ed. New York: Random House.

———, and O. D. DUNCAN. 1967. *The American Occupational Structure.* New York: John Wiley.

BLOOM, DAVID E. 1986. "Women and work." *American Demographics,* September, pp. 24–30.

———, and NEIL G. BENNETT. 1986. "Childless couples." *American Demographics,* August, pp. 22–25, 54.

BLUM, JOHN M., EDMUND S. MORGAN, WILLIE LEE ROSE, ARTHUR M. SCHLESINGER, JR., KENNETH M. STAMP, and C. VAN WOODARD. 1981. *The National Experience: A History of the United States.* 5th ed. New York: Harcourt Brace Jovanovich.

BLUMBERG, PAUL. 1980. *Inequality in an Age of Decline.* New York: Oxford University Press.

BLUMER, HERBERT. 1946. "Collective behavior." In Alfred McClung Lee (ed.), *Principles of Sociology.* New York: Barnes & Noble.

BLUMSTEIN, PHILLIP, and PEPPER SCHWARTZ. 1983. *American Couples.* New York: Morrow.

BOLLEN, KENNETH, and DAVID P. PHILLIPS. 1982. "Imitative suicides: A national study of the effects of television news stories." *American Sociological Review, 47,* pp. 802–809.

BOSE, CHRISTINE E., and PETER H. ROSSI. 1983. "Gender and jobs: Prestige standings of occupations as affected by gender." *American Sociological Review, 48,* pp. 316–330.

BOTTOMORE, T. B. 1966. *Classes in Modern Society.* New York: Pantheon.

BOWEN, EZRA. 1985. "For learning and ethnic pride?" *Time,* July 8, pp. 80–81.

BOWEN, EZRA. 1988. "Getting tough." *Time,* February 1, pp. 52–58.

BOWLES, SAMUEL, and HERBERT GINTIS. 1976.

Schooling in Capitalist America: Educational Reform and the Contradictions of Economic Life. New York: Basic Books.

BRENNER, M. HARVEY. 1977. "Personal stability and economic security." *Social Policy, 8,* May/June, pp. 2–4.

1984 Britannica Book of the Year. 1983. Chicago: Encyclopaedia Britannica Inc.

BRONFENBRENNER, U. 1970. *Two Worlds of Childhood.* New York: Russell Sage Foundation.

BROWN, DEE. 1978. *Bury My Heart at Wounded Knee.* New York: Holt, Rinehart and Winston.

BROWN, LESTER R. 1974. *In the Human Interest.* New York: Norton.

———, and ERIK P. ECKHOLM. 1974. *By Bread Alone.* New York: Praeger.

BROWN, ROGER W. 1954. "Mass phenomena." In Gardner Lindzey (ed.), *Handbook of Social Psychology.* Cambridge, Mass.: Addison-Wesley.

BROWN, SUSAN. 1984. "Changes in laws governing divorce: An evaluation of joint custody presumptions." *Journal of Family Issues, 5,* June, pp. 200–223.

BULLOUGH, VERN L. 1973. *The Subordinate Sex.* Chicago: University of Chicago Press.

BURCHINAL, LEE G., and LOREN E. CHANCELLOR. 1963. "Survival rates among religiously homogamous and interreligious marriages." *Social Factors, 41,* pp. 353–362.

BURNS, JAMES MACGREGOR, J. W. PELTASON, and THOMAS E. CRONIN. 1981. *Government by the People.* 11th ed. Englewood Cliffs, N.J.: Prentice-Hall.

BUTTERFIELD, FOX. 1979. "In the new China, 1 + 1 can = 4–No more." *New York Times,* November 11, p. E7.

BYLINSKY, GENE. 1988. "Technology in the year 2000." *Fortune,* July 18, pp. 92–98.

BYRNE, D. 1971. *The Attraction Paradigm.* New York: Academic Press.

CALDWELL, JOHN C. 1976. "Toward a restatement of demographic transition theory." *Population and Development Review, 2.*

CAMERON, WILLIAM BRUCE. 1966. *Modern Social Movements: A Sociological Outline.* New York: Random House.

CANETTI, ELIAS. 1978 (1960). *Crowds and Power.* New York: Seabury Press.

CANTRIL, HADLEY. 1940. *The Invasion From Mars: A Study in the Psychology of Panic.* Princeton, N.J.: Princeton University Press.

CAPDEVIELLE, P., and D. ALVAREZ. 1981. "International comparisons of trends in productivity and labor costs." *Monthly Labor Review,* December, p. 15.

Carnegie Council on Policy Studies in Higher Education. 1979. "Giving youth a better chance: Options for education, work, and service." *Chronical of Higher Education,* December 3, pp. 11–13.

Carnegie Foundation. 1979. *Report.* Berkeley, Calif.: Carnegie Foundation.

CARSTENS, KENNETH. 1978. "The churches in South Africa." In Ian Robertson and Phillip Whitten (eds.), *Race and Politics in South Africa.* New Brunswick, N. J.: Transaction Books.

CHALMERS, DAVID. 1980. "The rise and fall of the invisible empire of the Ku Klux Klan." *Contemporary Review,* **237,** August, pp. 57–64.

CHAMBLISS, WILLIAM J. 1973. "Elites and the creation of criminal law." In William J. Chambliss (ed.), *Sociological Readings in the Conflict Perspective.* Reading, Mass.: Addison-Wesley.

CHERLIN, ANDREW. 1981. *Marriage, Divorce and Remarriage.* Cambridge, Mass.: Harvard University Press.

CHI, KENNETH S., and SHARON K. HOUSE-KNECHT. 1985. "Protestant fundamentalism and marital success: A comparative approach." *Sociology and Social Research,* **69,** pp. 351–375.

CHOMSKY, N. 1975. *Language and Mind.* New York: Harcourt Brace Jovanovich.

CLAYTON, RICHARD B., and HARWIN L. VOSS. 1977. "Shacking up: Cohabitation in the 1970s." *Journal of Marriage and the Family,* **39,** May, pp. 273–283.

COHEN, ALBERT K. 1955. "A general theory of subculture." In *Delinquent Boys: The Culture of the Gang.* New York: Free Press.

COHEN, YEHUDI A. 1981. "Shrinking households." *Society,* **18,** January/February, p. 51.

———. 1974. "Pastoralism." In Y. A. Cohen (ed.), *Man in Adaptation: The Cultural Present.* 2nd ed. Chicago: Aldine.

COLE, STEWARD G., and MILDRED WIESE COLE. 1954. *Minorities and the American Promise.* New York: Harper & Row.

COLEMAN, JAMES S. 1977. *Parents, Teachers, and Children.* San Francisco: San Francisco Institute for Contemporary Studies.

———. 1966. *Equality of Educational Opportunity.* Washington, D.C.: U.S. Government Printing Office.

COLLINS, RANDALL. 1979. *The Credential Society: An Historical Sociology of Education and Stratification.* New York: Academic Press.

———. 1975. *Conflict Sociology: Toward an Explanatory Science.* New York: Academic Press.

Common Cause Magazine. 1981. February, p. 11.

———. 1981. April, p. 12.

COMTE, AUGUSTE. 1968 (1851). *System of Positive Policy.* Vol. 1. Trans. John Henry Bridges. New York: Burt Franklin.

CONGER, J. J. 1980. "A new morality: Sexual attitudes and behavior of contemporary adolescents." In P. Mussen, J. Conger, and J. Kagan (eds.), *Readings in Child and Adolescent Psychology: Contemporary Perspectives.* New York: Harper & Row.

Congressional Quarterly. 1980. 2nd ed. Washington, D.C.: U.S. Government Printing Office.

COOLEY, C. H. 1909. *Social Organization.* New York: Scribner.

COSER, L. A. 1977. *Masters of Sociological Thought.* 2nd ed. New York: Harcourt Brace Jovanovich.

———. 1967. *Continuities in the Study of Social Conflict.* New York: Free Press.

———. 1956. *The Functions of Social Conflict.* Glencoe, Ill.: Free Press.

CRANO, WILLIAM D., and JOEL ARONOFF. 1978. "A cross-cultural study of expressive and instrumental role complementarity in the family." *American Sociological Review,* **43,** August, pp. 463–471.

CRESSEY, D. R. 1969. *Theft of the Nation: The Structure and Operations of Organized Crime in America.* New York: Harper Torchbooks.

CRISPELL, DIANE. 1987. "Navigating with ship." *American Demographics,* September, p. 56.

CROSSON, PIERRE R. 1975. "Institutional obstacles to expansion of world food production." *Science,* **188,** pp. 519–524.

CULLINGFORD, CEDRIC. 1984. *Children and Television.* New York: St. Martin's Press.

CUMMINGS, MILTON C., and DAVID WISE. 1981. *Democracy Under Pressure: An Introduction to the American Political System.* 4th ed. New York: Harcourt Brace Jovanovich.

CURTISS, S. 1977. *Genie: A Psycholinguistic Study of a Modern-Day Wild Child.* New York: Academic Press.

CUZZORT, R. P., and E. W. KING. 1980. *Twentieth Century Social Thought.* 3rd ed. New York: Holt, Rinehart and Winston.

DAHRENDORF, R. 1959. *Class and Conflict in Industrial Society.* Stanford, Calif.: Stanford University Press.

———. 1958. "Out of Utopia: Toward a reorientation of sociological analysis." *American Journal of Sociology,* **64,** September.

DALTON, GEORGE. 1971. *Modernizing Village Economics.* Toronto: Addison-Wesley Module.

D'ANDRADE, ROY G. 1966. "Sex differences and cultural institutions." In Eleanor Emmons Maccoby (ed.), *The Development of Sex Differences.* Stanford, Calif.: Stanford University Press.

DANZIGER, SHELDON. 1976. "Explaining urban crime rates." *Criminology,* **14,** August, pp. 291–296.

DARWIN, CHARLES. 1964 (1859). *On the Origin of Species.* Cambridge, Mass: Harvard University Press.

DAVIDSON, LAURIE, and LAURA KRAMER GORDON. 1979. *The Sociology of Gender.* Chicago: Rand McNally.

DAVIS, F. JAMES. 1979. *Understanding Minority-Dominant Relations.* Arlington Heights, Ill: AHM Publishing.

DAVIS, KINGSLEY. 1976. *America's Children.* Washington, D. C.: National Council of Organizations for Children and Youth.

——— (ed.). 1973. *Cities: Their Origin, Growth and Human Impact.* San Francisco: W. H. Freeman.

———. 1966. "The world's population crisis." In Robert K. Merton and Robert Nisbet (eds.), *Contemporary Social Problems.* 2nd ed. New York: Harcourt Brace Jovanovich.

———. 1949. *Human Society.* New York: Macmillan.

———. 1940. "Extreme social isolation of a child." *American Journal of Sociology,* **45,** pp. 554–565.

———, and W. E. MOORE. 1945. "Some principles of stratification." *American Sociological Review,* **10,** pp. 242–249.

DE BEAUVOIR, S. 1972. "Old age: End product of a faulty system." *Saturday Review of Society,* April 8.

DERSHOWITZ, ALAN. 1982. *The Best Defense.* New York: Random House.

DEVORE, I. (ed.) 1965. *Primate Behavior: Field Studies of Monkeys and Apes.* New York: Holt, Rinehart and Winston.

DOLAN, EDWIN G. 1980. *Basic Economics.* 2nd ed. Hinsdale, Ill.: Dryden Press.

DOMHOFF, G. WILLIAM. 1983. *Who Rules America Now?* Englewood Cliffs, N.J.: Prentice-Hall.

———. 1967. *Who Rules America?* Englewood Cliffs, N.J.: Prentice-Hall.

DUBERMAN, LUCILE. 1976. *Social Inequality.* New York: Harper & Row.

DUKERT, JOSEPH M. 1983. "Who is poor? Who is truly needy?" *Public Welfare,* **41,** Winter, pp. 16–22.

DUMANOSKI, D. 1981. "Youth unemployment: Who's to blame?" *Boston Globe,* January 11, p. C2.

DURANT, WILL. 1954. "Our Oriental heritage." In *The Story of Civilization.* Vol. I. New York: Simon & Schuster.

———. 1944. *Caesar and Christ.* New York: Simon & Schuster.

DURKHEIM, EMILE. 1961 (1917). *The Elementary Forms of Religious Life.* New York: Collier Books.

———. 1960a (1893). *The Division of Labor in Society.* Trans. G. Simpson. New York: Free Press.

———. 1960b (1893). *Montesquieu and Rousseau.* Ann Arbor, Mich.: University of Michigan Press.

———. 1958 (1895). *The Rules of Sociological Method.* Glencoe, Ill.: Free Press.

———. 1954 (1917). *The Elementary Forms of Religious Life.* Trans. J. W. Swain. New York: Free Press.

———. 1951 (1897). *Suicide: A Study in Sociology.* Trans. J. A. Spaulding and G. Simpson. New York: Free Press.

———. 1950 (1894). *Rules of Sociological Method.* New York: Free Press.

EDMONDSON, BRAD. 1986. "The political sell." *American Demographics,* November, pp. 26–29, 63–69.

EHRLICH, PAUL. 1974. *The End of Affluence.* New York: Ballantine.

———, and ANN H. EHRLICH. 1972. *Population, Resources, Environment.* San Francisco: W. H. Freeman.

———, and S. SHIRLEY FELDMAN. 1978. *The Race Bomb: Skin Color, Prejudice, and Intelligence.* New York: Quadrangle.

EHRLICH, ISAAC. 1975. "The deterrent effect of capital punishment: A question of life and death." *American Economic Review,* **65,** pp. 397–417.

EISENBERG, RICHARD. 1982. "Robots and your job." *Money,* May, p. 196.

ELDER, GLEN H. 1975. "Adolescence in the life cycle: An introduction." In Sigmund E. Dragastin and Glen H. Elder, Jr. (eds.), *Adolescence in the Life Cycle*. New York: Halsted Press.

ELIOT, T. S. 1917. "The Love Song of J. Alfred Prufrock." In *Prufrock and Other Observations*.

ELKIND, DAVID. 1981. *The Hurried Child*. Reading, Mass.: Addison-Wesley.

ELLUL, J. 1964. *The Technological Society*. New York: Knopf.

EMBER, CAROL R., and MELVIN EMBER. 1981. *Anthropology*. 3rd ed. Englewood Cliffs, N.J.: Prentice-Hall.

ENGELS, FRIEDRICH. 1942 (1884). *The Origin of the Family, Private Property and the State*. New York: International Publishing.

———. 1973. *The Condition of the Working Class in England in 1844*. Moscow: Progress Publishers.

ENOS, DARRYL D., and PAUL SULTAN. 1977. *The Sociology of Health Care: Social, Economic, and Political Perspectives*. New York: Praeger.

ERIKSON, ERIK H. 1968. *Identity, Youth and Crisis*. New York: Norton.

———. 1964. *Childhood and Society*. New York: Norton.

ERIKSON, KAI T. 1966. *Wayward Puritans: A Study in the Sociology of Deviance*. New York: John Wiley.

EXTER, THOMAS. 1987. "How many Hispanics?" *American Demographics*, May, pp. 36–39, 67.

EXTER, THOMAS, and FREDERICK BARBER. 1986. "The age of conservatism." *American Demographics*, November, pp. 30–37.

FARB, PETER. 1978. *Humankind*. Boston: Houghton Mifflin.

Federal Committee on Standard Metropolitan Statistical Areas. 1979. *The Metropolitan Statistical Area Classification*. Washington, D.C.: U.S. Department of Commerce, Bureau of the Census, pp. 33–36, 38, 39, 44, 336, 351, 355.

FERHOLT, J. B., D. E. HUNTER, and J. M. LEVENTHAL. 1978. "Longitudinal research on the causes and effects of child maltreatment." Unpublished manuscript.

FERREE, MYRA MARX, and BETH B. HESS. 1985. *Controversy and Coalition: The New Feminist Movement*. Boston: G. K. Hall and Company.

FESTINGER, LEON, HENRY W. RIEKEN, and STANLEY SCHACTER. 1956. *When Prophesy Fails*. New York: Harper Torchbooks.

FINN, CHESTER E, JR. 1987. "The high school dropout puzzle." *Public Interest*, Spring, pp. 3–22.

FIRTH, RAYMOND. 1963. *Elements of Social Organization*. Boston: Beacon Press.

FISCHLER, STAN. 1980. "Garden security and return of the Bruins." *New York Times*, March 2, p. 25.

FISHER, JEFFREY D., and D. BYRNE. 1975. "Too close for comfort: Sex differences in response to invasions of personal space." *Journal of Personality and Social Psychology*, **32**, July, pp. 15–21.

FISHER, ROBERT. 1984. *Let the People Decide: Neighborhood Organizing in America*. Boston: G. K. Hall and Company.

FISKE, EDWARD B. 1988a. "Schools fall short despite drive for improvements, Bennett says." *New York Times*, April 25, p. A1.

———. 1988b. "Schools' back-to-basics drive found to be wanting in math." *New York Times*, June 8.

———. 1988c. "Racial shifts challenge U.S. schools." *New York Times*, June 22, p. A16.

———. 1982. "Rising tuitions signal shift in education costs." *New York Times*, May 16, p. A1.

FLANNERY, KENT V. 1968. "Archaeological systems theory and early Mesopotamia." In Betty J. Meggars (ed.), *Anthropological Archaeology in the Americas*. Washington, D.C.: Anthropological Society of Washington.

———. 1965. "The ecology of early food production in Mesopotamia." *Science*, **147**, pp. 1247–1256.

FOGEL, WALTER A. 1979. *Mexican Illegal Alien Workers in the United States*. Los Angeles: Institute of Industrial Relations, University of California.

———. 1975. "Immigrant Mexicans and the U.S. work force." *Monthly Labor Review*, **98**, May, pp. 44–46.

FORBES. 1980. "The 100 Largest U.S. multinationals." July 7, p. 102.

FORD, CLELLAN S. 1970. "Some primitive societies." In Georgene H. Seward and Robert C. Williamson (eds.), *Sex Roles in Changing Society*. New York: Random House.

FORTES, M., R. W. STEEL, and P. ADY. 1947. "Ashanti survey, 1945–46: An experiment in social research." *Geographical Journal*, **110**, pp. 149–179.

FRANKFORT, H. 1956 (1951). *The Birth of Civilization in the Near East*. Garden City, N.Y.: Doubleday/Anchor.

FREDRICKSON, GEORGE M. 1971. *The Black*

Image in the White Mind. New York: Harper & Row.

FREED, STANLEY A., and RUTH S. FREED. 1985. "One son is no sons." *Natural History,* January, p. 10.

FREEMAN, JAMES M. 1974. "Trial by fire." *Natural History,* **83,** January, pp. 54–63.

FREITAG, PETER. 1975. "The Cabinet and big business: A study of interlocks." *Social Problems,* **2,** December 23, pp. 137–152.

FREUD, SIGMUND. 1930. "Civilization and its discontents." *Standard Edition of the Complete Psychological Works of Sigmund Freud.* Vol. 29. London: Hogarth Press.

———. 1928. *The Future of an Illusion.* New York: Horace Liveright and the Institute of Psychoanalysis.

———. 1923. "The ego and the id." *Standard Edition of the Complete Psychological Works of Sigmund Freud.* Vol. 19. London: Hogarth Press.

———. 1920. "Beyond the pleasure principle." *Standard Edition of the Complete Psychological Works of Sigmund Freud.* Vol. 14, London: Hogarth Press.

———. 1918. *Totem and Taboo.* New York: Moffat, Yard & Co.

FRIED, MORTON. 1967. *The Evolution of Political Society.* New York: Random House.

FRIEDL, ERNESTINE. 1962. *Vasilika: A Village in Modern Greece.* New York: Holt, Rinehart and Winston.

FRIEDMAN, MILTON, and ROSE FRIEDMAN. 1980. *Free to Choose: A Personal Statement.* New York: Harcourt Brace Jovanovich.

FRIEDRICH, CARL J., and ZBIGNIEW BRZEZINSKI. 1965. *Totalitarian Dictatorship and Autocracy.* Vol. 2. Cambridge, Mass.: Harvard University Press.

FRIEZE, IRENE H., J. E. PARSONS, P. B. JOHNSON, DIANA N. RUBLE, and GAIL L. ZELLMAN. 1975. *Women in Sex Roles: A Social Psychological Perspective.* New York: Norton.

FUGUITT, GLENN V. 1984. "The nonmetropolitan population turnaround." *Annual Review of Sociology,* **21,** pp. 259–280.

GALDIKAS, BIRUTE M. F. 1980. "Living with the great orange apes." *National Geographic,* **157,** June, pp. 830–853.

GALLUP, GEORGE, JR., and JIM CASTELLI. 1987. *The American Catholic People: Their Beliefs, Practices, and Values.* Garden City, N.Y.: Doubleday and Company, Inc.

Gallup Opinion Index. 1976. *Religion in America.*

Gallup Organization. 1982. "Religion in America, 1981." Gallup Opinion Index. Princeton, N.J.: Gallup Organization and Princeton Research Center.

Gallup Report, 1981. "Religion in America: The Gallup Opinion Index, 1981." The Gallup Organization, Inc., and The Princeton Religion Research Center, Inc. Report No. 184, January, pp. 65–66, 75.

Gallup Report, 1988. "Religion in America." Report No. 259. Gallup Opinion Index. Princeton, N.J.: Gallup Organization and Princeton Research Center.

GANS, HERBERT J. 1979. "Deception and disclosure in the field." *The Nation,* **228,** May, pp. 507–510.

———. 1977. "Why exurbanites won't reurbanize themselves." *New York Times,* February 12, p. 21.

———. 1968. *People and Plans.* New York: Basic Books.

———. 1962. *The Urban Villagers.* New York: Free Press.

GARDNER, HOWARD. 1978. *Developmental Psychology.* Boston: Little, Brown.

GARFINKEL, HAROLD. 1972. "Studies of the routine grounds of everyday activities." In David Snow (ed.), *Studies in Social Interaction.* New York: Free Press.

———. 1967. *Studies in Ethnomethodology.* Englewood Cliffs, N.J.: Prentice-Hall.

GARGAN, EDWARD A. 1988. "Beijing admits easing of birth limits." *New York Times,* November 2, p. 3A.

GEERTZ, C. 1973. *The Interpretation of Cultures.* New York: Basic Books.

GERSICK, KELIN E. 1979. "Fathers by choice: Divorced men who receive custody of their children." In George Levinger and Oliver C. Moles (eds.), *Divorce and Separation: Context, Causes, and Consequences.* New York: Basic Books.

GERTH, HANS, and C. WRIGHT MILLS. 1953. *Character and Social Structure.* New York: Harcourt Brace Jovanovich.

GESMONE, J. 1972. "Emotional neglect in Connecticut." *Connecticut Law Review,* **5,** pp. 100–116.

GIBB, G. A. 1969. "Leadership." In G. Lindzey and E. Aronson (eds.), *The Handbook of Social Psychology.* Reading, Mass.: Addison-Wesley.

GIESE, ALENKA S., and WILLIAM A. TESTA. 1988. "Targeting high tech." *American Demographics,* **10,** May, pp. 38–41.

GILLIGAN, CAROL. 1982. *In a Different Voice.* Cambridge, Mass.: Harvard University Press.

GINSBERG, MORRIS. 1958. "Social change." *British Journal of Sociology,* **9,** pp. 205–229.

GIST, NOEL P., and SYLVIA FLEIS FAVA. 1974. *Urban Society.* 6th ed. New York: Crowell.

GLAZER, NATHAN, and DANIEL P. MOYNIHAN (eds.). 1975. *Ethnicity: Theory and Experience.* Cambridge, Mass.: Harvard University Press.

GLICK, PAUL C. 1984. "How American families are changing." *American Demographics,* **6,** January.

————. 1979. *The Future of the American Family.* Current Population Reports Series P-23, no. 78. Bureau of the Census, Special Studies. Washington, D.C.: U.S. Government Printing Office.

————, and ARTHUR J. NORTON. 1977. "Marrying, divorcing, and living together in the United States today." *Population Bulletin,* **32,** October, pp. 2–38.

————, and EMMANUEL LANDAU. 1950: "Age as a factor in marriage." *American Sociological Review,* **15,** August, pp. 517–529.

GLUECK, S., and E. GLUECK. 1956. *Physique and Delinquency.* New York: Harper & Row.

GNESSOUS, MOHAMMED. 1967. "A general critique of equilibrium theory." In Wilburt E. Moore and Robert M. Cooke (eds.), *Readings on Social Change.* Englewood Cliffs, N.J.: Prentice-Hall.

GOFFMAN, E. 1971. *Relations in Public.* New York: Basic Books.

————. 1963. *Behavior in Public Places.* New York: Free Press.

————. 1961a. *Asylums: Essays on the Social Situation of Mental Patients and Other Inmates.* Chicago: Aldine.

————. 1961b. *Encounters: Two Studies in the Sociology of Interaction.* Indianapolis: Bobbs-Merrill.

————. 1959. *The Presentation of Self in Everyday Life.* Garden City, N.Y.: Doubleday.

GOLDBERG, PHILLIP. 1968. "Are women prejudiced against women?" *Transaction,* **5,** pp. 28–30.

GOODE, W. J. 1963. *World Revolution and Family Patterns.* New York: Free Press.

————. 1960. "A theory of role strain." *American Sociological Review,* August 25.

GOODMAN, P. 1962. *Growing Up Absurd.* New York: Random House.

GORDON, M. M. 1975 (1961). "Assimilation in America: Theory and reality." In Norman R. Yetman and C. Hoy Steele (eds.), *Majority and Minority: The Dynamics of Racial and Ethnic Relations.* Boston: Allyn & Bacon.

————. 1964. *Assimilation in American Life.* New York: Oxford University Press.

————. 1947. "The concept of subculture and its application." *Social Forces,* **26,** pp. 40–42.

GOUGH, KATHLEEN. 1961. "Nayar: Central Kerela." In David M. Schneider and Kathleen Gough (eds.), *Matrilineal Kinship.* Berkeley and Los Angeles: University of California Press.

————. 1952. "Changing kinship usages in the setting of political and economic change among the Nayars of Malabor." *Journal of Royal Anthropological Institute of Great Britain and Ireland,* **82,** pp. 71–87.

GOULD, H. 1971. "Caste and class: A comparative view." *Module,* **11,** pp. 1–24.

GOULD, STEPHEN JAY. 1976. "This view of life: Biological potential versus biological determinism." *Natural History,* **85,** May.

GOULDNER, ALVIN W. 1970. *The Coming Crisis of Western Sociology.* New York: Avon.

GREELEY, ANDREW M., WILLIAM MCCREADY, and KATHLEEN MCCOURT. 1975. *Catholic Schools in a Declining Church.* New ed. Mission, Kans.: Sheed Andrews & McMeel.

GREENBERG, J. 1980. "Ape talk: More than pigeon English?" *Science News,* **117,** pp. 298–300.

GUMPLOWICZ, LUDWIG. 1899. *The Outlines of Sociology.* Philadelphia: American Academy of Political and Social Sciences.

GURR, TED ROBERT. 1970. *Why Men Rebel.* Princeton, N. J.: Princeton University Press.

HALL, EDWARD T. 1974. *Handbook for Proxemic Analysis.* Washington, D.C.: Society for the Anthropology of Visual Communication.

————. 1969. *The Hidden Dimension.* New York: Doubleday.

HALL, R. H. 1963–1964. "The concept of bureaucracy: An empirical assessment." *American Journal of Sociology,* **69,** pp. 32–40.

HARE, PAUL A. 1976. *Handbook of Small Group Research.* 2nd ed. New York: Free Press.

HARLAN, JACK R. 1971. "Agricultural origins: Centers and noncenters." *Science,* **174,** pp. 468–474.

HARLOW, HARRY F. 1975. "Love among the monkeys." *Science News,* **108,** December 20, pp. 389–390.

————. 1959. "Love in Infant monkeys." *Scientific American,* **200,** June, pp. 68–74.

————, and M. HARLOW. 1962. "The heterosexual affectional system in monkeys." *American Psychologist,* **17,** 1–9.

HARRIS, C. D., and E. L. ULLMAN. 1945. "The nature of cities." *Annals of the American Academy of Political and Social Science,* **242,** p. 12.

HARRIS, MARVIN. 1980. *Cultural Materialism: The Struggle for a Science of Culture.* New York: Random House.

——. 1975. *Culture, People, and Nature: An Introduction to General Anthropology.* 2nd ed. New York: Crowell.

——. 1966. "The cultural ecology of India's sacred cattle." *Current Anthropology,* **7,** pp. 51–63.

HARRIS, SARAH. 1971. *Father Divine.* New York: Macmillan.

HART, C. W. M., and ARNOLD R. PILLING. 1960. *The Tiwi of North Australia.* New York: Holt, Rinehart and Winston.

HARTLEY, SHIRLEY FOSTER. 1972. *Population: Quantity Versus Quality.* Englewood Cliffs, N.J.: Prentice-Hall.

HAUB, CARL. 1987. "Understanding population projections." *Population Bulletin,* December.

HAUSER, PHILLIP, and ROBERT GARDNER. 1982. "Urban future: Trends and prospects." In Philip Hauser et al., *Population and the Urban Future.* U.N. Fund for Population Activities, Albany, N.Y.: SUNY Press.

HAWLEY, AMOS. 1981. *Urban Society.* 2nd ed. New York: John Wiley.

HEER, DAVID M. 1980. "Intermarriage." In *Harvard Encyclopedia of American Ethnic Groups.* Pp. 513–521. Cambridge, Mass.: Harvard University Press.

HELMORE, KRISTIN. 1988. "In Third World, desire to limit family size far exceeds available help." *Christian Science Monitor,* July 21, p. 10.

HENRY, J. 1963. *Culture Against Man.* New York: Random House.

HERBERS, JOHN. 1986. *The New Heartland.* New York: Time Books.

——. 1981. "Census finds more blacks living in suburbs of nation's large cities." *New York Times,* May 31, pp. 1, 48.

——. 1981. "1980 Census finds sharp decline in size of American households." *New York Times,* May 5, pp. A1, A18.

HILLER, E. T. 1941. "The community as a social group." *American Sociological Review,* **6,** pp. 189–202.

HILLERY, G. A., JR. 1955. "Definitions of com-

munity: Areas of agreement." *Rural Sociology,* **20,** pp. 111–123.

HODGE, R. W., P. M. SIEGEL, and P. H. ROSSI. 1964. "Occupational prestige in the United States." *American Journal of Sociology,* **70,** pp. 286–302.

——, D. J. TREIMAN, and P. H. ROSSI. 1966. "A comparative study of occupational prestige." In R. Bendix and S. M. Lipset (eds.), *Class, Status and Power.* 2nd ed. New York: Free Press.

HOEBEL, E. ADAMSON. 1960. *The Cheyennes: Indians of the Great Plains.* New York: Holt, Rinehart and Winston.

HOFFMAN, ABBIE. 1968. *Revolution for the Hell of It.* New York: Dial Press.

HOLLINGSHEAD, AUGUST B. 1951. "Age relationships and marriage." *American Sociological Review,* **16,** August, pp. 492–499.

——. 1949. *Elmtown's Youth.* New York: John Wiley.

——, and F. C. REDLICH. 1958. *Social Class and Mental Illness.* New York: John Wiley.

HOLT, JOHN. 1972. "The little red prison." *Harper's,* **244,** June, pp. 80–82.

HOMANS, G. C. 1950. *The Human Group.* New York: Harcourt.

HORNER, MATINA S. 1972. "Toward an understanding of achievement-related conflicts in women." *Journal of Social Issues,* **28,** pp. 157–175.

HOROWITZ, L. I. 1976. *The Rise and Fall of Project Camelot.* Cambridge, Mass.: MIT Press.

HOSTETLER, J. A., and G. E. HUNTINGTON. 1967. *The Hutterites in North America.* New York: Holt, Rinehart and Winston.

HOWE, IRVING. 1976. *World of Our Fathers.* New York: Simon & Schuster.

HOYT, H. 1943. "The structure of American cities in the postwar era." *American Journal of Sociology,* **48,** pp. 475–492.

HUMPHREY, J. A., and M. E. MILAKOVICH. 1981. *The Administration of Justice.* New York: Human Sciences Press.

INKELES, ALEX, and DAVID H. SMITH. 1974. *Becoming Modern: Individual Changes in Six Developing Countries.* Cambridge, Mass.: Harvard University Press.

ITARD, J. 1932. *The Wild Boy of Aveyron.* Trans. G. Humphrey and M. Humphrey. New York: Appleton-Century-Crofts.

JACOBS, J. 1961. *The Death and Life of Great American Cities.* New York: Vintage.

JACOBSON, PAUL. 1959. *American Marriage and*

Divorce. New York: Holt, Rinehart and Winston.

JANIS, I., and L. MANN. 1976. *Decision Making.* New York: Free Press.

——, DWIGHT W. CHAPMAN, JOHN P. GILLIN, and JOHN P. SPIEGEL. 1964. "The problem of panic." In Duane P. Schultz (ed.), *Panic Behavior.* New York: Random House.

JARMULOWSKI, VICKI. 1985. "The blended family: Who are they?" *Ms.,* **13,** February, pp. 33–34.

JEFFRIES, V., and H. E. RANSFORD. 1980. *Social Stratification: A Multiple Hierarchy Approach.* Boston: Allyn & Bacon.

JENCKS, C., M. SMITH, H. ACLAND, J. J. BANE, D. COHEN, H. GINTIS, B. HEYNS, and S. MICHELSON. 1972. *Inequality: A Reassessment of the Effect of Family and Schooling in America.* New York: Holt, Rinehart and Winston.

JENSEN, A. R. 1969. "How much can we boost I.Q. and scholastic achievement?" *Harvard Educational Review,* **39,** Winter, pp. 1–123.

JOHNSON, NICHOLAS. 1971. "Television and violence: Perspectives and proposals." In Bernard Rosenberg and David Manning White (eds.), *Mass Culture Revisited.* New York: Van Nostrand Reinhold.

JORGENSON, JOSEPH G. 1971. "Indians and the metropolis." In Jack O. Waddell and O. Michael Watson (eds.), *The American Indian in Urban Society.* Boston: Little, Brown.

JOSLYN, RICHARD. 1984. *Mass Media and Elections,* Reading, Mass.: Addison-Wesley.

JUDSON, DAVID, and DAVID OLSON. 1984a. "Birth records say Stebbins kin whites." *Stockton Record,* January 17, pp. 1, 4.

——. 1984b. "Uproar over Stebbins' roots echoes far from District 9." *Stockton Record,* April 1, pp. 1, 4.

KAHL, J. A. 1960. *The American Class Structure.* New York: Holt, Rinehart and Winston.

KASARDA, J. D., MICHAEL D. IRWIN, and HOLLY L. HUGHES. 1986. "The South is still rising." *American Demographics,* June, pp. 32–35, 38–39, 70.

KASARDA, J. D., and M. JANOWITZ. 1974. "Community attachment in mass society." *American Sociological Review,* **39,** pp. 328–339.

KASINITZ, PHILIP. 1984. "Gentrification and homelessness: The single room occupant and the inner city revival." *Urban and Social Change Review,* **17,** Winter, pp. 9–14.

KATZ, ELIHU. 1957. "The two-step flow of communication: An up-to-date report on an hy-pothesis." *Public Opinion Quarterly,* **21,** pp. 61–78.

KENNEDY, JOHN F. 1961. "Introduction." In William Brandon (ed.), *The American Heritage Book of Indians.* New York: Dell.

KENNEY, MICHAEL. 1980. *Boston Globe,* January 7.

KERCKHOFF, ALAN C., and KURT W. BACK. 1968. *The June Bug.* New York: Appleton-Century-Crofts.

KERLINGER, F. N. 1973. *Foundation of Behavioral Research.* 2nd ed. New York: Holt, Rinehart and Winston.

KHALDUN, IBN. 1958. *The Mugaddimah, Bollingen Series XLIII.* Princeton, N.J.: Princeton University Press.

KLEIMAN, DENA. 1979. "New York: Suburbs have trouble too." *New York Times,* October 23, p. 6E.

KOENIG, FREDERICK. 1985. *Rumor in the Marketplace: The Social Psychology of Commercial Heresy.* Dover, Mass.: Auburn House.

KOHLBERG, LAWRENCE. 1969. "Stage and sequence: The cognitive-developmental approach to socialization." In David A. Goslin (ed.), *Handbook of Socialization Theory and Research.* Chicago: Rand McNally.

——. 1967. "Moral and religious education in the public schools: A developmental view." In T. Sizer (ed.), *Religion and Public Education.* Boston: Houghton Mifflin.

KOHN, HANS. 1956. *Nationalism and Liberty: The Swiss Example.* London: Allen and Unwin.

KOHN, MELVIN L. 1969. *Class and Conformity.* Homewood, Ill.: Dorsey Press.

——, and CARMI SCHOOLER. 1983. *Work and Personality: An Inquiry Into the Impact of Social Stratification.* New York: Ablex Press.

KOTELCHUK, D. 1976. *Prognosis Negative: Crisis in the Health Care System.* New York: Vintage.

KOTKIN, JOEL, and YORIKO KISHIMOTO. 1988. *The Third Century: America's Resurgence in the Asian Era.* New York: Crown Publishers, Inc.

KRAUSE, AUREL. 1956. *The Tlingit Indians.* Seattle: University of Washington Press.

KRAUSE, MICHAEL. 1966. *Immigration: The American Mosaic.* New York: Van Nostrand Reinhold.

KROEBER, ALFRED A. 1963 (1923). *Anthropology: Culture Patterns and Processes.* New York: Harcourt Brace Jovanovich.

KROEBER, T. 1961. *Ishi in Two Worlds.* Berkeley and Los Angeles: University of California Press.

KUMMER, H. 1971. *Primate Societies: Group Technologies of Ecological Adaptation.* Chicago: Aldine.

KUPER, HILDA. 1963. *The Swazi: A South African Kingdom.* New York: Holt, Rinehart and Winston.

KURIAN, GEORGE T. 1984. *The New Book of World Rankings.* New York: Facts on File Publications.

KUTNER, LAWRENCE. 1988. "For children and stepparents war isn't inevitable." *New York Times,* June 30, p. C8.

KUTSCHER, RONALD E. 1988. "An overview of the year 2000." *Occupational Outlook Quarterly,* **32,** Spring, pp. 3–9.

LAING, R. D. 1967. *The Politics of Experience.* New York: Ballantine.

LANCASTER, JANE B., and PHILLIP WHITTEN. 1980. "Family matters." *The Sciences,* **20.**

LANG, KURT, and GLADYS LANG. 1961. *Collective Dynamics.* New York: Crowell.

LANTZ, HERMAN R. 1982. "Romantic love in the premodern period: A sociological commentary." *Journal of Social History,* **15,** Spring, pp. 349–370.

LASCH, CHRISTOPHER. 1979. *The Culture of Narcissism.* New York: Warner Books.

———. 1977. *Haven in a Heartless World: The Family Besieged.* New York: Basic Books.

LASLETT, P. 1965. *The World We Have Lost: England Before the Industrial Age.* New York: Scribner's.

———, and PHILLIP W. CUMMINGS. 1967. "History of political philosophy." In Paul Edwards (ed.), *The Encyclopedia of Philosophy.* Vols. 5, 6. New York: Macmillan.

LASSWELL, THOMAS. 1965. *Class and Stratum.* Boston: Houghton Mifflin.

LATANE, J., K. WILLIAMS, and S. HARKINS. 1979. "Many hands make light the work: The causes and consequences of social loafing." *Journal of Personality and Social Psychology,* **37,** June, pp. 822–832.

LAZARSFELD, PAUL F. 1971. "Introduction." In Bernard Rosenberg and David Manning White (eds.), *Mass Culture Revisited.* New York: Van Nostrand Reinhold.

———, BERNARD BERELSON, and HAZEL GAUDET. 1968. *The People's Choice.* 3rd ed. New York: Columbia University Press.

LEAKEY, RICHARD E. 1981. *The Making of Mankind.* New York: Dutton.

———, and ROGER LEWIN. 1977. *Origins.* New York: Dutton.

LE BON, GUSTAVE. 1960 (1895). *The Crowd: A Study of the Popular Mind.* New York: Viking.

LEE, ALFRED MCCLUNG. 1978. *Sociology for Whom?* New York: Oxford University Press.

LEE, GARY R. 1981. "Marriage and aging." *Society,* **18,** January/February, pp. 70–71.

LEE, M. 1966. *Multivalent Man.* New York: George Braziller.

LEE, RICHARD BORSHAY. 1980. *The !KungSan.* Berkeley and Los Angeles: University of California Press.

———. 1969a. "Kung bushmen subsistence: An input-output analysis." In A. P. Vayda (ed.), *Environment and Cultural Behavior.* Garden City, N.Y.: Natural History Press.

———. 1969b. "A naturalist at large: Eating Christmas in the Kalahari." *Natural History,* **78,** December, p. 5.

LEMERT, EDWIN. 1972. *Human Deviance, Social Problems and Social Control.* 2nd ed. Englewood Cliffs, N.J.: Prentice-Hall.

LENIN, VLADIMIR I. 1949 (1917). *The State and Revolution.* Moscow: Progress Publishers.

LENSKI, GERHARD. 1966. *Power and Privilege: A Theory of Social Stratification.* New York: McGraw-Hill.

———, and JEAN LENSKI. 1982. *Human Societies.* 4th ed. New York: McGraw-Hill.

LEONARD, IRA M., and R. D. PARMET. 1971. *American Nativism, 1830–1860.* New York: Van Nostrand Reinhold.

LESLIE, GERALD R. 1979. *The Family in Social Context.* 4th ed. New York: Oxford University Press.

LEVIN, JACK, and WILLIAM C. LEVIN. 1980. *Ageism: Prejudice and Discrimination Against the Elderly.* Belmont, Calif.: Wadsworth.

LEVINE, ADELINE, and JANICE CRUMRINE. 1975. "Women and the fear of success: A problem in replication." *American Journal of Sociology,* **80,** pp. 964–974.

LEVINE, IRVING M., and JUDITH HERMAN. 1974. "The life of white ethnics." In Charles H. Anderson (ed.), *Sociological Essays and Research.* Homewood, Ill.: Dorsey Press.

LEVINSON, DANIEL J., with CHARLOTTE N. DARROW, EDWARD B. KLEIN, MARIA H. LEVINSON, and BRAXTON MCKEE. 1978. *The Seasons of a Man's Life.* New York: Ballantine.

LEVY, FRANK, 1987. "The middle class: Is it really vanishing?" *Brookings Review,* Summer, pp. 17–21.

LEWIN, KURT. 1948. *Resolving Social Conflicts.* New York: Harper.

LEWIS, MICHAEL. 1972. "Culture and gender roles: There's no unisex in the nursery." *Psychology Today,* **5,** pp. 54–57.

LEWIS, O. 1960. *Tepotzlan: Village in Mexico.* New York: Holt, Rinehart and Winston.

———. 1951. *Life in a Mexican Village: Tepotzlan Revisited.* Urbana, Ill.: University of Illinois Press.

LIEBERT, R. M., and R. W. POULOS. 1972. "TV for kiddies—Truth, goodness, beauty, and a little bit of brainwash." *Psychology Today,* November.

LINDESMITH, ALFRED R., and ANSELM L. STRAUSS. 1956. *Social Psychology.* New York: Holt, Rinehart and Winston.

LINK, R. 1980. "The *Literary Digest* poll: Appearances can be deceiving." *Public Opinion Quarterly,* February/March, p. 55.

LINTON, R. 1936. *The Study of Man.* New York: Appleton-Century-Crofts.

———. 1915. *The Cultural Background of Personality.* Westport, Conn.: Greenwood Press.

LIPSET, SEYMOUR M. 1960. *Political Man.* Garden City, N.Y.: Doubleday.

LIPSEY, R. G., and P. D. STEINER. 1975. *Economics.* New York: Harper & Row.

LOMBROSO-FERRERO, GINA. 1972. *Criminal Man.* Reprint ed. Montclair, N.J.: Patterson Smith.

LONGFELLOW, CYNTHIA. 1979. "Divorce in context: Its impact on children." In George Levinger and Oliver C. Moles (eds.), *Divorce and Separation: Context, Causes and Consequences.* New York: Basic Books.

LOULS, ARTHUR M. 1982. "The bottom line on ten big mergers." *Fortune,* May 3, p. 89.

LYNCH, K. 1960. *The Image of the City.* Cambridge, Mass.: MIT Press.

LYNN, DAVID B. 1969. *Parental and Sex Role Identification: A Theoretical Formulation.* Berkeley, Calif.: McCutchan.

MACCOBY, ELEANOR EMMONS, and CAROL NAGY JACKLIN. 1975. *The Psychology of Sex Differences.* Stanford, Calif.: Stanford University Press.

MACMURRAY, V. D., and P. H. CUNNINGHAM. 1973. "Mormons and gentiles." In Donald E. Gelfand, and Russell D. Lee (eds.), *Ethnic Conflicts and Power: A Cross-National Perspective.* New York: John Wiley.

MADSEN, WILLIAM. 1973. *The Mexican-Americans of South Texas.* 2nd ed. New York: Holt, Rinehart and Winston.

MALINOWSKI, BRONISLAW. 1954. *Magic, Science and Religion.* New York: Free Press.

———. 1922. *Argonauts of the Western Pacific.* New York: Dutton.

MANDLE, JOAN D. 1979. *Women and Social Change in America.* Princeton, N.J.: Princeton Books.

MANNING, WENDY, and WILLIAM O'HARE. 1988. "The best metros for Asian-American businesses." *American Demographics,* August, pp. 34–37, 59.

MANSNERUS, LAURA. 1988. "In happiness quotient, the unmarried gain." *New York Times,* June 15, pp. C1, C8.

MARCUSE, H. 1955. *Eros and Civilization: A Philosophical Inquiry Into Freud.* New York: Vintage Books.

MARTIN, K. M. 1976. "The evolution of social forms." In D. E. Hunter and P. Whitten (eds.), *The Study of Anthropology.* New York: Harper & Row.

———. 1974. The Foraging Adaptation: Uniformity or Diversity? Addison-Wesley Modular Publication No. 56. Reading, Mass.: Addison-Wesley.

———, and B. VOORHIES. 1975. *The Female of the Species.* New York: Columbia University Press.

MARX, KARL. 1968. "Wage, labour and capital." In Karl Marx and Friedrich Engels, *Selected Works in One Volume.* New York: International Publishers.

———. 1967a (1867). *Capital: A Critique of Political Economy.* Ed. Friedrich Engels. New York: New World.

———. 1967b (1867). *Das Kapital.* 3 vols. Ed. Friedrich Engels. New York: International Publishing.

———. 1964 (1844). *The Economic and Philosophical Manuscripts of 1844.* New York: International Publishers.

———. 1959 (1847). In Ralf Dahrendorf (ed.), *Class and Class Conflict in Industrial Society.* Stanford, Calif.: Stanford University Press.

———, and FRIEDRICH ENGELS. 1961 (1848). "The Communist Manifesto." In Arthur P. Mendel (ed.), *Essential Works of Marxism.* New York: Bantam Books.

MASON, KAREN OPPENHEIM. 1987. "The impact of women's social position on fertility in developing countries." *Sociological Forum,* **2,** Fall.

MAUSS, ARMAND L. 1975. *Social Problems of Social Movements.* Philadelphia: Lippincott.

MCCONNELL, J. V. 1977. *Understanding Human*

Behavior. 2nd ed. New York: Holt, Rinehart and Winston.

MCFEE, MALCOLM. 1976. "Social organization I: Marriage and the family." In David E. Hunter and Phillip Whitten (eds.), *The Study of Anthropology.* New York: Harper & Row.

MCLAUGHLIN, LORETTA. 1980 "China's last word on children: One." *Boston Globe,* September 6, pp. 1, 2.

MCNEILL, WILLIAM H. 1976. *Plagues and People.* New York: Anchor/Doubleday.

MEAD, G. H. 1934. *Mind, Self, and Society.* Ed. C. W. Morris. Chicago: University of Chicago Press.

MEAD, MARGARET. 1970. *Culture and Commitment.* New York: Doubleday.

———. 1943. "Our educational emphases in primitive perspectives." *American Journal of Sociology,* **48,** pp. 633–639.

———. 1935. *Sex and Temperament in Three Primitive Societies.* New York: Morrow.

MEADOWS, DONELLE H., DENNIS L. MEADOWS, JORGAN RANDERS, and WILLIAM W. BEHRENS, III. 1972. *The Limits of Growth: A Report of the Club of Rome's Project on the Predicament of Mankind.* New York: Universe Books.

MEGGARS, B. J. 1972. *Prehistoric America.* Chicago: Aldine.

MERTON, R. K. 1968 (1949). *Social Theory and Social Structure.* 2d ed. New York: Free Press.

———. 1938. "Social structure and social action." *American Sociological Review,* **3,** pp. 672–682.

———, LEONARD BROOM, and LEONARD S. COTTRELL, JR. 1959. *Sociology Today: Problems and Prospects.* New York: Basic Books.

METRAUX, RHODA. 1955. "Implicit and explicit values in education and teaching as related to growth and development." *Merrill-Palmer Quarterly,* **2,** pp. 27–34.

MICHELS, R. 1966 (1911). *Political Parties.* Trans. Eden Paul and Adar Paul. New York: Free Press.

MILLS, C. WRIGHT. 1963. *Power, Politics and People.* New York: Ballantine.

———. 1959. *The Sociological Imagination.* New York: Oxford University Press.

———. 1956. *The Power Elite.* New York: Oxford University Press.

MILLS, T. M. 1967. *The Sociology of Small Groups.* Englewood Cliffs, N.J.: Prentice-Hall.

MOLOTSKY, IRVIN. 1988. "New and old school chiefs differ on issues and styles." *New York Times,* September 22, p. A22.

MONTAGU, ASHLEY (ed.). 1973. *Man and Aggression.* 2nd ed. London: Oxford University Press.

——— (ed.). 1964a. *The Concept of Race.* New York: Collier Books.

———. 1964b. *Man's Most Dangerous Myth: The Fallacy of Race.* New York: Meridian.

MOORE, WILBERT E. 1965. *The Impact of Industry.* Englewood Cliffs, N.J.: Prentice-Hall.

MORRIS, DESMOND. 1970. *The Human Zoo.* New York: McGraw-Hill.

MOSCA, GAETANO. 1939. *The Ruling Class.* New York: McGraw-Hill.

MOSKOS, C. C. JR. 1975. "The American combat soldier in Vietnam." *Journal of Social Issues,* **31,** pp. 25–37.

MOULIK, MONI. 1977. *Millions More to Feed.* Rome: Food and Agriculture Organization of the United Nations.

MURDOCK, GEORGE P. 1949. *Social Structure.* New York: Macmillan.

———. 1937. "Comparative data on the division of labor by sex." *Social Forces,* **15,** pp. 551–553.

MUSON, H. 1979. "Moral thinking—Can it be taught?" *Psychology Today,* February.

MYRDAL, GUNNAR. 1969. *Objectivity in Social Research.* New York: Pantheon.

———. 1944. *An American Dilemma.* New York: Harper.

National Institute of Mental Health. 1982. *Television and Behavior: Ten Years of Scientific Progress and Implications for the Eighties.* 2 vols. Washington, D.C.: Government Printing Office.

National Opinion Research Center (NORC). 1977. *Cumulative Codebook for the 1972–77 General Social Surveys.* Chicago: NORC, University of Chicago.

NEUGARTEN, BERNICE L. 1979. "Time, age, and the life cycle." *American Journal of Psychiatry,* **136,** pp. 887–894.

New York Times. 1988a. "Sailor's death spurs review of training." May 18, p. A22.

———. 1988b. "Hearing begins into death of Naval recruit." June 6, p. A15.

———. 1988c. "Officer defended in drowning." June 9, p. A24.

———. 1988d. "U.S. school breakfast program lifts test scores." June 22, p. B7.

NICKELS, M. K., D. E. HUNTER, and P. WHITTEN. 1979. *The Study of Physical Anthropology and Archeology.* New York: Harper & Row.

NILUFER, R. AHMED. 1981. "Family size and sex preference among women in rural Bangladesh." *Studies in Family Planning,* **12.**

NISBET, R. A., and R. G. PERRIN. 1977. *The Social Bond: An Introduction to the Study of Sociology.* 2nd ed. New York: Knopf.

NOVAK, MICHAEL. 1972. *The Rise of the Unmeltable Ethnics.* New York: Macmillan.

NOVIT-EVANS, BETTE, and ASHTON WESLEY WELCH. 1983. "Racial and ethnic definition as reflections of public policy." *Journal of American Studies,* **17,** pp. 417–435.

OBERG, KALERNO. 1973. *The Social Economy of the Tlingit Indians.* Seattle: University of Washington Press.

OBERSCHALL, ANTHONY. 1968 (1965). "The Los Angeles Watts riot of August 1965." *Social Problems,* **15,** Winter, pp. 297–341.

OGBURN, WILLIAM F. 1964a. *On Culture and Social Change.* Chicago: University of Chicago Press.

———. 1964b (1950). *Social Change: With Respect to Culture and Original Nature.* Magnolia, Mass.: Peter Smith.

O'HARE, WILLIAM. 1988. "How to read poverty statistics." *American Demographics,* May, pp. 42–43.

———. 1987. "Separating welfare fact from fiction." *Wall Street Journal,* December 14, p. 24.

———. 1986. "The eight myths of poverty." *American Demographics,* May, pp. 22–25.

ORTNER, SHERRY. 1974. "Is female to male as nature is to culture?" In Michelle Zimbalist Rosaldo and Louise Lampheres (eds.), *Woman, Culture and Society.* Stanford, Calif.: Stanford University Press.

ORWELL, GEORGE. 1954. *Animal Farm.* New York: Harcourt Brace.

OTTERBEIN, KEITH. 1973. "The anthropology of war." In John J. Honigmann (ed.), *Handbook of Social and Cultural Anthropology.* Chicago: Rand McNally.

———. 1970. *The Evolution of War.* New Haven, Conn.: Human Relations Area Files.

OUCHI, WILLIAM G. 1981. *Theory Z: How American Business Can Meet the Japanese Challenge.* Reading, Mass.: Addison-Wesley.

PALEN, JOHN J. 1987. *The Urban World.* New York: McGraw-Hill.

PARK, R., E. BURGESS, and R. MCKENZIE (eds.). 1925. *The City.* Chicago: University of Chicago Press.

PARKE, R. D., and C. W. COLLMER. 1975. "Child abuse: An interdisciplinary analysis." In E. M.

Hetherington (ed.), *Review of Child Development Research.* Vol. 5. Chicago: University of Chicago Press.

PARKES, HENRY BAMFORD. 1968. *The United States of America: A History.* 3rd ed. New York: Knopf.

PARKINSON, C. NORTHCOTE. 1957. *Parkinson's Law.* Boston: Houghton Mifflin.

PARMET, IRA M., and ROBERT D. PARMET. 1971. *American Nativism, 1830–1860.* New York: Van Nostrand Reinhold.

PARSONS, TALCOTT. 1971. *The System of Modern Societies.* Englewood Cliffs, N.J.: Prentice-Hall.

———. 1966. *Societies: Evolutionary and Comparative Perspectives.* Englewood Cliffs, N.J.: Prentice-Hall.

———. 1954. *Essays in Sociological Theory.* Rev. ed. New York: Free Press.

———. 1951. *The Social System.* New York: Free Press.

———. 1937. *The Structure of Social Action.* New York: McGraw-Hill.

———, and ROBERT F. BALES. 1955. *Family Socialization and Interaction Process.* New York: Free Press.

——— and E. A. SHILS. 1951. *Toward a General Theory of Action.* Cambridge, Mass.: Harvard University Press.

PAULSEN, MONRAD. 1967. "Role of juvenile courts." *Current History,* **53,** August, pp. 70–75.

PAVLIK, Z. 1986. *Family Policy and Population Climate in the CSSR.* Conference on the Demographic Impact of Political Action, March.

PAVLOV, I. P. 1927. *Conditioned Reflexes.* Trans. G. V. Anrep. New York: Oxford University Press.

PAYER, LYNN. 1988. *Medicine and Culture.* New York: Henry Holt and Company.

PERRY, JOSEPH B., JR., and M. D. PUGH. 1978. *Collective Behavior: Response to Social Stress.* St. Paul, Minn.: West Publishing.

PETER, L. J., and R. HULL. 1969. *The Peter Principle.* New York: Morrow.

PETERSEN, WILLIAM. 1975. "On the subnations of western Europe." In Nathan Glazer and Daniel P. Moynihan (eds.), *Ethnicity: Theory and Experience.* Cambridge, Mass.: Harvard University Press.

PETTIGREW, THOMAS F., and ROBERT C. GREEN. 1975. "School desegregation in large cities: A critique of the Coleman 'white flight' thesis." *Harvard Educational Review,* **46,** pp. 1–53.

PHILLIPS, DAVID P. "The deterrent effect of capital punishment: New evidence on an old controversy." *American Journal of Sociology,* **86,** July, pp. 139–148.

PIAGET, J., and B. INHELDER. 1969. *The Psychology of the Child.* New York: Basic Books.

PILEGGI, N. 1981. "Open city." *New York,* January 19, pp. 20–26.

PIPES, RICHARD. 1975. "Reflections on the nationality problems in the Soviet Union." In Nathan Glazer and Daniel P. Moynihan (eds.), *Ethnicity: Theory and Experience.* Cambridge, Mass.: Harvard University Press.

PLATT, JOHN. 1987. "The future of AIDS." *Futurist,* November/December, pp. 10–17.

POSTMAN, NEIL. 1985. *Amusing Ourselves to Death.* New York: Viking Press.

PROVENCE, SALLY. 1972. "Psychoanalysis and the treatment of psychological disorders of infancy." In S. Wolman (ed.), *A Handbook of Child Psychoanalysis: Research, Theory, and Practice.* New York: Van Nostrand Reinhold.

———, and R. LIPTON. 1963. *Infants in Institutions.* New York: International University Press.

Public Opinion Quarterly. 1980. December/January, p. 35.

———. 1978. November/December, p. 33.

PUTKA, GARY. 1984. "As Jewish population falls in U.S., leaders seek to reverse trend." *Wall Street Journal,* April 13, pp. 1, 10.

QUINNEY, RICHARD. 1974. *Critique of Legal Order.* Boston: Little, Brown.

RACHMAN, DAVID J., and MICHAEL H. MESCON. 1982. *Business Today.* 3rd ed. New York: Random House.

RAINES, HOWELL. 1988. "British government devising plan to curb violence by soccer fans." *New York Times,* June 17, p. A1.

REDFIELD, R. 1960. *The Little Community.* Chicago: University of Chicago Press.

———. 1947. "The folk society." *American Journal of Sociology,* **52,** pp. 293–308.

———. 1941. *Folk Culture of Yucatan.* Chicago: University of Chicago Press.

———. 1934. "Culture changes in Yucatan." *American Anthropologist,* **36,** pp. 57–59.

———. 1930. *Tepotzlan: A Mexican Village.* Chicago: University of Chicago Press.

REICHEL, P. L. 1975. "Classroom use of a criminal activities checklist." *Teaching Sociology,* **3,** October, pp. 85–86.

REID, SUE TITUS. 1981. *The Correctional System.* New York: Holt, Rinehart and Winston.

———. 1979. *Crime and Criminology.* 2nd ed. New York: Holt, Rinehart and Winston.

REIMANN, JEFFREY H. 1979. "The rich get richer and the poor get prison." In *Ideology, Class, and Criminal Justice.* New York: John Wiley.

REINHOLD, ROBERT. 1988. "California intensifies planning for the big quake." *New York Times,* May 11, p. A11.

REISS, IRA L. 1980. *Family Systems in America.* 3rd ed. New York: Holt, Rinehart and Winston.

RIESMAN, D. 1950. *The Lonely Crowd.* New Haven, Conn.: Yale University Press.

ROBEY, BRYANT. 1984. "Black votes, black money." *American Demographics,* May, pp. 4–5.

ROBINSON, JACOB. 1976. "The Holocaust." In Yisrael Gutman and Livia Rothkirchen (eds.), *The Catastrophe of European Jewry.* Jerusalem: Yad Veshem.

ROBINSON, JOHN P. 1979. "Toward a postindustrious society." *Public Opinion Quarterly,* August/September, pp. 41–46.

ROGERS, WILLARD L., and ARLAND THORNTON. 1985. "Changing patterns of first marriage in the United States." *Demography,* **22,** pp. 265–279.

ROPER, BURNS W. 1985. "Early election calls: The larger dangers." *Public Opinion Quarterly,* **49,** Spring, pp. 5–9.

ROSALDO, MICHELLE ZIMBALIST. 1974. "Woman, culture and society: A theoretical overview." In Michelle Zimbalist Rosaldo and Louise Lamphere (eds.), *Woman, Culture and Society.* Stanford, Calif.: Stanford University Press.

ROSE, A. 1967. *Power Structure: Political Process in American Society.* New York: Oxford University Press.

ROSE, JERRY D. 1982. *Outbreaks: The Sociology of Collective Behavior.* New York: The Free Press.

ROSEN, GEORGE. 1968. *Madness in Society.* New York: Harper Torchbooks.

ROSENBERG, BERNARD, and DAVID MANNING WHITE (eds.). 1971. *Mass Culture Revisited.* New York: Van Nostrand Reinhold.

ROSENTHAL, R., and L. JACOBSON. 1966. "Teachers' expectancies: Determinants of pupils' I.Q. gain." *Psychological Reports,* **18,** pp. 115–118.

ROSS, CATHERINE. 1972. "Sex-role socialization in picture books for preschool children." *American Journal of Sociology,* **77,** May, pp. 1125–1150.

ROSSI, ALICE. 1985. *Gender and the Life Course.* New York: Aldine.

———. 1977. "A biosocial perspective on parenting." *Daedalus,* **106,** pp. 1–31.

ROSSIDES, D. W. 1976. *The American Class System.* Boston: Houghton Mifflin.

ROSZAK, T. 1969. *The Making of a Counterculture.* Garden City, N.Y.: Anchor/Doubleday.

RUMBERGER, RUSSELL W. 1987. "High school dropouts: A review of issues and evidence." *Review of Educational Research,* Summer, **57,** pp. 101–121.

RYAN, WILLIAM. 1971. *Blaming the Victim.* New York: Pantheon.

SAGARIN, EDWARD. 1978. *Sociology: The Basic Concepts.* New York: Holt, Rinehart and Winston.

SAHLINS, MARSHALL D. 1972. *Stone Age Economics.* Chicago: Aldine.

———, and ELMAN R. SERVICE (eds.). 1960. *Evolution and Culture.* Ann Arbor: University of Michigan Press.

SALAS, RAFAEL M. 1987. "Urban population growth: Blessing or burden?" *USA Today,* **116,** July, pp. 74–77.

SALHOLZ E, R. SANDZA, and A. COHEN. 1988. "A death by drowning." *Newsweek,* May 23, p. 25.

SALZMAN, P. C. 1967. "Political organization among nomadic peoples." *Proceedings of the American Philosophical Society,* **3,** pp. 115–131.

SAMOVAR, LARRY A., RICHARD PORTER, and NEMI C. JAIN. 1981. *Understanding Intercultural Communication.* Belmont, Calif.: Wadsworth.

SAMUELSON, PAUL A. 1976. *Economics.* 10th ed. New York: McGraw-Hill.

SANDBURG, CARL. *Chicago Poems.* 1916.

SAPIR, EDWARD. 1961. *Culture, Language and Personality.* Berkeley and Los Angeles: University of California Press.

SANDERS, ALVIN J., and LARRY LONG. 1987. "New sunbelt migration patterns." *American Demographics,* January, pp. 38–41.

SCARPITTI, FRANK. 1980. *Social Problems.* 3rd ed. New York: Holt, Rinehart and Winston.

SCHMID, CALVIN F., and CHARLES E. NOBBE. 1965. "Socioeconomic differentials among nonwhite races." *American Sociological Review,* **30,** December, pp. 909–922.

SCHUMPETER, JOSEPH A. 1950. *Capitalism, Socialism and Democracy.* 3rd ed. New York: Harper Torchbooks.

SCHUR, EDWIN M., and HUGO A. BEDAU. 1974. *Victimless Crimes: Two Sides of a Controversy.* Englewood Cliffs, N. J.: Prentice-Hall.

SCHWARTZ, JOE. 1988. "Hispanics in the eighties." *American Demographics,* January, pp. 42–45.

Science News. 1979. "World population decline documented." August.

SEBOLD, HANS. 1986. "Adolescents' shifting orientation toward parents and peers: A curvilinear trend over recent decades." *Journal of Marriage and the Family,* February, pp. 5–13.

SECORD, PAUL F., and CARL W. BACKMAN. 1974. *Social Psychology.* New York: McGraw-Hill.

SELIGMAN, DANIEL. 1984. "Pay equity is a bad idea." *Fortune,* **109,** May 14, pp. 133–140.

SELZNICK, P. 1948. "Foundations of the theory of organization." *American Sociological Review,* **13,** pp. 25–35.

SERVICE, ELMAN R. 1975. *Origins of the State and Civilization.* New York: Norton.

SHARP, LAURISTON. 1952. "Steel axes for stone-age Australians." *Human Organization,* **11,** pp. 17–22.

SHATTUCK, R. 1980. *The Forbidden Experiment.* New York: Farrar, Straus & Giroux.

SHAW, CLIFFORD R., and HENRY D. MCKAY. 1942. *Juvenile Delinquency and Urban Areas.* Chicago: University of Chicago Press.

———. 1931. "Social factors in juvenile delinquency." Vol. 2. In National Committee on Law Observance and Law Enforcement, *Report on the Causes of Crime.* Washington, D.C.: U.S. Government Printing Office.

SHELDON, W. H., E. M. HARTL, and E. MCDERMOTT. 1949. *The Varieties of Delinquent Youth.* New York: Harper.

———, and S. S. STEVENS. 1942. *The Variety of Temperament.* New York: Harper.

———, and W. B. TUCKER. 1940. *The Varieties of Human Physique.* New York: Harper.

SHELLOW, ROBERT, and DEREK V. ROEMER. 1965. "The riot that didn't happen." *Social Problems,* **14,** pp. 221–233.

SHEPARDSON, MARY. 1963. *Navajo Ways in Government.* Manasha, Wis.: American Anthropological Association.

SHIBUTANI, TAMOTSU. 1966. *Improvised News: A Sociological Study of Rumor.* Indianapolis: Bobbs-Merrill.

SHILS, EDWARD. 1971 (1960). "Mass society and its culture." In Bernard Rosenberg and David Manning (eds.), *Mass Culture Revisited.* New York: Van Nostrand Reinhold.

———. 1968. *Political Development in the New States.* The Hague: Mouton.

———. 1950. "Primary groups in the American army." In R. K. Merton and P. F. Lazarsfeld (eds.), *Continuities in Social Research*. New York: Free Press.

SHIN-SHAN HENRY TSAI. 1986. *The Chinese Experience in America*. Bloomington, Ind.: Indiana University Press.

SILBERMAN, C. E. 1978. *Criminal Violence—Criminal Justice: Criminals, Police, Courts and Prisons in America*. New York: Random House.

———. 1971. *Crisis in the Classroom: The Remaking of American Education*. New York: Random House.

SIMMEL, GEORG. 1957. "Fashion." *American Journal of Sociology,* **62,** pp. 541–588.

———. 1955. "The web of group affiliations." In *Conflict: The Web of Group Affiliations*. Glencoe, Ill.: Free Press.

———. 1950 (1917). *Sociology of Georg Simmel*. Trans. Kurt Wolff. Glencoe, Ill.: Free Press.

SIMON, JULIAN L., and HERMAN KAHN (eds.). 1984. *The Resourceful Earth: A Response to Global 2000*. New York: Basil Blackwell.

SIMPSON, GEORGE E., and MILTON YINGER. 1972. *Racial and Cultural Minorities: An Analysis of Prejudice and Discrimination*. 4th ed. New York: Harper & Row.

SJOBERG, GIDEON. 1965. *Preindustrial City: Past and Present*. New York: Free Press.

SKINNER, B. F. 1971. *Beyond Freedom and Dignity*. New York: Knopf.

SKOCPOL, THEDA. 1979. *States and Social Revolutions*. New York: Cambridge University Press.

SKOLNICK, ARLENE. 1973. *The Intimate Environment: Exploring Marriage and the Family*. Boston: Little, Brown.

SLATER, P. 1970. *The Pursuit of Loneliness: American Culture at the Breaking Point*. Boston: Beacon Press.

———. 1966. *Microcosm: Structural, Psychological, and Religious Evolution in Groups*. New York: John Wiley.

SMELSER, NEIL J. 1971. "Mechanisms of change and adjustment to change." In George Dalton (ed.), *Economic Development and Social Change*. Garden City, N. Y.: Natural History Press.

———. 1962. *Theory of Collective Behavior*. New York: Free Press.

SMITH, ADAM. 1969 (1776). *An Inquiry Into the Nature and Causes of the Wealth of Nations*. 2 vols. Chicago: University of Chicago Press.

SMITH, TOM. 1984. "America's religious mosaic." *American Demographics,* June, pp. 19–23.

SNYDER, Z. 1971. "The social environment of the urban Indian." In Jack O. Waddell and O. Michael Watson (eds.), *The American Indian in Urban Society*. Boston: Little, Brown.

SOLECKI, RALPH. 1971. *Shanidar: The First Flower People*. New York: Knopf.

SOLHEIM, W. G. 1972. "An earlier agricultural revolution." *Scientific American,* **226,** April, pp. 34–41.

SOROKIN, PITIRIM A. 1937. *Social and Cultural Dynamics*. New York: American Books.

SOSIN, MICHAEL. 1986. *Homelessness in Chicago*. School of Social Service Administration, University of Chicago.

SPAIN, DAPHNE. 1988. "Women's Demographic Past, Present and Future," Radcliffe Conferences on Women in the 21st Century, Cambridge, Mass. December.

SPANIER, GRAHAM B. 1983. "Married and unmarried cohabitation in the United States: 1980." *Journal of Marriage and the Family,* **45,** May, pp. 277–288.

SPATES, JAMES L., and JOHN J. MACIONIS. 1987. *The Sociology of Cities*. Belmont, Calif.: Wadsworth.

Special Task Force to the Secretary of Health, Education and Welfare. 1973. *Work in America*. Cambridge, Mass.: MIT Press.

SPENGLER, OSWALD. 1932. *The Decline of the West*. New York: Knopf.

SPICER, EDWARD H. 1962. *Cycles of Conquest*. Tucson: University of Arizona Press.

SPINDLER, GEORGE D. 1955. "Education in a transforming American culture." In George D. Spindler (ed.), *Education and Culture: Anthropological Approaches*. New York: Holt, Rinehart and Winston.

SPIRO, MELFORD E. 1960. "Addendum, 1958." In Norman W. Bell and Ezra F. Vogel (eds.), *A Modern Introduction to the Family*. Glencoe, Ill.: Free Press.

SPITZ, RENE A. 1945. "Hospitalism: An inquiry into the genesis of psychiatric conditions in early childhood." In Anna Freud et al. (eds.), *The Psychoanalytic Study of the Child*. New York: International Universities Press.

SQUIRE, PEVERILL. 1988. "Why the 1936 *Literary Digest* poll failed." *Public Opinion Quarterly,* **52,** Spring, pp. 125–133.

STABLER, KEN. 1986. "Bear Bryant." *Esquire,* June, p. 67.

STAIRES, GRAHAM L., ROBERT P. QUINN, and LINDA J. SHEPARD. 1976. "Occupational sex discrimination." *Industrial Relations,* **15,** pp. 88–98.

STARK, RODNEY, and CHARLES Y. GLOCK. 1968. *American Piety: The Nature of Religious Commitments.* Berkeley and Los Angeles: University of California Press.

STARK, RODNEY, and WILLIAM SIMS BAINBRIDGE. 1985. *The Future of Religion: Secularization, Revival, and Cult Formation.* Berkeley, Calif.: University of California Press.

STEWARD, JULIAN H. 1955. *The Theory of Culture Change: The Methodology of Multilineal Evolution.* Urbana, Ill.: University of Illinois Press.

STOLLER, R. J. 1967. "Effects of parents' attitudes on core gender identity." *International Journal of Psychiatry,* p. 57.

STONER, JAMES A. F. 1982. *Management.* 2nd ed. Englewood Cliffs, N.J.: Prentice-Hall.

STOUFFER, SAMUEL A. (ed.). 1950. *The American Soldier.* Princeton, N.J.: Princeton University Press.

STRAUS, MURRAY A., RICHARD J. GELLES, and SUZANNE K. STEINMETZ. 1980. *Behind Closed Doors.* New York: Anchor/Doubleday.

STULGOE, JOHN R. 1984. "The suburbs." *American Heritage,* **35,** February/March, pp. 21–36.

SUDMAN, SEYMOUR. 1985. "Do exit polls influence voting behavior?" *Public Opinion Quarterly,* Spring, pp. 332–333.

SULLIVAN, JOSEPH F. 1979. "New Jersey: Assaults are a daily occurrence." *New York Times,* October 23, p. 6E.

SUMNER, W. G. 1906. *Folkways: A Study of the Sociological Importance of Usages, Manners, Customs, Mores, and Morals.* Boston: Ginn.

Surgeon General's Scientific Advisory Committee on Television and Social Behavior. 1972. *Television and Growing Up: The Impact of Televised Violence.* Washington, D.C.: U.S. Government Printing Office.

SUTHERLAND, EDWIN H. 1961. *White Collar Crime.* New York: Holt, Rinehart and Winston.

———. 1940. "White collar criminality." *American Sociological Review,* **40,** pp. 1–12.

———. 1924. *Criminology.* New York: Lippincott.

———, and D. R. CRESSEY. 1978. *Principles of Criminology.* 10th ed. Chicago: Lippincott.

SUTTER, LARRY E., and HERMAN P. MILLER. 1973. "Income differences between men and career women." *American Journal of Sociology,* **78,** January, p. 965.

SUTTLES, G. 1972. *The Social Construction of Communities.* Chicago: University of Chicago Press.

———. 1968. *The Social Order of the Slum.* Chicago: University of Chicago Press.

SUTTON, W. A., and J. KOLAJA. 1960. "The concept of community." *Rural Sociology,* **25,** pp. 197–203.

SZYMANSKI, ALBERT T., and TED GEORGE GOERTZEL. 1979. *Sociology: Class, Consciousness, and Contradictions.* New York: Van Nostrand Reinhold.

TAEUBER, CYNTHIA M., and VICTOR VALDISERA. 1987. "Women in the American economy." *Current Population Reports, Special Studies,* Series P-23, No. 146.

TEITELBAUM, MICHAEL S., and JAY M. WINTER. 1985. *The Fear of Population Decline.* Orlando, Fla.: Academic Press.

TERRACE, H. S., L. A. PETITTO, R. J. SANDERS, and T. G. BEVER. 1979. "Can an ape create a sentence?" *Science,* **206,** pp. 891–902.

THOMAS, EVAN. 1986. "Peddling influence." *Time,* March 3.

THOMAS, W. I. 1928. *The Child in America.* New York: Knopf.

THOMPSON, LAURA. 1950. *Culture in Crisis.* New York: Harper.

THOMPSON, WARREN S. 1929. "Population." *American Journal of Sociology,* **34,** pp. 959–975.

TIGER, LIONEL, and ROBIN FOX. 1971. *The Imperial Animal.* New York: Holt, Rinehart and Winston.

Time. 1980. March 31.

———. 1979. "Cracking down on the big ones." December 31, p. 63.

———. 1979. "Nobody influences me!" December 10, pp. 29–34.

———. 1979. September 10.

———. 1979. August 6.

———. 1979. July 16.

———. 1979. "Save us! Save us!" July 9, pp. 28–32.

———. 1977. December 26.

TISCHLER, LINDA. 1988. "On the trail blazed by grandmas." *Boston Herald,* August 27, pp. 27–29, 31.

TOFFLER, ALVIN. 1970. *Future Shock.* New York: Random House.

TONNIES, FERDINAND. 1935 (1887). *Gemeinschaft und Gesellschaft: Grundbegnffeder Reinem Soziologie.* Leipzig.

TORREY, E. FULLER. 1988. "Homelessness and mental illness." *USA Today,* **116,** March, pp. 26–27.

TOWNSEND, BICKLEY. 1987. "Back to the future." *American Demographics,* March, p. 10.

TOYNBEE, ARNOLD. 1946. *A Study of History.* New York and London: Oxford University Press.

TRACHTENBERG, JOSHUA. 1961. *The Devil and the Jews.* New York: Meridian Books.

TREIMAN, DONALD J. 1977. *Occupational Prestige in Comparative Perspective.* New York: Academic Press.

TUMIN, M. 1953. "Some principles of stratification: A critical analysis." *American Sociological Review,* **18,** pp. 385–394.

TURNBULL, COLIN. 1972. *The Mountain People.* New York: Simon & Schuster.

TURNER, RALPH H. 1964. "Collective behavior." In R. E. L. Faris (ed.), *Handbook of Modern Sociology.* Chicago: Rand McNally.

———, and LEWIS M. KILLIAN. 1972. *Collective Behavior.* 2nd ed. Englewood Cliffs, N.J.: Prentice-Hall.

TYLOR, E. 1958 (1871). *Primitive Culture: Researches into the Development of Mythology, Philosophy, Religion, Art and Custom.* Vol. 1. London: John Murray.

———. 1889. "On a method of investigating the development of institutions applied to laws of marriage and descent." *Journal of the Royal Anthropological Institute,* **18,** pp. 245–269.

UDY, S. H., JR. 1959. "'Bureaucracy' and 'rationality' in Weber's organizational theory: An empirical study." *American Sociological Review,* **24,** pp. 791–795.

ULC, OTTO. 1975 (1969). "Communist national minority policy: The case of the Gypsies in Czechoslovakia." In Norman R. Yetman and C. Hoy Steele (eds.), *Majority and Minority: The Dynamics of Racial and Ethnic Relations.* Boston: Allyn & Bacon.

UHLENBERG, PETER. 1987. "How old is 'old age'?" *Public Interest,* Summer, pp. 67–79.

U.S. Bureau of the Census. 1988a. *Money Income of Households, Families, and Persons in the United States: 1986.* Current Population Reports Series P-60, No. 159. Washington, D.C. U.S. Government Printing Office.

———. 1988b. *Statistical Brief: December 1986.* Source: Occupational Outlook Quarterly.

———. 1987. *Statistical Abstract of the United States: 1988.* Washington, D.C., U.S. Government Printing Office.

———. 1985. Fertility of American Women. June, *Current Population Reports,* Series P-20, No. 406.

———. 1982. *Money Income and Poverty Status.*

———. 1981a. *Households and Family Characteristics.* Current Population Reports, Series P-20, no. 371. Washington, D.C.: U.S. Government Printing Office.

———. 1981b. *Marital Status and Living Arrangements.* Current Population Reports, Series P-20, no. 366. Washington, D.C.: U.S. Government Printing Office.

———. 1981c. *Money Income of Households in the United States.* Washington, D.C.: U.S. Department of Commerce.

———. 1981d. *1980 Census of Population.* Washington, D.C.: U.S. Department of Commerce.

———. 1981e. *U.S.A. Statistical Brief 1981: A Statistical Abstract Supplement.* Washington, D.C.: U.S. Bureau of the Census.

———. 1977. *Statistical Abstracts for States and Metropolitan Areas.* Washington, D.C.: U.S. Government Printing Office.

———. 1976. *Historical Statistics of the United States: Colonial Times to 1970.* Washington, D.C.: U.S. Government Printing Office.

U.S. Bureau of Justice Statistics. 1988a. *BJS Data Report.*

———. 1988b. *Households Touched by Crime, 1987.*

———. 1987. *Lifetime Likelihood of Victimization.*

U.S. Bureau of Labor Statistics. 1985. *Monthly Labor Review,* November.

U.S. Department of Commerce, Bureau of the Census. 1989. *Statistical Abstract of the United States, 1989.* Washington, D.C.: U.S. Government Printing Office.

———. 1988. *Statistical Abstract of the United States, 1987.* Washington, D.C.: U.S. Government Printing Office.

———. 1980a. *Social Indicators III.* Washington, D.C.: U.S. Government Printing Office.

U.S. Department of Justice. 1989. *Uniform Crime Report, 1988.* Washington, D.C.: U.S. Government Printing Office.

———. 1988. *Uniform Crime Report.* Washington, D.C.: Government Printing Office.

———. 1983. *Report to the Nation on Crime and Justice.* Washington, D.C.: Government Printing Office.

U.S. Department of Labor, Bureau of Labor Statistics. 1980. *Perspective on Working Women: A Databook.* Bulletin 2080, Table 62.

U.S. News & World Report. 1988. "Internationalization of crime in the United States." January 18.

———. 1988. "The Rochester experiment:

School reform, school reality." June 20, pp. 58–63.

——. 1982a. "Why the cost of health care won't stop rising." March 8, p. 67.

——. 1982b. "The ever-present hand of government." April 26, pp. 43–45.

USEEM, MICHAEL. 1984. *The Inner Circle: Large Corporations and the Rise of Business Political Activity in the U.S. and U.K.* New York: Oxford University Press.

VAN DE KAA, DIRK J. 1987. "Europe's second demographic transition." *Population Bulletin,* March.

VAGO, STEVEN. 1980. *Social Change.* New York: Holt, Rinehart and Winston.

VANFOSSEN, BETH E. 1979. *The Structure of Social Inequality.* Boston: Little, Brown.

VAN LAWICK-GOODALL, J. 1971. *In the Shadow of Man.* Boston: Houghton Mifflin.

VEBLEN, THORSTEIN. 1899. *The Theory of the Leisure Class.* New York: Macmillan.

VELTFORD, HELENE, and GEORGE E. LEE. 1943. "The Coconut Grove fire: A study in scapegoating." *Journal of Abnormal and Social Psychology,* Clinical Supplement, **38,** April, pp. 138–154.

VERBA, SIDNEY. 1972. *Small Groups and Political Behavior: A Study of Leadership.* Princeton, N.J.: Princeton University Press.

VON FRISCH, K. 1967. *The Dance Language and Orientation of Bees.* Cambridge, Mass.: Belknap.

Walker Commission. 1968. *Rights in Conflict: The Violent Confrontation of Demonstrators and Police in the Parks and Streets of Chicago During the Week of the Democratic National Convention of 1968.* Washington, D.C.: U.S. Government Printing Office.

WALSH, DORIS L. 1986. "What women want." *American Demographics,* June, p. 60.

WARNER, W. L. and P. LUNT. 1941. *The Social Life of a Modern Community.* New Haven, Conn.: Yale University Press.

WARREN, R. L. 1972. *The Community in America.* 2nd ed. New York: Rand McNally.

WATSON, J. B. 1925. *Behavior.* New York: Norton.

WEBER, MAX. 1962. *Basic Sociology.* Secaucus, N. J.: Citadel Press.

——. 1958a (1921). *The City.* New York: Collier.

——. 1958b. "Class, status, and party." In Hans H. Gerth and C. Wright Mills (eds.), *Max Weber: Essays in Sociology.* New York: Oxford University Press.

——. 1957. *The Theory of Social and Economic Organization.* New York: Free Press.

——. 1956. "Some consequences of bureaucratization." In J. P. Mayer (trans.), *Max Weber and German Politics.* 2nd ed.

——. 1949. *Max Weber on the Methodology of the Social Sciences.* Trans. and ed. Edward A. Shils and Henry A. Finch. N.Y.: Free Press.

——. 1947. *Max Weber: Essays in Sociology.* New York: Oxford University Press.

——. 1930 (1904–05). *Protestant Ethic and the Spirit of Capitalism.* Trans. Talcott Parsons. New York: Scribner.

——. 1922. *Economy and Society.* Trans. Ephraim Fischoff. New York: Bedminster Press, 1968.

WEISMAN, STEVEN R. 1988. "Pakistani women take lead in drive against Islamization." *New York Times,* June 17, pp. A1, A10.

WEISS, ROBERT S. 1979a. *Going It Alone: The Family Life and Social Situation of the Single Parent.* New York: Basic Books.

——. 1979b. "Issues in the adjudication of custody when parents separate." In George Levinger and Oliver C. Moles (eds.), *Divorce and Separation: Context, Causes, and Consequences.* New York: Basic Books.

WEISSBERG, ROBERT. 1981. *Understanding American Government.* Alternate ed. New York: Holt, Rinehart and Winston.

WEITZMAN, LENORE J. 1985. *The Divorce Revolution: The Unexpected Social and Economic Consequences for Women and Children in America.* New York: The Free Press.

WEITZMAN, LENORE J., and RUTH B. DIXON. 1980. "The transformation of legal marriage through no-fault divorce." In Arlene S. Skolnick and Jerome H. Skolnick (eds.), *Family in Transition: Rethinking Marriage, Sexuality, Child Rearing and Family Organization.* 3rd ed. Boston: Little, Brown.

WEITZMAN, LENORE J., DEBORAH EITLER, ELIZABETH HOKADA, and CATHERINE ROSS. 1972. "Sex-role socialization in picture books for preschool children." *American Journal of Sociology,* May, pp. 1125–1150.

WESTOFF, CHARLES F., and ELISE F. JONES. 1977. "The secularization of Catholic birth control practice." *Family Planning Perspectives,* **9,** September/October.

WHEELWRIGHT, PHILIP. 1959. *Heraclitus.* Princeton, N. J.: Princeton University Press.

WHITE, THEODORE H. 1982. *America in Search of Itself: The Making of the President, 1956–80.* New York: Harper & Row.

WHITE, W. F. 1943. *Street Corner Society.* Chicago: University of Illinois Press.

WHORF, B. 1956. *Language, Thought, and Reality.* Cambridge, Mass.: MIT Press.

WHYTE, W. H. 1956. *The Organization Man.* New York: Simon & Schuster.

WICKMAN, PETER, PHILLIP WHITTEN, and ROBERT LEVEY. 1980. *Criminology: Perspectives on Crime and Criminality.* Lexington, Mass.: Heath.

WIEBE, GERHART D. 1971. "The social effects of broadcasting." In Bernard Rosenberg and David Manning White (eds.), *Mass Culture Revisited.* New York: Van Nostrand Reinhold.

WILLIAMS, J. ALLEN, JOETTA A. VERNON, MARTHA WILLIAMS, and KAREN MALECHA. 1987. "Sex-role socialization in picture books: An update." *Social Science Quarterly,* March, pp. 148–156.

WILLIAMS, M. J. (ed.). "The 500: The *Fortune* directory of the largest U.S. industrial corporations." **105,** May 3, pp 258–286.

WILLIAMS, R. 1970. *American Society: A Sociological Interpretation.* 3rd ed. New York: Knopf.

WILLIAMSON, NANCY E. 1983. "Parental sex preferences and sex selection." In N. G. Bennett (ed.), *Sex Selection of Children.* New York: Academic Press.

WILLMOTT, PETER, and MICHAEL DUNLOP YOUNG. 1973. *The Symmetrical Family.* New York: Pantheon Books.

WILLNER, ANN RUTH. 1984. *The Spellbinders: Charismatic Political Leadership.* New Haven, Conn.: Yale University Press.

WILSON, BARBARA FOLEY. 1984. "Marriage's melting pot." *American Demographics,* **6,** July, pp. 34–37, 45.

WILSON, BARBARA FOLEY, and KATHRYN A. LONDON. 1987. "Going to the chapel." *American Demographics,* **9,** December, pp. 26–31.

WILSON, EDMUND. 1969. *The Dead Sea Scrolls 1947–1969.* Rev. ed. London: W. H. Allen.

WILSON, EDWARD O. 1979. *Sociobiology.* 2nd ed. Cambridge, Mass.: Belknap.

———. 1978. *On Human Nature.* Cambridge, Mass.: Harvard University Press.

———. 1975. *Sociobiology: The New Synthesis.* Cambridge, Mass.: Harvard University Press.

WILSON, JAMES Q. 1980. *American Government.* Lexington, Mass.: Heath.

WILSON, JOHN. 1973. *Introduction to Social Movements.* New York: Basic Books.

WIRTH, LOUIS. 1944. "Race and public policy." *Scientific Monthly,* **58,** April, pp. 302–312.

———. 1938. "Urbanism as a way of life." *American Journal of Sociology,* **64,** pp. 1–24.

WISSLER, CLARK. 1911. *The Social Life of the Blackfoot Indians.* Anthropological Papers of the American Museum of Natural History. American Museum of Natural History.

WITOLD, RYBCZYNSKI. 1983. *Taming the Tiger: The Struggle to Control Technology.* New York: Viking.

WOLF, ERIC. 1969. *Peasant Wars of the Twentieth Century.* New York: Harper & Row.

WOLFE, LINDA. 1981. "The good news." *New York,* December 28, pp. 33–35.

WOLFGANG, MARVIN, ROBERT M. FIGLIO, and THORSTEN SELLIN. 1972. *Delinquency in a Birth Cohort.* Chicago: University of Chicago Press.

WOODROW, KAREN A., JEFFREY S. PASSEL, and ROBERT WARREN. 1987. "Recent immigration to the United States—Legal and undocumented: An analysis of data from the June 1986 current population survey," paper presented at the meetings of the Population Association of America, Chicago.

World Bank. 1987. *World Development Report 1987.* Washington, D.C.: World Bank.

———. 1984a. *The Development Data Book.* Washington, D.C.: World Bank.

———. 1984b. "Measuring the Value of Children," World Development Report 1984, New York: Oxford University Press, pp. 122–123.

———. 1984c. *World Development Report, 1984.* New York: Oxford University Press.

YINGER, J. MILTON. 1970. *The Scientific Study of Religion.* New York: Macmillan.

———. 1960. "Contraculture and subculture." *American Sociological Review,* **25,** pp. 625–635.

ZEITLIN, I. N. 1981. *Social Condition of Humanity.* New York: Oxford University Press.

ZELNIK, MELVIN, and KANTNER. 1979. "Probabilities of intercourse and conception among U. S. teenage women 1971 and 1976." *Family Planning Perspectives,* **2,** May/June, pp. 177–183.

———. 1972. "Sexuality, contraception and pregnancy among young unwed females in the United States." In *U. S. Commission on Population Growth and the American Future: Demographic and Social Aspects of Population Growth.* Washington, D. C.: U. S. Government Printing Office.

ZIMBARDO, P. G. 1972. "Pathology of imprisonment." *Society,* **9,** April, p. 4.

PHOTO CREDITS

SUBJECT INDEX

Terms in **boldface** type are defined in the margin on the text pages indicated by boldface numbers.

Abortions, sex-selection, 630
Abstract ideals, 386
Academic skills, 416–417
Achieved statuses, 141
Acting crowd, 594
Adaptation, 78; biological (evolution), 75–76; cultural, 76–78, 98–99; and cultural lag, 78–79, 620–621; deviant modes of, 201–202; mechanisms of, 76–79; Merton's typology of individual modes of, 201–202
Adolescence, and gender-role socialization, 324, 326; peer group as influence in, 116–117, 118. *See also* Youth
Adoption, international, 280–281
Adult socialization, 118–120; aging and society, 124; career and identity, 121, 124; and gender identity, 326–327; marriage and responsibility, 120; and parenthood, 121
Adultery: An Analysis of Love and Betrayal, 312
Adultery, as gender issue, 312
Affiliation, 101–102
Age, and health, 548; and mate selection for marriage, 353
Age-specific death rates, 528–529
Aging, and socialization, 124; society in United States, 628–629, 631. *See also* Elderly
Agricultural societies, 150–151
AIDS (Acquired Immune Deficiency Syndrome), 548–552; and premarital sex, 361; and research, 37–38; and socialization in school, 114
Alcoholism, 9–10
Alienation, in bureaucracies, **177;** religion as tool in, **394**
Alternative life-styles, 370–374, 376
Altruism, 98–99
Altruistic suicide, 20
American Medical Association (AMA), as competition barrier, 231–232; and national health insurance, 547–548
American Revolution, 501, 502
American Sign Language (ASL), and animals, 84
Americanization Movement, 289–290
Analysis, 50–53
Anglo conformity, 278–279, 289–290; future pressure for, 305; in schools, 421
Animals, and culture, 83–85; study of behavior of, 314

Animism, 385
Annihilation, 283–285
Anomic suicide, 20–21
Anomie, and return to religion, 393; as theory of deviance, **201**
Apartheid, 294–295, 511; explained, 217, 276–277; justification of, on religious grounds, 392; as social inequality, 217
Aristocracy, 493
Ascribed statuses, 140
Asian Americans, 300–303; discrimination of, 274; in inner-city schools, 426; in labor force, 626
Asians, as immigrants, 286, 288
Assimilation, 278–279, 282; reverse, 279
Associations, 172–173; formal structure of, 173, 176; informal structure of, 173–174
Attitudes, family-related, survey on, 44
Authoritarian leader, 165
Authority, charismatic, 492; in groups, **163;** legal-rational, 491; and power, **490;** traditional, 491–492
Autism, 99
Autocracy, 493, 494–495

Baby boom generation, 357; as Catholics, 403; as conservatives, 512–513; future of, 628–629; in labor force, 361, 363, 480
Back-to-basics movement, 416–417, 430–431
Beagle (British ship), 63–64
Belief systems, 380, 383; Freud's view of, 389; as widespread, 398
Bias, design, 54; researcher, 49–50; sample, 47, 49
Bilateral system, 347
Bilocal residence, 352
Biology, and culture, 65–68; and socialization, 96–99
Birth Dearth, The, 536
Blacks, 291–295; American underclass of, 236–237; discrimination of, 274; forced migration of, 282; in labor force, 626; legal definition of, 270; as political force, 293, 508–510; population projections for, 296; poverty levels of, 249–250; reaction against Anglo conformity, 290; in schools, 276, 426–427, 429; segregation of, 282; and social Darwinism after the Civil War, 19; social definition of, 270–271; and standardized test bias,